Social Security and Retirement
around the World

A National Bureau
of Economic Research
Conference Report

Social Security and Retirement around the World

Edited by   Jonathan Gruber and
David A. Wise

 The University of Chicago Press

Chicago and London

JONATHAN GRUBER is professor of economics at the Massachusetts Institute of Technology and director of the Children's Program at the National Bureau of Economic Research. DAVID A. WISE is the John F. Stambaugh Professor of Political Economy at the John F. Kennedy School of Government, Harvard University, and the director for Health and Retirement Programs at the National Bureau of Economic Research.

The University of Chicago Press, Chicago 60637
The University of Chicago Press, Ltd., London
© 1999 by the National Bureau of Economic Research
All rights reserved. Published 1999
Printed in the United States of America
08 07 06 05 04 03 02 01 00 99   1 2 3 4 5
ISBN: 0-226-31011-6 (cloth)

Library of Congress Cataloging-in-Publication Data

Social security and retirement around the world / edited by Jonathan
    Gruber and David A. Wise.
        p.   cm. — (A National Bureau of Economic Research confer-
    ence report)
    Includes bibliographical references and index.
    ISBN 0-226-31011-6 (cloth)
    1. Social security—Congresses.   2. Retirement income—Con-
gresses.   3. Old age pensions—Congresses.   4. Aged—Economic
conditions—Congresses.   I. Gruber, Jonathan.   II. Wise, David A.
II. Series: Conference report (National Bureau of Economic Research)
HD7090.S583 1999
368.4—dc21   98-22488
                                                                  CIP

Contents

Preface

This volume consists of papers presented at a conference held at Château Beychevelle, Saint Julien, France, in May 1997. The papers are part of an ongoing project on social security and labor supply organized through the Program on the Economics of Aging at the National Bureau of Economic Research. Funding for organizing the project was provided by National Institute on Aging grant P20-AG12810 to the National Bureau of Economic Research. Funding for individual papers is noted in specific paper acknowledgments.

Any opinions expressed in this volume are those of the respective authors and do not necessarily reflect the views of the National Bureau of Economic Research or the sponsoring organization.

Introduction and Summary

Jonathan Gruber and David A. Wise

In almost every industrialized country, the population is aging rapidly, and individuals are living longer. These demographic trends have placed enormous pressure on the financial viability of the social security systems in these countries. The financial pressure is compounded by another trend. In virtually every country, employees are leaving the labor force at younger and younger ages. In some countries, the labor force participation rates of sixty- to sixty-four-year-old men have fallen by 75 percent over the past three decades.

What accounts for the striking decline in labor force participation? One explanation is that social security provisions themselves provide enormous incentive to leave the labor force early, thus by their very structure exacerbating the financial problems they face. It is this aspect of social security plan provisions that is emphasized in this volume. By considering the relation between plan provisions, on the one hand, and labor force participation rates, on the other, we hope to draw attention to the important role that social security can play in the labor force decisions of older persons.

This volume contains analyses based on evidence from eleven industrialized countries. In this summary, we attempt to distill key conclusions that can be drawn from the collective findings of the individual papers. The project relies on analyses of social security provisions and labor force participation conducted by a number of economists in their own countries: Pierre Pestieau and Jean-Philippe Stijns in Belgium, Jonathan Gruber in Canada, Didier Blanchet

Jonathan Gruber is professor of economics at the Massachusetts Institute of Technology and director of the Children's Program at the National Bureau of Economic Research. David A. Wise is the John F. Stambaugh Professor of Political Economy at the John F. Kennedy School of Government, Harvard University, and the director for Health and Retirement Programs at the National Bureau of Economic Research.

The authors acknowledge the support of the National Institute on Aging through grant 5 P20 AG12810 to the National Bureau of Economic Research.

and Louis-Paul Pelé in France, Axel Börsch-Supan and Reinhold Schnabel in Germany, Agar Brugiavini in Italy, Naohiro Yashiro and Takashi Oshio in Japan, Arie Kapteyn and Klaas de Vos in the Netherlands, Michele Boldrin, Sergi Jimenez-Martin, and Franco Peracchi in Spain, Mårten Palme and Ingemar Svensson in Sweden, Richard Blundell and Paul Johnson in the United Kingdom, and Peter Diamond and Jonathan Gruber in the United States.

The central feature of the project is an attempt to present comparable descriptive data and analytic calculations for each of these eleven countries. The country studies all follow the same format. Each begins with a description of the historical evolution of labor force participation and then presents data on the current age-specific activities and income sources of men and women in terms of the following: (1) labor force participation rates by age interval between 1960 and the present; (2) the proportion of employees covered by the public pension system, and the proportion of persons over age fifty-five receiving public pensions, from 1960 to the present; (3) replacement rates under the public pension system from 1960 to the present; (4) current labor force participation rates by age; (5) labor force status (employed, unemployed, disabled, retired); (5) proportion receiving various public "pensions" (e.g., old age, disability, survivor) by age; (6) proportions receiving employer-provided pensions by age; (7) source of household income by age; and (8) retirement and public pension hazard rates by age. In some instances, the presentation is adjusted to match individual country circumstances; in other cases, additional information is presented that is particularly important for a specific country. Each study then describes the institutional features of the country's social security system, highlighting any interactions with other public and private programs that might also influence retirement behavior. Finally, the core of each study is a detailed analysis of the retirement incentives inherent in the provisions of the given country's retirement income system. By making the same analytic calculations, and by presenting the same simulations for each of the countries, the individual studies provide a means of comparing retirement incentives among nations.

We begin this introduction by describing the dramatic fall in labor force participation rates over the past three decades, the phenomenon that provides the primary motivation for this project. We then describe the decline in labor force participation with age that is reflected in current labor force patterns. We draw attention in particular to the forgone productive capacity implicit in the low participation rates of older persons. We then use data from several countries to illustrate the relation between social security provisions and withdrawal from the labor force. These illustrative country data are also used to explain the key methods used in each of the country papers. We also point out important ways in which public and private policies differ among the countries, differences that must be kept in mind when making comparisons between countries. Finally, we present a summary of key findings for all the coun-

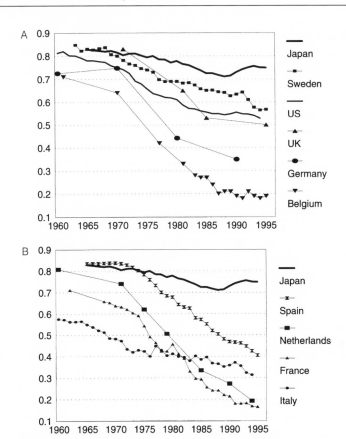

Fig. 1   Labor force participation trends for men aged 60 to 64

tries, emphasizing the relation between social security provisions and retirement patterns.

Labor Force Participation

The Decline since 1960

The decline in the labor force participation of older persons is one of the most dramatic features of labor force change over the past several decades. The decline has been striking in all but one of the countries studied here. The labor force participation rates of men aged sixty to sixty-four for the years 1960–66 are shown for each of the eleven countries in figure 1. The decline was substantial in each country but was much greater in some than in others. In the early 1960s, the participation rates were above 70 percent in each country and above 80 percent in several. By the mid-1990s, the rate had fallen to below 20 percent in Belgium, Italy, France, and the Netherlands, to about 35 percent in Germany, and to 40 percent in Spain. Although U.S. analysts have often emphasized the "dramatic" fall in that country, the decline in the United States from 82 to 53 percent was modest in comparison to the much more precipitous decline in these European countries. The decline to 57 percent in Sweden was also large, but modest when compared to the fall in other countries. Japan stands out with the smallest decline of all the countries, from about 83 to 75 percent. The labor force participation rates of forty-five- to fifty-nine-year-old men, as well as of those age sixty and older, have also declined substantially, and these trends can be seen in the individual country papers.

Each of the country papers presents completely parallel labor force and other data for men and women, including current labor force participation and departure rates by age, which are key components of the analysis in this volume. To simplify the exposition, and to limit the number of figures presented, we emphasize the data for men here. In addition, the cross-country comparisons, which are made toward the end of the introduction, are more easily interpreted for men than for women. In some respects, however, the labor force trends for older women are just as dramatic as those for men. Although the labor force participation rate of women of *all ages combined* has been increasing, this is not the pattern for older women. In seven of the ten countries for which data are available, the labor force participation rates of women aged sixty to sixty-four have been *declining* in the past three decades—in some cases by a factor of two—even though the participation rate of women started from a much lower base in the early 1960s. In no country has there been a general increase in this age group, in spite of the sharp trend toward increasing participation rates of women at younger ages. In some countries—the Netherlands and Belgium, for example—the participation rate since 1960 of women in this age group has never exceeded 10 percent! With the possible exception of one of the countries, the labor force participation rates of women at older ages—which have always been lower than the participation rates of men—are now declining. Most important, the current labor force departure rates for women at older ages are quite consistent with the departure rates for men, as explained below. Perhaps most important, by looking at the individual country papers, it is clear that the same within-country incentives that affect the retirement patterns of men apply equally to women. Indeed, women tend to leave the labor force at earlier ages than men. That is, women who are in the labor force at age sixty, for example, are typically more likely than men to retire at that age. In some countries, benefits are available at younger ages for women than for men. The incentives to leave the labor force—discussed in detail below—and the actual labor force departures at older ages appear to be at least as important for women as for men.

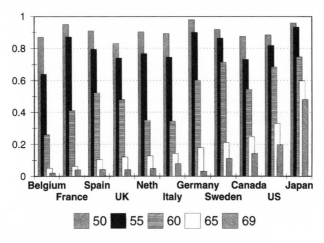

Fig. 2   Labor force participation by country and age

The Decline with Age and "Unused Productive Capacity"

The current relation between labor force participation and age for men is shown for each of the countries in figure 2. The countries are ordered by labor force participation at age sixty-five. At age fifty, approximately 90 percent of men are in the labor force in all the countries. The decline after age fifty varies greatly among countries. By age sixty-nine, virtually no men in Belgium are working; in Japan, almost 50 percent are still in the labor force. Indeed, most men in Belgium are no longer in the labor force at age sixty-five, and only about 25 percent are working at age sixty. In Japan, on the other hand, 60 percent are working at age sixty-five and 75 percent at age sixty.

There are many implications of the withdrawal of older men from the workforce. Some have to do with the differential political influence of older and younger voters. Some have to do with the psychological well-being of older persons as they age. We emphasize here the forgone productive capacity of older employees who leave the workforce. Figure 3a helps explain this idea and provides a simple way of comparing the extent of labor force withdrawal of older men across countries. This figure shows the labor force participation of men aged fifty to sixty-nine in three countries: Japan, Spain, and Belgium. For Japan, consider the height above the LFP (labor force participation) curve, which is the proportion of men not working at a given age (1 − LFP). Loosely speaking, we can refer to this measure as the *unused productive capacity* at that age. If the unused capacity is added up over all ages, we find the area above the LFP curve. Dividing by the total area of the figure (1 × 19) yields a rough measure of the unused capacity over the age range fifty to sixty-nine as a percentage of the total labor capacity in that age range. In Japan, the value of the unused capacity measure is 22 percent. It is clear from the figure that

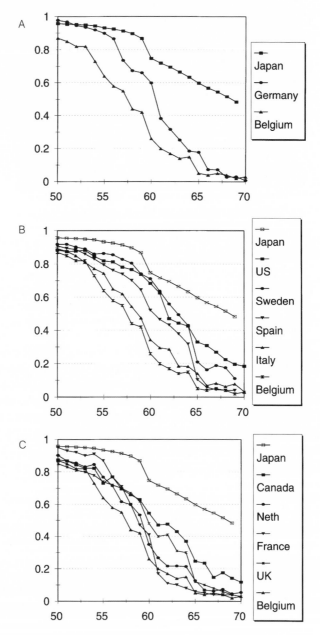

Fig. 3   Labor force participation of men by age and country

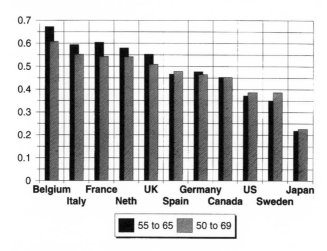

Fig. 4   Unused productive capacity

many more older men are out of the labor force in Belgium, where the unused capacity measure is 61 percent. In Spain, the unused capacity measure is 48 percent.

We emphasize that these are only relative measures; there is no reason to assume that all men who are not working should, or could, work. In particular, this measure might differ across countries because of differences in health status. Or unused capacity may be higher in countries in which a larger proportion of jobs are physically demanding.[1] Nevertheless, these enormous differences across fairly similar industrialized countries are striking.

The labor force participation profiles for the other countries are shown in figure 3*b*, *c*. For comparison, the profiles for Japan and Belgium are shown in each panel. The unused productive capacity measures for all the countries are shown in figure 4. For the entire age range from fifty to sixty-nine, the unused capacity measures range from a high of 61 percent in Belgium to a low of 23 percent in Japan. In the age range fifty-five to sixty-five, unused capacity ranges from 67 percent in Belgium to 22 percent in Japan. We consider below how this relative measure is related to the provisions of the social security programs in the countries.

1. In addition, our measure of unused capacity is crude. A more refined measure would account not only for participation but also for the nature of that participation, i.e., hours of work. It would account as well for the fact that moving from higher-paying (marginal product) jobs to lower-paying (marginal product) jobs increases unused capacity. For example, the higher labor force participation of older men in Japan may be due to less rigorous work in the secondary sector; we would therefore understate unused capacity for that country. Moreover, some of what is called *unused productive capacity* may include nonmarket work, such as off-the-books handiwork or volunteer labor; this would lower measured unused capacity. An appropriate measurement of unused capacity across countries is an important priority for future work.

The Incentive Effects of Plan Provisions

The key feature of each of the chapters in this volume is the highly detailed computation of plan retirement incentives. In this section, we provide a very brief overview of the provisions of social security plans that can create large retirement incentives. We then present evidence on how these incentives appear to be reflected in retirement behavior.

Two features of social security plans have an important effect on labor force participation incentives. The first is the age at which benefits are first available. This is called the *early retirement age*. The "normal" retirement age is also important, but, as the data will show, it is typically much less important than the early retirement age. It may once have been that most people were expected to retire at the normal retirement age; now, in most countries, few people work until the normal retirement age.

The extent to which people continue to work after the early retirement age is closely related to the second important feature of plan provisions, the pattern of benefit accrual. Suppose that, at a given age, a person has acquired entitlement to future benefits on retirement. The present discounted value of these benefits is the person's social security wealth at that age (SSW_a). The key consideration for retirement decisions is how this wealth will evolve with continued work. If a person is age fifty-nine, for example, what is the change in social security wealth if he retires at age sixty instead of age fifty-nine? The difference between social security wealth if retirement is at age a and social security wealth if retirement is at age $a + 1$, $SSW_{a+1} - SSW_a$, is called *social security wealth accrual*.

We compare social security wealth accrual to net wage earnings over the year. If the accrual is positive, it adds to total compensation from working the additional year; if the accrual is negative, it reduces total compensation. The ratio of the accrual to net wage earnings is an implicit tax on earnings if the accrual is negative and an implicit subsidy to earnings if the accrual is positive. Thus, a negative accrual discourages continuation in the labor force, and a positive accrual encourages continued labor force participation. This accrual rate, and the associated tax rate, is a key calculation that is made in the same way for each of the countries considered here. As it turns out, the pension accrual is typically negative at older ages: continuation in the labor force means a loss in the present value of net pension benefits, which imposes an implicit tax on work and provides an incentive to leave the labor force.[2]

The magnitude of social security wealth accrual and the corresponding tax or subsidy differ greatly from country to country and are determined by several provisions. The most important determinant of accrual is the adjustment to

---

2. While several authors have compared social security provisions in several countries—e.g., Kohli, Rein, Guillemard, and van Gunsteren (1991) and OECD (1995a, 1995b)—there has been no analytic calculation of the incentive effects of plan provisions whose results were comparable across countries.

benefits if a person works for another year. An additional year of work means a delay in receiving benefits, which will be received for one less year. In some countries, an "actuarial" adjustment is made, increasing benefits to offset the fact that they are received for fewer years. But, in other countries, no such adjustment is made. The greater the adjustment, the greater the inducement to continue working. If the adjustment is not large enough to offset the fewer years that benefits are received, however, there is an incentive to leave the labor force. Second, a person who continues to work must pay social security taxes on earnings, lowering net social security accrual. These tax payments make retirement more attractive. Third, the additional year of earnings is often used to recompute social security benefits, which are typically based on some measure of lifetime average earnings. Since earnings are often higher later in life than earlier, this may raise net accrual, making retirement less attractive. This effect may be especially important for the younger old, who are not fully "vested" in their social security systems until they have paid in for some minimal number of years. Finally, a delay in receiving benefits raises the odds that the worker might die before being able to collect any benefits. This lowers net social security accrual and may be an important consideration for the oldest workers.

In addition to social security plan provisions, other government and private programs may also affect the relation between social security plan provisions and observed retirement patterns. One is the availability of employer-provided pension plans. For example, half the employees in the United States are covered by employer-provided plans, about half of which are "defined-benefit" plans that have substantial retirement incentive effects, as emphasized by Stock and Wise (1990a, 1990b) and Lumsdaine, Stock, and Wise (1991, 1992, 1994). In most European countries, employer-provided plans are much less prevalent; the most important exceptions are the United Kingdom and the Netherlands. The other programs that may have an important effect on retirement are unemployment and disability insurance. In many European countries, these programs essentially provide early retirement benefits before the official social security early retirement age. While these other programs affect the comparisons that are made here, the basic relation between social security plan provisions and retirement is typically quite clear. In cases where these plans are especially important, the country studies have incorporated them into the "social security" incentive calculations.

Country-Specific Examples

To illustrate the relation between social security plan provisions and retirement behavior, we draw on the data for three countries: Germany, France, and the United States. The analysis of incentive effects presented in this volume pertains primarily to current country social security systems or to the systems as they existed until recently. Data for these three countries, however, allow a simple within-country comparison of change in plan provisions over time and the corresponding change in the labor force participation of older people. The experience of these countries also highlights a feature of retirement that is common to all countries, the concentration of retirement at social security early and normal retirement ages. These three examples also help draw attention to the features of other social programs—disability and unemployment, in particular—that often interact with the social security program in a country. In the final section, we discuss the overall evidence from the eleven countries and draw general conclusions on the basis of between-country comparisons.

The German Case

The German experience provides a clean example: a large fraction of employees is covered by the social security system, but few employees are covered by employer-provided pension plans, and such plans that do exist typically provide small benefits. On the other hand, "retirement" is to some extent encouraged in Germany by liberal disability and unemployment programs in addition to the social security plan provisions.

Before 1972, the social security retirement age in Germany was sixty-five, except for disability, and there was no social security early retirement age. But 1972 legislation provided for early retirement at age sixty for women and at age sixty-three for men (given the accumulation of required social security work years). In addition, the liberal use of disability and unemployment benefits effectively expanded the early retirement option. In a large fraction of cases, social security early retirement benefits were made available with no reduction in benefits; benefits taken at the early retirement age were the same as if they were taken at the normal retirement age. This greatly increased the net tax on work since delaying retirement simply reduced the number of years that one could receive benefits, without increasing the annual benefit.

In fact, there was a dramatic response to this increase in retirement incentives. Over the next few years, the mean retirement age of white-collar workers was reduced by 5.5 years, as shown in figure 5.[3]

The correspondence between plan provisions and retirement can also be demonstrated by considering the relation between retirement and social security provisions at a point in time. The detailed provisions of the 1972 legislation are mirrored in retirement rates by age. Figure 6 shows the proportion of men employed at a given age who retire at that age—the *hazard*, or *departure*, rate. The ages of key plan provisions are also noted on the figure so that the correspondence between provisions and retirement can be easily seen. Men who are "disabled" or "unemployed" at age sixty and have been employed for a certain number of years under the social security system are eligible for early retirement at that age. There is a corresponding large jump in the retirement rate at that age. Men who have been employed for thirty-five years are eligible for

---

3. The mean retirement age is the average age of persons retiring in a given year.

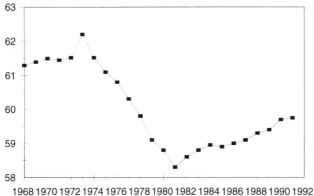

Fig. 5   Mean retirement age in Germany

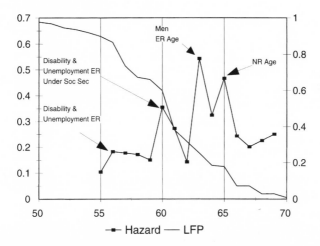

Fig. 6   Hazard and labor force participation rates for Germany
Note: ER = early retirement; NR = normal retirement.

early retirement at age sixty-three, and there is a corresponding jump in the retirement rate at that age. The normal retirement age is sixty-five, and there is a corresponding spike at that age as well. By age sixty-five, however, fewer than 29 percent of men are still in the labor force. In addition, even before age sixty, liberal interpretation of disability and unemployment plan provisions effectively serves to provide early retirement benefits (discussed further below).

But retirement eligibility may not by itself induce retirement. In Germany, a high price is paid for not retiring if eligible. Consider, for example, the prospects faced by a man with median earnings whose wife is three years younger than he is and who—like 40 percent of older German workers—would be

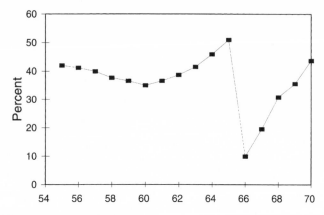

Fig. 7   Tax rates on work in Germany

eligible for disability benefits were he to leave the labor force. Suppose he could retire at age sixty but was considering postponing retirement until age sixty-five. The receipt of benefits for five fewer years would not be offset by larger benefits. Indeed, the present value of benefits if taken at age sixty-five would be much less than the present value of benefits if taken at age sixty; that is, the social security accrual rate is negative. Were retirement postponed by five years, the present value of the benefits would fall by almost 18 percent. Delaying retirement from age sixty to age sixty-one would reduce benefits by over 4 percent. This large negative accrual rate implies a substantial tax on additional work. The 4 percent reduction in benefits from delaying retirement to age sixty-one is equivalent to a tax of roughly 35 percent on the net wage earnings from working an additional year. This represents an enormous disincentive to continued work.

The tax rates on earnings for each additional year in the labor force from age fifty-five to age seventy are shown in figure 7. It is clear that the cost of postponing retirement is very large; a large fraction of what would be gained in wage earnings if the person worked between age sixty and age sixty-five, for example, is lost by way of reduced pension benefits. Thus, a large fraction of employees retire as soon as they are eligible.

The net effect on labor force participation is illustrated in figure 8, which describes the labor force status of men by age.[4] Retirement under the social security plan begins at age sixty, and labor force participation declines rapidly thereafter; by age sixty-five, virtually all men are retired under the social security retirement system.

---

4. Note that the labor force participation figures given here do not correspond exactly to the hazard rates shown earlier. The labor force status estimates are based on a nationally representative micro-data survey, while the hazard rate estimates are taken from administrative data on pension receipt.

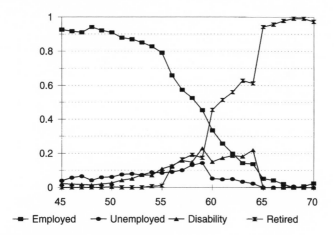

Fig. 8   Status of men by age in Germany

This figure also illustrates the interaction of the social security system and other programs. The labor force participation of men starts to fall well before the social security early retirement age. Indeed, at age fifty-nine—just before the social security early retirement age—only about 50 percent of employees are still in the labor force. The fall coincides with the increase in the proportion of men who are receiving unemployment benefits and the proportion receiving disability benefits. These programs in effect provide retirement benefits before the social security early retirement age. At age sixty, most of those receiving unemployment, and many of those receiving disability benefits, switch to receiving social security benefits instead. At age sixty-five, all those receiving disability benefits switch to social security.

The French Case

The experience in France provides another illustration of the effect of changes in plan provisions. Prior to 1972, the normal social security retirement age in France was sixty-five, and early retirement provisions were uncommon. In the early 1970s, early retirement provisions were introduced by way of a guaranteed income for persons age sixty and over who lost their jobs. In 1983, sixty became the *normal* retirement age. In addition, guaranteed income was provided for persons age fifty-seven and older who lost their jobs.

The effect of this series of reforms is easily seen in the panels of figure 9, which show the *distribution* of social security retirement ages of several cohorts—those attaining age sixty in 1972, 1978, 1982, and 1986, respectively. (These figures must be distinguished from those in, for example, fig. 6 above for Germany, which shows hazard or departure rates; fig. 9 shows the distribution of retirement ages.) In the early 1970s, the modal retirement age was sixty-five, as shown for the cohort that reached age sixty in 1972 (and age sixty-five

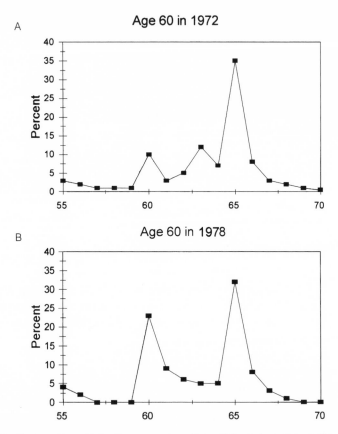

Fig. 9 Retirement ages in France: *a*, Age 60 in 1972; *b*, Age 60 in 1978; *c*, Age 60 in 1982; *d*, Age 60 in 1986

in 1977). But, as early as 1963, special allowances were provided for some workers who became unemployed at age sixty or older, perhaps reflected in the small spike at age sixty. Beginning in 1972, a "resource maintenance" program provided grants equal 60–70 percent of last earnings to persons who became unemployed between age sixty and age sixty-four. The effect of these programs seems to be reflected in the increasing proportion of workers retiring at age sixty, as shown in the second and third (1978 and 1982) panels of figure 9. Such allowances were also provided for younger workers in some industry sectors. In addition, early retirement before age sixty-five was available under some pension plans. In 1983, sixty became the normal social security retirement age (and guaranteed income was provided for persons age fifty-seven and older who lost their jobs). Shortly after that, the modal retirement age did indeed become sixty, as shown in the panel for the cohort reaching age sixty in 1986.

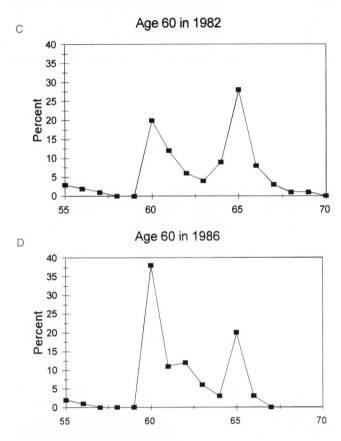

Fig. 9 (cont.)   Retirement ages in France

As in Germany, the current labor force departure rates in France also correspond closely to social security provisions. And, like the German provisions, the French social security provisions also impose a large tax on continued employment past the early retirement eligibility age, as shown in figure 10. The implicit tax on continued labor force participation earnings at age sixty is close to 70 percent. The negative tax rates (large subsidy) prior to age fifty-eight reflect the sharp increases in social security entitlement for continuing in the labor force during these years; workers receive much lower social security benefits unless they work until that age. But the incentive to stay in the labor force provided by this accrual is largely canceled by the guaranteed income for persons who become unemployed at age fifty-seven and older. The age-specific rates of departure from the labor force in France are shown in figure 11. Approximately 60 percent of employees who remain in the labor force until the social security early retirement age—sixty—retire then. But, even before that

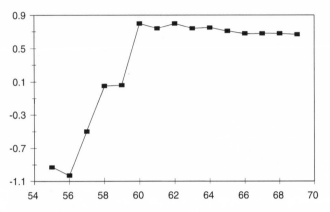

Fig. 10   Tax rates on work in France

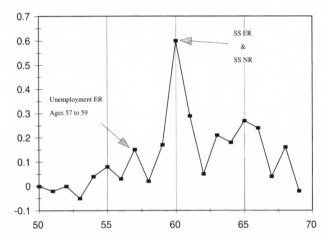

Fig. 11   Hazard rates for France
Note: ER = early retirement; NR = normal retirement; SS = social security.

age, departure rates are substantial, apparently reflecting the guaranteed income provisions for employees who become unemployed, even if they are not
eligible for social security benefits. Thus, as in Germany, there is a large incentive to take retirement benefits once they are available.

The U.S. Case

As in Germany and France, changes in the age of eligibility for social security benefits in the United States had a large effect on retirement behavior. This
pattern is illustrated in figure 12, which shows the hazard rates out of the labor
force for men in 1960, 1970, and 1980 (from Burtless and Moffitt 1984). In
1960, the normal retirement age was sixty-five, and there was no opportunity
for early retirement under social security. In that year, the hazard rate was low

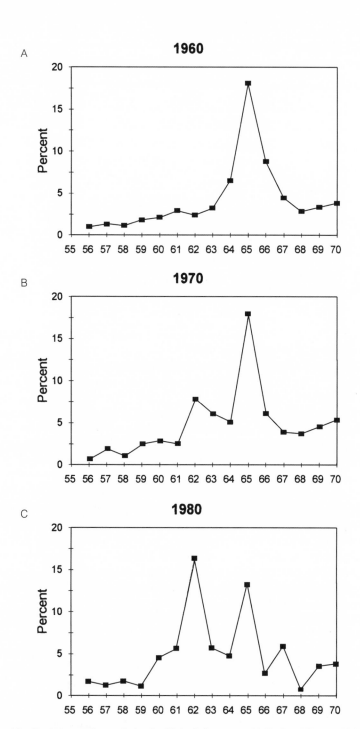

Fig. 12 Retirement hazards in the United States: *a*, 1960; *b*, 1970; *c*, 1980
Source: Burtless and Moffitt (1984).

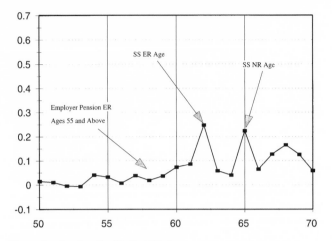

Fig. 13   Hazard rates for the United States
Note: ER = early retirement; NR = normal retirement; SS = social security.

until age sixty-five, when the departure rate jumped precipitously, reflecting the availability of social security benefits.

In 1961, early eligibility for retirement benefits for men at age sixty-two was introduced.[5] The effect of the introduction of early retirement on labor force departure rates is striking. Starting in 1970, and visible most clearly in 1980, there was a dramatic increase in the departure rate at age sixty-two and a corresponding decrease at age sixty-five. As a result, since 1980, the highest rate of labor force departure has been at age sixty-two.[6] Thus, as in Germany and France, in the United States the data suggest a very strong influence of social security incentives on retirement.

There is also, as in France and Germany, a strong, contemporaneous correspondence in the United States between social security early and normal retirement ages and departure from the labor force, as shown in figure 13. But there is a noticeable difference between the U.S. departure rates and those in France and Germany; the departure rates in the United States are much lower. Whereas, in France and Germany, the departure rates at the social security early retirement age are approximately 60 percent, in the United States the departure rate is only about 25 percent.

The difference corresponds to large differences in the tax on continued wage earnings. The tax in the United States is shown in figure 14. At age sixty-two, the tax rate in the United States is essentially zero, whereas in France the tax at the early retirement age (sixty) is close to 70 percent. In Germany, the tax rates just at and after the early retirement age are about 40 percent.

5. It had been introduced for women in 1956.
6. This evolution proceeded fairly slowly. A similar pattern is seen in Canada, as documented by Baker and Benjamin (1996): early retirement at age sixty was introduced in 1987, but not until the early 1990s was it reflected in a limited way in retirement behavior.

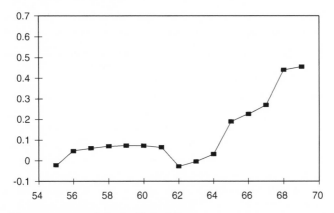

Fig. 14   Tax rates on work in the United States

There are four reasons why the tax rate at the early retirement age is so much lower in the United States. First, the "replacement rate" is much lower in the United States; thus, wage earnings exceed social security benefits by much more than in Germany or France. At age sixty-two, social security replaces about 41 percent of previous earnings on average, whereas, at age sixty, the replacement rate is 62 percent in Germany and 91 percent in France. Aside from other features of the programs, higher replacement rates increase the retirement incentives in Germany and France. The benefit forgone is much lower in the United States. Second, between age sixty-two and age sixty-five, the U.S. system provides an actuarial adjustment to benefits if their receipt is delayed, which offsets to a large extent the fewer years benefits are received. There is no actuarial adjustment in Germany or France.[7] Third, payroll tax rates to finance the program are much lower in the United States, which lowers the tax on additional work. Finally, the U.S. system allows higher earnings later in life to replace low earnings in earlier years; this is not true in Germany, but it can occur in France.

After the normal retirement age (sixty-five), however, tax rates become much higher in the United States, approaching 50 percent by age seventy. This is primarily because the actuarial adjustment after age sixty-five is much less than the "fair" rate—that which would be required to equate the expected present value of benefits if their initial receipt is delayed.

Finally, figure 13 shows an increase in departure rates around age fifty-five, well before the social security early retirement age. A similar but much more pronounced pattern is evident in figures 6 and 11 above for Germany and France, respectively. In those countries, the increase is associated with the receipt of unemployment and/or disability benefits. In the United States, on the other hand, the increase is apparently associated with employer-provided pension plan early retirement ages, which are common at fifty-five and are typi-

---

7. Reforms in 1992 introduced such an adjustment in Germany.

cally between fifty-five and sixty. The estimated hazard rates in figure 13 are imprecise, however, and thus do not show a precise increase at age fifty-five.[8]

To summarize, these three country illustrations make clear the very close correspondence between retirement ages and the statutory social security eligibility for early and normal retirement benefits. In all three cases, there are large jumps in labor force departure rates at the early retirement age in particular and at the normal retirement age as well. The correspondence is demonstrated most convincingly by within-country changes in retirement behavior over time, which follow on changes in statutory provisions. In addition, the jump in departure rates, at the early retirement age in particular, appears to be much greater in countries where the tax on continued work is large (Germany and France) than in countries where it is smaller (the United States). We turn now to an overview of the conclusions that seem warranted on the basis of the combined results in all eleven countries.

All Countries

In distilling the evidence from all the countries studied in this volume, three features of the data stand out. First, as in the three country illustrations, there is a strong correspondence between early and normal retirement ages and departure from the labor force. Second, the social security provisions in most countries place a heavy tax burden on work past the age of early retirement eligibility and thus provide a strong incentive to withdraw from the labor force early. Third, the tax—and thus the incentive to leave the labor force—varies substantially among countries. So does retirement behavior. Thus, by considering comparisons across the countries, we are able to draw general conclusions about the relation between the tax penalty on work and retirement behavior. Although the between-country comparisons suggest a rather strong relation between these provisions and retirement—in particular, the unused capacity measure—we do not attempt to assign quantitative magnitudes to the effects. We will try to summarize the results for all the countries, however, in a way that makes clear that economic incentives to retire are indeed associated with early departure from the labor force. More precise quantitative estimates of the effects of specific provisions must await more formal analysis.[9]

Early Retirement Provisions and Departure Rates

Perhaps the easiest way to see the relation between departure rates and early retirement provisions is to consider graphs of hazard rates for each of the countries, like those shown above for Germany, France, and the United States.

8. This jump in the hazard rate is more apparent in longitudinal data, as shown in Welch and Peracchi (1994).

9. Some analyses are reviewed on a country-by-country basis in appendices to the individual country papers.

These are shown for men in the first of the two panels that are presented for each country individually in figures 15*a* through 15*k*. The top panel for each country also shows the labor force participation rates by age for each country. It is evident that there is typically a strong correspondence between retirement plan provisions and labor force departure rates. In virtually every country, there is a sharp jump in the departure rate at the social security early retirement age, when employees are first eligible for benefits.[10] In every country, there is also a jump in departure at the normal retirement age. We emphasize the early retirement age, however, because in most countries only a small fraction of men remain in the labor force until the normal retirement age. Thus, the large departure rates at the normal retirement age apply to only a small fraction of employees.

Although the social security early retirement age is the most critical of plan provisions, as emphasized above, in many countries unemployment and disability programs effectively provide early retirement at younger ages. The effects of these programs are reflected in the departure rates before the social security early retirement ages. To understand the implications of departure rates, it is useful to have in mind a few illustrations of their cumulative effect: if 5 percent of those still employed leave each year, after five years 24 percent will have left. If 10 percent leave each year, 41 percent will have left over five years; if 20 percent leave each year, 67 percent will have left over five years. The effects of unemployment and disability programs seem especially evident in Belgium, France, the Netherlands, and Germany, where labor force departure rates approach or exceed 20 percent before the social security early retirement age. (These programs are also labeled on the first panels of fig. 15.) In contrast, in Sweden—which has no early retirement and normal retirement at sixty-five—departure rates before age sixty are typically well below 5 percent. Departure rates before the social security early retirement age are also much smaller in the United States and Canada, although in these countries employer-provided pension plans—with typical early retirement ages between fifty-five and sixty—provide incentive for some employees to retire at earlier ages.

To understand further the importance of unemployment and disability programs, the proportion of men reporting that they are unemployed or disabled is shown in the lower panel for each country in figure 15. These panels also show the proportion of men who are employed and the proportion who are retired. At age fifty-nine, for example, 22 percent of men are receiving unemployment or disability benefits in Belgium, 21 percent in France, 27 percent in the Netherlands, 33 percent in the United Kingdom, and 37 percent in Germany. Even in Sweden, where departure rates are relatively low before age sixty, 24 percent are receiving unemployment or disability benefits at age

10. In the Netherlands, the jump is not in fact at the social security retirement age but at the common employer plan early retirement age. In the Netherlands, employer plans are virtually universal and are mandated by law.

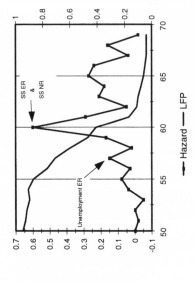

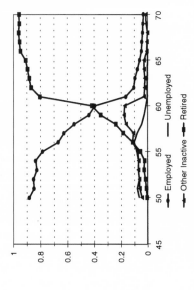

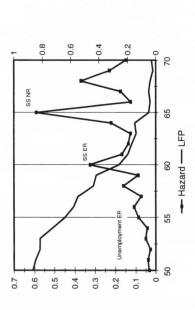

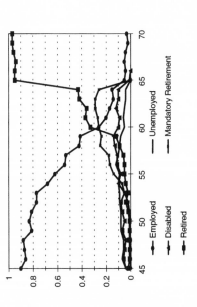

Fig. 15A Hazard and labor force participation rates (*top*), and status of men by age (*bottom*), Belgium

Fig. 15B Hazard and labor force participation rates (*top*), and status of men by age (*bottom*), France

Note: ER = early retirement; NR = normal retirement; SS = social security.

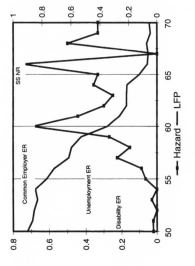

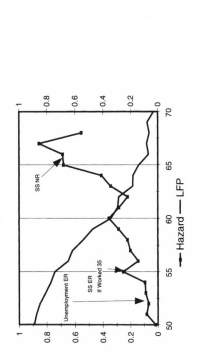

Fig. 15C Hazard and labor force participation rates (*top*), and status of men by age (*bottom*), Italy

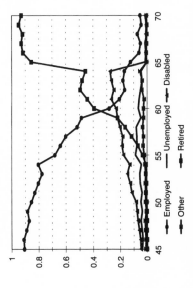

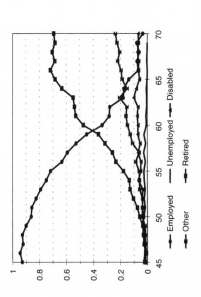

Fig. 15D Hazard and labor force participation rates (*top*), and status of men by age (*bottom*), the Netherlands

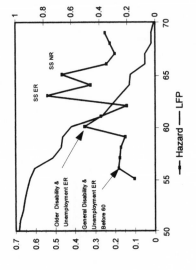

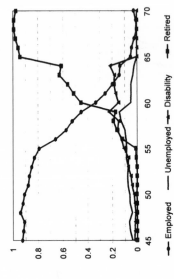

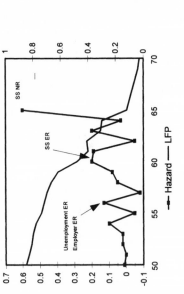

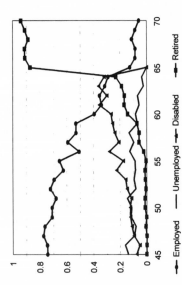

Fig. 15E Hazard and labor force participation rates (*top*), and status of men by age (*bottom*), the United Kingdom

Fig. 15F Hazard and labor force participation rates (*top*), and status of men by age (*bottom*), Germany

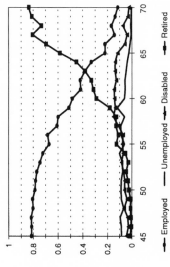

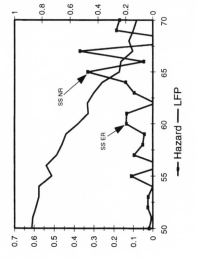

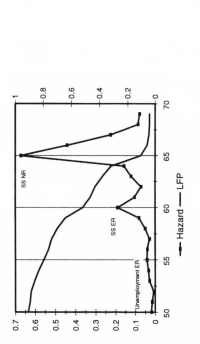

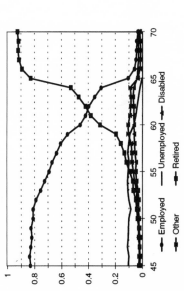

Fig. 15G Hazard and labor force participation rates (*top*), and status of men by age (*bottom*), Spain

Fig. 15H Hazard and labor force participation rates (*top*), and status of men by age (*bottom*), Canada

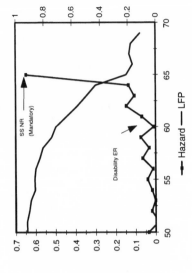

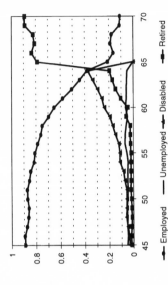

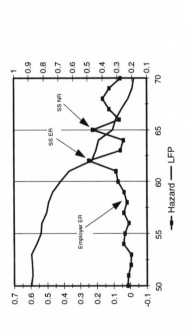

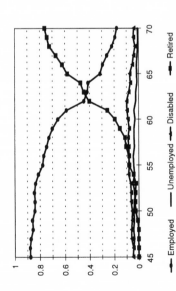

Fig. 15J Hazard and labor force participation rates (*top*), and status of men by age (*bottom*), Sweden

Fig. 15I Hazard and labor force participation rates (*top*), and status of men by age (*bottom*), the United States

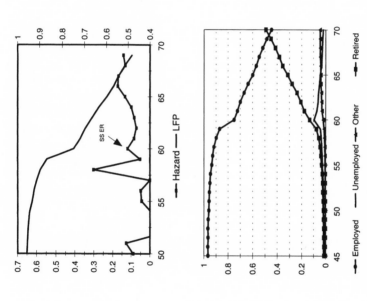

Fig. 15K **Hazard and labor force participation rates** (*top*), **and status of men by age** (*bottom*), **Japan**

fifty-nine. In the United States and Japan, on the other hand, only about 12 percent are receiving unemployment or disability benefits at age fifty-nine.

The relation between these programs and social security is made clear in these figures as well. For example, in France, almost all those who are unemployed at age sixty begin to receive social security benefits at that age and thereafter are officially classified as retired. In the Netherlands, the United Kingdom, Germany, and Sweden, the large fraction of persons receiving disability benefits before age sixty-five then starts to receive social security benefits and is classified as retired.

In short, the conclusion is clear: as was apparent in the more detailed data for Germany, France, and the United States, the collective evidence for all countries combined shows that statutory social security eligibility ages contribute in important ways to early departure from the labor force. In addition, unemployment and disability programs serve as early retirement programs in many countries.

Implicit Tax Rates and Incentives to Retire

The three illustrative country descriptions also suggested that the jump in the departure rate at the social security early retirement age is magnified by greater implicit tax penalties on wage earnings after social security eligibility. In particular, in France and Germany, with large taxes on continued work, the departure rate was much greater than in the United States, with a much smaller implicit tax on work. We explore this relation further here, drawing on the broader evidence from all the countries in the study. Labor force participation and retirement incentives for all eleven countries are summarized in table 1. The countries are ordered by the unused productive capacity of men between the ages of fifty-five and sixty-five, which is explained above and shown in figure 4 above. The panels of figure 15 follow the same order.

We emphasize, first, that, once employees are eligible for social security benefits, a heavy tax burden is often imposed on persons who continue to work. The third to last column of the table shows the implicit tax rate on labor earnings at the early retirement age for each country. It is clear that, in many countries, these tax rates are extremely high, in particular, in those countries at the top of the table—those with the greatest unused labor capacity. Thus, it is evident that the implicit tax on earnings can provide a strong incentive to leave the labor force.

The fourth column of the table shows replacement rates at the early retirement age, which are also very large in many countries, especially those with the greatest unused labor capacity.

Casual perusal of this table suggests a strong relation between unused labor capacity and the tax rate on continued work. To see the relation more clearly, it is useful to divide the countries into three groups: (1) those with high unused capacity (Belgium, France, Italy, the Netherlands, and the United Kingdom); (2) those with medium unused capacity (Germany, Spain, and Canada); and

Table 1   Unused Labor Capacity, Key Plan Features, and the Retirement Rate at Early Retirement Age, by Country

Country	Unused Labor Capacity, 55–65	Men Out of Labor Force, Age 59	Early Retirement Age	Replacement Rate at Early Retirement Age (%)	Accrual in Next Year (%)	Implicit Tax on Earnings in Next Year (%)	Tax Force Early Retirement Age to 69	Hazard Rate at Early Retirement Age (%)
Belgium	67	58	"60"	77	−5.6	82	8.87	33
France	60	53	60	91	−7.0	80	7.25	65
Italy	59	53	"55"	75	−5.8	81	9.20	10
The Netherlands	58	47	"60"	91	−12.8	141	8.32	70
The United Kingdom	55	38	60	48	−10.0	75	3.77	22
Germany	48	34	60	62	−4.1	35	3.45	55
Spain	47	36	60	63	4.2	−23	2.49	20
Canada	45	37	60	20	−1.0	8	2.37	32
The United States	37	26	62	41	0.2	−1	1.57	25
Sweden	35	26	60	54	−4.1	28	2.18	5
Japan	22	13	60	54	−3.9	47	1.65	12

Note: In some countries, the effective early retirement age is ambiguous. The ages in quotation marks are intended to signal cases where the ambiguity is perhaps the greatest, but the availability of unemployment and disability benefits creates ambiguities in other cases as well. The calculations presented in this table and in fig. 17 below are taken from the individual country papers and pertain to the following cases:

Belgium: The social security early retirement age is 60, but employees who are laid off are eligible for large benefits at younger ages. Thus, the accrual, implicit tax, and tax force measures treat unemployment benefits as early retirement benefits available at age 55.

France: Counting social security benefits, available at age 60, but not accounting for guaranteed income benefits for those losing their jobs at age 57 or older.

Italy: Social security benefits for private-sector employees, available at age 60, not counting disability availability.

The Netherlands: In addition to public social security benefits, the calculations account for virtually universal employer private pension benefits. The employer plan is assumed to provide for early retirement at age 60. There is no social security early retirement in the Netherlands, but employer early retirement benefits are commonly available at age 60.

The United Kingdom: Based on social security benefits only, but counting "incapacity" benefits at age 60 as early retirement benefits.

Germany: Counting social security benefits and assuming that a person is eligible for "early" disability benefits.

Spain: Based on Régimen General de la Seguridad Social (the main social security program).

Canada: Counting social security benefits only.

The United States: Counting social security benefits only.

Sweden: Counting social security benefits only. The hazard rate at the early retirement age is the average of the rates between age 59 and age 61.

Japan: Assuming the "diminishing-earnings" profile described in Yashiro and Oshio (chap. 6 in this volume). The employment option is to work in the primary firm until age 60 and then a secondary firm, where the worker would be eligible for the 25 percent wage subsidy were his earnings low enough.

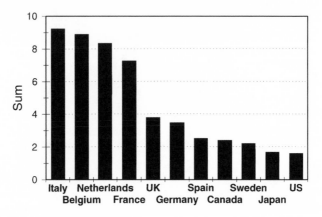

Fig. 16   Sum of tax rates on work

(3) those with low unused capacity (the United States, Sweden, and, in particular, Japan). The average replacement rate at early retirement in the first group is 76.6 percent of median earnings and the average tax on continued labor earnings in that year 91.8 percent. In the third group—with the least unused labor capacity—the average replacement rate at the early retirement age is 50 percent and the tax rate on continued earnings 24.7 percent. These comparisons point to a strong correlation between social security incentives and unused capacity.

There is no completely satisfactory way to summarize the country-specific incentives for early retirement. One crude measure is based on the implicit taxation of labor earnings once a person is eligible for social security benefits. We sum the implied tax rates on continued work beginning with the early retirement age—when a person is first eligible for social security benefits—and running through age sixty-nine. We call this the *tax force* to retire. This measure is reported in the second to last column of table 1. The measure is shown in figure 16, in which the countries follow the same order as in table 1. This figure suggests once again that there is a strong relation between social security penalties on work and retirement. The average tax force to retire is 7.5 in the first group of countries in table 1 and 1.8 in the third group.

The relation is formalized in figure 17, which presents scatter plots of the tax force to retire and unused labor capacity between age fifty-five and age sixty-five. Figures 17a and 17b are based on the sum of tax rates from the early retirement age through age sixty-nine. Japan is included in figure 17a but excluded from figure 17b. Figure 17c is based on the sum of tax rates from age fifty-five to age sixty-nine in all countries. In either case, the relation is clear; there is a strong correspondence between the tax force to retire and unused labor capacity. The relation is nonlinear, however. Thus, in the lower panels of each figure, unused capacity is plotted against the logarithm of the tax force. The solid line in these panels shows the "fit" of the data by a regression of unused capacity on the logarithm of the tax force. About 81 percent of the variation in unused capacity can be explained by the early retirement to age sixty-nine tax force to retire when Japan is included, and 86 percent can be explained when Japan is excluded. When the age fifty-five to age sixty-nine tax force measure is used, 82 percent of the variation is explained, including Japan.[11] Thus, these data suggest a strong relation between social security incentives to quit work and the labor force departure of older workers.

The correspondence between the two should be understood in a broader context, however. There are two distinct issues. First, while it seems apparent that social security provisions do affect labor force participation, it also seems apparent from the country papers that, in at least some instances, the provisions were adopted to encourage older workers to leave the labor force. For example, anecdotal evidence suggests that, in some countries, it was thought that withdrawal of older employees from the workforce would provide more job opportunities for young workers. This possibility does not by itself bring into question a causal interpretation of the relation between plan provisions and retirement. To the extent that it is true, it simply says that, in some instances, the provisions were adopted for a particular reason. And the data show that they worked.

The second issue, however, must temper a causal interpretation of the results. It could be argued that, to some extent at least, the social security provisions were adopted to accommodate existing labor force participation patterns, rather than the patterns being determined by the provisions. For example, early retirement benefits could be provided to support persons who are unable to find work and thus already out of the labor force. While this is surely possible, the weight of the evidence suggests otherwise. The German, French, and U.S. illustrations provide strong evidence that changes in plan provisions induced subsequent changes in retirement rates, not the other way around.

The data in the second column of table 1 above can be interpreted in the light of both these issues. These data show the proportion of men who have left the labor force by age fifty-nine. This is before the official social security early retirement age in all countries, with the exception of Italy, where the early retirement age is younger in some instances. The nonparticipation rate at age fifty-nine varies from a high of 58 percent in Belgium to a low of 13 percent in Japan. A large part of the difference across countries can apparently be ascribed to differences in disability and unemployment insurance provisions. One might think of the labor force participation at this age as the level at which the force of the official social security provisions is first felt. As emphasized above, however, in many instances, these other programs effectively provide

---

11. Japan appears to be an outlier when the first tax force measure is used, although not when the second tax force measure is used. That Japan appears to be an outlier in one version may reflect a weakness of our summary measure of unused capacity. A rather high share of Japan's labor force is self-employed and not covered by the social security system, and the very high participation rate at older ages in Japan is largely in the secondary sector and is often part-time.

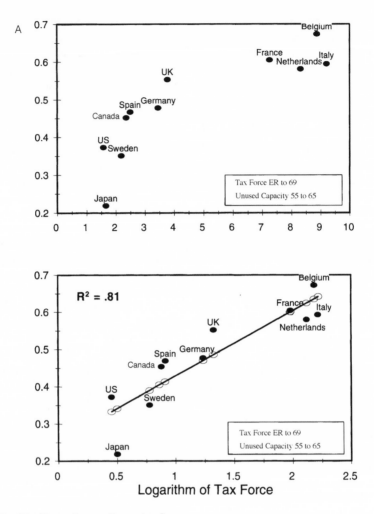

Fig. 17   Unused capacity vs. tax force
Note: ER = early retirement.

early retirement at younger ages than the official social security early retirement age. It is perhaps not surprising that these levels are also strongly related to the unused capacity measures.

Why were these provisions adopted? One possibility, consistent with the first issue above, is that they were part of an effort to facilitate the early withdrawal of older employees from the labor force. And, like the social security provisions themselves, they worked. Again, this does not by itself question the causal relation between the provisions and retirement; to the extent that it is

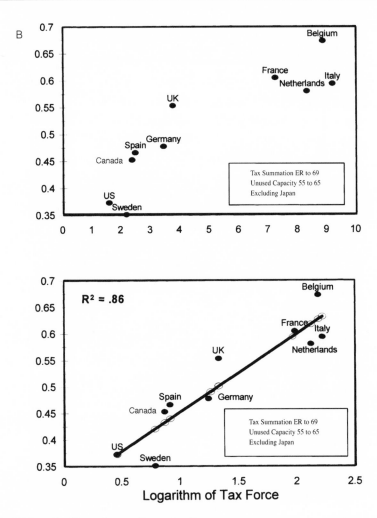

Fig. 17 (cont.)   Unused capacity vs. tax force

true, it suggests a reason for adopting the provisions. But these pseudo–early retirement programs could also have been adopted to accommodate preexisting labor force departure rates, and this possibility must temper a causal interpretation of the relation between program provisions and retirement. Again, however, the data for the three illustrative countries provide strong evidence of a causal link between provisions and retirement. Ultimately, the extent of any reverse causality cannot be determined by these descriptive statistics; it can be addressed only with more detailed analysis.

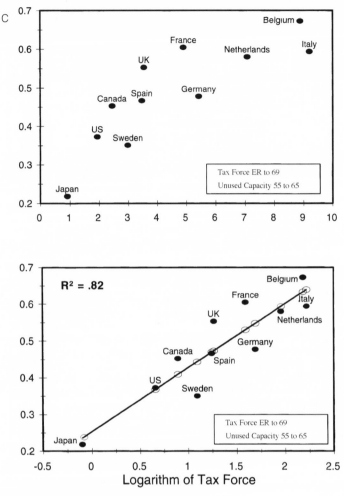

Fig. 17 (cont.)   Unused capacity vs. tax force

Conclusions

The populations in all industrialized countries are aging rapidly, and individual life expectancies are increasing. Yet older workers are leaving the labor force at younger and younger ages. In several countries in our study, participation rates for men aged sixty to sixty-four have fallen from over 70 percent in the early 1960s to less than 20 percent now. This decline in labor force participation magnifies population trends, further increasing the number of retirees relative to the number of persons who are working. Together, these trends have put enormous pressure on the financial solvency of social security systems around the world. Ironically, we argue, the provisions of the social security systems themselves typically contribute to labor force withdrawal.

It is clear that there is a strong correspondence between the age at which benefits are available and departure from the labor force. Social security programs often provide generous retirement benefits at young ages. In addition, the provisions of these programs often imply large financial penalties on labor earnings beyond the social security early retirement age. Furthermore, in many countries, disability and unemployment programs effectively provide early retirement benefits before the official social security early retirement age. We conclude that social security program provisions have indeed contributed to the decline in the labor force participation of older persons, substantially reducing the potential productive capacity of the labor force. It seems evident that, if the trend toward early retirement is to be reversed, a move that will almost surely be dictated by demographic trends, changing the provisions of social security programs that induce early retirement will play a key role.

References

Baker, Michael, and Dwayne Benjamin. 1996. Early retirement provisions and the labour force behavior of older men: Evidence from Canada. University of Toronto, Department of Economics. Mimeo.

Burtless, Gary, and Robert Moffitt. 1984. The effect of social security benefits on the labor supply of the aged. In *Retirement and economic behavior,* ed. H. Aaron and G. Burtless. Washington, D.C.: Brookings.

Kohli, M., M. Rein, A.-M. Guillemard, and H. van Gunsteren, eds. 1991. *Time for retirement: Comparative studies of early exit from the labor force.* Cambridge: Cambridge University Press.

Lumsdaine, Robin L., James H. Stock, and David A. Wise. 1991. Fenêtres et retraites. *Annales d'economie et de statistique* 20/21:219–42.

———. 1992. Three models of retirement: Computational complexity versus predictive validity. In *Topics in the economics of aging,* ed. D. Wise. Chicago: University of Chicago Press.

———. 1994. Pension plan provisions and retirement: Men and women, Medicare, and models. In *Studies in the economics of aging,* ed. D. Wise. Chicago: University of Chicago Press.

OECD. 1995a. The labor market and older workers. Social Policy Studies Series, no. 17. Paris.

———. 1995b. The transition from work to retirement. Social Policy Studies Series, no. 16. Paris.

Stock, James H., and David A. Wise. 1990a. The pension inducement to retire: An option value analysis. In *Issues in the economics of aging,* ed. D. Wise. Chicago: University of Chicago Press.

———. 1990b. Pensions, the option value of work, and retirement. *Econometrica* 58, no. 5:1151–80.

Welch, Finis, and F. Peracchi. 1994. Trends in labor force transitions of older men and women. *Journal of Labor Economics* 12, no. 2:210–42.

1 Social Security and Retirement in Belgium

Pierre Pestieau and Jean-Philippe Stijns

The future of Belgian social security is gloomy for a number of reasons pertaining to macroeconomic, demographic, and political factors. The unemployment rate is about 10 percent and should remain at that level for some time. In spite of recurrent programs to correct the marked imbalance in public finances, the ratio of debt to GNP is still about 130 percent. The ratio between those over sixty years of age and those of working age is expected to double between now and 2030. Finally, the Belgian political process makes any long-term policy reform difficult.

Social security benefit payments in 1990 amounted to 10.60 percent of GDP; this can be contrasted with 5.75 percent in 1961 and 6.46 percent in 1970. In 2048, all other things being equal, the aging of the population will push social security expenditure up by 63 percent. If such an increase cannot be supported, benefits will have to be cut drastically. It is forecast that the poverty rate among elderly people could then jump from the current 4.5 percent to 40 percent by 2040 (Delhausse, Perelman, and Pestieau 1996).

Among the reform options contemplated is a range of measures aimed at increasing the effective participation rate of people over age fifty and eventually raising both the age at which one can draw social security benefits (sixty) and the mandatory retirement age (sixty-five). In that respect, it is crucial to understand the interaction between social security and more generally social

Pierre Pestieau is professor of economics at the University of Liège and a research associate at the Center for Operations Research and Econometrics (CORE) and Delta, Paris. Jean-Philippe Stijns is a researcher at the Centre de Recherche en Economie Publique et de la Population (CREPP), University of Liège.

The authors are grateful to Etienne de Callataÿ, Bernard Delhausse, Arnaud Dellis, Sergio Perelman, and the members of the National Bureau of Economic Research project for helpful comments and to the Belgian Science Foundation (SSTC) for financial support.

insurance, on the one hand, and the labor force behavior of older Belgians, on the other hand. The purpose of this paper is to provide such an understanding.

This paper is divided into three sections. First, we present the relevant evidence on the labor market for older persons in Belgium. Second, we survey the main features of the Belgian social security system, providing some key figures, summarizing the relevant institutional details, and relating the latter to labor market evidence. In the third section, we present a simulation model aimed at assessing the retirement incentives underlying the Belgian social security system. In the appendix, we provide information on data sources, present a brief cross-country comparison, review previous empirical studies, and give an illustration of the fiscal treatment of retirement income.

Before proceeding, two remarks are in order. First, it is important to note that sections 1.1 and 1.3 do not rely on the same institutional setting. Section 1.3 is based on the current social security system after its most recent reform, outlined in section 1.2. The labor market behavior described in section 1.1 is influenced by institutional features some of which have now disappeared (for further discussion, see the appendix).

Second, two types of data are utilized in this study: those from surveys and those from administrative sources. In the first the observation unit is the individual or the household, in the second the benefit received: pension, unemployment compensation, or disability insurance payment. In the latter case, there is the possibility of double-counting as the same individual can draw benefits from two or even three retirement schemes.[1] In order to work with these figures, we had to normalize them.

1.1   The Labor Market Behavior of Older Persons in Belgium

1.1.1   Historical Trends

Figures 1.1 and 1.2 graph the labor force participation rates of men and women in different age groups since 1947. We focus on four age groups. For men, there is a decline in the labor force participation of all these groups. However, since the early 1990s, one observes a slight upturn. The most important drop concerns the age group sixty to sixty-four and to a lesser extent the age group fifty-five to fifty-nine. Note that, for both men and women over age sixty, the participation rate is negligible, at least as officially recorded. As we show below (figs. 1.7 and 1.8), most of the decline in participation rates before age sixty is due to mandatory early retirement programs (*prépension*) (for further discussion, see sec. 1.2.6).

The female labor force experienced a contrasting evolution. Indeed, there

---

1. Most commonly, pension receipts from public and private social security systems. However, the various types of social insurance are mutually exclusive in Belgium.

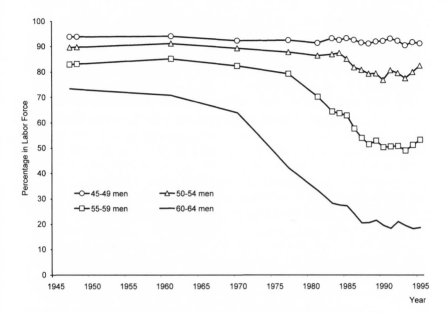

Fig. 1.1   Historical trends in the labor force participation of older men
Source: Federal Planning Bureau and Institut National de Statistique.

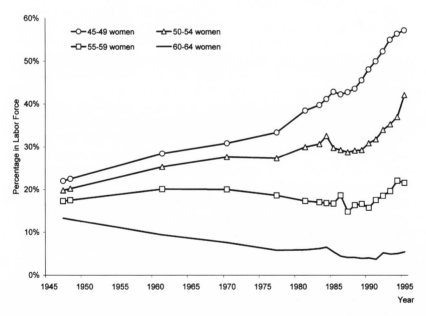

Fig. 1.2   Historical trends in the labor force participation of older women
Source: Federal Planning Bureau and Institut National de Statistique.

are two opposite trends: a structural trend of increasing participation and a downward trend similar to that of men that is the result of an explicit policy aimed at forcing elderly workers out of the labor force. For the youngest age groups, those between age forty-five and age fifty-four, participation is rising; for the oldest group, it is declining. For the intermediate age group, fifty-five to fifty-nine, one observes a contrasting evolution: a decline up to the mid-1980s, then an increase. The increase in the labor force participation of women aged fifty-five to fifty-nine is particularly marked since 1992. Whereas before 1992 women were allowed to retire as early as age fifty-five and retirement was mandatory at age sixty, in 1992 the early retirement age was raised to sixty and the mandatory retirement age to sixty-five—an attempt to restore parity to the rules governing men's and women's retirement behavior.

To explain this trend in labor market participation, it is tempting to consider the extent of social security generosity and particularly its evolution over time. Two remarks here are in order. First, given that in general there is no way to draw social security benefits before age sixty, earlier retirement is financed by unemployment insurance, disability insurance, or mandatory sectoral programs of early retirement. Second, such low participation rates can be explained not only in terms of secular trends witnessed elsewhere but also as a consequence of an unprecedentedly high level of unemployment.

In Belgium, since 1956, the entire workforce is covered by the social security system and more generally by the various social insurance schemes. To measure the generosity of social insurance, we can use the increasing percentage of men (fig. 1.3) and women (fig. 1.4) drawing social security, disability insurance, and mandatory early retirement benefits. The increase is impressive. Fewer than 40 percent of men and 37 percent of women over age fifty-five in 1961 drew such benefits, whereas more than 80 percent of men and 66 percent of women over age fifty-five in 1995 did so.

Another way to assess the generosity of benefit payments over time is to consider the evolution of the replacement rate. We use as an indicator of gross replacement the ratio of average full career pension over average wage (see the appendix). This is far from giving an accurate picture of what is going on, however. Hence, in figure 1.5 we also give the net replacement rate for a couple with one wage earner—which is much higher than the gross rate. In 1994, the gross rate was 0.55 and the net rate 0.85. Wage incomes are subject to high payroll taxes and progressive income taxes, whereas pension benefits are hardly taxed (there is an important tax exemption on the income tax and a very small payroll tax). As shown in figure 1.5, the net replacement rate was quite steady until 1982 and then increased rapidly. Lately, there has been a trend toward taxing retirement income. One can thus expect that the gap between net and gross replacement rates will narrow.

Table 1.1 provides net replacement rates for alternative cases with respect to wage level and marital status. It clearly appears that the net replacement rate reaches its highest level for low-wage, single-earner households (0.91). High-

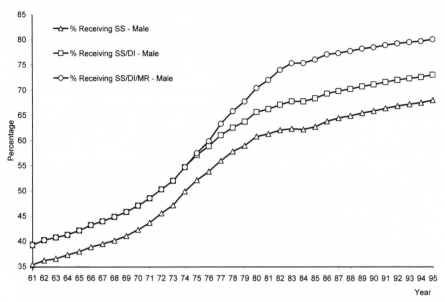

Fig. 1.3   Receipt of social security (SS), disability insurance (DI), and mandatory retirement (MR), age 55 and over, males

Source: Bouillot and Perelman (1995); own computations.

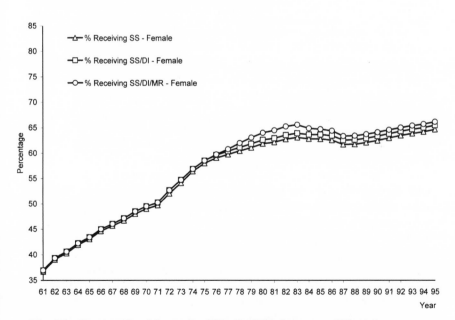

Fig. 1.4   Receipt of social security (SS), disability insurance (DI), and mandatory retirement (MR), age 55 and over, females

Source: Bouillot and Perelman (1995); own computations.

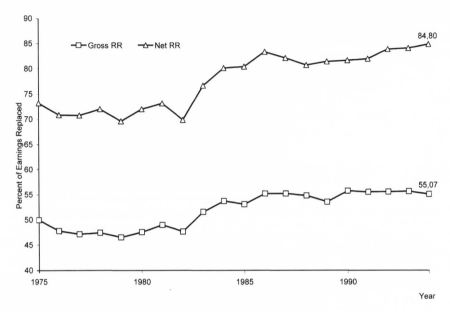

Fig. 1.5   Social security replacement rates (RRs) over time
Source: Own computations.

Table 1.1   **Net Rates of Replacement in 1991, Complete Career**

	Workers in the Household[a]					
	2			1		
Wage ratio to average wage	⅔	1	2	⅔	1	2
Replacement ratio (%)	81	73	53	91	80	60

Source: EUROSTAT (1992).
[a]The rate is the same for a single and for a married person whose spouse works as well.

wage households where the wage earner is single or where both the husband and the wife work show a much lower replacement ratio (0.53).

Comparing the time-series patterns of labor force participation and those of net replacement rates yields a mixed picture. On the one hand, there is some negative correlation between the generosity of the program and the labor force participation of men and, to a lesser extent, women aged sixty to sixty-five, but the correlation is far from perfect. Furthermore, one must look elsewhere for the reasons for the decline in labor force participation among those aged fifty to sixty. As we shall see, over the last several decades Belgium has induced or even forced large numbers of older workers to retire in order to open up jobs for the young.

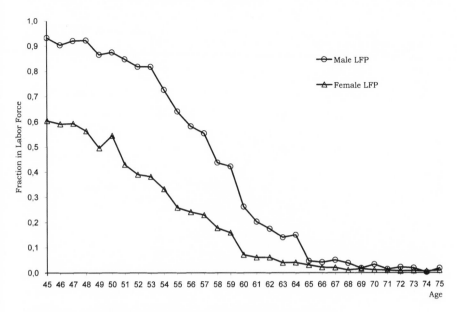

Fig. 1.6   Labor force participation (LFP) rates by age and sex
Source: Institut National de Statistique.

1.1.2   Labor Market Behavior in 1995

By focusing on the most recent period, one can get a clearer and more complete picture of labor market behavior as well as of the generosity of social security and other programs. The age pattern of participation for men and women is depicted in figure 1.6. At age forty-five, the participation rate of men is close to 94 percent, much higher than that of women (60 percent). There is then a continuous gradual decline for women; for men, the decline is slow until age fifty-two, at which point the pace steepens. Hence, the participation gap closes substantially by age sixty. By age seventy, participation rates are negligible for both sexes.

Figure 1.7 considers in more detail the allocation of time among men as they age, by distinguishing alternative social insurance statuses: (i) employed; (ii) unemployed; (iii) disabled; (iv) benefiting from an early retirement scheme; and (v) retired. The bottom line shows the share of men employed. The rate of employment declines slowly after age forty-eight, then at a higher pace after age fifty-three, reaching 50 percent at age fifty-seven. Mainly the self-employed work beyond age sixty-five.

First, from age forty-six to age sixty-five, the rate of unemployment appears quite stable. In reality, relatively more older workers than younger workers are unemployed, but most workers over age fifty-five are not included in government unemployment statistics. Nonemployment is also taken care of by disability insurance and particularly mandatory early retirement programs, to

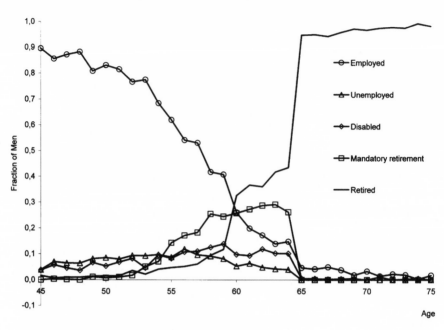

Fig. 1.7   Distribution of activities of men by age
Source: Institut National de Statistique, Labor Force Survey 1995.

which we return in section 1.2.6. The percentage of retirees under age sixty may be surprising (although still low). Apart from the usual statistical noise found in surveys, the majority of unemployed persons age fifty-five and over are not included in unemployment statistics and are classified as retired. Naturally, the number of pensioners increases quickly between age sixty and age sixty-five.

The same exercise is repeated for women in figure 1.8. Not surprisingly, the rate of employment is much lower for women than for men and declines quickly over age sixty. First, while women over age sixty are legally permitted to work, many are entitled to full benefits. Second, unemployment benefits are not available to women over age sixty, no matter how many years of service they have on record. Since until 1992 women could draw retirement benefits as early as age fifty-five, the share of pensioners in 1995 is still important for women aged fifty-eight and over. Another interesting feature is the share of women classified in other "statuses," most likely housework.

1.1.3   Income Sources of Older Persons

Figure 1.9 graphs the various sources of income of older households. Since our data come from the CSB (Centrum voor Sociaal Beleid, Universiteit Antwerpen) Panel of Belgian Households, the unit is the household, and the age is that of the head of the family. We consider the distribution of income across

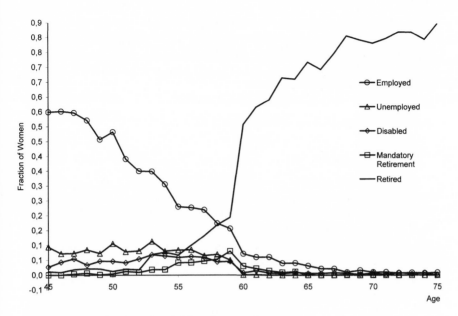

Fig. 1.8   Distribution of activities of women by age
Source: Institut National de Statistique, Labor Force Survey 1995.

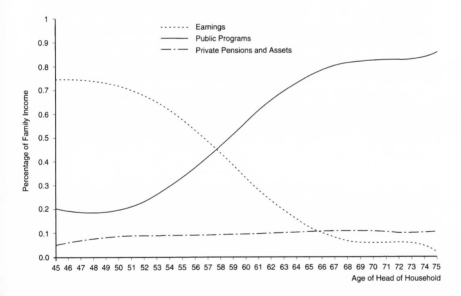

Fig. 1.9   Breakdown of source of family income
Source: Own computations; Centrum voor Sociaal Beleid, Universiteit Antwerpen.

three sources: earnings, social security and maintenance income, and capital income including private (occupational) pensions. Private pension income is indeed very small and cannot be distinguished from the return on other financial investments. The predominance of public programs among the resources of older persons is quite striking.

1.2   Key Features of the Belgian Social Security System

1.2.1   A Complex System

Belgium has three major pension schemes, one for public employees, one for the self-employed, and one for employees in the private sector (see also OECD 1994; and de Callataÿ and Turtelboom 1997). These are supplemented by a welfare scheme guaranteeing a minimum old age pension and by mandatory early retirement programs. Although these schemes operate under quite different rules for benefits and contributions, they are characterized by heavy government intervention and are financially unfunded.

In addition to these schemes, which are known as the first pillar of the pension system, private retirement accounts are also available; they are funded and financed by employers (the second pillar) or individual savings (the third pillar). These parallel schemes benefit from tax breaks; they are by no means obligatory. In any case, so far they have been limited in size: assets of private pension funds amount to only about 10 percent of GDP (EEC 1994), whereas social security pension rights represent more than 250 percent (Bouillot and Perelman 1995; OECD 1994). Table 1.2 provides data on average benefits and number of pensioners for the three major social security schemes plus the guaranteed minimum pension and the mandatory early retirement schemes.

Private-sector employees represent by far the most important category in terms of overall benefits and number of pensioners. They are the main focus of our study. Civil servants have on average the highest retirement benefits.

Table 1.2   Categories of Pensions Schemes, 1995

	Benefits as % of GDP	Number of Pensioners (1,000)[a]	Average Amount in Relative Terms
Private-sector employees	5.72	1,347	87.3
Self-employed	.71	246	59.1
Mandatory early retirement	.64	128	102.8
Minimum old age pensioners	.14	50	56.7
Public-sector employees	3.38	405	170.7
All schemes	10.59	2,175	100.0

Sources: Bouillot and Perelman (1995); own calculations.

[a]Including surviving spouses. There is the possibility of double-counting.

1.2.2   Private-Sector Employees

Employee pensions were organized in the private sector much later than in the public sector. Prior to 1924, an optional insurance subsidized by the government allowed interested workers to accumulate capital in a savings bank, the Caisse d'Epargne et de Retraite (CGER). In 1926, a compulsory funded scheme came into effect. After the Second World War, this system was gradually replaced, first by a mixed system, then by an exclusively pay-as-you-go system in 1967.

Private-sector pensions are financed mainly by payroll taxes and marginally by government transfers (the latter represent about 11 percent of overall benefits). In contrast to benefits, there is no limit on contributions. Payroll tax rates are 7.5 percent for employees and 8.86 percent for employers.

Private-sector employees can retire between the ages of sixty and sixty-five; they are entitled to a pension provided that they have fulfilled two-thirds of a complete career of forty-five years, that is, provided that they have worked for at least thirty years. The pension is based on salary during the entire career, length of the career, and an accrual factor that depends on marital status when retired. The pension benefit formula for private-sector employees can be sketched by the following equation, which assumes no employment history interruption but a career of x (≤ 45) years:

$$B_m = \frac{x}{45}0.75y, \quad \text{for married pensioners with only one pension,}$$

or

$$B_s = \frac{x}{45}0.60y, \quad \begin{array}{l}\text{for a household with more than one pension,}\\ \text{or for a single pensioner,}\end{array}$$

where y is the average of earnings duly indexed. In x as in y, years of unemployment or of sickness are accounted for as "years of career."[2] Surviving spouses receive B_s; they are treated as a single pensioner.[3] There are floors and ceilings: in 1996, the minimum household pension amounted to 56 percent of average net wages, and pensionable earnings are subject to a low ceiling, only 20 percent above average gross wages.

Both pensions and the ceiling are indexed to consumer prices. Occasional discretionary increases reflect wage growth; the last such increase was granted in 1991. The frequency of discretionary increases is unclear. Whether they must occur every other year is very rarely debated. This is not the only instance

---

2. Before 1996, women received a full pension for a forty-year career; they are now subject to the same regulations as men but will enjoy a transition period (of thirteen years). Before 1992, the pension was reduced by 5 percent for each year of retirement before the official retirement age.

3. Survival benefits are prorated with respect to the maximum number of years the late worker could have possibly worked from the age of twenty (relative maximum and minimum numbers apply, however).

when ambiguity is built into the system for political reasons. Minimum pensions are also linked to the consumer price index and are increased regularly.

1.2.3   Public-Sector Pensions

The social security scheme for public employees is the oldest.[4] Pensions are paid out of the general government budget. Public employees are taxed for the survivor's pension scheme at a rate of only 7.5 percent. Civil servants' retirement benefits are viewed as deferred income.

The mandatory retirement age is now sixty-five for both men and women. However, it is possible to opt for an incomplete career and take retirement at age sixty. Further, the legal retirement age is sixty or even younger for certain sectors of the workforce (e.g., teachers, military personnel).

Pension benefits are the product of the reference salary (the average salary for the five years preceding retirement), the number of years of service, and a benefit accrual factor (*tantième*), which ranges from one-thirtieth for university professors and magistrates to one-sixtieth for most civil servants. The product of career length and the accrual factor represents the nominal replacement rate, which cannot exceed 75 percent of the reference salary.

In addition to this limit, the civil servants' pension cannot exceed an absolute ceiling, about three times average net wages in 1995. There is also a floor equivalent to 56 percent of mean net wages for a single civil servant and 70 percent for a married civil servant. Except when computing this minimum pension, the household structure does not matter.

Finally, public-sector pensions are automatically indexed to salaries (*péréquation*); in other words, public-sector pensioners share in the economic growth that occurs during their retirement.

1.2.4   The Self-Employed

In 1956, compulsory insurance was set up for the self-employed, with proportional contributions giving the right to a fixed pension based on the number of years worked. In 1984, this fixed-rate system was replaced by one calculated proportionally on actual earnings. Expenses are covered by individual contributions[5] and an annual government transfer of funds (37 percent of overall benefits) from general revenues.

Pensions can be taken as early as age sixty, but the pension for men is reduced by 5 percent annually up to age sixty-five. The self-employed are also still subject to the rules applied to private-sector employees before 1992, except that imputed incomes are still used for years prior 1984.

---

4. Dating back to the law of 21 July 1844 covering civil and ecclesiastical pensions. The scheme as it stands today covers civil servants in the federal government and in the regional and local authorities and employees in certain public enterprises.

5. The rate is 16.7 percent for incomes below BF 1.8 million and 12.27 percent for incomes above.

1.2.5 Fiscal Treatment of Pension Benefits

Direct taxes on social security income are low in Belgium owing to the allowance of a large tax deduction. Payroll taxes are very low and concern only very high pensions. Beneficiaries receiving the highest pension benefits in the private sector are subject to an average tax rate of 9.8 percent—if there is no other income. First, note that public-sector retirees draw relatively higher benefits and pay much higher taxes. Second, the 9.8 percent rate applies only to households without additional sources of income. (The appendix provides more details.)

1.2.6 Mandatory Early Retirement

Compared to the United States and, to a lesser extent, other European Union countries, the social treatment of elderly workers in Belgium has two main original features: mandatory early retirement plans are widespread for those under sixty, the age of eligibility for social security benefits, and civil servants (by law) and public-sector employees (by collective agreement) cannot work after the mandatory retirement age of sixty-five. The minimum legal age for mandatory early retirement is sixty for workers in industries without a collective agreement (involving employers'/employees' joint responsibilities) and fifty-eight for workers covered by newly concluded collective agreements. If a preexisting collective agreement is renewed, lower minimum mandatory retirement ages are allowed than would be imposed by current law. The employer is normally required to hire one (usually younger) unemployed worker in the place of each retired worker.

The minimum age for mandatory retirement can be lowered to fifty in industries experiencing structural problems. These industries also need not replace the retired worker—an exemption granted by the government on a case-by-case basis.

This somewhat ad hoc system leads to a large variety of mandatory early retirement ages. In any case, mandatory early retirement implies that workers cannot draw social security benefits before the age of sixty-five (sixty for female workers).[6] Benefits are, however, computed as if workers had kept their jobs until the regular retirement age. These schemes are cofinanced by the employer and the government through unemployment compensation. The employer must pay the worker half the difference between unemployment compensation and the worker's former net wages.[7]

Table 1.3 shows the evolution of mandatory retirement as a percentage of population since 1985. Mandatory retirement programs concern only private-sector employees. They date back to 1976; their overall importance has been

6. The difference in the treatment of female and male workers will disappear, as a result of the 1996 reform, as the social security rules are gradually changed to achieve parity across genders.
7. Pensionable earnings are subject to a ceiling, and minimum benefits are defined by collective agreement. Fiscal rules are applied, but payroll taxes are low, and a large deductible is granted.

Table 1.3   Early Retirement in Percentage of Age-Group Population

	1985	1986	1987	1988	1989	1990	1991	1992	1993	1994	1995
55–64:											
Men	7.24	5.79	9.59	10.10	10.48	10.93	10.93	10.74	10.78	10.71	10.42
Women	1.12	.81	1.64	1.71	1.73	1.74	1.67	1.51	1.35	1.22	1.19
Total	4.10	3.06	5.52	5.81	6.01	6.25	6.22	6.05	6.00	5.91	5.76
55–59:											
Men	11.57	13.78	15.19	15.58	15.86	16.46	16.15	15.15	15.42	15.64	15.49
Women	2.53	3.33	4.10	4.43	4.58	4.74	4.81	4.60	4.43	4.22	4.15
Total	6.91	8.41	9.49	9.85	10.08	10.45	10.35	9.76	9.82	9.82	9.72
60–64:											
Men	16.82	18.80	20.50	21.49	22.54	23.86	24.59	25.53	26.01	26.50	26.52
Women	.00	.00	.00	.00	.00	.00	.00	.00	.00	.00	.00
Total	7.93	8.84	9.65	10.16	10.68	11.32	11.68	12.16	12.40	12.67	12.70

Source: Office National pour l'Emploi.

quite steady since 1987. Yet, over the last five years, one can observe a slightly contrasting evolution across age groups. Whereas the rate of early retirement between age fifty-five and age fifty-nine has recently declined, that for those aged sixty to sixty-four has increased.

Indeed, mandatory retirement is now progressively phased out. Over the last decade, the legal minimum age for mandatory retirement in the case of a new collective agreement has steadily increased from fifty to fifty-eight. In 1992, retirement at age sixty was made more attractive (see the appendix) with a view to switching from mandatory early retirement to so-called flexible retirement. However, in 1995, mandatory early retirement still represented about 15 percent of men aged fifty-five to fifty-nine and 25 percent of men aged sixty to sixty-four.

Very few women are covered by these programs, and, if they are, they are under age sixty. The reason is simple: the mandatory retirement age for private-sector female employees was sixty prior to 1996, and, furthermore, early retirement involved mainly the traditional industrial sectors (e.g., coal, steel, and glass), in which the majority of workers are men.

1.2.7   Guaranteed Minimum Old Age Income

The guaranteed minimum old age income program was initiated in 1946 and was extended, taking its current form, in 1969. No personal contributions are required as it is fully financed by the government. It is a means-tested welfare program. This program supplies assistance to all persons who have reached the legal pension age. From table 1.2 above, one can see that the benefits provided by this scheme are equivalent to 56 percent of average social security receipts.

1.2.8   Social Security and the Labor Market

An alternative means of analyzing labor force trends is through the evolution of the hazard rates that provide at each age the percentage increase of the labor force retiring from work (relative to the participation rate of workers at the previous age). Figure 1.10 shows the hazard rate for men. In it one observes a number of spikes. Those after age sixty-five are not relevant: they are generated by a very small labor force (negligible denominator) and cannot be accounted for by any feature of the social security system. The increase in the number of workers leaving the labor force at age sixty, the age of eligibility for social security, is striking. The spike at age sixty-five corresponds to the mandatory retirement constraint. The spike at age fifty-eight coincides with the standard age of mandatory early retirement.

In figure 1.11, the hazard rate for women is plotted. Focusing again on the relevant spikes, we note that the most pronounced spike occurs at age sixty, the mandatory retirement age for private-sector female employees before 1996. The spike at age sixty-five is occasioned by the civil servants who retire at that age. Before 1992, women were eligible for early retirement as early as age

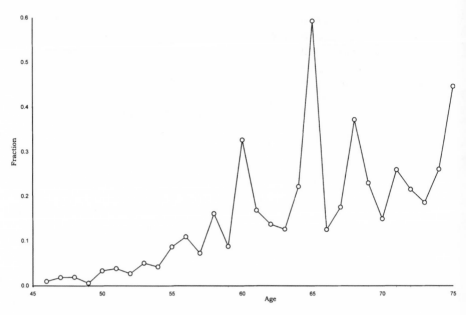

Fig. 1.10   Hazard rate out of the labor force for men
Source: Institut National de Statistique, Labor Force Survey.

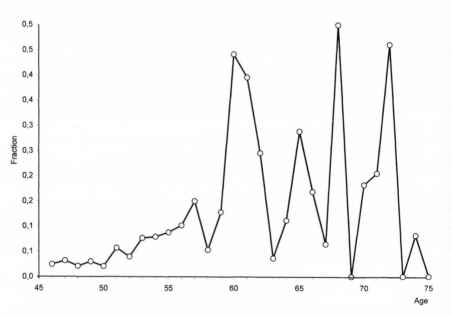

Fig. 1.11   Hazard rate out of the labor force for women
Source: Institut National de Statistique, Labor Force Survey.

fifty-five;[8] this, combined with mandatory early retirement schemes, can explain the small spike at age fifty-eight. Finally, Pepermans (1992) has shown that women in Belgium tend to retire the same year as their husbands, that is, at an average age that is three years younger than their husbands' age at retirement.

1.2.9   The Future

Will Belgium be able to afford its publicly financed social security system, operating entirely on a pay-as-you-go basis, in the first half of the next century? This question is clearly at the heart of political debate in Belgium, as it is in many other countries. To answer it, two approaches have been used.

The first consists in assessing the cost of the benefits to which the system is currently committed, that is, the present value of current and future benefits and contributions. According to Bouillot and Perelman (1995), gross commitments—which cover the social security wealth of all workers—have risen from 164.4 percent of GDP in 1961 to 292.5 percent of GDP in 1985 and will amount to 388.8 percent of GDP in 2040. Bouillot and Perelman measure gross commitments as the present value of the rights to benefits that living generations have acquired during their careers. This approach identifies as the most important characteristic of the Belgian social security system the fact that it is a defined-benefit system. Taking another point of view, the OECD (1994) estimates the present value of future pension expenditures in 1990 to be equal to 571 percent of GDP. On the other hand, the present value of future contributions ceteris paribus would represent only 406 percent of GDP, thus leaving Belgium with net commitments of merely 165 percent of GDP in 1990.

The second approach consists in projecting the annual increase in pension benefits under the assumption that the replacement rate is kept constant. According to the Belgian Planning Bureau, under plausible hypotheses private-sector pension expenditures, which represent about 6.6 percent of GDP, would jump to about 11 percent by 2030 (Englert, Fasquelle, and Weeman 1994). Note that these figures do not encompass civil servants' pensions. This oversight introduces a downward bias since former public-sector employees will undoubtedly constitute a growing share of retirees in the future. Indeed, in a recent study, de Callataÿ and Turtelboom (1997) show in their baseline projection that public-sector pension benefits would more than double as a percentage of GDP from 1995 to 2030.

Among the reform options debated, the increased participation of older workers is often stressed. As de Callataÿ and Turtelboom (1997, 30) write: "Labor market participation in Belgium is currently so low—and, correspondingly, the elderly dependency ratio so high—that any return to labor market participation and unemployment rates seen in other industrialized countries

---

8. Albeit with a 5 percent benefit reduction per year of anticipation on top of the current prorated rate, i.e., the same system as that applied to men before 1992.

will soften the demographic impact on pension expenditures. This underscores the critical contribution to the public finances that could be made by policy measures that would strengthen labor market performance in Belgium over the coming years."

1.3   Retirement Incentives

In this section, we use a simulation model aimed at assessing the incentives that the social security system gives workers to retire (this methodology is described in Diamond and Gruber, chap. 11 in this volume). We first focus on social security per se, which provides benefits only at age sixty. However, section 1.3.3 investigates the case of a worker who is entitled to unemployment benefits.

1.3.1   Base-Case Results

Table 1.4 shows the base-case results. The base-case worker was born in 1930. Having begun to work at age twenty, his career (forty-five years) will be complete in 1995. His wage profile is given in figure 1A.1 below in the appendix. He is entitled to social security benefits from 1990 on, that is, when he reaches the age of sixty. His wife is three years younger than he is and has never worked. He no longer has dependent children and is receiving standard fiscal deductions.

Consider first the replacement-rate column. From age fifty-five to age fifty-nine, pension benefits are not available, but payroll taxes must, of course, be

Table 1.4   **Base-Case Incentive Calculations**

Last Year of Work	Replacement Rate	SSW[a]	Accrual[a]	Accrual Rate	Tax/ Subsidy
Age 54	. . .	4,193,746	0	0	0
Age 55	. . .	4,247,922	54,176	.013	−.129
Age 56	. . .	4,304,178	56,256	.013	−.134
Age 57	. . .	4,365,004	60,826	.014	−.145
Age 58	. . .	4,427,306	62,302	.014	−.148
Age 59	.749	4,493,147	65,841	.015	−.157
Age 60	.771	4,285,110	−208,037	−.046	.496
Age 61	.794	4,076,567	−208,543	−.049	.497
Age 62	.817	3,870,541	−206,026	−.051	.491
Age 63	.839	3,665,171	−205,370	−.053	.489
Age 64	.863	3,466,790	−198,381	−.054	.473
Age 65	.874	3,244,903	−221,888	−.064	.529
Age 66	.882	3,027,124	−217,779	−.067	.519
Age 67	.890	2,827,248	−199,876	−.066	.476
Age 68	.898	2,632,906	−194,342	−.069	.463
Age 69	.905	2,448,357	−184,549	−.070	.440

[a]Both SSW (social security wealth) and ΔSSW (accrual) are in Belgian francs ($1.00 ≈ BF 32.00).

paid in the case of continued work. At age sixty, the first year benefits can be claimed, the replacement rate is roughly 75 percent. The level of pension increases between the ages of sixty and sixty-four because of career completion and between the ages of sixty-five and sixty-nine because low-earnings years are replaced by higher-earnings years. This explains the overtime profile of the replacement rate. Note that, at age sixty-five, it is equal to 0.863 and close to the one given in figure 1.5 and table 1.1 above.[9] The next three columns show the evolution of social security wealth.

Additional years of work affect the computation of social security wealth in five ways: (i) Payroll taxes are paid (negative effect). (ii) As long as the career lasts for fewer than forty-five years, benefits are increased by a factor of one-sixtieth (i.e., $0.75 \times 1/45$) (positive effect). (iii) An additional year of work can replace a previous low-earnings year (positive effect). (iv) An additional year of work at age sixty and beyond implies fewer years over which benefits can be claimed (negative effect). (v) There is always some chance that the worker and/or his spouse will die (negative effect). These five effects operate differently between the ages of fifty-five and fifty-nine, between the ages of sixty and sixty-four, and over age sixty-four:

	i	ii	iii	iv	v
55–59	−	+	0	0	0
60–64	−	+	0	−	−
65+	−	0	+	−	−

The period from age sixty to age sixty-five is one during which the system is actuarially unfair. Working one additional year brings for a couple a gross benefit increase of $1/45 \times 0.75$ for all coming years but a loss of a full year's pension benefits. It is, therefore, not surprising that, during this period, social security wealth decreases rapidly. Naturally, beyond age sixty-five, when the work career is complete, social security wealth declines even more quickly. One must add, however, that very few people have the opportunity of working beyond age sixty-five; in other words, there is no real choice beyond that age.

Between the ages of fifty-five and fifty-nine, the effect ii dominates effect i. Consequently, social security wealth increases moderately, and workers are subject to small subsidy rates. Therefore, one cannot rely solely on social security incentives to explain retirement between age fifty-five and age fifty-nine. In Belgium, most cases of retirement between those ages are induced by existing social insurance schemes: unemployment, disability, sickness, etc. We return to this point in section 1.3.3 below. Of course, mandatory early retirement also plays an important role here, as explained above.

9. There is a 6 percent difference between our results and those of EUROSTAT. This difference is the result of the fact that the reference for wages is the median for us and the mean for EUROSTAT.

Table 1.5   **Incentive Calculations—Single Worker**

Last Year of Work	Replacement Rate	SSW[a]	Accrual[a]	Accrual Rate	Tax/Subsidy
Age 54	...	2,742,452	0	0	0
Age 55	...	2,740,106	−2,346	−.001	.006
Age 56	...	2,740,954	848	.000	−.002
Age 57	...	2,744,944	3,990	.001	−.010
Age 58	...	2,752,092	7,148	.003	−.017
Age 59	.696	2,762,366	10,274	.004	−.024
Age 60	.713	2,531,229	−231,137	−.084	.551
Age 61	.726	2,283,319	−247,910	−.098	.590
Age 62	.736	2,030,821	−252,498	−.111	.601
Age 63	.746	1,785,965	−244,857	−.121	.583
Age 64	.756	1,548,965	−237,000	−.133	.564
Age 65	.756	1,292,551	−256,414	−.166	.611
Age 66	.756	1,049,869	−242,681	−.188	.578
Age 67	.756	820,740	−229,129	−.218	.546
Age 68	.756	604,909	−215,832	−.263	.514
Age 69	.756	402,269	−202,640	−.335	.483

[a]Both SSW (social security wealth) and ΔSSW (accrual) are in Belgian francs ($1.00 ≈ BF 32.00).

Over age sixty, the accrual rate steadily decreases from −5 percent to −7 percent, with a corresponding tax rate turning around 50 percent. This shock is explained by the sudden availability of benefits coupled with increasing mortality. Working at the age of sixty-five corresponds to the largest negative accrual since, above that age, effect iii is the only potentially positive effect on social security wealth.

1.3.2 Other Cases

Table 1.5 explores the same questions for a single worker. In this case, payroll taxes are the same as before, but the expected benefits are lower. The theoretical gross replacement rate for a married couple is 0.75 and for a single person only 0.60. Further, the life expectancy of a woman who is three years younger than her husband exceeds that of her husband by seven years. It is, therefore, not surprising that both social security wealth and replacement rates are consistently lower for a single worker than for a married couple the husband of which is working. Thus, over age fifty-five, additional work is but very little subsidized. Over age sixty, tax rates are consistently higher for single than for married workers. It is striking to compare the levels of social security wealth across these two tables, which reveal a quite high implicit tax imposed on single male workers.

Table 1.6 considers an alternative earnings history. We assume that the worker started to work at age twenty-five and that he has an incomplete earnings history through age seventy. We further assume that he contemplates

Table 1.6   **Incentive Calculations—Incomplete Earnings Profile**

Last Year of Work	Replacement Rate	SSW[a]	Accrual[a]	Accrual Rate	Tax/ Subsidy
Age 54	. . .	3,414,293	0	0	0
Age 55	. . .	3,475,489	61,196	.018	−.146
Age 56	. . .	3,537,615	62,126	.018	−.148
Age 57	. . .	3,600,628	63,013	.018	−.150
Age 58	. . .	3,664,527	63,899	.018	−.152
Age 59	.609	3,729,189	64,662	.018	−.154
Age 60	.626	3,568,662	−160,527	−.043	.382
Age 61	.644	3,408,441	−160,221	−.045	.382
Age 62	.661	3,249,660	−158,781	−.047	.378
Age 63	.679	3,092,053	−157,607	−.048	.375
Age 64	.696	2,951,595	−140,458	−.045	.335
Age 65	.713	2,819,284	−132,311	−.045	.315
Age 66	.731	2,689,043	−130,240	−.046	.310
Age 67	.748	2,566,851	−122,192	−.045	.291
Age 68	.766	2,444,245	−122,606	−.048	.292
Age 69	.783	2,327,145	−117,100	−.048	.279

[a]Both SSW (social security wealth) and ΔSSW (accrual) are in Belgian francs ($1.00 \approx$ BF 32.00).

working that long even though we know that in Belgium this is almost impossible. With such a history, before age sixty there is an important work subsidy, and at age sixty and after the tax for working one more year is lower than in the base-case calculation.

In table 1.7, we summarize the results obtained under alternative assumptions about lifetime earnings, the discount rate, survival probability, and the gender-age gap. Not surprisingly, these assumptions lead to expected differences in terms of the replacement rate and social security wealth. For example, with an older wife or with a higher mortality risk, social security wealth is lower; with higher lifetime income, the replacement rate is lower, and social security wealth is higher. Yet the tax rate is relatively steady for all these cases, ranging from 0.382 (incomplete history) to 0.583 (tenth percentile). Figures 1.12–1.16 present the tax-subsidy age profile for these alternative assumptions.

1.3.3 Incentive Computations for a Worker Entitled to Unemployment Benefits

Entitlement to unemployment benefits[10] is available to workers in case of (involuntary) layoff. It has consequences both in terms of replacement income and in terms of pension rights. We have taken unemployment insurance net

10. We have chosen unemployment compensation as replacement income. We could have chosen instead early mandatory retirement or disability benefits. But, in general, mandatory early retirement is not chosen voluntarily and implies retirement at age sixty-five. Disability benefits are in principle subject to some screening.

Table 1.7 **Incentive Calculations—Summary of Other Cases (last year of work is age 59)**

Case	Replacement Rate	SSW[a]	Accrual[a]	Accrual Rate	Tax/ Subsidy
Base case	.771	4,285,110	−208,037	−.046	.496
Single worker	.713	2,531,229	−231,137	−.084	.551
Diminishing earnings	.764	3,802,341	−219,650	−.055	.535
Incomplete history	.626	3,568,662	−160,527	−.043	.382
10th percentile	.894	3,919,982	−195,212	−.047	.583
90th percentile	.695	5,420,567	−372,833	−.064	.564
Discount = 6%	.771	2,345,182	−195,993	−.077	.467
Discount = 1%	.771	6,229,508	−195,272	−.030	.465
Higher mortality risk	.771	3,831,585	−207,276	−.051	.494
Lower mortality risk	.771	4,651,405	−195,056	−.040	.465
Wife born 1927	.771	3,684,036	−212,455	−.055	.506
Wife born 1939	.771	4,608,155	−195,316	−.041	.465

[a]Both SSW (social security wealth) and ΔSSW (accrual) are in Belgian francs ($1.00 ≈ BF 32.00).

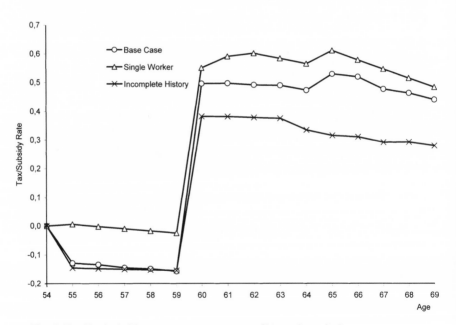

Fig. 1.12   Tax/subsidy rates across career profiles and marital status

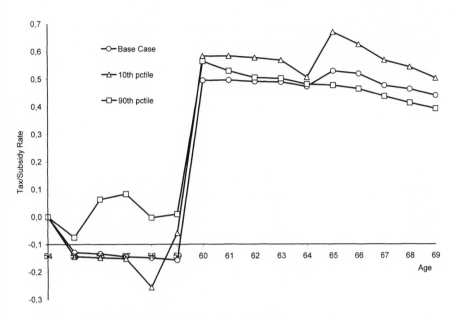

Fig. 1.13 Tax/subsidy rates across earnings profiles

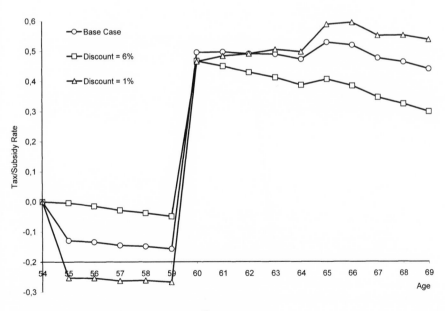

Fig. 1.14 Tax/subsidy rates across discount rates

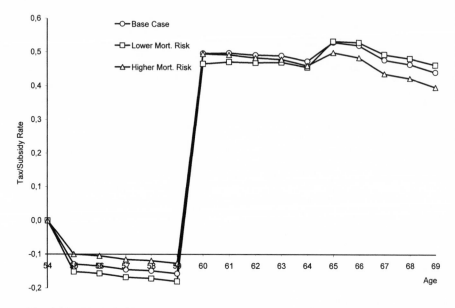

Fig. 1.15   Tax/subsidy rates across mortality risk

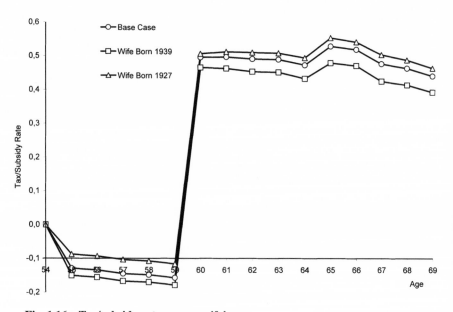

Fig. 1.16   Tax/subsidy rates across wife's age

Table 1.8   **Net Replacement Rates (%) with Unemployment Benefits, 1994–95**

	Single	Married[a]
First year	79	70
Following years	55	64

Source: Martin (1996).

[a]Spouse not working.

Table 1.9   **Base-Case Incentive Calculations, Worker Entitled to Unemployment Benefits**

Last Year of Work	Replacement Rate	SSW[a]	Accrual[a]	Accrual Rate	Tax/ Subsidy
Age 54	...	6,173,342	0	0	0
Age 55	...	5,828,691	−344,651	−.056	.821
Age 56	...	5,488,842	−339,849	−.058	.809
Age 57	...	5,157,398	−331,444	−.060	.789
Age 58	...	4,833,646	−323,752	−.063	.771
Age 59	.749	4,493,147	−340,500	−.070	.811
Age 60	.771	4,285,110	−208,037	−.046	.496
Age 61	.794	4,076,567	−208,543	−.049	.497
Age 62	.817	3,870,541	−206,026	−.051	.491
Age 63	.839	3,665,171	−205,370	−.053	.489
Age 64	.863	3,466,790	−198,381	−.054	.473
Age 65	.874	3,244,903	−221,888	−.064	.529
Age 66	.882	3,027,124	−217,779	−.067	.519
Age 67	.890	2,827,248	−199,876	−.066	.476
Age 68	.898	2,632,906	−194,342	−.069	.463
Age 69	.905	2,448,357	−184,549	−.070	.440

[a]Both SSW (social security wealth) and ΔSSW (accrual) are in Belgian francs ($1.00 \approx$ BF 32.00).

replacement rates directly from Martin (1996). Table 1.8 summarizes the results of interest for this paper. Years of unemployment benefits are fully taken into account for pension computation. Besides, the worker is imputed his last wages for these years.

Table 1.9 presents the base-case results (corresponding to table 1.4 above) while assuming that the worker is entitled to unemployment benefits. Only rows corresponding to the last year of work for ages fifty-four to fifty-eight change since, once pension benefits are available, workers are assumed to opt for them if they stop working. The observed increase in social security wealth stems from the accounting of unemployment benefits. One also observes that, between the ages of fifty-five and fifty-nine, there is an important tax on continued work. Indeed, the worker now forgoes unemployment insurance benefits, while his pension rights are left almost unchanged whether he works or not. In the same way, tables 1.10 and 1.11 duplicate tables 1.5 and 1.6 above for single

Table 1.10   **Incentive Calculations—Single Worker, Worker Entitled to Unemployment Benefits**

Last Year of Work	Replacement Rate	SSW[a]	Accrual[a]	Accrual Rate	Tax/ Subsidy
Age 54	. . .	4,371,072	0	0	0
Age 55	. . .	4,050,244	−320,828	−.073	.764
Age 56	. . .	3,738,690	−311,553	−.077	.742
Age 57	. . .	3,434,903	−303,788	−.081	.724
Age 58	. . .	3,144,095	−290,808	−.085	.693
Age 59	.696	2,762,366	−381,729	−.121	.909
Age 60	.713	2,531,229	−231,137	−.084	.551
Age 61	.726	2,283,319	−247,910	−.098	.590
Age 62	.736	2,030,821	−252,498	−.111	.601
Age 63	.746	1,785,965	−244,857	−.121	.583
Age 64	.756	1,548,965	−237,000	−.133	.564
Age 65	.756	1,292,551	−256,414	−.166	.611
Age 66	.756	1,049,869	−242,681	−.188	.578
Age 67	.756	820,740	−229,129	−.218	.546
Age 68	.756	604,909	−215,832	−.263	.514
Age 69	.756	402,269	−202,640	−.335	.483

[a]Both SSW (social security wealth) and ΔSSW (accrual) are in Belgian francs ($1.00 ≈ BF 32.00).

Table 1.11   **Incentive Calculations—Incomplete Earnings Profile, Worker Entitled to Unemployment Benefits**

Last Year of Work	Replacement Rate	SSW[a]	Accrual[a]	Accrual Rate	Tax/ Subsidy
Age 54	. . .	5,312,097	0	0	0
Age 55	. . .	4,983,382	−328,715	−.062	.783
Age 56	. . .	4,663,627	−319,755	−.064	.762
Age 57	. . .	4,351,954	−311,673	−.067	.742
Age 58	. . .	4,051,148	−300,806	−.069	.716
Age 59	.609	3,729,189	−321,959	−.079	.767
Age 60	.626	3,568,662	−160,527	−.043	.382
Age 61	.644	3,408,411	−160,221	−.045	.382
Age 62	.661	3,249,660	−158,781	−.047	.378
Age 63	.679	3,092,053	−157,607	−.048	.375
Age 64	.696	2,951,595	−140,458	−.045	.335
Age 65	.713	2,819,284	−132,311	−.045	.315
Age 66	.731	2,689,043	−130,240	−.046	.310
Age 67	.748	2,566,851	−122,192	−.045	.291
Age 68	.766	2,444,245	−122,606	−.048	.292
Age 69	.783	2,327,145	−117,100	−.048	.279

[a]Both SSW (social security wealth) and ΔSSW (accrual) are in Belgian francs ($1.00 ≈ BF 32.00).

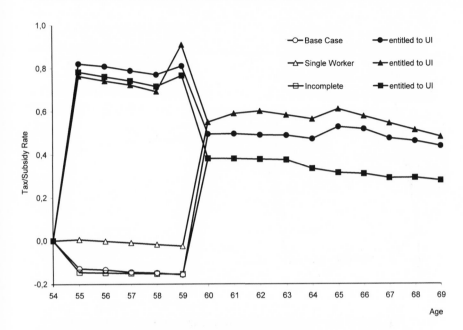

Fig. 1.17   Tax/subsidy rates with and without entitlement to unemployment insurance (UI), base, single, and incomplete career case

workers and the incomplete earnings profile cases when workers who stop working before age sixty are entitled to unemployment compensation. In both instances, continued work before ages fifty-five and fifty-nine appears to be heavily penalized. Again, this is not surprising and explains why so many workers withdraw from the labor force at those ages.

Figure 1.17 contrasts tax/subsidy rates with and without unemployment benefits for the base, single, and incomplete career cases. Single workers face lower tax rates between age fifty-four and age fifty-eight since unemployment insurance net replacement rates are lower for them. However, at age fifty-nine, this worker is subject to a higher tax rate on further work as singles have a 79 percent net replacement rate on their first year of unemployment. Naturally, a worker whose career can be completed faces a lower tax rate on continued work than does the base-case worker.

Figure 1.18 investigates the same issue while varying income level. Interestingly, the lower the income level, the higher the tax rate on continued work. Indeed, workers with higher wages still see their social security wealth increase thanks to real-wage growth, while lower-wage earners have hit the minimum pension threshold and are imputed years of career anyway.

What can be concluded from these results? Once a worker has been laid off, he is given very little monetary incentive to get back to work. Indeed, for low-

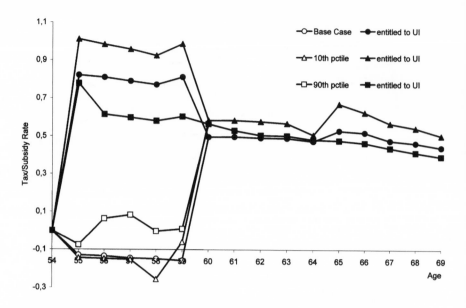

Fig. 1.18   Tax/subsidy rates with and without entitlement to unemployment insurance (UI), varying income level

income (first-decile) workers, tax rates between the ages of fifty-four and fifty-nine are around 100 percent! This again reflects the pervasive government policy of pushing older workers out of labor force, even prior to the legal age of retirement. However, these figures should not be used to explain why one would wish to leave the labor force voluntarily.

1.4   Conclusion

Belgian social insurance—in particular, the treatment of retirement age—is at a crossroads. On the one hand, because of the huge unemployment problem among young people, the government tends to force workers out of the labor market earlier than governments elsewhere. At the same time, those who retire at the normal and the early retirement ages enjoy a level of welfare equivalent to if not higher than that enjoyed by those in other age classes.

On the other hand, the fact of an aging population implies that social security expenditures will double by 2040 if the replacement ratio is kept constant and the mandatory retirement age maintained at its current level. Irrespective of the forecast methods used, Belgium is faced with steeply rising expenditures on retirement and health care. Although the outlook is similar in other European countries, the problem in Belgium is aggravated by the marked size of the public debt. It seems inevitable that social security benefits will become less generous and that, above all, the effective retirement age will have to be raised. Unfortunately, drastic reforms of social security and of the civil servants' pension schemes have been viewed as quasi suicidal by all recent Belgian governments.

Appendix

Data Appendix

Historical Data

Historical Trends in Labor Force Participation of Older Men and Women (Figs. 1.1 and 1.2 above)

Sources. Our sources here are Institut National de Statistique, decennial census until 1981; Institut National de Statistique, Labor Force Survey from 1983 until 1995.

Social Security, Disability Insurance, and Mandatory Retirement Receipt of Older Men and Women (Figs. 1.3 and 1.4 above)

Sources. Our sources here are Bouillot and Perelman (1995) and our own computations. Results come from administrative data. Percentages have been adjusted so that the percentage of the population receiving social security, disability insurance, or mandatory retirement compensation (males and females) corresponds to that given by the Labor Force Survey in 1993. Note that, from 1961 until 1987, actual data (see below) have been used; from 1988 to 1995, the Belgian Federal Planning Bureau's projections are reported, after the above-mentioned adjustment.

Data. Pension outlays and number of pensioners (private sector) are taken from Office National des Pensions, *Statistique annuelle des bénéficiaires de pensions.* Number of pensioners (public sector) is taken from Ministère de la Prévoyance Sociale, *Annuaire statistique de la sécurité sociale.* The breakdown by age of pensioners (private sector) is taken from Institut National de Maladie Invalidité, *Rapport général,* pt. 3, *Rapport statistique.* The minimum guaranteed income to the elderly (welfare) is taken from Office National des Pensions, *Statistique annuelle des bénéficiaires de pension.* Total population is taken from Institut National de la Statistique, *Statistiques démographiques.* The number taking mandatory retirement is taken from June issues of the *Bulletin mensuel* (Office National pour l'Emploi) and from information supplied by various individuals in the Office Natonal pour l'Emploi.

*Social Security Replacement Rates (Gross and Net) over Time
(Fig. 1.5 above)*

Source. Our source is our own computations. Mean gross pension receipts have been computed for a worker with a complete career on the year of his or her retirement. This mean pension is a weighted average of single and married pension earners. Mean gross wages of private-sector workers (thus including the self-employed) have been computed. The ratio of these two means defines our gross replacement rate. Our net replacement rate corresponds to the ratio of mean net pension receipts over mean net wages. Taxes on replacement earnings have been accounted for. Both payroll and income taxes have been deducted from mean gross wages. Income taxes have been computed using the average tax rate.

Data. The average income tax rate is taken from Institut National de la Statistique, *Statistiques financières.* Average pension receipts for a complete career are taken from Office National des Pensions, *Statistique annuelle des bénéficiaires de pension.* Average wages and payroll taxes are taken from Office National de la Sécurité Sociale, *Rapport annuel.*

Contemporaneous Data

General Remarks

Most data come from the Labor Market Survey conducted in Belgium by the Institut National de Statistique and published by EUROSTAT. The following main distinctions apply.

Computations related to labor force participation (e.g., fig. 1.6 above) have been undertaken using the following ILO definitions: *working active:* had a paid job for at least one hour during the survey week; accomplished nonpaid help in the family company or farm; *unemployed:* has no job (i.e., worked less than an hour during the survey week); is actively seeking a job; is available for work within the fifteen days following the interview; *active:* working active or unemployed. Note that this classification scheme proceeds from subjective answers.

The following categories of (in)activity (figs. 1.7 and 1.8 above) are distinguished: *employed; unemployed; disabled; mandatory early retired; retired;* and *other.* Here, the surveyed person determines which category best describes himself or herself with regard to the labor market. Therefore, adding up the employed and the unemployed will not necessarily give back what the ILO definitions imply.

The Labor Market Survey is so constructed that, for characteristics concerning more than 5 percent of the active population, the standard deviation at the NUTS 2 (regional) level does not exceed 8 percent (taking account of the sampling for unemployment). Numbers regarding smaller groups have to be considered with some care, as in the case of specific *age-to-age* figures.[11]

Labor Market Participation Rates by Age and Sex in 1995 (Fig. 1.6 above) and Distribution of Activities of Men and Women by Age in 1995 (Figs. 1.7 and 1.8 above)

Source. Our source is Institut National de la Statistique, 1995 Labor Force Survey.

Breakdown of Source of Family Income (Fig. 1.9 above)

Source. Our source is our own computations. Series have been smoothed with a (sixth-degree) polynomial.

Data. Data are taken from the Household Survey, Center voor Sociaal Beleid, Universiteit Antwerpen, and from our own computations.

Hazard Rate Out of the Labor Force for Men and Women (Figs. 1.10 and 1.11 above)

Source. Our source is Institut National de la Statistique, 1992–95 Labor Force Surveys. Three pairs of years have been used: 1992–93, 1993–94, and 1994–95. The mean hazard rate over these years is reported while substituting a zero in the case of a negative hazard rate. The purpose of this substitution is to eliminate cohort effects from labor market data and get rid of negative hazard rates.

Studying Retirement Incentives in Belgium

Simulations (Figs. 1.12–1.18 above)

Earnings patterns come from figure 1A.1. Note that, in our computations, we have assumed that, once granted, social security benefits are indexed to the CPI. Since January 1976, they are no longer indexed to wage growth (this is in contrast to the system prevailing for public-sector employees, the so-called *péréquation*). Limited discretionary increases were granted in 1990 and 1991. There is no particular reason to believe that this will happen again in the near future.

We decided to present a consistent social security system throughout the years covered by our simulations. Recall that, in our case-study approach, our worker is supposed to be age sixty-five in 1995. In the Belgian system, he is hence allowed to retire at any time between 1990 and 1995. In fact, public policy changed in 1992. First, in Belgium, past income record is indexed to

11. There were 77,689 responses to the 1992 survey, 81,219 to the 1993 survey, 81,281 to the 1994 survey, and 80,319 to the 1995 survey. The nonresponse rate is about 10 percent. Nonresponses are not accounted for.

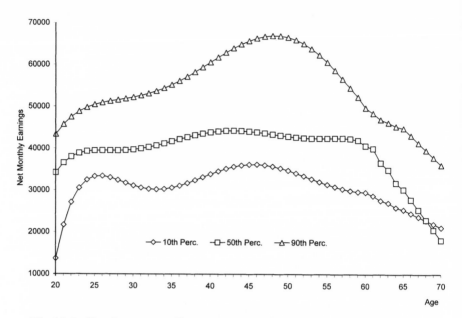

Fig. 1A.1   Earnings-age profile
Source: Own computations; Center voor Sociaal Beleid, Universiteit Antwerpen.

the CPI but also adjusted on a discretionary basis to account for wage growth. However, there has been no adjustment since 1992. Note that this wage-growth adjustment played a role in the retirement decisions reached by workers turning age sixty or sixty-one in 1990 and 1991. We have left out of our analysis this potential incentive to delayed retirement. Second, during these very two years, however, the former system still prevailed, and pensions were reduced by 5 percent for each year of early retirement. This factor acted in the opposite way, providing incentives for early retirement. We have also left out of our analysis this potential incentive to early retirement. We can assume that, on the whole, these two factors counterbalanced each other.

Further, as explained above, benefits are capped with respect to the income stream to be considered. This ceiling is itself adjusted to the CPI and also to wage growth on a discretionary basis. Again, since 1992, there has been no such adjustment. We have again voluntarily neglected this factor for 1990–91. At the time of writing, an automatic adjustment mechanism is being introduced. It does not, however, concern the period under investigation.

These three conventions are natural in the case of Belgium. Indeed, de Callataÿ and Turtelboom (1997) rely on the same hypotheses. This, in fact, enables us to frame all our computations in real terms, rather than hazarding the future real and nominal growth rates as well as the share of growth that the labor factor will be able to capture.

Benefit computation is, in fact, based on gross earnings. We have therefore

Table 1A.1   **Labor Participation and Unemployment**

	Participation Rate, Men Aged 55–64		Unemployment Rate, 1995
	1979	1994	
The United States	70.8	62.6	5.5
Japan	81.5	81.2	3.1
Germany	63.2	45.0	8.2
France	67.0	39.1	11.6
Italy	36.8	30.7	12.2
The United Kingdom	70.2	64.5	8.7
Belgium	44.5	33.0	9.4
The Netherlands	63.2	40.7	6.5
Spain	73.8	48.6	22.7
Sweden	77.8	68.8	9.2

Source: OECD (1996).

used the Belgian income tax rules in 1992 to convert net monthly earnings into gross yearly income. Net monthly income was obtained anew while using the 1992 fiscal rules as an approximation. Indeed, fiscal rules were not indexed during the period covered by our investigation.

Comparisons with Other Countries

One of the main motivations for early retirement is reducing unemployment. Table 1A.1 provides the labor force participation rate for men aged fifty-five to sixty-four and the rate of unemployment in a number of OECD countries. One sees that countries with high unemployment rates tend to have low labor force participation rates among elderly workers. This evidence can be interpreted in two ways. First, it could imply that policies promoting early retirement do not work. Second, it could simply imply that, without such policies in place, unemployment would be even higher.

Earlier Studies of Flexible Retirement in Belgium

Luttgens and Perelman (1987) studied the retirement behavior of a sample of male blue-collar workers who reached age sixty during the period 1973–77. During that period, a full-career worker with a career of z years gets a yearly pension equal to

$$y \frac{45 - z}{45} \times \left(1 - \frac{5z}{100} \right)$$

of the pension he would get retiring at age sixty-five. Luttgens and Perelman show that social security did not have a significant influence on the early retire-

Table 1A.2   **Aggregate Taxation Rate on Social Security Benefits (%)**

	Relative Gross Amount	Global Taxation Rate	Relative Net Amount
Maximum pension[a]	168	9.8	152
(Floor + max)/2	134	4.0	129
Highest zero tax pension	127	.0	127
Floor[b]	100	.0	100

Source: Own calculations.

[a]Married worker having received ceiling wages from age 20 to age 64.

[b]Married worker with a complete career (45 years).

ment decision, and they justify their result by means of the actuarial neutrality of social security.

More recently, Pepermans (1992) addressed the same problem using a sample of individuals aged fifty to seventy in 1985. On the basis of his model, he computes the relevant probability that a typical worker (male, married, with a nonworking spouse) will retire before age sixty-five, the legal retirement age: 0.196 at age sixty, 0.396 at age sixty-three, and 0.917 at age sixty-five. There is a clear bias in his study since, in that period, most workers retiring early did not choose to do so. As noted above, since 1991 voluntary early retirement has been made more attractive.

The Average Tax Rate for Private-Sector Retirees

Table 1A.2 provides the average tax rate on social security benefits for a couple only one of whom is a wage earner. There are three components: a health care payroll tax of 3.55 percent; a "solidarity" income tax of at most 2 percent; and the personal income tax, which can be very high (the marginal rate is 25 percent). However, for those whose reported income is restricted to social security benefits, there is a tax exemption, which amounts to about 90 percent of mean household income.

Table 1A.2 also shows that the exemption amounts to 130 percent of the minimum household pension. The average tax rate on the maximum private-sector pension is lower than 10 percent. A pension in between the minimum and the maximum is taxed at 4 percent. Note, however, that these reasonable tax rates hold for pensioners who are relying solely on social security. Although, as has been shown in section 1.1.3, this is a reasonable assumption for most aged people, we can conjecture than pensioners receiving high social security benefits may in fact be subject to higher tax rates owing to additional sources of income.

References

Bouillot, L., and S. Perelman. 1995. Evaluation patrimoniale des droits à la pension. *Revue belge de sécurité sociale* 37, no. 4:803–31.

de Callataÿ, E., and B. Turtelboom. 1997. Pension reform in Belgium. *Cahiers économiques de Bruxelles,* no. 156:371–412.

Delhausse, B., S. Perelman, and P. Pestieau. 1996. Retirement and growing old: Which model of protection? In *International perspective on supplementary pensions: Actors and issues,* ed. E. Reynaud, L. Roberts, B. Davies, and G. Hugues. London: Quorum.

Englert, M., N. Fasquelle, and S. Weeman. 1994. Les perspectives d'évolution à très long terme de la sécurité sociale (1991–2050). Planning Paper no. 66. Brussels: Planning Bureau.

European Economic Commission (EEC). 1994. Supplementary pension in the European Union. Development Report by the European Commission's Network of Experts on Supplementary Pensions. Brussels.

EUROSTAT. 1992. Rapport entre revenu de retraite et revenu d'activité au moment du départ à la retraite. Luxembourg.

Luttgens, A., and S. Perelman. 1987. Public pensions, health status and other determinants of retirement: A case study on Belgian aged workers. University of Liège, Department of Economics. Mimeo.

Martin, J. 1996. Indicateurs de taux de remplacement aux fins de comparaisons internationales. *Revue economique de l'OECD* (Paris) 26, no. 1:116–32.

OECD. 1994. *OECD economic survey: Belgium, Luxembourg.* Paris.

———. 1996. *Employment in Europe.* Brussels: European Commission.

Pepermans, G. 1992. Retirement decision in a discrete choice model and implications for the government budget: The case of Belgium. *Journal of Population Economics* 5, no. 3:229–43.

2   Social Security and Retirement in Canada

Jonathan Gruber

Government transfers to older persons in Canada are one of the largest and fastest-growing components of the government budget. Total expenditures on the four primary transfer programs for older Canadians amounted to $41 billion in 1995, which was 23 percent of the federal budget and 5.3 percent of GNP in that year. In 1970, total expenditures were only $2 billion, amounting to just 14 percent of the federal budget and 2.3 percent of GNP. Moreover, unless the system is changed, rapid growth appears likely for the near future. The ratio of persons age sixty-five and over to persons age twenty to age sixty-four is projected to grow from its current level of 19 percent to over 40 percent by the year 2075. As a result, the payroll tax necessary to finance the major social insurance program for older persons, the Canada/Quebec Pension Plan (CPP/QPP), is projected to grow from its current level of 5.6 percent of wages to over 14 percent by the year 2075 (Office of the Superintendent of Financial Institutions Canada 1993). Similar cost increases are in store for the other three major transfer programs to older Canadians, programs financed from general revenues: the Old Age Security (OAS) demogrant and the means-tested Guaranteed Income Supplement (GIS) and Spousal Allowance (SPA) programs.

As a result of this growing fiscal imbalance, Canada may be required to consider a number of reforms to its social security system over the coming years. But, for understanding the implications of any potential reforms, it is critical to understand how this complicated web of programs affects the retirement decisions of older Canadians. Public income support is the dominant feature of the opportunity set facing households over age sixty-five in Canada. For the median household where the head is over age sixty-five, these social

Jonathan Gruber is professor of economics at the Massachusetts Institute of Technology and director of the Children's Program at the National Bureau of Economic Research.

The author is grateful to Sue Dynarski and especially Courtney Coile for excellent research assistance and to the National Institute on Aging for financial support.

security programs represent 61 percent of total family income; for 23 percent of such households, they provide more than 90 percent of family income.[1] As a result, it seems likely that the structure of the social security program has important effects on the life-cycle savings and labor supply decision making of households and in particular on their retirement decisions. But little empirical analysis has been conducted of either the retirement incentives under the Canadian system or the effects of those incentives on behavior.

The purpose of this paper is to provide an overview of the interaction between social security and the labor force behavior of older persons in the Canada. I do so in four steps. First, in section 2.1, I document the pertinent facts about the labor market behavior of older persons in Canada, both today and over time. Then, in section 2.2, I describe the structure of the system of income support programs for older persons in Canada, summarizing the relevant institutional details for thinking about retirement behavior. Finally, in section 2.3, I present the results of a simulation model designed to document the retirement incentives inherent in these programs for current cohorts of retirees. Section 2.4 concludes by considering the implications of my findings.

2.1   The Labor Market Behavior of Older Persons in Canada

As in most industrialized nations, the second half of the twentieth century in Canada has been marked by a declining attachment to the labor force of older persons. In 1960, 87 percent of men aged fifty-five to sixty-four and 30 percent of men age sixty-five and above were participating in the labor force; by 1993, these ratios had fallen to 61 and 10 percent, respectively. One possible explanation for this shift is the increasing generosity of the income support programs for older Canadians. But, before addressing the effects of these programs, it is useful to provide some more background on the labor market behavior of older men and women.

The historical and contemporaneous facts presented in this section are drawn from a number of different data sources. These are summarized in the appendix. In the appendix, I also provide a brief overview of the databases that are used by researchers in Canada to study retirement behavior.

2.1.1   Historical Trends

Figures 2.1 and 2.2 graph the labor force participation rates of men and women in different age groups since 1960. I focus on three age groups: forty-five to fifty-four; fifty-five to sixty-four; and over sixty-five. For men, there is a decline in the labor force participation of all these groups. The decline for the youngest group is slight, while the decline for the other groups is much more precipitous. The percentage decline is most dramatic for those age sixty-five and over, who by the end of the sample period were very rarely participating in the labor force.

---

1. Author's tabulations of the 1992 Survey of Consumer Finances.

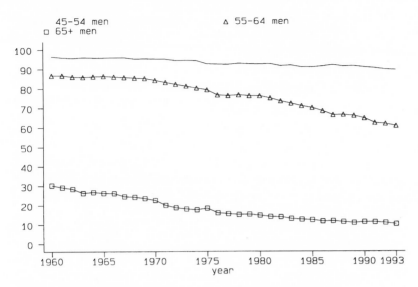

Fig. 2.1   Historical trends in labor force participation of older men

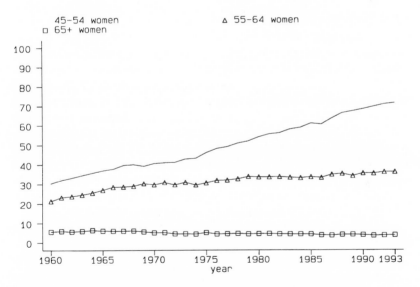

Fig. 2.2   Historical trends in labor force participation of older women

For women, the pattern is quite different: any trend toward earlier retirement is dominated by increased labor force participation. For the two younger groups, participation is rising; for the oldest group, it declines slightly.

One first-pass approach to considering whether social security is associated with these labor force trends is to examine related trends in social security

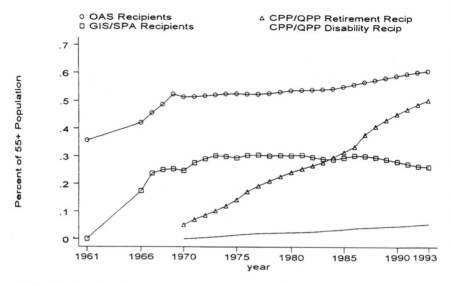

Fig. 2.3   Receipt of public retirement income

generosity. I do so in two ways. First, in figure 2.3, I show the share of the population over age fifty-five receiving various sources of retirement income. I consider four types of income: OAS; GIS or SPA; CPP/QPP retirement benefits; and CPP/QPP disability benefits. I do not have data on age-specific receipt rates before 1981, so I simply normalize total receipt by the age fifty-five and over population. This is not a problem for all the retirement programs, which are restricted to those age sixty and above; this will slightly overstate the size of the disability program since some recipients are under age fifty-five.

There has been a steady growth in receipt of OAS income and disability benefits. There has been a much more rapid growth in receipt of CPP/QPP retirement benefits, rising from zero to roughly half the over fifty-five population by 1993. Perhaps owing to the growth in this income source, there was little growth in GIS/SPA benefits after 1975 and even a decline after 1985.

Figures 2.4 and 2.5 explore this time series in more detail, focusing on the period after 1980, for which I have data on receipt rates by age and sex for the CPP only. Each figure has four lines, representing OAS receipt, GIS/SPA receipt, CPP retirement receipt, and receipt of any of these benefits, including CPP disability. These figures parallel figure 2.3 above: slightly rising OAS receipt (more so for women than for men), more rapidly rising CPP retirement receipt, and a somewhat offsetting decline in GIS/SPA receipt. Of particular interest in these graphs is the jump in CPP retirement receipt in 1987; as discussed below, in this year, early eligibility at age sixty was made available. Overall, there is a steady rise in receipt of income from these programs, with a jump in 1987.

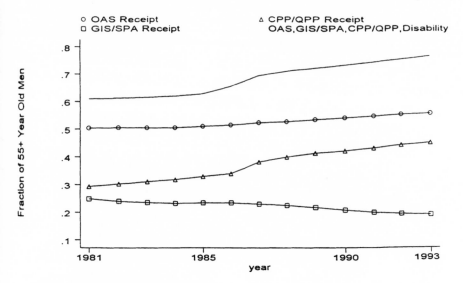

Fig. 2.4   Program receipt for men

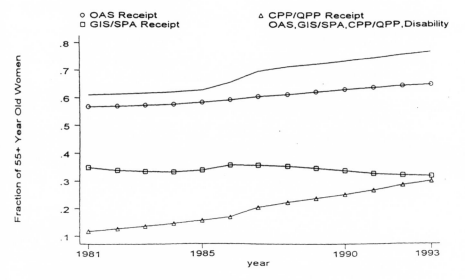

Fig. 2.5   Program receipt for women

Second, in figure 2.6, I show the change in generosity of benefits payments over time. I show the replacement rate through all these four income support programs from 1960 to 1991 for low-, medium-, and high-earnings workers. These replacement rates are computed (according to the algorithm described in the simulation section below) for a sixty-five-year-old man in 1995 with a

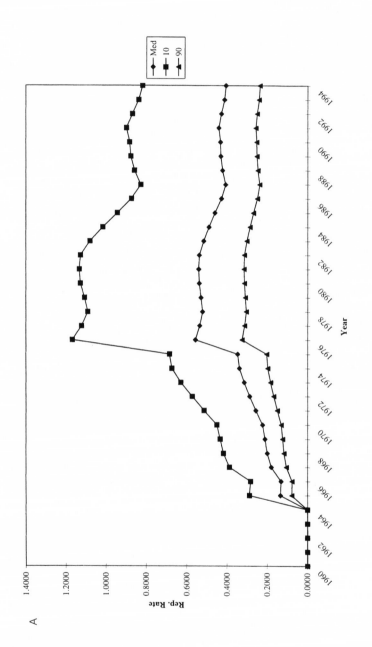

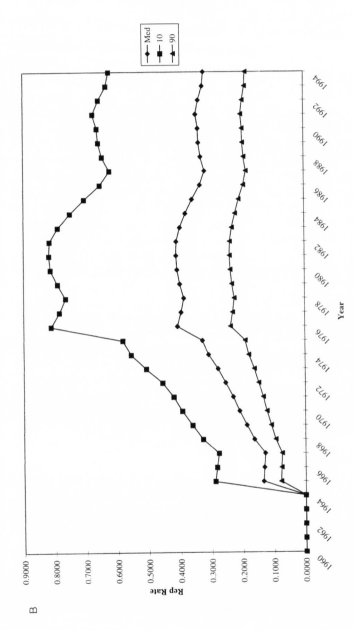

Fig. 2.6 Replacement rates: *a*, without asset income; *b*, with asset income

sixty-two-year-old wife.[2] A key consideration in computing replacement rates is the level of other income (i.e., asset income) available to potential retirees since the GIS and SPA programs are means tested. As a result, I consider two cases: a couple with no asset income (fig. 2.6a) and a couple with $4,818 in other income (in 1990 dollars), which is the median level of nongovernment income available in 1990 for families where the head is over age sixty-five (fig. 2.6b).

Replacement rates grow substantially over time. In all cases, they start at zero until 1965 since OAS benefits were restricted to those age seventy and over until that year. Then, in 1966, CPP/QPP benefits were introduced; as described below, this program was phased in over a ten-year period; in 1967, the GIS program was introduced as well. As a result of these two features, the replacement rate grew steadily until 1975, reaching roughly 35 percent in that year for the median earner. In 1975, the SPA program was introduced, leading to a discrete jump in replacement rates due to the fact that the couple in our example has an eligible wife. Replacement rates then declined somewhat over time, as the growth rate in earnings exceeded inflation by a substantial amount in the mid-1980s.[3] The replacement rates for the tenth and ninetieth percentiles follow a pattern similar to that of the median case, although more pronounced for the tenth percentile; in the late 1970s, replacement rates exceeded one for this sample.

In figure 2.6b, I consider the effect of introducing asset income. This substantially lowers replacement rates by reducing the benefits received through the means-tested GIS and SPA programs. But the time-series pattern is similar to that in figure 2.6a.

These time-series patterns yield a mixed picture of the influence of social security. Clearly, there is a strong correlation between the size of the program and the labor force participation rate of older men. But the decline in participation of older men has continued unabated in the 1980s and 1990s, even as program generosity has declined.

2.1.2   Labor Market Behavior in 1993

For a more detailed understanding of the time pattern of labor force participation in recent times, I turn to the April 1992 and 1993 Survey of Consumer Finances (SCF). The SCF is a large, nationally representative survey that asks individuals about their labor force attachment at both the point of the survey and the previous year as well as about income in the previous year. I pool two years of the SCF for added precision in my estimates of labor force participation by age.

The age pattern of nonparticipation for men and women is depicted in figure 2.7. At age forty-five, the participation of men is significantly higher, although

---

2. I use the earnings from the median, tenth, and ninetieth percentiles of the earnings distribution of the 1930 cohort that is used in the simulation model.

3. Moreover, the earnings of the sample family head are tied to the earnings base for CPP taxation, which grew especially fast in the mid-1980s.

Fig. 2.7   Participation rates by age and sex

almost 80 percent of forty-five-year-old women are working. There is then a gradual parallel decline for men and women until age fifty-five, at which point the pace steepens; this is particularly true for men, with the result that the participation gap closes substantially by age sixty-five. By age seventy, participation has dropped quite low, with fewer than 10 percent of men or women participating in the labor force.

Figure 2.8 considers in more detail the allocation of time among men as they age, by dividing activities at each age into employment, unemployment, disability, and retirement. There is a steady decline in employment among men. Most of this decline is reflected in an increase in retirement and in an increase in disability after age fifty-five; unemployment rates are fairly constant until age sixty. After age sixty, employment falls more rapidly, and unemployment falls as well; disability begins to fall after age sixty-five. These declines are reflected in rapid increases in retirement. This same exercise is repeated for women in figure 2.9. The patterns are similar, with the exception that a much larger share of women is not pursuing any of these activities (these women are out of the labor force for other reasons).

2.1.3   Income Sources of Older Persons

Figures 2.10 and 2.11 examine the incidence of public and private retirement income for older persons. Figure 2.10 graphs two series for men only: the rate of receipt of OAS, CPP/QPP, and GIS/SPA and the rate of receipt of other public assistance through the unemployment insurance and social assistance (means-tested welfare) programs. This figure highlights the fact that, even before retirement, a large share of men are receiving public assistance. As a re-

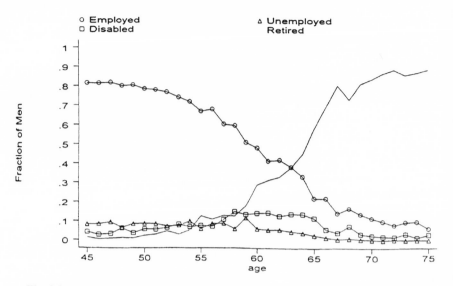

Fig. 2.8   **Distribution of activities of men by age**

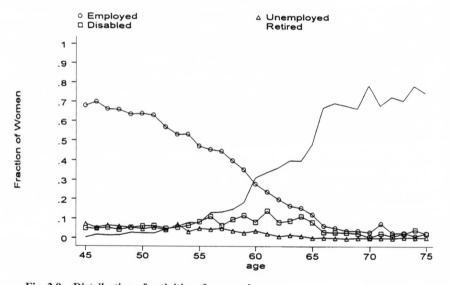

Fig. 2.9   **Distribution of activities of women by age**

sult, the dramatic increase in retirement income receipt after age sixty is to some extent offsetting other government transfer payments. By age sixty-five, there is no receipt of other transfers, and all men are receiving some form of retirement income.

Figure 2.11 displays the percentage of men and women at each age who are receiving private pension income. This grows fairly rapidly from age fifty-five

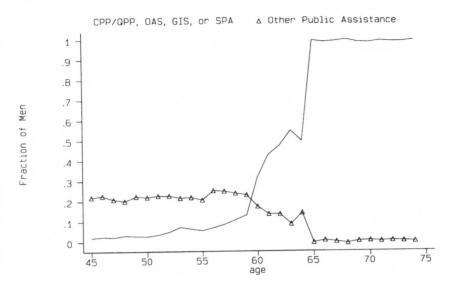

Fig. 2.10   Public income recipiency for men

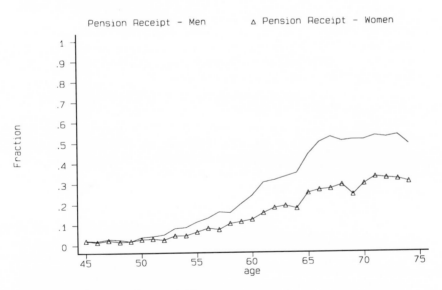

Fig. 2.11   Private pension receipt by sex

on, particularly for men, so that by age sixty-seven more than half the male population is receiving pension income. Pension receipt for women at older ages is only about two-thirds as common. At the same time, however, many women will be benefiting from these income streams through their husband's pension.

Finally, figure 2.12 shows the distribution of income sources for couples,

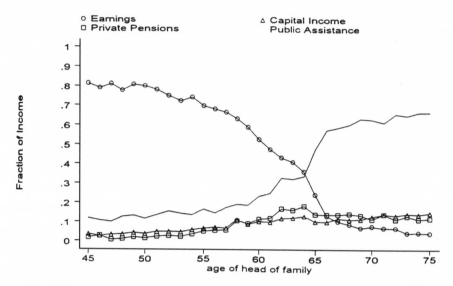

Fig. 2.12   Distribution of family income by source

arrayed by the age of the head of the family.[4] I consider the distribution of income across four sources: earnings, capital income, private pensions, and public-sector income (predominantly retirement income for older couples, as shown in fig. 2.10 above). Earnings is the dominant source of family income until age fifty-five, at which point the earnings share begins to decline rapidly; even from age forty-five to age fifty-five, however, public assistance plays a nontrivial role (mirroring the results in fig. 2.10). The decline in earnings after age fifty-five is compensated for by increases in each of the other elements, most important among which is public income. By age seventy, public assistance income accounts for over 70 percent of family income.

2.2   Key Features of the Income Security System

2.2.1   The Old Age Security System

The oldest component of the income security system for older Canadians is the Old Age Security (OAS) system, which was put in place in 1952, replacing a provincially run means-tested benefits system that had existed since 1927. This program is available to anyone age sixty-five or over who meets certain residence requirements.[5] The program originally provided benefits to

4. This differs somewhat from previous figures, where the unit of observation is the older person; this is because these income concepts are best measured at the family level.
5. Individuals must have been a Canadian citizen or legal resident of Canada at some point before application and have resided in Canada for at least ten years (if currently in Canada) or twenty years (if currently outside Canada).

those age seventy or over, and the age of eligibility was dropped to sixty-five in 1965.

The OAS pension itself is a uniform demogrant that was equal to $387.74 (19 percent of median monthly earnings of twenty- to sixty-four-year-old males in Canada) in 1995. Individuals who do not meet residence requirements are entitled to a partial OAS benefit. OAS benefits have been indexed to the consumer price index since 1972. OAS benefits are fully subject to both federal and provincial income taxes. In addition, there is a clawback of OAS benefits from very high-income individuals: in 1993, the OAS for a single individual was reduced by fifteen cents per dollar of net income exceeding $53,215. OAS benefits are financed from general taxation revenues.

2.2.2   The Canada/Quebec Pension Plan

The largest component of the income security system is the Canada Pension Plan (CPP) and the Quebec Pension Plan (QPP). These programs began on 1 January 1966 and are administered separately by Quebec and the rest of Canada.

The plan is financed by a payroll tax of 2.7 percent each on both employers and employees. This payroll tax is levied up to the year's maximum pensionable earnings (YMPE), $34,900 in 1995 (or 145 percent of median annual earnings). The YMPE is indexed to the growth in average wages in Canada. In addition, earnings up to the year's basic exemption (YBE) are exempted from the computation; this is defined as 10 percent of the YMPE.

Eligibility for this plan is conditioned on contributions for at least one calendar year during the contributory period, which is the period from attainment of age eighteen or 1 January 1966 if later. Benefits are then computed in several steps. First, the number of months used to compute the retirement pension is computed by subtracting from the number of months in the contributory period (a) months receiving a disability pension, (b) months spent rearing small children,[6] (c) months between age sixty-five and the commencement of the pension, and (d) 15 percent of the remaining months. The last three of these conditions are subject to the provision that they not reduce the contributory period below 120 months minus months of disability pension receipt. In addition, excess earnings in one month above one-twelfth of the YMPE may be applied to months in the same year where earnings are below one-twelfth of the YMPE.

Second, the remaining months of earnings history are converted to current dollars, using as a deflator the ratio of the YMPE in each year to the average of the YMPE over the three years prior to (and including) the year of pension receipt. Finally, the benefit is computed as 25 percent of the average of this real earnings history. This 25 percent ratio has been in place since 1976; from 1967 to 1976, the program was phased in, with the share of average earnings paid out in benefits rising from 2.5 percent in 1967 to 25 percent in 1976. In

---

6. This is defined as months where there was a child younger than seven years of age and the worker had annual earnings of at least one-twelfth of the YBE. This provision was introduced in 1983.

addition, before the YMPE reached the average industrial wage in 1986, it was rising more rapidly than average wages (12.5 percent per year).

Until 1984 for the QPP and 1987 for the CPP, benefits could not be claimed before the sixty-fifth birthday, and there was no actuarial adjustment for delayed claiming. Beginning at these times, individuals were allowed to claim benefits as early as age sixty, with an actuarial reduction of 0.5 percent for each month of early claiming (before age sixty-five) and an actuarial increase of 0.5 percent for each month of delayed claiming (after age sixty-five).

Until 1975, receipt of benefits under the CPP and QPP was conditioned on low earnings levels, with earnings above these ceilings taxed away at high rates. In 1975, these earnings tests were eliminated. With the introduction of early retirement in 1984 and 1987, however, an earnings test was reintroduced: workers can claim early benefits only if their annual earnings do not exceed the maximum retirement pension payable at age sixty-five for the year in which the pension is claimed ($713.19, or 36 percent of median monthly earnings, in 1995). This earnings test is applied only at the point of application, however; after that point, there is no additional check on the individual's earnings.[7] Moreover, the earnings test does not apply any more once the individual reaches age sixty-five.

CPP/QPP benefits are independent across spouses and are a function of an individual spouse's earnings history only.[8] But there is an interdependence through survivor benefits (as well as the interdependences through the means-tested programs described below). Spouses are eligible for survivor pensions if the deceased contributor made contributions for at least 10 years or one-third the number of years in the contributory period and if the spouse is over age thirty-five or has dependent children. For spouses under age sixty-five, the survivor pension is a combination of a flat-rate portion plus 37.5 percent of the earnings-related pension of the deceased spouse. For spouses age sixty-five and over, the survivor's pension is equal to 60 percent of the earnings-related pension. The pension used to calculate the survivor benefit is not subject to actuarial adjustment. If the surviving spouse is receiving his or her own earnings-related pension, then the combination of the two pensions cannot exceed the maximum retirement pension available in the year that the later of these two pensions commences. Children of deceased contributors are also entitled to a survivor benefit if under eighteen or a full-time student between the ages of eighteen and twenty-five; this benefit is a flat amount. There is also a lump-sum death benefit, which is generally equal to half the annual CPP/QPP pension amount.

Benefits are legislated to increase with the consumer price index (since 1973), average over the twelve-month period ending with October of the preceding year. Benefits are fully subject to federal and provincial income taxes.

---

7. Earnings after the initial receipt of a CPP/QPP pension are not included in the subsequent average earnings used to compute future benefits.

8. Couples do have the option of sharing their benefits for income tax purposes since taxation is at the individual level.

2.2.3   The Guaranteed Income Supplement and Spousal Allowance

The Guaranteed Income Supplement (GIS) is a means-tested supplement available to recipients of OAS that was introduced in 1967. Individuals must reapply for the GIS each year, and the means test for eligibility (and benefit) levels is repeated. The income level for means testing is defined in the same way as for income tax purposes, with the important exclusion of OAS pension income. Unlike OAS or CPP/QPP benefits, GIS benefits are based on family income levels.

There are separate single and married guarantee levels for the GIS; in 1995, these were $460.79 for singles and $300.14 (each person) monthly for married couples (23 percent and 15 percent of median monthly income, respectively). Benefits are then taxed away as income rises at a rate of 50 percent, although a couple with one member over age sixty-five and one under age sixty is taxed at only 25 percent with an initial amount of income exempted.

The Spousal Allowance (SPA), which was introduced in 1975, is a means-tested monthly benefit available to sixty- to sixty-four-year-old spouses of OAS recipients and to sixty- to sixty-four-year-old widows/widowers. For the spouse of an OAS recipient, the benefit is equal to the OAS benefit plus GIS at the married rate; the OAS portion is then taxed at 75 percent as income rises until it is reduced to zero, and then the combined GIS benefits are taxed at 50 percent. For a widowed spouse, the benefit is equal to the OAS plus the GIS at the widowed rate and is taxed equivalently. Both the GIS and the SPA guarantees are also indexed to inflation, and neither source of income is subject to either the federal or the provincial tax system.

2.2.4   Hazard Rates

One natural question is whether the labor force behavior of older Canadians lines up with the incentives inherent in the systems described above. I explore this in figures 2.13 and 2.14, which show hazard rates out of the labor force for men and women, respectively. This is measured as the increase in the rate at which workers leave the labor force from the previous age, relative to the stock of workers participating at the previous age.

For men, there is clear evidence of a dramatic increase in the rate at which workers leave the labor force at age sixty-five, which is the age of normal retirement for CPP/QPP and of entitlement to OAS benefits. Fully 40 percent of the men who remain in the labor force at age sixty-five leave during that year. There is also evidence of a response to the CPP/QPP early retirement age of sixty, but it is not particularly strong relative to the hazards in surrounding years. This is consistent with the notion that the response to early retirement entitlements emerges only slowly, as documented by Burtless and Moffitt (1986) for the United States. For women, the pattern is similar: a pronounced spike at age sixty-five, with some evidence of a response around age sixty, but nothing particularly pronounced.

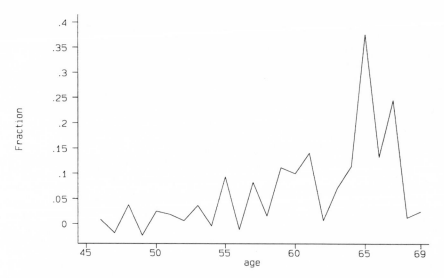

Fig. 2.13   Hazard rate out of labor force for men

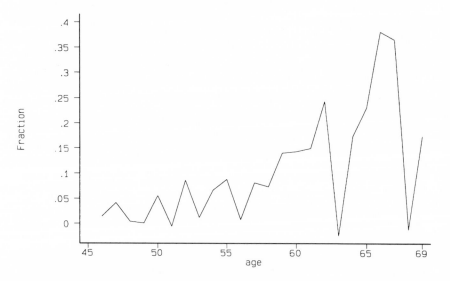

Fig. 2.14   Hazard rate out of labor force for women

2.2.5   Other Public Programs

In addition to the federal retirement programs, there are a variety of provincial programs that provide supplements to low-income retirees. For example, a program in Ontario provides $80.00 per month to Ontario residents who are recipients of the GIS; but these funds are taxed back at 50 percent as other (non-OAS or -GIS) income rises.

A final program that is important for considering retirement incentives is the disability insurance program that is operated through the CPP/QPP. This program provides benefits to those workers unable to work owing to disability. The basic benefits structure consists of two portions: a flat-rate portion, which is a lump sum paid to all disabled workers, and an earnings-related portion, which is 75 percent of the applicable CPP/QPP retirement pension, calculated with the contributory period ending at the date of disability. This program is fairly stringently screened, and fewer than 5 percent of older Canadian men are on disability insurance. Nevertheless, recent research shows that the benefit structure of this program has important effects on labor supply (Gruber 1996).

2.2.6   Private Pension Coverage

Another important feature of the retirement landscape is private pensions. Defined-benefit pension plans share many of the same incentive features as public insurance plans. In fact, many Canadian workers are covered by occupational pensions, or RRPs. In 1992, 47.5 percent of paid workers were covered by occupational pensions, with coverage being slightly higher for males than for females. Ninety percent of plan members were in defined-benefit plans, although the share in defined-contribution plans has been growing recently. Defined-contribution plans may also affect retirement through income effects, but there should not be tax/subsidy effects on the work decision since the payout is not dependent on work patterns.

2.2.7   The Retirement Effects of Income Support Programs in Canada

While a large U.S. literature on social security and retirement exists (for a review, see Diamond and Gruber, chap. 11 in this volume), much less work has been done in the Canadian context. Recently, Baker and Benjamin (1996) have explored the effects of the introduction of the early retirement option under the QPP in 1984 and the CPP in 1987. They found that there was little effect of this policy change on the labor force behavior of sixty- to sixty-four-year-olds in the short run. But there is some suggestion of a longer-run response, as a "spike" in the rate at which workers leave the labor force has emerged at age sixty in recent years (as shown in fig. 2.13 above). Baker and Benjamin (1997) explore another important policy change, the removal of earnings tests under the CPP and QPP in the 1970s. They find that the removal of earnings testing was associated with a significant shift from part-time to full-time work among older workers.

2.3   Retirement Incentives

2.3.1   Simulation Modeling

In this section, I use a model of benefits determination under these four programs to assess the incentives of social security on retirement through accrual rate effects. Given the similarities of the CPP and QPP programs, the incentives are calculated for the representative CPP worker. This program embeds the benefits computation and clawback structure of these four programs to compute benefits for a worker, given his age, spouse's age, earnings history, and date of retirement. I use the base-case assumptions about the CPP for wage and price growth, as well as assumptions about the growth of the program contribution rate, to model incentives. The program computes benefits for the worker and survivor and death benefits for the case where the worker has died.

The next step in the simulation is to take these monthly benefit entitlements and compute an expected net present discounted value of social security wealth (SSW); this includes the future entitlements from all four programs. This requires projecting benefits out until workers reach age one hundred and then taking a weighted sum that discounts future benefits by both the individual discount rate and the prospects that the worker will live to a given future age. The methodology for doing so is described in Diamond and Gruber (chap. 11 in this volume). For the worker himself, this is fairly straightforward; it is simply a sum of future benefits, discounted backward by time preference rates and mortality rates. For survivor benefits, it is more complicated since I must account for the joint likelihood of survival of the worker and the dependent. In the base case, I use a real discount rate of 3 percent, although I vary this below. To adjust for mortality prospects, I use sex/age-specific life tables for 1990 from Statistics Canada. Finally, to compute net social security wealth, I subtract out the CPP payroll tax payments that the individual would make during any continued work. I add both the employee and the employer shares of the payroll tax, under the assumption that the employer shares fully borne by the worker in the form of lower wages. All figures are discounted back to age fifty-five by both time preference rates and mortality risk.

For the output of the simulations, I calculate three different concepts. The first is the net of tax replacement rate, the rate at which social security replaces the (after-tax) earnings of the worker should he continue working in that year. It is important to do this calculation on an after-tax basis in order to account for the facts that (*a*) OAS, GIS, and SPA benefits are not taxable and (*b*), even for taxable CPP benefits, the individual may be in a lower tax bracket when retired. I model the average tax rate faced by earners of different earnings levels in each year, assuming that the tax system stays constant into the future (with the same rate structure and indexed tax brackets). The second concept is the accrual rate, the percentage change in social security wealth from the previous year.

Finally, I compute a tax/subsidy rate, which is the absolute change in social security wealth over the potential earnings from working that next year. This represents the implicit tax on or subsidy to continued work, in terms of the net change in social security wealth that is implied by that additional year of work. The numerator of this tax/subsidy rate is the opposite of the change in social security wealth from working the additional year. The denominator is the potential earnings over that additional year. Thus, if this figure is positive, it implies that the social security system causes a disincentive to additional work through forgone social security wealth. This is the relevant concept for the worker who is trading off leisure (on social security) against continued work.

Note that, in computing these concepts, I use the unconditional mortality risk beyond age fifty-five; that is, there is some probability that the worker may be dead at each year after his fifty-fifth birthday. An alternative approach would be to use conditional life tables at each year: for example, for the worker considering retiring on his sixty-third birthday, I discount the future by the age sixty-three–conditional life table. The correct approach here depends on the perspective from which this computation is taken. My approach is appropriate if the computation is taken from the perspective of the forward-looking fifty-four-year-old who is considering the retirement incentives at all future ages. The alternative would be appropriate for year-by-year decision making on retirement. Since I discount all the dollar figures back to age fifty-five by both time preference and mortality risk, both concepts yield the same tax/subsidy effects (since both numerator and denominator are deflated); however, they will yield somewhat different values of social security wealth and therefore different accrual rates.

To produce the base-case numbers, I use a typical individual who was born in January 1930 and thus turned age sixty-five in January 1995. In theory, in order to calculate benefits for a worker, I would need his entire earnings history since 1966. In practice, I use a "synthetic" earnings history, which uses the median earnings of a cohort through time. As a first step in creating this synthetic earnings history, I have computed information on the median earnings by calendar year and age cohort from the 1973–93 Survey of Consumer Finance (SCF data).[9] More specifically, I take the median earnings for a sixty-two-year-old in 1992, for a sixty-one-year-old in 1991, and so on, back through the survey years. To backcast from 1973 to 1966, before cross-sectional survey data are available, I first estimate cross-sectional age-earnings profiles in the 1973 survey. I then apply these estimates to "un-age" the workers in the 1975 survey back to 1966 and deflate these pre-1975 profiles by average wage growth by region, using data from Gruber and Hanratty (1995). To project earnings beyond 1992, I use the growth in the YMPE (actual to 1995, projected thereafter).

In pursuing this calculation, I found a relatively steep decline in median earnings after about age fifty, which presumably reflects the fact that more and more of the earning population is working only part-time. However, the synthetic individual is considering the decision to work full-time for an additional

9. These data are collected annually at the individual level from 1981 on. Before then, they were collected biannually at the family level; I use the information for male heads of household.

year, so this skews the true nature of the underlying earnings history. As a result, I use this synthetic earnings profile through age fifty and then assume that earnings stay constant in real terms from age fifty-one on.

For the purposes of the simulations presented below, I assume that workers claim social security benefits at the point of their retirement or when they become eligible if they retire before the point of eligibility. I assume initially that the worker's wife is exactly three years younger than he. I also assume that she has never worked. Finally, a critical parameter is the level of outside (i.e., asset) income available to the worker since the GIS and SPA benefits are means tested. Following the computation of replacement rates above, I consider two cases: zero outside income and outside income of $4,818.

2.3.2   Base-Case Results

Table 2.1 shows the base-case results, with zero asset income. Each row represents the age of the worker in the last year that he worked; that is, the first row represents the effect of working during the fifty-fourth year and retiring on the fifty-fifth birthday (1 January 1985). The first column shows the net replacement rate. This concept is not defined until the worker can actually claim benefits, which occurs if his last year of work is at age fifty-nine so that he retires at age sixty.

At that first point of possible claiming, the replacement rate is roughly 18 percent. The replacement rate then rises slowly to age sixty-five, as workers increase their social security benefits by delaying claiming. At age sixty-five, there is a large discrete jump, as the OAS benefit begins, and then a continued slow rise from actuarial adjustment. Then, at age sixty-eight, there is another

Table 2.1   Base-Case Incentive Calculations, No Outside Income

Last Year of Work	Replacement Rate	SSW	Accrual	Accrual Rate	Tax/ Subsidy
54	...	148,138	0	0	0
55	...	149,053	916	.0062	−.0415
56	...	148,944	−109	−.0007	.0051
57	...	148,188	−756	−.0051	.0355
58	...	147,437	−751	−.0051	.0365
59	.1760	146,685	−753	−.0051	.0380
60	.1964	145,232	−1,453	−.0099	.0771
61	.2116	143,667	−1,565	−.0108	.0848
62	.2520	142,162	−1,505	−.0105	.0848
63	.2806	140,528	−1,634	−.0115	.0962
64	.6037	137,502	−3,025	−.0215	.1859
65	.6124	131,793	−5,709	−.0415	.3672
66	.6212	125,678	−6,115	−.0464	.4128
67	.9285	120,112	−5,565	−.0443	.3955
68	.9545	115,755	−4,357	−.0363	.3269
69	.9838	111,473	−4,282	−.0370	.3403

discrete jump from the wife's OAS benefit and a continued rise from actuarial adjustment. Thus, for the worker who works through his sixty-ninth year and collects on his seventieth birthday, social security replaces roughly all his after-tax earnings.

The next three columns show the evolution of social security wealth over time. In order to understand these results, it is useful to recap the five mechanisms through which additional work affects the computation of social security wealth: (1) The worker must pay social security taxes on his earnings, lowering net social security wealth. (2) The additional year of earnings is used in the recomputation of social security benefits, replacing a previous low (or zero) earnings year (besides the 15 percent of lowest months that have already been excluded). Additional work raises net social security wealth through this channel. But this is true only if these additional years of earnings are above the YMPE and some earlier years of earnings were below. For the median worker, in fact, all years of earnings are above the YMPE. (3) The additional year of work, for work at ages sixty-two and beyond, implies a delay in claiming. This raises future benefits through the actuarial adjustment, but it implies fewer years over which benefits can be claimed. As a result, there is an ambiguous effect on net social security wealth. (4) The additional year of work will lower GIS and SPA benefits through means testing, both of the income from work and of the higher CPP benefit that results from additional work. (5) For each year into the future that I consider, there is some chance that the worker will die, lowering his net social security wealth. Thus, it is unclear ex ante whether the social security system will tax or subsidize additional work in any given case.

As table 2.1 shows, a worker who retires on his fifty-fifth birthday has accumulated $148,138 in social security wealth. There is then a small increase in social security wealth for work during the fifty-fifth year. This is because the worker still has not completed his earnings history, with the result that additional years of work therefore replace a zero in the benefits computation. Similarly, the system is neutral with respect to work during the fifty-sixth year since roughly (in this example) six months of work in that year are required to complete the earnings history. After this point, additional earnings do not affect average earnings, as noted above, since earnings in every year are above the YMPE. From age fifty-seven on, therefore, social security wealth uniformly declines, with the result that the system is placing a net tax on work. As a result, the accrual rate is negative in all years except the first.

The final column shows the tax/subsidy rate. There is a slight subsidy to work of 4.2 percent in the fifty-fifth year, as noted above, and then taxes on work thereafter. This tax is lower than the payroll tax that finances the CPP through age sixty since earnings below the YBE and earnings above the YMPE are exempted from tax. But there is no other form of tax/benefit linkage in this range since there is no benefit recomputation for additional work for a worker whose earnings each year were above the YMPE.

Table 2.2   Base-Case Incentive Calculations, Outside Income

Last Year of Work	Replacement Rate	SSW	Accrual	Accrual Rate	Tax/ Subsidy
54	...	124,391	0	0	0
55	...	125,406	1,015	.0082	−.0488
56	...	125,336	−70	−.0006	.0034
57	...	124,580	−756	−.0060	.0374
58	...	123,829	−751	−.0060	.0383
59	.1817	123,076	−753	−.0061	.0397
60	.2017	121,938	−1,138	−.0092	.0629
61	.2165	120,759	−1,179	−.0097	.0662
62	.2449	119,668	−1,091	−.0090	.0636
63	.2695	118,501	−1,167	−.0097	.0709
64	.5078	115,824	−2,677	−.0226	.1694
65	.5182	111,513	−4,311	−.0372	.2849
66	.5268	106,841	−4,672	−.0419	.3234
67	.8496	103,284	−3,557	−.0333	.2587
68	.8805	100,629	−2,654	−.0257	.2034
69	.9142	97,805	−2,824	−.0281	.2287

Beginning in the sixtieth year, tax rates on continued work rise more rapidly. There is actually an increase in the underlying value of the man's CPP wealth over the range of work in the sixtieth through the sixty-third years. But this is overshadowed by the scheduled rise in the CPP tax rate and the reduction in GIS/SPA benefits.

Beginning with work during the sixty-fourth year, the tax rates rise substantially as the (constant) actuarial adjustment becomes insufficient to compensate for delayed claiming of benefits.[10] In addition, beginning in the sixty-fifth year, there is a much larger tax rate through the GIS/SPA program. This is due to the fact that the GIS benefit kicks in once the worker is age sixty-five and receiving the OAS. The tax rate then declines again beginning with work during the sixty-seventh year. This is because the wife is turning sixty-five and therefore moving out of the range of eligibility for the (means-tested) SPA benefit. As a result, there is less of a disincentive for earnings for the husband.

Table 2.2 presents analogous results for the case with outside income. In this case, the pattern of tax rates is quite similar through age sixty. From age sixty on, however, the tax rates on continued work are somewhat lower, with tax rates peaking at 32 percent (instead of the 41 percent tax rate with zero asset

10. The relatively large jump at age sixty-four is due to the particulars of this example. There is a much larger rise in the CPI from 1992 (when the worker is age sixty-two) to 1993 (age sixty-three) than from 1993 to 1994 (age sixty-four). As a result, the increase in benefits is unusually large from age sixty-two to age sixty-three and unusually small from age sixty-three to age sixty-four. Thus, there is little change in the tax rate on continued work from age sixty-two to age sixty-three and a large change from age sixty-three to age sixty-four; in other years, the change from age sixty-two to age sixty-four would be spread across both years.

Table 2.3   **Single Worker, Outside Income**

Last Year of Work	Replacement Rate	SSW	Accrual	Accrual Rate	Tax/ Subsidy
54	. . .	68,957	0	0	0
55	. . .	69,648	691	.0100	−.0352
56	. . .	69,456	−192	−.0028	.0100
57	. . .	68,700	−756	−.0109	.0390
58	. . .	67,949	−751	−.0109	.0397
59	.1551	67,196	−753	−.0111	.0409
60	.1705	66,469	−727	−.0108	.0413
61	.1826	66,427	−42	−.0006	.0024
62	.2002	66,622	195	.0029	−.0116
63	.2211	66,884	262	.0039	−.0162
64	.3616	65,278	−1,606	−.0240	.1036
65	.3752	63,202	−2,076	−.0318	.1396
66	.3884	60,804	−2,398	−.0379	.1686
67	.4032	58,435	−2,369	−.0390	.1748
68	.4175	55,777	−2,658	−.0455	.2062
69	.4320	52,951	−2,826	−.0507	.2315

income). This pattern is a simple reflection of the implicit tax on work put in place by the GIS and SPA programs. With more outside income, these programs are irrelevant. As a result, raising CPP benefits through working to an older age is relatively more attractive since doing so does not reduce the means-tested entitlement. Thus, the net effect of the Canadian retirement income system on work incentives is fairly sensitive to whether the family is in the range where means-tested benefits are relevant.

2.3.3 Other Cases

Table 2.3 explores these same results for a single worker for the case with outside income. Until age sixty, the pattern of incentives for the single worker is very similar to that for the married worker. From age sixty on, however, the tax rates are dramatically lower for the single worker than for the base-case married worker. This reflects the fact that there is no implicit taxation through the SPA program in this case since there is no spouse who can benefit from that program. That is, these findings illustrate that the CPP system itself is very close to being actuarially fair after the age of early eligibility but that the large tax rates that we saw earlier arose from the means-tested transfers that were in place through the SPA system. If there is no outside income for this single worker, however, there are nontrivial taxes after age sixty (on the order of 8 percent), reflecting the clawback of GIS benefits.

For retirement from age sixty-five on, however, there is once again a substantial tax for the single worker, owing to unfair actuarial adjustment of the CPP benefit. These taxes rise steadily with age, as the actuarial adjustment becomes increasingly unfair. At the oldest ages in my computations, the results

Table 2.4   Tenth Percentile Earner, No Outside Income

Last Year of Work	Replacement Rate	SSW	Accrual	Accrual Rate	Tax/ Subsidy
54	...	140,871	0	0	0
55	...	141,388	517	.0037	−.0474
56	...	141,377	−12	−.0001	.0011
57	...	141,042	−335	−.0024	.0322
58	...	140,696	−346	−.0025	.0348
59	.2810	140,344	−352	−.0025	.0369
60	.3141	139,124	−1,220	−.0087	.1362
61	.3373	137,743	−1,381	−.0099	.1580
62	.4143	136,422	−1,321	−.0096	.1584
63	.4608	135,014	−1,408	−.0103	.1771
64	1.2210	132,699	−2,315	−.0171	.3057
65	1.2427	128,110	−4,589	−.0346	.6377
66	1.2650	123,311	−4,799	−.0375	.7035
67	1.7663	118,940	−4,370	−.0354	.6776
68	1.8110	115,124	−3,816	−.0321	.6276
69	1.8596	111,432	−3,692	−.0321	.6548

are once again similar for married couples and singles as wives have moved out of the range of SPA eligibility.

One particularly interesting dimension of heterogeneity is the lifetime earnings of workers. Tables 2.4 and 2.5 contrast the case of a worker whose earnings are at the tenth percentile of the earnings distribution with that of one whose earnings are at the ninetieth percentile. In doing this calculation, I assume that the age-earnings profiles of both workers are the same; I simply shift the intercept at age fifty for these profiles. For the tenth-percentile worker, I assume no outside income; for the ninetieth-percentile case, I assume the median outside income.

Before age sixty, these cases yield fairly similar results. One interesting finding is that the tax rates on *both* high and low earners are lower than those on the base-case worker. This is because more of the earnings of the high earner are above the YMPE and therefore exempt from taxation; similarly, more of the earnings of the low earner are below the YBE and also exempt from taxation. But these differences are fairly slight.

But, from age sixty on, a striking difference emerges. For the low-income worker, this system is very generous, replacing 28 percent of his income if he retires after his fifty-ninth year, 122 percent of his income if he retires after his sixty-fourth year, and 186 percent of his income if he retires after his sixty-ninth year. At the same time, the tax rates in place are very large; they reach a peak of *over 70 percent* for retirement on the seventieth birthday. Thus, the worker with low lifetime earnings and no outside income faces a large disincentive in considering further work after age sixty and particularly from age sixty-five on.

Table 2.5   **Ninetieth Percentile Earner, Outside Income**

Last Year of Work	Replacement Rate	SSW	Accrual	Accrual Rate	Tax/ Subsidy
54	...	124,391	0	0	0
55	...	125,406	1,015	.0082	−.0318
56	...	125,336	−70	−.0006	.0022
57	...	124,580	−756	−.0060	.0239
58	...	123,829	−751	−.0060	.0243
59	.1146	123,076	−753	−.0061	.0250
60	.1264	121,938	−1,138	−.0092	.0394
61	.1355	120,759	−1,179	−.0097	.0414
62	.1529	119,668	−1,091	−.0090	.0397
63	.1679	118,501	−1,167	−.0097	.0441
64	.3152	115,824	−2,677	−.0226	.1050
65	.3207	111,513	−4,311	−.0372	.1761
66	.3251	106,841	−4,672	−.0419	.1993
67	.5228	103,284	−3,557	−.0333	.1591
68	.5404	100,629	−2,654	−.0257	.1247
69	.5594	97,805	−2,824	−.0281	.1398

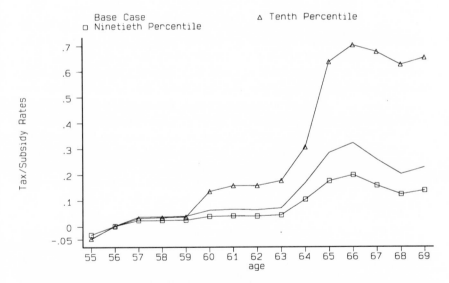

Fig. 2.15   Tax/subsidy rates by earnings level

For workers with higher lifetime earnings, the replacement rates through the system are much lower, as are the implicit tax rates. Even at their peak, the tax rates on continued work are below 20 percent. These patterns are compared in figure 2.15, which illustrates these differences: similar tax rates until age sixty, with a growing divergence thereafter.

Finally, table 2.6 considers a different permutation to the earnings history:

Table 2.6   Incomplete Earnings History, Outside Income

Last Year of Work	Replacement Rate	SSW	Accrual	Accrual Rate	Tax/ Subsidy
54	...	117,249	0	0	0
55	...	118,264	1,015	.0087	−.0488
56	...	119,252	988	.0084	−.0487
57	...	120,247	995	.0083	−.0492
58	...	121,237	990	.0082	−.0505
59	.1783	122,213	977	.0081	−.0515
60	.1995	121,293	−920	−.0075	.0508
61	.2155	120,387	−906	−.0075	.0509
62	.2450	119,462	−925	−.0077	.0539
63	.2696	118,295	−1,167	−.0098	.0709
64	.5085	115,617	−2,678	−.0226	.1695
65	.5186	111,257	−4,361	−.0377	.2882
66	.5275	106,582	−4,675	−.0420	.3236
67	.8497	102,978	−3,604	−.0338	.2621
68	.8807	100,323	−2,654	−.0258	.2034
69	.9143	97,499	−2,824	−.0281	.2287

assuming that the worker was unemployed for four years and that he therefore has an incomplete earnings history (for the case with outside income). This offers an incentive for the worker to retire later since additional years of work replace zeros in the computation of CPP benefits. This is illustrated by the sizable subsidy to work through age fifty-nine; this subsidy arises because of the replacement of zero values in the earnings history. From age sixty to age sixty-two, there is a tax rate on continued work, but it is smaller than in the base case. Then, from age sixty-three on, the tax rate is the same as in the base case as the earnings history has been completed.

2.4   Conclusions

The system of retirement income provision in Canada is a critically important feature of the opportunity set of older workers who are considering retirement. This set of four programs provides a large source of income support for retired workers, but it also potentially taxes continued work among those who wish to work beyond the age of early retirement eligibility. I have documented that there is clearly an important effect of these programs on the timing of retirement. Future work on retirement in Canada could usefully explore the effect of program generosity on retirement behavior. In particular, it is important to assess the role that these (often quite large) implicit taxes play in determining retirement decisions, both on average and across groups of workers that face very different incentives, for example, high and low earners.

Appendix
Data Sources

Historical Data

Labor force participation data are from Statistics Canada's CANSIM CD-rom. Data were also provided directly by Statistics Canada. Population data are from Economic Council of Canada (1976), Denton and Ostry (1967), and Statistics Canada (1995). Data on program receipt are from Human Resources Development Canada (1996).

Contemporaneous Data

All contemporaneous figures were tabulated by the author from April SCF data for 1992 and 1993.

References

Baker, Michael, and Dwayne Benjamin. 1996. Early retirement provisions and the labour force behaviour of older men: Evidence from Canada. University of Toronto, Department of Economics. Mimeo.

———. 1997. How do retirement tests affect the labor supply of older men? University of Toronto, Department of Economics. Mimeo.

Burtless, Gary, and Robert Moffitt. 1986. Social security, earnings tests, and age at retirement. *Public Finance Quarterly* 14:3–27.

Denton, Frank D., and Sylvia Ostry. 1967. *Historical estimates of the Canadian labour force.* Ottawa: Dominion Bureau of Statistics.

Economic Council of Canada. 1976. *People and jobs: A study of the Canadian labor market.* Ottawa: Information Canada.

Gruber, Jonathan. 1996. Disability insurance benefits and labor supply of older persons. Massachusetts Institute of Technology, Department of Economics. Mimeo.

Gruber, Jonathan, and Maria Hanratty. 1995. The labor market effects of introducing national health insurance: Evidence from Canada. *Journal of Economics and Business Statistics* 13, no. 2 (April): 163–74.

Human Resources Development Canada. 1996. *Statistics related to income security programs.* Ottawa.

Office of the Superintendant of Financial Institutions Canada. 1993. *Canada Pension Plan: Fifteenth actuarial report.* Ottawa.

Statistics Canada. 1995. *Historical labor force statistics.* Ottawa.

3 Social Security and Retirement in France

Didier Blanchet and Louis-Paul Pelé

Very few studies exist concerning the economic determinants of retirement age in France. Three main reasons may account for this situation. First, a common idea is that the French pension system offers little flexibility concerning choice of retirement age, with the result that little room is left for estimating economic models of retirement behavior. A second explanation is the complexity of the pension system, which renders data collection extremely difficult and discourages efforts to build systematic behavioral models. Third, age at exit from the labor force is determined not only by individual preferences and the structure of the pension system itself but more and more often by parallel systems such as preretirement schemes or specific dispositions of unemployment insurance targeted toward older workers, and the development of these schemes reflects both supply- and demand-side effects on the labor market; it may therefore appear meaningless to develop behavioral models that remain generally limited to supply-side considerations.

All these explanations are valid, but only partially. Flexibility in the choice of retirement age is not great, but still exists: in fact, the basic general regime offers the possibility of retirement between the ages of sixty and sixty-five. The problems raised by the complexity of the system can then be bypassed, in a first attempt, by concentrating on this general regime and associated complementary schemes. Finally, if it is indisputable that interactions between supply and demand factors in a context of low employment complicate the analysis of

Didier Blanchet is head of the Ecole Nationale de la Statistique et de l'Administration Economique. At the time this work was initiated, he was head of the Redistribution et Politiques Sociales division at the Institut National de la Statistique et des Etudes Economiques. Louis-Paul Pelé is a member of the Redistribution et Politiques Sociales division at the Institut National de la Statistique et des Etudes Economiques.

The authors are grateful to David Wise and Jonathan Gruber for leading the International Social Security Comparisons project and giving many helpful suggestions. They also acknowledge useful comments from other participants in the project.

retirement behavior, this implies at the same time that this analysis is particularly worthwhile. The extension of preretirement schemes in France is probably one of the major aspects of our current pension problems; it may limit the feasibility of policies aimed at raising the average retirement age, with the result that the question of the structure of incentives generated by this system is of particular importance, whatever the channels through which these incentives finally affect behavior, that is, directly through individuals or indirectly through employers.

It is with these elements in mind that we present here some results concerning the labor force participation of older workers in France and their link with the organization of the pension system. We proceed in three steps: (1) a general description of trends in labor force participation, pension levels, and pension coverage; (2) a precise description of the way pensions are computed in the basic general regime and the two most important complementary schemes; and (3) the simulation of incentives implied by these computation rules. This latter section illustrates how simple computations of future benefits help clarify the properties of pension rules. But it also shows the importance of what remains to be done to give a full explanation of labor force participation at older ages and the way that participation could be affected by future or ongoing reforms of retirement or preretirement schemes.

3.1   The Labor Market Behavior of Older Persons in France

This section is devoted to an analysis of labor force participation trends around retirement age. We first place recent developments in a long-term perspective. Then, concentrating on what has happened since 1968, we show that this period has been characterized by an acceleration of the long-run decline of the average retirement age and at the same time by the increasing complexity of the pattern of transition from activity to retirement.

3.1.1   Long-Term Trends in Labor Force Participation

We first provide figures—focusing on male workers to avoid the offsetting trends resulting, for women, from increased activity at median ages—for labor force participation since the 1920s. Figure 3.1 shows that the decline in labor force participation at older ages has been a long-term trend. It must be noted that this trend has been observed despite the fact that the French population has been aging for most of the century. But this apparent paradox can be easily explained by general economic growth. Economic progress resulted in a collective income/leisure trade-off in favor of a longer retirement period, which had no difficulty outweighing the consequences of a moderate aging process, and this trade-off was largely mediated by the development of pension schemes.

Actually, this decline in labor force participation at older ages occurred in a context of increased coverage and generosity of the pension system. Direct measures of coverage ratios are difficult to obtain: owing to the fragmentation

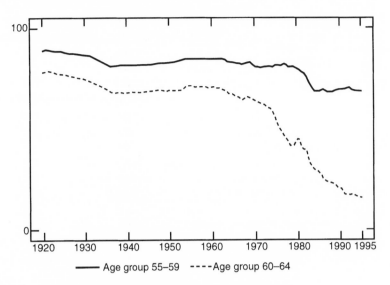

Fig. 3.1   Participation rate of older men, France, long term
Source: Marchand and Thélot (1991); Bordes and Guillemot (1994).

of the pension system in France, there are no systematic series giving numbers of beneficiaries or contributors in the whole population. Adding up series that exist for the major schemes, we nevertheless get the overall upward trend displayed in figure 3.2. In fact, since 1974, when affiliation with a pension system became mandatory, we can consider that coverage is complete. The remaining gap between total employment and the number of contributors that appears in figure 3.2, therefore, means not that some people remain uncovered but simply that they are covered by basic schemes that do not belong to the list of nine major schemes taken into account for this graph.

A similar evolution can be observed on the pensioners' side, as displayed in figure 3.3. It should be noted that the interpretation of this figure is complicated by the fact that one individual may, over his career, have been covered (successively) by more than one basic regime.[1]

Evidence of the increased generosity of the pension system is also given by the very crude computation of the ratio of total old age expenditures, divided by the number of inactive persons over age sixty, to the average net wage in the labor force, which is displayed in figure 3.4. The ratio of average benefits to average wages increased by about 60 percent between 1950 and 1974 and continued to increase after the complete generalization of coverage after 1974, for various reasons: the maturing of the systems, changes in computation rules for the main regimes, and an active policy of revaluation of benefits.

---

1. In 1993, the average French pensioner received benefits from 1.4 different basic schemes plus an average of 1.1 benefits derived from complementary schemes. Figure 3.3 covers beneficiaries only from the first category of regimes.

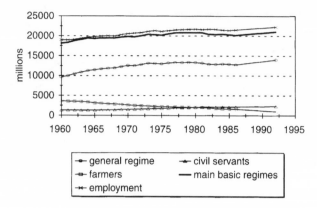

Fig. 3.2   Contributors to pension regimes

Note: In this figure, the category *main basic regimes* includes nine basic regimes, which cover almost the entire employed population. The figure also shows separate figures for three regimes: the general regime, which covers wage earners from the private sector, the regime for farmers, and the civil servants' pension scheme.

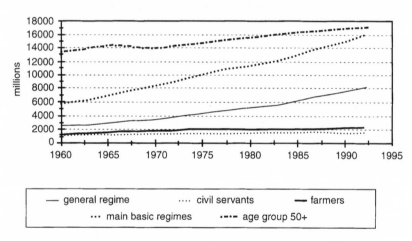

Fig. 3.3   Pensioners in the basic regimes

Note: The figure shows the number of pensioners in the different basic regimes. As in fig. 3.2 above, the total number refers to the nine basic regimes. As is discussed in the text, a retiree may receive pensions from several basic regimes (the average number of basic pensions is 1.4). Therefore, the last category shows the total number of pensions but overstates the total number of retirees.

Yet these general and progressive changes do not account for the evolution of labor force participation rates since the 1980s, which must be more narrowly linked to changes in the legal retirement age and to the extension of other forms of exit from the labor force, that is, the development of preretirement schemes.

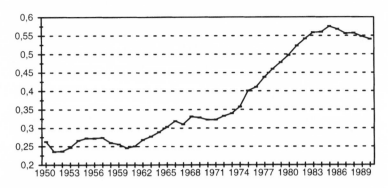

Fig. 3.4 Ratio of average old age benefit to average wage

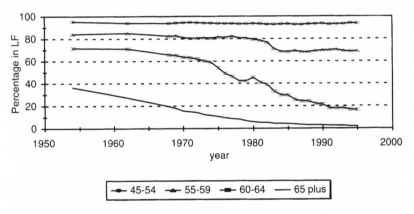

Fig. 3.5 Historical trends in the labor force participation of older men (LF = labor force)
Source: Bordes and Guillemot (1994).

3.1.2 Detailed Trends since 1960

During this period, the participation rate among workers over age fifty-five decreased by more than 50 percent, from 31.5 to 15 percent. Among workers over age sixty, it fell from 22.5 to 4.8 percent. Such dramatic decreases in the participation rates of older workers had never been observed before.

Their first consequence is that hardly any individuals over age seventy are employed. For instance, the participation rate of men between the ages of seventy and seventy-four was divided by ten between 1970 and 1995 (from 15.2 to 1.5 percent). The age group sixty-five to sixty-nine also disappeared from the labor force almost completely: rates amount to 3.7 percent for men and 2.5 percent for women, as opposed to, respectively, 30.6 and 15 percent in 1968. Second, the age group sixty to sixty-four experienced the most substantial decrease in the participation rate over the same period, from 65.7 to 16.5 percent among men (fig. 3.5) and from 32.4 to 14.6 percent among women (fig. 3.6).

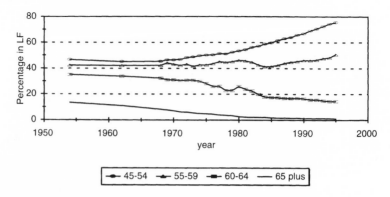

Fig. 3.6   Historical trends in the labor force participation of older women (LF = labor force)
Source: Bordes and Guillemot (1994).

Finally, the participation rate for men between the ages of fifty-five and fifty-nine decreased from 82.5 to 68.9 percent.

Rates for women have long been fluctuating, with a continuous increase in female activity at median ages counteracting the effect of earlier exit from the labor force. The second effect dominated in the age group sixty to sixty-four until recently, while the first one dominated constantly in the age group fifty-five to fifty-nine (fig. 3.6).

On the whole, the average age of people withdrawing from the labor force fell by 4.5 years between 1969 and 1993, from 62 to 58.5. Figures 3.7 and 3.8 also show the specific role played by preretirement schemes and unemployment insurance in explaining the drop among men of employment rates (not only labor force participation rates) in these age groups. They played the major role in the decline of employment between the ages of sixty and sixty-four until the mid-1980s, after which they have been taken over by the progressive application of retirement at age sixty. It was during the same period that preretirement before age sixty developed, affecting about 20 percent of the age group. Rates of preretirement have remained at this level since the end of the 1980s.

3.1.3   The Current Situation

The current situation is summarized in figures 3.9–3.12. Detailed profiles of occupation and labor force participation by age are given in figures 3.9 and 3.10. Activity and employment both start declining around age fifty-five, doing so in a quasi-linear fashion until age sixty, at which point their values are between 30 and 40 percent. They then drop rapidly, only a small portion of the population remaining at work after age sixty-two, which proportion quits the labor force very progressively until ages sixty-five to seventy.

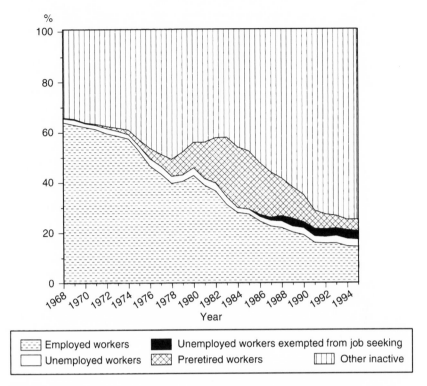

Fig. 3.7   Status of active male workers aged 60–64 from 1968 to 1995
Source: Blanchet and Marioni (1996).

Figures 3.11 and 3.12 give more details concerning the link between age and status between the ages of fifty and seventy-five. Inactive people are broken down into retired and other inactive; for men, the latter category includes a large fraction of preretired people between the ages of fifty-five and sixty. Active people are broken down into employed and unemployed, the latter category peaking at age fifty-six, then declining progressively until age sixty, with transfers from this category to the categories of retired or preretired. Parallel patterns exist for women, with the difference that a larger share can be classified as other inactive at all ages, even after the normal retirement age. It must be noted, however, that the data for these two graphs are obtained from self-declarations on the Employment Survey, the categories of which do not perfectly coincide with administrative definitions of unemployment, preretirement, or retirement.

Moving to the measurement of income resources for households whose head is retired, table 3.1 gives the distribution between work income, pension benefits, minimum old age benefits, and capital income, according to previous

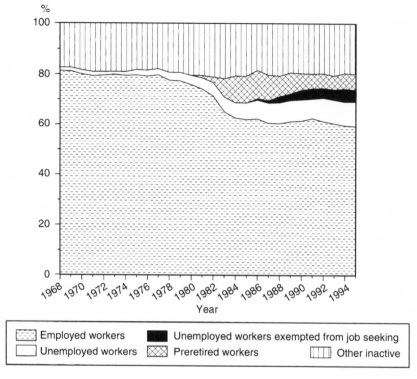

Fig. 3.8 Status of active male workers aged 55–59 from 1968 to 1995
Source: Blanchet and Marioni (1996).

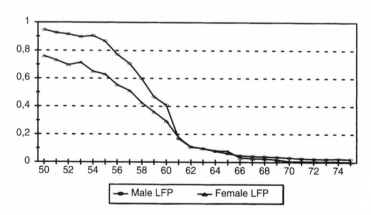

Fig. 3.9 Labor force participation (LFP) rates by age and sex
Source: Employment Survey 1996.

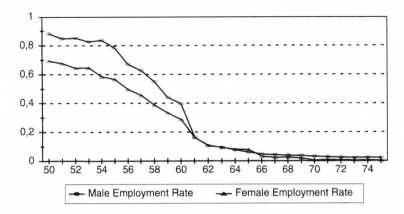

Fig. 3.10   Employment rates by age and sex
Source: Employment Survey 1996.

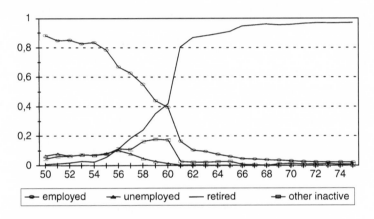

Fig. 3.11   Distribution of activities of men by age
Source: Employment Survey 1996.

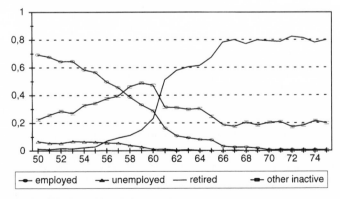

Fig. 3.12   Distribution of activities of women by age
Source: Employment Survey 1996.

Table 3.1   Distribution of Household Income by Source (households whose head
                   is inactive)

	Share of Each Source in %			
	Activity Earnings	Pensions	Minimum Pension	Property Income
Total	6.1	76.2	5.3	12.4
Former status of head:				
Farmer	6.1	59.8	17.9	16.2
Independent worker	6.2	54.1	4.8	34.9
Wage earner	6.0	82.4	2.8	8.8
Other	6.9	65.5	12.1	15.5

Source: Taxable Earnings Survey 1984.

activity. Various pension income or other public subsidies constitute the major part of total income for households whose head was previously a wage earner. Capital income plays a larger role for former self-employed workers and workers from the agricultural sector, the latter also relying heavily on minimum old age benefits. In all cases, by construction (household head is retired), work income plays a minor role.

On the whole, these various income sources result in an average standard of living for retired households that is roughly equal to the average standard of living of active households. This contrasts with the situation that prevailed up to the 1970s and that led to the strong policy in favor of pension revaluation illustrated in figure 3.4 above.

3.2   Structure and Rules of Retirement Schemes

Two difficulties arise when one attempts to describe the French pension system. The first is due to its complexity, that is, the coexistence of many different regimes covering various segments of the population. We give a brief overview of the various regimes, but we then concentrate on the system that concerns the majority of the population, the combination of the basic general regime and mandatory complementary schemes organized on a socioprofessional basis (ARRCO [Association de Regimes de Retraite Complémentaires] and AGIRC [Association Générale des Institutions de Retraite des Cadres]), all of them being pay-as-you-go systems.

The second difficulty comes from the fact that the rules of these systems are not fixed but change over time. We concentrate here on the rules that prevailed at the beginning of the 1990s. Concerning the general regime, these rules essentially resulted from a reform introduced in 1983 that allowed retirement at a full rate at age sixty.

We then complete this presentation by providing information on (*a*) the system of preretirement, which, beside the rules governing normal pensions, plays a large role in shaping labor force participation rates between the ages of fifty-five and fifty-nine, and (*b*) the reforms introduced since 1993, starting with a reform of the general regime whose consequences should progressively affect new cohorts of retirees until the first decade of the next century.

3.2.1   The Different Regimes

The French system is often considered to be complex, but its structure can nevertheless be summed up simply in the following way:

For most of the population (wage earners from the private sector), the pension relies on two pillars: (1) The first is the basic general regime, which offers benefits corresponding to the share of wages below a social security ceiling.[2] We hereafter use the term *social security* to describe this segment of the system, even if it does not exactly correspond to the French conventions.[3] In 1992, 70.5 percent of people over age sixty received a social security pension. On the contributors' side, the same year, the general regime covered 64.8 percent of the labor force. (2) The second pillar is complementary schemes, organized on a socioprofessional basis. These schemes developed between 1946 and the mid-1960s. They consist of a large number (about 180) of specific regimes, but these regimes are federated in two main organisms ensuring interregime demographic compensation: (*a*) AGIRC for executive workers and only for the fraction of their wages over the social security ceiling and (*b*) ARRCO for other workers and executives' wages below the ceiling. In 1972, contributing to a complementary scheme became compulsory. Today, complementary schemes provide 40 percent of retirement pensions for wage earners in the private sector (Join-Lambert et al. 1994, 366).

Beside this simple two-pillar structure, the complexity of the French system, in fact, is principally due to the existence of a large number of exceptions to this general rule of organization. These exceptions are the result of two factors. When social security was created in 1945, people who already benefited from more generous dispositions refused to join the new system (e.g., people belonging to the public sector). Some categories preferred, on the other hand, to adopt cheaper systems offering lower protection because they thought that a large part of their retirement needs was likely to be covered by other sources, such as professional capital for the self-employed. Beside the two-pillar system constituted by the general regime and ARRCO/AGIRC, we therefore have a multiplicity of special regimes and regimes for self-employed workers applying specific rules. For instance, there are about 120 first-pillar retirement

2. In 1994, the gross value of the social security ceiling was Fr 12,760, while the average gross wage was Fr 12,280.

3. In the French system, the term *social security* (*sécurité sociale*) is used to characterize all the basic social insurance schemes that were set up in 1945: health insurance, family allowances, work injuries, and basic pensions. The French social security system does not limit itself, as does social security in the United States, to the public pension scheme. We use *social security* here to describe the intersection of the pension field and the field of *sécurité sociale* in the French sense of the term.

schemes other than the general regime. In particular, it must be observed that civil servants are not really covered by an autonomous pension system since their pensions are paid directly through the state budget.

For all categories of people, there is, at last, a system of minimum pension (*minimum vieillesse*), which is a means-tested allowance. The size of the population benefiting from this minimum pension has regularly declined in the past, owing to the increasing maturity of normal pensions. It is now a little over 1 million, as opposed to 2.55 million in 1959 (Commissariat Général du Plan 1995).

3.2.2 Benefits and Contributions: General Regime and Complementary Schemes

We now give more details about the calculation of pensions for the general regime and complementary schemes.

Benefits from the General Regime

The general regime offers contributory benefits corresponding to the share of wages below the social security ceiling. We consider the rules that prevailed between 1983 and the beginning of the 1990s and that, until now, have been only little affected by changes introduced in 1993, whose application will be very progressive. Under these rules, the pension was computed on the basis of several criteria. It was proportional to the number of years contributed (truncated to 37.5 years) and to a reference wage, which used to be the average wage of the ten best years of the pensioner's career (past nominal wages being reevaluated at time of liquidation according to a set of retrospective coefficients). The formula was therefore

$$\text{(1)} \qquad \text{pension} = \alpha \times \left(\frac{\text{no. of years, truncated to 37.5}}{37.5} \right)$$

$$\times \text{ (average wage of the 10 best years),}$$

the proportionality coefficient α being itself modulated. It was maximal when the pensioner left, at age sixty, with 37.5 years of contributions or more; in that case, its value was set at 50 percent, and this exactly ensured a replacement rate of the reference wage (not necessarily the last wage) equal to 50 percent. The same value of α also applied, whatever the number of years of contributions, when the individual left at age sixty-five. In all other cases, the coefficient was reduced either by 1.25 percentage point for each term missing to reach the value of 150 terms or by 1.25 percentage point for each term missing to reach age sixty-five, the formula to be used being the one that lead to the most favorable outcome.

This system means that the number of years of contributions affects the pension level in two ways, which may imply, in some cases, a very strong dependency between age at retirement and pension level. To provide a full under-

Table 3.2   **Replacement Rate Provided by the General Regime for Three Reference Cases**

Age	Number of Years of Contributions	α (%) (1)	Number of Years/37.5 (2)	Replacement Ratio (%) (1) × (2)
Individual A:				
60	25	25	.667	16.7
61	26	30	.693	20.8
62	27	35	.720	25.2
63	28	40	.747	29.9
64	29	45	.773	34.8
65	30	50	.800	40.0
Individual B:				
60	30	25	.800	20.0
61	31	30	.827	24.8
62	32	35	.853	29.9
63	33	40	.880	35.2
64	34	45	.907	40.8
65	35	50	.933	46.7
Individual C:				
60	35	37.5	.933	35.0
61	36	42.5	.960	40.8
62	37	47.5	.987	46.9
63	38	50	1.000	50.0
64	39	50	1.000	50.0
65	40	50	1.000	50.0

standing of this interaction, table 3.2 shows the consequences of this system for three reference cases with individuals arriving at age sixty with, respectively, twenty-five, thirty, and thirty-five years of contributions.

The first person must wait until age sixty-five to retire at a full rate α (50 percent). Even so, however, his pension will be reduced by the fact that he has only thirty years of contributions at this age. His replacement ratio will therefore be equal only to 30/37.5 of the maximum replacement ratio, which is equal to 50 percent. Note that, at each age under sixty, the downward adjustment of α is computed on the basis of the number of years shy of age sixty-five, rather than the number of years shy of a value of $N = 37.5$, since the rule consists in applying the most favorable of the two adjustments.

The second individual must also wait until age sixty-five to retire at the full rate α but will benefit at this age by a higher replacement rate, equal to 35/37.5 times the maximum replacement ratio of 50 percent. In this case, again, the downward adjustment before age sixty-five is based on the number of years shy of age sixty-five.

The third individual will not have to wait until age 65. He will benefit from the maximum replacement rate as soon as he reaches a cumulated number of years of contributions equal to 37.5, that is, at age 62.5. If he decided to leave between the ages of 60 and 62.5, the downward adjustment would be computed according to the number of years shy of the total of 37.5 years of contributions, rather than the number of years shy of age 65, since the first rule is now the most generous. Note also that, for this individual, working past age 62.5 does not bring any further advantage in terms of pension level.

Some additional observations must be added to this presentation of the general regime. First, some people have been successively affiliated with different schemes, especially in older cohorts: for instance, people moving from agriculture or self-employment to the status of wage earner in industry or services. These people will collect two basic pensions, one from their initial regime and one from the general regime. The latter will be proportional to the number of years spent in this regime, according to formula (1), yet coefficient α will be evaluated taking into account the *total* number of years of contributions, whatever the regime. Reductions in α, furthermore, do not apply in certain cases: veterans, disabled workers, and female workers who have twenty-four years of contributions and have raised three children.

Formula (1) also implies that, at the time they are claimed, pensions are computed in current nominal French francs. They are then reevaluated each year on a discretionary basis. During the 1970s and early 1980s, the general policy was to overindex these pensions in order to make up for the initial gap between the standard of living of workers and that of pensioners. Since the mid-1980s, the practice has instead consisted in an indexation on prices.

Benefits from Complementary Schemes: ARRCO and AGIRC

These schemes are almost fully contributive. Pensions are computed according to a system of points. Points are accumulated during the worker's career in proportion to his contributions: the contribution rate is fixed, and one franc contributed in year t is considered equivalent to the formal buying of $1/$RW points, where RW, in the system terminology, constitutes the reference wage (*salaire de référence,* which is in fact the price of one point). The pension is then equal to the total number of points accumulated over the pensioner's career, multiplied by a coefficient V (*valeur du point*), which is fixed every year.

For a pensioner who began working at time t_0 and stopped at time t_1, the formula for pension at time t can therefore be written as

$$(2) \qquad \text{pension} = V(t) \cdot \sum_{t'=t_0}^{t_1} \frac{\tau(t')w(t')}{RW(t')},$$

where $\tau(t')$ and $w(t')$ are, respectively, the contribution rate and the worker's wage at time t'. As explained above, only a fraction of the wage is taken into account for computing contributions and points accumulated each year: for nonexecutives, the wage is truncated to three social security ceilings, and contributions are collected by ARRCO; for executives, contributions are collected

Table 3.3   **Current Features of Complementary Schemes (1993)**

	ARRCO	AGIRC
Contractual contribution rate (% of gross wages)	5	13
Reference wage (Fr)	21.18	19.69
Value of point (Fr)	2.24	2.36

by ARRCO for the part of the wage below the ceiling and by AGIRC for the segment of the wage falling above the ceiling up to four times the ceiling.

Contribution rates, reference wages, and values of points that prevail are not the same in both schemes. Table 3.3 gives levels for 1993.

Concerning retirement age in these complementary schemes, the normal retirement age remains theoretically sixty-five, even after the 1983 reform, which introduced retirement at age sixty in the general regime. For retirement under age sixty-five, a quasi-actuarial adjustment is supposed to be applied. But, since the 1983 reform, this adjustment is not applied to people who fulfill the conditions for a basic retirement at the full rate (more than 37.5 years of contributions). The resulting extra expenditures for the complementary schemes are supported by a specific entity, financed through various contributions: the Association pour la Structure Financière. This simply means that complementary schemes have been de facto transformed in schemes where normal retirement is at age sixty, but without bearing its cost (or bearing it only in terms of forgone contributions).

Taxation, Contributions, Earnings Tests

Taxation rules differ for pensions and wages. A certain number of contributions concern *only* wage earners. Pensioners are exempted from these contributions. This is the case for contributions to unemployment insurance, at a rate of about 3.2 percent. This is also the case for contributions to pension schemes, at the following rates: for the general regime, 6.55 percent of the fraction of the wage below the social security ceiling; for complementary schemes (ARRCO and AGIRC), 2 percent of the wage below three times the social security ceiling to ARRCO for nonexecutives and 2 percent of the wage below the social security ceiling to ARRCO and 4.68 percent of the fraction of the wage between one and four times the social security ceiling to AGIRC for executives.

It must be added that, concerning complementary schemes, these basic contribution rates—which are the ones used to compute the accumulation of points and future entitlements—are now systematically affected by majoration coefficients, which are now equal to 125 percent in both regimes. This is an additional tax, meaning that points are, in fact, purchased 25 percent above their face value.

We next have contributions that concern *both wage earners and pensioners,*

Table 3.4   **Some Contribution Rates (%)**

	Employer	Employee or Protected Person	Total
General regime:			
Health:			
Workers	12.8	6.8	19.6
Pensioners	. . .	1.4	1.4
Preretired	. . .	5.5	5.5
Family	5.4	. . .	5.4
Old age:			
Wages below the ceiling	8.2	6.55	14.75
Full wage	1.6	. . .	1.6
Unemployment insurance:			
Below ceiling	5.34	3.22	8.56
From 1 to 4 times ceiling	5.47	3.86	9.34
Complementary pensions:[a]			
Executives:			
Below ceiling (ARRCO)	3 ($\times$ 1.25)	2 ($\times$ 1.25)	5 ($\times$ 1.25)
From 1 ceiling to 4 times ceiling (AGIRC)	9.36 ($\times$ 1.21)	4.68 ($\times$ 1.21)	14.04 ($\times$ 1.21)
Others (AARCO):			
Below 3 times ceiling	3 ($\times$ 1.25)	2 ($\times$ 1.25)	5 ($\times$ 1.25)

Sources: Join-Lambert et al. (1994); Legros (1995).

[a]The multiplicative coefficient refers to the concept *calling rates* (*taux d'appel*); i.e., there is a basic statutory contribution rate, but the real contribution rate is obtained after multiplication by the calling rate, which was lower than one during the first decades of existence of the system and now increases more or less regularly.

but at *different rates.* This is the case of contributions to health insurance, whose rates are 6.8 percent on wages, 1.4 percent on pensions from the general regime, and 2.4 percent on complementary pensions.

We then have taxes or contributions that are *similar for both sources of income.* These are the generalized social contribution (CSG), introduced in 1988, whose rate is now equal to 2.4 percent and whose aim is to finance a certain number of noncontributive allowances, and the personal income tax, which is progressive and whose rules are almost the same for pensions and wages (the only difference consists in a tax allowance on wages whose aim is to compensate for expenditures linked to professional activity).

Table 3.4 shows these different rates. In addition, it gives the rates for contributions paid by employers.

Concerning at last earnings tests in the attribution of pensions, the rules differ across regimes, but we can generally consider that they strongly discourage the continuation of activity after the claiming of the pension. Concerning the general regime, there is no formal impossibility of combining benefits with labor income, but claiming pension rights implies the interruption of the labor relation with the current employer. The only possibility is then to combine benefits with independent work or to work for another employer, a possibility that will concern only a small minority. Furthermore, concerning complementary schemes, starting a new activity generally leads to the interruption of benefits.

3.2.3 Preretirement

Preretirement systems developed in France in several steps. We can distinguish between two main periods, before and after the lowering of the normal retirement age to sixty in 1983.

Preretirement During the 1970s

The first period was dominated by measures concerning workers between the ages of sixty and sixty-four. The first measure dates back as early as 1963, when a specific allowance (ASFNE, a special allowance from the National Fund for Employment) was created to help workers aged sixty or over who had been laid off. This allowance has been progressively replaced, starting in 1972, by a system of resource maintenance (*garanties de ressources*). It ensured that workers over age sixty who lost their jobs would receive 60–70 percent of their last income up to age sixty-five, which was then the normal retirement age. This system was extended considerably in 1983, covering up to 400,000 people, roughly one-quarter of the population in the age bracket sixty to sixty-four. Some allowances were also introduced for workers under age sixty, but only in specific sectors suffering from very large employment problems, such as the iron industry.

It is in this context that retirement at age sixty was introduced in 1983. One implication of this highly symbolic reform is that it acted primarily as a pure substitution process, normal pensioners progressively replacing people benefiting from resource maintenance programs. This explains why the reform did not produce any significant break in the evolution of activity, as can be seen by reference to figures 3.1 and 3.5 above.

This does not mean, however, that the reform was completely neutral. First, it changed considerably the nature and the reversibility of the protection that was offered: there was a shift from a kind of unemployment insurance to a quasi-universal pension system. Second, this change created a further impulse to a lowering of activity rates before age sixty. The introduction of retirement at age sixty was initially expected to eliminate the necessity of any form of preretirement. But, in the face of a still rising rate of unemployment, and in a period of rapid industrial reconversion, it quickly became apparent that it would be necessary to reintroduce some form of special safety net for workers younger than the normal retirement age.

Preretirement since 1983

In the second period, preretirement developed along two lines, in proportions that have varied over time and that reflect the fluctuating desire of the state to control the process. The first measure taken was the reactivation of the

ASFNE: people who are entitled to such benefits have left their firms under specific conditions resulting from negotiations between the firm and the state. The second measure, which implies much less control, consists in specific dispositions of the French system of unemployment insurance. Under the common rule, people falling into unemployment are entitled to compensation for a limited period of time; since 1992, this compensation decreases with the duration of unemployment. But these rules do not apply to people who lose their jobs after a certain age (fifty-seven until mid-1993, now fifty-eight), who can benefit from full compensation until they are able to take the normal pension at the full rate. This system is not officially described as preretirement, and it differs from a pension system in that people are eligible to receive benefits under it only if they have been laid off by their employer.

It must be noted that the coexistence of these two systems generates problems for the measurement of labor force participation rates for these age groups: Truly preretired people are naturally counted as inactive. However, those collecting unemployment insurance can be considered both as active and, since they are generally exempt from actively seeking jobs, as inactive (according to international conventions). The situation is even more ambiguous when labor force status is self-declared, as was the case for some of the statistics given in section 3.1 above.

3.2.4   Recent or Ongoing Reforms

A reform of the general regime was enacted in 1993 the main features of which are the following: (*a*) After liquidation, pensions will be indexed on prices instead of on either net or gross wages. This measure will have the effect of reducing the relative standard of living of older pensioners. In fact, this measure essentially establishes as official what had become the standard practice over the last decade. Nevertheless, in the case of rapid increases of net wages (high productivity growth), some occasional and discretionary reindexation could be introduced (*clause de rendez vous*). (*b*) Retirement at age sixty will remain possible, but, in order to receive the full rate, the number of years of contributions will be raised from 37.5 under the current rule to 40 in 2003. (*c*) The reference wage used in the formula (1) above will progressively be computed on a greater number of years, from the best ten years initially to the best twenty-five years in 2008.

No similar reform has been applied, at this stage, to any of the special regimes. The attempted extension of these new rules—now suspended—to some of these regimes was in fact one of the reasons behind the controversy that arose in November 1995 over the Juppé Plan.

Measures to reform complementary schemes have so far consisted mainly in increasing contractual rates (a policy that has the drawback of increasing future rights), in increasing calling rates (this policy does not have the same drawback: it generates receipts without generating new rights), and in moderating the value of the point. Certain noncontributory advantages were also reduced. But a different policy, increasing the reference wage, is now being implemented. This policy amounts to reducing future benefits without changing the current level of contributions. It is equivalent to an anticipation of future reductions of the value of the point.

3.3   Retirement Incentives

Is behavior consistent with the incentives generated by the pension system and especially with the incentives generated in 1983 by the introduction of retirement at age sixty? We look first at the informal evidence given by hazard rates derived from the profiles given in section 3.1 and from other sources. We then move to more formal computations of social security entitlements at different ages. Given the difficulty of dealing with special regimes, we limit ourselves to the "normal" case of a worker affiliated with the general regime and compulsory complementary schemes of the ARRCO/AGIRC group.

3.3.1   Informal Evidence

Figures 3.13–3.16 reveal patterns of behavior that seem qualitatively consistent with the main features of the pension systems that have just been described. Figure 3.13 and 3.14 give, for men and women, rates of exit from the labor force directly derived from the labor force participation rates used in figure 3.9 above. These transition rates have been computed using two successive realizations of this survey, in 1995 and 1996. They show that exits from the labor force occur continuously between the ages of fifty-five and sixty, when they can be attributed to preretirement schemes, then peak with entry into normal retirement at age sixty. There are residual exits after age sixty, probably people who are not eligible to retire at the full rate at age sixty; the

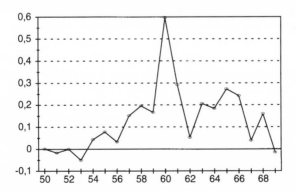

Fig. 3.13   Hazard rate out of the labor force for men
Source: Employment Survey 1995, 1996.

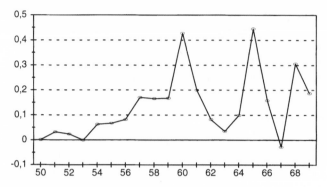

Fig. 3.14   Hazard rate out of the labor force for women
Source: Employment Survey 1995, 1996.

relative importance of such cases is apparently greater for women, who, owing to shorter careers, are less likely to arrive at age sixty with 37.5 years of past contributions and who are then forced to wait until age sixty-five to retire.

Figure 3.15 gives more details concerning the link between age and the probability of claiming one's benefits, rather than exit from the labor force. The data are derived from a panel of pensioners established in 1986 by SESI (the statistical office of the French Ministry of Social Affairs). Data for five cohorts of pensioners, born in 1906, 1912, 1918, 1922, and 1926, were collected directly from pension funds. The ages at which these successive cohorts entered normal retirement are available. This sample allows us to assess the effect of the 1983 reform. Before 1983, some workers could retire from the labor force at age sixty, but most had to make due with preretirement schemes, and the age at which they claimed benefits from the general regime remained equal to sixty-five—hence the predominant peak at sixty-five for the 1912 cohort. The 1983 reform, which lowered the normal retirement age to sixty, made these preretirement schemes pointless, and workers began claiming benefits from the general regime at age sixty. Hence, the age at which benefits were claimed decreased, with a progressive shift to a situation where the predominant spike is at age sixty, after a transition period characterized by bimodal profiles.

Figure 3.15 relies on the distribution of retirement age within each cohort. From these data, we can compute hazard rates giving, at each age, the instantaneous probability of retiring. Figure 3.16 shows hazard rate profiles within the same four cohorts. Here again, the ages of sixty and sixty-five play a specific role. The spike at age sixty-five remains high over time, with retirement occurring then for at least 70 percent of workers still working at this age. If the 1983 reform did not change this behavior, it strongly increased the probability of claiming at age sixty, the corresponding hazard rate rising from about 10 percent in the 1912 cohort to 40 percent in the 1926 cohort. Thus, after the

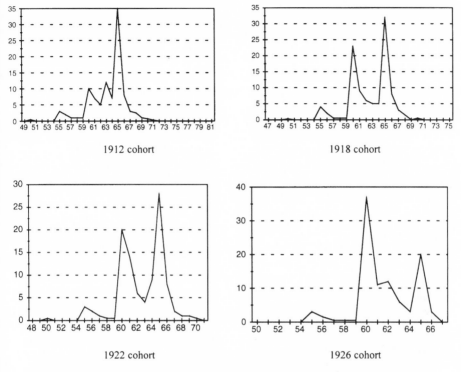

Fig. 3.15   Age of entry into normal retirement within four cohorts (percentage retiring at each age)
Source: Dangerfield (1994).

reform, fewer workers stay in the labor force until age sixty-five, even though sixty-five remains the upper bound of the retirement age. More people are eligible to receive a full pension and therefore retire before age sixty-five, notably at age sixty.

3.3.2   Simulation Modeling

Our analysis focuses on workers' entitlements from social security (including mandatory complementary schemes). Precisely, social security wealth (SSW) is defined as the weighted sum of future pensions and contributions, all terms being discounted from the time of evaluation by both a discount rate for time preference and the worker's survival probability at each date. All computations are supposed to apply to a worker aged fifty-five years. Thus, probabilities are defined conditionally on survival at age fifty-five. All amounts are evaluated at this age, which allows comparisons of social security wealth at different dates. The detailed formula for social security wealth is given in the appendix.

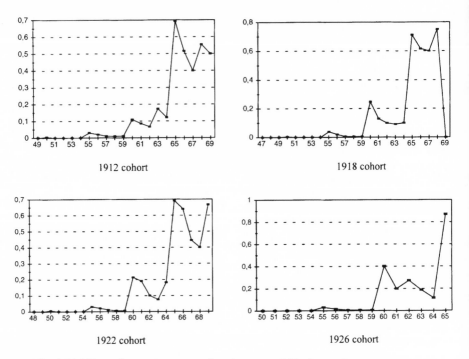

Fig. 3.16   Hazard rates into normal retirement within four cohorts
Source: Dangerfield (1994).
Note: These hazard rates are calculated from distribution data contained in fig. 3.15 above.

Several elements enter the calculation of social security wealth. In order to determine the level of pensions, we follow the rules of the general regime to compute benefits for the worker and his survivor. Here, computations are run only on a yearly basis (not a monthly one). Each year, pensions are revised according to the price index (up to 1982, they used to be indexed on the mean gross wage, which was more favorable). We follow standard assumptions about the future values of price and wage growth. We use specific sex-cohort-age life tables to adjust for survival prospects. We subtract contributions[4] to social security and complementary schemes while the worker is still working.

In France, receiving a pension from the general regime requires that one stop working for one's current employer; the result is that we can assume that the age at exit from the labor force cannot be higher than the age at which a pension is claimed. Can it be lower? Two cases must be considered: (*a*) For people retiring after age sixty, we assume that the two ages exactly coincide.

---

4. We consider here contributions from both the worker and the employer since, whatever their origin, contributions entail a decrease in present earnings in order to obtain entitlements to future pensions.

As in the United States, these decisions are not systematically the best insofar as, if the worker is not entitled to a pension at the full rate at an early age, he may increase his entitlements simply by waiting to retire. Nevertheless, empirically, most workers are entitled to a pension at the full rate at the time of retirement, and there is therefore no profit in postponing claiming benefits. (*b*) On the contrary, we assume that people leaving work before age sixty delay claiming their pension until age sixty. Since sixty is the youngest age at which a pension can be claimed, at least under the general regime, this is the only reasonable assumption that can be made.

We run our computations for different types of worker. In the base case, we consider a worker from the 1930 cohort and reconstitute his earnings history as follows. From empirical data, we evaluate the median wage of male workers from the 1930 cohort between 1967 and 1994. We complete this profile backward according to the mean wage index. From the data, we get a profile up to age sixty-four. But, owing to a rapid decrease in the participation rate, a nonnegligible selection bias[5] affects the estimation of the median wage after age fifty-five. For this reason, we follow the correction suggested in Diamond and Gruber (chap. 11 in this volume), assuming that earnings stay constant in real terms from age fifty-one on.

In the base case, the real discount rate for time preference is set to 3 percent. The worker's wife was born in 1933. We assume that she did not work during her life and that she cannot therefore claim a pension in her own right. As a survivor, she is entitled to a pension that amounts to slightly over 50 percent of her husband's.

Besides social security wealth, we can compute other indicators varying with the retirement age. First, we calculate replacement rates, after the deduction of social contributions and income taxes. To take into account taxes on income, we must make assumptions about household composition since, in France, the level at which taxes are levied depends on the number of dependents. We consider the simple situation of a "fiscal household" with no children, the family comprising either a single worker or a couple.

We then compute accrual values, defined as the difference between the values of social security wealth in two following years. We describe below the different factors accounting for the change in social security wealth between two years. We compare this accrual to the value of social security wealth by computing the accrual rate. Finally, in order to measure incentives to retire, we compare the accrual value to the earnings of the last year of work: the opposite

---

5. Contrary to what is observed in the United States, the earnings profile observed in France after age sixty does not decline but increases. Two reasons may explain this fact. First, there are few part-time workers at this age since everyone is eligible to receive a pension, at least a minimum pension from the welfare state, and getting this pension implies stopping work. Second, in the framework of an earnings-leisure trade-off, incentives to continue working after age sixty are strong for high-earnings workers.

Table 3.5   **Base-Case Incentive Calculations**

Last Year of Work	Replacement Rate	SSW	Accrual	Accrual Rate	Tax/ Subsidy
54	...	792,068	...	...	...
55	...	886,083	94,015	.12	−.91
56	...	986,531	100,447	.11	−.97
57	...	1,034,081	47,551	.05	−.46
58	...	1,029,771	−4,310	.00	.04
59	.92	1,024,586	−5,185	−.01	.05
60	.91	954,881	−69,705	−.07	.67
61	.92	892,339	−62,542	−.07	.60
62	.91	826,880	−65,459	−.07	.63
63	.92	768,327	−58,552	−.07	.56
64	.92	710,313	−58,014	−.08	.56
65	.93	656,799	−53,514	−.08	.52
66	.94	607,337	−49,461	−.08	.48
67	.95	559,482	−47,855	−.08	.46
68	.96	513,035	−46,447	−.08	.45
69	.96	468,382	−44,652	−.09	.43

value of the ratio is called the tax/subsidy rate. When the tax/subsidy rate is positive, working one more year entails a decline in social security wealth, which somehow represents a tax on last year's earnings.

Results for the different cases are presented in sections 3.3.3 and 3.3.4 below.

3.3.3   Base-Case Results

Table 3.5 gives figures for the base case. Each row corresponds to the last year of work, ranging from age fifty-four to age sixty-nine. If, at the end of this last year of work, the individual is younger than sixty, we assume that he waits until age sixty to claim his pension (sixty is the minimum retirement age). In other cases, retirement is assumed to start just after the end of the last year worked.

Table 3.5 first shows replacement rates that appear to be very high (more than 90 percent). This finding is consistent with empirical observations from various surveys, and the high rates result from several factors. First, benefits include (mandatory) complementary pensions; thus, replacement rates can exceed the 50 percent full rate from the general regime. Second, pensions bear fewer social security taxes than do wages (about 20 percent on wages as opposed to less than 5 percent on pensions). Third, income taxes are progressive, and subtracting income taxes therefore raises the replacement ratio. The combination of all these factors eventually leads to a situation where after-tax pensions are very close to after-tax wages. Besides, in this base case, the worker is entitled to a full-rate pension from the general regime at age sixty; that is

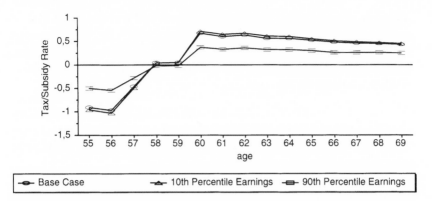

Fig. 3.17 Tax/subsidy rate across earnings profiles

why the replacement rate is already very high at this age and then slowly increases with complementary pensions.

If we turn to social security wealth and its variations with age, we must refer to the interplay between age at claiming and the number of years of contributions, which was already illustrated in table 3.2 above.[6] In the base case, workers are assumed to have contributed since age twenty. This implies the following dependency between age at exit from the labor force and social security wealth: (*a*) Between the ages of 55 and 57.5, one more year of contributions has two positive effects: it increases the coefficient α by 5 percentage points,[7] and it increases parameter *N* (number of years of contributions) by about one-thirty-fifth, or 3 percent. This increases the future level of the pension by an amount that is roughly 6–7 percent of the average wage. Multiplied by the length of retirement, which is roughly twenty years, this implies an accrual of social security wealth of more than 100 percent of the wage, which easily dominates the loss that results from the fact that the individual will pay one more year of contributions. This results in the large "subsidy" observed in the last column and depicted in figure 3.17. (*b*) At the ages of fifty-eight and fifty-nine, working one more year does not bring any new entitlements to the general regime and only a few more entitlements to complementary schemes. It does not change the length of the retirement period, but it costs one more year of contributions. The result is a slight decrease in social security wealth and a moderate implicit taxation of labor. (*c*) The picture is the same after age sixty: almost no new entitlements and one more year of contributions, but with the

6. Remember that three elements enter into the computation of the basic pension: the average wage over the ten best years; the rate α (from 25 to 50 percent, when age rises from sixty to sixty-five or when the number of years of contributions increases from 32.5 to 37.5); and the ratio of the number of years of contributions over 37.5. The full rate is defined as α being equal to 50 percent.

7. Last year of work at age fifty-seven increases α by only 2.5 percent because the full rate is obtained at age 57.5, after 37.5 years of contributions.

difference that delaying exit from the labor force now reduces the duration of retirement. Therefore, one more year of work reduces social security wealth not only by the amount of contributions but also by the value of forgone pension. This loss in social security wealth induces an implicit taxation of labor, whose rate tends toward the order of magnitude of the replacement ratio.[8]

What is the consistency between the results of these computations and actual labor force participation rates, reported earlier? Taken literally, these theoretical computations would suggest that the optimal age at departure is fifty-eight years. But actual hazard rates show that real behavior differs in various ways: either people leave earlier than this age or later.

Leaving the work force earlier than age fifty-eight is sometimes the result of incentives under specific regimes where very early retirement is possible, but in most cases it can also be explained by the importance of preretirement schemes or the specific rules applying to unemployment benefits at later ages. As explained earlier, workers who are laid off before age sixty can benefit, under specific conditions, from preretirement schemes or unemployment insurance until they are eligible to receive a full-rate social security pension (at at least age sixty). Years spent in one of these schemes are validated as years contributing to the basic regime; therefore, pension entitlements increase even if the worker is no longer active. In terms of future pensions, workers are not penalized.

Table 3.6 illustrates the consequences of this latter possibility for an individual who, between his exit from employment and his access to a pension from the general regime at the full rate, would receive unemployment benefits, this implying, of course, that his exit from employment results from being laid off and is not voluntary.[9] This table shows an apparent incentive to leave the labor force between the ages of fifty-six and fifty-seven. Of course, this applies only to those individuals who are fired at this age, and the decision to fire an employee is made by the employer, not the employee. In order to explain the low activity rates beyond this age, we must therefore assume that employers also derive benefits from these early exits. But this additional condition is probably fulfilled since these early exits offer employers a convenient means of solving the problem of excess labor capacity at low social cost.[10]

8. Nevertheless, the tax/subsidy rate differs from the replacement ratio (pensions/wage) for several reasons. First, the loss includes contributions in addition to forgone pensions. Then, we relate this loss to the gross wage since all taxation rates apply to the gross wage (referring to the net wage would yield higher tax/subsidy rates). Finally, in the computation of social security wealth, values are affected by the survival probability of the worker, which makes the absolute value of the accrual decrease with age, contrary to the replacement rate.

9. The coverage of preretirement schemes was very briefly extended, around 1980, to those voluntarily leaving a job, but this resulted in an explosion of preretirement expenditures, and the scheme was quickly abandoned.

10. This induces a potential risk of collusion between employers and employees, and some specific measures have been introduced to try to prevent it. For example, firms are asked to make additional contributions to unemployment insurance for people fired after a given age (Delalande contribution, after the measure's creator). Ex ante control is exerted by the state over other forms

Table 3.6   **Incentive Calculations—Unemployment Benefits between Work and Retirement**

Last Year of Work	Replacement Rate	SSW	Accrual	Accrual Rate	Tax/ Subsidy
54	. . .	1,065,913	. . .	. . .	. . .
55	. . .	1,100,430	34,516	.03	−.33
56	. . .	1,143,812	43,383	.04	−.42
57	. . .	1,136,666	−7,146	−.01	.07
58	. . .	1,079,952	−56,713	−.05	.55
59	.93	1,024,586	−55,366	−.05	.53
60	.92	954,881	−69,705	−.07	.67
61	.93	892,339	−62,542	−.07	.60
62	.92	826,880	−65,459	−.07	.63
63	.93	768,327	−58,552	−.07	.56
64	.93	710,313	−58,014	−.08	.56
65	.94	656,799	−53,514	−.08	.52
66	.95	607,337	−49,461	−.08	.48
67	.96	559,482	−47,855	−.08	.46
68	.96	513,035	−46,447	−.08	.45
69	.96	468,382	−44,652	−.09	.43

On the other hand, those who neither benefit nor suffer from these provisions generally leave the workforce after age fifty-eight and generally at age sixty (see the hazard rates shown in fig. 3.13 above). This is due to the fact that sixty remains the minimum age at which normal pension benefits can be claimed. What the results outlined above show means only that, from the point of view of the ratio of benefits to contributions, it would be optimal to stop contributing at age fifty-eight and then start receiving benefits at age sixty. But this would mean no source of income at all between the ages of fifty-eight and sixty, a solution that can be ruled out a priori for individuals who, generally, are liquidity constrained and cannot consider the possibility of having no income source for two years.

Is there an alternative way to compute social security accrual rates that would be more consistent with this behavior? One possibility would be to forbid any lag between interruption of activity and the claiming of pension rights. For people leaving the workforce before age sixty, this would imply social security wealth equal to zero (and even less than zero after subtracting contributions) since these people would receive no pension at all. This way of computing social security wealth has not been used here because the results would have been both trivial and unrealistic: an individual who would be forced to

---

of preretirement (FNE), the attribution of these kinds of preretirement benefits being conditional on the existence of a social plan prepared by the firm including some compensatory measures: e.g., firms must commit to recruiting a certain number of young workers or to employing middle-aged workers for a certain duration, and so on.

leave the workforce before age sixty will, of course, whatever his liquidity constraint, wait until age sixty to claim his pension.

3.3.4   Other Cases

Tables 3.7–3.10 show variations from the base case. Whatever the situation, we observe both the importance of the rate of the pension and high values for replacement rates.

In the case of a single worker (table 3.7), the level of social security wealth is smaller than in the base case, simply because there are no survivor benefits. Besides, although pensions and wages are the same as in the base case, replacement rates are slightly different because income taxes depend on the number of people in the household. However, incentives to retire are the same, with a maximum social security wealth for the last year of work at age fifty-seven and a high tax on wages for work beyond age sixty.

Table 3.8 and figure 3.17 above present the results of a wage profile at the tenth percentile of the wage distribution. Replacement rates are slightly higher than in the base case. The results for social security wealth and the tax/subsidy rate are similar to previous results, with positive accrual as long as the level of pensions increases, a small decrease at ages fifty-eight and fifty-nine, and then a huge decrease after age sixty resulting from forgone benefits.

In table 3.9, and again in figure 3.17 above, we examine the case of a worker at the ninetieth percentile of the wage distribution. Replacement rates are much lower than in the base case because of the high level of wages. Wages taken into account in the computation of pensions are capped, in the basic general regime (by the social security ceiling) as well as in complementary schemes

Table 3.7   **Incentive Calculations—Single Worker**

Last Year of Work	Replacement Rate	SSW	Accrual	Accrual Rate	Tax/ Subsidy
54	...	666,801	...	...	...
55	...	740,221	73,420	.11	−.71
56	...	817,607	77,386	.10	−.75
57	...	851,928	34,321	.04	−.33
58	...	841,109	−10,819	−.01	.10
59	.92	830,107	−11,002	−.01	.11
60	.91	756,702	−73,405	−.09	.71
61	.93	688,481	−68,221	−.09	.66
62	.92	621,819	−66,662	−.10	.64
63	.93	559,498	−62,321	−.10	.60
64	.93	498,909	−60,589	−.11	.58
65	.94	441,338	−57,571	−.12	.56
66	.94	388,614	−52,724	−.12	.51
67	.95	337,712	−50,901	−.13	.49
68	.96	288,461	−49,252	−.15	.48
69	.96	241,174	−47,287	−.16	.46

Table 3.8   **Incentive Calculations—Tenth Percentile Wage**

Last Year of Work	Replacement Rate	SSW	Accrual	Accrual Rate	Tax/ Subsidy
54	. . .	527,363	. . .	. . .	. . .
55	. . .	589,645	62,282	.12	−.96
56	. . .	656,541	66,896	.11	−1.03
57	. . .	688,575	32,033	.05	−.49
58	. . .	685,953	−2,622	.00	.04
59	.97	682,757	−3,196	.00	.05
60	.96	636,651	−46,106	−.07	.71
61	.97	594,697	−41,954	−.07	.65
62	.96	551,248	−43,449	−.07	.67
63	.97	511,754	−39,494	−.07	.61
64	.97	473,039	−38,715	−.08	.60
65	.98	437,188	−35,851	−.08	.55
66	.98	404,200	−32,988	−.08	.51
67	.99	372,531	−31,669	−.08	.49
68	1.00	342,151	−30,380	−.08	.47
69	1.00	313,030	−29,121	−.09	.45

Table 3.9   **Incentive Calculations—Ninetieth Percentile Wage**

Last Year of Work	Replacement Rate	SSW	Accrual	Accrual Rate	Tax/ Subsidy
54	. . .	1,128,847	. . .	. . .	. . .
55	. . .	1,239,107	116,260	.10	−.50
56	. . .	1,365,077	125,970	.10	−.54
57	. . .	1,430,006	64,929	.05	−.28
58	. . .	1,435,511	5,505	.00	−.02
59	.61	1,440,303	4,792	.00	−.02
60	.61	1,353,627	−86,676	−.06	.37
61	.62	1,275,728	−77,899	−.06	.33
62	.62	1,192,814	−82,914	−.06	.36
63	.63	1,119,002	−73,812	−.06	.32
64	.63	1,045,122	−73,879	−.07	.32
65	.64	976,418	−68,704	−.07	.30
66	.65	915,054	−61,364	−.06	.26
67	.66	854,800	−60,254	−.07	.26
68	.67	795,283	−59,517	−.07	.26
69	.68	737,552	−57,732	−.07	.25

(by a higher ceiling). For this reason, even in after-tax values, pensions amount to less than 70 percent of wages. However, incentives show the same profile as in the base case.

The next case again stresses that incentives to go on working are strong until the worker is entitled to a full-rate pension. Table 3.10 describes results for a

Table 3.10   Incentive Calculations—Incomplete Earnings History

Last Year of Work	Replacement Rate	SSW	Accrual	Accrual Rate	Tax/ Subsidy
54	. . .	460,363	. . .	. . .	. . .
55	. . .	461,053	690	.00	−.01
56	. . .	463,250	2,197	.00	−.02
57	. . .	464,443	1,193	.00	−.01
58	. . .	504,618	40,175	.09	−.39
59	.58	586,050	81,432	.16	−.79
60	.65	626,648	40,598	.07	−.39
61	.74	665,157	38,509	.06	−.37
62	.81	693,905	28,748	.04	−.28
63	.86	681,341	−12,564	−.02	.12
64	.86	627,596	−53,745	−.08	.52
65	.88	577,934	−49,662	−.08	.48
66	.88	532,095	−45,839	−.08	.44
67	.89	487,866	−44,228	−.08	.43
68	.90	445,182	−42,684	−.09	.41
69	.91	404,001	−41,181	−.09	.40

worker with an incomplete earnings history. We suppose that the worker began to work at age 26 and is therefore not entitled to a full pension at age 60. Before age 58.5, the rate of the pension—not available before age 60—is 25 percent. Between the ages of 58.5 and 63.5, the rate increases by 5 percent per year,[11] from 25 to 50 percent, but, for each year of work after age 60, the worker forgoes one year of benefits. Thus, the accrual rate is positive at ages 58 and 59, remains positive between the ages of 60 and 62 (although smaller than before), becomes negative at age 63 because of the limited increase in the rate (2.5 percent), and remains negative later. In this case, the relatively small increase in the pension induced by work at age 63 does not offset the loss of one year's pension and thus leads to a decrease in social security wealth. Therefore, the maximum value of social security wealth is obtained for a last year of work at age 62, that is, for leaving the workforce at age 63, before reaching eligibility for the full rate, which is obtained at age 63.5. In fact, if computations were made on a quarterly basis, we would observe that social security wealth reaches its maximum right at age 63.5: here again, there are strong incentives not to retire at a reduced rate, even if delaying after age 60 implies giving up some pension. Finally, after reaching the full rate, we observe, as in previous cases, a heavy tax on work.

As for the replacement rate, values increase quickly up to the full rate, then keep going up slowly. Values are lower than in the base case because of the

11. As above, work at ages 58 and 63 induces only a 2.5 percent increase in the pension rate since the rate rises only after age 58.5 (32.5 years of contributions) and reaches its maximum at age 63.5 (37.5 years of contributions).

shorter career: the worker accumulated fewer points for complementary schemes. Nevertheless, the replacement rate eventually reaches 90 percent.

In all cases, we get similar results across the board. Rules of retirement schemes imply that social security wealth is maximized when the pension is obtained at the full rate. Early retirement at a reduced rate implies a reduction in social security wealth, which means that the system is not actuarially fair. The evidence is particularly clear in the case of an incomplete earnings history, where, between the ages of sixty and sixty-two, when it is possible immediately to claim a pension, it is still profitable to delay retirement in order to increase the pension level. On the other hand, beyond the full rate, further work entails a decrease in social security wealth, which acts as a tax on earnings.

3.4   Conclusion

There is little doubt that the question of knowing what determines age at retirement in France and what may drive its future evolution is particularly important. France has labor force participation rates at older ages that are among the lowest among similar developed countries, and, like all these countries, France is faced with the prospect of a rapidly aging population during the first half of the next century, a problem whose partial solution may lie in an increase in the retirement age.

This paper provides a partial explanation of current labor force participation rates in France. The age at which benefits are claimed is roughly consistent because of the conjunction of two elements: the possibility of retiring, under certain conditions, and receiving a full pension at age sixty and the fact that a majority of people are presently able to do so.

Although we did not attempt to make any projections, these kinds of computations may prove useful in assessing the effect of future changes in these two elements. The first change is that, over the next decade, future cohorts will face a progressive strengthening of the conditions that must be fulfilled in order to take full retirement at age sixty, following the implementation of the Balladur reform of 1993. The second change is that these cohorts will be characterized by new patterns of labor force participation over their whole life cycles, and especially a later age at entry into the labor force, that will make it harder to meet these conditions. These two changes will interact cumulatively to lower the probability of being able to retire at age sixty. We did not attempt to simulate this aspect because to do so would involve a full projection of labor histories at the individual level,[12] but it is clear that it is along the lines explored here that such simulations should be developed.

On the other hand, it remains true that the simulation of labor force participation around age sixty goes further than the computation of incentives pro-

---

12. A long-run dynamic micro-simulation model is currently being developed to deal with this question, but the results remain too preliminary to be included here.

vided by the single pension system. Interaction with unemployment insurance, preretirement schemes, the general situation of the labor market, and the behavior of firms are other aspects of a complex problem that deserve specific treatment and that were touched on here only briefly.

Appendix

We first present a general formula to evaluate social security wealth (SSW), defined as the present discounted value of social security benefits for a worker of age a_0 and considering retirement at age r, denoted SSW(a_0, r). We use the following notation:

a_0 = worker's age at evaluation of SSW;

r = age at retirement;

max age = maximum potential age;

δ = age difference between the worker and his spouse ($\delta > 0$ when the spouse is younger);

$p(a)$ = probability of worker's survival at age a conditional on survival at age a_0;

$q(a_f)$ = probability of spouse's survival at age a_f conditional on survival when the worker is a_0;

$B(a)$ = amount of retirement benefits at age a conditional on retirement at age r;

$C(a)$ = amount of contribution at age a to social security and complementary schemes (depends only on the wage at age a);

$R(a_f/a)$ = amount of survivor benefits at spouse's age a_f conditionally to end of worker's activity at age a; and

ρ = discount rate.

We decompose SSW into three elements:

PB(a_0, r) = present value at age a_0 of future benefits if retirement occurs at age r;

SSC(a_0, r) = present value at age a_0 of social security contributions until retirement at age r; and

SuB(a_0, r) = present value at age a_0 of survivor benefits if the worker retires at age r.

$$PB(a_0, r) = \sum_{a=r}^{a=\text{max age}} p(a)B(a)\frac{1}{(1 + \rho)^{a-a_0}},$$

$$SSC(a_0, r) = \sum_{a-a_0}^{a=r-1} p(a)C(a)\frac{1}{(1 + \rho)^{a-a_0}},$$

$$SuB(a_0, r) = \sum_{a-a_0}^{a=r-1} [p(a) - p(a + 1)]\frac{1}{(1 + \rho)^{a+1-a_0}}$$

$$\times \left[\sum_{a_f=a+1-\delta}^{a_f=\text{max age}} R(a_f/a)q(a_f)\frac{1}{(1 + \rho)^{a_f-(a+1-\delta)}} \right]$$

$$+ \sum_{a=r}^{a=\max age} [p(a) - p(a + 1)]\frac{1}{(1 + \rho)^{a+1-a_0}}$$

$$\times \left[\sum_{a_f=a+1-\delta}^{a_f=\max age} R(a_f/r - 1)q(a_f)\frac{1}{(1 + \rho)^{a_f-(a+1-\delta)}} \right],$$

$$SSW(a_0, r) = PB(a_0, r) + SuB(a_0, r) - SSC(a_0, r).$$

References

Blanchet, D., and P. Marioni. 1996. L'activité après 55 ans: Évolutions récentes et éléments de prospective. *Economie et statistique,* no. 300:105–19.

Bordes, M. M., and D. Guillemot. 1994. *Marché du travail—séries longues.* INSEE Résultats, Emploi-revenus, 62–63. Paris: Institut National de la Statistique et des Etudes Economiques.

Commissariat Général du Plan. 1995. *Perspectives à long terme des retraites.* Paris: La Documentation Française.

Dangerfield, O. 1994. Les retraités en 1993: Des situations très différentes selon les parcours professionels. *Solidarité santé,* no. 4:9–21.

Join-Lambert, M. T., et al. 1994. *Politiques sociales.* Paris: Presses de la Fondation Nationale des Sciences Politiques et Dalloz.

Legros, F. 1995. La protection sociale dans les pays développés. In *RAMSES 96: Synthèse de l'actualité mondiale,* ed. Thierry de Montbrial and Pierre Jacquet. Paris: Dunod/Institut Français des Relations Internationales.

Marchand, O., and C. Thélot. 1991. *Deux siècles de travail en France: Population active et structure sociale, durée et productivité du travail.* INSEE etudes. Paris: Institut National de la Statistique et des Etudes Economiques.

4 Social Security and Retirement in Germany

Axel Börsch-Supan and Reinhold Schnabel

Old age social security benefits represent the largest part of the German social budget. In 1993, social security benefits amounted to 10.3 percent of GDP, a share more than two and a half times larger than in the United States. Social security income represents about 80 percent of household income of households headed by a person aged sixty-five and over.

The German social security system (the Gesetzliche Rentenversicherung and its equivalents)[1] is large because it is mandatory for every worker except the self-employed and those with very low incomes. In addition, the German social security system is very generous in two respects. First, the system has a very high replacement rate, generating net retirement incomes that are currently about 72 percent of preretirement net earnings for a worker with a forty-five-year earnings history and average lifetime earnings.[2] This is substantially higher than, for example, the corresponding U.S. net replacement rate of about 53 percent.[3] Second, the system has very generous early retirement provisions, including easy ways to claim disability benefits, increasing the number of ben-

Axel Börsch-Supan is professor of economics at the University of Mannheim and a research associate of the Center for Economic Policy Research and the National Bureau of Economic Research. Reinhold Schnabel is assistant professor at the University of Mannheim.

Matthias Fengler, Ulrich Finke, Isabel Gödde, Jens Köke, and Christian Wessels provided helpful research assistance. The authors are grateful to Joachim Winter, Peter Schmidt, and Edgar Kruse for fruitful discussions. Research in this paper was supported by the National Institute on Aging and the Deutsche Forschungsgemeinschaft, Sonderforschungsbereich 504, at the University of Mannheim.

1. For example, the retirement system of civil servants.

2. *Replacement rate* is here defined as the current pension of a retiree with a forty-five-year average earnings history divided by the current average earnings of all dependently employed workers. A different definition of *replacement rate* is used in app. B. *Replacement rate* is also defined differently when used relative to the most recent earnings of a retiring worker, which are usually higher than the lifetime average.

3. Using the same replacement rate concept as in n. 2 above.

eficiaries. The average retirement age is quite young in West Germany (about age fifty-nine) and even younger in East Germany.[4] The prevalence of early retirement comes in addition to a population that is already quite old and has contributed to a significantly higher ratio of pensioners to workers than in other countries. Currently, one hundred German workers pay for sixty-four pension recipients, as opposed to only twenty-five pension recipients per hundred workers in the United States.[5]

The tendency toward early retirement is particularly problematic in times of population aging. The proportion of persons aged sixty and older will increase from 21 percent in 1995 to 36 percent in the year 2035, when population aging will peak in Germany. With Switzerland and Austria, this will be the highest proportion in the world. The old age dependency ratio will almost double, from 57 percent in 1995 to 102 percent in 2035. As a consequence, the German social security contribution rate is expected to increase dramatically and substantially to exceed the rates in other industrialized countries. While, in 1997, the contribution rate stood at about 20 percent of gross income,[6] even conservative estimates put the contribution rate significantly above 30 percent of gross income at the peak of population aging if the current system and current retirement behavior remain as they are. Population aging will dramatically reduce the rate of return of the German retirement system. Estimates vary by the way benefits and contributions will be adjusted; rates of return will be around zero for cohorts born after 1970 (see Börsch-Supan 1997; and Schnabel 1997). Key questions for public policy are, therefore, How much of the large and increasing retirement burden can be attributed to the incentive effects of the public pension system, and which features should be changed to accommodate population aging?

This paper presents a descriptive analysis of the incentive effects of the German old age social security system on retirement decisions. In section 4.1, we summarize the labor market behavior of older German men and women between 1960 and now. In section 4.2, we provide a general description of the German public pension system. In section 4.3, we conduct a detailed analysis of retirement incentives. Specifically, we compute accrual rates of social security wealth and show that they have actually been negative for those who have not retired early. In section 4.4, we provide a brief survey of the empirical literature that attempts to link the incentives of the social security system with retirement behavior in West and East Germany. We then synthesize our findings and conclude.

---

4. The average retirement age in a given year is the average age of those workers receiving a public pension income for the first time.

5. There is some double-counting in both countries as persons can receive more than one pension.

6. As of 1 January 1997, the total contribution rate is 20.3 percent; 10.15 percent is deducted from the employee's gross pay, another 10.15 percent paid by the employer.

4.1   Labor Market Behavior

In this section, we first depict historical trends in labor force participation, participation in the public pension system, and coverage of the elderly by old age social security, then we more closely investigate labor market status and retirement patterns in the early 1990s.

As will be explained in section 4.2 below, we include in the public pension system all branches of the Gesetzliche Rentenversicherung (i.e., blue collar, white collar, and mining) and also the separate retirement system for civil servants. We distinguish old age, disability, and survivor benefits within the public pension system.

Data for the historical trends come from the German population survey (Mikrozensus, MZ) and the German Department of Labor and Social Affairs (Bundesministerium für Arbeit und Sozialordnung, BMAS). Cross-sectional data for recent years have mainly been drawn from the German Socio-Economic Panel (GSOEP) and from statistics supplied by the German association of public pension providers (Verband der deutschen Rentenversicherungsträger, VdR). These data sources are described in more detail in appendix A.

4.1.1   Historical Trends

Germany shares the rapid decrease in old age labor force participation with most other industrialized countries (fig. 4.1).[7] This decrease accelerated after 1970. In section 4.4, we argue that the dramatic decline after 1970 is at least partly due to the introduction of "flexible" retirement arrangements in 1972 that did not adjust benefits according to actuarial tables. It is interesting to note that male labor force participation declined from 1970 to 1990 for all ages over fifty and increasingly so for older persons. Female labor force participation increased for all ages under sixty. The increase for the age range from fifty to fifty-nine is noteworthy because it contrasts to the decline in male labor force participation due to a high share of disability claims among male workers.

The German public pension system is mandatory for every worker except the self-employed and those with very low earnings (see sec. 4.2 below). Hence, coverage by the public pension system is high and has steadily increased from 77 percent in 1960 to a plateau of almost 90 percent around 1980 (fig. 4.2). The increase in the 1960s and 1970s stemmed from the declining share of the self-employed and farmers in the labor force, while the slight decrease in very recent years was caused by the increase in part-time jobs that do not require participation in the social safety net.

In accordance with coverage, the number of beneficiaries also increased sharply from 1960 to 1995 (fig. 4.3). Among those age fifty-five and older, 85 percent received pensions from the public system in 1995, while this share was

---

7. Tables for all figures in this paper are available on request.

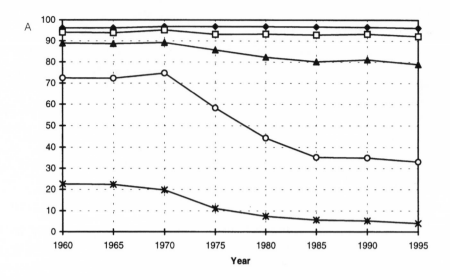

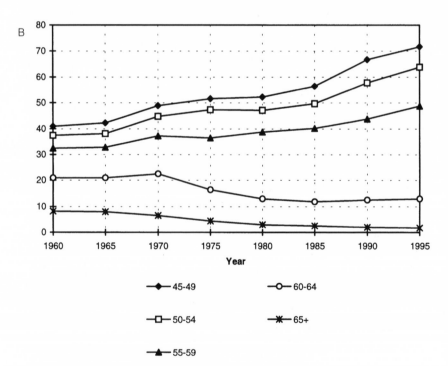

Fig. 4.1   Labor force participation rates: *a*, males; *b*, females
Source: Mikrozensus (StatBA 1990, FS1, R4.1.1: S.51, 55; StatJB 1966: S. 149; StatJB 1971: S.121; StatJB 1976: S. 148; StatJB 1981: S.94; StatJB 1986: S. 97).

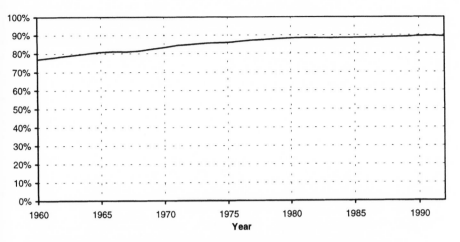

Fig. 4.2   Share of workers covered by the German public pension system

Sources: Stat. Bundesamt, FS1/4.1.1, based on Mikrozensus; own calculations.

Note: Share of white-collar workers, blue-collar workers, miners, and civil servants in total labor force. Not included are those self-employed who are voluntary members of the public pension system.

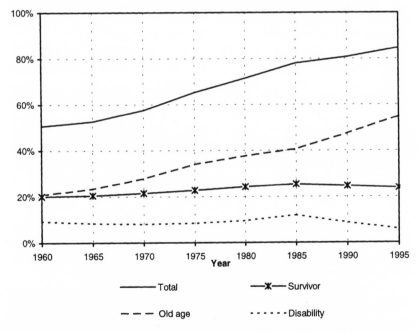

Fig. 4.3   Share of persons aged 55 and older receiving public pensions

Sources: VdR; own calculations.

Note: By definition, all persons receiving old age pensions are age 60 and above. Percentage receiving disability pensions: share of those aged 55 and over estimated from 1992 share. Persons receiving survivor benefits: some double-counting; very small number of persons below age 55 included. Note that table 4.3 below represents the stock of retirees and that fig. 4.29 below shows the flow into retirement.

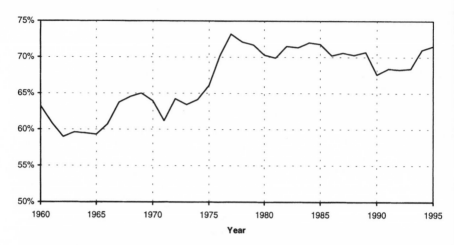

Fig. 4.4   Replacement rate of the German public pension system
Source: BMAS.
Note: Pension after 45 years average contribution as percentage of average net wage. The 1990 rate is low because East German pensions were not yet adjusted to the West German level.

only a little above 50 percent in 1960. Figure 4.3 distinguishes three kinds of pensions: old age and disability pensions based on contributions from own earnings and survivor pensions. Most of those who receive a public pension receive an old age pension. Disability benefits rose particularly fast in the early 1980s, until more stringent requirements were put in place. Survivor benefits remained about steady.

The replacement rate of the German public pension system is very generous. It increased from 63 percent in 1960 to 72 percent currently (fig. 4.4). Note that the replacement rate varied in the short term as indexation to gross wages (more recently, net wages) was not automatic but at the discretion of the legislature. The drop after 1990 is due to the inclusion of the initially very low East German pensions, which were subsequently raised to the West German level.

4.1.2   Labor Market Behavior in Recent Years

In order to investigate recent labor market behavior in more detail, we pool the 1993, 1994, and 1995 waves of the GSOEP. The data cover some seventeen thousand persons annually in East and West Germany. We also use VdR data for the number of beneficiaries of the public pension system.

Figure 4.5 shows the rapid decline in labor force participation around age sixty for both female and male workers and the large share of persons who exit the labor force even earlier. Particularly sharp declines in labor force participation are visible at ages fifty-six (male only), sixty, and sixty-five. By age sixty-six, male labor force participation has dropped below 7.5 percent.

Figure 4.6 looks more closely at the employment status of males and females in Germany. *Employment status* is defined as actual occupation. *Retired*

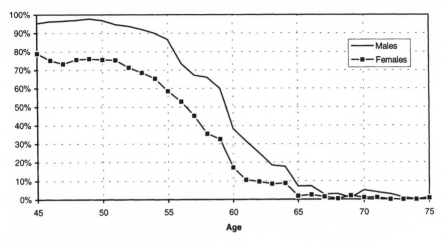

Fig. 4.5   Labor force participation rates
Sources: GSOEP 1993–95; own calculations.
Note: Percentage of sample persons of given age.

in this figure refers to persons who call themselves retired regardless of whether they receive some kind of pension. The category includes disabled persons and persons having retired before being eligible for a public pension. *Unemployed* refers to the registered unemployed who are still seeking work. Unemployment increases with age and peaks immediately before age sixty. The category *unemployed* does not include those who receive unemployment benefits but are actually retired. As will be explained in section 4.2 below, unemployment is one of the many pathways to early retirement and has been encouraged by the government in official and, even more so, in unofficial "preretirement" schemes (*Vorruhestand*).

Figure 4.7 links the labor force status of figure 4.6 with the receipt of public pensions. After age fifty-five, a substantial number of workers enter early retirement without receiving a public pension (old age or disability). These are the above-mentioned workers who receive some combination of unemployment benefits and severance pay under several preretirement schemes. Eventually, by age sixty-five, almost all male and most female preretirees will receive a public pension. Preretirement is high: it peaks between the ages of fifty-six and fifty-nine at 20 percent for men and 25 percent for women.

Figure 4.8 yields a closer look at the different kinds of public pensions that were displayed in figure 4.7. About 95 percent of elderly German men and 85 percent of women receive public old age and disability pension benefits as a result of their own contributions from earnings. In addition, a large share of women (strongly increasing with age, peaking at 60 percent for women aged seventy-five and older) and a small share of men receive survivor benefits.

Benefits before age sixty are disability benefits. These disability pensions

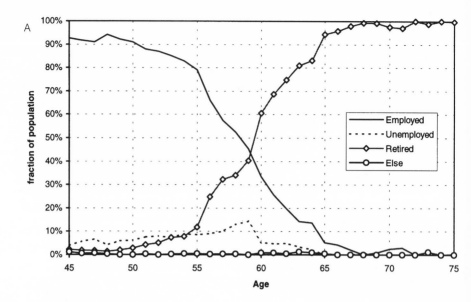

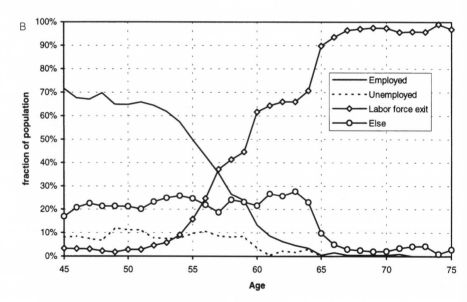

Fig. 4.6   Labor force status: *a*, **males;** *b*, **females**

Source: GSOEP 1993–95.

Note: Percentage of sample persons at given age. Unemployed = registered unemployed who are willing to work.

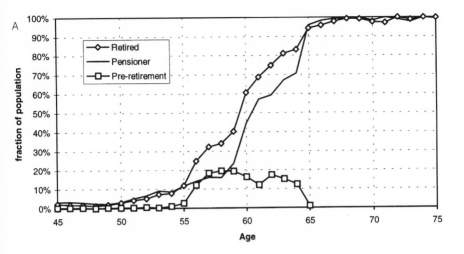

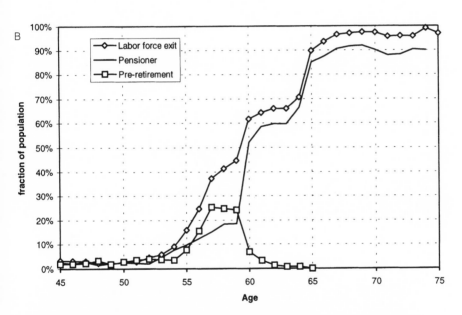

Fig. 4.7   Labor force status and receipt of own pension: *a*, **males;** *b*, **females**

Source: GSOEP 1993–95.

Note: Labor force exit = retired from labor market (includes persons who receive pensions and persons with preretirement status); pensioner = receives old age or disability pension; preretirement = retired from labor market (1) receiving unemployment benefits and/or (2) receiving compensating payments from (former) employer while at zero hours of work.

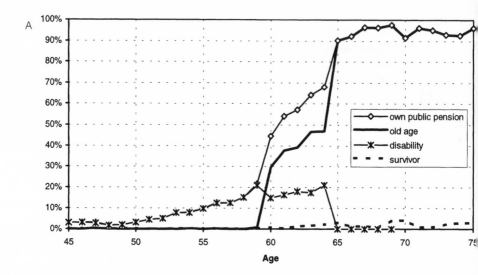

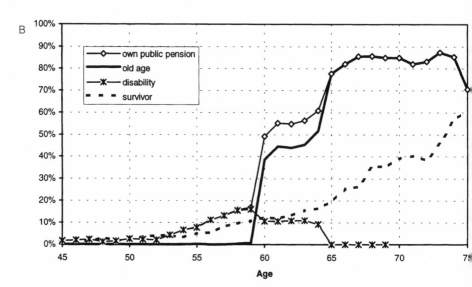

Fig. 4.8 Recipients of public pension income: *a*, males; *b*, females

Sources: GSOEP 1993–95; own calculations.

Note: Survivor, old age, disability, and civil servant pension recipients as share of sample persons at given age.

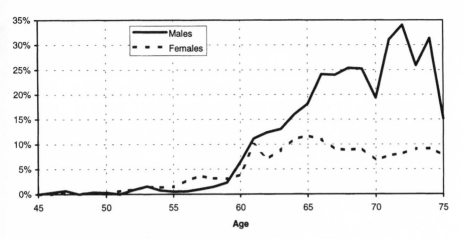

Fig. 4.9   Recipients of firm pensions by age
Sources: GSOEP 1993–95; own calculations.
Note: Firm pensions as share of sample persons at given age.

are converted between the ages of sixty and sixty-five to old age pensions. The sharp increase in beneficiaries between the ages of sixty and sixty-five mirrors the rapid decline in labor force participation at that age, as seen in figure 4.7. The sharp decline of own pensions among women aged seventy-five and older is not a true age effect. Rather, the decline reflects a cohort effect because female workers aged seventy-five and over had very low labor force participation.

About a quarter of the male elderly (aged sixty-five and over) receive private firm pensions (fig. 4.9). This pension comes generally in addition to the public pensions depicted in figure 4.8. The share is low relative to British and American standards, and it is even smaller for the female elderly. Firm pensions have been popular and were used to create internal company funds until the very favorable corporate income tax treatment was abolished. The "age" pattern in figure 4.9 therefore displays strong cohort effects in addition to true age effects.

Not only do a relatively small number of persons receive private firm pensions, but firm pensions are also relatively low. They account for less than 5 percent of total retirement income among elderly households, the bulk of whose income is provided by public pensions (about 80 percent). This can be seen in figure 4.10. Private asset income also plays a much smaller role than in the United States and the United Kingdom and never exceeds 10 percent on average at any age.

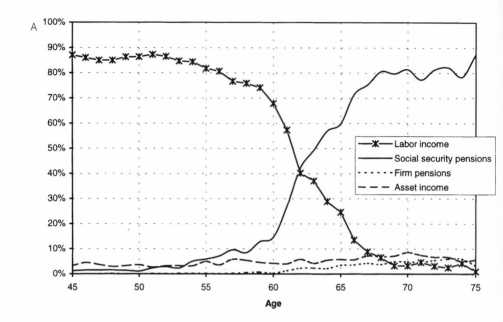

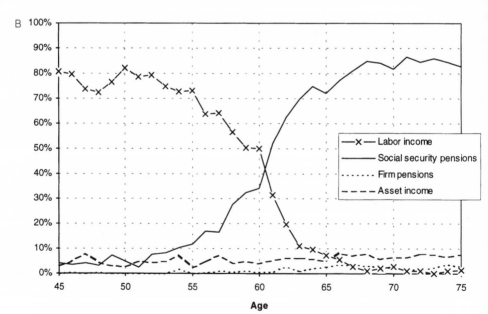

Fig. 4.10   Source of household income by age of householder: *a*, **male head of household;** *b*, **female head of household**

Sources: GSOEP 1993–95; own calculations.

4.2   Key Features of the German Pension System

4.2.1   The History of Retirement Insurance in Germany

Germany has the oldest formal social security system, introduced in 1889 by Chancellor Bismarck. Originally a fully funded disability insurance program, the system became a mandatory retirement insurance program (Gesetzliche Rentenversicherung, GRV), which was converted to a pay-as-you-go scheme after its capital stock was severely eroded during the Great Depression and World War II. In the 1960s and 1970s, the German system evolved into one of the most generous pension systems in the world in terms of both its replacement rate and its early retirement provisions. Germany now faces the most dramatic population aging among the industrialized countries, which severely jeopardizes the social security system in its current, generous form.

As opposed to those in many other countries (such as the United Kingdom and the Netherlands), public pensions in Germany are designed to extend the standard of living that was achieved during an individual's work life into retirement.[8] Public pensions are roughly proportional to labor income averaged over the life course and incorporate only few redistributive properties (much fewer than, e.g., in the United States). This is the reason that the German pension system is termed *retirement insurance* rather than *social security,* as in the United States, and most workers still understand their contributions as *insurance premia* rather than *taxes,* although this appears to be changing in the face of the severe benefit cuts currently being discussed in response to population aging.

The retirement insurance system consists of several programs, each providing benefits that can be accumulated in certain cases. The system combines old age pensions, disability pensions, and survivor pensions. East Germany is now fully integrated in the West German retirement system, although a few transitional rules still apply. Strictly speaking, German retirement insurance is not part of the government budget but a separate entity that is subsidized by the federal government. Were there a surplus, social security contributions could not legally be used to decrease the government deficit, as they can in the United States.

Until 1972, the system was very inflexible and permitted retirement only at age sixty-five, except for disability, which, however, made up for roughly 50 percent of new retirement entries (see fig. 4.29 below).[9] The landmark 1972 pension reform introduced the opportunity to retire at different ages during the so-called window of retirement without a direct adjustment of retirement

---

8. Hauser (1995) provides an overview and comparison of European old age social security systems.

9. We use *retirement* in this section to refer to the receipt of a public pension for the first time unless we also discuss labor force exit in the same context. The reader is reminded that there is substantial "preretirement" without public pension income (see fig. 4.7 above).

benefits.[10] At the same time, the reform indexed benefits to the gross wage bill, laying the groundwork for a system of pensions that increased faster than net wages and much faster than inflation. In the face of increasing budget problems, these two generous provisions were replaced by the second landmark 1992 pension reform. This reform enacted a more actuarially fair formula, and indexation was changed to net rather than gross wages. Since the 1992 reform, the retirement insurance system has been modified in a continuous flurry of small reform steps. Several loopholes were closed, and partial retirement was introduced. Normal retirement age, which remained at age sixty-five for men, will gradually be increased by the year 2004 to age sixty-five for women as well. Nevertheless, it has become increasingly clear that the 1992 pension reform did not solve the demographic challenge to come. The discussion was still ongoing in the spring of 1997; proposals were converging toward a severe reduction of benefits accompanied by more reliance on private savings.

This constant change makes it difficult to describe *the* German retirement insurance system. Moreover, the 1992 reform and its recent modifications will be fully effective only after the year 2004 because most workers are still "grandfathered" by the pre-1992 legislation. We focus our description of the German system on (*a*) the system features between 1972 and 1992 because they describe the behavior of retirees until about the year 2000 and (*b*) the system features after the 1992 reform with all modifications that have been enacted, including the budget reconciliation act of June 1996.

4.2.2   Coverage and Contributions

The German pay-as-you-go public pension system features very broad mandatory coverage of workers. Only the self-employed (8.9 percent of the labor force) and workers with earnings below the official minimum earnings threshold (*Geringfügigkeitsgrenze,* 15 percent of average monthly gross wage— about 5.6 percent of all workers) are not subject to mandatory coverage.[11]

Roughly 80 percent of the budget of German public retirement insurance is financed by contributions that are administrated like a payroll tax, levied equally on employees and employers. Total contributions in 1997 represented 20.3 percent of the first DM 8,200 of monthly gross income (the upper earnings threshold, *Beitragsbemessungsgrenze,* about 180 percent of the average monthly gross wage).[12] Technically, contributions are split evenly between employees and employers: 10.15 percent is deducted from the employee's gross wages, and another 10.15 percent is paid directly by the employer. While the

---

10. There was an adjustment for retiring at ages sixty-six and sixty-seven (see below).

11. Some professions, most notably civil servants, have their own mandatory retirement system. Although implicit, these systems effectively mimic the general public pension system and are included in it here.

12. Monthly gross household income in Germany was DM 5,300 in 1996, corresponding to a purchasing power of U.S.$30,300 annually (based on the OECD purchasing power parity of DM 2.10 per U.S.$1.00).

contribution rate has been fairly stable since 1970, the upper earnings threshold has been used as a financing instrument. The latter is anchored to the average wage and has increased considerably faster than inflation.

Social security benefits are essentially tax free.[13] Pension beneficiaries do not pay contributions to the pension system or to unemployment insurance.[14] However, pensioners must pay the equivalent of the employee contribution to the mandatory medical insurance. The equivalent of the employer's contribution to health insurance is paid by the pension system.

The remaining approximately 20 percent of the social security budget is a subsidy from the federal government. This subsidy is also used to fine-tune the pay-as-you-go budget constraint, which has a minimal reserve of one month's worth of benefits.

4.2.3 Public versus Private Pensions

Public pensions provide the major source of income after retirement. Although firm pensions exist in Germany, their role is small. In 1993–95, 21 percent of the male elderly and less than 9 percent of the female elderly received private pensions. Moreover, private pension income is small. The average share of private firm pensions in total retirement income is less than 5 percent for elderly German households (see fig. 4.9 above). One can therefore essentially abstract from private pensions and contribute all incentive effects on retirement behavior to the public pension system. This is quite different from the situation in the United Kingdom or the United States and considerably facilitates the analysis of retirement behavior in Germany.

4.2.4 Benefit Types

The German public pension system (or, as it is referred to in Germany, the retirement insurance system) provides *old age pensions* for workers age sixty and older, *disability benefits* for workers under age sixty that are converted to old age pensions at the latest at age sixty-five, and *survivor benefits* for spouses and children. In addition, preretirement (i.e., retirement before age sixty) is possible through several mechanisms using the public transfer system, mainly unemployment compensation. We begin by describing old age pensions.

4.2.5 Eligibility for Benefits and Retirement Age for Old Age Pensions

Eligibility for benefits and the minimum retirement age depend on which type of pension the worker chooses. The German public retirement insurance system distinguishes five types of old age pensions, displayed in table 4.1, corresponding to normal retirement and four types of early retirement.

This complex system was introduced by the 1972 social security reform.

---

13. Technically, the return on the pay-as-you-go system is taxable. The return is deemed a fixed share of the pension benefits that is below the general income tax exclusion unless the household has substantial nonpension income.

14. An exception is the very few "partial retirees" who pay taxes on their labor income.

Table 4.1   **Old Age Pensions (1972 legislation)**

Pension Type	Retirement Age	Years of Service	Additional Conditions	Earnings Test
A. Normal	65	5		No
B. Long service life ("flexible")	63	35		Yes
C. Women	60	15	10 of those after age 40	Yes
D. Older disabled	60	35	Loss of at least 50% earnings capability	(Yes)
E. Unemployed	60	15	1.5–6 years of unemployment (has changed several times)	Yes

One of the key provisions was the introduction of "flexible retirement" after age sixty-three with full benefits for workers with a long service history. In addition, retirement at age sixty with full benefits is possible for women, the unemployed, and older disabled workers.[15] *Older disabled workers* refers to those workers who for health or labor market reasons cannot be appropriately employed and are age sixty or older. In order to claim old age disability benefits, one must either (1) be physically disabled (at least 50 percent), (2) pass a strict earnings test, or (3) pass a much weaker earnings test. The strict earnings test is passed if the earnings capacity is reduced below the minimum earnings threshold for any *reasonable* occupation (about 15 percent of the average gross wage)—*erwerbsunfähig.*[16] The weaker earnings test is passed when no vacancies corresponding to the worker's *specific* job description are available and the worker faces at least a 50 percent loss in earnings when changing to a different job—*berufsunfähig.* As opposed to disability insurance for workers under age sixty (see below), full benefits are paid in all three cases.

With the 1992 social security reform and its subsequent modifications, the age limits for types B and C of early retirement will gradually be raised to sixty-five. These changes will be fully phased in by the year 2004. The only distinguishing feature of types B and C of "early retirement" will then be the possibility of retiring up to five years earlier than age sixty-five if a sufficient number of service years (currently thirty-five) have been accumulated. As opposed to the pre-1992 regulations, benefits will be adjusted to a retirement age below sixty-five in a fashion that we describe below.

15. This *old age* pension for disabled workers is different from the *general* disability pension for younger workers.
16. The earnings tests are described below. For a detailed description of disability regulations, see Riphahn (1995).

4.2.6 Benefits

Benefits are strictly work related. The German system does not have the kinds of benefits for spouses that exist in the United States. Benefits are computed on a lifetime contribution basis and adjusted according to type of pension and retirement age. They are the product of four elements: (1) the employee's relative contribution position, (2) the years of service life, (3) adjustment factors for pension type and (since the 1992 reform) retirement age, and (4) the average pension. The first three factors make up the "personal pension base," while the fourth factor determines the income distribution between workers and pensioners in general.

The employee's relative contribution position is computed by averaging his or her annual relative contribution positions over the entire earnings history. In each year, the relative contribution position is expressed as a multiple of the average annual contribution (roughly speaking, the relative income position). A first element of redistribution was introduced in 1972 when this multiple could not fall below 75 percent for contributions before 1972 provided a worker had a service life of at least thirty-five years. A similar rule was introduced in the 1992 reform: for contributions between 1973 and 1992, multiples below 75 percent are multiplied by 1.5 up to the maximum of 75 percent, effectively reducing the redistribution for workers with income positions below 50 percent.

Years of service life are years of active contributions plus years of contributions on behalf of the employee and years that are counted as service years even when no contributions were made at all. These include, for instance, years of unemployment, years of military service, three years for each child's education (deductible by one of the parents),[17] some allowance for advanced education,[18] etc., introducing a second element of redistribution. The official government computations, such as the official replacement rate (*Rentenniveau*), assume a forty-five-year contribution history for what is deemed a "normal earnings history" (*Eckrentner*). In fact, the average number of years of contributions is slightly under forty. Unlike in the United States, neither is there an upper bound of years entering the benefit calculation, nor can workers choose certain years in their earnings history and drop others.

Since 1992, the average pension is determined by indexation to the average net labor income. This solved some of the problems that were created by indexation to gross wages between 1972 and 1992. Nevertheless, wage rather than cost-of-living indexation makes it impossible to finance the retirement burden by productivity gains. The average pension has provided a generous benefit level for middle-income earnings. Table 4.2 shows replacement rates and compares them to those in the United States. Note that Germany has much less

17. Three years after the 1992 reform. The number of years has been changed frequently.
18. This allowance used to be very generous but has been dramatically reduced recently.

Table 4.2   Replacement Ratios of Social Security Old Age Pensions
                   (1972 legislation)

	Net Replacement Ratio (%)	
Relative Income	United States	West Germany
50	61	67
75	55	66
100	53	71
150	45	77
200	41	75
300	30	53

Source: Casmir (1989, 508, 512).

Note: Relative income is expressed as a percentage of the net wage of an average production worker with forty years of service. Married couple supplement not included.

redistribution than the United States. The low replacement rates for high incomes result from the upper limit at which earnings are subject to social security contributions.

Before 1992, the *adjustment of benefits to retirement age* was only implicit via years of service.[19] Because benefits are proportional to years of service, a worker with fewer years of service will get lower benefits. With a constant income profile and forty years of service, each year of earlier retirement decreased pension benefits by 2.5 percent, and vice versa.

The 1992 social security reform changed this. Age sixty-five now acts as the "pivotal age" for benefit computations. For each year of earlier retirement up to five, and provided that the appropriate conditions outlined in table 4.1 above are met, benefits will be reduced by 3.6 percent (in addition to the effect of fewer service years). The 1992 reform also introduced rewards for *later* retirement in a systematic way. For each year of retirement postponed past the minimum age indicated in table 4.1, the pension is increased by 6 percent in addition to the "natural" increase caused by number of service years.

Table 4.3 displays the retirement age–specific adjustments for a worker who has earnings that remain constant after age sixty. The table relates the retirement income for retirement at age sixty-five (normalized to 100 percent) to the retirement income for retirement at earlier or later ages and compares the implicit adjustments after 1972 with the total adjustments after the 1992 social security reform is fully phased in. As references, the table also displays the corresponding adjustments in the United States and actuarially fair adjustments at a 3 percent discount rate (see Börsch-Supan 1992).[20]

19. Curiously, before 1992 the German system provided a large increase in retirement benefits for work at ages sixty-six and sixty-seven. However, the incentive proved ineffective because it was far offset by the inducements to early retirement.

20. The actuarially fair adjustments equalize the expected social security wealth defined in app. B for a worker with an earnings history starting at age $S = 20$. A higher discount rate yields steeper adjustments.

Table 4.3   **Adjustment of Public Pensions by Retirement Age**

Pension as % of the Pension One Would Obtain Had One Retired at Age 65

Age	Germany		United States		Actuarially Fair[e]
	Pre-1992[a]	Post-1992[b]	Pre-1983[c]	Post-1983[d]	
62	100.0	89.2	80.0	77.8	80.5
63	100.0	92.8	86.7	85.2	86.3
64	100.0	96.4	94.4	92.6	92.8
65	100.0	100.0	100.0	100.0	100.0
66	107.2	106.0	103.0	105.6	108.1
67	114.4	112.0	106.0	111.1	117.2
68	114.4	118.0	109.0	120.0	127.4
69	114.4	124.0	112.0	128.9	139.1

Sources: Börsch-Supan (1992); and own calculations.
[a]Gesetzliche Rentenversicherung, 1972–92.
[b]Gesetzliche Rentenversicherung after 1992 reform has been fully phased in.
[c]Social security (OASDHI) until 1983.
[d]Social security (OASDHI) after 1983 social security reform has been fully phased in.
[e]Evaluated at a 3 percent discount rate, 1992/94 mortality risks of West German males, and an average increase in net pensions of 1 percent per year.

While neither the German nor the American system was actuarially fair prior to the reforms, the public retirement system in Germany as enacted in 1972 was particularly distorting. There was less economic incentive for Americans to retire before age sixty-five and only a small disincentive to retire later than age sixty-five after the 1983 reform, while the German social security system tilted the retirement decision heavily toward the earliest retirement age applicable. The 1992 reform diminished but did not abolish this incentive effect.

4.2.7   Related Social Security Programs

Until now, we have discussed *old age benefits.* Contributions to German retirement insurance also finance *disability benefits* to workers of all ages and *survivor benefits* to spouses and children.

In order to be eligible for *disability benefits,* a worker must pass one of the two earnings tests mentioned earlier for the old age disability pension. If the stricter earnings test is passed, full benefits are paid (Erwerbsunfähigkeitsrente, EU). If only the weaker earnings test is passed and some earnings capability remains, disability pensions before age sixty are only two-thirds of the applicable old age pension (Berufsunfähigkeitsrente, BU). In the 1970s and early 1980s, the German courts interpreted both rules very broadly, in particular the applicability of the first rule. Moreover, jurisdiction also overruled the earnings test (see below) for earnings during disability retirement. This lead to a share of EU-type disability pensions of more than 90 percent of all disability pensions. Because both rules were used to keep unemployment rates down, their generous interpretation has only recently led to stricter legislation.

Survivor pensions are paid at 60 percent of the husband's applicable pension if the spouse is age forty-five and over or if children are in the household (*große Witwenrente*); otherwise they are paid at 25 percent (*kleine Witwenrente*). Survivor benefits represent a large component of the public pension budget and of total pension wealth, as will be shown in section 4.3 below. Certain earnings tests apply if the surviving spouse has her own income, for example, her own pension. This is relevant only for a very small share of widows—fewer than 10 percent. Only recently have male and female survivors been treated equally. As mentioned above, the German system does not have a married couple supplement for spouses of beneficiaries. However, most wives acquire their own pension by active and passive contribution (mostly years of advanced education and years of child education).

4.2.8 Preretirement

In addition to benefits through the public pension system, transfer payments (mainly unemployment compensation) enable what is referred to as "preretirement." As was shown in figure 4.7 above, labor force exit before age sixty is frequent: about 45 percent of all men call themselves "retired" at age fifty-nine. Only about half of them retire because of disability; the other 50 percent make use of one of the many official and unofficial preretirement schemes.

Unemployment compensation has been used as preretirement income in an unofficial scheme that induced very early retirement. Before workers could enter the public pension system at age sixty, they were paid a negotiable combination of unemployment compensation and supplemental or severance pay. At age sixty, a pension of type E (see table 4.1 above) could be claimed. As the rules of pensions of type E and the duration of unemployment benefits changed, so did the "unofficial" retirement ages. Age fifty-six was particularly frequent in West Germany because unemployment compensation is paid up to three years for elderly workers; it is followed by the lower unemployment aid. Earlier retirement ages could be induced by paying the worker the difference between the last salary and non-means-tested unemployment compensation for three years and for further years the difference between the last salary and means-tested unemployment aid—all depending on the so-called social plan that a firm would negotiate with workers before restructuring the workforce.

In addition, early retirement at age fifty-eight was made possible under an official preretirement scheme (Vorruhestand), in which the employer received a subsidy from unemployment insurance if a younger employee was hired in his or her place. While the first (and unofficial) preretirement scheme was very popular and a convenient way to overcome the strict German labor laws, few employers used the second, official scheme.

4.2.9 Partial Retirement

The 1992 reform also introduced the concept of partial retirement. Partial retirement is possible at the one-third, half, and two-thirds levels. During par-

tial retirement, all rules and regulations apply in proportion, for example, benefits and earnings limits. For instance, if retired at the one-third level, the worker
receives only one-third of the benefits, and only one-third of the earnings are
applied to the earnings test. In fact, partial retirement is extremely rare.

4.2.10   Earnings Tests

Earnings tests apply only to early retirement (types B–E in table 4.1 above)
and only for the time between early retirement and age sixty-five. Normal pensions (type A in table 4.1) are paid in full irrespective of other wage or non-
wage income. To receive benefits before age sixty-five, one must pass the strict
earnings test with a relatively small earnings limit (the minimum earnings
threshold mentioned earlier, about 15 percent of average gross wages).

If the earnings limit is exceeded, the benefit reduction makes use of the
somewhat complicated mechanism of partial retirement. As just mentioned,
this case is very rare. For instance, if actual earnings are between two and three
times the strict earnings limit, the worker will be considered one-third retired.
Hence, the worker receives one-third of the benefits in addition to his or her
other earnings. Earnings between 150 and 200 percent of the earnings limit
permit the receipt of 50 percent of benefits, earnings between 100 and 150
percent of the earnings limit two-thirds of full benefits. After age sixty-five,
the earnings tests no longer apply, and full benefits are paid irrespective of the
type of pension.

4.2.11   Resulting Retirement Patterns

The regulations of the German pension system are perfectly reflected in the
distribution of the ages at which workers receive a public pension for the first
time, depicted in figure 4.11. There are essentially three ages for entry (as a
beneficiary) into the German public pension system: sixty, sixty-three, and
sixty-five. Very few people enter at other ages. This bundling is entirely created
by the institutional provisions of the public pension system. By 1995, sixty had
become the most popular entry age for male and female workers. For male
workers sixty-three is the next important entry age, while for female workers
it is sixty. There is no spike at age sixty-three because women may receive
public pensions at age sixty unless they have a service life of fewer than fifteen
years. This is unlike the pattern among male workers, who may receive a public
pension at age sixty only if they are unemployed or disabled. In turn, there are
more women receiving a public pension for the first time at age sixty-five because more women than men have short earnings histories.

Figure 4.12 displays an estimate of the related hazard rate, defined as new
beneficiaries of the public pension system (from fig. 4.11) divided by the total
number of workers in the labor force. Unfortunately, currently no reliable data
exist with which to compute the number of "persons at risk" for a true hazard
rate. While there are data on dependent workers who are currently employed
and are eligible for public pension benefits, there is a large number of so-called

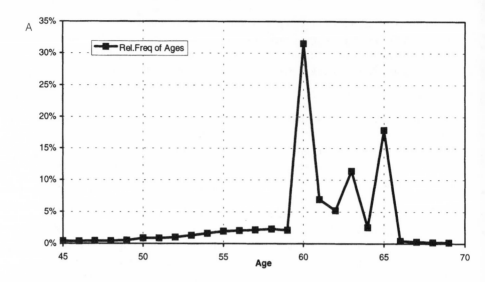

A

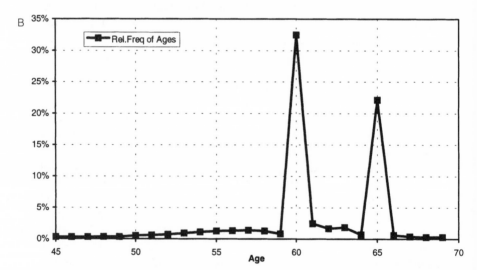

B

Fig. 4.11   Distribution of public pension retirement ages: *a*, **males;** *b*, **females**
Source: VdR data (complete enumeration of entries into retirement).
Note: Distribution of age of workers receiving benefits for the first time in 1995.

latently insured persons who have acquired some claim on public pensions.
Many of these persons will eventually receive a public pension. For example,
all self-employed persons who have served in the military as a conscript or
who have done an apprenticeship earlier in their career are technically
"insured." The problem is particularly severe for women; thus, we do not
display hazard rates for women. For men, our estimate in figure 4.12 shows

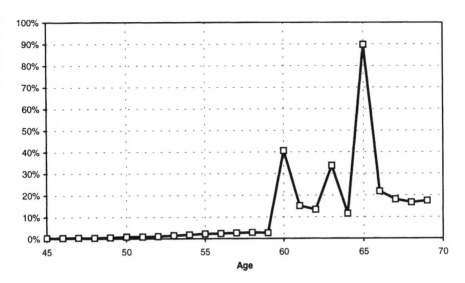

Fig. 4.12   Retirement hazard rates by age—males
Source: VdR data (complete enumeration of entries into retirement).
Note: Hazard rates have been estimated from the empirical distribution of males claiming retirement benefits (disability and old age) for the first time in the year 1995. Numbers (derived from flows) do not match perfectly with fig. 4.7 above, which is based on survey data on stocks.

three "spikes" at ages sixty, sixty-three, and sixty-five. Fifty percent of eligible males receive their first pension at age sixty; of those who continue to work until age sixty-three, 70 percent enter the public pension system at that age; virtually no one postpones entry into the public pension system beyond age sixty-five.

Figures 4.11 and 4.12 relate retirement to receiving a public pension for the first time. Figure 4.13 relates it to labor force exit. The figure displays the age distribution of labor force exits, together with the age distribution of public pension entries, on the basis of GSOEP survey data. Figure 4.13 shows that the spikes in public pension entry can be accounted for only partially by labor force exits. They are also partially due to "conversions" from other out-of-the-labor-market states (preretirement schemes) to public pensions. Preretirement has a spike at age fifty-six, as described above. Note that figure 4.13 corresponds to figure 4.7 above, which showed stocks rather than flows. The pattern of public pension entries in figure 4.13 is virtually the same as in figure 4.11, although the former is based on a sample, while the latter is a complete count of all new beneficiaries.

4.2.12   The Integration of East Germany

Since January 1992, Germany has a unified public pension system with the same replacement ratios and the same adjustment factors for new pensioners. This does not imply the same level of pensions, however, because the replace-

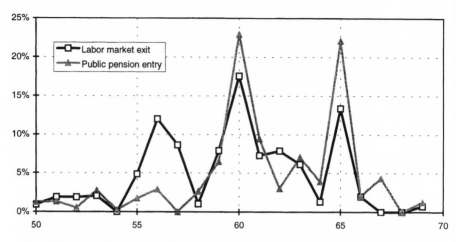

Fig. 4.13   Age distribution of labor force exit and public pension receipt—males
Sources: GSOEP 1993–95; own calculations.

ment rates refer to the relative wage level in either part of the country. Before January 1992, the situation is complicated by the transition of the old East German system to the West German one. Between 1990 and 1992, existing pensions in East Germany were revalued several times. In the rest of this section, we describe this process and briefly comment on some of the problems that arose during the transition process.[21]

The entire East German social security system was organized in one comprehensive institution (Sozialversicherung),[22] financed in equal parts by the state budget and by contributions from workers. This system had to be integrated into the western one, which consists of three independent institutions: social health, unemployment, and retirement insurance, each of which is separately financed by earnings-related contributions and only relatively modestly subsidized by the federal budget.

As opposed to the West German system described above, the comprehensive East German social security system aimed to reintegrate people into the labor force and to keep them working as long as possible. As a consequence, the relative position of pensioners in East Germany was poor by international standards, although most comparisons do not account for the high subsidy of everyday goods in the former East Germany.

The retirement system of the former East Germany included a mandatory and a voluntary part, which made the transition to the completely mandatory

21. For details of the transition, see Schmähl (1991, 1992).
22. More precisely, there were two institutions, the Sozialversicherung der Arbeiter und Angestellten and the Sozialversicherung bei der staatlichen Versicherung der DDR.

western system even more problematic. The mandatory part covered the first M 600 of income, about 45 percent of the average East German income. In 1971, a voluntary part of the public insurance was introduced (Freiwillige Zusatzrentenversicherung). In addition, there existed more than sixty supplementary insurance schemes for certain sectors (e.g., doctors, teachers, and—controversial after unification—the police, the army, and the intelligence service). Taking mandatory and voluntary insurance together, the typical replacement rate varied between 49.9 percent for workers retiring in 1970 and 62.7 percent for workers retiring in 1990.[23] Retirement age had been fixed at sixty for women and sixty-five for men.

As a result of the different supplementary insurance schemes, existing pensions in East Germany were partly higher, partly lower than they would have been had they been calculated under West German rules. The transition process involved two simultaneous changes. First, pensions had to be recalculated on the basis of the West German law. The level so obtained had to be revalued with respect to the currency exchange rate and the relative income standard in East Germany. These revaluations were governed by political, not economic, decisions. Pensions lower than their West German equivalents were immediately raised to the level in West Germany, at least to the level of social assistance. Pensions that were higher than their West German equivalents were reduced in a stepwise fashion to the level in West Germany. This reduction was achieved by at least partly excluding the workers involved from the general income increases in the process of wage and pension revaluation.

Taking both adjustments together, East German pensions on average increased by about 60 percent between mid-1990 and mid-1991, the first year after the introduction of the deutsche mark. The average pension in East Germany is now essentially equal to the West German average.[24] Only two-thirds of this increase was covered by payroll contributions, with the result that a considerable subsidy had to be paid out of the West German federal budget (Schmähl 1992).

At the same time, the fixed retirement age in the former East Germany was abolished in favor of the West German 1972 window rules, as described above. Moreover, special regulations to keep the statistical unemployment rate down (*Vorruhestandsregelungen*) were introduced, permitting retirement at age fifty-five in East Germany with a net replacement rate of about 65 percent.

23. Comparing standard workers with equal income and years of service (Schmähl 1992, table 1).

24. This is due to two compensating effects: average service life was much longer in East Germany (forty-seven years for men) than in West Germany (thirty-nine years for men); average earnings, however, were about 20 percent lower in the East. In addition, female labor force participation in the East was dramatically higher than in the West, raising the average pension for East German women to almost 30 percent above the pension for West German women.

4.3   Retirement Incentives: Accrual Rates of Pension Wealth

As emphasized in the previous section, German retirement insurance creates strong incentives to retire early. Postponing retirement by one year has two negative effects on social security wealth: the worker must give up one year of (net) pensions, and he must pay contributions of about 20 percent of his current gross earnings. On the other hand, postponing retirement raises pensions by 3.6 percent through the adjustment factor (after the 1992 reform has been fully phased in). This increase is less than the actuarially fair adjustment of between 6.5 and 8 percent per year (depending on the age of the worker), which is required to compensate for mere waiting. The additional year of contributions raises the future pension income profile and the expected value of survivor benefits by roughly one-fortieth.

The incentives to retire are conveniently expressed as accrual rates of social security wealth. *Accrual* is defined as the expected gain in social security wealth by postponing retirement one year. Accrual rates express the relative gain, that is, the accrual of postponing retirement one year relative to social security wealth in a given year. We define *social security wealth* as the expected net present value of social security benefits minus any contributions to the public pension system during the retirement window, here defined as the age range from fifty-five through seventy. Contributions before age fifty-five are sunk. All calculations use 1992/94 mortality tables, conditioned on survival until age fifty-five. In computing present discounted values, we use a 3 percent discount rate as a baseline. Precise definitions can be found in appendix B. As long as social security wealth accrual is positive, it is rational to postpone retirement unless labor/leisure preferences or similar considerations dominate the expected gain in social security wealth. Negative accrual rates from a certain age on are sufficient (although not necessary) for retirement at that age.

We use the benefit and contribution rules described in the previous section to compute pension wealth for synthetic income profiles of different types of households. Applying (historical or projected) contribution rates and limits, we compute the social security contributions of households in each year. Contributions are converted to relative contribution positions for each year and are accumulated over time. This yields the first element in the benefit formula, a life-cycle measure of relative contributions. Once the worker is eligible for retirement benefits, we multiply the relative contribution position by years of service and apply the adjustment factors of table 4.3 above. Finally, the personal pension base is multiplied by the average pension. We compute accrual rates of social security wealth from age fifty-five on, although—assuming that the worker does not apply for disability pensions—he will not be able to receive old age social security benefits at that age.

After 1996, we assume a real increase in average pensions equal to the (projected) real net wage increase.

Up to the year 1996, we use historical data on contributions, average wages, and pensions. After 1996, we have to use projected real wage increases and projected social security contribution rates. In the basic scenario, net wages are assumed to grow by 1 percent annually in real terms,[25] and contributions are computed using the budget constraint of the pay-as-you-go system, based on the median demographic projection by the Federal Statistical Office of Germany.[26]

As a base case, we consider a married couple with a husband born in 1930 and a wife born in 1933.[27] We assume that the husband is the main income earner and that the wife is eligible for full survivor benefits.[28] Our base-case earnings history starts in 1950, when the worker has reached age twenty. In 1985, this worker is age fifty-five.[29] Our base-case worker has an average labor income history and an age-earnings profile that is increasing until age fifty-five.[30] Thus, the average earner is earning less than the average aggregate labor income in his early work life (72 percent at age twenty) and more than that later on (112 percent from age fifty-five). The average aggregate labor income is drawn from the GRV administration records. We also do the same calculation for workers with 0.7 and 1.77 times the average income, corresponding to the mean labor income of the lowest and the highest labor income decile.[31]

The accrual rates for the base case are displayed in figure 4.14 below. Figures 4.15–4.20 below compare the accrual rates of variations of the base case. In figure 4.14, we present accrual rates that would have prevailed had the 1972 law still been in place. We then show accrual rates for a 1 percent and a 6 percent discount rate. Then we vary mortality. In the high-mortality case, we multiply the probability that a person dies at each given age by 1.16 until survivor rates are zero; in the low-mortality case, we multiply by 0.84. Finally, we present accrual rates for the low- and high-income cases. Detailed numerical results are available on request.

Figure 4.14 shows the accrual rates for our base case, the average earner. It is a hypothetical case as we apply the social security rules as if the 1992 reform had been fully phased in. Before age sixty, the worker is not eligible for public pension benefits. Working a year longer at age fifty-five yields a pension that is one-thirty-fifth higher (one additional year of average earnings, relative to

25. The increase between 1985 and 1995 was 4 percent per year. In 1996, however, the increase was 0.5 percent.
26. Eighth coordinated population projection, medium scenario (see Sommer 1994).
27. Using the 1985–95 waves of the GSOEP, we estimated the average age difference—controlling for age and cohort effects—for this cohort to be approximately three years at retirement age.
28. The means test for survivor benefits is very weak. Only 10 percent of widows' own pensions fall above the means test, and only 40 percent of the amount exceeding the limit is deducted from the survivor benefit.
29. By choosing age twenty as the start of the worker's earnings history, we assume that the worker has accumulated enough years of service to qualify for type B ("flexible") early retirement up to five years before age sixty-five.
30. The earnings profiles have been estimated using the 1 percent sample from the West German social security records and are taken from Fitzenberger et al. (1995).
31. Based on the labor earnings distribution drawn from the 1995 GSOEP.

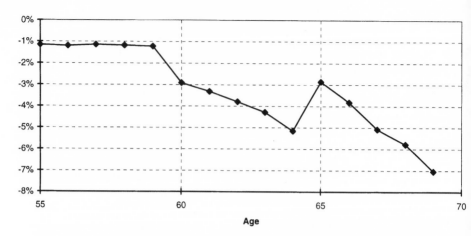

Fig. 4.14   Accrual rates of social security wealth (base case)

Note: Accrual of social security wealth when retiring one year later as percentage of net social security wealth (for a precise definition, see app. B). Figures 4.15–4.20 below display accrual rates for alternative simulations.

thirty-five years of past earnings history). At a 3 percent discount rate and about a 1 percent chance of dying at that age, accrual of expected social security wealth is slightly negative. At age sixty, the worker becomes eligible for pension benefits according to the 1992 reform, although at reduced benefits. Postponing retirement from age sixty to age sixty-one increases pensions by 3.6 percent. However, this is more than offset by a 3 percent discount rate, a chance of dying now of 1.5 percent, and a reduction of the length of retirement by about 5.5 percent (based on a life expectancy of 18.3 years at age sixty). With the increase in mortality risk, accrual rates become more and more negative until age sixty-five, the "normal retirement age." After age sixty-five, benefits are increased by 6 percent for each year of postponement. This raises the accrual rates dramatically. However, with the exception of postponing retirement from sixty-five to sixty-six, all further accrual rates remain negative.

Figure 4.14 clearly shows that the adjustments of pension benefits to retirement age established in the 1992 pension reform (see table 4.2 above) are not sufficient to offset the shorter period of retirement, the quickly increasing mortality risk, and the additional years of contributions.

Figure 4.15 compares the 1992 law with the regulations that applied between 1972 and 1992. Because the 1992 law will not be fully implemented until the year 2004, this simulation more closely represents the current retirement incentives. While the pattern is qualitatively similar to that in figure 4.14, all accrual rates are lower and negative. The magnitudes are relatively large: postponing retirement between the ages of sixty-two and sixty-five by one year corresponds to a loss of more than 6 percent. The 1972 law thus yields a very strong incentive to retire as early as possible. The 1992 reform did not do away

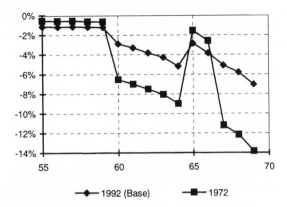

Fig. 4.15   1972 vs. 1992 legislation

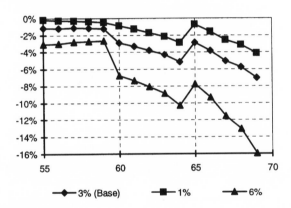

Fig. 4.16   Discount rates

with these incentives, although it substantially reduced them. Most significantly, accrual rates are still negative until age sixty-five. Hence, even the reformed system encourages workers to retire early.

A lower discount rate reduces the penalty of postponing retirement. Figure 4.16 displays this effect, based on the 1992 legislation. The incentive to postpone retirement before age sixty-five remains negative even at very small discount rates. With a high discount rate, the incentives to retire late are strongly negative throughout.

The sensitivity to mortality is similar and shown in figure 4.17. Lower mortality raises the accrual rates, while higher mortality lowers them. Even at very optimistic mortality assumptions, however, the incentives to postpone retirement between the ages of sixty and sixty-five remain negative.

Figure 4.18 changes the relative income position. Accrual rates are insensitive to income variations within the lowest and the highest deciles as they

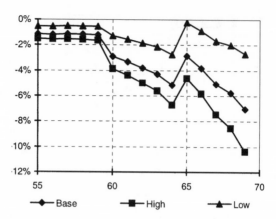

Fig. 4.17   Mortality

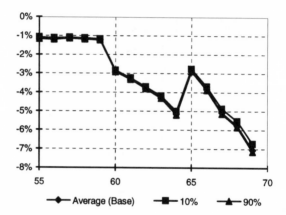

Fig. 4.18   Income by percentile

change benefits and contributions in proportion. This is due to the condensed income distribution in Germany, where the lowest decile is represented by 30 percent less and the highest less than 80 percent more than the average labor income. The income redistribution mechanism in the form of a lower bound of the relative contribution position alters the accrual rates only for extremely low incomes, although the strong incentive effects to retire early remain essentially in place.

These negative incentive effects are even stronger for singles. Figure 4.19 varies marital status; single corresponds to a single male earner. The main reason for this sensitivity is the leverage added by survivor benefits. The younger the wife, the higher total expected benefits. The penalty for postponing retirement varies roughly in proportion to the sum of expected benefits. Hence, increasing the differences in the age of husband and spouse works like the decrease in mortality depicted in figure 4.17 above.

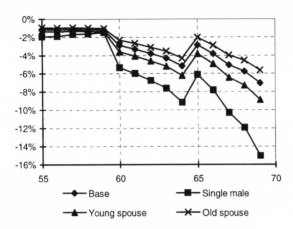

Fig. 4.19   Marital status

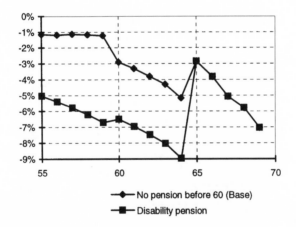

Fig. 4.20   Disability

Finally, figure 4.20 shows the difference between being able and not being able to claim disability benefits before age sixty. In the first case, benefits are not adjusted to retirement age at all. In addition, the earnings record is augmented by fictitious earnings of one-third of the preretirement average annual earnings for each year of disability until age sixty. Thus, the accrual rates are strongly negative, creating a strong incentive to seek disability status, for example, by invoking one of the labor market conditions described in section 4.2 above.

Figures 4.21–4.27 below translate social security wealth accrual into a more convenient metric: they relate the accrual of social security wealth by postponing retirement to projected earnings during postponement. If this accrual is positive, the workers of the same age remaining in the workforce subsidize

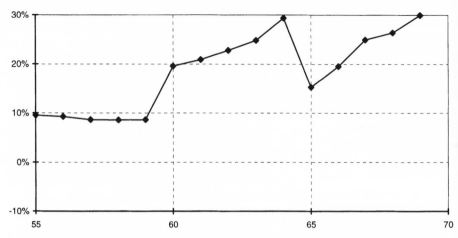

Fig. 4.21   Tax/subsidy rates (base case)

Note: Loss of social security wealth when retiring one year later as percentage of predicted earnings (for a precise definition, see app. B). Figures 4.22–4.27 below display tax rates for alternative simulations.

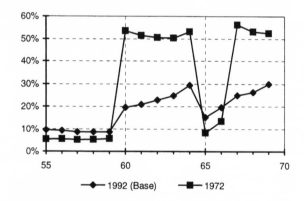

Fig. 4.22   1972 vs. 1992 legislation

those who have already retired. Figures 4.21–4.27 actually display negative accrual divided by projected earnings, hence the tax rate by which an additional year of work is taxed relative to a year of retirement.

As figure 4.21 shows, additional work is indeed taxed and at relatively high rates, reaching almost 30 percent at age sixty-four. Under the 1972 legislation, these implicit tax rates were even higher, exceeding 50 percent between age sixty and age sixty-four and again after age sixty-seven (see fig. 4.22). Tax rates are even positive before age sixty when a worker retires without receiving pension benefits until age sixty. This is because the increase in the pension that

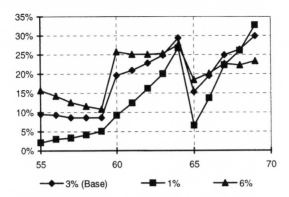

Fig. 4.23   Discount rates

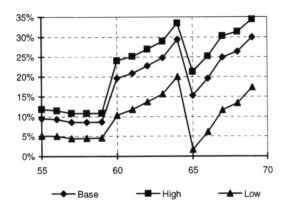

Fig. 4.24   Mortality

the worker will eventually receive at age sixty is less than the loss in wealth due to the additional contributions.

Figures 4.23–4.26 show variations in the discount rate, mortality, income level, and marital status. They repeat the patterns already shown in the accrual rates. Postponing retirement is virtually always a bad economic proposition. Only under a very low discount rate, very low mortality, or a very large age differential between husband and spouse is the accrual of social security wealth between age sixty-five and age sixty-seven smaller than the projected earnings during this postponement period.

Finally, figure 4.27 shows the benefit of claiming disability status. In this case, the implicit tax rate on additional work exceeds 50 percent between the ages of fifty-five and sixty-four. The additional pension wealth gained by disability status is DM 148,000 (almost 2.5 years of average annual gross wages).

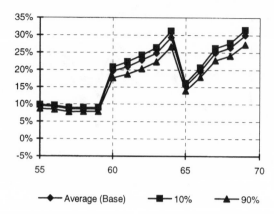

Fig. 4.25   Income by percentile

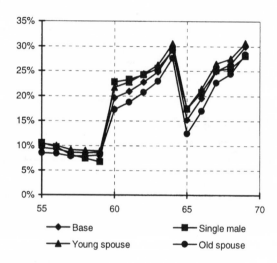

Fig. 4.26   Marital status

These simulations show quite clearly that retirement incentives are strong in Germany. The following section looks at the actual evidence in Germany.

4.4   Effects of Social Security on Retirement: Evidence in Germany

The German retirement patterns depicted in section 4.1 above, and the spikes in the hazards to retire visible in figures 4.11 and 4.13 above, suggest a strong relation to the provisions of the German retirement system that were described in the previous section, specifically, to the lack of actuarial adjustment of benefits to the various forms of early retirement. This section collects further evidence in this direction. We first look at the few "natural experi-

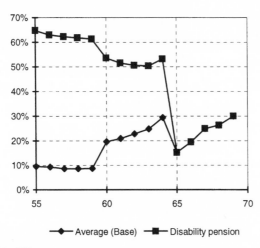

Fig. 4.27   Disability

ments" that have taken place in the German retirement system: the 1972 social security reform, subsequent modifications in particular of the requirements to claim disability benefits, and the transition in East Germany to the West German pension system. We then summarize the evidence from the available microeconometric studies of the German pension system.

The sharp decline in labor force participation between 1970 and 1980, which was depicted in figure 4.1 above, is associated with a steep decline in the average retirement age, defined as the average age of all new social security claimants in a given year. Figure 4.28 plots the average retirement age against the time axis. It shows clearly the effects of the introduction of early retirement at full benefits that were introduced in the 1972 German social security reform. The reform was enacted in the beginning of 1973. Retirement age declines sharply from age 63 to age 58.5 after 1973. The spike in 1973 is due to a composition effect: the average retirement age within both categories of retirement dropped significantly (from 57.8 to 57.1 for disability and from 65.1 to 64.5 for old age retirement). At the same time, the number of old age retirements increased in absolute numbers and relative to disability retirement due to the introduction of early retirement at age sixty-three without a health test.

Also, this new possibility to retire early initially substituted for claiming disability. As figure 4.29 shows, disability is one of the major pathways to retirement in Germany.[32] Note that figure 4.29 distinguishes two kinds of disability: disability claims before and after age sixty. In 1972, immediately before the pension reform, about 50 percent of all new retirees claimed disability. This percentage dropped by almost 15 percent in the single year after the 1972 reform. Claims for disability benefits then began increasing again and peaked

---

32. The notion of "pathways" to retirement is borrowed from Jacobs, Kohli, and Rein (1990).

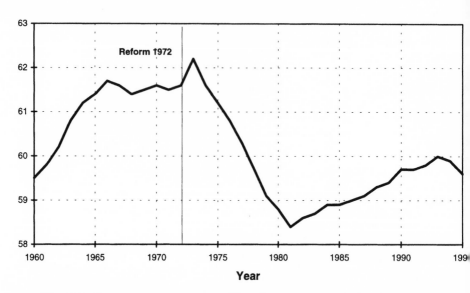

Fig. 4.28   Average retirement ages—West German men
Source: VdR (1997).
Note: Average age of retirement in given year (disability and old age). The spike in 1973 is due to a composition effect: the 1972 reform introduced retirement at age 63, which increased dramatically the number of old age retirements relative to disability retirements. At the same time, average retirement age dropped in both old age and disability retirements.

in 1981, when more than 70 percent of new retirees used one of the two disability pathways. From 1981 on, the requirements for disability benefits were made gradually tighter, and the proportion of disability claimants declined to some 45 percent in 1995.

The other pathways to retirement include an increasing share of early retirement due to unemployment. Because of an increase in interrupted earnings histories, the share of "normal" retirees at age sixty-five also increased since the mid-1980s.

Figure 4.30 presents a closer look at the effects of the 1972 pension reform. It shows most clearly the change in the frequency of specific retirement ages chosen. The introduction of the window replaced the almost universal retirement age of sixty-five before 1972 by an almost even split between age sixty-three and age sixty-five within the first years after the reform. By 1980, sixty became the most frequent age of retirement.

The patterns in figures 4.28 and 4.29 above suggest a causal relation between retirement incentives and behavior. More formal econometric analyses were carried out by Börsch-Supan (1992), Schmidt (1995), and Börsch-Supan and Schmidt (in press). These studies used microeconometric option value analyses to compute the incentive effects of the nonactuarial adjustment of benefits in the German social security system on early retirement. The option value of

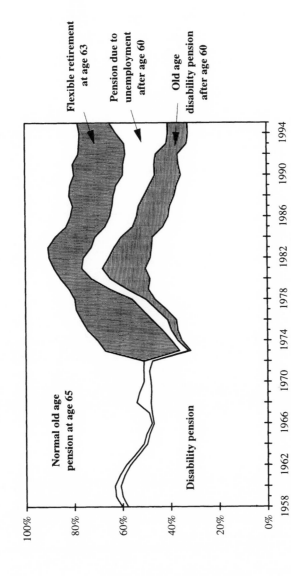

Fig. 4.29 Pathways to retirement—males
Source: VdR (1997).
Note: Share of new entries into public pension and disability insurance.

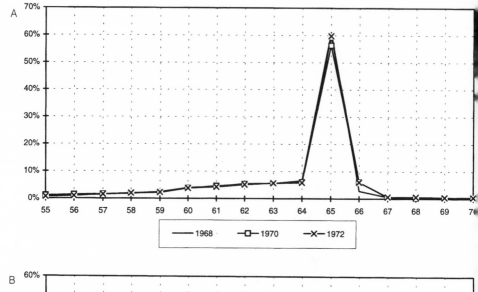

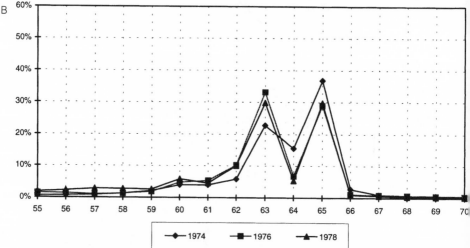

Fig. 4.30   Distribution of retirement ages: *a*, **before the 1972 reform;** *b*, **after the 1972 reform;** *c*, **1970–80**

Source: VdR Rentzugangsstatistik (white-collar workers, male).

Note: After 1980, the distribution of retirement ages remained relatively stable.

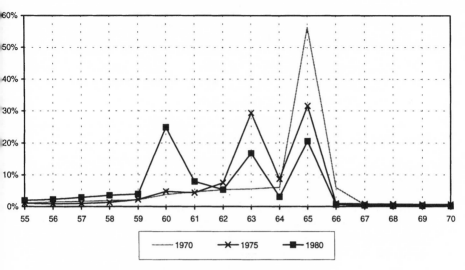

Fig. 4.30 (cont.)   Distribution of retirement ages

postponing retirement is computed according to Stock and Wise (1990) and inserted as an independent variable in a binary logit regression of labor force participation (Börsch-Supan 1992) and various hazard models of the retirement age (Schmidt 1995; Börsch-Supan and Schmidt, in press). The models are applied to West and East German panel data (GSOEP 1984–90 in West Germany, GSOEP 1990–92 in East Germany).

Both methodologies produce almost identical results. The option value has strong predictive power; its coefficient is highly significant and large. The authors use these results in several micro-simulation models to predict retirement ages under alternative retirement age–dependent adjustment formulas. For each sample person, the option value is changed from its actual value to the value that results from inserting alternative adjustment factors in the pension computation formula (see table 4.3 above).

Table 4.4 summarizes the results in terms of average retirement ages and the percentage taking very early retirement (before age sixty). The first row gives the baseline retirement age under the old German public pension system as observed in 1984. The low average retirement age is due to (physical and economic) disability retirement. The second row predicts the effects of the 1992 German social security reform. This reform will remove some, but by no means all, of the distortions toward early retirement when it is finally fully implemented in 2004. It will increase the average retirement age by about half a year. The micro simulation also reveals that retirement before age sixty is reduced from 32.2 to 28.2 percent.

Table 4.4   Simulated Retirement Age and Early Retirement

	Mean Retirement Age	Early Retirement (%) (retirement age < 60)
System before 1992 reform	58.5	32.2
After 1992 reform	59.0	28.2
Nondistorting system	60.6	17.8

Sources: Börsch-Supan (1992); and Börsch-Supan and Schmidt (in press).

The third row shows the effect of switching to a nondistorting system with adjustment factors computed for the discount rate estimated in the retirement probability model (see table 4.3 above). The simulation reveals a strong reaction to this change in the social security system. A nondistorting system would shift the retirement age by more than two years. The effects of a nondistorting system are most powerful in the reduction of early retirement, that is, retirement before the official window period. Retirement at ages fifty-nine and below would drop from the current 32.2 percent to 17.8 percent.

Riphahn (1995) has analyzed the disability provisions of the German retirement insurance system and found strong incentive effects. While she used a small data set derived from the German panel (GSOEP), she confirms the aggregate time-series results of Jacobs, Kohli, and Rein (1990) that show that the proportion of disability pensions varied strongly and positively with the generosity of the disability provisions.

Riphahn and Schmidt (1995) and Jacobs, Kohli, and Rein (1987) attempt to disentangle labor supply from labor demand effects, using aggregate data. While the results obtained by Jacobs, Kohli, and Rein are not fully conclusive, the analysis by Riphahn and Schmidt shows a dominance of supply effects, largely introduced by the incentives of an actuarially unfair pension formula.

Finally, unification provided another "natural experiment" to identify the incentive effects of the German retirement system. The introduction of the deutsche mark at a one-to-one exchange rate resulted in a massive increase in unit labor cost in East Germany, leading to a dramatic decrease in labor demand. The result was huge unemployment. In addition, labor force participation decreased sharply across all ages, but particularly so for ages fifty and over (table 4.5A). Rates of transition into early retirement were exceptionally high: around five times as high as in the western part of the country (table 4.5B). This resulted in a mean retirement age in East Germany more than three years younger than in West Germany (table 4.5C).

Most of this early retirement appears to have been induced by the very generous early retirement provisions in East Germany mentioned at the end of section 4.2 above. Börsch-Supan and Schmidt (in press) investigate the magnitude of this inducement effect. Their paper uses the methodology mentioned earlier in this section: for a large sample of West and East German workers,

Table 4.5   **Labor Force Transition in East Germany**

A. The Rapid Decline in Labor Force Participation in East Germany (%)

	1990	1991	1992
Full-time employed	56.9	44.5	37.4
Not in labor force	33.6	48.3	59.1
Observations	3,764	3,456	3,328

B. Transitions out of the Labor Force in East and West Germany

	West Germany, 1984–90			East Germany, 1990–92		
	Male	Female	Total	Male	Female	Total
Initially in labor force	1,589	780	2,369	483	482	965
Transitions per year	65.3	46.9	101.3	95.0	105.0	200.5
Transitions rate (%)	4.1	6.0	4.3	19	21	20.0

C. Mean Age at Labor Force Exit, 1984–90

	Men	Women	Total
East Germany	55.4	56.3	55.8
West Germany	58.3	56.5	57.7

Sources: Börsch-Supan and Schmidt (in press); 1990–92 waves of the East German SOEP based on all panel members of age forty-four and above in 1990.

the paper computes the option value of postponing retirement and inserts this value alongside other sociodemographic variables in a hazard model of retirement. In spite of the even greater generosity of early retirement provisions and the very different circumstances in East Germany, the authors estimate strikingly similar effects of the retirement incentives as measured by the respective coefficients of the option values in the East and West German regressions. Hence, *conditional on the different incentives* in East and West Germany, the response to these incentives is rather similar and very strong in both parts of the country.

4.5 Outlook

The responsiveness of the choice of retirement age to the incentives offered by the pension system has strong policy implications. Not only does the public pension system in Germany dispense with using the retirement age–dependent adjustments as policy instruments for balancing the budget of the pension system, but it even yields incentives that work against this because the adjustments are not actuarially fair. Rather than rewarding later retirement to moderate the labor supply disincentives created by rapidly rising social security taxes, social security regulations in Germany have encouraged early retirement, thus aggravating the imbalance between the number of workers and pensioners in times of population aging.

The 1992 German social security reform will only moderately remove some of these distortions when fully phased in (in 2004). It is predicted to increase the average retirement age by only about half a year. A truly age-neutral system would shift the retirement age by up to four times as much.

The renewed social security debate in Germany, only a few years after the most recent reform, focuses on further changes in the benefit structure and applicable retirement ages. Major changes, such as a transition from the current pay-as-you-go system to a partially or fully funded system, are not seriously debated among government officials. While such considerations as meeting the Maastricht criteria and reducing the high unemployment rate dominate the current social security debate in Germany, one should keep in mind that changing the retirement system later will become more complicated by the change in the politics of the social security system: the political power will shift from the working population to the retired population, that is, to an electorate that is unlikely substantially to change the balance between per capita benefits and contributions.

Appendix A
Data Sources

Mikrozensus

Since 1957, the Federal Statistical Office conducts a yearly survey called the Mikrozensus (MZ), which is comparable to the American Current Population Survey. The MZ is the main source of official population and labor market statistics in Germany.

The MZ is a 1 percent random sample of the residential population in Germany, stratified by regional variables (state, size of city/county, etc.). The primary sampling units are households. All household members age sixteen and older are personally interviewed. Before German unification, sample size was approximately 250,000 households and 600,000 persons. The questionnaire is regulated by federal law and includes information on demographics, household structure, labor market status, and sources of income. Unfortunately, until very recently, access to the raw data was extremely limited owing to restrictive data protection regulations. The latest versions are now available as public-use files on submission of a research proposal to the Federal Statistical Office in Wiesbaden.

The Federal Statistical Office publishes extensive tabulations of results based on the MZ and also conducts specific analyses on request (analyses for which it charges). Our historical data are based on publications of the Federal

Statistical Office: the statistical yearbooks and the more detailed series called *Fachserien*.

Verband deutscher Rentenversicherungsträger Data

The Verband deutscher Rentenversicherungsträger (VdR) is a federal institution that represents the twenty-three social security agencies of the German states (Landesversicherungsanstalten), the federally organized social security branch for white-collar workers (Bundesversicherungsanstalt für Angestellte), and some occupation-specific organizations (e.g., the mining industry). By federal law, one of the tasks of the VdR is to provide statistics on the German social security system.

The VdR data on social security pensions include all employees who are enrolled in the public pension system (as contributors and as beneficiaries) and are based on the individual social security accounts and the payments of pensions through the postal service (Deutsche Post AG, formerly Deutsche Bundespost). Each individual record consists of some hundred variables, such as demographic information, complete contribution history, years of service, retirement age, type of pension, and pension income. These data are not available to researchers outside the VdR. The VdR publishes for each year tabulations of stock and flow data on pensions and retirement. Our hazard rates of retirement are based on the VdR publications on retirement (by age) and on the number of employees covered by the social security system (by age).

Unfortunately, the number of persons retiring also includes persons who were self-employed or not working previous to retirement. This reduces the value of the VdR data in computing retirement hazard rates. Almost every German has a social security record and thus some ("latent") pension claims that will eventually lead to some pension payments. Women often change from an "out-of-labor-market status" into retirement. Thus, one cannot calculate reliable hazard rates without knowing the labor force status before retirement for women. The bias of hazard rates for men is less severe because the number of self-employed men is small and one can correct the number of males in the labor force by using the Mikrozensus data.

The available VdR data have no intertemporal links. Hence, one cannot identify where a new entrant into the public pension system comes from. We use the GSOEP data to link labor force exit with public pension entry.

Publications by the Department of Labor and Social Affairs

The German Department of Labor and Social Affairs (Bundesministerium für Arbeit und Sozialordnung, BMAS) publishes historical data on the German public pension system. These include contribution rates, contribution limits, average earnings, average pension, net and gross replacement rates, the volume of contributions and benefits by type of pension, and the number of contributors and beneficiaries. These data are contained in several publications that are available on request (BMAS 1990, 1996a, 1996b).

The German Socio-Economic Panel

The German Socio-Economic Panel (GSOEP) is an annual panel study of some six thousand households and some fifteen thousand individuals. Its design closely corresponds to the U.S. Panel Study of Income Dynamics (PSID). The panel was begun in 1984; twelve waves were available in 1997. Response rates and panel mortality are comparable to the PSID. The GSOEP data provide a detailed account of income and employment status. The data are used extensively in Germany, and increasing interest in the United States prompted the construction of an English-language user file available from Richard Burkhauser and his associates at Syracuse University. Burkhauser (1991) reports on the usefulness of the German panel data and provides English-language code books as well as an internationally accessible GSOEP version.

Already in 1990, the West German panel was augmented by an East German sample. This permitted a fascinating account of the transition in East Germany.

The sample size of GSOEP waves is considerably smaller than that of the MZ waves or the VdR enumerations. The GSOEP analyses in this paper are based on cells by age and gender that contain roughly three to four hundred persons aged forty-five to sixty, roughly two to three hundred persons aged sixty to sixty-seven (male) and sixty to seventy-two (female), and otherwise roughly one to two hundred persons.

Appendix B
Computation of Social Security Wealth

Social security wealth is defined as expected present discounted value of benefits minus applicable contributions. Seen from the perspective of a worker who is S years old and plans to retire at age R, social security wealth (SSW) is computed as follows:

$$\text{SSW}_s(R) = \sum_{t=R}^{\infty} \text{YPEN}_t(R) \cdot a(s)_t \cdot \delta^{t-S} - \sum_{t=S}^{R-1} c_t \cdot \text{YLAB}_t \cdot a(s)_t \cdot \delta^{t-S},$$

where SSW = present discounted value of retirement benefits (= social security wealth); S = planning age; R = retirement age; YLAB_t = labor income at age t; $\text{YPEN}_t(R)$ = pension income at age t for retirement at age R; c_t = contribution rate to pension system at age t; $a(s)_t$ = probability of surviving at least until age t given survival until age S; and δ = discount factor = $1/(1 + r)$.

The calculations for a couple are more complicated. They include benefits for the surviving spouse, weighted by the survival probability of the spouse.

For a formal description, see Diamond and Gruber, chap. 11 in this volume, app.).

The accrual rate of social security wealth between age $t - 1$ and age t is defined as

$$ACCR_{55}(t) = [SSW_{55}(t) - SSW_{55}(t - 1)] / SSW_{55}(t - 1).$$

Note that these rates are computed from the perspective of a fifty-five-year-old worker ($S = 55$).

Replacement rate denotes the ratio of the pension (YPEN) that the worker would receive if he would retire at that age to the approximate net wages (YLAB^{NET}) he would earn if he would postpone retirement. Note that the mortality risk does not enter this calculation:

$$REPL(t) = YPEN_t(t) / YLAB_t^{NET}.$$

Tax rate refers to the ratio of the negative social security wealth (SSW) accrual to the approximate net wages (YLAB^{NET}) that the worker would earn if he would postpone retirement. Note that SSW is an expected present value including discounting and mortality risk and that YLAB ignores the probability that the worker could die before age seventy:

$$TAXR(t) = -[SSW_{55}(t) - SSW_{55}(t - 1)] / YLAB_t^{NET}.$$

A negative tax rate represents a "subsidy" to the pensioner.

References

Börsch-Supan, Axel. 1992. Population aging, social security design, and early retirement. *Journal of Institutional and Theoretical Economics* 148:533–57.

————. 1997. Germany: A social security system on the verge of collapse. Working paper. University of Mannheim, Department of Economics.

Börsch-Supan, Axel, and Peter Schmidt. In press. Early retirement in East and West Germany. In *Employment policy in the transition to free enterprise: German integration and its lessons for Europe,* ed. R. Riphahn, D. Snower, and K. Zimmermann. Heidelberg: Springer.

Bundesminister für Arbeit und Sozialordnung (BMAS). 1990. *Die Rentenreform 1992.* Bonn: Bundespresseamt.

————. 1996a. *Die Rente.* Bonn: Bundespresseamt.

————. 1996b. *Sozialpolitische Informationen 4.* Bonn: Bundespresseamt.

Burkhauser, Richard. 1991. An introduction to the German Socio-Economic Panel for English speaking researchers. Working Paper no. 1. Syracuse University, Center for Policy Research.

Casmir, B. 1989. *Staatliche Rentenversicherungssysteme im internationalen Vergleich.* Frankfurt: Lang.

Fitzenberger, Bernd, Reinhard Hujer, Thomas E. MaCurdy, and Reinhold Schnabel.

1995. The dynamic structure of wages in Germany, 1976–1984—a cohort analysis. Discussion Paper no. 533-95. University of Mannheim, Department of Economics.

Hauser, Richard. 1995. Stand und Entwicklungstendenzen der Annäherung der sozialen Sicherung in der Europäischen Union: Das Beispiel der Alterssicherung. In *Internationalisierung von Wirtschaft und Politik,* ed. Winfried Schmähl. Baden-Baden: Nomos.

Jacobs, K., M. Kohli, and M. Rein. 1987. Testing the industry-mix hypothesis of early exit. Discussion paper. Wissenschaftszentrum Berlin.

———. 1990. Germany: The diversity of pathways. In *Time for retirement: Comparative studies of early exit from the labor force,* ed. M. Kohli, M. Rein, A.-M. Guillemard, and H. van Gunsteren. Cambridge: Cambridge University Press.

Riphahn, Regina T. 1995. Disability retirement among German men in the 1980s. Münchner Wirtschaftswissenschaftliche Beiträge, no. 95-20. Munich: Ludwig Maximilians Universität.

Riphahn, Regina T., and Peter Schmidt. 1995. Determinanten des Ruhestandes: Lockt der Ruhestand oder drängt der Arbeitsmarkt? Discussion Paper no. 95-10. Mannheim: Zentrum für Wirtschaftsforschung.

Schmähl, Winfried. 1991. Alterssicherung in der DDR und ihre Umgestaltung im Zuge des deutschen Einigungsprozesses—Einige verteilungspolitische Aspekte. In *Sozialpolitik im vereinten Deutschland,* ed. G. Kleinhenz. Berlin: Duncker & Humblot.

———. 1992. Public pension schemes in transition: Germany's way to cope with the challenge of an aging population and the German unification. University of Bremen, Centre for Social Policy Research. Mimeo.

Schmidt, Peter. 1995. *Die Wahl des Rentenalters—Theoretische und empirische Analyse des Rentenzugangsverhaltens in West- und Ostdeutschland.* Frankfurt: Lang.

Schnabel, Reinhold. 1997. Internal rates of return of the German pay-as-you-go social security system. Working paper. University of Mannheim, Department of Economics.

Sommer, Bettina. 1994. Entwicklung der Bevölkerung bis 2040: Ergebnis der achten koordinierten Bevölkerungsvorausberechnung. *Wirtschaft und Statistik* 7:497–503.

Stock, James H., and David A. Wise. 1990. The pension inducement to retire: An option value analysis. In *Issues in the economics of aging,* ed. David A. Wise. Chicago: University of Chicago Press.

Verband deutscher Rentenversicherungstraeger (VdR). 1997. *Rentenversicherung in Zeitreihen.* 4th ed. Frankfurt am Main.

5 Social Security and Retirement in Italy

Agar Brugiavini

Italy is now experiencing one of the lowest fertility rates among developed countries, while life expectancy has improved dramatically over the past few years.[1] This aging process is partly counterbalanced by a significant increase in the size and frequency of immigration flows into the country. However, even the most optimistic scenarios suggest that this inflow will not be enough to reverse the demographic pattern shown by the data. In particular, figures 5.1–5.3 show a dramatic increase in the share of older people and in the dependency ratio over past decades.[2] Furthermore, the positive effects of the baby-boom generation were already fading by 1984, and the ratio of old people and very young people to the working-age population stayed roughly constant after that year (fig. 5.3). Demographic projections suggest that, by 2030, each adult individual will support 0.4 elderly individuals and that this rate may

Agar Brugiavini is assistant professor in the Department of Economics of the University of Venice and a research associate of the Institute for Fiscal Studies in London.

The author is indebted to Jonathan Gruber, David Wise, and the participants in the International Social Security Comparisons project for their helpful comments. Thanks are due to Onorato Castellino, Maria Cozzolino, Elsa Fornero, Giovanni Martinengo, and Massimo Rostagno for many useful insights on the Italian social security system and to Luana Gava, Roberta Marcolin, and Franco Mariuzzo for patiently setting up the data. The author is grateful to the Istituto Nazionale per la Previdenza Sociale administration and the Bank of Italy for providing individual level data and the Consiglio Nazionale delle Richerche (CNR) (grant 96.01418.CT10) and the European Community Training and Mobility of Research Network (contract ERBFMRXCT960016) for financial support. The usual disclaimer applies.

1. In 1990, estimates were (i) an average of 1.3 children per woman of child-bearing age and (ii) life expectancy at birth of 73.6 years for men and 80.2 years for women (Ministero del Tesoro 1996). The Italian Central Statistical Office (ISTAT) has more recently (1996) estimated (i) an average of 1.18 children per woman and a life expectancy at birth of 75.3 years for men and 81.7 years for women (Ministero del Tesoro 1997).

2. This is the ratio of old people to people of working age. The ratio based on the actual labor force figures (appearing as the denominator) may be misleading as labor force series show a jump in 1977 owing to a change in the Labor Force Survey questionnaire.

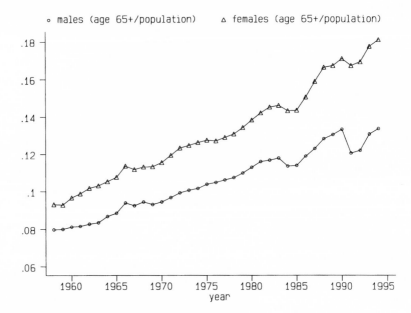

Fig. 5.1 **Share of the population age 65 and over**

Fig. 5.2 **Dependency ratio—old**

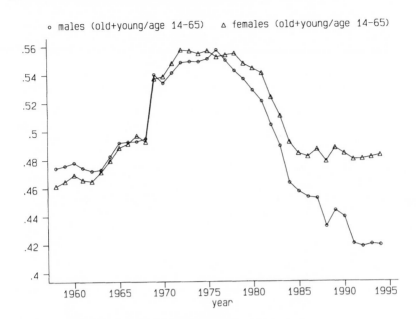

○ males (old+young/age 14-65)   △ females (old+young/age 14-65)

Fig. 5.3   Dependency ratio—old and young

increase to 0.56 by 2050 (fig. 5.4) (Livi Bacci 1995a, 1995b; Ministero del Tesoro 1997).

This demographic trend is coupled with a sizable social security program. In 1995, approximately 17 percent of GDP was devoted to old age and other public assistance outlays (Ministero del Tesoro, *Relazione generale sulla situazione economica del paese,* 1996). Estimates of the size of the Social Security Administration liabilities for the payment of future benefit rights in terms of net social security wealth amount to 300 percent of GDP in 1993 (Beltrametti 1996). From the point of view of households, this corresponds to a large share of their assets being in the form of social security wealth: estimates based on micro data suggest that, on average, social security wealth holdings are as large as private wealth holdings.[3] Not surprisingly, these stylized facts have prompted economists to investigate more closely both the financial viability of the social security system and the effects of the incentives provided by the social security program on households' behavior. As a result, two major reforms have been implemented in very recent years aimed at reducing the level of benefits and restricting eligibility criteria for retirees.

One of the key elements both in evaluating future budget outlays and in

3. In 1993, households held, on average, L 349 million in private wealth and L 382 million in pension wealth, corresponding, on average, to nine and ten times, respectively, the after-tax household income of that year (estimates based on my own calculations from Bank of Italy cross-sectional data). Note that U.S.$1.00 was equivalent to L 1,610 in January 1995.

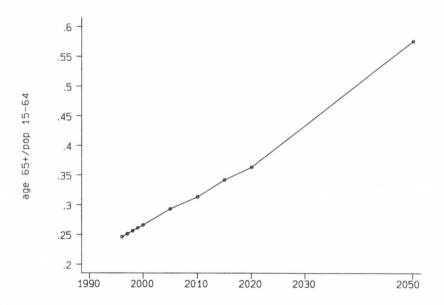

Fig. 5.4   Projected demographic trends, share of population over 65 over working-age population

assessing the effect of social security on households' choices is the effect of the retirement decision on the labor market. In fact, understanding the link between social security–related incentives and labor supply can help explain some features of the labor market structure (e.g., the increasing detachment of older people from the labor force). This in turn provides some idea of how the budget will be affected by a given labor market configuration, that is, by the relation between the number of social security taxpayers and benefit recipients. Italy is a very interesting example in this context. First, because virtually all retirement income is provided to individuals by the social security system, pension funds and private annuities play a negligible role. Second, until 1995 replacement rates were very high (roughly 80 percent of last wage), and therefore the retirement decision involved a large fraction of the household's resources. In particular, when considering whether to work an additional year, the individual sets against the earnings of one extra year almost the same amount of income not collected as social security benefits. Third, the existence of an early retirement provision, which attracts no actuarial penalty, greatly distorts choices in favor of early retirement. Finally, different groups in the population belong to different social security funds characterized by different benefit payouts and eligibility criteria. This causes redistribution between individuals, and, given the variety of incentives provided across these groups, it generates different behavioral responses to policy changes (e.g., the recent reforms), which can be exploited for applied economic analysis.

This paper addresses the issues outlined above by first documenting the stylized facts characterizing the labor market both over the recent past and over the life cycle of individuals (sec. 5.1). Section 5.2 describes the structure of the Italian social security program and summarizes the relevant institutional details. Section 5.3 is devoted to a simulation model designed to better understand the incentive effects of social security on current cohorts of retirees. Section 5.4 draws some conclusions.

5.1   The Labor Market Behavior of Older Persons in Italy

The Italian labor market has been characterized by a declining attachment to the labor force of older persons, but different patterns are observed for men and for women. After World War II, the Italian social security system became increasingly more generous, particularly with regard to early retirement. There is now a consistent body of evidence that this increased generosity is closely related to a reduction in household savings (Rossi and Visco 1995; Attanasio and Brugiavini 1997). This prompts the question of whether observed changes in labor supply behavior could be explained by the growth of the Italian social security program over those years. An interesting twist in the investigation of this issue in the Italian case is that, owing to the lack of actuarial penalties on early retirement, the workers exhibiting these trends may still be relatively young.

The historical and contemporary facts presented in this section are drawn from a number of different data sources. These are summarized in appendix A.

5.1.1   Historical Trends

Figures 5.5 and 5.6 map out the labor force participation rates of men and women of different age groups since 1958. Four age groups are selected: forty to fifty, fifty to sixty, sixty to sixty-five, and over sixty-five.[4]

From these aggregate figures, a marked difference emerges between the labor market behavior of older men in the age groups over sixty. Figure 5.5 indicates that, for these groups, participation starts low (e.g., 60 percent in 1958 for the age group sixty to sixty-four) and declines sharply (to about 30 percent in 1994 for the age group sixty to sixty-four). These figures can be contrasted with the age group fifty to sixty, which is characterized by a greater attachment (90 percent share in 1958) and an almost comparable drop (to about 70 percent) in recent years.

The same distinction can be drawn for female labor force participation (fig. 5.6): for older women, participation declines slightly but steadily, while, for younger women, higher and increasing participation is observed. The decline

---

4. The choice of age groups is constrained by data availability. However, these age groups are consistent, for men, with the social security configuration that set the normal retirement age at sixty.

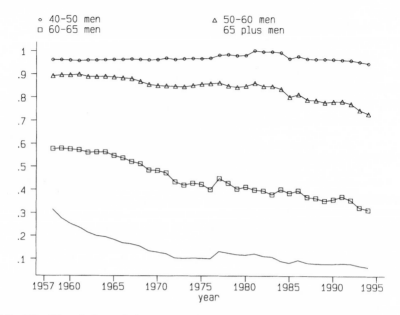

Fig. 5.5   Historical trends in the labor force participation of older men

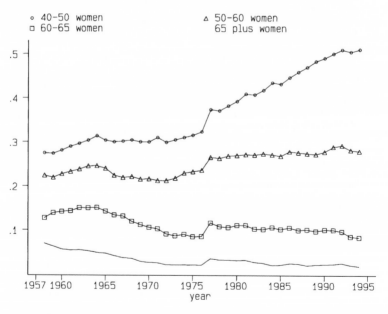

Fig. 5.6   Historical trends in the labor force participation of older women

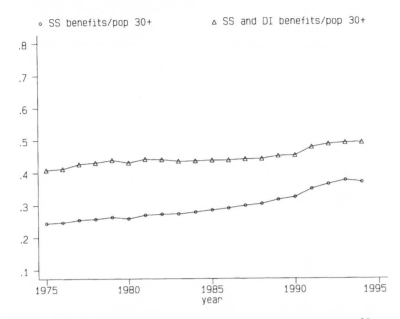

Fig. 5.7   Social security and disability insurance benefit recipients, age 30 and over

in the labor force participation rate observed for older women in recent years is less sharp than that for men because of a more marked increase over time in participation in the labor force among younger cohorts.[5]

In order to explore possible correlations between the labor market evidence and the developments in the social security program, a number of graphs are presented that document the increasing generosity of the social security system over time.

A first graph looks at the share of the population over age thirty receiving benefits (fig. 5.7).[6] These are distinguished in two time series: the first series shows the share of old age social security benefits (inclusive of early retirement benefits) and benefits to survivors paid to the population in the age group over

5. There is a noticeable jump of all the series in fig. 5.6 above (and also in fig. 5.5 above, although the jump is less sharp) in the year 1977. This is due to a change in the definition of the labor force occurring in that year, which is described in more detail in app. A.

6. The choice of this wide age group is determined by the availability of data on disability insurance benefits recipients. In fact, disability insurance benefits are not distinguished by age for every social security fund. It is possible to infer from INPS data (a subset of the social security program, mainly excluding the public sector) that not many disability insurance benefits are paid out before age thirty, hence making this age the natural cutoff point. Alternatively, I could have shown, for the INPS fund alone, the share of disability insurance recipients age fifty over the population age fifty; however, this provides a misleading picture as in some years there was a disproportionate number of disability insurance benefits paid out to those self-employed in agriculture.

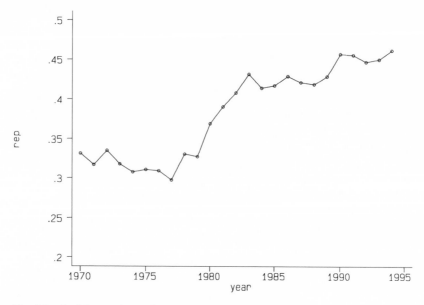

Fig. 5.8   Social security replacement rate over time, FPLD (private-sector employees)

thirty; the second series is based on the share of old age social security benefits, survivor benefits, and disability insurance benefits paid to the population of the same age group. It should be pointed out straight away that, in this graph, although the legend reads *benefit recipients,* it is actually the number of benefits that is recorded, as the number of recipients is not generally available. The two figures may differ significantly as each person may receive more than one type of benefit.[7] Both lines increase sharply from 1960 up to the first half of the 1970s, following a more moderate trend thereafter. What is striking is the incidence of disability insurance benefits in this group of the population and how this feature evolves over time. However, the two series tend to converge for most recent years as screening for disability insurance benefits eligibility gets tighter; for example, in 1993, roughly 14 percent of disability insurance benefits were paid out to this age group.[8]

Figure 5.8 shows the change in generosity over time by plotting the aggregate replacement rate (for the private-sector employees fund only). This is

7. For example, some people may claim a survivor benefit and an old age pension. Unfortunately, I could not distinguish between males and females because of lack of data.
8. In sec. 5.2 below, I explain how disability insurance benefits played the role of unemployment/poverty safety net until 1984, when a law was passed by Parliament greatly limiting eligibility and increasing the frequency and quality of screening. To get a general picture, it could be added that, in 1993, disability insurance benefits paid by the INPS administration (i.e., excluding the public sector) covered approximately 7 percent of the resident population.

available for years since 1970, and it is much lower than the "theoretical" replacement rate (roughly 80 percent) because it is obtained as the average benefit level (all types of benefits) over the average of earnings computed on the basis of the payments made to the Social Security Administration. There is a clear pattern of increase over the last few decades, with a huge jump between 1980 and 1985.

5.1.2   Labor Market Behavior in 1995

In order to explore more recent facts about the labor market and to analyze patterns of labor force attachment and benefit receipt over the life cycle, it may be useful to turn to micro evidence. I use the Bank of Italy Survey (SHIW), which is a nationally representative survey of Italian households based on questions about consumption, saving, demographic structure, and labor supply asked of each member of the household (see app. A). The responses given by each adult member of the household concern current labor supply behavior as well as some retrospective information on employment. Unfortunately, the whole work history of each worker cannot be reconstructed as there are no questions about spells of unemployment or previous detachments from the labor force. I exploit the data both in its cross-sectional component and in its panel component for the years 1989, 1991, and 1993.[9] For the graphs contained in this section, cross-sectional data are better suited: I decided to work with the three cross sections, rather than just use the 1993 one, as the year 1993 is considered to have been affected by a brief, yet sharp, recession that could provide misleading results. The panel dimension is used to construct the hazard rate out of the labor force, to be discussed in section 5.3 below.

The age pattern of participation for men and women is given in figure 5.9. There is a striking difference between the two curves. They both peter out after age sixty, but, while for men we observe a participation rate close to unity at age forty-five, which runs down to 0.44 by age sixty (normal retirement age under the pre-1992 legislation), women have a participation rate close to 0.5 at age forty-five, which decreases steadily afterward. The most precipitous drop for males seems to occur between age fifty-five and age sixty-two: early retirement seems a natural explanation of this finding.

Figure 5.10 shows how men allocate their time among different activities as they age. There are four categories of activity: employment, unemployment, disability, and retirement. While disability insurance characterizes a nonnegligible fraction of men at all ages, there is a downward trend in the numbers of the employed population that exactly parallels the labor force attachment pro-

---

9. I also have social security data (INPS archive) in panel form over twenty years; these are also described in app. A. However, this latter data set covers only private-sector employees, and it is an unbalanced panel: in order to provide a general description of the labor market, I therefore opted for the Bank of Italy data. This also allowed me to present some interesting comparisons between private- and public-sector employees pursued further in app. B.

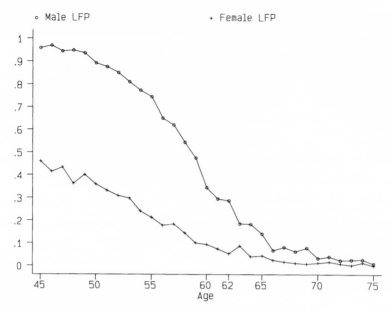

Fig. 5.9   Participation rates by age and sex

file.[10] The age pattern of the share of the retired is most striking: retirement absorbs a huge share of men in a relatively short time, starting with approximately 1 percent at age fifty and reaching 70 percent at age sixty-six.[11] Figure 5.11 shows the results of the same split for women: the underlying trends are very different from those observed for men: while the share of employed women starts low and declines steadily over time, the share of retired women grows dramatically over time and reaches a peak at age sixty-five. For example, at age fifty, a negligible fraction has retired, while, at age sixty-five, roughly 50 percent have quit work, mainly reflecting different statutory retirement ages for men and for women. Disability insurance is claimed by a nonnegligible

10. There is a discrepancy between the line representing disability insurance recipients derived from this data source and the one derived from official statistics, shown in fig. 5.7 above. First, it should be noticed that fig. 5.7 refers to the share of the population of over age thirty (both males and females) receiving disability insurance benefits. Furthermore, aggregate data count the number of benefits, not the number of recipients. I have attempted the same calculation using micro data in producing fig. 5.10, however, not every income earner reports her or his second or third pension, and respondents do not always report receiving a disability insurance benefit if they work. Finally, as I explain in app. A, the Bank of Italy data, a very rich data source, tends to oversample wealthy households slightly, probably underestimating the number of disability insurance recipients. In any case, if I cumulate the share of disability insurance benefit recipients from age thirty on, I obtain approximately the same result.

11. For the "retired" curve, I consider only individuals receiving an old age social security benefit or an early retirement social security benefit, excluding all other social security benefits, e.g., the "basic pension" (an income maintenance benefit).

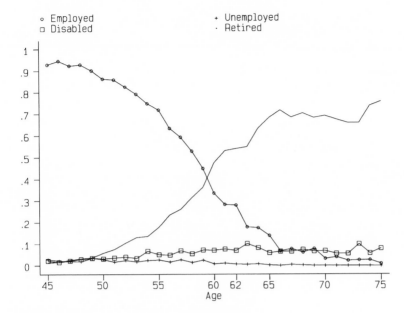

Fig. 5.10 Distribution of activities of men by age

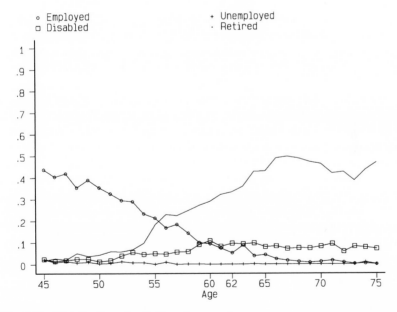

Fig. 5.11 Distribution of activities of women by age

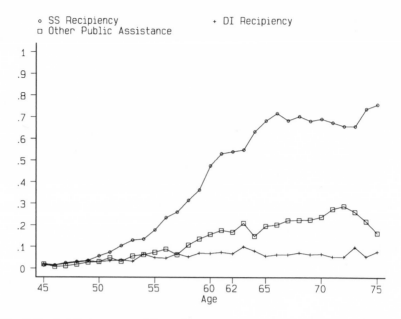

○ SS Recipiency   + DI Recipiency
□ Other Public Assistance

Fig. 5.12   Public income recipiency for men

fraction of women, starting at age fifty and continuing until advanced old age. It should be stressed that all graphs are much below the value of 100 percent as many women are not engaged in paid working activities during the life cycle.[12]

5.1.3   Income Sources of Older Persons

Figure 5.12 plots social security and disability insurance receipt for men. It shows a marked increase, over the life cycle, of social security benefits and, to a lesser extent, of other public assistance benefits. In figure 5.13, this aspect is further investigated by looking at the percentage of men and women receiving a social security benefit.[13] This share grows rapidly after age fifty-five: between the ages fifty and fifty-nine, the percentage is higher for women (who are more likely to benefit from a survivor pension); after that age interval, there is a stable gender gap. The growing importance of social security over the life cycle is confirmed by figure 5.14, which shows that the share of family income coming from earnings declines rapidly after age fifty-five, that the share of income from capital remains relatively stable, and that there is a corresponding increase in social security benefits and public transfers (see n. 13).

12. Because I am excluding non-work-related social security benefits (as explained in n. 11 above), the share of women receiving some benefits would be much higher (approximately 90 percent) at later ages, when women become more likely to receive a survivor benefit or a basic pension.

13. Any sort of social security benefit, even if it is not the main source of income.

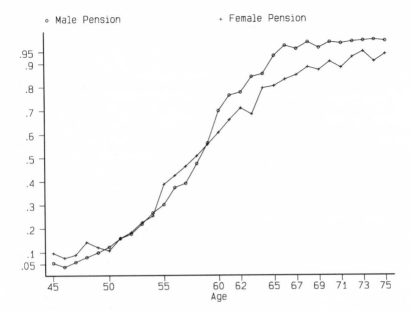

Fig. 5.13   Share receiving pension

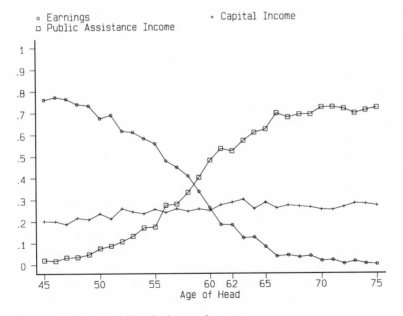

Fig. 5.14   Distribution of family income by source

5.2   Key Features of the Italian Social Security System

5.2.1   History of the Social Security System in Italy

Old age insurance originated in Italy in the public sector in the nineteenth century for employees in the army, while private-sector blue-collar workers had their first (fully funded and nonmandatory) fund set up in 1889 (for a complete and detailed history of the Italian social security system, see Castellino 1976). By 1960, the National Institute for Social Security (Istituto Nazionale per la Previdenza Sociale, or INPS) was collecting mandatory social security payroll taxes from a large share of private-sector employees (under the heading Private-Sector Employees Fund, FPLD) as well as from an increasing number of the self-employed (workers in agriculture and commerce). Hence, INPS, and particularly FPLD, established itself as the main social security fund administration in the country, followed by the public-sector employees' fund.[14] However, many other groups of workers kept (or set up) their own independent funds, each group taking the view that its fund should have its own special conditions. Hence, it was at a very early stage that the social security program took the form of a patchwork of independent schemes, typically characterized by different rules concerning payroll taxes, benefit payout, and eligibility requirements.

While a pay-as-you-go (PAYGO) financing method had been gradually introduced since the 1950s, it was only in 1969 that the financial distress of the funded schemes caused by the events of World War II and the desire to set up a modern welfare state finally led to a definite move toward a PAYGO system for the major funds. Almost simultaneously, three further important changes were introduced for the private-sector employees' fund: (1) benefit computation became of a "final salary" type (average of the last five years of employment, as explained below) in place of the previous career average measure; (2) a means-tested income maintenance scheme was introduced for each individual over age sixty-five not covered by old age insurance (the so-called *pensione sociale*); (3) social security benefits became automatically linked to a price-growth index. Finally, the early retirement option was introduced for private-sector employees: this would allow a retiree to claim old age benefits conditional on having "completed" thirty-five years of social security tax payments, but with no constraint on age. It should be added that the early retirement option had been available to government employees since 1956: throughout the 1960s and 1970s, it was made even more generous for this group as men could claim the early retirement benefit having made only twenty years' social security tax payments while married women needed to contribute to the public-sector employees fund for as few as fifteen years. The public sector also re-

14. I am not describing the self-employed INPS fund, although this had an interesting evolution and is becoming increasingly important.

ceived preferential treatment in another relevant respect: benefit computation was based on a "pure final salary" in place of an average of the last five years' earnings. More recently (1976), social security benefits for private-sector employees were automatically linked to real-wage growth as well as price growth.

These facts show that, after World War II, acts of Parliament enacted piecemeal changes that went almost invariably in the direction of increasing generosity, with no concern about the long-term effects of these amendments. The Italian experience seems even more peculiar considering that, for forty years, this trend continued uninterrupted and then two major reforms were passed by Parliament within a period of three years, both aimed at improving the social security budget—the first in 1992 (referred to as the Amato reform), the second in 1995 (known as the Dini reform).

5.2.2 Current Features of the Social Security System

In this section I describe in detail the legislation governing the social security system in 1992. In fact, the evidence presented in section 5.1 concerns the features of the social security system before the reforms. I therefore provide only a brief overview of the system after the reforms.

The Italian social security system relies on three "pillars": (i) mandatory old age insurance, also providing insurance to survivors and disability benefits; (ii) pension funds; and (iii) private annuities. The first covers the majority of the working population (almost all private-sector employees) and is financed by a PAYGO method,[15] while the remaining forms of insurance provide additional coverage outside (or, in a few cases, as substitutes for) the public program. Pension funds are generally fully funded and nonmandatory (unless they substitute for the public program, as happens for employees in some banks and financial institutions).

In this study, I consider the social security system to be a mandatory public insurance program collecting payroll taxes from both employers and employees to provide old age benefits, survivor benefits, and disability insurance to its members.[16] I disregard pension funds and private annuities as they play a negligible role. The social security program is based on a number of institutions administering public pensions. A vast majority of the population is insured with the INPS. This is itself responsible for a number of separate and independent funds, the most important of which is the FPLD. Although a description of the INPS-FPLD gives a fairly good idea of the system as a whole, it should be borne in mind that a wide variety of cases actually exist. Table 5.1

---

15. That is, an unfunded method of financing.

16. The Italian social security system has played a major role in providing a safety net for low-income households both explicitly (through special provisions that are part of the INPS administration, e.g., income maintenance provisions for the needy and very old) and implicitly (through disability benefits). Although these income maintenance provisions are not included in this study, they have certainly contributed to the inflation of the INPS budget and are relevant in explaining the aggregate data.

Table 5.1   Number of Pensions and Number of Workers for Some Major Social Security Funds, 1993

	Pensions (thousand)	Workers (thousand)	Ratio
INPS, total	14,814	16,345	.91
Private-sector employees, FPLD	10,141	11,250	.90
Self-employed	3,634	4,347	.84
Agriculture	2,038	893	2.28
Arts and crafts	816	1,798	.45
Commerce	780	1,655	.47
Other INPS	314	748	.42
Public-sector employees	2,171	3,776	.57
Others	284	969	.29

summarizes some of the main indicators for the private-sector employees' fund (INPS-FPLD), the public-sector employees' fund,[17] and the INPS-managed fund for the self-employed.

Table 5.1 shows clearly that INPS provides insurance to a large fraction of the working population; public-sector employees account for only 15 percent of total INPS workers and 20 percent of the INPS-FPLD group.

Payroll Social Security Taxes

The inflow of resources into the system comes from employers' and employees' contributions: when outlays exceed revenue, the deficit is financed by the central government, which has come under increasing pressure to pay for pensions. For example, it is estimated that the theoretical equilibrium payroll tax (i.e., the payroll tax that would balance the budget) was, in 1991, between 35 and 44 percent, according to whether full imputation is made for income maintenance benefits. This is much higher than the actual payroll tax (26.4 percent in 1991): the difference is an estimate of the tax levied on the entire population of income tax payers in order to finance pensions (INPS, *Le pensioni domani,* 1993).

The payroll tax is unevenly shared between employer and employee. In 1983, for INPS-FPLD, the total payroll tax was 24.51 percent of gross earnings, of which 7.15 percent fell on the employee. In 1995, this grew to 27.17 percent, of which 8.34 percent was paid by the worker. In contrast, social security taxes for public-sector employees and the self-employed have been lower, although gradually converging to the private-sector ones.[18] A further 7.41 per-

---

17. I am referring to the public-sector employees fund as one entity, but there are two major groups: Central Government Employees and Istituto Nazionale Previdenza e Assistenza Dipendenti Amministrazioni Pubbliche (other civil servants [e.g., local government employees], teachers in primary education, etc.); this latter group was formerly known as the Treasury Fund.

18. There is no split between what is paid for old age benefits and for the other benefits. It should be noted that, for public-sector employees, various rules apply. In particular, for government employees, no explicit social security tax is paid by the employer.

cent should be added in the private sector for a "severance-pay fund," referred to as TFR. This is retained by the employer and builds up in a fund, directly managed by the employer, that provides a lump-sum benefit at the time of retirement. I discuss this provision in more detail below; however, it should be noted that an additional 0.8 percent tax is related to the TFR provision in a complex fashion. This additional 0.8 percent social security tax is paid by the employer on a monthly basis, but it does not accrue to the severance pay fund (a fraction of this tax goes to the National Health Service and a fraction to the social security fund). At the end of the year, the employer takes from his employees' TFR fund a rebate equivalent to the additional tax he paid, which is therefore effectively paid by the employees.

The tax base is not capped: this is a point long debated in the literature, as social security benefits are capped. There is a limit to earnings under which the social security tax due stays constant: in 1995, social security tax had to be paid on at least L 720,000 of yearly earnings (which is approximately 3 percent of mean individual earnings of that year and is below the value of the bottom 5 percent of the distribution of earnings). This limit is known as the *minimum amount subject to social security tax.*

Eligibility

Eligibility requirements are met when a man reaches age sixty (a woman fifty-five) and has contributed for at least fifteen years.[19] However, the early retirement option often makes the age requirement irrelevant as a worker in the private sector can claim early retirement benefits at any age if thirty-five years' tax payments have been completed. For a male public-sector employee, twenty years' tax payments are required (fifteen years for a married woman). (However, it should be added that, in the pre-1995 legislation, the normal retirement age for the public sector is sixty-five for both men and women [for full details, see table 5.2].) In general, a year of work is completed if fifty-two weeks of social security tax payments have been recorded by the Social Security Administration. However, since 1984, only yearly earnings above a threshold (e.g., L 13 million in 1995, approximately 37 percent of mean earnings) count as full: lower earnings lead to a proportional reduction in the recorded number of weeks.[20] This limit is known as the *minimum eligibility level.* A relevant aspect in discussing incentives to labor supply provided by the social security program is the retirement earnings test. In fact, in Italy, workers can

---

19. Retirement is not mandatory, but individuals who intend to work beyond the normal retirement age are not protected by law and could be fired. However, before the 1992 reform, a worker could postpone retirement (up to age sixty-five in the private sector) if this would allow him to complete forty years' tax payments. The 1992 reform encouraged workers to postpone retirement (until age sixty-five) even if forty years' contributions had been completed by providing a slightly higher return in the benefit computation formula. Claiming and receiving a pension are often separate events. The delays in paying different types of benefits vary: in most cases, benefits are received one month later than the date of the claim (the latter usually coincides with the worker's birthday).

20. Allowance is made for special cases: e.g., maternity leave.

Table 5.2   Eligibility Criteria for Retirement and Early Retirement

	Private Sector		Public Sector		Self-Employed	
	Male	Female	Male	Female	Male	Female
Pre-1992 regime:						
Old age benefit (age)	60	55	65	65	65	60
Early retirement (years of tax payments)	35	35	20	15	35	35
Post-1992 regime:						
Old age benefit (age)	65	60	65	65	65	60
Early retirement (years of tax payments)	35	35	35	35	35	35
Post-1995 regime:						
Old age benefit (age)	57–65	57–65	57–65	57–65	57–65	57–65

draw a pension and earn income at the same time. However, there are earnings cutoffs that make this choice less attractive. The earnings cutoffs have changed over time and have been heavily affected by the reforms. I focus attention solely on the rules applying to private-sector employees prior to 1992: Old age social security benefits could be claimed while receiving earnings. In this case, benefits could be claimed only within the amount given by the minimum benefit plus half the difference between the actual benefit and the minimum benefit. Early retirement benefits could not be claimed along with earnings.

From this brief description of the eligibility criteria, there emerges a picture of a social security system that is actuarially unfair and enacts, willingly or unwillingly, redistribution of resources across the population. In particular, there is an incentive to early retirement as no actuarial penalty applies to early retirees. For example, a private-sector employee who started work at age sixteen could retire at age fifty-one, while the same worker could retire at age thirty-six in the public sector. This might explain why detachment from the labor force increases significantly over time in the age group fifty to sixty as well (see fig. 5.5 above).

Benefit Computation

For a private-sector employee (INPS-FPLD), benefits are computed by first averaging the last five years' earnings (prior to the retirement age): this gives the level of "pensionable earnings." Actual earnings of each year are taken before tax and converted to real amounts by means of a consumer price index.[21] Pensionable earnings are converted to social security benefits by applying a 2 percent factor (referred to as the *rate of return*) for each year of social security

21. This is an index provided by the Central Statistical Office (ISTAT) in which weights applied to prices are taken from a large sample of the Italian population on the basis of a sampling frame of blue- and white-collar employees (Indice dei Prezzi al Consumo per le Famiglie di Operai e Impiegati).

tax payment up to a maximum of forty years. Hence, a worker can get at most 80 percent of his pensionable earnings. If retirement is postponed, additional years of work beyond a total of forty do not count for benefit computation; however, they are included in pensionable earnings as they replace earnings of earlier years. The system is highly progressive both because of earnings caps and because of old age minimum benefit levels. Earnings entering the benefit computation are capped. Between 1969 and 1988, pensionable earnings would be set against a given limit, and the amount in excess of that limit would not contribute to the benefit formula. For example, in 1985, pensionable earnings in excess of L 32 million (1.6 times the average earnings for that year) would not be included in benefit calculations. After 1988, the constraint was less stringent, as a lower "rate of return" was applied to pensionable earnings in excess of a given limit. In 1995, a 2 percent rate applied to the first L 57 million (again, 1.6 times the average earnings) and a 1.5 percent rate to pensionable earnings in excess of that figure but below L 76 million (2.2 times the mean earnings), and the returns fell to 1.25 percent for pensionable earnings between L 76 and L 95 million (2.7 times the mean earnings). Finally, the top earnings bracket attracted a 1 percent return.

The system is much more generous to low-income workers by providing a *minimum benefit,* that is, a "floor" benefit level.

It is worth recalling that public-sector employees have their benefit level based on final salary rather than average earnings over the last five years. For all funds, benefits increase at regular intervals with nominal wages, that is, consumer price growth plus real earnings growth. The former is measured by the consumer price index but is implemented in a slightly staggered fashion (e.g., if the social security benefit amounts to more than three times the "minimum benefit," indexing is based on 75 percent of the price change). Wage growth is measured by changes in real wages in both the private and the public sectors.[22]

Minimum Benefit

The minimum benefit is a relevant concept in the Italian social security system both because the number of retirees involved is nonnegligible and because the minimum benefit is often used as a benchmark against which to set incomes for other provisions. In practice, if the benefit formula gives a retiree a benefit level below a given threshold, the benefit itself is set in line with that threshold. Up to 1983, this provision could be applied to more than one pension for the same retiree, while it now affects only one pension for each retiree, leaving the other benefits at their computed level. This income transfer to low-income retirees is conditional on means testing: up to 1992, this test involved only the

---

22. Indexation to nominal wage started, for INPS-FPLD, in 1975: the legislation has changed several times in the last few decades, tending to extend this feature to more groups of the working population. The timing of indexation has also changed several times: during the 1970s, it was done quarterly.

claimant's income and excluded the income of the spouse. Hence, for example, in 1985, the means test had a cutoff at twice the minimum level (roughly L 4.7 million that year, which was 17 percent of mean household income). More recently, a similar limit applies to singles, but for married couples what matters is the sum of the incomes of both spouses, which must be below four times the minimum level (in 1995, approximately L 8 million, which was 18 percent of mean household income).

Taxation

While social security taxes are not subject to income taxes (as these are paid after the social security tax), social security benefits are taxed at current tax rates.

Survivor Benefits

While survivor benefits to widows were part of the insurance contract at a very early stage, it was only in 1977 that several household members were entitled to claim such benefits, eligibility extending from widows and children younger than age eighteen to include widowers and children older than age eighteen in full-time education. More recently, beneficiaries include (i) the surviving spouse, (ii) children younger than age twenty-one if in secondary school and younger than age twenty-six if attending college working toward a degree or of any age if disabled, and (iii), conditional on none of the above being alive, dependent parents or single dependent sisters and brothers. In order to claim the survivor benefit, the worker should have had a full five years' tax payments. Survivor benefits can also originate from the disability insurance benefit of the worker (described below). The actual benefit is a percentage of the old age benefit that the deceased worker would receive at that age—60 percent for the lone surviving spouse, 20 percent to each child if one of the spouses is alive, and 40 percent to each child if orphaned, up to a total amount not exceeding the initial old age benefit of the worker. Parents, brothers, and sisters receive, if eligible, 15 percent of the old age benefit each, up to grand total of 100 percent of the old age benefit itself. The Italian social security system does not envisage a dependent wife benefit: the only advantages to married couples are to those drawing minimum-level pensions (described above).

Other Social Security Programs

In recent years, the social security program has been under scrutiny, the financial distress within the system leading to calls for a reduction in both benefit levels and eligibility. This also focused the attention of policy makers on a global social security reform in order to achieve a much-needed realignment of the treatment of different groups of workers. This process started with two important changes brought about in 1984 and in 1989, the former relating to disability insurance provision and the latter trying to regulate those benefits aimed at the redistribution of income. One of the key elements in the debate that took place at the time was the insistence on clearly distinguishing between benefits relating to an income maintenance program (implementing redistributive policies, which would therefore be financed by the entire population) and old age insurance benefits (which were more properly financed by the working population).

A typical income maintenance provision, in which the role of the central government predominated over that of the Social Security Administration, was the means-tested *basic pension* (*pensione sociale*) granted to individuals over age sixty-five (even if they had made no social security tax payments). To be eligible, a single person cannot have an income above the level of the basic pension itself (the basic pension in 1995 was L 4.6 million, 13 percent of mean earnings), while a couple cannot have an income above L 19 million in 1995 (54 percent of mean earnings). The benefit is granted with no penalty in the absence of other incomes, and it is awarded only partially if some resources are available within the income cutoff. Another interesting example is the unemployment benefit, paid in the form of an early retirement benefit (*prepensionamento*), granted to workers of firms in specific industries going through a recession. This benefit can be claimed by the worker five years earlier than the normal retirement age and could be regarded as a form of "involuntary" early retirement. However, not only does this apply only to a limited number of occupational sectors in the economy, but it is also becoming less frequent.

Disability Insurance

The most striking feature in this debate is the role of disability insurance, which is still part of the social security program. There are at present two possible disability insurance benefits: (i) the "disability insurance pension," provided under the legislation that applied up to 1984, and (ii) the "disability insurance provision" (*assegno di invalidità*), which can be claimed under the post-1984 legislation. The former was granted to workers who proved that they were physically unable to carry out their job (with their earnings ability reduced by two-thirds) and who had completed five years' tax payments. *Earnings ability* was, however, a rather loose concept, involving the doctor's judgment of the general welfare level of the claimant, not just his or her health quality. Disability insurance pensions were computed by following the general rules of eligibility and of benefit calculation and by computing pensionable earnings as the average of actual earnings prior to the date of the claim. After 1984, the existing disability insurance pensions were not terminated or modified, except in cases in which the beneficiary had an income exceeding three times the minimum benefit. Starting in 1984, the disability insurance provision was the new form of disability insurance benefit; it was granted under the same eligibility requirements as before, with the important difference that *loss of earnings ability* was defined much more strictly. Furthermore, the disability insurance provision was temporary, and a new claim was required for renewal

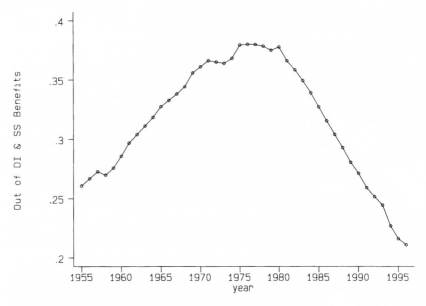

Fig. 5.15   Share of disability insurance benefit receipts, FPLD (private-sector employees)

every three years, which entailed new medical examinations. Screening of the health status of disability insurance recipients is now carried out randomly. The disability insurance provision is to be brought in line with the minimum benefit whenever the calculated benefit is below that level.

This brief description of the disability insurance benefit and its evolution over time highlights the strong incentive provided to claim disability insurance in order to achieve early retirement in those cases where the early retirement option was not available. However, the 1984 law had a major effect in reversing this trend: figure 5.15 shows that the share of disability insurance benefits over total benefits peaked in the years 1975–80 and declined sharply thereafter. In figure 5.16 the same pattern emerges from the ratio of disability insurance benefits to insured workers: by relating disability insurance benefits to the working population (insured with INPS-FPLD), it is possible to appreciate how the steepest decline came in 1987, when the new disability insurance legislation of 1984 had its full effect.[23] More interestingly, disability insurance benefits over total benefits dropped dramatically for the age group fifty to fifty-nine, the age group immediately preceding normal retirement age (fig. 5.17).

23. This ratio can be computed only since 1975. Therefore, in fig. 5.16, I have also shown again the ratio of DI benefits over total benefits for this subperiod (provided in fig. 5.15 for a longer spell) in order to draw a comparison.

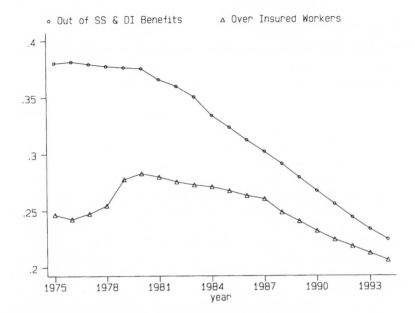

Fig. 5.16 Share of disability insurance benefit receipts, FPLD (private-sector employees)

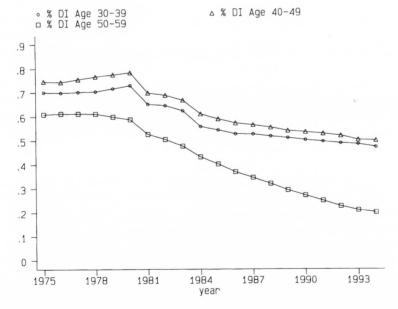

Fig. 5.17 Share of disability insurance benefit receipts as a fraction of total social security and disability insurance benefits, FPLD (private-sector employees)

The Severance Pay Fund, TFR

This provision applies to both private- and public-sector employees. In the private sector, a nonnegligible fraction of annual earnings (7.41 percent) is earmarked by employers for an end-of-job one-time payment. This money does not contribute to any pension fund but is directly managed by the firm, which uses it as internal funds. This appears as another key feature of the system in analyzing the incentives of social security with regard to retirement: the prospect of cashing in a lump sum at retirement (which would otherwise earn a low rate of interest) may induce a worker to leave the labor force earlier than the normal retirement age.

The TFR was originally set up in the private sector and was regarded by workers as a form of unemployment benefit; firms encouraged the growth of this fund in order both to reduce workers' mobility and to create an extra source of internal financing (Di Vezza 1990). The legislation concerning the lump-sum benefit computation differs from sector to sector and, prior to 1982, from occupation to occupation within the private sector. In particular, prior to 1982, the lump sum would, for the vast majority of private-sector employees, correspond to a share of 8.33 percent (i.e., one-twelfth) of the final wage adjusted according to the number of years in employment with the same firm. Hence, the fund would effectively grow at the wage-growth rate for each year up to 1982, and each year the employer would retain 8.33 percent of the gross wage of his employees. After 1982, for all employees in the private sector, the fund built up each year was capitalized at a rate given by the sum of two components: a fixed 1.5 percent plus 75 percent of the growth in prices recorded in the month of December of the previous year. In periods of high inflation, this growth rate would be below the price-growth rate and much below nominal wage growth. For this reason, it is often argued that workers would be better off if they could invest that money with a financial institution. While 7.41 percent of gross earnings is retained by the employer for the TFR fund in the manner described above, a further 0.8 percent of the worker's gross earnings is paid by the employer to the INPS administration, which does not contribute to the employee's TFR.[24] The employer collects a full rebate on this additional payroll tax by reducing the TFR of his employees for an equivalent amount at the end of the year. Hence, this additional tax is effectively paid by the employee with no corresponding TFR benefit.

While the TFR payroll tax is not subject to any income tax, the worker pays separate income tax on the TFR lump-sum benefit at reduced tax rates.[25]

---

24. I have already described under the heading *Social Security Tax* how this additional payroll tax mainly goes to the National Health Service to provide health insurance for retirees.

25. Income tax is paid on the TFR only above a given minimum level. This tax-exempt level changes over time.

Old Age Insurance through Private Schemes

Saving through pension funds is available for only a limited number of individuals in specific occupational sectors and is almost invariably a voluntary additional supplement to the basic pension. More recently, the need to alleviate part of the burden of pension provision that falls on social security has shifted attention to a system in which, in addition to the public pension scheme, there should exist a non-own-managed pension fund and possibly a private old age insurance contract. The recent reforms intend to channel the enforced "low-return" savings of the TFR into pension funds for newly hired employees, provided that the firm/industry and the fund itself abide by a number of requirements. It is still being debated whether this change will increase or decrease workers' welfare, the debate hinging on a number of factors (including the behavior of firms in setting wages).

5.2.3 The Recent Reforms

Some of the issues raised in the description given above of the social security system have been tackled by the recent reforms. The first reform (known as the Amato reform) was passed by Parliament in 1992. Once phased in, it reduced pension outlays and ironed out major differences between various sectors and occupations. However, this left the rules governing the early retirement provision almost untouched and, according to many, did not produce the much-needed savings in the social security budget. Hence, the second reform (known as the Dini reform) of 1995 totally changed some of the basic rules for granting benefits to future retirees and attempted to harmonize the actuarial rates of return for early and late retirees. For the purpose of this study, I focus on the 1995 reform, passing over the 1992 reform and the transitional phase between the two reforms. This choice is motivated by my intention of highlighting the features of long-term equilibria. However, as shown in appendix B, the Amato reform had a major effect on retirement behavior as it was the first signal of a coherent redesigning of the social security system. In table 5.3, some of the key features of the three regimes are summarized.

The post-1995 reform adopts a "contribution-based" method of benefit calculation. It should be stressed that this applies only to benefit computation, while financing is still on a PAYGO basis. The social security benefit is the annuity equivalent to the present value (at retirement) of past payroll taxes, updated by means of a five-year moving average of the nominal GDP growth rate. The relevant tax rate is 33 percent, and an age-related actuarial adjustment factor is applied to the resulting figure.[26] As for the early retirement provision, the 1992 reform ironed out differences between programs (contributions had to be paid for at least thirty-five years, irrespective of type of occupation, sector, etc.), with no adjustment of retirement benefits, while the 1995 reform

---

26. Hence, the benefit is (33%) × (adjustment factor) × (present value of social security taxes).

Table 5.3   Some Key Features of the Pre-1992 Regime, the Post-1992 Regime, and the Post-1995 Regime (having completed the transition)

	Pre-1992	Post-1992	Post-1995
Normal retirement age	60 (men), 55 (women)	65 (men), 60 (women)	57–65 (men), 57–65 (women)
Transitional period		2032	2035
Pensionable earnings	Average of final five years' real earnings (converted to real values through price index)	Career average earnings (converted to real values through price index + 1%)	Not applicable
Pension benefit	2% (pensionable earnings) × (t), where t is the number of years in the system (at most 40 years)	2% (pensionable earnings) × (t), where t is the number of years in the system (at most 40 years)	Annuity based on stock of Social Security payroll tax; past taxes converted to real values through nominal GDP growth rate
Indexation of pension	Cost of living plus real earnings growth	Cost of living	Cost of living
Pension to survivor	60% to spouse, 20% to each child, 40% to each child (if no spouse)	Same	Same, but 70% to lone child + means test
Years of contributions for eligibility	15	20	5
Early retirement provision	Any age if 35 years' social security taxes	Any age if 35 years' social security taxes	Flexible within the window

introduced a *window* of pensionable ages with actuarially based adjustment of pensions. These vary between age fifty-seven and age sixty-five with "actuarial adjustment factors" between 4.720 and 6.136 percent, respectively. Contribution requirements changed from the initial fifteen years to just five years after 1995. Payroll taxes jumped to 32.7 percent of gross earnings (to be split between the employer and the employee): the increase (from approximately 27 percent in 1995) was partly artificial as it was simply the result of relabeling under one social security tax rate several contribution items. The other provisions were basically unchanged, although, following the new eligibility requirements and benefit formula, the rules governing "minimum benefits" became tighter. The basic pension (*pensione sociale*) was replaced by a basic provision (*assegno sociale*), which was to be financed by the central government and was granted under stricter means testing.

Table 5.3 summarizes some of the key features of three regimes: the regime prevailing before the Amato reform (denoted as the pre-1992 regime), the one prevailing at the steady state after the Amato reform (the post-1992 regime), and the one prevailing after the Dini reform (the post-1995 regime). However, both reforms are characterized by a rather long transitional period affecting all the cohorts of post-1992 retirees: the provisions for the transitional periods involve a pro rata method of establishing eligibility and benefit computation criteria. This method allows the legislation of the old regime to apply to the share of years in employment under that regime, while the remaining share is regulated by the new rules. This meant that, in practice, during the transitional phase a retiree could have his eligibility and his social security benefits computed according to three different systems of legislation.[27]

5.2.4   The Hazard Rate out of the Labor Force

From the brief description of the social security system in place before 1993, it is clear that there were many loopholes that allowed workers to retire earlier than the normal retirement age. The early retirement option, which attracted no actuarial penalty, was the leading candidate in explaining some of the facts observed at the aggregate level. Other social security provisions have played a major role: for example, disability insurance benefits may have contributed to the increasing detachment of young workers from the labor force, owing to the poor screening methods implemented prior to 1984. However, a more detailed description of the dynamic nature of the retirement choice could be gained by looking at hazard rates. These are constructed by using the panel dimension of the Bank of Italy data over three years of interviews, 1989, 1991, and 1993.

---

27. For example, for someone retiring at age sixty-two in 1995, benefits in the transitional period were based on two regimes as follows. A weighted average of final salaries was computed by distinguishing two components: for a portion the average of the last five years' real earnings and for a portion the last six years' real earnings (plus a further six months). This average was the pensionable earnings measure. To this, a return of 2 percent per year (up to a maximum of forty years) was applied, provided that pensionable earnings were below a given limit; a reduced rate applied to earnings above the limit.

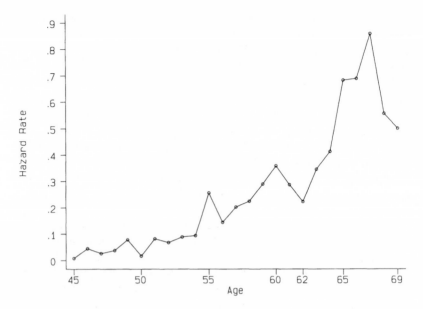

Fig. 5.18   Hazard rate out of labor force for men

Although the panel component is a small random sample (about three thousand households, roughly eight thousand earner units per year), it is useful in controlling for compositional effects (for a description of the data, see app. A).

The hazard rate out of the labor force for men is depicted in figure 5.18. There are several interesting spikes in this diagram: at ages sixty, fifty-five, and sixty-six. The first peak is easily explained by recalling that the normal retirement age prevailing before 1992 in the private sector was sixty for men. The spike occurring at age fifty-five is, however, of almost comparable size: this corresponds to recipients of either early retirement provisions or disability insurance benefits. The huge spike at age sixty-six is partly due to a small denominator and partly due to the fact that private-sector employees represent only a fraction of the labor force.[28] From figure 5.19, it is possible to gauge the different labor force attachment of women: the early spike at age fifty-three to fifty-five corresponds to the normal retirement age in the private sector. By age sixty-five, virtually all women in the sample are out of the labor force. However, a nonnegligible fraction gradually exits the labor force by age fifty-five.

In order to obtain a sharper description of the relation between institutional features and actual behavior, I have computed hazards for the two subsamples private- and public-sector employees. The limited sample size did not allow me to distinguish between males and females. There is a clear distinction between the behavior of the two groups. In figure 5.20, the hazard for

28. It should be recalled that, although retirement is not mandatory, there is virtually no possibility of working beyond age sixty-five.

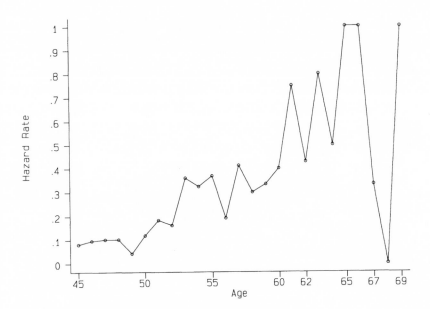

Fig. 5.19   Hazard rate out of labor force for women

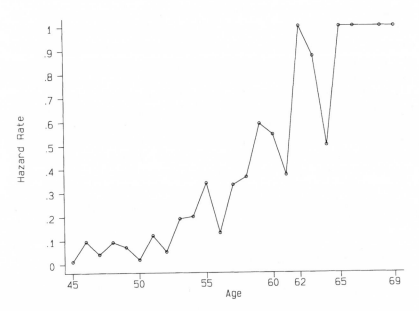

Fig. 5.20   Hazard rate out of labor force, private-sector employees

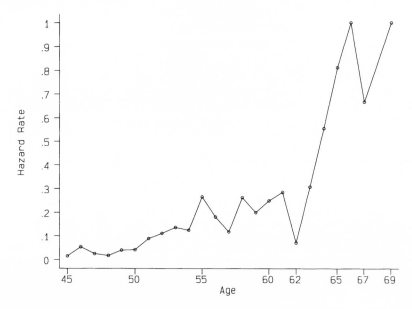

Fig. 5.21   Hazard rate out of labor force, public-sector employees

private-sector employees shows that there is a progressive detachment from the labor force at three crucial ages: fifty-five (presumably early retirement), sixty (normal retirement age), and sixty-three. Public-sector employees (fig. 5.21) also show an early peak at age fifty-five; however, many seem to carry on working until the normal retirement age (sixty-five).

These findings are confirmed by the frequency distribution of actual retirement ages presented in figures 5.22–5.24. The pictures are based on actual retirement ages of retirees who answer a retrospective question on which was the year of their retirement. I use four cross sections of the Bank of Italy Survey (see app. A) for the years 1989, 1991, 1993, and 1995 and compute the frequency distribution of the various retirement ages relative to the total number of retirees. These figures show that institutional features greatly affected retirement decisions: two peaks occur for men, at ages sixty and sixty-five, while for women there are three peaks, at ages fifty-five, sixty, and sixty-five.

5.3   Retirement Incentives

5.3.1   Simulation Model

The simulation model that I use to assess the incentives of social security on retirement computes net social security wealth for a married individual who was born in January 1930 and turned sixty-five in January 1995. The simulation is carried out for a "base case" and for a number of alternative cases in

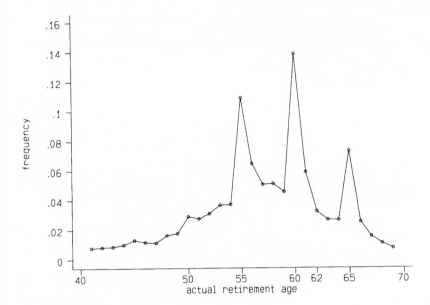

Fig. 5.22   Retirement age, all

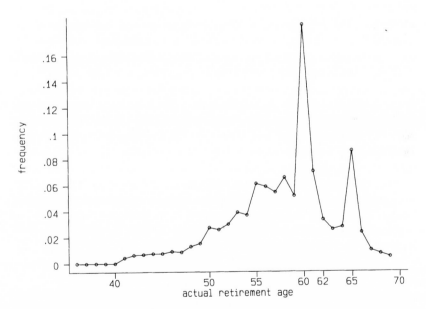

Fig. 5.23   Retirement age for men

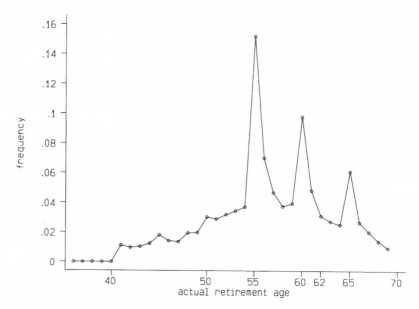

Fig. 5.24   Retirement age for women

which the sensitivity of the results to the parameter configuration is assessed. Retirement is analyzed between the ages of fifty-five and sixty-nine, and it is assumed that the median worker claims benefits under the pre-1992 legislation.[29] In fact, two major reforms of the Italian social security system took place within this period, one in 1992 and one in 1995, both characterized by a long transitional period, as described in section 5.2 above. On the one hand, the pre-1992 legislation seems the relevant regime on which to base the model in order to explain the features of the time-series data on labor force attachment; on the other hand, from 1993 on, individuals have experienced a gradual move toward a different system, one that is not described in the simulation. However, since the transitional phase, starting in 1993, has been characterized by a pro rata method of benefit computation, which only marginally affected individuals on the verge of retirement, the use of the pre-1992 legislation seems appropriate.[30]

The simulation computes retirement old age benefits, benefits to survivor (wife) if the worker has died, and net pension wealth for a married employee in the private sector (i.e., insured with INPS-FPLD). It should be stressed that,

29. An alternative case is presented in which the post-1995 legislation (i.e., after the most recent reform of the Italian social security system) is analyzed at the steady state.

30. The pro rata method corresponds to a benefit computation where the pre-1992 legislation applies to the fraction of years for which the worker has been contributing under the old regime and the post-1992 legislation applies to the remaining fraction. Hence, for our cohort, the effect of the new legislation is felt only for at most sixth-fortieths of the computational period. The 1995 reform also entails a similar pro rata method starting in 1996 for the transitional period: this would be even less relevant to the results of the base-case simulation.

as shown in section 5.2 above, the private-sector employees' fund, INPS-FPLD, is representative of the insured population in terms of both size and its historical relevance; however, the other funds (particularly the government employees' and INPS self-employed funds) are of nonnegligible size and of growing importance. I neglect disability insurance benefits since the worker becomes eligible to claim benefits in 1985, when the new screening rules were in place and disability insurance benefits could no longer be a substitute for early retirement, as was the case prior to 1984. I take into account the "severance pay fund" provision (TFR).

The basic assumption is that this individual worked continuously in a full-time job during his active life. In almost all cases, the worker is assumed to enter the labor force at age twenty, but, in one case, an incomplete earnings history is modeled.

It should be noted immediately that Italy has experienced wild variations in wage-growth and price-growth rates over the past decades: it seemed reasonable to assume a constant earnings growth rate, constant inflation rate, and tax brackets fixed in real terms throughout the simulation. I present only one case at the end of this section where I have adopted the actual earnings profile and actual tax brackets as a counterfactual. All these assumptions will be described in more detail below.

The simulation involves a number of steps:

Computation of the Benefit Level at the Chosen Retirement Age

This step requires computing a sort of "final salary" formula, which is obtained by averaging the last five years' gross earnings (inflation indexed)—this average is referred to as *pensionable earnings*. The retiree will receive in his first year of retirement 2 percent on pensionable earnings, for each year of contributions, up to a maximum of forty years' contributions. Cappings apply to the computation of pensionable earnings, and benefit levels that do not reach a given minimum threshold are brought up to that level (for details, see sec. 5.2 above and app. A). Net benefits are obtained by subtracting the income tax applying in the given year.

Computation of Expected Social Security Wealth

Net social security wealth is the present discounted value of future benefits up to age one hundred. This is the weighted sum of projected benefits, with weights given by male survival probability, and the individual discount rate. The pre-1992 legislation applies a "double indexation" of benefits that grow with both inflation and real wages.[31] I compute a stream of future benefits in nominal terms. This allows me to set the nominal benefits against the actual

---

31. As explained in sec. 5.2 above, inflation is measured by the consumer price index, while real wage growth should be measured by increases in contractual minimum wages. In all the simulations, I have adopted a 1.5 percent real wage growth and a 3.5 percent price growth. In the counterfactual, where actual earnings are used, I have adopted real earnings growth in the industrial sector up to 1995 and earnings growth equal to GDP growth afterward.

level of the minimum benefit in each year when considering the incentives for a low-earnings individual. In fact, although everything else grows with the economy, I use actual parameters as far as the social security features are concerned. In particular, the historical levels for capping of earnings, for the minimum benefit levels, and for the social security tax rate are adopted. This also makes it easier to compute after–income tax benefits on the basis of the nominal benefit. In fact, income taxes apply to pension income as well as to earnings.[32] Hence, all figures are then discounted back to age fifty-five at a nominal rate based on a 3 percent real discount rate plus a 3.5 percent inflation rate. The mortality prospect is given by the Italian sex/age-specific life tables ("Tavole di mortalita' per sesso e per eta', anno 1985," in ISTAT, *Annuario statistico italiano, 1988*). The life table is kept unchanged over the years; that is, the perspective is taken of a fifty-five-year-old forward-looking worker who plans for his retirement at each future age up to age sixty-nine. To compute net social security wealth, I take out, along with income taxes, the social security payroll tax that the individual would pay during any continued work. Hence, if the worker evaluates the possibility of postponing retirement for one year, his social security wealth is net of the present value (at age fifty-five) of the social security payroll tax that he and his employer would pay in that year.[33] Because income tax rates and social security tax rates (plus the severance pay fund tax rates) affect earnings and social security wealth calculation in a complex fashion, I provide below a sketch of the steps taken in the simulation to include these different tax rates.

Pension Wealth to the Surviving Wife

The Italian social security system provides a pension to survivors (in this simulation, the surviving wife), although no benefit is provided to the dependent wife.[34] Hence, a joint likelihood of the death of the worker and the survival of the wife is computed for each year beyond the chosen retirement age. In the base case, the worker's wife is three years younger and has never worked.

Severance Pay Fund Benefit (TFR)

This involves computing the lump-sum benefit at the age of retirement corresponding to the 7.41 percent of gross earnings earmarked by the employer for this fund. While the lump-sum benefit is added to social security wealth, the

---

32. It should be noted that the Italian tax system is progressive, highly nonlinear, and subject to marked changes over the years: hence, in general it would be inappropriate simply to extrapolate income taxes and rebates from one year to the next. In practice, since I am assuming constant growth rates and a tax system that grows with the economy in all relevant simulations, the after–income tax benefits could be computed starting from real benefits as well.

33. Social security taxes in Italy are particularly high (see sec. 5.2 above) and have also changed over the years.

34. As explained in the previous section, special allowance is made for a dependent wife only in those cases where the pension is topped up to a minimum level and the retiree is allowed to receive earnings at a higher level than in a "single-household" case. In this exercise, I have ignored the fact that a pension to survivors exists both during the worker's active life and during retirement. The present simulation accounts only for the wife of the retiree claiming benefits.

TFR tax from additional work reduces net social security wealth. I have made two simplifying assumptions throughout all the simulations in order to compute the TFR:

1. The relevant rules for benefit computation are those in place after 1982 (see sec. 5.2 above). This implies that the same rate is used to capitalize the TFR fund each year (1.5 percent plus 75 percent of the inflation rate), hence underestimating the value of the fund accumulated up to 1982. In fact, up to 1982, the fund would basically grow at the nominal growth rate of the worker's wage.[35]

2. I do not apply income tax to the TFR benefit: this omission overestimates the actual benefit. Since the average income tax rate on the TFR benefit is, for a median worker, approximately between 10 and 15 percent, this should be almost equivalent to the underestimation discussed above. Hence, the two biases should roughly cancel each other out.[36]

5.3.2 Methodological Issues

The results of the simulation are the net of tax replacement rate, the accrual rate, and the tax/subsidy rate from additional work. The *net of tax replacement rate* is the rate at which the net social security benefit replaces the worker's (after-tax) earnings should he continue to work in that year. The other two measures of the incentives provided by the social security program require the computation of net social security wealth. This is the present value of future pension benefits (after income tax) net of the present value of any additional contribution from continued work. Hence, the *accrual rate* can be computed as the relative change in net social security wealth from the previous year. Finally, the *implicit tax/subsidy* is the absolute change in net social security wealth over the potential earnings from working an additional year. The implicit tax/subsidy should be interpreted as an implicit tax, via social security entitlements, on an additional year of work. The numerator is the opposite of the numerator used in the accrual rate, and it measures the change in social security wealth looking at one additional year of work. Hence, a positive number indicates a disincentive to (a tax on) work through social security wealth that the worker forgoes.

Both the net replacement rate and the implicit tax/subsidy require a measure of earnings from additional work: since the income tax system and the social security tax system interact in a complex way, it is best to provide some notation at this stage.

Replacement Rate

Both the social security benefit and the earnings of the additional year of work are subject to income taxes. In accordance with the Italian tax system,

---

35. However, as I explained in sec. 5.2 above, these rules would vary across different occupational groups within the private sector.

36. The underestimation is generated by the difference in the compounded rates based on $r_1 = 1.5\% + (0.75) \times (3.5\%)$ in each year, as opposed to $r_2 = [(1.015) \times (1.035) - 1]$ in each year.

the relevant measure of earnings is obtained by subtracting first social security taxes and then income taxes as social security contributions are not subject to income tax. A further complication arises when considering the TFR tax.[37] This is a fraction of gross earnings retained by the employer that is not recorded in the available gross earnings data (neither is the employer social security tax). Hence, under the assumption that the employer social security tax payment and the TFR tax are reflected in a lower wage, a grossing-up procedure is required in order to obtain the theoretical gross earnings figure.

Let us assume that the tax system can be described by one tax rate τ_I (in fact, there are several tax rates, tax exemptions, and tax rebates). Let τ_W be the worker social security tax rate, τ_E the employer social security tax rate, and τ_{TFR} be the TFR tax rate, while Y represents earnings before income tax and employee social security tax but after the TFR tax and after social security taxes have been paid by the employer.[38] Hence, Y represents earnings as recorded by the available survey data.

The replacement rate is based on after–income tax and after–social security tax earnings, on the one hand, and after–income tax social security benefits, on the other hand. Hence, obviously, the lump-sum TFR benefit (a stock value) should not appear in the numerator of the replacement rate. As for net earnings, these are given by[39]

$$YN = (1 - \tau_W - \tau_I)Y.$$

Implicit Tax/Subsidy

In measuring earnings, which appear in the denominator of the implicit tax/subsidy, I add back to after–income tax earnings both the employee and the employer contributions. In fact, these have already been taken out of net social security wealth. In other words, earnings (YTS), which appear in the denominator of the implicit tax/subsidy, are obtained by grossing up as follows:

$$YTS = YN + \tau_W Y + \tau_E Y + \tau_{TFR} Y.$$

5.3.3 Assumptions for the "Base Case"

In the "base-case" simulation, the worker is characterized by a "synthetic earnings history." This is obtained by projecting backward and forward the 1994 median earnings of a particular year-of-birth cohort of workers. Median earnings are computed on a panel of workers (private-sector employees) in

37. Strictly speaking, this is not a tax as the employer retains part of the gross wage from his employees, which is not paid to any social security fund. However, I call it the *TFR tax* for simplicity.

38. Notice that, throughout the exercise, I am ignoring an additional 0.8 percent social security tax paid by the employee as this has no corresponding benefit (see sec. 5.2 above).

39. Although I am showing a computation carried out in one step, the actual computation in the simulation requires two separate steps, taking out first the social security tax, then income taxes, which are highly nonlinear.

continuous employment, drawn from the private-sector social security workers archive. The data available go from 1974 to 1994.[40] Although it would seem appropriate to focus on the cohort that was born in 1930, I have defined a cohort within a ten-year age band (from 1927 to 1936): this is in order to allow for both a reasonable sample size within each cell and comparability with other data sets.[41]

Because wages for all cohorts, and particularly for the cohort in which I am interested, show marked changes over the sample period (due mainly to price changes), and since income taxes greatly affect net earnings in a nonlinear fashion over the years, the simulation results based on historical earning profiles and historical tax rates proved hard to interpret. It seemed appropriate to turn to an economy where wages and taxes grow at constant rates. Hence, I used the 1994 median earnings figure and the 1994 tax system as a starting point. To project earnings both forward and backward, I used the assumptions on inflation, wages, and GDP growth adopted by the Italian government in making its forecasts on future social security government expenditure.[42] The choice of a cohort of full-time employees in continuous employment provides a misleading estimate of median earnings of that cohort: part-time work and, more important, incomplete earnings histories are quite common in the Italian labor market. However, this characterization of the base case is then compared with an alternative case where an incomplete earnings history is modeled explicitly. Finally, I adopt the historical values for social security tax rates, while the TFR retention rate is assumed to be constant throughout, for the reasons given above.

5.3.4 Base-Case Results

Table 5.4 shows the base-case results. Each row represents the age of the worker in the last year that he works. Hence, the first row presents results for a married man who has worked during the year 1984 and retired on his fifty-fifth birthday (1 January 1985). The first column is the net replacement rate described above. The row for age fifty-five represents the first year of eligibility. The next three columns show the evolution of net social security wealth over time. Finally, marginal retirement incentives are captured by the rates presented in the last two columns. It is worth recalling at this stage the aspects of

40. The series is projected backward to 1950 by making use of earnings growth rates drawn from Rossi, Sorgato, and Toniolo (1993).
41. In particular with the Bank of Italy cross-sectional survey. For details, see app. A.
42. In particular, I have used a 1.5 percent annual rate for both real earnings growth and real GDP growth and a 3.5 percent rate for annual inflation. Since these growth rates had been chosen for future projections, in order to obtain steady earnings I also used the same rates in retrospective extrapolation—even if this resulted in gross underestimation of true growth figures. Government actuaries have actually run future projections on the effects of the social security reform by making use of a number of different scenarios. The motivation for the choice of parameters in this exercise is twofold: on the one hand, adopting the same real growth rate for both GDP and earnings gives a simple benchmark; on the other hand, there is evidence that, in the last twenty years, there has not been a marked difference, on average, between the two rates (see also Rostagno 1996).

Table 5.4   **Base-Case Incentive Calculations**

Last Year of Work	Replacement Rate	Social Security Wealth	Accrual	Accrual Rate	Tax/ Subsidy
54	. . .	285,353	0	0	0
55	.726	280,477	−4,876	−.017	.245
56	.744	274,486	−5,990	−.021	.308
57	.761	268,066	−6,420	−.023	.338
58	.780	261,160	−6,907	−.026	.372
59	.798	253,918	−7,242	−.028	.401
60	.799	241,677	−12,241	−.048	.697
61	.804	229,536	−12,141	−.050	.711
62	.805	217,643	−11,893	−.052	.718
63	.805	205,963	−11,680	−.054	.729
64	.809	194,396	−11,568	−.056	.746
65	.809	183,099	−11,296	−.058	.756
66	.809	172,011	−11,088	−.061	.772
67	.809	161,167	−10,844	−.063	.787
68	.809	150,577	−10,590	−.066	.803
69	.809	140,269	−10,308	−.068	.818

the social security system that determine the figures in table 5.4, in particular, the tax implicit in postponing retirement by one year:

a) The pre-1992 regime allowed a private-sector employee to benefit from early retirement, with no age requirement, provided thirty-five years' contributions had been completed. Hence, although the normal retirement age for a man in the private sector was sixty, the base-case individual could actually claim retirement as early as his fifty-fifth birthday. It should also be noted that, although retirement is not mandatory, in practice very few can retire after age sixty-five (on this point, see sec. 5.2 above).

b) For each additional year of work, the worker must pay social security taxes: in Italy, these have grown in discrete jumps. Hence, net social security wealth is affected in a nonlinear fashion over time.

c) The additional year of earnings enters the benefit computation formula both because pensionable earnings are an average taken over the last five years' earnings and because, up to age sixty, any such additional year increases the fraction of years of contributions accounted for in the computation itself.[43] After age sixty, the fraction of pensionable earnings that is converted into a pension stays constant at 80 percent. The effect on social security wealth of adding one year to the benefit computation then depends on real earnings growth and inflation; in fact, past earnings are converted to current figures by means of price indexation.

43. Having completed forty years' contributions to the system, the retiree receives a first benefit of 80 percent of pensionable earnings (i.e., a fraction of 2 percent for each year of contribution).

d) For an additional year of work, there are fewer years over which benefits are claimed, lowering social security wealth. On the other hand, the TFR fund accumulates for one more year; but the rate of return on this fund is below nominal earnings growth and has no actuarial adjustment.

e) Finally, for each future year, there is a chance that the worker will die, lowering his social security wealth.

The first result to notice in table 5.4 is that the replacement ratios are very high at all ages. This is an important feature of the Italian system to be kept in mind in order to explain all subsequent results. Although the benefit computation formula suggests that the social security benefit should replace at most 80 percent of pensionable earnings, the actual figures show replacement ratios that range from 0.735 to 0.803. This is both because pensionable earnings differ from earnings coming from an additional year of work and because the tax system affects both the numerator and the denominator in a progressive fashion. The variation over time of the replacement ratio is totally explained by the social security tax figures: the same rate computed before social security tax earnings would give simply two levels, one before age sixty and one after age sixty.

Table 5.4 shows that a typical worker starts with a net pension wealth (inclusive of the TFR benefit) of L 285 million, reaching L 183 million at age sixty-five (going from approximately fifteen times to seven times his respective median earnings). There is a steady decline in social security wealth over the life cycle; however, a careful inspection of accrual rates reveals a significant fall between age fifty-nine and age sixty. This means that there is no incentive to delay retirement, particularly at the normal retirement age (because in that year the individual completes forty years' tax payments and reaches "full contribution history").

The final column shows the tax/subsidy rate. This is a very high number: the tax on working one additional year is roughly between 25 and 82 percent of after–income tax earnings of that year. The main reason for such a remarkable result is the large replacement ratio implied by the pre-1992 social security system. Similarly to the accrual rate, the implicit tax shows a jump at age sixty, and it then grows steadily for later ages (a graph is provided in fig. 5.25).

Finally, it should be noted that, while the severance pay fund provision (TFR) affects the level of social security wealth, it does not have significant effects on the marginal changes in social security wealth or on the shape of the implicit tax/subsidy profile.[44] Further simulations (not shown here) imply that the implicit tax is higher in the presence of the TFR provision than in its absence, providing one more reason to retire early. This is because the return on this fund is lower than earnings growth.

---

44. For the median worker of the base case, the TFR benefit at retirement is roughly 23 percent of total net social security wealth.

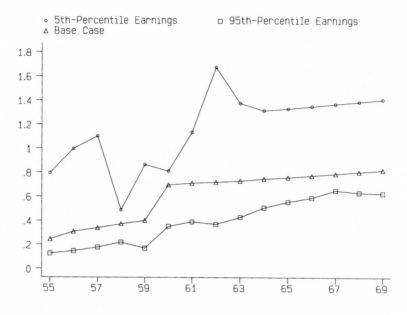

Fig. 5.25   Tax/subsidy rate across earnings profiles after social security tax, constant earnings/tax growth

5.3.5   Other Cases

In this section, some sensitivity analysis is carried out by allowing for both permutations in the age-earnings profile and variations in the parameters.

Table 5.5 looks at a *single man* who considers retirement at different future ages, starting at age fifty-five. The results for the replacement rate differ only slightly from the base-case scenario. In fact, under the assumption that the wife never worked, old age pension benefits for a couple are based on the man's earnings profile. However, the income tax system differs in the two cases, entailing a tax rebate for couples that could affect both social security benefits and earnings. The replacement rate is lower than for a married man (apart from the first figure at age fifty-five), hence suggesting that the income tax rebate weighs more on the earnings of an additional year of work than on social security benefits. Social security wealth is at a lower level than for a married man because there is no pension to the surviving spouse. Results for the accrual rate are simply a rescaled version of the finding obtained for a married man at a slightly lower level (hence becoming more negative). The implicit tax is lower throughout for a single man (apart from the first figure) than for the married man, again because of the income tax system. A slight divergence between the implicit tax paths for a couple and for a single worker occurs toward the end of the working life, owing to the effect of the wife's survival probability becoming important in the net social security wealth calculation. This similarity across

Table 5.5   Incentive Calculations—Single Worker

Last Year of Work	Replacement Rate	Social Security Wealth	Accrual	Accrual Rate	Tax/ Subsidy
54	...	236,380	0	0	0
55	.735	230,997	−5,383	−.023	.282
56	.736	225,293	−5,704	−.025	.301
57	.754	219,247	−6,045	−.027	.326
58	.773	212,808	−6,439	−.029	.356
59	.791	206,140	−6,668	−.031	.378
60	.793	195,449	−10,691	−.052	.623
61	.797	184,917	−10,532	−.054	.632
62	.799	174,681	−10,237	−.055	.633
63	.799	164,705	−9,975	−.057	.638
64	.803	154,893	−9,812	−.060	.648
65	.803	145,393	−9,500	−.061	.651
66	.803	136,142	−9,251	−.064	.660
67	.803	127,152	−8,991	−.066	.668
68	.803	118,427	−8,725	−.069	.677
69	.803	109,978	−8,449	−.071	.687

the two cases is explained by (*a*) the lack of additional benefits for the dependent wife and (*b*) the fact that benefits to the surviving spouse are provided with no age limit (only means testing).

Table 5.6 describes the results for a worker with an *incomplete earnings history*. Unlike the base case, he starts working at age twenty-four (in 1954); hence, when considering retirement on his fifty-fifth birthday, he would have completed only thirty-one of forty years of his social security tax history and would reach full eligibility only at age sixty-four (working at age sixty-three). This variation on the base case has interesting implications for the incentive results. First, the replacement rate is lower than in the base case up to age sixty-four, after which it coincides. The tax/subsidy path is shifted to the right at a much lower level for ages below sixty-five. This is because, at that point, full eligibility is reached in both cases; hence, up to that age, there is a higher incentive to work for someone who entered the labor force later. After age sixty-five, the two paths do not overlap exactly because of the TFR provision, which stays constantly lower for the case of an incomplete earnings history.

Further variations to the base case are obtained by changing the age-earnings profile and the institutional setup. The results are summarized in table 5.7, where findings across different simulations are shown for significant ages only.

The first permutation is made in the earnings profile, by including both ends of the distribution of earnings. In the Italian social security system, there is both capping on pensionable earnings and topping up of low benefit levels; hence, interesting cases may be explored when earnings reach the roof or the floor of social security benefits. Experimenting with the data revealed that the two interesting cases lie in the top 95 percent and the bottom 5 percent of

Table 5.6   Incentive Calculations—Incomplete Earnings History

Last Year of Work	Replacement Rate	Social Security Wealth	Accrual	Accrual Rate	Tax/ Subsidy
54	...	249,356	0	0	0
55	.638	245,988	−3,368	−.014	.169
56	.656	241,570	−4,418	−.018	.227
57	.674	236,698	−4,871	−.020	.257
58	.692	231,316	−5,382	−.023	.290
59	.710	225,575	−5,741	−.025	.318
60	.729	219,396	−6,179	−.027	.352
61	.751	212,772	−6,624	−.030	.388
62	.770	205,864	−6,908	−.032	.417
63	.788	198,653	−7,210	−.035	.450
64	.809	191,057	−7,596	−.038	.490
65	.809	179,911	−11,147	−.058	.746
66	.809	168,972	−10,939	−.061	.762
67	.809	158,276	−10,696	−.063	.776
68	.809	147,834	−10,442	−.066	.792
69	.809	137,674	−10,161	−.069	.807

Table 5.7   Incentive Calculations—Summary of Other Cases, Last Year of Work Is Age 61

Case	Replacement Rate	Social Security Wealth	Accrual	Accrual Rate	Tax/ Subsidy
Base case	.804	229,536	−12,141	−.050	.711
Single worker	.797	184,917	−10,532	−.054	.632
Incomplete history	.751	212,772	−6,624	−.030	.388
5th percentile	1.357	87,029	−4,382	−.048	1.135
95th percentile	.580	408,138	−15,660	−.037	.390
Post-1995 regime	.547	148,423	−1,073	−.007	.063
Actual earnings	.840	165,975	−9,613	−.055	.648

the distribution of earnings.[45] These two points of the distribution were obtained, for the year 1994, from the same panel data set used in constructing median earnings. In both cases, I then applied the same earnings growth rate (backward and forward) used for the median earnings profile. For the earnings capping level and the "minimum benefit," I take actual figures; however, for the years after 1995, figures are calculated on the basis of economic growth.

These permutations show some inherent redistributional features of the Italian social security system, and they explain how these provide incentives for

45. While the tenth and ninetieth percentiles were almost untouched by the roof and floor of the social security system, the fifth and ninety-fifth percentiles almost invariably hit these barriers: while these may be extreme cases, they are useful in describing how these upper and minimum levels operate.

intertemporal decisions by individuals. Obviously, replacement rates are on average much higher for the *fifth percentile* and much lower for the ninety-fifth percentile than in the base case: an example for age sixty-one can be found in the first column of table 5.7. Accrual rates and the tax/benefit of continued work look very different in the base case than they do for the low-earnings and high-earnings individual. Some interesting insights can be gained from the comparison. In fact, while capping on pensionable earnings applies to pensionable earnings, topping up of benefits applies directly to the benefit level. The tax/subsidy pattern for the bottom 5 percent of the distribution shows large fluctuations (fig. 5.25 above). This is because the minimum benefit grows roughly in line with actual historical earnings. The implicit tax levels are very high (reaching a peak of 180 percent of potential earnings at age sixty-two). In fact, there is a large transfer component from the system to the individual that the individual forgoes if he postpones retirement. Opposite results are obtained for the top *ninety-fifth percentile.* The replacement rate is lower than for the base case, and the implicit tax pattern is constantly lower than the base case. This is explained by a high level of potential earnings (in the denominator) that is not fully reflected in the benefit computation (in the numerator). Moreover, the ninety-fifth percentile tax pattern is not as smooth as the age-tax profile obtained for the base case, again because actual earnings capping changes over time in discrete jumps.

A further set of results is based on the *post-1995 legislation.* The assumption is made that the 1995 reform of the Italian social security system has been completely phased in—and this naturally means that one should be extremely careful in interpreting the findings. In fact, as explained in section 5.2 above, the transitional period of the 1995 reform is a very long one (ending in 2035), while, in my simulation, the legislation is considered when implemented for a worker retiring between the years 1985 and 2000.

At this stage, it is useful to give a brief recap of a few crucial features of the post-1995 (steady-state) legislation, as they differ radically from those of the base-case scenario:

a) The post-1995 reform adopts an average-earnings-based method of benefit calculation. First, the present value (at retirement) of past payroll taxes is determined. This is obtained by taking a 33 percent share of past earnings for each year in which the worker and the employer paid payroll taxes and weighing each past wage by means of a five-year moving average of the nominal GDP growth rate. This stock measure is then converted into an annuity by applying an age-related actuarial adjustment factor, given below.

b) The 1995 reform enacts a window of pensionable ages with an actuarially based adjustment of pensions: the ages are between fifty-seven and sixty-five, with factors ranging between 4.72 and 6.136 percent, respectively. Before age fifty-seven, I have used a constant factor 4.72 percent and, after age sixty-five, a constant factor 6.136 percent.

c) Future benefits then grow with prices only.

d) Finally, the TFR provision abides by the same rules as in the old regime.

Table 5.8   **Incentive Calculations—Post-1995 Regime**

Last Year of Work	Replacement Rate	Social Security Wealth	Accrual	Accrual Rate	Tax/ Subsidy
54	. . .	159,881	0	0	0
55	. . .	156,914	−2,968	−.019	.149
56	. . .	153,398	−3,516	−.022	.181
57	.463	152,557	−842	−.005	.044
58	.482	151,386	−1,170	−.008	.063
59	.502	150,151	−1,235	−.008	.068
60	.523	149,496	−655	−.004	.037
61	.547	148,423	−1,073	−.007	.063
62	.570	146,543	−1,881	−.013	.114
63	.593	144,000	−2,543	−.017	.159
64	.622	140,868	−3,132	−.022	.202
65	.628	134,420	−6,448	−.046	.432
66	.634	127,868	−6,553	−.049	.456
67	.640	121,318	−6,549	−.051	.475
68	.646	114,879	−6,439	−.053	.488
69	.652	108,342	−6,537	−.057	.519

It is obvious that the crucial features of this benefit calculation method are (1) the difference between the (smoothed) GDP growth rate and the earnings growth experienced by each individual and (2) the actuarial adjustment factor. Individuals cannot withdraw from the labor force before their fifty-seventh birthday or after their sixty-fifth birthday; however, as with the base case, I have carried out the simulation from age fifty-four (last year of work) to age sixty-nine.

From table 5.8, there immediately emerges a striking contrast with the pre-1992 regime with regard to the replacement rate figures (now ranging between 0.463 and 0.652) and the net social security wealth figure (roughly L 160 million at age fifty-four, i.e., ten times the median earnings). This is because workers only gradually build up an increasing stock of social security taxes. Accrual rates are negative throughout; however, they do not follow the pattern observed for the base case. Perhaps the most interesting comparison with the base case is that concerning the implicit tax (fig. 5.26). While the implicit tax is much lower than in the base case, the new regime does not particularly encourage work beyond age fifty-seven (the age of eligibility). Between age sixty-four and age sixty-five, the implicit tax jumps because there is no further increase in the adjustment factor. After age sixty-five, the implicit tax grows almost in line with that in the base case: this is because, in both cases, all the relevant parameters remain constant. However, while in the pre-1992 regime benefits grow with earnings (with no fund buildup), in the new regime benefits grow with prices, but the stock of social security taxes builds up. The behavior of the implicit tax between the ages of fifty-seven and sixty-five is not as smooth as one would expect, given the emphasis placed by the reform on producing

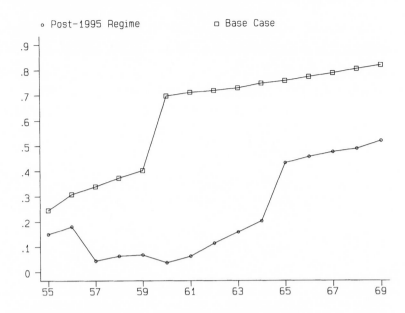

Fig. 5.26   Tax/subsidy rate across regimes after social security tax, constant earnings/tax growth

an "actuarially fair system," and given that the simulation is based on constant growth rates. This may be explained by the calibration of the actuarial adjustment factor, which is based on a slightly different life table from the one used in this study, and by the use of a different discount factor. In fact, the actuarial adjustment of the benefits that, under the new regime, apply at the different retirement ages was calibrated by government actuaries in order to achieve actuarial fairness across retirement ages for an individual who is sixty-two in 1996 and by assuming a real discount rate of 1.5 percent.[46]

Finally, it is interesting to compare the base case with a counterfactual case where the *actual earnings profile* and actual income taxes have been used to produce a "realistic case."

Earnings are computed by taking medians from the given year-of-birth cohort of employees by calendar year. To follow this cohort back through time (i.e., before 1977), I used the growth rate of gross earnings, at current prices, for employees in the industrial sector. The age-earnings profile of the "typical actual worker" does not show an appreciable decline until the last available years: the stable growth in earnings for this group is explained both by the fact that we are following a true cohort of full-time male employees through time and by the fact that my definition of this cohort covers a wide age band. This

46. This calibration procedure is designed so that an individual aged sixty-two in 1996 is indifferent between the prereform and the postreform regimes.

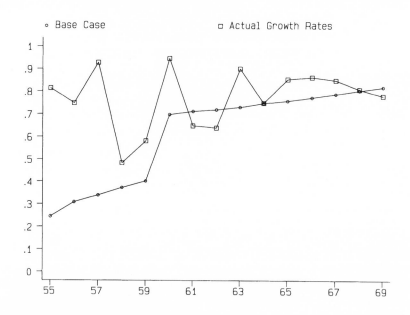

Fig. 5.27   Tax/subsidy rate across growth rates after social security tax, actual earnings/tax growth

implies that part-time work should be excluded from the sample by definition and that sample numerosity becomes a problem only for the last few years, when many members of the cohort have retired. Hence, it is only from age sixty (1990) that I have replaced actual earnings with their projection, obtained by letting earnings increase at the same growth rate as nominal wages in the industrial sector. For this case, I provide information at age sixty-one (in table 5.7 above) and the implicit tax profile (fig. 5.27). It is clear that the results for the "actual earnings" profile are totally dominated by changes in earnings growth rates and income taxes. The highest disincentive to supply labor for an extra year is for those aged fifty-seven, sixty, and sixty-three; after age sixty-seven, there is a steady decline in the implicit tax. While the peak at age sixty can again be explained by, among other things, full eligibility, the spike at age fifty-seven is partly due to a decline in the earnings growth rate, immediately followed by a sharp increase (the former affects the numerator, while the latter affects the denominator). This is also reflected in a relatively low replacement rate for age fifty-seven. This early spike is a particularly interesting feature of the system as it happens to coincide almost exactly with a peak in the male hazard rate out of the labor force.

5.4   Conclusions

The Italian social security system is characterized by strong incentives to early retirement. These have certainly had an effect on individual intertemporal

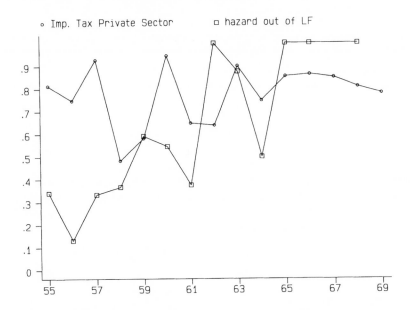

Fig. 5.28   Tax/subsidy rate against hazard, private-sector employees, actual earnings/tax growth

decisions, particularly those concerning labor supply. Both time-series data and micro data provide support for the view that there is a causal relation between the increased generosity of the social security system and its eligibility criteria and the timing of retirement. Moreover, the simulation exercise carried out in this study shows that these incentives differ across groups of the population according to such characteristics as individual earnings profiles and work experience. The tax on additional work implied by forgone social security wealth is almost invariably large, and it usually peaks at the ages when the empirical evidence shows the highest detachment rates from the labor force. For example, the male hazard shown in figure 5.18 above and the distribution of actual retirement ages (fig. 5.23 above) suggest that there are three typical ages for leaving the labor force: a first peak is observed at age fifty-five, then a significant peak at age sixty (corresponding to the normal retirement age in the private sector), while the third exit from the labor force occurs around age sixty-five. This is in line with the incentives provided by the social security system as measured by the implicit tax/subsidy. In fact, the tax/subsidy profile (table 5.4 above) suggests that the system encourages workers to leave the labor force at all ages, and certainly to retire no later than age sixty. The existence of these incentives in the social security program is even more evident in the tax/subsidy profile computed under "realistic assumptions" with regard to the earnings profile and the income tax system (fig. 5.28). This exercise points out not only that the social security benefit formula is actuarially unfair but also that it is totally dominated by the behavior of wages and prices immediately before the year chosen to retire. As a result, the median worker of this exercise would find it very costly to postpone retirement after age fifty-seven. This suggests that a simple cost/benefit analysis might have induced many to take advantage of early retirement, which in Italy has been widely available with no actuarial penalty. The social security reforms of 1992 and 1995, aimed at reducing benefit outlays, have affected workers' behavior in many respects. There is a direct effect on savings, related to the substantial reduction in household pension wealth due to reduced benefit levels and restricted eligibility criteria. While the effects on labor supply decisions are harder to gauge, the econometric evidence presented in appendix B suggests that the 1992 reform was regarded by many as a breaking point, after which the social security system could no longer be as generous as it had been in the past. Hence, many reacted to the reform by moving up their expected retirement age (particularly young people in the private sector).

Appendix A
Data Sources

Historical Data

Labor Force Participation by Age and Sex

This is based on ISTAT's *Annuario del lavoro e dell'emigrazione* (1958–80) and *Supplemento al bollettino mensile di statistica* (1975–85). For subsequent years, the series on labor force participation can be derived from ISTAT's *Rilevazione nazionale delle forze di lavoro* (1986–94). The jump in the series in 1976, also discussed in Casavola and Sestito (1994), was produced by a change in the definition of both *unemployment* and *employment*. After that year, these two terms covered people actively seeking work even if not previously employed and people who did not regard themselves as employed but who worked during the survey week.

Share of Workers

This is based on ISTAT's *Annuario del lavoro e dell'emigrazione* (various issues), *Rilevazione nazionale delle forze di lavoro* (various issues), *Supplemento al bollettino mensile di statistica* (1975–85), and *Collana di informazione* (1986–95); and Ministero del Tesoro, *Relazione generale sulla situazione economica del paese* (several issues). Survival probabilities are drawn from "Tavole di mortalità," in ISTAT's *Annuario statistico italiano* (1989, 1995).

Benefit Receipt and Insured Population

The figures based on historical data for benefit receipt are drawn from ISTAT's *Statistiche dei trattamenti pensionistici* (1985–94) and *Supplemento al bollettino mensile di statistica* (1975–84); and INPS, *Notizie statistiche*

(1977–80). However, more details can be found in CENSIS/CER, *Rapporto sulla situazione sociale del paese*. The Treasury has published some special reports on projections for future pension outlays: Ministero del Tesoro, *Tendenze demografiche e spesa pensionistica* (1996), and *Sanità, scuola e pensioni* (1997).

Contemporaneous Data

All figures tabulated by the author are drawn from the Bank of Italy Survey, 1989–93 (see below).

Studying Retirement in Italy

There are two main sources available at a micro level:

Bank of Italy Cross-sectional Data

The Bank of Italy provides cross-sectional data at regular intervals. This is a nationwide survey that collects detailed information on Italian households concerning their saving/consumption decisions, earnings of each member of the family, and demographic variables. I have used several cross sections of the survey: the waves available since 1984 (i.e., 1984, 1985, 1986, 1987, 1989, 1991, and 1993) plus the waves that are part of the Bank of Italy Historical Archive (annually from 1977 to 1983). The two sets of samples differ in many respects: the former (i.e., more recent waves) has a larger number of observations (around eight thousand, as opposed to four thousand or fewer for previous years), there is less detailed information on working status (e.g., the age at which the individual started working is missing), and, most important, age is recorded in ten- and fifteen-year bands that are kept fixed over the years. In this study, I have used only the 1989, 1991, and 1993 surveys; however, I have carried out comparisons with the other available source (see the next subsection). To this end, I constructed year-of-birth cohorts for both sources, which I kept fixed throughout the study.

I assigned individuals to different year-of-birth cohorts on the basis of their age and the year of the survey. For all the observations where age was recorded in intervals (surveys for the years 1977–83), I randomly assigned individuals to year-of-birth cohorts by assuming a uniform distribution within the age interval. Each age band may contain up to three cohorts.

In order to cope with the scarcity of observations resulting for some cells, and given the restriction imposed by the recording of age before 1984, I defined cohorts over year-of-birth bands as follows: cohort 1, before 1911; cohort 2, between 1912 and 1926; cohort 3, between 1927 and 1936; cohort 4, between 1937 and 1946; cohort 5, between 1947 and 1956; cohort 6, between 1957 and 1959; cohort 7, between 1960 and 1963; and cohort 8, after 1963. Besides questions regarding the characteristics of those already retired, there are some retrospective questions posed to both retirees and workers (e.g., age at which they started work). However, a full work history cannot be constructed. There are also questions about expected retirement age and, in just one survey, expected social security benefit.

The INPS Database

I use an unbalanced panel running for twenty years (1974–94), drawn from the INPS Archive 01/M, that records information about workers on the basis of a form sent yearly to the INPS by employers. The information available concerns age, sex, occupation, wage, and changes of job characteristics, but no information on education or household structure is available. I constructed cohort gross earnings profiles for the simulation on the basis of this sample according to age bands. The relevant age band for the median worker is year of birth between 1927 and 1936.

Appendix B
The Effects of Social Security on Retirement: Survey of the Literature and Econometric Estimates

Here, I first give a brief review of the literature on incentives within the social security program affecting individuals' behavior. I then move on to some new empirical evidence that tries to measure behavioral responses to changes in social security provisions directly.

Existing Literature

While a great deal of research has been carried out both on the effects of the reforms and on the relation between saving behavior and social security wealth, very little attention has been devoted to the effects of social security security arrangements on labor supply. There are a few notable exceptions: in particular, Geroldi (1993), Peracchi and Rossi (1995), and Padoa Schioppa Kostoris (1996). The work carried out by Peracchi and Rossi tries to assess the overall effect of the 1995 reform, stressing, among other aspects, how there are some distinct patterns in the time-series data clearly generated by the increasing generosity of the social security system. In particular, the authors note that labor force participation in Italy is lower than in other countries, particularly for the age group fifty-five to fifty-nine (immediately prior to the normal retirement age). The authors also point out that the existence of the early retirement option is a very likely explanation of the fact that the average employment rate for the age group fifty to fifty-seven falls with each year of age. The results presented in sections 5.1 and 5.3 above confirm these facts. A more direct question is raised by the work of Padoa Schioppa Kostoris (1996), who evaluates the potential financial gains from the 1995 reform under different scenarios by simulating potential quits from the labor force. Another relevant approach to assessing the importance of the labor supply incentives of social security is to turn attention away from the "median worker" to other cases. A very detailed study by Rostagno (1996) shows that incomplete earnings histories may play a crucial role in evaluating the effects of the reforms and that these cases may be much more common than previously thought. This might help explain some features of the hazard rates out of the labor force shown in section 5.2 above because, while many retire well before the normal retirement age, there is still action in the data after age sixty caused by people who want to reach full contribution.

An important test of the effects of changes in the institutional setting is the analysis of the behavioral responses of individuals and households. Following Feldstein's seminal paper (1974), a very stimulating empirical literature on the effects of the social security system on the saving patterns of Italian households has developed. After early papers that estimated a very low degree of substitutability between pension wealth and private wealth (Brugiavini 1987; and Jappelli 1995) on households' micro data, a number of contributions have challenged that finding. Rossi and Visco (1994, 1995) argue that much of the decline in the Italian saving rate in the 1970s was due to the increased generosity of the social security system over those years, and time-series estimates suggest that about one-third of Italian accumulated capital stock may have been lost because of this exceptional growth. More recently, Attanasio and Brugiavini (1997) have adopted a "natural experiment" approach in using micro data to evaluate the differential effect of the 1992 reform on the saving behavior of households. In particular, the authors distinguish between groups of the population that are likely to be affected in different ways by the reform and then look at the mean variation (between the postreform and the prereform value) in savings across these groups. It emerges that, between 1991 and 1993, the groups that were most affected by the reform in terms of benefit cuts or stricter eligibility rules also tended to save more.

Redistributional Effects of the Social Security System and Econometric Estimates of Changes in Expected Retirement Age

One distinct feature of the Italian social security system is the difference existing in the arrangements of the different funds. I have already discussed how the public-sector, as opposed to private-sector, employees' fund was privileged in many respects by the pre-1992 legislation, particularly because of the early retirement option (more generous for the public sector) and because of the benefit computation formula (of a pure final salary type in the public sector). Castellino (1994) estimates that a large stock of resources was redistributed across generations and across funds because of these different features. One way to look at how these differences affect labor supply decisions is to contrast the hazard rate of public- and private-sector employees, as I have done in figures 5.20 and 5.21 above. In the private sector, three relevant peaks were pointed out: age fifty-six (early retirement), age sixty (normal retirement), and age sixty-four (possibly incomplete earnings history). In the public sector, there is also evidence of early retirement between the ages of fifty-five and sixty-one, but then virtually every worker has retired by age sixty-five (the normal retirement age).

Turning to the econometric evidence, I present some estimates of changes in expected retirement ages drawn from the Bank of Italy panel of household-level data. The methodology adopted is a "difference-in-difference" estimator and draws heavily on the work of Attanasio and Brugiavini (1997) described above. In particular, the basic identifying assumption is that the 1992 reform is the only relevant change (as far as differential labor supply decisions are concerned), and I therefore exploit the reform to measure behavioral responses before and after the event. The first difference is the time difference, the second that between groups. Groups in the population are assumed to be exogenously determined, and, given the availability of panel data, I can control for individuals' characteristics throughout (Venti and Wise 1995). Hence, membership in a group can be interpreted as an instrument (control). I allocate individuals to groups according to the characteristics observed at the beginning of the sample (year 1989) and discard those who later cross groups, particularly if they change employment status and type of occupation. A careful selection of the sample is crucial to this methodology because of the identification issues described above. In the end I was left with approximately fifteen hundred men and seven hundred women.

Given that the panel is partly rotating—that is, some households are replaced after two years—there are at least two data points for each individual, which allowed me to compute differences in the expected retirement age. I selected six groups, three according to occupation (employee in the private sector, employee in the public sector, and other occupations) and two according to experience (less than fifteen years' social security tax payments in 1993 and more than fifteen years' tax payments in 1993). This is because the 1992 reform relies on a pro rata method (described earlier) that leaves the rules to be adopted for the latter group almost unchanged while it greatly affects the eligibility criteria and benefit calculation for the former group. However, in constructing the variable *experience,* I had to rely on information regarding the age at which work started, which may be a noisy measure. A slightly different selection criteria based on year-of-birth cohorts provided almost identical results in the estimates. It is worth recalling at this stage that the Amato reform of 1992 has gradually postponed the normal retirement age but has not tackled the early retirement option, apart from restricting eligibility requirements in the public sector.[47]

---

47. The normal retirement age gradually moves from sixty to sixty-five for men. The early retirement option is available, but public-sector employees need thirty-five years of contributions

Table 5B.1   **Mean Expected Retirement Age: Panel Data, 1989–95**

Group	1989	1991	1993	1995
Males, young (1959–74)	59.19	60.06	59.89	61.14
Males, old (1922–58)	60.24	60.68	59.94	60.07
Females, young (1959–74)	56.58	57.23	56.74	58.40
Females, old (1922–58)	57.30	57.93	57.90	59.17

Table 5B.2   **Yearly Changes in Expected Male Retirement Age: Panel Data, 1989–95 (baseline regression, groups defined by age)[a]**

	Δ Years	S.E.
Occupation:		
Private-sector employee:		
Generation 1	.957	.359
Generation 2	.197	.194
Public-sector employee:		
Generation 1	.644	.673
Generation 2	.756	.297
Others:		
Generation 1	−.050	.586
Generation 2	.494	.268
	F	Prob > F
Hypothesis 1	.17	.680
Hypothesis 2	2.49	.115

Note: Generation = 1 if years of tax payments in 1993 < 15 and 2 if years of tax payments in 1993 ≥ 15. Hypothesis tests: hypothesis 1: private-sector employees of generation 1 = public-sector employees of generation 1; hypothesis 2: private-sector employees of generation 2 = public-sector employees of generation 2.

[a]Number of observations = 1,896.

Table 5B.1 presents mean expected retirement age for some groups of the population. While the figures are suggestive of a reduction occurring between 1991 and 1993, it is hard to place any statistical significance on this finding.

Tables 5B.2 and 5B.3 show the econometric estimates. In table 5B.2, the regression is carried out for males, the dependent variable is the change (in years) in expected retirement age, and the explanatory variables are group dummies that take the value one if the individual belongs to that group and zero otherwise. In this case, OLS estimates automatically deliver an efficient estimator of mean changes in the dependent variable. In fact, variations in sample numerosity across groups suggest that it is possible to improve on simple arithmetic means.

---

to become eligible in place of the previous twenty years (fifteen for married women). In the public sector, normal retirement age has been sixty-five throughout.

Yearly Changes in Expected Male Retirement Age: Panel Data, 1989–95 (groups defined by age)[a]

	Δ Years	S.E.
Occupation:		
Private-sector employee:		
Generation 1	1.387	.453
Generation 2	.254	.253
Public-sector employee:		
Generation 1	.792	.831
Generation 2	1.129	.371
Others:		
Generation 1	−.483	.774
Generation 2	.762	.305
Private-sector employee in 1993:		
Generation 1	−2.570	.910
Generation 2	−.567	.469
Public-sector employee in 1993:		
Generation 1	.480	1.671
Generation 2	−.854	.749
Others in 1993:		
Generation 1	.963	1.444
Generation 2	−1.295	.777
Private-sector employee in 1995:		
Generation 1	.753	.887
Generation 2	.442	.527
Public-sector employee in 1995:		
Generation 1	−1.792	1.805
Generation 2	−1.434	.845
Others in 1995:		
Generation 1	1.283	1.466
Generation 2	−.217	.866

	F	Prob > F
Hypothesis 1	.36	.530
Hypothesis 2	3.79	.050
Hypothesis 3	2.57	.109
Hypothesis 4	.11	.745
Hypothesis 5	1.63	.200
Hypothesis 6	3.54	.061

Note: Generation = 1 if years of tax payments in 1993 < 15 and 2 if years of tax payments in 1993 ≥ 15. Hypothesis tests: hypothesis 1: private-sector employees of generation 1 = public-sector employees of generation 1; hypothesis 2: private-sector employees of generation 2 = public-sector employees of generation 2; hypothesis 3: private-sector employees in 1993 of generation 1 = public-sector employees in 1993 of generation 1; hypothesis 4: private-sector employees in 1993 of generation 2 = public-sector employees in 1993 of generation 2; hypothesis 5: private-sector employees in 1995 of generation 1 = public-sector employees in 1995 of generation 1; hypothesis 6: private-sector employees in 1995 of generation 2 = public-sector employees in 1995 of generation 2.

[a]Number of observations = 1,896.

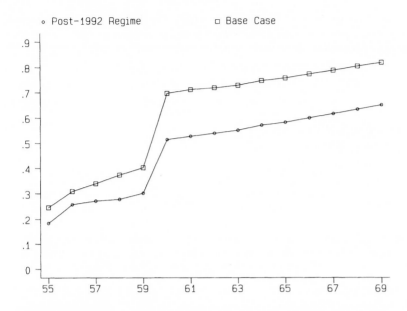

Fig. 5B.1   Tax/subsidy rate across regimes after social security tax, constant earnings/tax growth

The results of table 5B.2 give the baseline specification. Expected retirement age seems to have increased between 1989 and 1995, particularly for young individuals working in the private sector. However, the results of table 5B.3 suggest that the reforms have had an effect on expected retirement age: in 1993, young individuals working both in the private sector and in the public sector tended to reduce their expected retirement age. This is in line with the common belief that, while postponing normal retirement age (in the private sector), the 1992 reform has mainly affected younger workers. In particular, young workers in the private sector tended to reduce their retirement age by approximately 2.5 years, and there is evidence of a significant difference in the behavior of private- and public-sector employees.

Interpretation of Results

It is hard to provide a clear-cut interpretation of the results outlined above, particularly because the event *retirement* may be quite far in the future for many workers in the sample and the expected retirement age could be a noisy variable. The 1992 reform did not remove the early retirement option; hence, it would still be possible, in both the private and the public sectors, to reduce retirement age even though the reform did postpone the statutory retirement age. Young workers have been greatly affected by the 1992 reform as their social security wealth has been reduced by a considerable amount. The implicit tax profile, corresponding to the 1992 reform (see fig. 5B.1), shows that the implicit tax on work is still positive and high over the life cycle, hence providing an incentive to retire early. What seems to emerge (also from table 5B.1 above) is that, before the reform, many thought of their retirement age as the normal retirement age and that the reform has focused the attention of workers on this issue. The 1992 reform also made it clear that the system could no longer be as generous as it has been in the past and that, given the incentive system discussed in this paper, on average workers want to get out of the program as soon as they can.

References

Attanasio, Orazio P., and Agar Brugiavini. 1997. L'effetto della riforma amato sul risparmio delle famiglie italiane. In *Ricerche quantitative per la politica economica, 1995, convegno Banca d'Italia–Centro Interdipartimentale di Econometria*. Rome: Servizio Studi, Banca d'Italia.

Banca d'Italia. Various issues. I bilanci delle famiglie italiane negli anni 1977–1993. *Supplementi al bollettino statistico (note metodologiche ed informazioni statistiche).*

Beltrametti, Luca. 1996. *Il debito pensionistico in Italia*. Bologna: Il Mulino.

Brugiavini, Agar. 1987. Empirical evidence on wealth accumulation and the effects of pension wealth: An application to Italian cross-section data. Discussion Paper no. 20. London School of Economics, Financial Market Group.

Casavola, P., and Paolo Sestito. 1994. L'indagine ISTAT sulle forze del lavoro. *Lavoro e relazioni industriali*, no. 1:179–95.

Castellino, Onorato. 1976. *Il labirinto delle pensioni*. Bologna: Il Mulino.

———. 1994. La riforma del sistema previdenziale ovvero il rapporto che non fu scritto. *Moneta e credito* 188:515–40.

Centro Studi Investimenti Sociali (CENSIS)/Centro Europa Ricerche (CER). Various issues. *Rapporto sulla situazione sociale del paese*. Rome.

Di Vezza, Luigi. 1990. *La giungla delle liquidazioni*. Rome: Edizioni Lavoro.

Feldstein, Martin. 1974. Social security induced retirement and aggregate capital accumulation. *Journal of Political Economy* 82:905–26.

Geroldi, Gianni. 1993. Età legale ed età effettiva di pensionamento. In *Le pensioni domani: Primo rapporto sulla previdenza in Italia*, ed. Istituto Nazionale per la Previdenza Social. Bologna: Il Mulino.

Istituto Nazionale per la Previdenza Sociale (INPS). 1993. *Le pensioni domani: Primo rapporto sulla previdenza in Italia*. Bologna: Il Mulino.

———. 1994. *Banche dati statistiche: Archivio 01/M*. Rome.

———. Various years. *Notizie statistiche: Raccolta di studi su AGO*. Rome.

Istituto Nazionale di Statistica (ISTAT). Various years. *Annuario del lavoro e dell'emigrazione*. Rome.

———. Various issues. *Annuario statistico italiano*. Rome.

———. Various years. *Collana di informazione*. Rome.

———. 1989. *I conti economici nazionali di occupazione e redditi da lavoro dipendente*. Collana d'Informazione. Rome.

———. 1993. *Rapporto annuale: La situazione economica del paese*. Rome.

———. Various years. *Rilevazione nazionale delle forze di lavoro*. Collana di Informazione. Rome.

———. Various issues. *Statistiche dei trattamenti pensionistici.* . . . Collana di Informazione. Rome.

———. Various issues. Statistiche della previdenza, della sanità e della assistenza sociale. *Annuario.* Rome.

———. Various issues. *Statistiche del lavoro.*

———. Various years. *Supplemento al bollettino mensile di statistica.* Rome.

Istituto Poligrafico e Zecca dello Stato. 1995. *Riforma del sistema pensionistico obbligatorio e complementare.* Gazzetta Ufficiale della Repubblica Italiana, Legge 08/08/1995 n. 335. Rome.

Jappelli, Tullio. 1995. Does social security reduce wealth accumulation? Evidence from Italian survey data. *Ricerche economiche* 49, no. 1:1–32.

Livi Bacci, Massimo. 1995a. Evoluzione demografica e sistema pensionistico. *Economia italiana* 1:19–40.

———. 1995b. Popolazione, trasferimenti e generazioni. In *Le pensioni difficili: La previdenza sociale in Italia tra crisi e riforme,* ed. O. Castellino. Bologna: Il Mulino.

Ministero del Tesoro. Various years. *Relazione generale sulla situazione economica del paese,* vol. 3. Rome.

Ministero del Tesoro. Ragioneria Generale dello Stato. Ufficio Statistico. 1996. *Tendenze demografiche e spesa pensionistica: Alcuni possibili scenari.* Quaderno Monografico no. 9 de "Conti Pubblici e Congiuntura Economica." Rome.

———. 1997. *Sanità, scuola e pensioni: Le nuove previsioni basate sugli scenari demografici I.S.T.A.T.* Quaderno Monografico no. 13 de "Conti Pubblici e Congiuntura Economica." Rome.

Padoa Schioppa Kostoris, Fiorella. 1996. La riforma italiana delle pensioni di anzianità e vecchiaia del 1995 e gli effetti di finanza pubblica. Documenti di lavoro (discussion paper) no. 37/96. Rome: Istituto per la Programmazione Economica.

Peracchi, Franco, and Nicola Rossi. 1995. Nonostante tutto, è una riforma. In *Frontiere della politica economica,* ed. F. Giavazzi, A. Penati, and G. Tabellini. Milan: Il Sole 24 Ore.

Rossi, Nicola, Andrea Sorgato, and Gianni Toniolo. 1993. I conti economici degli italiani: Una ricostruzione statistica (1890–1990). *Rivista di storia economica* 10:1–21.

Rossi, Nicola, and Ignazio Visco. 1994. Private saving and government deficit. In *Saving and the accumulation of wealth: Essays on Italian household and government saving behaviour,* ed. A. Ando, L. Guiso Luigi, and Ignazio Visco. Cambridge: Cambridge University Press.

———. 1995. National saving and social security in Italy. *Ricerche economiche* 49: 329–56.

Rostagno, Massimo. 1996. *Il percorso della riforma, 1992–1995: Nuovi indicatori di consistenza e di sostenibilità per il Fondo Pensioni Lavoratori Dipendenti.* Rome: Banca d'Italia.

Venti, Steven F., and David A. Wise. 1995. Individual response to a retirement saving program: Results from U.S. panel data. *Ricerche economiche* 49:235–54.

6 Social Security and Retirement in Japan

Naohiro Yashiro and Takashi Oshio

While the aging of the population is a common feature in many industrial countries, the most striking feature in the case of Japan is the high speed at which the process is occurring. The reason for this is closely related to Japan's rapid economic development, which has triggered equally rapid social changes, namely, falling fertility ratios and rising life expectancies. As a result, the ratio of elderly people—usually defined as those who are age sixty-five or over—to the working-age population (aged twenty to sixty-four) rose from .10 in 1930 to .24 in 1995 and is projected to rise to .48 in 2025. This will lead to a large expansion of social expenditures in the coming decades.

Japan's social security expenditures in 1994 amounted to ¥57 trillion, which was 11.9 percent of Japan's GDP in that year, doubling its share of GDP in the past twenty years. Public pension benefits accounted for a large share of total social security expenditures (51.3 percent), followed by medical insurance benefits (38.2 percent). Public pension benefits also account for over 50 percent of the total family income of the average household whose head is age sixty-five or over. Thus, like other industrial countries, the benefit structure of the public pension program is likely to have important effects on the retirement decisions of older persons.

Nevertheless, there are several important characteristics particular to the case of Japan. One is the high household saving rate, which was 13.2 percent of disposable income in 1994, compared with 3.8 percent in the United States. According to opinion polls, the major incentive (even among older persons) to save is preparing for retirement. Another characteristic is the high level of labor force participation (LFP) of older persons. The average labor force participa-

Naohiro Yashiro is professor of economics at the Institute of International Relations at Sophia University. Takashi Oshio is professor of economics at Ritsumeikan University.

The authors thank David Wise, Jonathan Gruber, and seminar participants for helpful discussions.

tion ratios of males aged sixty to sixty-four and sixty-five to sixty-nine were 75 and 54 percent, respectively. The high labor force participation of older persons in Japan is one factor behind the high levels of household saving as it is likely that people continue to save as long as they work. To what extent these high ratios of both labor force participation and savings on the part of older persons in Japan are affected by the social security system remains a source of much controversy.

The purpose of our paper is to provide an overview of the interaction between social security (in particular, the public pension scheme) and the labor force behavior of older persons in Japan. The structure of the paper is in line with that of Diamond and Gruber (chap. 11 in this volume), who conduct a similar study for the U.S. social security system. In section 6.1, we examine several key features of the labor market behavior of older persons with specific reference to the recent reversal of the previous trend toward earlier retirement.[1] In section 6.2, we describe the basic structure of the public pension system in Japan, focusing on the recent major changes in the institutional details concerning retirement behavior. In section 6.3, we estimate the social security wealth of the average employee in Japan and document the retirement incentives inherent in the current social security system. Finally, we discuss several country-specific social security and labor market issues that are closely related to social security wealth.

6.1   The Labor Market Behavior of Older Persons

One of the common features in the labor markets in many OECD countries in the postwar period, including Japan, has been the declining participation of older persons. In 1960, almost 70 percent of men aged sixty-five to sixty-nine were participating in the labor force. By 1997, this figure had fallen to 53 percent—a figure that is nevertheless still high by international standards. There are various factors affecting these declines in labor market participation, among which improvement in social security benefits is significant. In this section, we provide some background on the labor market behavior of older persons.

6.1.1   Historical Trends

Figures 6.1 and 6.2 show the historical trends of the labor force participation rates of men and women from 1960 to 1996, respectively. For men, the labor force participation rates of those aged sixty to sixty-four and sixty-five and above declined, while the rate for those aged forty-five to fifty-nine was virtually flat. For women, the pattern is quite different—for age groups younger

1. What *retirement* means in Japan is usually retirement from the primary firm in which one used to work for a long time and not necessarily retirement from the labor market per se. Many older Japanese persons continue to work after mandatory retirement from the primary firm, moving to smaller firms with no mandatory retirement but less favorable working conditions.

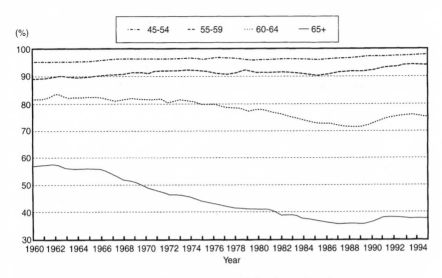

Fig. 6.1   Historical trends of labor force participation rates of men

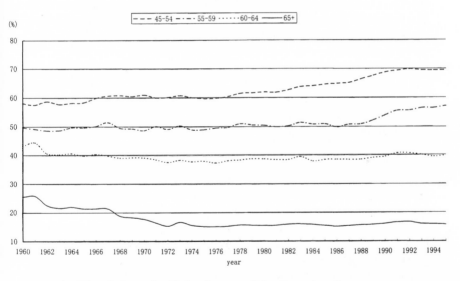

Fig. 6.2   Historical trends of labor force participation rates of women

than sixty, labor force participation increased, while, for age groups over sixty, the trend toward earlier retirement dominates—although the changes are much less pronounced than in the case of men.

This decline in the labor force participation rates of older persons in Japan is mainly due to the declining share of the self-employed and improved pension benefits. In the postwar period, the share of the self-employed (including unpaid family workers) among total workers fell from 47 to 18 percent between 1960 and 1996. This is mainly due to the decline of the agricultural sector and the migration of the population from rural to urban areas. However, in 1996, the share of the self-employed among total employment was still 35 and 57 percent in the age groups sixty to sixty-four and sixty-five or above, respectively, partly accounting for the high labor market attachment of older persons. As the average labor market participation of the self-employed is higher than that of employees, the shrinking self-employed sector is one factor behind the falling average labor force participation ratios. Another factor behind the decline in labor force participation is an increasing trend toward greater pension benefits (see below).

As for the participation ratio in the pension plans, enrollment in a public pension plan is compulsory for everyone in the workforce, including the self-employed. However, whereas the social security premiums of employees are automatically deducted from wages along with taxes, about 30 percent (excluding those who are exempted from paying premiums) of the self-employed and other nonemployees do not participate in a pension plan, a situation due mainly to the lack of an enforcement mechanism. Also, the public pension benefits of the self-employed have little effect on their labor force participation. This is because eligibility for benefits is not linked to retirement and because pension benefits are granted at age sixty-five and are not means tested. Also, the average benefit level is approximately one-quarter that for employees. The pension benefits of employees, however, are significantly higher and are subject to an earnings test. Thus, with the rising share (53 percent of all workers in 1960, 84 percent in 1996) of employees, who are more affected by public pension policies, public pension benefits figure more importantly in the retirement decisions of older Japanese workers (fig. 6.3).

6.1.2   Reversal of the Trend toward Earlier Retirement

Another interesting feature of the labor force participation of older persons in Japan is the fact that the long-run pattern of decline reversed between 1988 and 1993 and that participation thereafter remained steady at its 1993 level. This is particularly prominent among men aged sixty to sixty-four, but a similar pattern is observed for the group aged sixty-five or over, too (see fig. 6.1 above). Although many attribute older people's high levels of labor market participation in Japan to such supply-side factors as insufficient social security benefits, such factors do not plausibly explain the reversal of the trend as Japan's social security benefits have not declined in comparison to earnings over time. A key cause of the reversal lies in demand. If we compare the labor force participation of men aged sixty to sixty-four and the unemployment rate of the same age group, reflecting the tightness of the labor market for older persons, the period of the increase in labor force participation also saw a falling unemployment rate. Estimating the labor force participation of men aged sixty to

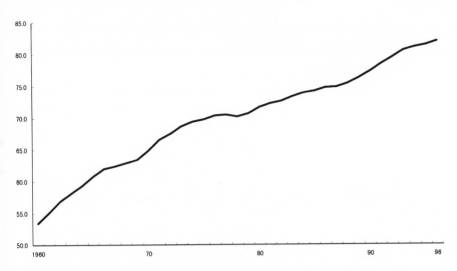

Fig. 6.3   Share of employees in total employed

sixty-four by adding the corresponding unemployment rate to the average replacement ratio resulted in a better explanation of rising labor force participation in the late 1980s (fig. 6.4).[2] While the strong demand for employment
resulting in the rising labor force participation of older persons in the late
1980s was mainly due to cyclic factors, such demand may well be seen again
in the near future. This is because the size of the working-age population (between the ages of fifteen and sixty-four) has already started to shrink as of
1995, and this trend is projected to continue through the twenty-first century:
with a constant labor force participation rate for each age group, Japan's labor
force will decline by 7.6 percent in 2020 from the 1993 level. This overall
decline in the labor force may well stimulate the labor force participation of
older persons by providing them with good job opportunities.

Figure 6.5 indicates social security replacement rates over time. The replacement ratio here is defined as the ratio of the monthly pension benefits of a
married couple in the representative public pension scheme for private-sector

2. The OLS estimated results with and without the unemployment rate are as follows:

$$\text{LFP} = 88.18 - 0.311 \text{ replacement ratio,} \quad R^2 = .0775,$$

$$(46.64) \ (-10.83)$$

$$\text{LFP} = 86.37 - 0.0852 \text{ replacement ratio} - 1.896 \text{ unemployment rate,} \quad R^2 = 0.884.$$

$$(62.74) \ (-1.87) \qquad\qquad\qquad (-5.58)$$

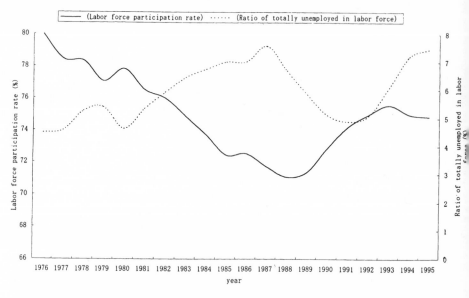

Fig. 6.4   Labor force participation of men aged 60–64 and unemployment rate

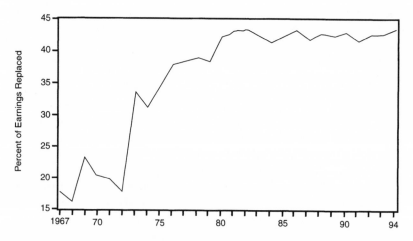

Fig. 6.5   Social security replacement rates (monthly earnings including bonus)

employees to average monthly earnings, including biannual bonus payments. There was a sudden jump in 1974 when the public pension scheme was reformed, including the introduction of wage indexation, resulting in a doubling of benefits in subsequent periods. After the 1980s, the replacement rates have increased steadily over time.

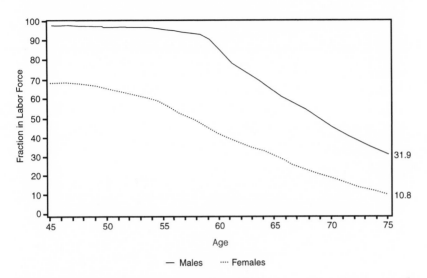

Fig. 6.6   **Participation rates by age and sex (%)**

6.1.3   Recent Labor Market Behavior

To obtain a more detailed understanding of the time pattern of labor force participation in recent years, we use the national census data for 1990. The national census asks all individuals in the country about their labor force participation at the time the survey is conducted. Also, this is the only survey that publishes labor force participation data broken down by age-by-age changes.

The age pattern of participation for men and women is shown in figure 6.6. At age forty-five in 1990, the participation rate of men is close to full capacity, while only 70 percent of women worked. There is then a gradual decline for men until age fifty-five, at which point the pace accelerates. There is a sharp drop in participation at age sixty, which is the typical mandatory retirement age for major Japanese firms. But even after the mandatory retirement age, labor market attachment is relatively strong, and 32 percent of males still work even at age seventy-five. It should be noted that, among elderly males, the share of the self-employed who are voluntary part-time workers is much higher than the male average (16 percent), accounting for 34 and 47 percent of total employment for the age groups sixty to sixty-four and sixty-five to sixty-nine, respectively. This implies that the actual capacity of human resources at older ages in Japan may well be overestimated if one accounts for their shorter working hours. Participation falls more rapidly for women in their fifties than it does for men, although the pace is almost unchanged up to the eighties, with the result that the participation gap between the genders closes beyond age sixty. As most older women in the labor market are self-employed, the mandatory retirement system affects the participation of women much less than it does that of men.

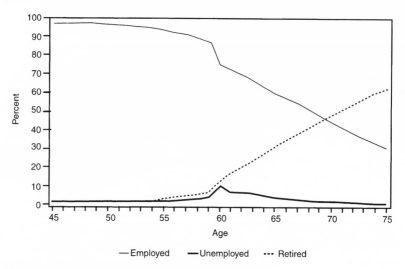

Fig. 6.7   Distribution of activities of men by age (%)

Figure 6.7 shows in more detail the allocation of time among men as they age, dividing their activity status into employment, unemployment, and retirement. From the available statistics, it is difficult to determine whether those who are not in the workforce are retired or simply not working. Thus, retired persons are considered to be those who are not in the labor force and do not either engage in household work, go to school, and seek jobs. This same exercise is repeated for women in figure 6.8. Particularly to be noted among Japanese women aged forty to fifty is the high ratio of homemakers; they account for a substantial portion even at age sixty and beyond.

6.1.4   Income Sources of Older Persons

In figure 6.9, we examine the public retirement incomes of older persons on the basis of the Basic Survey on People's Life, conducted by the Ministry of Welfare. The figure shows the rate at which public pension and other public assistance mainly from the income maintenance program is received. Beginning at age sixty, the rate of collection of social security benefits increases sharply, driven by the collection of the public pension, until it is over 90 percent for those over age sixty-five. Private pensions are not popular in Japan, partly because there are few tax incentives to encourage enrolling in such pensions. On the contrary, large lump-sum severance payments made at the time of retirement, a substitute for the firm pensions offered in the United States, play an important role in saving for retirement (for details, see the section below on country-specific practices).

Private pensions have become an important source of retirement income. The size of the accumulated assets of private pensions in the financial markets

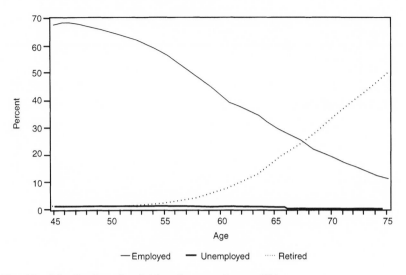

Fig. 6.8   Distribution of activities of women by age (%)

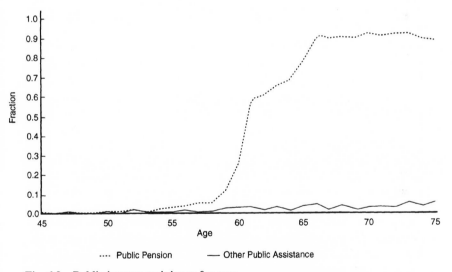

Fig. 6.9   Public income recipiency for men

exceeded that of firm pensions in the 1990s even though the tax benefits are quite limited. While the official data on private pensions are scant, an ad hoc survey based on a small sample by the Ministry of Post and Telecommunication indicates that the ratio of families having private pensions has risen over the last few years (fig. 6.10).

Finally, figure 6.11 shows the distribution of income sources of individuals

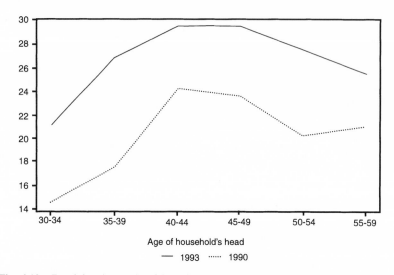

Fig. 6.10   Participation ratio of families to private pensions

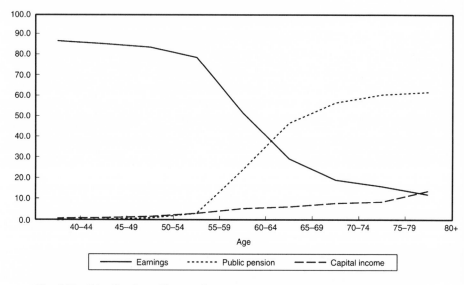

Fig. 6.11   Distribution of income by source

between the ages of forty-five and seventy-five on the basis of the Basic Survey on People's Life. We consider the distribution of income across three sources: earnings, capital income, and public pensions. Earnings are the dominant source of family income until age sixty, accounting for about 80 percent of total household income. Beginning at age sixty, earnings decline, and public pensions grow as a major source of the income of the elderly, accounting for about 80 percent of the total. It should be noted that these data on the incomes of elderly individuals are not available from the conventional household surveys, which are based on the age of the household's head. More than half the elderly age sixty-five or over live with their relatives, including their children's family, and the ratio is particularly high for the poor elderly. Thus, those who are economically dependent on their children tend to drop from the household surveys, leaving the relatively rich elderly as the head of the household in statistics (Yashiro 1997). Also, even when an elderly individual maintains the position of the household's head, the inclusion of children's earnings in the family income may underestimate the role that pension benefits play in the total income of the elderly. Thus, an international comparison of the economic position of the elderly needs to account for the difference in family structure.

6.2 Key Features of the Social Security System

6.2.1 A History of the Social Security System in Japan

The current public pension for private-sector employees originated from the Rodosha Nenkin Hokenhou (Pension Insurance for Workers) Act in 1942, following the establishment of the National Health Insurance Act of 1938. Although the major purpose of social security insurance was to secure workers' standard of living, such extensive social security reform was possible only in wartime, when the government needed all the manpower it could muster in exchange for an assurance that minimum living standards would be maintained.

Japan's social security program, which consists of public pension and health insurance schemes and covers everyone, including those who are self-employed or not working, was established in 1961. Since then, the size of social security expenditures increased at a much faster pace than did the economy as a whole, growing from 4.9 percent of national income in 1960 to 14.1 percent in 1996. A major reform of social security occurred in 1973. The pension reform included the introduction of automatic increases in benefits with increases in inflation and wages: monthly pension benefit levels are set at 60 percent of wages when the funding scheme is fully matured, and revaluation of the benefit levels occurs every five years; benefits are also adjusted annually to keep pace with increases in the CPI. Also, there is a scheme providing special benefits for the elderly who have not contributed long enough to receive pension benefits. On the other hand, the health insurance scheme was also reformed mainly to improve benefits. Medical costs covered by health insurance have increased from 50 to 70–90 percent of the total. Also, 100 percent of expensive medical care is covered by the insurance, and those aged seventy and above are covered by separate health insurance, under which medical services are provided at minimal fixed cost.

However, 1973 also saw the oil price hike and a deceleration of economic growth, ending the high-growth period of 10 percent average annual economic growth prevailing since the early 1950s. Moreover, the total fertility ratio started to decline again in 1975, from about 2.1 to 1.4 in 1996, while male and female life expectancy at age sixty-five has increased substantially, from 13.7 and 16.6 years to 16.7 and 21.0 years, respectively. Both economic and demographic factors have worked against the social security fiscal balance by reducing the number of contributors and increasing beneficiaries and placing strong pressure on the system in the form of increasing fiscal deficits.

The most recent public pension reform in 1994 was meant to mitigate the demographic pressure on the social security program. First, pension premiums are to be raised to a level slightly lower than 30 percent of monthly wages by the year 2025. Second, pension benefits are linked not to gross wages but to wages net of taxes and social security premiums; that is, the higher the taxes and social security premiums imposed on the working generation, the lower the pension benefits of the retired, thus balancing the equality between the generations. Third, the eligibility age for the flat pension component of the employees' pension is scheduled to be raised from the current sixty to sixty-five beginning in 2001, one year every three years.

6.2.2 Major Features of the Public Pension Scheme

Japan's public pension scheme consists basically of two pillars: one is the basic pension mainly for the self-employed and other nonemployees; the other is for employees in both the public and the private sectors. The pension benefits for employees consist of two parts: the basic pension, which they have in common with the self-employed, and the earnings-related pension.

The basic pension is mainly for the self-employed, unpaid family workers, and nonworkers (the unemployed, students age twenty or over, homemakers). It is a simple scheme based on a flat tax and a flat benefit structure, and it is managed by local authorities. It is organized on an individual-unit basis—that is, both husband and wife pay premiums and receive benefits individually—thus, there are benefits for neither dependent spouses nor survivors. The eligibility age is sixty-five, but one can collect the benefits as early as age sixty with a certain reduction in rates. The basic pension has little effect on retirement decisions mainly because the benefits are relatively small (the average benefit was ¥43,000 per month in 1995). Benefits are not subject to any earnings criteria.

On the other hand, the pension schemes for employees are organized on a family-unit basis, and dependent spouses are covered by the pension of the head of the household. In addition, dependent spouses are provided as individuals with the basic pension from age sixty-five and survivor pension benefits, equivalent to two-thirds of the full pension. The earnings-related pension is designed to maintain an individual's standard of living after retirement, and payments are proportional to contributions related to wages in the past, subject to a certain ceiling. The average amount of the benefits was ¥168,000 per month in 1995. Unlike the pension scheme for the self-employed, the employee pension can greatly affect the retirement decision of an individual, particularly at age sixty to sixty-four, when the benefits are reduced on the basis of amount of earnings. Thus, in the following sections, our discussion will center around the pension schemes for employees.

6.2.3   Pension Schemes for Employees

There are eight public pension schemes covering various types of employees, and the Kosei Nenkin Hoken (KNH, Employees Pension Insurance) dominates as the largest public pension scheme for private-sector employees, covering 85 percent of all employees. Thus, we use the KNH to represent the earnings-related pension for employees. The public pension for employees is financed by premiums that are paid by employees and employers in equal proportions, and the total premium paid was 16.5 percent of monthly wages[3] in 1995 (i.e., the employee and the employer paid 8.25 percent each).

An additional contribution of 8 percent of monthly wages is devoted to health insurance for private-sector employees. The social security fund, consisting mostly of pension funds and the surplus, equivalent to 3.5 percent of GDP in 1995, receives interest from the Fiscal Investment and Loan Program (FILP).[4] In addition, there are government transfers financed by general taxes equivalent to one-third of the total benefits of the basic pension and administrative expenses. Although the public pension fund is subsidized by the central government, its budget is kept completely separate from the general budget, and the surplus in the pension fund cannot be used to reduce the government deficit.

Eligibility for a public pension is based on age. All individuals between twenty and fifty-nine years of age are obliged to participate in their respective public pension programs. Most of the contributions (and income taxes) are automatically deducted from wages by the company, except in certain small firms. However, those aged sixty and over are not automatically qualified to enroll in a public pension scheme even though they may continue to work.[5] Individual pension assets can be transferred to other schemes when one changes jobs, as in principle an individual is eligible to receive only one pension.

6.2.4   Pension Benefits

An individual's benefit amount is determined by the following steps. A worker's monthly wages (excluding semiannual bonuses) are converted into

---

3. The monthly standard wage excludes semiannual bonuses, accounting for a quarter of annual earnings. The replacement rate of pension benefits to annual earnings is slightly below 50 percent, which is on a comparable basis to that prevailing in other OECD countries.

4. FILP is the government financing program directed mainly at public infrastructures supported mainly by funds from the public pension funds and postal savings. FILP has played an important role in providing funds for social capital, particularly during the high-growth period.

5. Even after age sixty-five, an individual can voluntarily contribute to the earnings-related pension unless he already receives pension benefits.

hyoujun houshuu getsugaku (HHG), the standard average monthly earnings), indexed by the national wage average. HHG is divided into thirty brackets that range from ¥92,000 to ¥590,000. This wage history is averaged over the employee's entire period of coverage up to age sixty-four. A particular characteristic of the Japanese pension system is that the total length of the contributing periods for the earning-related portion of the KNH is not fixed (regardless of how many years one has worked) and that only a limitation on age (age sixty-five) exists.[6]

In this sense, the additional years' work plays an important role in increasing the benefits in the earning-related component of the employee's pension. For example, a worker who left his firm at age sixty and continues to work in another firm at much lower wages can still increase his pension benefits as the positive effect on the pension benefits from an additional year of work will more than offset the negative effect arising from the lowered average contribution.

Workers can claim KNH benefits at the normal retirement age of sixty-five, before the full pension is granted at age sixty-five. Between the ages of sixty and sixty-four, the payment of pension benefits is subject to an earnings test (see below). Beyond age sixty-five, the recipient is eligible to receive the full pension with no earnings test and has the option of delaying receipt of the full pension. For workers reaching age sixty-five in 1996, an additional 12 percent of pension benefits is paid for each year that the collection of benefits is delayed. This amount will steadily increase until the additional rate reaches 88 percent at age seventy.

6.2.5   The *Zaishoku* (Early Retirement) Pension

While one can claim the *zaishoku* pension benefits as early as age sixty, the receipt of social security benefits is conditional on passing the "earnings test" on wages (but not on other income or assets) until age sixty-five. This scheme corresponds to the early retirement systems in many other OECD countries. That is, if one earns more than a certain floor level, social security benefits (PENW_t) are reduced for each additional dollar of earnings (W_t) until, at high earnings, one may not qualify at all. For example, if an individual earns even a small amount, the benefits are automatically reduced by 20 percent. Benefits are reduced for any earnings above ¥220,000 per month by 50 percent of the full pension benefits (PENF60) for each additional increment of earnings. Benefits are reduced by 100 percent for anyone who earns more than ¥340,000.[7] The formula is

---

6. There is a maximum number of years of contributions—forty—in the flat pension for the self-employed.

7. This rate of reduction of pension benefits with higher wages has been lowered substantially since 1995 to prevent it from acting as a disincentive for older workers, but a de facto 50 percent effective income tax still remains.

$$\text{PEN}W_t = \text{PENF60} \quad \text{for } W_t = 0,$$

$$= 0.8 \times \text{PENF60} \quad \text{for } 0 < W_t < 22 - 0.8 \times \text{PENF60},$$

$$= 11 - W_t/2 + 0.4 \times \text{PENF60} \quad \text{for } 22 - 0.8$$

$$\times \text{PENF60} < W_t < 34,$$

$$= 28 - W_t0.4 \times \text{PENF60} \quad \text{for } 34 < W_t < 28 + 0.4 \times \text{PENF60},$$

$$= 0 \quad \text{for } 28 + 0.4 \times \text{PENF60} < W_t.$$

These thresholds on the earnings test increase every five years with average earnings in the economy.

6.2.6   The Full Pension

The full KNH pension for which one is eligible at age sixty-five is generous by international standards. First, the pension benefits are not subject to an earning tests, and even full-time workers can receive full pension benefits. Second, no contributions from the earnings of those age sixty-five and over are required even if the individuals concerned are working full time. Third, income tax law favors pension benefits over earnings, and most benefit recipients are exempt from income taxes. Thus, receiving full pension benefits at age sixty-five does not exert much influence on retirement decisions.

6.2.7   Benefits to Dependent Spouses

There are additional pension benefit provisions for those who have dependent families. Dependent spouses of social security beneficiaries receive additional benefits: the *kakyu* (a supplementary pension), the dependent spouse's own basic pension, and survivor benefits.[8] First, *kakyu* pension benefits for the dependent spouse are ¥226,000 per year; the same amount is provided for the first two dependent children under the age of eighteen and ¥75,300 for any younger children.[9] Second, dependent spouses are entitled to their own basic pension from age sixty-five with no additional contributions, unlike singles or economically independent spouses with the same income levels. This measure protects dependent spouses who divorce at older ages and have no individual pension on which to rely. Third, surviving spouses receive three-quarters of full pension benefits, beginning at age sixty. Dependent children, parents, grandchildren, and grandparents are eligible for these benefits as well.

The situation involving dependent spouses who have their own earnings is somewhat complicated because they therefore are entitled to pensions based

8. A dependent spouse is one who earns less than ¥1.3 million annually and is not obliged to pay premiums.
9. The *frikae* (replacement) pension benefit is replaced by the *kakyu* pension when dependent spouses reach age sixty-five. The *kakyu* pension benefit is a temporary provision for older persons and is subject to a reduction in rates based on year of birth. The more recently the spouse was born, the less she receives, and those born after 1965 receive nothing.

on their own contributions. Economically independent spouses are obliged to choose between survival benefits and their own pension benefits. Since 1995, however, they have had the option of receiving half of each.[10] This raises equality issues about possibly significant differences in the lifetime pension benefits collected by workers who have the same level of earnings but who may or may not have dependent spouses because, beyond a certain income ceiling, they lose various pension benefits granted to nonworking homemakers. In addition, the system may well discourage dependent spouses from working full-time. Indeed, several studies indicate that dependent spouses deliberately restrain their annual earnings in order to maintain their status (Higuchi 1995).

6.2.8   Disability Pension

The disability pension is the income that workers physically unable to participate in the labor market will receive to sustain their standard of living. Those who qualify for the disability pension are eligible to receive benefits regardless of age after age twenty. The benefits are calculated in a similar way to retirement pensions, and additional benefits of 25 percent are provided to those who are considered to have a major disability. Also, one can collect a disability basic pension amounting to ¥785,500 per year regardless of the length of contributing periods. One can choose either of two disability pensions.

In 1994, 285,000 people received a disability pension (3 percent of old age pension recipients), and the average benefit was ¥102,000 per month (60 percent of average old age pension benefits). Eligibility conditions for the disability pension are strict. Most disabilities must originate in injuries, and physical disabilities that occur with aging are not sufficient. Thus, in Japan, disability pensions cannot be used to finance earlier retirement, as such pensions can be in several European countries.

6.2.9   Hazard Rate

An effective indicator of the effects of the country-specific social security system on labor force participation trends is the "hazard rate" out of the labor force for men and women. This is measured as the increase from the previous age of those leaving the labor force relative to the stock of workers participating at the previous age. However, this indicator is susceptible to age-by-age population changes and is not an appropriate measure to use when examining the exit pattern of older persons in Japan.

Thus, we show instead an alternative hazard rate out of the labor force in terms of participation rates—the percentage point changes in the participation rates from the previous year—for men and women (fig. 6.12). We see a large

10. A rationale for this adjustment is that both survivor benefits and own pension benefits are subsidized by the government and receiving two subsidies instead of one is considered unfair. Households in which both husband and wife work were not nearly as prevalent at the time the earnings-related pension was first developed.

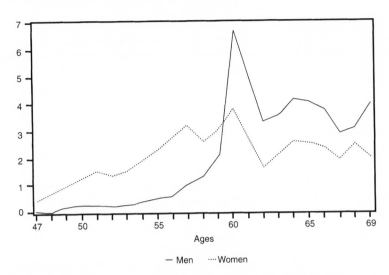

Fig. 6.12   Hazard rate out of the labor force (differences in labor force participation ratio)

jump at age sixty for men. This is obviously the result of the general practice of mandatory retirement. However, it also suggests that social security has a role in explaining the retirement behavior of men as sixty is the age of eligibility for the earlier retirement social security benefit, just as in the United States. In addition, there is another jump at age sixty-five, which corresponds to the eligibility age for receiving the full pension benefit without the earnings-test criteria. On the other hand, because many women in their fifties are part-time workers and social security benefits do not work as retirement incentives for older women, the jump at age sixty is less pronounced for women since retirement for women rising consistently through the fifties.

6.3   Survey of Previous Studies

Few empirical studies have been conducted in Japan concerning the interaction between social security benefits and retirement. This discussion draws on Takayama (1992), Seike (1993), and Tachibanaki and Shimono (1994). First, Takayama (1992) used the micro-data set from the National Survey on Family Income and Expenditure (1984) to estimate pension wealth and analyze the redistributional effects of the public pension. Takayama (1992) also examined the probability of retirement for dependent employees with various classes of pension benefits in the age group sixty to sixty-four, finding a significant negative relation. Moreover, the marginal effect of an increase in benefits on retirement is large for individuals at the low end of the benefit range. Similar results have been obtained by Tachibanaki and Shimono (1994).

Second, Seike (1993), following previous work by Ward (1984), estimated the pension wealth of an average employee having a dependent spouse and its annual changes. He found that changes in pension wealth as a proportion of annual earnings before retirement became negative at age sixty, when pension benefits are provided. This is consistent with a large drop in labor force participation. However, as Seike conceives social security wealth, premiums are not subtracted. Also, the expected value of the survivor pension is not taken into account as his concept of pension wealth is individual based, compared with ours, which accounts for the expected benefits of the wife. Further, there is room for argument as to the extent to which the concept of social security wealth should be broadened; we take a wider view, one that accounts for various factors affecting the retirement decision of an individual, including wage subsidies specific to the age group sixty to sixty-four.

6.4   Retirement Incentives

In this section, we use a representative household to assess the incentives of social security benefits on retirement through accrual rate effects; we also test variations under alternative assumptions. A major reform of the Japanese public pension scheme was introduced in 1994, but in this section we analyze the effects of the situation prevailing before the 1994 reform, postponing discussion of the effects of the 1994 reform until the country-specific analysis provided in section 6.5 below.

6.4.1   Modeling Social Security Benefits

In Japan, the Social Security Administration's official data that record the individual history of wage earnings and social security tax payments are not available to us. Thus, we use instead data reported in published sources. The basis for our analysis is the Basic Wage Survey by the Ministry of Labor. This survey is published annually, and each firm submits a report with data indicating the average worker's wage, age, years of work experience at the particular firm, and education as well as firm size, occupation, and industry. We apply the average monthly wage of a worker in the following way.

We present a typical Japanese household, headed by a man age sixty-five in 1995 (born on 1 April 1930 as the social security data are collected on a fiscal year basis, i.e., from April to March in the following year, in Japan) whose wife was born in 1933 and has no work experience. He is a high school graduate (as are about 50 percent of the male employees in 1995) and worked in the same firm from age twenty until the normal retirement age of sixty. At age sixty, he left that firm and started to work in another. We assume that he worked full-time in both firms. The couple's children are already grown and are now economically independent. This household head works for a typical Japanese company and is covered by the Kosei Nenkin Hoken (KNH) plan, the largest public pension scheme for private-sector employees (covering 85 and 71 percent of contributors among wage earners and beneficiaries, respectively).

There are other public pensions for employees in the public sector and specific groups of the private sector with different pension contributions and benefits schemes, but these are not considered here. Our household head is eligible for three components of KNH: the basic component, the earnings-related component, and the additional component for a dependent wife. Firm pensions and private pensions are not considered here.

On the basis of the assumptions outlined above, the following steps are necessary to compute social security wealth, which is the expected net present value of social security benefits through the individual's lifetime.

First, we derive the wage profile of a typical worker whose characteristics are given above. Since panel data are not available, we simply assume that the historical wage profile of an individual traces the same wage profile pattern in a given year adjusted by inflation, which is the same method taken by Seike (1993).

Second, the wage data contained in the Basic Wage Survey are adjusted to the scales of the standard wages on which the pension premium and benefits are based. The monthly social security benefits are the sum of the following components: (1) a fixed component, which is a certain unit price multiplied by the number of years worked, set at a maximum of 444 months; (2) years of contributions (which do not account for years of unemployment); (3) the base wage rate; and (4) an adjustment for a dependent spouse.

Third, the pension premium is imposed on the base wage, which is monthly wages including overtime payments but excluding bonuses. Thus, the wage data contained in the Basic Wage Survey are adjusted to a pension premium basis. In addition, the adjusted wage profiles are deflated by the historical wage series in the Ministry of Labor's Maitsuki Kinrotokei Chousa (Survey of Monthly Wages). We add both the employee's and the employer's share of the pension premiums, under the assumption that the employer's share is fully borne by the worker, for example, in the form of lower wages.

Using these procedures, we derive social security wealth (SSW), social security accrual (SSA), and taxes/subsidies, explaining the worker's retirement incentives. The average life expectancy is based on the Japan life tables from the Population Research Institute, Ministry of Health and Welfare, adjusting for the sex/age-specific mortality rate. Note that we use the "unconditional mortality risk" beyond age fifty-five, which is tantamount to disregarding the probability of death at each year after the fifty-fifth birthday.[11] We use this unconditional mortality assumption because, at the time of the computation of social security wealth, it is reasonable to base an analysis on the perspective of the forward-looking individual who, at age fifty-four, is considering retirement incentives at all future ages. In the base case, we use a real discount rate of 3 percent.

11. An alternative assumption is to vary the conditional mortality risk on the basis of the year of retirement.

6.4.2   Social Security Wealth

Social security wealth is the net discounted sum of lifetime pensions and other benefits at age fifty-five. We subtract the pension premiums that the individual would pay during any continued work and compute an expected net present value of social security wealth. Social security wealth is the sum of the expected pension benefits not only to an individual but also to his spouse, including the *zaishoku* (earlier retirement) pension, the full pension at age sixty-five, the addition for dependent spouses, survivor benefits, and the individual basic pension for dependent spouses aged sixty-five and over. The last benefit needs some additional explanation, since a dependent spouse is eligible for the basic pension on her own and it is not paid to the household head. Nevertheless, we include the pension benefits of the dependent spouse when determining the social security wealth of the household head as we did with survivor benefits. In addition, wage subsidies are added to social security wealth after the 1994 reform.

Comparing the discounted values of social security wealth at different ages, however, is not enough to predict the retirement decision. The accrual rate for work in a given year, which is the change in the worker's future social security benefits relative to what he would earn over the coming year, also figures in an individual's decision whether to work another year. Thus, social security accrual is defined as the difference in social security wealth: $SSA_t = SSW_t - SSW_{t-1}$.

Social security accrual is presented as a ratio, that is, the percentage change in social security wealth. Also, the change in social security wealth (i.e., social security accrual) relative to projected earnings over that year is defined as a tax/subsidy rate. If the change in social security wealth associated with an additional year of work is negative, the effect is that of a tax on work. If the change is positive, the effect is that of a subsidy to work.

6.4.3   Specific Characteristics of Retirement Incentives in Japan

The following two points about labor market conditions must be taken account of in any discussion of the retirement incentives of older persons in Japan. First, after retirement at age sixty, the wages of older persons tend to fall substantially—by 40 percent, on average—from the preretirement level. This is mainly because wages in the primary firm—the "internal labor market"— are seniority based while those with the new firm—the "external market"— are close to flat. Thus, unlike in the United States, the preretirement wage is not a realistic reference for the opportunity costs of one's retirement. We assume that this diminishing wage profile (which older persons over age sixty actually face) reflects the actual labor market situation in the base-case simulation.

Second, older persons between the ages of sixty and sixty-four can claim the *zaishoku* pension, and these benefits are dependent on wages. When wages are sufficiently low, the individual can receive both wages and pension benefits, subject to an earnings test. Thus, when deciding to work at that age, the individual compares a full-time wage, on the one hand, with a part-time wage and pension benefits, on the other. Also, at age sixty-five and beyond, individuals are eligible to receive a full pension with no earnings criteria; that is, full pension benefits are unconditional, and no premium is required.

6.4.4 The Base Case

The results of the base-case simulation are summarized in table 6.1. Each row represents the age of the worker in the last year he works. For example, the row for age fifty-four represents the effect of working until age fifty-four and retiring on the fifty-fifth birthday.

The first column shows the replacement rate, which is conventionally defined as the ratio of pension benefits to preretirement wage earnings. This concept is irrelevant until the worker can actually claim pension benefits, which occurs when his last year of work is fifty-nine and he retires on his sixtieth birthday. When he becomes eligible to claim a pension, the replacement rate is about 55 percent. This rate jumps to 80 percent in his sixtieth year because the preretirement wage—the denominator of the replacement rate—drops substantially after the mandatory retirement age of sixty.

The large drop in the replacement rate at age sixty-four is due to the fact that, after the sixty-fifth birthday, pension benefits are not conditional on an earnings test and the worker need not pay any pension premiums. He will see a small jump in the rate in his sixty-seventh year, when his wife, who is three years his junior, becomes eligible for her basic pension benefit.

Table 6.1   Base-Case Incentive Calculations

Last Year of Work	Replacement Rate	SSW (thousand yen)	Accrual (thousand yen)	Accrual Rate	Tax/ Subsidy
54	. . .	33,490	. . .	. . .	. . .
55	. . .	34,106	616	.018	−.195
56	. . .	34,734	628	.018	−.202
57	. . .	35,058	324	.009	−.106
58	. . .	35,390	333	.009	−.112
59	.552	35,662	272	.008	−.138
60	.800	35,018	−644	−.018	.338
61	.799	34,396	−622	−.018	.340
62	.802	33,792	−603	−.018	.342
63	.801	33,208	−584	−.017	.340
64	.438	32,719	−489	−.015	.204
65	.549	32,719	0	0	0
66	.547	32,719	0	0	0
67	.716	32,719	0	0	0
68	.608	32,719	0	0	0
69	.607	32,719	0	0	0

The next three columns show the evolution of social security wealth over time. If the worker retires on his sixtieth birthday, the net present value of his social security wealth would be ¥35.7 million. Social security wealth increases up to his sixtieth birthday because he cannot claim any benefits until then. If he works another year, however, social security wealth falls by 1.8 percent. Thus, for this individual, the public pension system is "actuarially unfair" as it penalizes work beyond age sixty by reducing future social security benefits. Social security wealth is unchanged beyond age sixty-five because, as mentioned above, there are no more contributions or opportunity costs for postponing retirement.

Social security accrual is the change in social security wealth from the previous period. Between the ages of fifty-five and fifty-nine, social security accrual is positive—an additional year of work gradually raises social security wealth with longer contribution periods, and this exceeds the negative effects of additional pension premiums. However, as the worker is eligible for the *zaishoku* pension benefits from age sixty, additional work until age sixty-four incurs the opportunity costs of a delay in claiming the benefits. In addition, the higher the earnings received, the more the pension benefits are reduced. For example, the benefits of the base-case worker are reduced by half. As a result, the social security accrual rate is negative; there is roughly a 2 percent decline in social security wealth each year due to continued work. Social security accrual becomes zero beyond age sixty-five, reflecting no change in social security wealth.

The final column shows the tax/subsidy rate. The tax/subsidy rate is the ratio of change in social security wealth to projected earnings over that year. The negative sign here indicates a subsidy, implying that a worker receives more than an actuarial adjustment for delaying his benefit claims and paying additional pension premiums. The worker keeps getting subsidies to work through his sixtieth birthday, but, beyond that point, he is forced to pay taxes on work through age sixty-four. This is because he loses social security benefits by continuing to work; besides, the pension benefits of most individuals are not taxed, while wages are. If a worker decides to work between the ages of sixty and sixty-four, forgone social security wealth amounts to nearly one-third of a year's earnings. This significant shift from subsidy to tax at age sixty is a major cause of the large drop in labor force participation. There is, however, no such tax disincentive effect beyond age sixty-five.

6.4.5   Other Cases

Table 6.2 shows these results for a single worker. The negative effect of delayed retirement is larger for a single than for a married worker. This is mainly because the single worker has no survivors and receives no other benefits for a dependent spouse (even though the premiums paid are equal given the same earnings). The social security wealth of a single worker at age fifty-nine is ¥21.9 million, 39 percent less than that of a married worker. Neverthe-

Table 6.2   **Incentive Calculations—Single Worker**

Last Year of Work	Replacement Rate	SSW (thousand yen)	Accrual (thousand yen)	Accrual Rate	Tax/ Subsidy
54	...	20,350	...	...	...
55	...	20,840	490	.024	−.158
56	...	21,338	498	.024	−.163
57	...	21,529	191	.009	−.064
58	...	21,727	198	.009	−.069
59	.516	21,864	137	.006	−.071
60	.751	21,164	−700	−.032	.376
61	.751	29,483	−681	−.032	.381
62	.754	19,821	−662	−.032	.384
63	.753	19,178	−643	−.032	.383
64	.425	18,630	−548	−.029	.244
65	.541	18,630	0	0	0
66	.538	18,630	0	0	0
67	.536	18,630	0	0	0
68	.534	18,630	0	0	0
69	.532	18,630	0	0	0

less, the difference in social security accrual between the married and the single individual is not very significant. This is due mainly to the fact that, while the social security wealth of the married worker at age sixty is much larger than that of a single worker, the change in social security benefits by working another year is almost exactly the same for the married and the single individual since the additional benefit for a spouse is largely fixed. The larger tax on the single worker, however, indicates that he will lose more from his decision to continue work than his married counterpart.

The incentive mechanism varies by wage level. Tables 6.3 and 6.4 show the effects of considering different earning histories for a married worker: We compare a worker at the ninetieth percentile of the earnings distribution (table 6.3) with a worker at the tenth percentile (table 6.4).[12] According to tables 6.3 and 6.4, the replacement rate is higher for the low-earnings worker. Also, the tax rate on the low-wage earner is twice that of the high-wage earner. This implies the redistributional mechanism in the basic pension (the fixed component), through which the low-wage earner loses more relative to his wage earnings by postponing retirement than does the high-wage earner.

Table 6.5 considers a different permutation to the earnings history for a worker who has an incomplete earnings history. Compared with the base case, where the worker has contributed for forty years at age sixty, the worker in this case is assumed to have started working five years later; he therefore needs to work an additional five years to be eligible for full pension benefits. According

12. Wages for these workers are obtained from the 1994 age/earnings profile.

Table 6.3   Incentive Calculations—Ninetieth Percentile Earnings

Last Year of Work	Replacement Rate	SSW (thousand yen)	Accrual (thousand yen)	Accrual Rate	Tax/ Subsidy
54	...	39,031	...	...	...
55	...	39,777	746	.019	−.150
56	...	40,545	768	.019	−.157
57	...	41,018	472	.012	−.099
58	...	41,507	489	.012	−.105
59	.425	41,907	400	.010	−.129
60	.618	41,178	−729	−.017	.244
61	.620	40,469	−709	−.017	.247
62	.624	39,777	−692	−.017	.250
63	.625	39,104	−673	−.017	.251
64	.391	38,575	−529	−.014	.156
65	.478	38,575	0	0	0
66	.476	38,575	0	0	0
67	.595	38,575	0	0	0
68	.527	38,575	0	0	0
69	.526	38,575	0	0	0

Table 6.4   Incentive Calculations—Tenth Percentile Earnings

Last Year of Work	Replacement Rate	SSW (thousand yen)	Accrual (thousand yen)	Accrual Rate	Tax/ Subsidy
54	...	29,547	...	...	...
55	...	30,082	535	.018	−.276
56	...	30,622	540	.018	−.283
57	...	30,853	230	.008	−.123
58	...	31,087	235	.008	−.129
59	.772	31,283	196	.006	−.143
60	.982	30,713	−571	−.018	.430
61	.981	30,163	−549	−.018	.432
62	.985	29,633	−531	−.018	.434
63	.982	29,121	−512	−.017	.432
64	.474	28,676	−444	−.015	.241
65	.606	28,676	0	0	0
66	.604	28,676	0	0	0
67	.825	28,676	0	0	0
68	.669	28,676	0	0	0
69	.669	28,676	0	0	0

to this table, the tax for working an additional year at ages sixty to sixty-four is less for the worker with an incomplete earnings history.

Figure 6.13 shows the time-series pattern of taxes on/subsidies to continued work for the base case and these two permutations of the different earnings histories. The subsidy is larger for the low-wage earner at ages under sixty. From age sixty to age sixty-four, there is a substantial tax on an additional year

Table 6.5   **Incentive Calculations—Incomplete Earnings History**

Last Year of Work	Replacement Rate	SSW (thousand yen)	Accrual (thousand yen)	Accrual Rate	Tax/ Subsidy
54	. . .	22,218	. . .	. . .	. . .
55	. . .	22,689	471	.021	−.197
56	. . .	23,175	486	.021	−.189
57	. . .	23,682	506	.022	−.201
58	. . .	24,194	512	.022	−.209
59	.409	24,664	470	.019	−.276
60	.581	24,533	−131	−.005	.079
61	.591	24,385	−148	−.006	.093
62	.603	24,219	−166	−.007	.107
63	.612	24,122	−96	−.004	.063
64	.387	24,084	−39	−.002	.020
65	.460	24,084	0	0	0
66	.458	24,084	0	0	0
67	.665	24,084	0	0	0
68	.546	24,084	0	0	0
69	.545	24,084	0	0	0

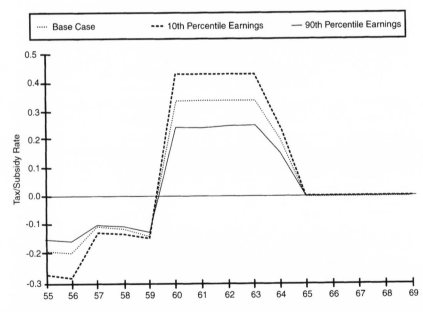

Fig. 6.13   **Tax/subsidy rates across earnings profiles**

Table 6.6   **Incentive Calculations—Summary of Other Cases for Last Year of Work Is Age 60**

Case	Replacement Rate	SSW (thousand yen)	Accrual (thousand yen)	Accrual Rate	Tax/ Subsidy
Base case	.800	35,018	−644	−.018	.338
Single worker	.751	21,164	−700	−.032	.376
90th percentile	.618	41,178	−729	−.017	.244
10th percentile	.735	30,169	−1,257	−.040	.671
Incomplete history	.581	24,533	−131	−.005	.079

of work on the small base of earnings at the tenth percentile. Also, table 6.6 summarizes various incentive calculations.

6.5   Country-Specific Issues

6.5.1   Lump-Sum Severance Payments

In Japan, one can get a substantial amount in severance payments when leaving a company. For example, a typical college graduate working at the same firm for thirty-five years receives a lump-sum payment equivalent to forty-eight months of wages in 1994, which is partly substitutable with the firm's pension. Usually, the amount increases with more years of service up to a certain number of years. However, the increase in the lump-sum payments becomes marginal when the worker is in his fifties, and the net gain from it declines over time. Many Japanese firms encourage earlier retirement by increasing lump-sum payments with a rate of the increase that declines with age. Also, they give higher payments to those employees who voluntarily leave the firm before the normal retirement age (Seike 1997).

6.5.2   Wage Subsidies

Another social insurance benefit that potentially interacts with the public pension program is the wage subsidies to working older persons, a program established in 1994 as part of the unemployment insurance scheme. The wage subsidy program intends to shift the recipients of unemployment insurance; beginning at age sixty, one can be eligible for a wage subsidy for as long as five years, compared to the maximum three hundred days for which older people can receive unemployment insurance. These subsidies of 25 percent of the current wage (W_t) are provided to those who are aged sixty to sixty-four years and receive a wage that is at least 15 percent lower than their wage at the (normal retirement) age of sixty (W_0), subject to a certain wage ceiling.[13]

---

13. The wage subsidy program was introduced in order to encourage older persons who receive unemployment compensation to work.

Wage subsidies (sub) to these older workers are determined on the basis of the following formulas:

$$\text{sub} = 0.25 \times W_t \quad \text{for } W_t < 0.64 \times W_0,$$

$$= (13.6 \times W_0 - 16W_t) / 21 \quad \text{for } 0.64 \times W_0 < W_t < 0.85 \times W_0,$$

$$= 0 \quad \text{for } 0.85 \times W_0 < W_t.$$

The first formula is the one that potentially applies to most older persons as their wages after mandatory retirement fall by about half on average.

The wage subsidy program is an entirely different scheme from the public pension, but its economic implications are similar to those of the *zaishoku* pensions for those aged sixty to sixty-four. Both are available to the same age group and are subject to certain earnings criteria, thus affecting retirement decisions. We treat this wage subsidy in the same way as we do pension premiums; both affect social security wealth, though in opposite directions. As the wage subsidy of 25 percent well exceeds the employee's share of pension premiums (8.25 percent), the combined effects would increase the net public pension assets of an individual.

6.5.3 Effects of the 1994 Pension Reform

In Japan, there was a major revision of the public pension scheme as well as of employment insurance in 1994. These two reforms are expected to have a desirable effect on work incentives for the elderly. First, the reform in the *zaishoku* (on-the-job) pension has lowered the "tax effect" on work for those aged sixty to sixty-four. Roughly speaking, after the 1994 reform, the worker with an additional two dollars in earnings will lose one dollar of pension benefits, instead of the two dollars he would have lost before the reform. Second, the wage subsidy equivalent to 25 percent of wage earnings is given to the same age group up to a certain ceiling of earnings. However, the wage subsidies are scheduled to be revised in 1998: for those who receive both a wage subsidy and pension benefits, an amount equivalent to 10 percent of wages is to be deducted from the pension benefits. We have already accounted for this revision in our calculations of taxes/subsidies after the 1994 reform.

As a result of the 1994 reform, the tax rate for an individual working an additional year at age sixty is estimated to have been lowered to approximately one-third of the prereform level (see table 6.7 as well as fig. 6.14). These two reforms in the social insurance schemes should reduce the disincentive effect of the public pension and stimulate the labor force participation of older persons.

6.6 Conclusion

This study reveals the incentive mechanism whereby the public pension affects the retirement decisions made in the Japanese labor market, a mechanism

Table 6.7   **Base-Case Incentive Calculations (after 1994 reform)**

Last Year of Work	Replacement Rate	SSW (thousand yen)	Accrual (thousand yen)	Accrual Rate	Tax/ Subsidy
54	...	33,490	...	...	...
55	...	34,053	563	.017	−.182
56	...	34,629	575	.017	−.188
57	...	34,901	272	.008	−.091
58	...	35,184	283	.008	−.097
59	.562	35,655	472	.013	−.187
60	.624	35,412	−244	−.007	.100
61	.627	35,164	−248	−.007	.106
62	.628	34,911	−253	−.007	.113
63	.633	34,649	−263	−.008	.117
64	.409	34,267	−381	−.011	.159
65	.549	34,267	0	0	0
66	.547	34,267	0	0	0
67	.716	34,267	0	0	0
68	.608	34,267	0	0	0
69	.607	34,267	0	0	0

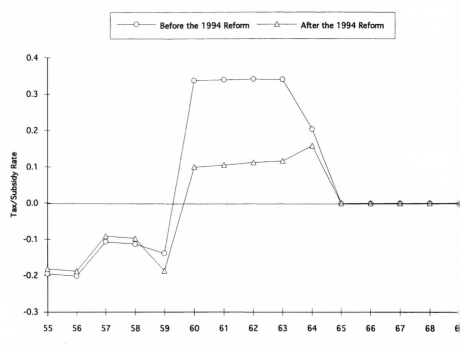

Fig. 6.14   Tax/subsidy rates before and after the 1994 reform

that has much in common with those in the United States and other OECD countries. Pension benefits are designed to be "actuarially unfair," and the decision to work between the ages of sixty and sixty-four is penalized. As the population is aging rapidly, it is wasteful to maintain such a disincentive mechanism. This study indicates the need to reform the public pension scheme to restore an actuarially fair principle.

Even given the disincentive effect outlined above, the labor market participation of older Japanese persons is quite high by international standards, and the trend toward earlier retirement has changed recently. This is partly due to the fact that there are a significant number of self-employed persons in their sixties in the labor market. Also, the sustained demand for labor should have helped raise the labor force participation rate of older persons. But the fact that the public pension is designed on more generous lines in Japan than in other industrialized countries is also important; for example, after age sixty-five, no more contributions or any earnings tests are required to determine eligibility for benefits. This partly explains why the labor market participation rate of older Japanese persons is high. The 1994 pension reform, which both mitigates the tax effect on the earlier retirement pension scheme and introduces a wage subsidy scheme, would further reduce the size in the expected loss in social security wealth with continued work between the ages of sixty and sixty-four, thus possibly stimulating older persons to work.

References

Higuchi, Yoshio. 1995. Sengyoushufu hogoseisaku no keizatekikiketsu (Economic consequences of the policy protecting nonworking housewives). In *Jyakusha hogo seisakuno keizai bunseki* (Economic analysis of the protection of the so-called economically disadvantaged), ed. Tatsuo Hatta and Naohiro Yashiro. Tokyo: Nihonkeizaishinbunsha.

Seike, Atsushi. 1993. *Koureika sakaino roudoushijyo* (The labor market in an aging society). Tokyo: Toyokeizai shimposha.

———. 1997. Labor market implications of social security: Company pension plans, public pensions, and retirement behavior of the elderly in Japan. In *The economic effects of aging in the United States and Japan,* ed. Michael Hurd and Naohiro Yashiro. Chicago: University of Chicago Press.

Tachibanaki Toshiaki and Shimono Keiko. 1994. Kojinchochikuto raifusaikuru (Savings and the life cycle). Tokyo: Nihonkeizaishimbunsha.

Takayama Noriyuki. 1992. *The graying of Japan: An economic perspective on public pensions.* Tokyo: Kinokuniya; Oxford: Oxford University Press.

Ward, M. P. 1984. The effect of social security on male retirement behavior. Santa Monica, Calif.: Rand Corp.

Yashiro, Naohiro. 1997. Economic position of the elderly in Japan. In *The economic effects of aging in the United States and Japan,* ed. Michael Hurd and Naohiro Yashiro. Chicago: University of Chicago Press.

7 Social Security and Retirement in the Netherlands

Arie Kapteyn and Klaas de Vos

The programs providing income to the elderly in the Netherlands may be characterized according to a limited number of salient features. First, there is a distinct cutoff at age sixty-five. Broadly speaking, all persons age sixty-five or over are entitled to the same general old age pension (AOW; we refer to this as *social security*). Most other benefits (e.g., disability, unemployment, welfare) expire when someone turns age sixty-five. Second, both over and under age sixty-five, next to the entitlement programs guaranteed by law, relatively many people who stop working are entitled to other benefits, for example, occupational pensions supplementing social security for persons over age sixty-five and early retirement pensions for persons under age sixty-five. Strictly speaking, benefits of the latter type are not part of the social security system. However, these benefits provide powerful incentives to retire next to the benefits provided by social security.

Until recently, studies about the incentives provided by social security to retire in the Netherlands were scarce (see sec. 7.2 below and app. B). In fact, most people no longer work when they reach age sixty-five. This may be ascribed partly to pressure by employers to take early retirement and partly to various other earnings replacement schemes for people under age sixty-five.

Like most other developed countries, the Netherlands is faced with an increasing share of elderly persons in the total population. The share of the population over age sixty-five has grown from 8 percent in 1950 to 13 percent in 1995 and is expected to rise to 21 percent by the year 2050. If nothing else

Arie Kapteyn is professor of econometrics at the CentER for Economic Research at Tilburg University. Klaas de Vos is research associate of Economics Institute Tilburg and the CentER for Economic Research at Tilburg University.

The efforts of Isolde Woittiez in providing information for appendix B and the comments made by participants in the NBER International Social Security Project are gratefully acknowledged. The authors take all responsibility for any errors.

changes, this will cause a considerable increase in social security expenditures. However, the fact that occupational pensions for persons over age sixty-five are fully funded gives the Netherlands a relative advantage over many other countries. A more immediate concern is the low participation rate for persons under age sixty-five and the costs of the programs providing income to these persons, both public programs, such as disability insurance, and occupational early retirement schemes. In recent years, the government has considerably limited access to and the attractiveness of disability insurance in order to limit the costs of the program. Moreover, many firms have started to negotiate reforms in early retirement programs because the financial burden of these programs is threatening profits.

The paper is organized as follows. In section 7.1, we present statistics about the labor market behavior of older people in the Netherlands, both cross sectionally and over time. In section 7.2, we describe the structure of the entitlement schemes for the elderly in the Netherlands and give a brief description of recent research in the Netherlands on the retirement incentives inherent in the system. Finally, in section 7.3, we present the results of simulating the retirement incentives inherent in the social security system, calculating the implicit tax on continued work for older people at different retirement ages.

7.1   The Labor Market Behavior of Older Persons in the Netherlands

The data used to obtain the figures presented in this section are drawn from a number of different sources. These are summarized in appendix A.

7.1.1   Historical Trends

Figures 7.1 and 7.2 graph the labor force participation rates of older men and women in different age groups since 1960. For older men, there is a decline in

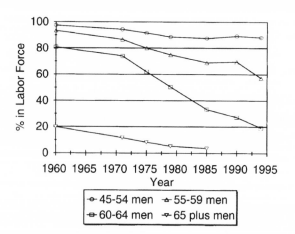

Fig. 7.1   Historical trends in the labor force participation of older men

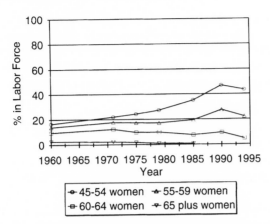

Fig. 7.2   Historical trends in the labor force participation of older women

labor force participation in all age groups. The decline is particularly dramatic for sixty to sixty-four-year-olds. In 1960, about 80 percent of this age group was in the labor force, as opposed to only 20 percent in 1994. For men aged sixty-five or over, labor force participation declined from about 20 percent in 1960 to about 3 percent in 1985. After that year, Statistics Netherlands stopped recording labor force participation for this age group.

For women, there is a notable increase in labor force participation in the age group forty-five to fifty-four (from less than 20 percent in 1960 to more than 40 percent in 1994). There is also a slight increase in the participation rate in the age group fifty-five to fifty-nine. The participation rates in the oldest age groups remained low.

It is clear that the changes in the social security system in the period concerned are not the main factor explaining the declining labor force participation rates since social security provides an income only to persons age sixty-five or older and the largest decline in labor force participation took place among persons younger than age sixty-five. Yet the proliferation of occupational pensions in addition to the basic pension provided by social security made it less and less likely that persons would continue to work after age sixty-five.

In the younger age groups, the relatively generous disability insurance scheme (introduced in 1967) offered an attractive way to retire before age sixty-five. In particular, in the 1970s and 1980s, when the Netherlands faced periods of rapidly increasing unemployment, the disability route to retirement for older employees became a very popular alternative to general layoffs. In 1968, 12 percent of the males between fifty-five and sixty-four years of age received a disability insurance benefit. From 1975 to 1985, this percentage increased from 21 to 37 percent. In 1995, about one-third of the males between the ages of fifty-five and sixty-four received a disability benefit.

In addition, in the face of continued pressure to decrease labor costs, many firms started to offer even more generous early retirement programs. In 1981, about 2 percent of the males between the ages of fifty-five and sixty-four received an early retirement (VUT) benefit; by 1987, this percentage had increased to about 10 percent and by 1995 to about 17 percent.[1]

7.1.2 Labor Market Behavior in 1994

For a more detailed picture of labor force participation in recent years, we use the 1993/1994 Housing Needs Survey (Woningbehoeftenonderzoek, WBO). The WBO is a large, nationally representative survey (fifty-five thousand households) that, among other things, records labor force attachment and income.

The age pattern of labor force participation for men and women in 1994 is depicted in figure 7.3. At age forty-five, almost 95 percent of men and about 55 percent of women participate in the labor force; that is, either they classify their main activity as paid work, or they call themselves unemployed. Among men, participation drops gradually to about 85 percent for fifty-four-year-olds and then starts dropping sharply, to about 55 percent for fifty-nine-year-olds. Between the ages of fifty-nine and sixty, there is a drop of another 20 percent to a level of 35 percent, and, up to age sixty-two, participation drops further to about 20 percent. At age sixty-five, there is a further drop to about 10 percent, and, over age sixty-five, only about 5 percent of the male population is in the labor force.

For women, participation gradually declines from 55 percent at age forty-five to about 22 percent at age fifty-nine. From age fifty-nine to age sixty, participation halves to about 11 percent. Above age sixty-five, hardly any woman considers herself to be part of the labor force.

Figures 7.4 and 7.5 further subdivide males and females into socioeconomic groups. Figure 7.4 shows that up to age fifty-five the group nonworking males consists mainly of the disabled. After age fifty-five, the percentage of the disabled still rises to about 25 percent between the ages of sixty and sixty-five,[2] but the percentage of retirees rises from almost zero at age fifty-four to almost 50 percent beyond age sixty. Beyond age sixty-five, a large majority of men consider themselves to be retired. Figure 7.5 shows that most nonparticipating women younger than age sixty-five are classified as "other." This pertains largely to housewives. The percentage of the disabled rises slightly from age forty-five to age sixty-four but remains clearly lower than the corresponding

1. These figures include only early retirement (VUT) benefits and do not take account of persons who received a regular old age pension before age sixty-five. In a limited number of occupations, the official pension age is younger than sixty-five. Moreover, some pension funds used to offer retirement after forty years of work if this number was reached before age sixty-five.

2. These numbers are lower than the numbers quoted above, where it is stated that about one-third of the males between the ages of fifty-five and sixty-four receive disability benefits. The numbers given above stem from registers. Apparently, the WBO underrepresents disability insurance recipients.

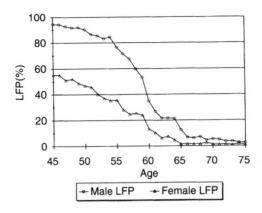

Fig. 7.3   Labor force participation (LFP) rates by age and sex

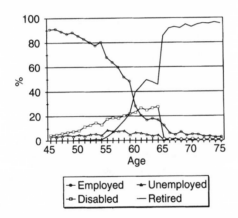

Fig. 7.4   Distribution of activities of men by age

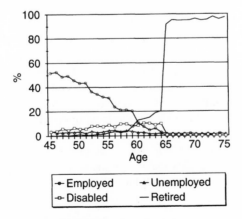

Fig. 7.5   Distribution of activities of women by age

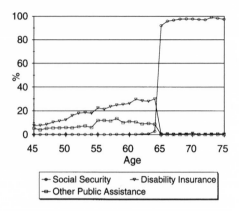

Fig. 7.6   Public income recipiency for men

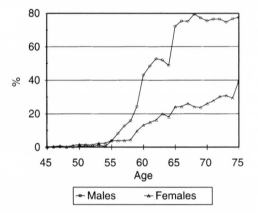

Fig. 7.7   Percentage receiving private pension by age and sex

percentage for men. The same holds for the percentage of retirees up to age sixty-four. After age sixty-five, almost all women call themselves retired.

Figures 7.6 and 7.7 examine the incidence of public assistance and private retirement income for older persons. Figure 6.6 graphs the percentage of men receiving social security, disability insurance, and any other kind of public assistance (excluding child benefits): the most important kinds of benefits are disability benefits, unemployment benefits, social assistance (welfare benefits), and social security. In principle, social security is paid to persons over age sixty-five, the other benefits mainly (in the case of disability insurance and unemployment benefits exclusively) to younger persons.

At age forty-five, about 12 percent of men receive some form of benefit. This percentage rises gradually to about 23 percent at age fifty-four and then shows a steep rise to about 35 percent at age fifty-five. Between the ages of

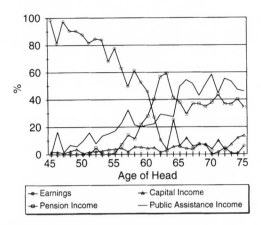

Fig. 7.8   Distribution of family income by source

fifty-five and sixty-four, the percentage of men receiving public assistance shows a small increase to about 40 percent, and then it explodes to about 95 percent at age sixty-five and above.

Figure 7.7 reports the percentages of men and women at each age who are receiving private pension income.[3] For men, this percentage increases from about 5 percent at age fifty-five to about 23 percent at age fifty-nine. Between the ages of fifty-nine and sixty, there is a fairly sharp increase of almost 20 percent to 42 percent. The percentage of males receiving private pensions increases further to about 50 percent at age sixty-two. Between the ages of sixty-four and sixty-five, there is again a sharp increase to almost 75 percent. Over age sixty-five, between 75 and 80 percent of men report that they receive private pensions.

For women, the percentages receiving private pensions after age fifty-five are considerably lower than they are for men. The increase to about 30 percent at age seventy-four is fairly smooth. The increase of about 10 percent between the ages of seventy-four and seventy-five is remarkable. It should be noted that many private pension funds in the Netherlands have an arrangement for widows' pensions. Therefore, the pensions received by women are not all due to their own labor market history.

Figure 7.8 shows the distribution of family income by source for couples, plotted against the age of the family head. Four sources of income are considered: earnings, capital income, private pensions, and public-sector income (mainly social security for persons age sixty-five or over, disability insurance, and other public benefits for younger persons). Below age fifty-three, more than 80 percent of income consists of earnings. Between the ages of fifty-eight and sixty-five, earnings decline from 60 to about 5 percent of income. Capital

---

3. This includes early retirement benefits.

income is not a large component in any of the age groups. Private pensions (including early retirement) start to make up a significant portion of total income at about age fifty-six, a portion that rises to more than 50 percent at some ages between sixty and sixty-five, which illustrates the importance of this component in the decision to retire before age sixty-five. After age sixty-five, private pensions make up about 35–40 percent of total income. The share of public benefits increases from about 5 percent for the age groups under fifty to about 25 percent for the age groups between the ages of sixty and sixty-five. Over age sixty-five, public benefits consist mainly of social security and make up about 50 percent of total income on average.

7.2   Key Features of the Social Security System

7.2.1   A History of the Social Security System in the Netherlands

The General Old Age Pension Law (Algemene Ouderdomswet, AOW, i.e., social security) was introduced in 1957. Its purpose was to guarantee a sufficient income to virtually all persons age sixty-five or over. The AOW was preceded by several earlier schemes, such as the so-called Drees Emergency Law (Noodwet Drees, 1949),[4] which provided less broad coverage. Since 1980, the level of social security benefits has been linked to the statutory minimum wage. Couples with a head over age sixty-five were entitled to a social security benefit equal to the after-tax minimum wage, and single persons over age sixty-five were entitled to a social security benefit equal to 70 percent of the (after-tax) minimum wage.

7.2.2   Current Features of the Social Security System

In 1994, the system was changed in such a way that each individual age sixty-five or over is now entitled to 50 percent of the minimum wage, with a supplement of 20 percent for single persons, of 40 percent for single parents with a dependent child under age eighteen, and of up to 50 percent for persons with a partner under age sixty-five (the percentage depends on the income of the partner).

Social security is financed purely on a pay-as-you-go basis by a payroll tax on taxable income of persons under age sixty-five. The associated tax rate is currently (1996) 15.4 percent levied on taxable income up to a maximum (of f 45,325 per year). Social security basically provides equal coverage for all persons over age sixty-five. An exception is those persons who spent part of their working life (age fifteen to sixty-four) abroad. In that case, social security benefits are reduced by 2 percent for every year spent abroad. In 1994, social security benefits amounted to about f 32 billion, or 5 percent of GDP. Cur-

---

4. Drees was the minister of social affairs at the time.

rently, about one in every five households in the Netherlands receives social security.

The entitlement to social security does not require retirement from the labor force.

7.2.3   Other Public Programs

A number of arrangements exist that enable persons to stop working before turning age sixty-five. The main ones are disability insurance, unemployment benefits, and various early retirement schemes. Together, these schemes induced the number of persons working in the age bracket sixty to sixty-five to drop dramatically over the last thirty-five years (cf. fig. 7.1 above).

One important benefit program is the Disability Insurance Act (Wet op de Arbeidsongeschiktheidsverzekering, WAO) introduced in 1967. Disability insurance covers all employees (except civil servants, who have their own, very similar, arrangements) against loss of earnings due to long-term sickness and disability. Until 1992, disability insurance guaranteed employees who lost more than 80 percent of their earnings capacity a benefit of 70 percent (80 percent before 1985) of their daily wage (up to a maximum) up to age sixty-five. Currently, disability benefits start at 70 percent of previous earnings (up to a maximum), but they fall to a lower level after a certain period (both the length of this period and the percentage depend on age). However, most employees have taken out additional insurance to cover the risk of the disability insurance benefit falling below 70 percent of their previous earnings.[5]

In the 1980s, disability insurance became a very popular arrangement, one that employers could use to get rid of elderly, less productive employees. Severe legal obstacles existed (and still exist) to laying off employees, and disability benefits were more generous than unemployment benefits.[6] As a result of this, both employers and employees had a preference for the disability route to unemployment. The ensuing rise in the costs of disability insurance induced the government to limit eligibility for disability insurance by tightening entry conditions and reducing benefit levels. Moreover, persons receiving disability benefits are now subject to a more rigorous screening of their loss of earnings capacity.

As mentioned above, unemployment benefits (Werkloosheidswet, WW) are less generous than disability benefits, mainly because they are paid for only a

5. It should be noted that, for single earners who lost more than 80 percent of their earnings capacity, disability benefits are always at least as high as the relevant social assistance (welfare) level (ABW/RWW), which, for a couple, is approximately equal to the after-tax minimum wage. In contrast to the entitlement to social assistance, household wealth is not taken into account.

6. Disability benefits continued until the individual receiving them reached age sixty-five. Unemployment benefits typically lasted for only two and a half years (but longer for older workers). Furthermore, while an individual was on disability, his pension rights often continued to accumulate as if he were still employed (the arrangements varied by pension fund), whereas the unemployed accumulated very few, if any, pension rights.

limited period (depending on the number of years worked before unemployment). However, most people age sixty or over who become unemployed can expect to receive unemployment benefits equal to 70 percent of their previous earnings up to age sixty-five.[7] Another relevant feature is that, over age 57.5, the unemployed no longer must register with an employment agency and thus de facto can retire from the labor market.

Households with a head younger than age sixty-five without other sources of income (and limited household wealth) are entitled to social assistance (ABW, or Algemene Bijstandswet [General Social Assistance Act], and RWW, or Rijksgroepsregeling Werkloze Werknemers [State Unemployment Act]). The level of the benefits is approximately equal to the level of social security for persons over age sixty-five. Since social security is linked to the minimum wage, this implies that, for employees earning low wages, the replacement rate is about 100 percent. Hence, in particular for those with low wages who are over 57.5 years of age and hence have no obligation to look for a job in order to qualify for benefits, early retirement does not involve a loss of income.

All public benefits for persons younger than age sixty-five are paid only to the extent that a person is not employed.[8]

7.2.4   Private Transfers

Next to social security, a majority of the population over age sixty-five is entitled to a supplementary occupational pension. Meuwissen (1993) estimates that about 80 percent of households with a head aged sixty-five or over received some form of additional pension in 1989. It can safely be assumed that this percentage has only increased since then. Of those households not receiving a pension, more than half draw additional income from other sources, for example, capital income. Typically, occupational pensions supplement social security to 70 percent of final pay for persons who have worked for forty years. After tax, the replacement rate is usually substantially higher.

In general, if an employer offers a pension scheme, then participation in such a scheme is compulsory. More than 99 percent of the pension schemes are of the defined-benefit type,[9] whereas the remainder (0.6 percent) are of the defined-contribution type. More than 72 percent of the pension benefits are defined on the basis of final pay, the remainder being a mixed bag of various combinations of final pay, fixed amounts, and average pay. Combining the effects of social security and private pension schemes leads to the following before-tax replacement rates for those individuals who have contributed for a sufficient number of years: 34 percent receive less than 60 percent, 27 percent between 60 and 69 percent, 20 percent between 70 and 79 percent, and 19

7. As with disability benefits, if necessary, the unemployment benefit is supplemented by welfare benefits to reach the social assistance level; household wealth is not taken into account. Hence, for single earners with low wages, the replacement rate can be almost 100 percent.

8. For those employed part-time, benefits may supplement their earnings.

9. The information in this paragraph stems from PN (1987).

percent at least 80 percent of final pay. One should keep in mind that after-tax replacement rates may be substantially higher.

Most large firms have their own pension fund; smaller firms usually participate in sectorwide pension funds. In the latter case, the contribution rates do not differ between firms, depending on the composition of the labor force.

Private pension arrangements usually require that people leave the job in which they accumulate pension rights at age sixty-five at the latest. There is no earnings test, however, and people may consider looking for secondary jobs once they retire.

Early retirement became increasingly common during the 1980s and was viewed as a means of reducing unemployment. In recent years, the costs of early retirement have increased considerably, and many firms are currently trying to reduce these costs by reducing entitlements or increasing the minimum age at which employees are eligible for early retirement. Typically, early retirement schemes guarantee an employee a benefit equal to 70 or 80 percent of previous earnings up to age sixty-five. In after-tax terms, replacement rates are even higher. Furthermore, while in early retirement, one often continues to accumulate pension rights, although possibly at a lower rate than when working.

Early retirement may be organized via the pension funds, which also provide the occupational pensions, or via the employer itself. Moreover, in contrast to these pensions, early retirement is usually financed on a pay-as-you-go basis. Early retirement usually requires ten years of employment with the same employer before the early retirement date, whereas old age pension rights remain valid if the worker changes jobs. The payment of an early retirement pension usually requires complete withdrawal from the labor market.

Figures 7.9 and 7.10 give the hazard rates of labor force exit for men and women, defined as the number of persons who leave the labor force at the specified age, relative to the size of the labor force a year earlier. These figures

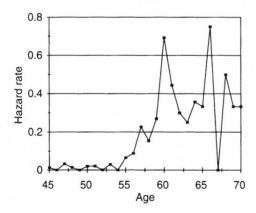

Fig. 7.9   Hazard rate out of the labor force for men—based on panel data

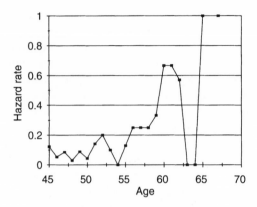

Fig. 7.10   Hazard rate out of the labor force for women—based on panel data

are based on 1992–93 Socio-Economic Panel data. Because of the size of the panel and the low participation rates over age sixty or so, the figures should be considered only illustrative. Nevertheless, for men, the figures suggest that the hazard rates of leaving the labor force surpass 20 percent around age fifty-seven and peak at age sixty, which is consistent with the proliferation of early retirement programs. For women, the figures are based on even smaller numbers of observations. Here, we find that leaving the labor force occurs more frequently at earlier ages but also peaks around age sixty.

It can be concluded that, in the Netherlands, there exists an elaborate system of income replacing transfers that can be expected to act as an incentive to leave the labor force on one's sixty-fifth birthday at the latest. Moreover, it should be noted that, whereas rather strict laws are in force that prevent employers laying off younger employees, reaching the age of sixty-five is a legal reason for discharge, and social insurance protecting against loss of earnings as a result of sickness, disability, or unemployment covers only employees younger than age sixty-five.

7.2.5   The Retirement Effects of Social Security—Empirical Evidence

Until recently, the literature on the retirement effects of social security, disability, or unemployment programs in the Netherlands was quite thin. Papers on this issue were usually descriptive and qualitative in nature. This situation has changed in the 1990s owing to an initiative of the so-called NESTOR program.[10] Under this program, a substantial grant was given to a group of researchers at the University of Leiden (who subsequently called themselves CERRA, the Centre for Economic Research on Retirement and Aging) to set

---

10. NESTOR is an acronym (in Dutch) for the Netherlands Program for Research on Aging. It is probably best compared with the National Institute of Aging in the United States, keeping in mind that NESTOR was only a temporary program.

up a panel of elderly households (at the time of the first wave, 1993, the head of the household had to be between forty-three and sixty-three years of age) as well as a research program using these data. A fair amount of the research produced by CERRA has been on retirement.[11]

An overview of the empirical literature on retirement in the Netherlands is given in appendix B. The literature brings out a number of salient, although perhaps not surprising, facts: There exist powerful incentives to retire early, and people usually retire as soon as they are eligible. Both unemployment and disability act as alternatives for early retirement. The choice between the three exit routes (unemployment, disability, and early retirement) is partly driven by the financial attractiveness of the routes. The dramatic fall in labor force participation among the elderly in the Netherlands can probably be explained largely by the introduction of additional incentives to retire over the last three decades.

7.3 Retirement Incentives

In this section, we estimate social security wealth and pension wealth for a number of stylized cases to assess the incentives of social security and private pensions through accrual rate effects. For simplicity of terminology, the term *social security wealth* will include pension wealth, unless explicitly stated otherwise.

7.3.1 Simulation

In the Netherlands, roughly after age sixty, the levels of unemployment and disability benefits (both until age sixty-five) and social security (after age sixty-five) do not depend on the age of retirement. After becoming unemployed or disabled, the worker can expect to keep the same level of benefits up to age sixty-five. After age sixty-five, social security is independent of work history. Hence, if we limit ourselves to these three benefit types, the implicit subsidy on retiring (the change in the worker's future benefits, relative to what he would earn in the coming year) will be equal to the replacement rate (the level of benefits in the coming year relative to his earnings in the coming year) plus the rates of contribution to the programs. The only way in which an employee's future income (after the coming year) may be affected by retiring one year earlier is via his or her private pension. Retiring before age sixty-five may affect the level of private pension to be received after age sixty-five by reducing the number of years counting toward pension benefits.

In this section, we compute social security and pension wealth, accrual rates, and implicit tax/subsidy rates for persons aged fifty-five in January 1985, depending on when they stop working (between 1985 and 2000, i.e., between their fifty-fifth and seventieth birthdays). As in Diamond and Gruber (chap. 11

---

11. A description of the research program can be found in CERRA (1996).

in this volume), accrual rates are defined as the change in the worker's social security and pension wealth relative to the social security and pension wealth obtaining if he retires one year earlier, and tax/subsidy rates are defined as the change in the social security and pension wealth relative to what he would earn over the coming year. Social security and pension wealth (the sum of which will be denoted by SSW) is calculated as the actuarially discounted sum of future benefits minus the discounted sum of future contributions to the programs involved when still at work. In our computations, we distinguish four baseline cases: (a) persons who receive an early retirement pension when they stop working at age sixty[12] or later and who will receive a private pension in addition to social security once they turn age sixty-five; (b) persons who receive a disability benefit when they stop working before age sixty-five and who will receive a private pension in addition to social security once they turn age sixty-five; (c) persons who will receive only social security when they turn age sixty-five; and (d) persons who receive a disability benefit when they stop working before age sixty-five and who will receive only social security when they turn age sixty-five.

As can be inferred from the data given in section 7.1 above, cases a and b are the most common ones. A large majority of employees are entitled to private pensions in addition to social security when they turn age sixty-five. Moreover, most firms have early retirement programs, and all employees have disability insurance. Early retirement usually requires ten years of continuous service with the same employer, which would mean that most elderly employees qualify. Access to the disability route is supposed to be limited to persons unable to work, which has been relatively easy to prove until fairly recently. Cases c and d are valid only for the (very small) groups of employees who, on retirement, are entitled to public benefits only.

For all entitlements, we assume zero growth in real terms after 1995.[13] For survival probabilities, we use the sex/age-specific survival tables of Statistics Netherlands (1992). We assume independence between the mortality rates of the worker and his spouse. We use a real discount rate of 3 percent. To compute net benefit and pension levels, we subtract payroll and income taxes. For the years after 1995, we use the tax schedule for 1995, keeping tax rates and brackets fixed in real terms.

To produce our baseline numbers, we consider a typical male who was born in January 1930 and thus turned age fifty-five in January 1985. We assume that his annual before-tax earnings in 1985 equal f 48,152, which is equal to the median earnings for males working more than thirty-two hours per week in the age group fifty to fifty-nine, as based on the Socio-Economic Panel (SEP) of

---

12. It should be noted that the early retirement age varies by employer or sector. In the calculations, we assume that early retirement is possible as of age sixty.

13. For disability, social security, and unemployment benefits, this is more or less in line with current government policy. Some private pension funds guarantee that pensions will grow with the increase in real wages, however.

1985. We assume that the worker's wife is three years younger than he is and that she has no earnings herself.

We assume that, between 1985 and 1995, the wage has moved with the index for the statutory minimum wage.

7.3.2   Base-Case Results

We consider a worker who may or may not be working another year between his fifty-fifth and seventieth birthdays. The results are shown in table 7.1, and the resulting tax/subsidy rates are graphed in figure 7.11. In general, working another year can affect social security wealth in different ways:

1. The worker younger than age sixty-five who chooses to work another year must pay payroll taxes toward social security, unemployment insurance, disability insurance, and, possibly, private pensions. This lowers net social security wealth.

2. The worker younger than age sixty-five may forgo a year of benefits (disability insurance, early retirement if over age sixty), which lowers net social security wealth.

3. At age fifty-nine, the worker would be entitled to early retirement only if he worked another year. This would considerably increase net social security wealth.

4. Working another year (up to age sixty-five) would imply accumulating another year of occupational pension rights, which increases net social security wealth.

5. Working another year after age sixty-five could imply forgoing a year of occupational pensions and receiving a lower amount of net social security benefits than without earnings. This would decrease net social security wealth.

The four baseline cases can be summarized as follows:

a) Persons who are entitled to an early retirement pension at age sixty would typically lose the right to an early retirement pension and stop accumulating pension rights when they stop working before that age. In the calculations, we assume that they go on accumulating pension rights until their sixty-fifth birthday if they take early retirement. Because, typically, entry in an occupational pension scheme is impossible before age twenty-five, we assume that individuals have started accumulating pension rights at age twenty-five.

As early retirement is assumed to be possible only as of age sixty, no replacement rate is reported in the table until the age at the last year of work is fifty-nine. Typically, early retirement pensions pay 80 percent of previous earnings; the after-tax replacement rate is about 90 percent. After age sixty-five, the occupational pensions supplement social security to 70 percent of final pay, which likewise results in an after-tax replacement rate of about 90 percent as a result of the fact that persons aged sixty-five or over no longer pay contributions to social security or other payroll taxes.

From age fifty-five to age fifty-eight, every additional year of work results in a decrease in social security wealth by about 7 percent. By working an

Table 7.1   **Incentive Calculations for the Base Case**

Age at Last Year of Work	Replacement Rate	SSW	Accrual	Accrual Rate	Tax/ Subsidy
			SS + ER + PP		
54	. . .	266,958	. . .	. . .	. . .
55	. . .	247,365	−19,593	−.073	.687
56	. . .	229,033	−18,332	−.074	.650
57	. . .	212,121	−16,912	−.074	.612
58	. . .	196,668	−15,453	−.073	.578
59	.910	296,367	99,699	.507	−3.777
60	.906	258,463	−37,903	−.128	1.410
61	.900	222,715	−35,748	−.138	1.384
62	.902	188,559	−34,157	−.153	1.339
63	.892	157,316	−31,242	−.166	1.280
64	.909	128,554	−28,762	−.183	1.222
65	.909	120,371	−8,183	−.064	.357
66	.909	112,631	−7,740	−.064	.347
67	.909	105,331	−7,300	−.065	.337
68	.909	98,468	−6,863	−.065	.327
69	.909	92,038	−6.430	−.065	.315
			SS + DI + PP		
54	.791	459,325	. . .	. . .	. . .
55	.789	417,164	−42,161	−.092	1.478
56	.787	376,878	−40,285	−.097	1.428
57	.788	338,751	−38,128	−.101	1.379
58	.782	303,010	−35,741	−.106	1.338
59	.761	269,520	−33,490	−.111	1.269
60	.761	237,690	−31,830	−.118	1.184
61	.759	207,718	−29,972	−.126	1.160
62	.762	179,121	−28,598	−.138	1.121
63	.758	152,290	−26,831	−.150	1.099
64	.909	128,554	−23,735	−.156	1.009
			SS Only		
54	. . .	197,610	. . .	. . .	. . .
55	. . .	183,590	−14,019	−.071	.475
56	. . .	170,062	−13,528	−.074	.464
57	. . .	157,316	−12,746	−.075	.447
58	. . .	145,269	−12,047	−.077	.436
59	. . .	134,189	−11,080	−.076	.407
60	. . .	122,498	−11,691	−.087	.421
61	. . .	111,459	−11,039	−.090	.415
62	. . .	100,220	−11,240	−.101	.431
63	. . .	89,981	−10,239	−.102	.410
64	.610	80,823	−9,158	−.102	.380
65	.610	78,045	−2,778	−.034	.118
66	.610	75,414	−2,632	−.034	.115

Table 7.1   (continued)

Age at Last Year of Work	Replacement Rate	SSW	Accrual	Accrual Rate	Tax/ Subsidy
67	.610	72,927	−2,487	−.033	.112
68	.610	70,584	−2,343	−.032	.109
69	.610	68,383	−2,200	−.031	.105
			SS + DI		
54	.764	389,976	. . .	. . .	. . .
55	.763	353,389	−36,587	−.094	1.239
56	.763	317,908	−35,481	−.100	1.217
57	.763	283,946	−33,962	−.107	1.191
58	.759	251,611	−32,334	−.114	1.171
59	.761	220,903	−30,708	−.122	1.129
60	.739	190,069	−30,834	−.140	1.111
61	.743	160,918	−29,150	−.153	1.096
62	.744	132,173	−28,745	−.179	1.103
63	.740	105,447	−26,726	−.202	1.069
64	.610	80,823	−24,624	−.234	1.022

Note: SS = social security; ER = early retirement; PP = private pension; SSW = social security wealth; DI = disability insurance.

additional year, an individual accumulates an additional year of pension rights, which increases the pension to be received after age sixty-five. However, the net present value of this is much lower than the contributions paid by the individual and his employer for social security, pensions, disability insurance, and unemployment insurance. In fact, there is an implicit tax of around 60 percent of net earnings on working an additional year.[14]

When an individual works until his sixtieth birthday, he is assumed to be entitled to early retirement. As a result of this, his social security wealth increases by more than 50 percent, and there is an implicit subsidy on his net earnings of more than 375 percent if on his fifty-ninth birthday he decides to work another year.

From age sixty on, by working another year, workers not only pay another year of contributions toward social security, pensions, etc. but also forgo a year of early retirement benefits. Their pension rights (as of age sixty-five) are not affected. As a result, working another year is implicitly taxed at a rate of around 130 percent of net earnings.

The calculations for the cases in which the persons retire on their sixty-sixth

14. It should be noted that one of the factors determining the accrual rates and the implicit tax rates is the contribution to be made to the occupational pension fund. These contributions vary considerably across pension funds. In the calculations, we have used the contributions valid for one of the largest private pension funds in the Netherlands (PGGM), operating mainly in the health sector.

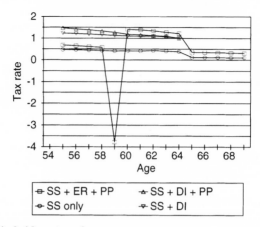

Fig. 7.11   Tax/subsidy rates—base cases

Note: SS = social security; ER = early retirement; PP = private pension; DI = disability insurance.

birthday or later are tentative, at best, because retirement at age sixty-five is virtually automatic if those involved have not retired earlier. In the calculations, we assume that an individual who works after age sixty-five is paid the same net earnings as before his sixty-fifth birthday and, in addition, receives social security. Moreover, it is assumed that he stops accumulating pension rights and is not entitled to (occupational) pensions as long as he keeps working.

Forgoing the occupational pension for a year results in a decrease of social security wealth by about 6.5 percent per year. This amounts to an implicit tax rate of about 33 percent on net earnings.

All in all, the figures suggest that there is a huge incentive to stop working at the early retirement age, especially if one looks at social security and pension wealth, the accrual rate, and the implicit tax rate. For most couples in the Netherlands, the replacement rate would be the most obvious decisive factor. Replacement rates of more than 90 percent make it likely that only very few persons would decide to work an extra year, for instance, if they derive high nonmonetary rewards from work.[15]

b) We assume that those who receive a disability benefit when they stop working before age sixty-five and an occupational pension in addition to social security after age sixty-five would stop accumulating pension rights once they receive disability benefits.

If these persons would receive disability benefits, they receive 70 percent of their previous earnings, or almost 80 percent after tax. By working an additional year, the worker would forgo a year of disability insurance benefits and pay an additional year of contributions. On the plus side, he would accumulate

15. It should also be noted that the loss of fringe benefits such as a company car might be taken into account in the decision whether to retire early.

additional pension rights. The net result is a decrease in social security wealth. This decrease in social security wealth drops from about f 42,000 in 1986 to f 24,000 in 1994, which amounts to an accrual rate increasing from −9 to −16 percent or an implicit tax rate on net earnings decreasing from almost 150 percent in 1985 to 101 percent in 1994.

The results for retiring between one's sixty-sixth and seventieth birthdays are equal to the results of base case *a*.

In this case, the figures suggest an incentive to retire into disability as soon as possible. The accrual rates and tax rates could be even higher if one keeps accumulating pension rights during disability (free of charge), as is the case in some pension schemes.

Again it should be mentioned that probably the most important incentive to retire is the replacement rate. Although the replacement rate in terms of gross earnings was reduced from 80 to 70 percent in January 1985, this does not appear to have affected the attractiveness of the scheme very much. The introduction of sharper criteria for disability in recent years appears to have been somewhat more successful in reducing the inflow.

c) We assume that those who receive only social security after age sixty-five would not receive any benefit until reaching age sixty-five if they retire voluntarily before that age.

Because they would not receive any benefit, the replacement rate is, in fact, zero. If they continue working, the payment of contributions for social security, disability insurance, and unemployment insurance causes social security wealth to decrease by 7–10 percent per year from 1985 to 1994, which implies an implicit tax rate of more than 47 percent of net earnings in 1985, which gradually decreases to 38 percent in 1994. In view of the replacement rate in this case, these numbers are probably not very relevant in practice.

If these individuals retire after age sixty-five, we assume that they would receive the same net earnings as before age sixty-six and, in addition, social security. The replacement rate of social security alone is about 61 percent. In this case, if they continue to work, they pay a higher income tax rate on their social security benefit than without earnings, which reduces social security wealth by about 3 percent per year (an implicit tax on earnings of about 11 percent).

Again, looking at social security wealth only, the incentive would seem to be to retire as soon as possible. However, without any earnings replacing benefits, the option of retiring would not be feasible for most persons.

d) For those who receive a disability benefit when they stop working before age sixty-five and receive social security after age sixty-five, there are two main differences from case *b* above. First, when working, they would not pay pension contributions toward the occupational pension scheme. Second, they would not receive an occupational pension after age sixty-five.

If these persons were to retire between their sixty-sixth and seventieth birthdays, the results would be equal to base case *c*.

Table 7.2   **Incentive Calculations for the Single Worker**

Age at Last Year of Work	Replacement Rate	SSW	Accrual	Accrual Rate	Tax/ Subsidy
			SS + ER + PP		
54	...	159,640	...	...	...
55	...	140,245	−19,395	−.121	.709
56	...	122,103	−18,141	−.129	.670
57	...	105,379	−16,724	−.137	.631
58	...	90,114	−15,265	−.145	.595
59	.905	186,501	96,387	1.070	−3.780
60	.918	149,038	−37,463	−.201	1.457
61	.909	113,675	−35,363	−.237	1.455
62	.908	79,981	−33,694	−.296	1.418
63	.898	49,195	−30,786	−.385	1.357
64	.920	20,866	−28,329	−.576	1.295
65	.920	9,409	−11,457	−.549	.535
66	.920	−1,424	−10,833	−1.151	.521
67	.920	−11,640	−10,216	...	.506
68	.920	−21,241	−9,602	...	.490
69	.920	−30,235	−8,993	...	.472
			SS + DI + PP		
54	.790	342,352	...	...	...
55	.788	301,321	−41,032	−.120	1.499
56	.787	262,126	−39,195	−.130	1.447
57	.789	225,044	−37,081	−.141	1.398
58	.784	190,286	−34,759	−.154	1.355
59	.750	157,612	−32,673	−.172	1.281
60	.763	126,428	−31,184	−.198	1.213
61	.758	97,060	−29,368	−.232	1.208
62	.758	69,134	−27,926	−.288	1.175
63	.754	43,911	−25,223	−.365	1.112
64	.920	20,866	−23,045	−.525	1.053
			SS Only		
54	...	94,825	...	...	...
55	...	80,806	−14,019	−.148	.494
56	...	67,278	−13,528	−.167	.483
57	...	54,532	−12,746	−.189	.465
58	...	42,485	−12,047	−.221	.454
59	...	31,405	−11,080	−.261	.421
60	...	19,080	−12,324	−.392	.464
61	...	7,430	−11,650	−.611	.466
62	...	−4,538	−11,969	−1.611	.493
63	...	−15,514	−10,976	...	.474
64	.462	−25,358	−9,844	...	.441
65	.462	−28,807	−3,449	...	.158
66	.462	−32,068	−3,261	...	.154

Table 7.2   (continued)

Age at Last Year of Work	Replacement Rate	SSW	Accrual	Accrual Rate	Tax/ Subsidy
67	.462	−35,143	−3,075	. . .	.149
68	.462	−38,033	−2,890	. . .	.144
69	.462	−40,740	−2,707	. . .	.139
		SS + DI			
54	.762	277,538	. . .	. . .	. . .
55	.762	241,882	−35,656	−.128	1.256
56	.762	207,301	−34,581	−.143	1.234
57	.762	174,197	−33,103	−.160	1.209
58	.759	142,656	−31,541	−.181	1.189
59	.725	112,570	−30,086	−.211	1.144
60	.742	82,177	−30,394	−.270	1.143
61	.742	53,412	−28,765	−.350	1.151
62	.742	25,103	−28,309	−.530	1.166
63	.738	−1,168	−26,270	−1.047	1.134
64	.462	−25,358	−24,191	. . .	1.083

Note: SS = social security; ER = early retirement; PP = private pension; SSW = social security wealth; DI = disability insurance.

Because these persons do not pay pension contributions, both the replacement rates and the implicit tax rates are slightly lower than in case *b* above. However, solely from the viewpoint of accrual rates and implicit tax rates, there is still a distinct incentive to retire as soon as possible.

7.3.3   Other Cases

Table 7.2 gives the analogous results for a single worker. The main differences between table 7.2 and table 7.1 above are the considerably lower amounts of social security wealth accumulated by a single worker. In most cases, the implicit tax rates are much the same as for a couple, while the accrual rates are higher because the denominator (social security wealth) is lower.

Similar to the case for couples, the single worker who could take early retirement would find it attractive to take it at the earliest possible age if he could afford an income loss of about 10 percent. The disability benefit option also appears to be very attractive.

The next two tables, tables 7.3 and 7.4, concern workers who are at the ninetieth and tenth percentiles of the earnings distribution, respectively (see also fig. 7.12). As is the case for the median, we take the ninetieth and tenth percentiles of the 1985 income distribution of full-time male workers between the ages of fifty and fifty-nine and assume that the time pattern of wages follows that of the statutory minimum wage.

Table 7.3   **Incentive Calculations for the 90th Percentile**

Age at Last Year of Work	Replacement Rate	SSW	Accrual	Accrual Rate	Tax/ Subsidy
		SS + ER + PP			
54	. . .	448,203	. . .	. . .	. . .
55	. . .	414,605	−33,599	−.075	.678
56	. . .	383,316	−31,288	−.075	.637
57	. . .	354,915	−28,401	−.074	.586
58	. . .	329,104	−25,811	−.073	.531
59	.924	512,294	183,189	.557	−4.031
60	.925	448,763	−63,530	−.124	1.394
61	.917	389,145	−59,618	−.133	1.366
62	.916	333,770	−55,375	−.142	1.305
63	.907	282,947	−50,824	−.152	1.249
64	.921	236,198	−46,748	−.165	1.196
65	.921	213,761	−22,438	−.095	.586
66	.921	192,537	−21,223	−.099	.571
67	.921	172,517	−20,020	−.104	.555
68	.921	153,694	−18,823	−.109	.537
69	.921	136,056	−17,637	−.115	.519
		SS + DI + PP			
54	.566	697,921	. . .	. . .	. . .
55	.566	636,243	−61,678	−.088	1.244
56	582	577,533	−58,710	−.092	1.195
57	.563	521,598	−55,935	−.097	1.154
58	.594	469,394	−52,204	−.100	1.073
59	.595	421,043	−48,351	−.103	1.064
60	.596	378,667	−42,376	−.101	.930
61	.598	338,622	−40,044	−.106	.917
62	.605	301,317	−37,305	−.110	.879
63	.605	267,455	−33,863	−.112	.832
64	.921	236,198	−31,256	−.117	.800
		SS Only			
54	. . .	197,610	. . .	. . .	. . .
55	. . .	174,209	−23,401	−.118	.446
56	. . .	151,300	−22,909	−.132	.442
57	. . .	129,860	−21,439	−.142	.420
58	. . .	109,485	−20,375	−.157	.399
59	. . .	90,816	−18,670	−.171	.393
60	. . .	74,362	−16,454	−.181	.349
61	. . .	59,183	−15,179	−.204	.336
62	. . .	44,271	−14,912	−.252	.342
63	. . .	30,191	−14,079	−.318	.336
64	.365	17,632	−12,560	−.416	.313
65	.365	12,684	−4,948	−.281	.126
66	.365	8,008	−4,676	−.369	.122

Table 7.3   (continued)

Age at Last Year of Work	Replacement Rate	SSW	Accrual	Accrual Rate	Tax/ Subsidy
67	.365	3.601	−4.406	−.550	.119
68	.365	−537	−4.139	−1.149	.115
69	.365	−4.410	−3.873	. . .	.111
		SS + DI			
54	.535	447.327	. . .	. . .	. . .
55	.536	395.847	−51.480	−.115	.980
56	.553	345.516	−50.331	−.127	.971
57	.537	296.543	−48.973	−.142	.960
58	.567	249.775	−46.768	−.158	.917
59	.595	205.460	−44.315	−.177	.932
60	.575	163.616	−41.844	−.204	.887
61	.581	124.488	−39.128	−.239	.865
62	.589	86.614	−37.874	−.304	.868
63	.589	50.693	−35.921	−.415	.858
64	.365	17.632	−33.061	−.652	.823

Note: SS = Social Security; ER = early retirement; PP = private pension; SSW = social security wealth; DI = disability insurance.

The replacement rates, accrual rates, and tax/subsidy rates for workers at the ninetieth percentile (table 7.3) who are entitled to early retirement are much the same as those for workers with a median wage. The main difference concerns the unlikely case of retiring after age sixty-five. Since, for high-income workers, occupational pensions make up a larger share of total income after age sixty-five, these workers would forgo a larger amount by continuing to work after age sixty-five. It should be remembered that the basic social security benefit is paid regardless of whether the worker has retired and that occupational pensions are paid only if the worker has left his job.

When ninetieth percentile workers receive disability insurance benefits, their replacement rate is considerably lower than that for the median worker as a result of the ceiling in the public disability insurance system. The rates of accrual and the implicit tax rates are also lower than those for the median worker. However, only the lower replacement rate suggests that, for these workers, retiring via the disability route is less attractive than for workers with lower wages.[16]

Ninetieth percentile workers who are not entitled to occupational pensions

16. It should be noted that, in a number of pension arrangements, the disability benefit for workers with wages above the public insurance ceiling is supplemented to 70 percent of previous earnings by the pension fund. For these workers, the replacement rate would be fairly close to that of the median worker.

Table 7.4　　　**Incentive Calculations for the 10th Percentile**

Age at Last Year of Work	Replacement Rate	SSW	Accrual	Accrual Rate	Tax/ Subsidy
			SS + ER + PP		
54	...	199,961	...	...	...
55	...	186,692	−13,269	−.066	.617
56	...	174,143	−12,549	−.067	.591
57	...	162,460	−11,683	−.067	.562
58	...	151,665	−10,795	−.066	.540
59	.878	213,951	62,286	.411	−3.157
60	.876	189,332	−24,619	−.115	1.284
61	.871	166,123	−23,209	−.123	1.261
62	.872	143,921	−22,202	−.134	1.209
63	.864	123,585	−20,335	−.141	1.151
64	.871	104,841	−18,744	−.152	1.100
65	.871	104,023	−819	−.008	.049
66	.871	103,249	−774	−.007	.048
67	.871	102,520	−729	−.007	.046
68	.871	101,836	−684	−.007	.045
69	.871	101,196	−640	−.006	.043
			SS + DI + PP		
54	.871	357,535	...	...	...
55	.869	325,515	−32,020	−.090	1.488
56	.866	294,784	−30,731	−.094	1.447
57	.867	265,573	−29,210	−.099	1.406
58	.854	238,085	−27,488	−.104	1.374
59	.866	212,255	−25,830	−.108	1.309
60	.867	188,023	−24,232	−.114	1.264
61	.861	165,145	−22,878	−.122	1.243
62	.863	143,282	−21,863	−.132	1.191
63	.856	123,282	−20,000	−.140	1.132
64	.871	104,841	−18,441	−.150	1.083
			SS Only		
54	...	197,610	...	...	...
55	...	189,610	−8,000	−.040	.366
56	...	181,812	−7,798	−.041	.362
57	...	174,439	−7,373	−.041	.350
58	...	167,410	−7,030	−.040	.345
59	...	160,898	−6,512	−.039	.325
60	...	154,346	−6,552	−.041	.336
61	...	148,153	−6,193	−.040	.330
62	...	141,899	−6,254	−.042	.336
63	...	136,276	−5,624	−.040	.314
64	.851	131,268	−5,008	−.037	.290
65	.851	130,598	−670	−.005	.040
66	.851	129,966	−632	−.005	.039

Table 7.4   (continued)

Age at Last Year of Work	Replacement Rate	SSW	Accrual	Accrual Rate	Tax/ Subsidy
67	.851	129,373	−594	−.005	.037
68	.851	128,817	−556	−.004	.036
69	.851	128,298	−519	−.004	.035
			SS + DI		
54	.858	355,184	...	...	...
55	.856	328,432	−26,752	−.075	1.224
56	.854	302,453	−25,980	−.079	1.206
57	.852	277,553	−24,900	−.082	1.183
58	.839	253,830	−23,723	−.085	1.166
59	.866	231,335	−22,495	−.089	1.121
60	.851	209,265	−22,070	−.095	1.132
61	.850	188,413	−20,852	−.100	1.112
62	.852	167,919	−20,494	−.109	1.102
63	.846	148,850	−19,069	−.114	1.066
64	.851	131,268	−17,582	−.118	1.020

Note: SS = social security; ER = early retirement; PP = private pension; SSW = social security wealth; DI = disability insurance.

after their sixty-fifth birthday or to any benefit before age sixty-five have lower social security wealth than median workers if they retire after age fifty-five as a result of the higher contributions to social security, disability insurance, and unemployment insurance made during the years they are still working. The accrual rates—the decrease in social security wealth as a result of working an additional year—are also higher than for median workers, in particular when they choose to continue working beyond age sixty. In that case, the amounts of payroll taxes paid toward social security, unemployment insurance, and disability insurance reduce social security wealth—the denominator in the accrual rate calculations—to such an extent that the accrual rates increase considerably, although the absolute amounts of the decrease remain limited. On the other hand, the implicit tax rates on net earnings are somewhat lower than for median workers because the contributions to social security, disability insurance, and unemployment insurance are subject to a ceiling. After age sixty-five, the replacement rate of social security only is about 36.5 percent for workers at the ninetieth percentile.

Ninetieth percentile workers who are entitled to disability insurance before age sixty-five and to social security only after age sixty-five also face lower replacement rates than median workers. Similar to the previous case, their accrual rates increase considerably when they continue to work, while the tax rates are somewhat lower than for median workers.

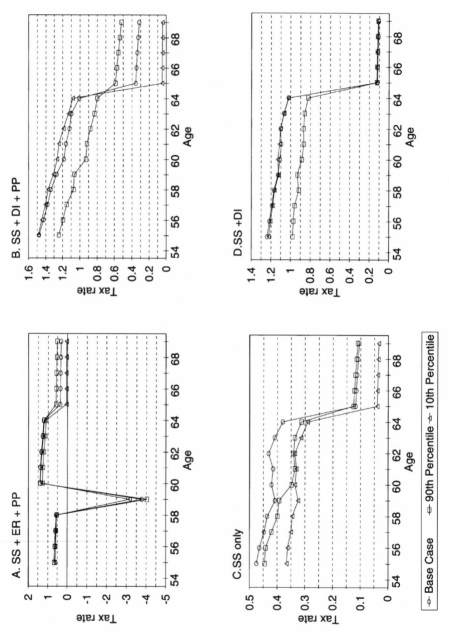

Fig. 7.12 Tax/subsidy rates across earnings profiles: *a*, social security + early retirement + private pension; *b*, social

Workers who are at the tenth percentile of the earnings distribution face slightly lower replacement rates than median workers if they are entitled to early retirement. This is because the increase in net income as a result of the fact that pension contributions and payroll taxes no longer have to be paid is lower at this level of income. The rates of accrual and the implicit tax rates are slightly lower than at the median.

In the case where these workers with low wages would receive disability insurance, their benefits would be equal to the social minimum. As a result of this, the replacement rates for persons retiring before age sixty-five are higher than those for the median worker. The accrual rates and the implicit tax rates are much the same as those for median workers.

For low-wage workers who, on reaching age sixty-five, are entitled only to social security, social security wealth is higher than for workers at the median. This is a result of the lower contributions to social security (and disability and unemployment insurance) made before retiring, which are not followed by lower benefits after age sixty-five.

The replacement rate for the worker entitled to social security only is only marginally lower than that for the worker who is also entitled to private pensions after age sixty-five (.851 as compared to .871), which shows that private pensions make up only a very small part of total income after retirement for low-wage workers.

Table 7.5 presents the results for persons with an incomplete earnings history. Social security benefits and disability benefits are not affected by the earnings history. With respect to occupational pensions, we assume that the persons have accumulated only thirty years of pension rights when working until age sixty-five instead of the maximum of forty. Apart from a reduction in social security wealth, this hardly appears to affect the results. In fact, in monetary terms, the accruals are exactly the same in most cases because the amounts paid for contributions are the same and the amounts forgone in pension receipts are also the same, the increase in before-tax pensions as a result of accumulating one more pension year leading to a constant increase in net pensions at the relevant range of pensions. The amounts of accrual differ only if the threshold for the statutory health insurance for the elderly is crossed.

As a result of having accumulated pension rights over thirty instead of forty years, the replacement rate of the pensions received after age sixty-five is reduced by about 7 percent, from .91 to .84. It should be noted that, in this case, the decrease for single workers would be higher (from .92 to .79), mainly because the occupational pension makes up a larger share of the income for a single retiree than for a couple.

Since, by working after age sixty-five, individuals forgo a lower amount of occupational pension, the amounts of accrual after age sixty-five are lower than those shown in table 7.1 above, as are the implicit tax rates.

Summarizing the results of these calculations, it can be seen that the Dutch system of social security, disability insurance, early retirement, and occupa-

Table 7.5   Incentive Calculations for an Incomplete Earnings History

Age at Last Year of Work	Replacement Rate	SSW	Accrual	Accrual Rate	Tax/ Subsidy
			SS + ER + PP		
54	...	243,842	...	...	...
55	...	224,249	−19,593	−.080	.687
56	...	205,917	−18,332	−.082	.650
57	...	189,005	−16,912	−.082	.612
58	...	173,551	−15,453	−.082	.578
59	.910	274,123	100,572	.579	−3.810
60	.906	236,220	−37,903	−.138	1.410
61	.900	200,472	−35,748	−.151	1.384
62	.902	166,315	−34,157	−.170	1.339
63	.892	135,073	−31,242	−.188	1.280
64	.838	106,311	−28,762	−.213	1.222
65	.838	99,460	−6,851	−.064	.298
66	.838	92,976	−6,484	−.065	.291
67	.838	86,856	−6,120	−.066	.283
68	.838	81,099	−5,757	−.066	.274
69	.838	75,701	−5,398	−.067	.265
			SS + DI + PP		
54	.791	436,209	...	...	...
55	.789	394,047	−42,161	−.097	1.478
56	.787	353,762	−40,285	−.102	1.428
57	.788	315,634	−38,128	−.108	1.379
58	.782	279,894	−35,741	−.113	1.338
59	.761	246,404	−33,490	−.120	1.269
60	.761	214,574	−31,830	−.129	1.184
61	.759	184,602	−29,972	−.140	1.160
62	.762	156,005	−28,598	−.155	1.121
63	.758	130,069	−25,936	−.166	1.062
64	.838	106,311	−23,758	−.183	1.010
			SS Only (not affected)		
54	...	197,610	...	...	...
55	...	183,590	−14,019	−.071	.475
56	...	170,062	−13,528	−.074	.464
57	...	157,316	−12,746	−.075	.447
58	...	145,269	−12,047	−.077	.436
59	...	134,189	−11,080	−.076	.407
60	...	122,498	−11,691	−.087	.421
61	...	111,459	−11,039	−.090	.415
62	...	100,220	−11,240	−.101	.431
63	...	89,981	−10,239	−.102	.410
64	.610	80,823	−9,158	−.102	.380
65	.610	78,045	−2,778	−.034	.118

Table 7.5   (continued)

Age at Last Year of Work	Replacement Rate	SSW	Accrual	Accrual Rate	Tax/ Subsidy
66	.610	75,414	−2,632	−.034	.115
67	.610	72,927	−2,487	−.033	.112
68	.610	70,584	−2,343	−.032	.109
69	.610	68,383	−2,200	−.031	.105
		SS + DI (not affected)			
54	.764	389,976	. . .	. . .	. . .
55	.763	353,389	−36,587	−.094	1.239
56	.763	317,908	−35,481	−.100	1.217
57	.763	283,946	−33,962	−.107	1.191
58	.759	251,611	−32,334	−.114	1.171
59	.761	220,903	−30,708	−.122	1.129
60	.739	190,069	−30,834	−.140	1.111
61	.743	160,918	−29,150	−.153	1.096
62	.744	132,173	−28,745	−.179	1.103
63	.740	105,447	−26,726	−.202	1.069
64	.610	80,823	−24,624	−.234	1.022

Note: SS = social security; ER = early retirement; PP = private pension; SSW = social security wealth; DI = disability insurance.

tional pensions results in great incentives to retire as early as possible, except in the case where the worker would be entitled to early retirement, in which case it would be attractive to wait until the early retirement age. These findings are fairly robust to changes in assumptions about earnings. Further calculations show that the results are also unaffected by changes in assumptions about discount rates, mortality, and wife's age. The fact that very few persons in the Netherlands work until their sixty-fifth birthday can be seen to be entirely consistent with these findings.

Nevertheless, some remarks are in order. First, it should be mentioned that the implicit tax rates take into account contributions to social security, disability insurance, unemployment insurance, and occupational pensions, which a worker in the Netherlands would hardly be able to estimate. In particular, pension and social insurance contributions made by the employer are often not mentioned on wage slips. Furthermore, payroll taxes are collected jointly with income taxes, and only a very well-informed worker would be able to identify them separately. In the end, what really seems to matter for the individual considering retirement is the replacement rate.

Second, the options open to workers depend on individual circumstances. Early retirement is currently a fairly general provision in most firms, but retirement via the disability route has been made more difficult in recent years.

7.4   Concluding remarks

In the Netherlands, the system of provisions for elderly people who (have to) stop working can be characterized by two main dimensions. First, there is a division by age, between people age sixty-five and older and those under age sixty-five. Second, both public and private schemes are important. For people under age sixty-five, publicly provided disability and unemployment benefits exist next to early retirement schemes provided by the employer. For most people over age sixty-five, private pensions supplement social security.

The labor force participation of the elderly, especially of males, has dropped considerably over the last thirty-five years. Between the ages of sixty and sixty-five, only about 20 percent of males are in the labor force; over age sixty-five, participation is considered to be too low to be of interest.

Combining public and private schemes, employees who stop working can mostly expect high replacement rates. The effect on future benefits of retiring now instead of working one more year is rather low. The resulting implicit tax rates of working one more year are very high. This in itself may provide a strong incentive to retire early. Yet, without further research, it would be hard to say which part of the drop in participation among older workers is due to those incentives and which part is involuntary, that is, due to real disability and involuntary unemployment. Empirical research available today suggests that the incentives described here provide the main explanation for the sharp drop in labor force participation among the elderly part of the labor force.

Appendix A
Data Sources

All data used come from Statistics Netherlands.

Historical Data

Data are from the census (1960, 1971) and Labor Force Surveys (1975, 1979, 1985, 1990, 1994). Figures are not adjusted for changes in definitions. Figures for labor force participation of persons aged sixty-five or over are not available after 1985.

Contemporaneous Data

For the detailed figures on labor force participation, we use the 1993/1994 Housing Needs Survey (Woningbehoeftenonderzoek, WBO). The WBO is a large, nationally representative survey (fifty-five thousand households) that records, among other things, labor force attachment and income.

The figures on hazard rates (fig. 7.9 and 7.10 above) are based on the 1992 and 1993 waves of the Socio-Economic Panel (SEP). The income composition figures (fig. 7.8 above) are based on the latest Socio-Economic Panel data (1993) and pertain to the year 1992. The SEP is a nationally representative household panel consisting of about five thousand households. The figures pertain to before-tax incomes. It should be noted that the subdivision into age groups causes the numbers of observations on which the figures are based to be rather small.

Appendix B
The Effect of Social Security on Retirement— Recent Evidence

As noted by Woittiez, Lindeboom, and Theeuwes (1994, 5), until recently there was "a paucity of empirical research" in the Netherlands on factors determining retirement. Contributions that they mention are Delsen (1989), who gives an overview of early retirement schemes in Europe; Bolhuis, Ottens, and Steenbeek-Vervoort (1987), who discuss the problem of the financial sustainability of early retirement schemes introduced in the early 1980s; and Henkens and Siegers (1990), who provide one of the first quantitative analyses of retirement decisions of males in the Netherlands. The most prominent study in this "earlier literature" is undoubtedly Aarts and de Jong (1992). Their monograph reports on a project covering more than a decade of research into the determinants of disability. Next to obvious health factors, financial considerations are found to play an important role. Indeed, this study was the first to document by means of quantitative analysis the fact that the disability scheme was both a financially attractive route into early retirement for the employee and a convenient way to lay off elderly employees.

In view of the tightening of the eligibility rules for disability, the reduction of disability benefit levels, and the simultaneous introduction of various generous early retirement schemes, one would expect a substitution of channels into retirement as a result of this. Woittiez, Lindeboom, and Theeuwes (1994) study precisely this point. By means of both multinomial logit and conditional logit models, they model the probability of finding elderly individuals (defined as being between forty-eight and sixty-two years of age) in one of four states: working, disabled, unemployed, or early retired. They find a significant role for financial incentives; that is, a state becomes more likely if the associated income level is higher. Simulations with their models show, for instance, that a 10 percent reduction of benefits in the nonworking states raises the percentage of individuals found working by a few percentage points. The authors also find evidence for stigma effects (cf. Moffit 1983) in their conditional logit model, indicating that the state of unemployment is valued below the state of disability and that both are valued below early retirement. This finding is partly supported by Woittiez and Theeuwes (1998), who use self-reported measures of life satisfaction as well as several measures of mental and physical health to find that, other things being equal, people who work are generally better off than those who do not, with early retirees running a close second. The disabled are the least satisfied with their life, whereas the unemployed are above the disabled and below the early retired. The key difference between the unemployed and the early retired lies in the involuntary nature of the former state. Indeed, the authors find that it is precisely this involuntary nature that explains most of the dissatisfaction of the unemployed.

In principle, early retirement can also have a involuntary nature as an employer may pressure an employee who is eligible for early retirement to leave the firm. Thio (1995) lumps together all exit routes considered so far (disability, early retirement, and unemployment) for a sample of household heads between the ages of fifty-three and sixty-three. Everyone not working in his sample has indicated whether the separation from the last job was involuntary (dismissal, forced by the firm, afraid of being laid off) or voluntary (had "worked long enough," etc.). He then uses a competing risks model to explain these different routes into retirement. He does find some evidence for involuntary early retirement, although this is not significant. Nevertheless, early retirement remains the favorite exit route out of employment. In Kerkhofs, Theeuwes, and Woittiez (1996), transitions out of a job are analyzed by means of a duration model. They also establish a substitution pattern in the choice of exit routes. When the early retirement route is available, it dominates the other exit routes.

As both eligibility rules and replacement rates for early retirement differ across firms (or sectors), one may suspect that employees and employers match to their mutual benefit. Workers with a preference for early retirement may match with firms that offer relatively low wages and the possibility of retiring early. Firms (or sectors) that need healthy young workers may decide to offer generous early retirement schemes. Thio and Woittiez (1996) investigate this issue by estimating a hedonic price relation in which the wage offered to an individual employee is related to characteristics determining worker productivity and early retirement benefits. The early retirement benefits are constructed on the basis of a wage-growth equation and specific information on the early retirement rules for the firm. These are converted into a ratio of the expected present value of early retirement to the expected present value of wages. It is found that there is a trade-off between wages and early retirement benefits, but not one for one; that is, the better early retirement benefits are not fully reflected in lower wages. This finding seems to be consistent with the behavior of employers in the Netherlands, who are increasingly anxious to change the early retirement rules as these turn out to be much more expensive than originally anticipated.

Clearly, for this type of study, the availability of data for both employees and employers is essential. Another study taking advantage of this is Theeuwes and Lindeboom (1995). These authors match firm and employee data to analyze the effect of exit routes on the number of elderly employees leaving the firm. They provide evidence that there is some, but not full, substitution between channels into retirement. This gives room for policy measures to reduce retirement. On the basis of employee data only, they find that eligibility requirements, rather than benefit levels, determine the moment of retirement. Heyma and Thio (1994) take up the issue of explaining differences in labor force participation among elderly workers between the United States and the Netherlands, exploiting the Health and Retirement Survey (HRS) and the CERRA samples. They first estimate standard probit participation equations as well as nonparametric variants. Next, they consider simple transition models. Qualitatively, the models are not very different across the two countries; parameter estimates generally have the same sign, with one major exception: (imputed) log wage has a positive effect on the probability of participation in the Netherlands and a negative effect in the United States. It is a bit hard to interpret this difference as no replacement ratios are given. The interesting part of Heyma and Thio's analysis is where they use U.S. estimates to predict participation in the Netherlands and vice versa. This shows that, if the Dutch had the American coefficients, labor force participation would even be higher than it is in the United States, whereas, if the Americans had the Dutch coefficients, labor force participation in the United States would be even lower than it is in the Netherlands. This suggests that the explanation for the observed differences between the United States and the Netherlands is not a matter of different characteristics of individuals but rather a matter of a different institutional environment. The two main features of this institutional environment are financial incentives and eligibility rules, both of which are not, or not fully, taken into account in the comparison in Heyma and Thio (1994).[17]

Heyma (1996) addresses both these elements in a dynamic programming model of retirement decisions. He takes into account the three exit routes mentioned earlier and allows for the possibility of layoffs. Except for working, all states (disability, unemployment, and retirement) are assumed to be absorbing states. He builds financial incentives and eligibility rules into his model. Having estimated the model, he simulates such policy changes as later eligibility for early retirement, raising the mandatory retirement age by two years, and lower early retirement benefits. The effects found are substantial. For example, if the early retirement benefits are set equal to disability benefits, the labor force participation of sixty-two-year-olds easily doubles. Heyma, Lindeboom, and Kerkhofs (1997) extend this model by using data on individual behavior,

---

17. The inclusion of log wages captures some financial incentive aspect, but, since no replacement ratios are used, it is not clear what to make of it.

survival rates, and private pensions and firm data. The effects are similar to those found in Heyma (1996). Emphasizing the institutional characteristics, they are able to explain many of the dynamics in retirement behavior.

The research reviewed here provides ample evidence for the dominant role of financial incentives and eligibility rules in the explanation of the low labor force participation rate among the elderly in the Netherlands. However, no study has yet fully quantified the part of the decrease in labor force participation among the elderly that can be ascribed to the changes in incentives and eligibility rules that have occurred over the last three decades.

References

Aarts, L., and Ph. R. de Jong. 1992. *Economic aspects of disability behaviour.* Amsterdam: North-Holland.

Bolhuis, E. A., S. J. Ottens, and M. A. Steenbeek-Vervoort. 1987. De VUT met pensioen. *Economisch statistische berichten* 72:726–28.

Centre for Economic Research on Retirement and Aging (CERRA). 1996. Economic aspects of aging. Working paper. University of Leiden.

Delsen, L. 1989. VUT-regelingen in Europa. *Economisch statistische berichten* 74: 924–26.

Henkens, K., and J. J. Siegers. 1990. The decision to retire: The case of Dutch men aged 50–64. Working paper. The Hague: Nederlands Interuniversitair Demografisch Instituut.

Heyma, A. 1996. Retirement and choice constraints: A dynamic programming approach. Research Memorandum no. 96.03. University of Leiden, Centre for Economic Research on Retirement and Aging.

Heyma, A., M. Lindeboom, and M. Kerkhofs. 1997. Retirement from the labour force: On the relative importance of supply and demand. Working paper. University of Leiden, Centre for Economic Research on Retirement and Aging.

Heyma, A., and V. Thio. 1994. Labour force participation of elderly men. Working paper. University of Leiden, Centre for Economic Research on Retirement and Aging.

Kerkhofs, M., J. J. M. Theeuwes, and I. Woittiez. 1996. Mobility and the older worker: A substitution of routes. Working paper. University of Leiden, Centre for Economic Research on Retirement and Aging.

Meuwissen, P. J. J. 1993. AOW-ontvangers en aanvullend (pensioen)inkomen. *Statistisch Magazine* 13, no. 1:11–13.

Moffit, R. 1983. An econometric model of welfare stigma. *American Economic Review* 73:1023–35.

Pensioenkaart van Nederland (PN). 1987. *Pensioenkaart van Nederland.* The Hague: Pensioenkamer.

Statistics Netherlands. 1992. *Life tables for the Netherlands, 1986–1990.* Voorburg.

Theeuwes, J. J. M., and M. Lindeboom. 1995. Arbeidsmarkt en Uittreding. In *Ouderen, wetenschap en beleid II,* ed. B. C. M. Nitsche. Utrecht: Nederlands Instituut voor Gerontologie.

Thio, V. 1995. Retirement: The distinction between quits and layoffs. Working paper. University of Leiden, Centre for Economic Research on Retirement and Aging.

Thio, V., and I. Woittiez. 1996. Wages and early retirement: An hedonic price approach. Working paper. University of Leiden, Centre for Economic Research on Retirement and Aging.

Woittiez, I., M. Lindeboom, and J. Theeuwes. 1994. Labour force exit routes of the Dutch elderly: A discrete choice model. In *The economics of pensions: The case of the Netherlands,* ed. L. Bovenberg. Rotterdam: Onderzoekcentrum voor Financieel Economisch Beleid, Erasmus University Rotterdam.

Woittiez, I., and J. Theeuwes. 1998. Well-being and labour market status. In *The distribution of welfare and household production: International perspectives (in honor of Aldi Hagenaars),* ed. S. Jenkins, A. Kapteyn, and B. M. S. van Praag. Cambridge: Cambridge University Press.

8   Social Security and Retirement in Spain

Michele Boldrin, Sergi Jimenez-Martin, and
Franco Peracchi

Public pensions represent the most important welfare program in Spain, absorbing almost 70 percent of the total expenditure for social protection programs, and representing about 11.5 percent of GDP in 1994. The average annual growth rate of public pension expenditures over the period 1980–95 has been 13.1 percent, about 1.5 times higher than the GDP growth rate.

All available studies indicate a progressive worsening of the financial situation of the social security system (*sistema de la seguridad social*), the most important public pension program in Spain. While we concentrate here on the retirement incentives provided by the current system without addressing the system's long-run viability, a brief overview of its aggregate evolution is useful to place the subsequent analysis in the proper perspective.

The fraction of annual social security expenditures that is covered through direct contributions, from either workers or employers, has decreased steadily from 89.4 percent in 1980 to 66 percent in 1995, the difference being made up by increasingly large transfers from the government. Even the most optimistic projections forecast a continuous increase in the current account deficit of the Spanish social security system. Normalizing to zero the deficit of the pension system in 1995, the deficit in 2010 is expected to range between 0.8 and 3.5 percent of GDP (Herce 1997). The worsening of the deficit reflects the expectation that the growth of social security revenues will not be able to keep up

Michele Boldrin is the Marc Rich Professor of Economics at Universidad Carlos III de Madrid and a research associate of the Center for Economic Policy Research. Sergi Jimenez-Martin is assistant professor of economics at Universidad Carlos III de Madrid. Franco Peracchi is professor of econometrics at the Università di Pescara.

The authors thank Jon Gruber and David Wise for their comments, Almudena Duran and Vincenzo Galasso for helpful discussions, and Luis Martin for research assistance. Financial support from the Direccion General de Investigacion Cientifica y Tecnica (project PB94-0378), the Comision Interministerial de Ciencia y Technologia (project SEC96-0738), the Fundación Banco de Bilbao Vizcaya, and the Fundación Marc Rich is gratefully acknowledged.

Table 8.1   **Annual Growth Rates of Real Pension Expenditures, Number of Pensions, and Real Average Pension (1994 prices), 1980–95**

	Type of Pension					
	Old Age	Disability	Widows	Orphans	Other Relatives	Total
Pension expenditures:						
1980–85	5.5	9.3	4.6	3.2	4.9	6.4
1985–90	5.9	3.5	7.8	2.2	3.5	5.5
1990–95	5.8	3.9	6.3	1.4	6.3	5.3
Number of pensions:						
1980–85	2.4	7.3	4.7	2.5	3.7	4.2
1985–90	2.9	1.6	4.0	1.0	3.0	2.8
1990–95	3.2	1.3	3.5	.7	12.1	2.8
Average pension:						
1980–85	1.8	1.3	−.9	.3	−1.1	1.1
1985–90	2.7	2.3	3.7	1.4	.9	2.6
1990–95	2.4	2.2	2.7	.3	−4.7	2.3

Source: Ministerio de Trabajo (1995).

with the strong increase in social security expenditures, which should grow in real terms between 2.5 and 3.2 percent annually over the next two decades.

As we explain in more detail below (sec. 8.2), the current social security system provides five types of contributory pensions: old age, disability, survivor, orphan, and other relatives. Over the three subperiods 1980–85, 1985–90, and 1990–95, total expenditure on each type of contribution-based pension has grown in real terms at annual rates given in table 8.1. The most important source of pension expenditure growth has been demographic change, followed by the widening of coverage and the increase in real average pensions. We now provide some aggregate indices of the more recent evolution of these three factors.

Life expectancy at birth has increased by seven years over the last three decades, from 69.9 years in 1960 to 76.9 in 1991. This, together with the concurrent sharp decline in birth rates and the effect of the aging baby boomers, is reflected in figure 8.1, which presents the basic trends in the structure of the population of working age (sixteen and over) over the last twenty years. We distinguish between three broad age groups: sixteen to twenty-four, twenty-five to fifty-four, and fifty-five and over. The fraction of the age group sixteen to twenty-four reached a peak between 1982 and 1987 and has been falling ever since. The fraction of the age group twenty-five to fifty-four declined until 1988 and is now rising as the baby boomers get older. On the other hand, the fraction aged fifty-five and over has been increasing steadily, although at a decreasing rate.

Over the three intervals 1980–85, 1985–90, and 1990–95, the annual growth

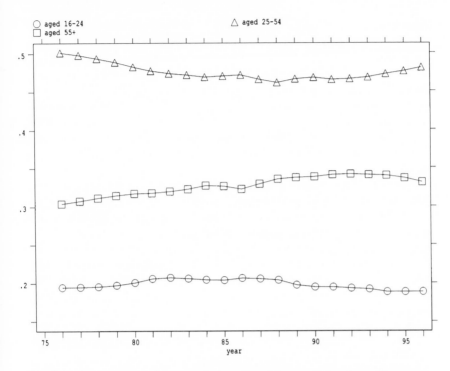

Fig. 8.1   Age structure of the population of working age (16 and over) by year

rate of the total number of public pensions has been equal to 4.2, 2.8, and 2.8, percent, respectively (table 8.1 above). As of 1994, the total number of contributory pensions outstanding was equal to 6.9 million, according to official social security records, of which 3.2 million are old age, 1.7 million disability, 1.8 million survivor, 168,000 orphan, and 42,000 other relatives.

The third factor, namely, the increase in the real value of average pensions, is also captured in table 8.1, which reports the annual growth rate of real average pensions for each group and time interval. Notice that Spanish pensions are not particularly generous, at least with respect to the European average. For example, the average pension in 1994 was equivalent to only 47 percent of per capita GDP, against a European average of 62 percent. In the same year, the average pension was equal to 63 percent of the average wage, and 70 percent of the pensions were below the minimum wage.

This fact suggests, as a tentative hypothesis, that the financial imbalance of the Spanish system may come not from its particular generosity but, instead, from other factors. The aggregate data reported above illustrate two of these other factors: the dramatic shift in the demographic structure and the rapid growth of the public pension system. As illustrated in section 8.2 below, the latter has come about since 1972 through the extension of coverage to various groups with either very short contribution histories or a very low contribution-to-pension ratio.

A third determinant of the system's financial imbalance is the loss of contributions and the increase in pension payments induced by the shortening of professional lives and the parallel growth of early retirement. In this study, we try to document the extent to which this third factor may be "endogenous" to the social security system. We show that Spanish social security legislation generates strong incentives to retire early and that Spanish workers tend to do so.

The rest of this paper is organized as follows. Section 8.1 presents some basic facts about labor market behavior and the social insurance use of older workers in Spain. Section 8.2 describes the evolution of the Spanish system since its inception and illustrates in relative detail its current institutional features. Section 8.3 presents a set of simulations that illustrate the incentive effects of the current system on labor market participation and retirement decisions. Section 8.4 offers some conclusions. Finally, appendix A describes the main data sets used and other sources of information about retirement behavior in Spain, and appendix B briefly reviews the recent literature about retirement in Spain.

8.1   The Labor Market Behavior and Social Insurance Use of the Elderly

8.1.1   Historical Trends

Figures 8.2 and 8.3 show the historical trends in labor force participation rates of older men and women for four age groups: forty-five to fifty-four, fifty-five to fifty-nine, sixty to sixty-four, and sixty-five and over. The data are taken from Fernández Cordón (1996) and consist of tabulations based on the Spanish labor force survey (Encuesta de Población Activa, or EPA) for the period 1965–94.

Male labor force participation rates have been falling for all age groups considered. The sharpest decline is for those aged sixty-five and over and sixty to sixty-four. While 40 percent of men aged sixty-five and over were labor force participants in 1965, by 1994 this percentage was down to about only 5 percent. The fall for those aged sixty to sixty-four starts a little later but is equally impressive, from about 85 percent in 1970 to a little over 40 percent in 1994. The decline for the other two age groups is less dramatic, although it is worth noticing that, by 1994, the labor force participation rate of men aged fifty-five to fifty-nine was down to about 70 percent and that the negative trend seems to be continuing.

Female labor force participation rates present a mixed picture, with a clear downward trend only for women aged sixty-five and over. For the other age

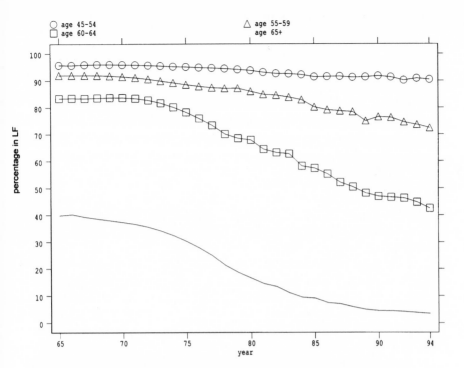

Fig. 8.2   Historical trends in the labor force participation of older men

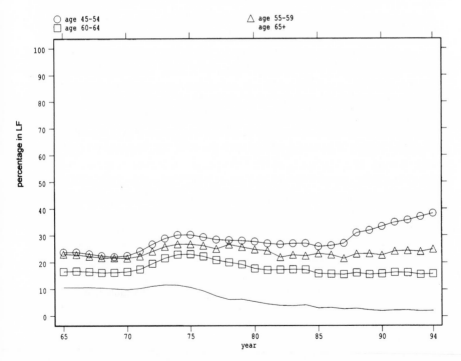

Fig. 8.3   Historical trends in the labor force participation of older women

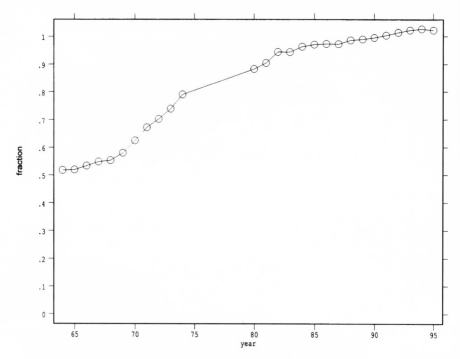

Fig. 8.4   Fraction of workers covered by the social security system

groups considered, we observe a small decline in the second half of the 1960s, followed by a rise in the first half of the 1970s and a subsequent slow decline lasting until the mid-1980s, when female labor force participation rates start increasing again, at least for women younger than age sixty.

Figure 8.4 shows the fraction of workers covered by the social security system. The denominator of the ratio is obtained by projecting to the population level the employment rate resulting from the EPA. The numerator is the number of workers contributing to the old age and disability insurance program (SOVI) for the period 1964–75 and the number of workers affiliated with the social security system (*en alta laboral*) after 1979. The data for the period 1976–79 are not reported because they are considered to be of poor quality and fundamentally unreliable.

In 1964, only half the workers were covered by mandatory insurance. Since then, the proportion covered has grown steadily. This is due mainly to the progressive integration into the social security system of a number of professional pensions schemes (*mutualidades*), to the legislation of mandatory public pension for many categories of self-employed workers, and to the widening of the coverage offered under the disability insurance plan. Historical details are provided in the next section.

Notice that the number of workers covered by social security has surpassed,

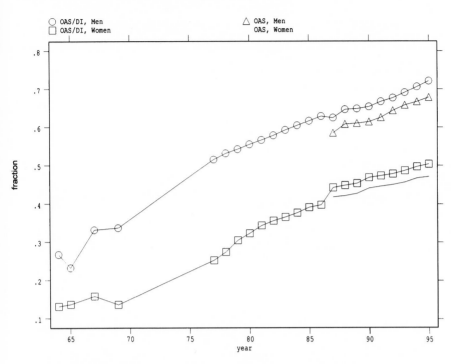

Fig. 8.5   Old age and survivor (OAS) and disability (DI) pension receipt among people aged 55 and over

in the most recent years, the official employment level. This provides strong support for the view that the EPA grossly underestimates the actual level of employment (and overestimates, consequently, the level of unemployment). For more details on this issue, see, for example, Villagarcía (1995).

Figure 8.5 shows the share of the population aged fifty-five and over receiving old age, disability, or some other type of pension. Data are again from the EPA, which asks respondents to report their status in the week before the survey, distinguishing between being retired, being permanently disabled, and receiving another pension different from old age or disability. The latter category is particularly important for women since it includes survivor pensions. The upper profile indicates the fraction of older men receiving public pensions. The profile immediately below indicates the fraction of older men receiving old age or survivor pensions. The lower profiles correspond to females.

The figure shows clearly the steady increase in pension receipt rates. The nature and the dynamics of the benefits, however, are quite different between the two sexes. Most men aged fifty-five and over receive old age or disability pensions, whereas survivor pensions are by far the most common type of benefit among women. In particular, for the years after 1986, for which a reliable comparison can be made, the growth rate of survivor pensions among females

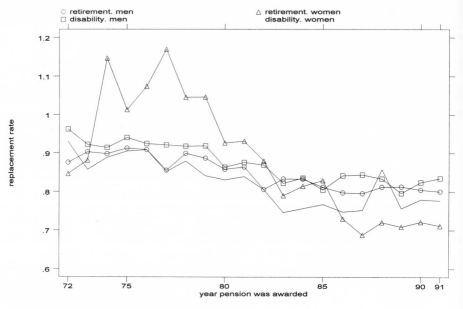

Fig. 8.6   Replacement rates

greatly outpaces the growth rate of both old age and disability pensions, the share of which remains stable at about 20 percent.

The difference between the two sexes in the relative importance of the various sources of pension income is readily understood by combining two factors. One is the increased coverage of males by means of old age or disability pensions; the other is the longer life expectancy of females, which transforms males' pensions into females' survivor benefits.

Although reliable estimates of replacement rates over time are not available, we were able to obtain some information using social security administrative records. The old age and disability pension replacement rates presented in figure 8.6 are computed as the ratio between the initial pension award and the benefit base or *base reguladora* (defined in sec. 8.2.4 below) at the time of retirement. Until 1985, the benefit base is a very good measure of preretirement earnings, being computed as the average salary over the last two years of work. After 1985, it is computed over the longer period of eight years before retirement (see below).

Female old age pension replacement rates surge to 100 percent in the early 1970s. This is due to the fact that, in the years immediately after the introduction of the current system, pensions were granted to individuals with very short work histories and, simultaneously, pensions were adjusted to their minimum level. Replacement rates decline rapidly after 1979 as female wages move closer to those of men. After 1986, the female replacement rates become indeed lower than the male replacement rates. In all other cases, the figure shows a steady decline of replacement rates over the period considered, which becomes more pronounced after the 1985 reform (see the next section). Because of the way in which the initial pension is computed (see sec. 8.2.3 below), this phenomenon suggests a continuous reduction in either the number of contributory years or the age of retirement or both. The existence of strong incentives to early retirement is, in our view, a critical feature of the Spanish social security system. We return to a detailed analysis of this issue in the last two sections of the paper, where we argue that the main incentive to early retirement comes from the generous mechanism determining the minimum pension.

8.1.2   Contemporaneous Age Patterns

This section focuses on the age range from forty-five to seventy-five. Unless indicated otherwise, the data are tabulations based on the pooled EPAs for the second quarters of the years 1993–95.

These results are consistent with the ones obtained using the 1990–91 Household Budget Survey (Encuesta de Presupuestos Familiares, or EPF), which we do not report.

Figure 8.7 compares cross-sectional labor force participation rates by age for men and women. At age forty-five, female labor force participation rates

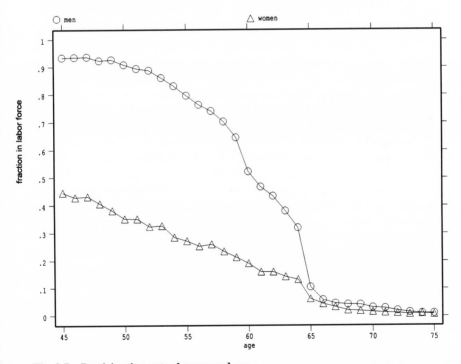

Fig. 8.7   Participation rates by age and sex

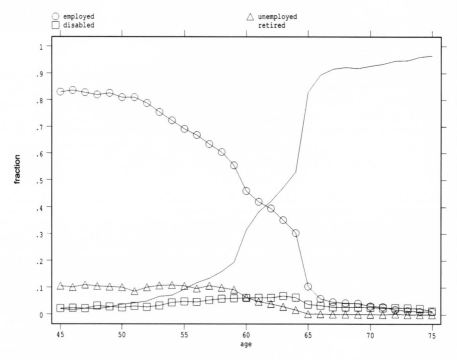

Fig. 8.8   Distribution of activities of men by age

are less than 50 percent, about half those of men. After that age, labor force participation rates decline steadily, with noticeable differences between the two sexes. For women, labor force participation rates decline linearly, with a sizable jump only at age sixty-five. For men, the decline tends instead to accelerate with age, at least until age sixty-five, and shows two noticeable jumps at ages sixty and sixty-five.

Figures 8.8 and 8.9 show, for each age, the distribution by main activity (employed, unemployed, disabled, and retired) separately by sex. Overall, the patterns of labor force participation rates are confirmed, but two interesting features appear, common to both men and women. First, the fraction of the population classified as unemployed declines rapidly with age. Second, the residual fraction of individuals not belonging to any of the previous four categories (not reported in the figures) increases steadily until age sixty-five, when it suddenly falls. This downward jump is due to the award of noncontributory old age pensions to people aged sixty-five who were previously out of the labor force or covered by other welfare programs (see below). After age sixty-five, there are almost no men left in the residual category, whereas the fraction of women classified in this category declines owing the increase in the fraction receiving survivor pensions.

The next set of figures is based on the Spanish Household Budget Survey

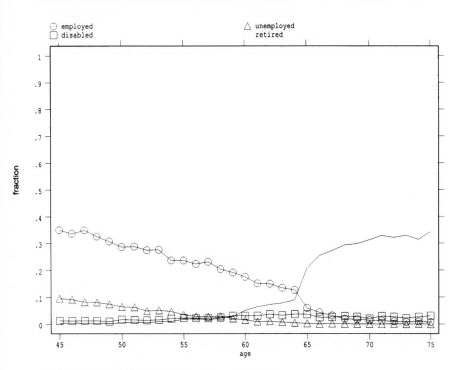

Fig. 8.9   Distribution of activities of women by age

(EPF) for 1990. These figures are meant to assess the extent to which transfers from the social security system affect the income of older men and women.

Figure 8.10 shows the fraction of men who receive some form of public income at each age. Public income, identified in the EPF with welfare payments (*prestaciones sociales*), is broken down into three categories: old age and survivor pensions, disability pensions, and other welfare payments.

The fraction of men receiving disability pensions increases sharply right before age sixty-five, suggesting a strategic use of this kind of pension to anticipate retirement and avoid the cuts that the legislation would otherwise impose on old age pensions. In fact, those who are declared disabled can stop working, collect a disability pension immediately, and still receive their old age pension in full once they reach age sixty-five. For individuals who have already cumulated thirty-five years of work, are younger than age sixty-five, belong to social security regimes that do not allow for early retirement, and do not expect any substantial real wage increase, the "disabled first, retired later" strategy is clearly a dominant one.

A precise assessment of the number of those who participate in or receive income from private pension schemes is very hard to come by, owing to the lack of data. Figure 8.11 reports data from the EPF and gives a breakdown of the sources of family income (earnings, assets, private pensions, and public

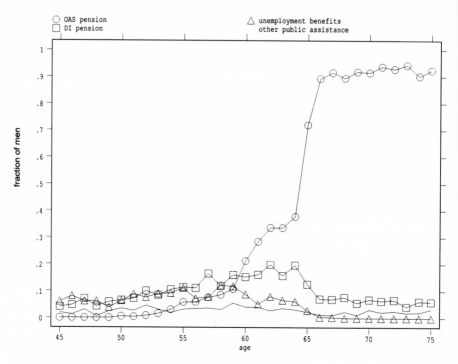

Fig. 8.10   Public income receipt by age for men

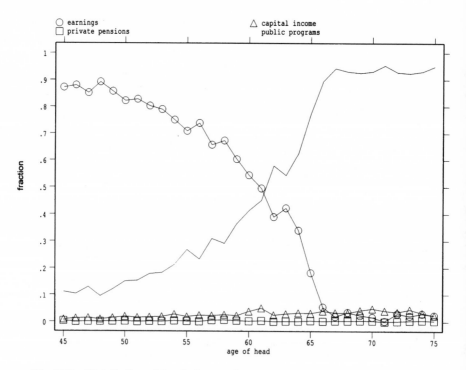

Fig. 8.11   Distribution of family income by source

transfers) by the age of the (male) family head. The graph suggests the irrelevance of private pensions. Notice that the fraction receiving such transfers, besides being almost negligible (less than 3 percent) for both men and women, remains practically constant at all ages.

8.2   Institutional Features of Social Security

8.2.1   Historical Evolution

Mandatory insurance for job-related accidents was introduced in 1900, through a bill that also authorized the creation of some funds, for public employees only, paying disability and retirement pensions.

In 1919, mandatory retirement insurance (*retiro obrero obligatorio*) was introduced for private-sector employees aged sixteen to sixty-five whose total annual salary was below a certain threshold. Contributions to the fund came from both the employer and the employee in a three-to-one ratio.

In 1926, a universal pension system for public employees (Régimen de Clases Pasivas, or RCP) was established, providing a minimum pension and the option of contributing, out of the salary and up to a maximum amount, toward a complementary pension. By the late 1930s, most Spanish employees were covered, in one form or another, by some minimal, government-mandated retirement insurance program.

With the end of the Republic and the advent of Franco's regime, a number of more or less connected changes were implemented. In 1939, workers' retirement (*retiro obrero*) was replaced by old age insurance (*seguro de vejez*). While the former was based on a capitalization system, the latter was from the beginning a completely unfunded, pay-as-you-go scheme. At the same time, the regime promoted the creation of complementary pension funds, called *mutualidades y montepíos laborales,* which were jointly managed by the Ministry of Labor and the regime-sponsored trade unions.

By 1950, the system had acquired its basic organization in two pillars, which remained essentially unchanged until the mid-1970s, when the collapse of the dictatorial regime brought about major changes. Public servants were all covered by the RCP, while private-sector employees with annual earnings below a certain ceiling were covered by old age insurance. Both public and private employees could also enroll in complementary pension plans (the *mutualidades*), which, despite their apparently private nature, were under complete government control.

Variability in benefit and tax rates across different professional groups and sectors of activity was not negligible. A ceiling on covered earnings was legislated in 1950 and updated more or less regularly after that. For most *mutualidades,* covered earnings were computed as the average annual salary over a period of twenty-four consecutive months chosen by the retiree within the last seven years of work.

8.2.2   Major Reforms since 1960

The 1963 Social Security Act (Ley de Bases de la Seguridad Social) eliminated the income ceiling for enrollment in old age insurance, unified the various contributions for retirement, disability, etc. in a general social security contribution, and modified the percentages contributed by the employer and the employee.

Another consequence of the 1963 reform was the creation of a very large number of special funds (*regímenes especiales*) next to the general scheme (*régimen general*), generating a jungle of special treatments and privileges for sectors and categories that either were politically close to the regime or enjoyed the support of a particularly strong trade union.

The 1963 act also defined, for each professional group and sector of activity, the tax base (*bases de cotización*) on which social security taxes were levied. This tax base, however, had little to do with actual earnings. The difference between the two increased sharply over time until the 1972 reform, which effectively linked the tax base to wages (overtime pay excluded).

Besides linking the tax bases to actual wages, the 1972 bill also loosened significantly the eligibility criteria and began undoing the system of *mutualidades* by establishing common replacement rates in place of the previous system, under which each category had its own. Finally, it established the principle that pensions should be indexed to both the cost of living and real wage growth.

In 1977, a reform bill made a first attempt at harmonizing the many existing funds by reducing the differences in the treatment they offered and by putting (in 1979) the administration of the whole system under the newly created National Social Security Institute (Instituto Nacional de la Seguridad Social, or INSS). Overall, this process increased the percentage of workers covered by the public social security system, as it is clearly reflected by the aggregate data reported in the previous section.

The last major reform process, which came to shape the current regime, began in 1985. Three important changes were introduced. First, eligibility criteria for disability pensions were tightened. Second, the minimum number of years of contributions required to obtain an old age pension was increased from eight to fifteen. Third, the number of years entering the computation of the benefit base was increased from two to eight. The reform also provided for a reduction in the number of existing special funds, either through their integration in the general scheme or by merging them together. This process, which began in 1986, is not yet completed as various small groups of public employees retain their privileges. Overall, the 1985 reform had a greater effect on the replacement rates than on the percentage of covered workers as the latter had already reached a very high level.

In 1986, the Spanish government established a public health insurance system (INSALUD) covering the whole population, which was largely financed by contributions to the social security system. This arrangement ended with the budget year 1989, when the whole cost of INSALUD was attributed to the general government budget. A set of regulations for complementary private pension plans was introduced in 1987 and further modified in 1995.

Another important change was the introduction, in 1990, of noncontributory pensions for elderly people aged sixty-five and over and for disabled people aged eighteen and over who live in households with incomes below a certain minimum and satisfy a residency requirement. The financing of these noncontributory pensions is attributed to the general government budget.

Finally, on 26 June 1997, after this paper had been completed, Parliament introduced a number of changes in the parameters to be used for the computation of benefit bases and pensions. The number of contributive years over which the benefit base is computed will progressively increase from the current eight to fifteen between now and 2001. The formula for the computation of the replacement rate α (see below) has also been made less generous, whereas the 8 percent per year penalty applied to early retirees between the ages of sixty and sixty-five is reduced to 7 percent for those individuals with forty or more years of contributions at the time of retirement.

8.2.3   The Current Situation

Under the current legislation, public contributory pensions are provided by the following programs:

a) The General Social Security Scheme (Régimen General de la Seguridad Social, or RGSS) and Special Social Security Schemes (Regímenes Especiales de la Seguridad Social, or RESS) cover all private-sector employees, self-employed workers, professionals, members of cooperative firms, employees of most public administrations other than the central government (e.g., municipalities, local corporations), the clergy, convicted individuals working while in jail, professional athletes, members of Parliament, and unemployed individuals who comply with the minimum number of contributory years when reaching age sixty-five. The general and the special schemes together covered 12.4 million workers in 1996, of which 8.7 million (70 percent) were covered by RGSS and the remaining 3.7 million (30 percent) by RESS.

The latter include five special schemes set up for particular classes of workers: (1) the self-employed (Régimen Especial de Trabajadores Autónomos, or RETA), covering 2.3 million workers on average during 1996; (2) agricultural workers and small farmers (Régimen Especial Agrario, or REA), covering about 1.2 million workers in 1996, of which 65 percent are employees and the remaining 35 percent self-employed; (3) domestic workers (Régimen Especial de Empleados de Hogar, or REEH), covering 144,000 individuals in 1996; (4) sailors (Régimen Especial de Trabajadores del Mar, or RETM), covering 82,000 workers in 1996, of which 84 percent are employees and the remaining 16 percent are self-employed; and (5) coal miners (Régimen Especial de la Minería del Carbón, or REMC), covering 28,000 workers in 1996.

b) The government employees scheme (Régimen de Clases Pasivas or RCP) includes public servants (both military and civil) currently employed by the central government and its local branches. It also covers, through a number of small special funds, all civil war veterans and survivors, a variety of semipublic employees, the victims of terrorist attacks, etc. The number of workers covered by RCP was 806,000 in 1994.

c) The Special Funds are the remnants of the old *mutualidades y montepios,* paying small supplementary pensions and providing basic health insurance to certain groups of civil servants (MUFACE), military personnel (ISFAS), and members of the judiciary system (MUCEJU). These pensions complement the basic ones paid by RCP or RGSS.

d) The Insurance Systems of Regional Governments and Local Administrations are small programs, covering employees of certain regional governments or local administrations, and are financed through transfers from the central government.

e) Finally, there exists a long array of small pension plans, covering employees of other institutions (e.g., the Bank of Spain, a number of formerly public banks, many local corporations, special branches of some regional governments, etc.), that managed to maintain their special treatments despite the process of homogenization started in the 1980s.

The legislation approved by Parliament on 26 June 1997 establishes the progressive elimination of all the special regimes by the year 2001. Aside from the pension scheme for public employees (RCP), the Spanish social security system will then be structured around only two "schemes" for the private sector: one for employees and one for the self-employed.

The number of workers affiliated with the general scheme increased from 6.7 million in 1982 to 8.7 million in 1996. As we have argued already, a large part of this growth simply reflects the progressive incorporation of a variety of previously autonomous funds. At the same time, the number of people affiliated with the special schemes decreased from 3.9 to 3.7 million. Overall, the number of people affiliated with social security (excluding RCP and the smaller funds) increased from 10.6 million in 1982 to the current 12.4 million.

Figure 8.12 shows the distribution of those affiliated with social security (excluding RCP) by program. The fraction affiliated with the general scheme grew from about 63 percent in 1982 to about 70 percent in 1996, with a corresponding decline in the fraction affiliated with the special schemes. It is interesting to note that all special schemes except that for the self-employed have lost affiliates. The decline has often been dramatic, as in the case of domestic workers and small farmers.

8.2.4 The General Scheme

This section describes the rules governing old age and survivor pensions under the general scheme (RGSS), the main social security program in Spain and the benchmark for our simulations. Many of these rules also apply to the

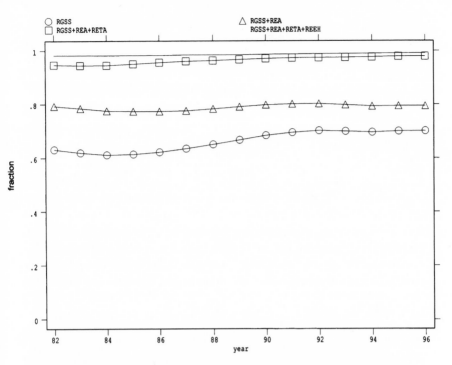

Fig. 8.12   Distribution of affiliation to social security by program (general scheme [RGSS], self-employed [RETA], agricultural workers and small farmers [REA], domestic workers [REEH]), annual averages, 1982–96

special schemes (RESS) and the scheme for government employees (RCP). The main differences will be noted below when we discuss these other programs.

Financing

RGSS is a pure pay-as-you-go scheme financed partly by contributions from earnings (about two-thirds in 1996) and partly by transfers from the government budget (about one-third in 1996).

Contributions are a fixed proportion of covered earnings, defined as total earnings, excluding payments for overtime work, between a floor and a ceiling that vary by broadly defined professional category. Currently, eleven categories are distinguished. For the first seven, floors and ceilings apply to monthly earnings. These floors and ceilings are shown in table 8.2 for the years 1990 and 1996. They are approximately equal to, respectively, the professional minimum wage and three times the professional minimum wage. For the last four categories, floors and ceilings apply to daily earnings and are not reported in the table.

As the table shows, a process of slow convergence between floors and ceil-

Table 8.2   **Floors and Ceilings on Monthly Earnings (PTA 1,000 at current prices)**

	1990		1996	
Professional Category	Floor	Ceiling	Floor	Ceiling
Engineers and college graduates	87.150	291.540	113.070	374.880
Technical engineers	72.270	291.540	93.780	374.880
Supervisors and foremen	62.820	291.540	81.510	374.880
Administrative assistants	58.350	291.540	75.690	374.880
Clerks	58.350	185.820	75.690	279.390
Janitors	58.350	164.400	75.690	279.390
Clerk assistants	58.350	164.400	75.690	279.390

ings and across categories is in place. This process is generated by asymmetrical inflation adjustments and an intentional effort to control total expenditures on pensions by slowing down the growth of the higher ones. Over time, these modifications have substantially weakened the link between covered earnings and lifetime wage and work effort, especially for workers earning relatively high wages and salaries.

Social security tax rates have fluctuated over time, being lowered in the early 1980s and increased afterward. The current tax rate is 28.3 percent (it was 29.3 percent until January 1995), of which 23.6 percent is formally attributed to the employer and the remaining 4.7 percent to the employee. A tax rate of only 14 percent is levied on most earnings from overtime work, of which 12 percent is paid by the employer and the remaining 2 percent by the employee.

Eligibility

Entitlement to an old age pension requires the number of years of contributions to be at least fifteen (only eight were required until 1985), of which at least two must be within the last eight years immediately before retirement.

As a general rule, recipiency is conditional on having reached age sixty-five and is incompatible with income from any employment that requires affiliation to social security.

Benefit Computation

Suppose that the eligibility conditions are met, and consider a person aged sixty-five or over who retires in month t after $n \geq 15$ years of contributions. His initial monthly pension P_t is computed as

$$P_t = \alpha_n \mathrm{BR}_t,$$

where the benefit base (*base reguladora*) BR_t is a weighted average of covered monthly earnings W_{t-j} over a reference period that consists of the last eight years before retirement,

$$BR_t = \frac{1}{112}\left(\sum_{j=1}^{24} W_{t-j} + \sum_{j=25}^{96} W_{t-j}\frac{I_{t-25}}{I_{t-j}}\right),$$

and I_{t-j} is the consumer price index for the jth month before retirement.

The replacement rate α_n depends on the number of years of contributions and is equal to

$$\alpha_n = \begin{cases} 0 & \text{if } n < 15, \\ .6 + .02(n - 15) & \text{if } 15 \leq n < 35, \\ 1 & \text{if } 35 \leq n. \end{cases}$$

It may be further adjusted in the case of early retirement, as described in the next section.

A few remarks are in order. First, after fifteen years of contributions, the pension is already equal to 60 percent of the benefit base. After thirty-five years of contributions, the pension is equal to the benefit base, and there is no direct advantage from contributing further, although contributions are mandatory until retirement.

Second, if there were no inflation and no wage growth in the reference period, that is, if W_{t-j} was constant over the last eight years, then the benefit base would be equal to $6/7 = .857$ of the last monthly social security wage. This is because pensions (and, usually, salaries) are paid in fourteen monthly installments, whereas monthly social security contributions are levied on yearly salaries divided by twelve. For a person with thirty-five years of contributions, the annual benefit base would then be equal to the last annual wage.

Third, earnings in the last two years before retirement are not adjusted for inflation. For earlier months, they are adjusted and converted to money equivalents of the twenty-fifth month before retirement. In periods of high inflation, these aspects of the benefit formula imply that the benefit base may be well below the average real wage in the last eight years.

Fourth, beginning 15 July 1997, the number of reference years will be increased by one every year until 2001 and could then be increased further up to fifteen years. Moreover, the formula for computing α_n has also been changed to

$$\alpha_n = \begin{cases} 0 & \text{if } n < 15, \\ .5 + .03(n - 15) & \text{if } 15 \leq n < 25, \\ .8 + .02(n - 25) & \text{if } 25 \leq n < 35, \\ 1 & \text{if } 35 \leq n. \end{cases}$$

In all our simulations, we obviously used the old formula, which was in place over the relevant sample period.

Early Retirement

The normal retirement age is sixty-five, but early retirement at age sixty is permitted for those who became affiliated with social security before 1967.

Table 8.3   Replacement Rates by Age and Number of Years of Contributions

Years of Contributions	Age					
	60	61	62	63	64	65+
15	.360	.408	.456	.504	.552	.600
20	.420	.476	.532	.588	.644	.700
25	.480	.544	.608	.672	.736	.800
30	.540	.612	.684	.756	.828	.900
31	.552	.626	.699	.773	.846	.920
32	.564	.639	.714	.790	.865	.940
33	.576	.653	.730	.806	.883	.960
34	.588	.666	.745	.823	.902	.980
35+	.600	.680	.760	.840	.920	1.000

Currently, more than one-third of those who retire under the general scheme take advantage of this possibility.

The current legislation distinguishes between two cases. The first one, representing the vast majority of those currently retiring between the ages of sixty and sixty-five (Durán 1995, 472), is the case of workers who started contributing as dependent employees to some *mutualidad laboral* before 1967. In this case, the replacement rate is reduced by 8 percentage points for each year under age sixty-five. Table 8.3 shows how replacement rates vary with age and the number of years of contribution. Notice the different incentive to work an extra year for a person aged sixty and one aged sixty-five, both with thirty-four years of contributions. In the former case, the pension increases from 58.8 to 68 percent of the benefit base, while, in the latter, it increases only from 98 to 100 percent. As of 15 July 1997, workers who retire after age sixty with forty or more years of contributions will be charged a penalty of only 7 percent for each year under age sixty-five.

The second case, representing about 10 percent of early retirees, is the case of workers with dangerous or unhealthy jobs (e.g., bullfighters; employees of railroads, public transportation companies, and airlines; etc.) or workers who were laid off for industrial restructuring regulated by special legislation. In this case, no reduction applies. Notice that these exemption rights are "portable" as the minimum retirement age without penalty, for an individual who was previously employed in one of the sectors deemed dangerous or unhealthy, is reduced in proportion to the number of years of work spent in such sectors.

Unless there are collective agreements that prescribe mandatory retirement, individuals may continue working after age sixty-five. There is no direct incentive for delaying retirement, however, at least for those individuals who have already reached thirty-five years of contributions at age sixty-five. The only indirect form of incentive would be the prospect of particularly high wage growth in the forthcoming years, as this would proportionally increase the ben-

Table 8.4 **Annualized Minimum Wage (SMI) and Minimum and Maximum Annual Pensions (PTA 1,000 at current prices)**

		Minimum Pension				
		With Dep. Spouse		Without Dep. Spouse		
Year	Annualized SMI	< 65	≥ 65	< 65	≥ 65	Maximum Pension
1985	520.380	353.530	406.000	336.490	384.860	2,631.300
1986	561.960	399.000	455.840	364.000	417.200	2,631.300
1987	590.100	430.920	492.310	412.860	442.260	2,631.300
1988	616.560	465.500	532.000	411.040	471.100	2,631.300
1989	650.720	520.870	595.350	441.490	505.960	2,710.400
1990	700.140	575.820	658.140	488.040	559.300	2,900.128
1991	745.500	614.460	702.240	520.800	596.820	3,094.448
1992	787.920	649.530	742.280	550.550	630.840	3,270.834
1993	819.420	682.710	780.150	578.690	663.040	3,437.644
1994	847.980	712.810	814.520	604.170	692.230	3,557.960
1995	877.800	744.240	850.360	630.770	722.750	3,714.508
1996	908.880	770.350	880.180	652.890	748.090	3,877.944

efit base (recall that only the last eight years of wages are taken into account in this computation). For those with fewer than thirty-five years of contributions, a small direct incentive to postpone retirement is provided by the fact that the ratio of the pension to the benefit base grows 2 percentage points per year of contribution until reaching 100 percent.

Maximum and Minimum Pension

Pensions are subject to a ceiling legislated annually and roughly equal to the ceiling on covered earnings. The 1996 ceiling corresponds to about 4.3 times the minimum wage (*salario mínimo interprofesional,* or SMI) and about 1.6 times the average monthly earnings in the manufacturing and service sectors. If the computed old age pension is below a minimum, then a person is paid a minimum pension legislated annually. Minimum and maximum pensions, as well as the annualized SMI, are reported in table 8.4. Other things being equal, minimum pensions are higher for those who are older than age sixty-five or have a dependent spouse.

In the last decade, minimum pensions grew at about the same rate as nominal wages, whereas maximum pensions grew at a lower rate that is about equal to the inflation rate. The ratio between the minimum old age pension and the minimum wage has been increasing steadily from the late 1970s (it was 75 percent in 1975) until reaching almost 100 percent in the early 1990s. On the other hand, the percentage of pensioners of the general scheme receiving the minimum pension has been declining steadily, from over 75 percent in the late 1970s to 27 percent in 1995.

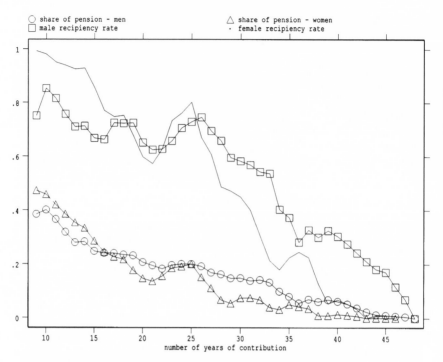

Fig. 8.13   Fraction of pensioners receiving complements to the minimum and share of the pension due to complements by number of years of contribution, 1993

In figure 8.13, we analyze the relative importance of complements to the minimum, that is, the difference between the actual pension amount and the "virtual" pension in the absence of minimum pension rules. The sample, from administrative social security records as of January 1993, includes people who retired before 1985 with only eight years of contributions.

The fraction of the total pension that comes from complements varies with the pension type. It is 10.1 percent for men and 12.5 percent for women in the case of old age pensions, 5.8 and 6.2 percent, respectively, in the case of disability pensions, and 19.4 percent in the case of survivor pensions. Not surprisingly, the fraction of pensioners who receive complements to the minimum and the share of the pension due to complements both decrease with the number of years of contributions. For example, people who retire with ten years of contributions get 40 percent of their pension from complements, whereas people who retire with thirty-five years get less than 10 percent from complements.

It is interesting to note that both indices are higher for men than for women for longer contributory lives. This result has to be interpreted with care, however, since there are very few women (fewer than 10 percent) among pensioners who contributed for thirty-five years or more, whereas women represent the majority among pensioners who have contributed for fifteen or fewer years.

Pension Indexation

Pensions are fully indexed to inflation, as measured by the consumer price index (*indice de precios de consumo,* or IPC). Until 1986, pensions were also indexed to real-wage growth.

It should be noted that indexation is to expected inflation, as defined annually by the central bank and the Treasury. If actual inflation is above expected inflation, then the difference is paid only to the pensions that are below the minimum wage. No adjustment is made, however, if actual inflation falls below expected inflation, as occurred during the last two years. Pensions that have already reached the legislated ceiling are not indexed but are automatically adjusted with the ceiling.

While this indexation mechanism could, at least theoretically, induce large reductions in the real value of higher pensions and a strong tendency to pension equalization, in practice this has occurred only to a limited extent.

Family Considerations

A pensioner receives a fixed annual allowance for each dependent child who is younger than age eighteen or disabled. In 1996, this allowance was equal to PTA 408,840, corresponding to about 45 percent of the annualized minimum wage. In addition, the minimum pension is increased by a fixed amount if a pensioner has a dependent spouse (table 8.4 above).

Survivors (spouse, children, other relatives) may receive a fraction of the benefit base of the deceased if the latter was a pensioner or died before retirement after contributing for at least five hundred days in the last five years. The benefit base is computed differently in the two cases. If the deceased was a pensioner, the benefit base coincides with the pension. If the deceased was a worker, it is computed as an average of covered earnings over an uninterrupted period of two years chosen by the beneficiary among the last seven years immediately before death. If death occurred because of a work accident or an illness contracted at work or because of working conditions, then the benefit base coincides with last earnings.

The surviving spouse gets 45 percent of the benefit base of the deceased. In the case of divorce, the pension is divided between the various spouses according to the length of their marriage with the deceased. Such a pension can be received in combination with labor income and any other old age or disability pension, but it is lost if the spouse remarries. As a point of interest, we point out here that the remarriage rate among Spanish widows is particularly low compared to the remarriage rate in other countries.

Surviving children get 20 percent each of the benefit base of the principal as long as they are younger than age eighteen or unable to work and stay unmarried. An orphan who is a sole beneficiary may receive up to 65 percent of the benefit base. If there are several surviving children, the sum of the pensions to the surviving spouse (if any) and children cannot exceed 100 percent of the benefit base.

A peculiarity of the Spanish system is the "pension in favor of family members." This pension entitles other surviving relatives (e.g., parents, grandparents, siblings, nephews, etc.) to 20 percent of the benefit base of the principal if they satisfy certain eligibility conditions (they are older than age forty-five, do not have a spouse, do not have other means of subsistence, have been living with and depending economically on the deceased for the last two years). To this pension one may add the 45 percent survivor pension if there is no surviving spouse or eligible surviving children.

There are specific minimum pensions for the different types of survivorship. In particular, the minimum pension to a surviving spouse was raised in 1992 and is now equal to the minimum old age pension for a person without a dependent spouse.

8.2.5 Special Schemes

In this section, we sketch the main differences between the general and the special schemes. Whereas rules and regulations for sailors and coal miners are very similar to the ones for the general scheme, special rules apply to the self-employed, farmers, agricultural workers, domestic servants, and a few other categories not discussed here, such as part-time workers, artists, traveling salespeople, and bullfighters. Besides differences in the social security tax rate and the definition of covered earnings, an important difference is the fact that those affiliated with the special schemes have no early retirement option (an exception is made for miners and sailors).

The rest of this section focuses on the special schemes for self-employed workers (RETA) and for farmers (REA), which together represent 93 percent of those affiliated with the special schemes and 86 percent of the pensions that they pay out.

The Self-Employed

While the social security tax rate is the same for RETA and the general scheme (28.3 percent in 1996), covered earnings are computed differently as the self-employed are essentially free to choose their covered earnings between a floor and a ceiling legislated annually. Not surprisingly in the light of the strong progressivity of Spanish personal income taxes, a suspiciously large proportion of self-employed workers report earnings equal to the legislated floor.

In 1996, the floor and the ceiling were equal to PTA 101,940 and PTA 374,880 per month, respectively, corresponding to 1.6 and 5.8 times the minimum wage and 0.5 and 1.9 times average earnings in manufacturing and services. For a self-employed individual aged fifty or over, the ceiling was only about half, namely, PTA 195,000 per month, which was about equal to average monthly earnings.

A crucial difference with respect to the general scheme is that, under RETA, receipt of an old age pension is compatible with maintaining self-employed status. This provision effectively configures RETA pensions as pure old age pensions, completely independent from labor market participation decisions.

Some other important provisions are the following. RETA requires only at least five years of contributions in the ten years immediately before the death of the principal in order to qualify for survivor pensions. Under RETA, the latter is 50 percent of the benefit base. If the principal was not a pensioner at the time of death, the benefit base is computed as the average of covered earnings over an uninterrupted period of five years chosen by the beneficiary among the last ten years before the death of the principal.

Farmers

In this case, both the social security tax rate and covered earnings differ with respect to the general scheme. Self-employed farmers pay 18.75 percent of a tax base that is legislated annually and is unrelated to actual earnings. In 1996, this was equal to PTA 80,490 per month, corresponding to 1.24 times the minimum wage and about 40 percent of average monthly earnings in the manufacturing and service sectors.

Farm employees, instead, pay 11.5 percent of a monthly base that depends on their professional category and is legislated yearly. In addition, for each day of work, their employer must pay 15.5 percent of a daily base that also varies by professional category and is legislated annually.

8.2.6   Government Employees

We now describe briefly the main differences between the general scheme and RCP, the pension fund for the employees of the central government.

Public servants are divided into five categories, A–E, corresponding loosely to decreasing schooling levels: A is college graduates (*doctor, licenciado, arquitecto o equivalente*), B people holding certain kinds of college diplomas (*ingeniero técnico, diplomado, etc.*), C high school graduates (*bachiller o equivalente*), D junior high school diplomas (*graduado escolar o equivalente*), and E individuals with lower education levels (*certificado de escolaridad*). There were many more categories before the 1985 reform. For each of these categories, the budget law defines every year a theoretical social security wage (*haber regulador*) that is used to compute social security contributions and pensions. The implied wage scale has remained relatively constant since 1985. So, for example, the ratio of level A to level E wages was equal to 2.39 between 1985 and 1989, dropped to 2.33 in 1990, and rebounced and remained constant at 2.45 afterward.

Social security contributions are the sum of three parts, each proportional to the legislated covered wage, according to proportionality factors legislated annually: (*a*) *derechos pasivos* (3.86 percent in 1995); (*b*) *cuota mensual de mutualidades* (1.89 percent in 1995); and (*c*) *aportación del estado* (paid by the government, it varies between 6 and 10 percent depending on the sector of the administration).

To parallel this three-part contribution structure, actual pensions are computed by adding up three sources of benefits: (*a*) the basic pension (*derechos pasivos*); (*b*) a portion directed to the pensioner's family (*ayuda familiar*); and (*c*) a complementary portion coming from the various *mutualidades* (ISFAS, MUFACE, MUCEJU).

The basic monthly pension of a public servant who retires in month *t* after contributing for *n* years to RCP is computed as $P_t = \alpha_n BR_t$, where the dependence of α_n on number of years worked has been changed quite frequently during the last ten years. For $n \geq 15$, the last table of proportionality factors, legislated in 1990, can be reasonably (but not exactly) approximated by

$$\alpha_n = \min[1, 1 - .0366(35 - n)].$$

The differences with respect to the general scheme are various. First, while entitlement to a pension still requires at least fifteen years of contributions, the replacement rate (the ratio of the pension to the benefit base) increases somewhat irregularly with seniority, up to 100 percent after thirty-five years. So, for example, fifteen years of service give the right to a pension equal to only 26.92 percent of the benefit base, against 60 percent of the general scheme. After thirty years, the same ratio has increased to 81.73 percent, against 90 percent for the general scheme. Historically, this replacement ratio has been unstable as it can be modified year by year through the budget law.

Second, the benefit base is computed as a weighted average of covered earnings, on which the worker paid the contributions, with weights equal to the percentage of the career spent at each level, that is,

$$BR_t = \sum_i p_i H_{it},$$

where p_i is the fraction of the career spent on level *i*, and H_{it} are the covered earnings corresponding to level *i*, as determined by the current law at time *t*.

Third, unlike the general scheme, RCP imposes mandatory retirement at age sixty-five. Exceptions are made for a few special categories, such as university professors and judges. On the other hand, RCP allows for early retirement at age sixty, without any penalty for public servants with at least thirty years of service (twenty for military personnel).

A fourth important difference with respect to the general scheme is compatibility between RCP pension receipt and income from continuing to work. In a number of special cases, RCP pensioners are allowed to keep a public-sector occupation as long as this does not provide them with a "regular flow of income" (e.g., this is the case of members of legislative bodies). More important, the legislation allows RCP pensions to be cumulated with earnings from employment in the private sector.

It should be noted that those who leave public administration after contributing the minimum number of years, but before reaching the retirement age, can claim an RCP pension once they reach age sixty-five. The benefit base used to compute such a pension does not refer to the time when the individual left public administration but is instead the one legislated for the year the individual turns sixty-five. Furthermore, any future modification in the law will have no effect on the pensions that are already being paid. The latter will be forever regulated by the legislation of the time when the individual earned the right to the RCP pension.

When a public servant is dismissed because of disability (and therefore starts drawing a disability pension) or dies (and the survivors are therefore entitled to a pension), the missing years between the person's age at the time of disability or death and sixty-five are counted as actual years of service in the computation of either the disability or the survivor pension. Should the disability be caused by an accident while on duty, the disability pension is doubled.

8.2.7   Disability Pensions

The social security system provides insurance against both temporary and permanent illness or disability.

Temporary Illness or Disability

The subsidy for temporary illness or disability (*incapacidad laboral transitoria*) was not regulated by the 1985 reform, and its provisions have undergone frequent changes.

Eligibility requires affiliation with the social security system for a minimum period that depends on the nature of the covered risk. Common illness requires only 180 days of contributions during the last five years, paid maternity/paternity leave requires at least nine months before the date of delivery and 180 days during the last twelve months, and no minimum eligibility criterion is imposed for work-related accidents or illnesses.

The benefit base depends on actual earnings during the last twelve months. In the case of common illness or an accident unrelated to work, the subsidy is equal to 60 percent of the benefit base for each day of absence between the fourth and the twentieth and to 75 percent of the benefit base afterward until the maximum period is reached. It is always equal to 75 percent in case of work-related accident or illness and maternity/paternity (only one of the partners being allowed to use the subsidy per each child). The maximum period for which the subsidy can be received is eighteen months, after which the worker must either return to work or be classified as permanently disabled.

Contributory Disability Pensions

Permanent disability pensions have played an important role in allowing Spanish workers to retire at ages younger than sixty. In particular, they were used extensively during the late 1970s and early 1980s as an early retirement mechanism for workers in restructuring industries (shipbuilding, steel, mining, etc.) or as substitutes for long-term unemployment subsidies in depressed regions. The total disability rate (as a percentage of the workforce) doubled in less than ten years, from about 0.7 percent in 1975 to 1.5 percent in 1983. By tightening the requirements, the 1985 reform managed to bring the phenomenon under partial control. Disability rates have since decreased, stabilizing at around 0.6 percent.

Disability pensions are divided into contributory and noncontributory. This section deals with contributory pensions. Noncontributory pensions are dealt with in the next section.

Eligibility and pension amounts depend on the level of disability. The 1985 reform distinguished four levels of permanent disability characterized by increasing severity. Since then, the legislation has formally reduced these levels to three but has also created a special subcase of the first level with the explicit purpose of using the disability funds to subsidize the dismissal of old workers from certain sectors or geographic areas.

The first level (*incapacidad permanente total para la profesión habitual,* or IPT) corresponds to inability to do the usual job. A special subcase (*incapacidad permanente total cualificada para la profesión habitual,* or IPTC) applies only to employees older than age fifty-five who are in particular socioeconomic situations. The second level (*incapacidad permanente absoluta,* or IPA) corresponds to inability to do any kind of job. The third level (*gran invalidez,* or GI) requires, in addition, continued attendance by other persons in order to carry out basic vital functions.

When disability is caused by an ordinary illness, eligibility for a pension requires from five to fifteen years of contributions, depending on the age at which the person fell ill and the seriousness of the disability. There is no contribution requirement when the disability is caused by an accident, regardless of whether it is work related, or by an illness contracted at work.

Eligibility requirements are fairly complicated. We try here to streamline their presentation. In the cases of IPA or GI, fifteen years of contributions are required, of which at least three must be during the last ten years. For the other two cases (IPT and IPTC), eligibility depends on age. For persons aged twenty-six or younger, the requirement is half the number of years between age sixteen and the age when disability began. For persons older than age twenty-six, the requirement is either five years or a fourth of the number of years between age twenty and the age when disability began, whichever is largest. Furthermore, at least a fifth of the required years of contributions must have occurred during the last ten years.

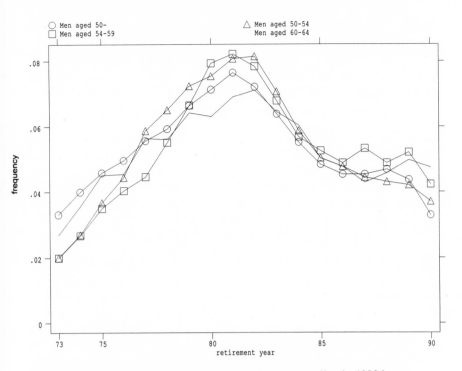

Fig. 8.14   Distribution of male disability pensions outstanding in 1993 by age group and year of award

The benefit base depends on the source of disability. In the case of ordinary illness, it is computed as for old age pensions. For accidents unrelated to work, it is the average annual wage over a period of twenty-four consecutive months chosen by the person within the last seven years of work. For work-related accidents or illnesses, it is the average wage in the last year of work.

The pension equals 55 percent of the benefit base under IPT and increases to 75 percent under IPTC. In the case of IPA, it is equal to 100 percent of the benefit base, whereas for GI it is equal to 100 percent of the benefit base plus another 50 percent covering the person taking care of the disabled individual.

Disability pensions are indexed to inflation like the other RGSS pensions. Unlike the latter, however, disability pensions may be kept while earning income from a job different from the one under which the disability (even a complete one) was contracted.

We mentioned earlier that disability pensions were awarded very generously until 1985. This is illustrated in figure 8.14, which reports the distribution of male disability pensions outstanding in 1993, by age and year of award, on the basis of social security administrative records. For all age groups, awards peak between 1980 and 1982, when the growth rate of the number of outstanding disability pensions reached 6 percent per year. Between 20 and 25 percent

Table 8.5   Percentage Ratio between the Number of Disability Pensions Paid and the Number of Workers Covered by the Various Social Security Programs, 1981–94: General Fund (RGSS), Self-Employed (RETA), Agricultural Employees (REAa), Farmers (REAb), Coal Miners (REMC), Sailors (RETM), Domestic Workers (REEH)

Year	RGSS	RETA	REAa	REAb	REMC	RETM	REEH	Total
1981	.79	1.06	2.29	2.14	2.33	...	2.32	1.10
1982	1.15	1.06	3.17	2.34	3.61	...	2.79	1.45
1983	1.31	1.03	3.02	2.33	3.21	...	2.88	1.54
1984	1.17	.83	2.41	2.14	2.91	...	2.57	1.33
1985	.72	.58	1.61	1.80	1.52	...	2.48	.90
1986	.62	.57	1.67	1.97	1.80	1.58	1.93	.83
1987	.55	.51	1.34	1.84	1.42	1.34	2.00	.72
1988	.52	.51	1.21	2.06	1.69	1.45	2.21	.70
1989	.43	.43	1.13	1.95	1.64	1.12	2.25	.60
1990	.44	.51	1.21	2.38	2.36	1.22	2.90	.62
1991	.41	.57	1.30	2.58	2.18	1.18	3.30	.62
1992	.47	.64	1.37	2.53	2.37	1.26	3.12	.67
1993	.47	.68	1.25	2.15	2.29	1.25	2.85	.64
1994	.44	.77	1.35	1.91	2.03	1.24	2.75	.61

of the outstanding disability pensions were granted during those years, which correspond to the most severe postwar recession in the Spanish economy. For women, a very similar picture is obtained.

The extent to which disability pensions may have been used as instruments to reduce employment in certain sectors of the Spanish economy is evident in table 8.5, which reports the percentage ratio between the number of disability pensions paid and the number of workers covered by the various social security programs for the years between 1981 and 1994.

While certain sectors are clearly characterized by a higher risk of work-related accidents, this fact cannot explain the persistently higher percentage of the disabled among domestic or agricultural workers or the strong countercyclic pattern of the disability ratios reported.

A second interesting element is the age distribution of new recipients of disability pensions. In 1994, for example, the average age of new recipients was 51.7 years, on average, with values of 50 for RGSS and 54, 55.6, and 57.9, respectively, for RETA, REA, and REEH. Table 8.6 shows, for each social security program and each level of disability, the fraction of new disability pensions awarded in 1994 to individuals aged fifty-five and over.

Criteria are now much more strict, although court rulings often recognize claims to a pension that have been rejected by the social security administration. At least in principle, a person receiving a disability pension may be subject to periodic checks in order to determine whether the conditions for a pension are still met.

| Table 8.6 | Fraction of New Disability Pensions Awarded (year 1994) to Individuals Aged 55 and over by Social Security Program and Level of Disability: Inability to Do the Usual Job (IPT), Inability to Do Any Kind of Job (IPA), Complete Inability (GI) |

Program	IPT	IPA	GI
RGSS	4.0	43.5	39.3
RETA	53.4	64.4	49.3
REA	58.5	63.7	68.9
REMC	.3	48.6	60.0
RETM	14.9	32.1	32.0
REEH	25.0	75.0	80.6

Noncontributory Disability Pensions

Noncontributory disability pensions are granted, through a special branch of the social security system called Instituto Nacional de Servicios Sociales (INSERSO), to disabled people aged eighteen to sixty-five who are ineligible for contributory pensions, have been legal residents of Spain for at least five years (of which at least two are immediately before applying for such a pension), and whose annual income is below a certain threshold. INSERSO also provides its beneficiaries with basic health insurance, free medicine, and other complementary social services.

In 1990, a number of preexisting noncontributory programs were rationalized and unified under INSERSO. As of 1995, the total annual budget of INSERSO was PTA 418 billion, of which 64 percent was direct government transfers, while the rest was financed through social security contributions. Just to give an idea of the relative magnitude of this program, which represents about 0.7 percent of Spanish GDP, notice that total expenditures for the public university system in 1995 were only slightly higher, at about 0.9 percent of GDP.

Of the total annual budget of INSERSO in 1995, about 39 percent was spent in either direct monetary transfers or services to disabled individuals, about the same amount went to noncontributory old age pensions (see the next section), 20 percent was transferred to the regional governments (*comunidades autónomas*) providing similar services, and 2 percent covered INSERSO administrative costs.

The basic annual disability pension paid by INSERSO in 1996 was PTA 498,120, corresponding to 55 percent of the minimum wage (SMI) and 19 percent of average monthly earnings during the same year. Such amounts may vary according to the economic and physical conditions of the individual and may be increased up to 50 percent.

At the end of 1995, there were about 163,000 recipients of noncontributory disability pensions residing in Spain, of which 36 percent were males and 64 percent females. Another 198,000 people (22 percent males and 78 percent females) received one of three other monetary subsidies also administered by INSERSO.

8.2.8   Other Transfer Programs

We now describe a few other transfer programs that are conditioned on age or for which the elderly can qualify solely on the basis of having a low income.

Unemployment Benefits

There exists a special subsidy for unemployed people who are older than age fifty-two, lack income sources, have contributed to unemployment insurance for at least six years in their life, and, except for age, satisfy all the requirements for an old age pension. This subsidy pays up to 75 percent of the minimum wage and may be received until the person reaches the age at which he or she can access an old age pension. Years spent unemployed count as years contributing toward an old age pension.

The Noncontributory Old Age Pension

A person aged sixty-five or over who does not qualify for an old age pension is entitled to a noncontributory pension (*pension de jubilación no contributiva*) if he or she has been a legal resident of Spain for the last ten years and his or her annual income is below a certain threshold. This program is also administered by INSERSO. Receipt of such a pension guarantees receipt of public health care assistance and other benefits available to social security pensioners.

The annual pension amount is equal to the minimum income threshold, and both depend on whether the person lives with others. If the person does not live with others, then the pension is equal to the basic amount paid out by INSERSO to disabled individuals. If the person lives with others, then the pension amount varies with the number of household members.

At the end of 1995, 186,000 people received a noncontributory old age pension from INSERSO. Of these, 14 percent were males and 86 percent females.

Other Programs Run by INSERSO

In addition to its duties in the field of disability and old age pensions, INSERSO runs a variety of other programs aimed at the elderly population. These programs include creating and maintaining residential and day-care centers open to retirees aged sixty and over and their spouses and managing the Social Thermal Program (Programa de Termalismo Social) and the Program for Elderly People's Holidays (Programa de Vacaciones Tercera Edad). The latter two programs offer paid or subsidized vacations to pensioners or people aged sixty-five or over as well as paid or subsidized stays at spas and thermal resorts within the country. The spouse of an eligible person is also covered by the program.

Recently, most regional governments have also begun to provide a number of services for retired people, ranging from subsidized holidays to a reduction in the cost of public transportation, special medical and psychological care, special houses for the elderly, etc.

8.2.9   Private Pensions

Private pension coverage is voluntary but not very widespread. Yet the number of participants in private pension plans has more than doubled in the last few years, from 628,000 in 1990 to 1,525,000 in 1994 (de las Fuentes and Gonzalo 1996, 255). The assets of private pension funds still represent only a small, but a growing, fraction of GDP, estimated to be 4.7 percent in 1997 (de las Fuentes and Gonzalo 1996, 251).

The main incentive to participate is tax deferral. Contributions can be entirely deducted from taxable income up to a maximum (equal to PTA 1 million in 1996, corresponding to 1.1 times the annualized minimum wage), provided that they do not exceed 15 percent of total annual income. On receipt, pension benefits are treated as regular components of labor income and taxed accordingly.

There are three forms of organization of a private pension plan. The first (*sistema asociado*), open to all members of the association that promotes the plan (e.g., a trade union), is rare. The second (*sistema de empleo*), open to all employees of the firm that promotes the plan, is confined to a few large firms, mainly publicly owned, in the banking and electricity sectors. The third (*sistema individual*) is open to everybody and is the predominant one, covering about 85 percent of the participants in private pension plans.

8.2.10   The Rights of Older Workers

Only public-sector employees are subject to mandatory retirement. The mandatory retirement age is normally sixty-five, but it can be earlier for certain categories (military, police, etc.). There is no mandatory retirement in the private sector unless it is specifically covered in collective agreements, a situation that occurs rarely.

In principle, age discrimination is prohibited by law. Indeed, a government attempt to introduce mandatory retirement at age sixty-nine was rejected by the Spanish Supreme Court on the ground that it would represent a form of age discrimination that violates constitutional principles.

8.3   Retirement Incentives under the Social Security System

We now present the results of calculations carried out to evaluate the retirement incentives provided by the Spanish social security system. These calculations refer only to the general scheme. We exclude disability insurance for two reasons. First, it is now more severely screened than it was during the 1980s. Second, the extent to which it is used as an early retirement device follows political criteria that vary greatly between regions and sectors and cannot be properly formalized. Private pensions are also excluded since they are voluntary and cover only a very small fraction of the workforce.

Replacement rates are net of social security contributions and personal income taxes. Although there is no difference in the tax treatment of labor earnings and pensions, our simulations take into account the effects of the highly progressive nature of the Spanish tax system. This does not affect the qualitative picture, but it has a sizable effect on the final magnitudes. In order to provide the reader with a clearer picture of the powerful role that, over and above the pension system, a very progressive income tax schedule may play in determining labor supply decisions, we also report simulation results gross of income taxes for some of the most significant cases.

Exact calculations of after-tax wealth and replacement rates are complicated by the fact that the number of bend points in the Spanish marginal tax schedule is high (thirty-four in 1985 and still seventeen in 1995). As an approximation, we proceeded as follows. We first used the 1995 tax schedule to trace out the relation between the average tax rate (net of standard deductions) and income (net of social security contributions paid by a worker). We then fitted by least squares a fourth-order polynomial to this relation. Finally, the estimated coefficients were used to determine after-tax income for all previous and subsequent years.

8.3.1 The Base Case

Our base case is a male employee, born on 1 January 1930, who has been contributing to social security without interruption since he turned twenty, on 1 January 1950. He reaches the early retirement age of sixty in 1990 and the normal retirement age of sixty-five in 1995. He is married to a woman who is three year younger than he is and has never worked. They have no dependent children, and their conditional survival probabilities at each age are equal to the ones obtained by the latest mortality tables published by the National Statistical Institute (INE) with reference to the year 1990. We assume that the survival probabilities of the husband and the wife are independent.

Our base-case worker has a real discount rate of 3 percent, and his age-earnings profile has been constructed as follows. First, using the EPF for 1980–81, we computed median annual earnings in 1980 for a full-time, nonagricultural male employee born in 1930. We then predicted annual earnings in all other years using the annual growth rate of nominal earnings, as computed by INSS. After 1995, we assumed an annual growth rate of nominal wages of 4.5 percent and an annual inflation rate of 3 percent. These assumptions are in line with the main macroeconomic scenarios summarized in Herce (1997).

Simulations start in year 1985, when our base-case worker turns age fifty-five and completes thirty-five years of contributions, and run for each year until he turns age seventy, in the year 2000. At age fifty-five, his benefit base is already equal to 100 percent of the average wage during the last eight years of work. For the period between 1985 and 1996, we use historical data for all the relevant social security parameters. For the subsequent years, social security tax rates are assumed to remain constant at their 1996 level, the pension is assumed to be perfectly indexed to price inflation, and the floors and ceilings on earnings, as well as the minimum and maximum pensions, are assumed to grow at the same rate as nominal wages.

Our basic hypotheses are the following. First, if the worker stops working before age sixty, then he elects to begin receiving his old age pension at age sixty, the earliest possible moment, whereas, if he stops working past age sixty, then he starts receiving his old age pension immediately. Second, if he stops working before age sixty, then he receives no benefits or unemployment compensation in the interim years until he starts drawing a pension. Third, the wealth calculations are all net present values as of 1 January 1995.

It may be worth summarizing the main qualitative effects of working one more year beyond age sixty in the simulations that we are about to present: (1) It may increase social security benefits by increasing the benefit base BR_t or the replacement rate α_n (see sec. 8.2.4 above). The benefit base increases if earnings from the extra year of work exceed average earnings during the last eight years. The replacement rate increases if the worker has contributed for fewer than thirty-five years, in which case an extra year of work buys an extra 2 percent of the benefit base. If the worker has already contributed for thirty-five years, as in the base case, only the effect on the benefit base is relevant. (2) It reduces the penalty for early retirement by 8 percentage points. (3) It reduces by one year the expected period over which the worker will receive a pension. (4) It implies paying additional social security contributions. (5) The marginal tax rate on labor income may turn out to be higher than the marginal tax rate on pension income, owing to the high progressivity of the Spanish income tax schedule. This effect is likely to be important for workers who are in the higher portion of the earnings distribution.

Table 8.7 presents our calculations of replacement rates, social security wealth, social security wealth accrual (the change in social security wealth with respect to one year earlier), social security wealth accrual rates (the rates of change in social security wealth), projected earnings, and the implicit tax/subsidy rates on continuing to work (minus the ratio between social security wealth accrual and projected earnings) at each age between fifty-four and sixty-nine. Both earnings and social security wealth are net of personal income taxes and are expressed in PTA thousands at 1995 prices.

Social security wealth starts up at PTA 11.3 million (about $87,000), but it loses about 15 percent of its value between age fifty-four and age fifty-nine because the growth of median wages during the period 1986–90 was not enough to compensate for the additional contributions paid. Social security wealth rises again between age fifty-nine and age sixty-three, mainly because of the progressive reduction in the penalty for earlier retirement (effect 2), but falls very rapidly after age sixty-four, when additional years of work add noth-

Table 8.7   Incentive Calculations for the Base Case (after-tax values in PTA
                   1,000 at 1995 prices)

Age at Last Year of Work	Replacement Rate	SSW	Accrual	Accrual Rate	Projected Earnings	Tax/ Subsidy
54	...	11,343.7	...	...	1,533.6	...
55	...	11,006.9	−336.8	−.030	1,557.5	.216
56	...	10,836.9	−170.0	−.015	1,572.4	.108
57	...	10,598.0	−238.9	−.022	1,558.8	.153
58	...	10,025.0	−573.1	−.054	1,582.3	.362
59	.590	9,566.8	−458.2	−.046	1,603.8	.286
60	.661	9,809.7	242.9	.025	1,625.2	−.149
61	.730	10,008.0	198.3	.020	1,648.2	−.120
62	.816	10,193.3	185.3	.019	1,648.6	−.112
63	.895	10,117.1	−76.2	−.007	1,649.4	.046
64	.996	9,860.6	−256.5	−.025	1,606.9	.160
65	.998	8,629.4	−1,231.3	−.125	1,627.5	.757
66	.996	7,364.4	−1,264.9	−.147	1,648.4	.767
67	.988	6,067.9	−1,296.5	−.176	1,669.6	.777
68	.981	4,815.7	−1,252.2	−.206	1,691.0	.741
69	.973	3,608.2	−1,207.5	−.251	1,712.7	.705

ing to the expected pension amount, while effects 3 and 4 become very strong. As a result of this, the implicit tax rate on continuing work increases rapidly between age fifty-four and age fifty-eight, when it reaches 36 percent. It turns negative (subsidy) between the ages of sixty and sixty-two as the penalty associated with early retirement is progressively reduced. The net tax or subsidy is almost zero at age sixty-three but becomes positive (tax) again and rapidly increasing afterward.

Notice that the net replacement rate increases from about 60 percent at age fifty-nine to about 100 percent at age sixty-five and declines slightly afterward. Also notice that social security wealth reaches its maximum value at age fifty-four, long before the worker is allowed to retire.

8.3.2 Other Cases

Table 8.8 presents the incentive calculations for the case of a single worker. The main difference with respect to the base case is that the household he represents (missing a female spouse) has smaller effective survival probabilities at each age, resulting in lower social security wealth. The age profile of tax/subsidy rates is not very different from the base case, except for the fact that there is hardly any subsidy for continuing work between age sixty and age sixty-three. In other words, the reduction in the expected length of time over which pension benefits will be received (effect 3) and the higher marginal tax rates on earnings completely wash out with the increase in the benefit base brought about by effects 1 and 2. Also in this case, social security wealth is maximized at age fifty-four.

Table 8.8   **Incentive Calculations for the Case of a Single Worker (after-tax values in PTA 1,000 at 1995 prices)**

Age at Last Year of Work	Replacement Rate	SSW	Accrual	Accrual Rate	Projected Earnings	Tax/ Subsidy
54	. . .	9,159.8	. . .	. . .	1,533.6	. . .
55	. . .	8,847.4	−312.4	−.034	1,557.5	.201
56	. . .	8,697.0	−150.4	−.017	1,572.4	.096
57	. . .	8,459.9	−237.1	−.027	1,558.8	.152
58	. . .	7,897.5	−562.4	−.066	1,582.3	.355
59	.590	7,449.4	−448.1	−.057	1,603.8	.279
60	.661	7,570.2	120.8	.016	1,625.2	−.074
61	.730	7,553.3	−17.0	−.002	1,648.2	.010
62	.816	7,501.2	−52.1	−.007	1,648.6	.032
63	.895	7,226.1	−275.1	−.037	1,649.4	.167
64	.996	6,802.1	−424.0	−.059	1,606.9	.264
65	.998	5,616.4	−1,185.7	−.174	1,627.5	.729
66	.996	4,421.8	−1,194.6	−.213	1,648.4	.725
67	.988	3,222.7	−1,199.1	−.271	1,669.6	.718
68	.981	2,078.4	−1,144.2	−.355	1,691.0	.677
69	.973	989.5	−1,088.9	−.524	1,712.7	.636

Table 8.9 presents the incentive calculations for the case of a median wage profile with an "incomplete" earnings history. This worker started working at age thirty and does not therefore fully qualify for a pension until he reaches age sixty-five in 1995. The high tax rate on continuing work at all ages between fifty-five and fifty-nine is counterintuitive, but it helps illustrate the dramatic importance of a sixth effect embedded in the Spanish social security system, the "minimum pension effect."

If the worker stops working at age fifty-five, with only twenty-five years of contributions, the pension that he will receive after turning sixty will be low and hit the lower bound on pensions when he reaches age sixty-four. Since minimum pensions grow at the same rate as nominal wages, there is no advantage in working one extra year in order to raise the initial pension, as the latter is in any case low and going to be equal to the minimum pension after just a few years. Notice that the situation is completely different if the worker considers retiring when he turns sixty. In this case, as shown in table 8.3 above, working one extra year until age sixty-one would increase his pension from 54 to 62.6 percent of the benefit base.

Table 8.10 differs from the base case because we used the tenth percentile of annual earnings as our 1980 anchor. Given the 1980 anchor, annual earnings for all other years are predicted as in the base case. Table 8.11 presents a parallel set of calculations using the ninetieth percentile of annual earnings as our 1980 anchor. Tax/subsidy rates for these two cases are also presented in figure 8.15 along with the base case.

We have already seen that the incentives to retire at the earliest possible date

Table 8.9   **Incentive Calculations for the Case of an Incomplete Earnings History (after-tax values in PTA 1,000 at 1995 prices)**

Age at Last Year of Work	Replacement Rate	SSW	Accrual	Accrual Rate	Projected Earnings	Tax/ Subsidy
54	...	10,446.4	...	...	1,533.6	...
55	...	10,022.4	−424.0	−.041	1,557.5	.272
56	...	9,664.3	−358.1	−.036	1,572.4	.228
57	...	9,406.9	−257.5	−.027	1,558.5	.165
58	...	9,005.5	−401.4	−.043	1,582.3	.254
59	.536	8,687.4	−318.1	−.035	1,603.8	.198
60	.613	8,886.4	199.0	.023	1,625.2	−.122
61	.691	9,253.5	367.1	.041	1,648.2	−.223
62	.787	9,670.8	417.3	.045	1,648.6	−.253
63	.880	9,851.4	180.6	.019	1,649.4	−.109
64	.996	9,860.6	9.3	.000	1,606.9	−.006
65	.998	8,629.4	−1,231.3	−.125	1,627.5	.757
66	.996	7,364.4	−1,264.9	−.147	1,648.4	.767
67	.988	6,067.9	−1,296.5	−.176	1,669.6	.777
68	.981	4,815.7	−1,252.2	−.206	1,691.0	.741
69	.973	3,608.2	−1,207.5	−.251	1,712.7	.705

Table 8.10   **Incentive Calculations for the Tenth Percentile Earnings Case (after-tax values in PTA 1,000 at 1995 prices)**

Age at Last Year of Work	Replacement Rate	SSW	Accrual	Accrual Rate	Projected Earnings	Tax/ Subsidy
54	...	10,621.0	...	...	889.8	...
55	...	10,334.2	−286.9	−.027	904.1	.317
56	...	10,052.2	−282.0	−.027	913.1	.309
57	...	9,776.9	−275.2	−.027	904.9	.304
58	...	9,513.9	−263.0	−.027	919.0	.286
59	.741	9,255.8	−258.1	−.027	931.9	.277
60	.731	8,444.5	−811.3	−.088	944.8	.859
61	.722	7,659.2	−785.3	−.093	958.6	.819
62	.810	6,954.4	−704.8	−.092	958.9	.735
63	.892	6,431.7	−522.7	−.075	959.3	.545
64	.996	6,070.7	−361.0	−.056	933.8	.387
65	.998	5,342.6	−728.1	−.120	946.2	.770
66	.996	4,604.1	−738.5	−.138	958.8	.770
67	.988	3,855.8	−748.4	−.163	971.5	.770
68	.980	3,132.6	−723.1	−.188	984.4	.735
69	.972	2,435.9	−696.7	−.222	997.4	.698

Table 8.11   **Incentive Calculations for the Ninetieth Percentile Earnings Case (after-tax values in PTA 1,000 at 1995 prices)**

Age at Last Year of Work	Replacement Rate	SSW	Accrual	Accrual Rate	Projected Earnings	Tax/ Subsidy
54	...	18,450.0	...	...	2,561.6	...
55	...	17,800.3	−649.7	−.035	2,603.0	.250
56	...	17,427.6	−372.7	−.021	2,630.5	.142
57	...	16,829.3	−598.3	−.034	2,610.5	.229
58	...	15,565.3	−1,264.0	−.075	2,631.4	.480
59	.561	14,789.6	−775.7	−.050	2,666.6	.291
60	.627	15,210.1	420.6	.028	2,701.7	−.156
61	.691	15,398.5	188.4	.012	2,739.6	−.069
62	.776	15,711.9	313.4	.020	2,740.2	−.114
63	.859	15,710.9	−1.5	.000	2,741.5	.000
64	.966	15,490.9	−219.4	−.014	2,671.6	.082
65	.982	13,769.4	−1,721.5	−.111	2,705.6	.636
66	.996	12,002.4	−1,767.0	−.128	2,739.9	.645
67	.988	9,802.4	−2,200.0	−.183	2,774.7	.793
68	.981	7,677.5	−2,124.9	−.217	2,809.9	.756
69	.973	5,628.5	−2,049.0	−.267	2,845.6	.720

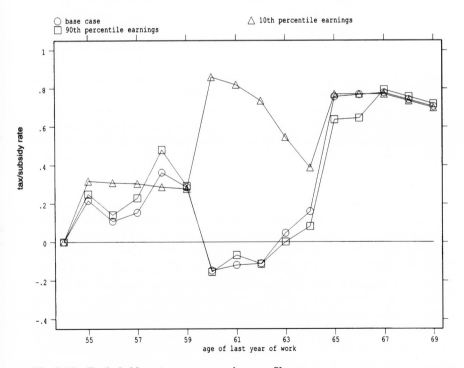

Fig. 8.15   Tax/subsidy rates across earnings profiles

Table 8.12   Tax/Subsidy Rates with and without Minimum Pensions

Age at Last Year of Work	Base Case		Incomplete History		10th Percentile	
	With	Without	With	Without	With	Without
55	.216	.172	.272	.058	.317	.150
56	.108	.050	.228	−.052	.309	.027
57	.153	.123	.165	−.000	.304	.101
58	.362	.372	.254	.217	.286	.355
59	.286	.284	.198	.141	.277	.267
60	−.149	−.221	−.122	−.331	.859	−.264
61	−.120	−.127	−.223	−.256	.819	−.172
62	−.112	−.112	−.253	−.254	.735	−.161
63	.046	.046	−.109	−.109	.545	.001
64	.160	.160	−.006	−.006	.387	.118
65	.757	.757	.757	.757	.770	.738
66	.767	.767	.767	.767	.770	.751
67	.777	.777	.777	.777	.770	.762
68	.741	.741	.741	.741	.735	.726
69	.705	.705	.705	.705	.698	.691

are much stronger for individuals with an incomplete earnings history. The bias of the system toward "forcing out" low-wage earners is confirmed by the different patterns of the tax/subsidy rate faced by individuals at the ninetieth and tenth percentiles of the wage distribution. Whereas for the former there is an incentive, stronger than for the base case, to keep working past age sixty and until about the age of sixty-three or sixty-four, for the latter the disincentive to do so peaks at age sixty, in terms of both accrual and tax/subsidy rates.

Figure 8.15 also shows that the tax rate for low-wage earners increases sharply in the age range sixty to sixty-four, contrary to what happens to high-wage earners. In other words, should a low-earnings individual be working at the age of, say, sixty-one, he would still find it advantageous to quit immediately, whereas this is not true for the base case or a high-earnings person.

Table 8.12 provides the reader with a further appraisal of the extent to which the minimum pension mechanism creates incentives to early retirement for low-wage earners. It reports tax/subsidy rates with and without minimum pensions in the base case, the incomplete earning history case, and the tenth percentile case.

The effect on the incentives to early retirement is very strong for the low-income individual. The variation caused by the minimum pension in the implicit tax from continuing to work is already very high at age fifty-five, peaks at age sixty, and remains substantial at much later ages as well. For a worker with an incomplete earnings history, the effect of the minimum pension provision is also relevant until age sixty but vanishes rapidly afterward. Instead, the difference caused by the existence of the minimum pension on the tax/subsidy for the base-case worker is always negligible.

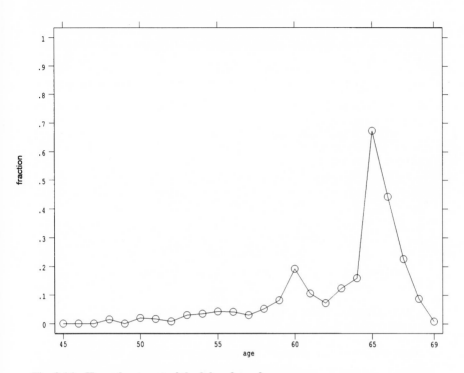

Fig. 8.16   Hazard rate out of the labor force for men

8.3.3   Discussion

Our first concern is with the relations between the incentive effects we have computed and the retirement facts available.

Figures 8.16 and 8.17 show hazard rates by age for men and women, respectively. The hazard rate is defined here as minus the percentage change in the cross-sectional age-participation profile. For men, the hazard increases smoothly with age and shows clear peaks at the ages of sixty and sixty-five, corresponding, respectively, to the Spanish early and normal retirement ages. This is consistent with our calculations, which show a strong incentive for low-income earners and/or workers with incomplete histories to retire as early as possible (age sixty) and for everybody else to retire at age sixty-five.

Among women, things are harder to judge. The behavior of the hazard rate for women is very erratic at almost all ages, and there are various small peaks at ages between fifty-two and sixty-one, followed by the prominent one at age sixty-five. Our reading of the data is that the only significant peaks in the hazard for women occur at ages sixty-one and sixty-five. All the other ones are likely to reflect pure sample noise, although one could rationalize the presence of a spike at age fifty-four through the interaction between eligibility requirements and minimum pension provisions.

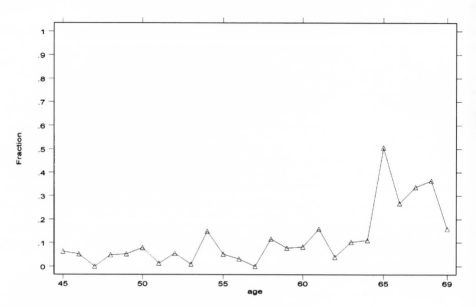

Fig. 8.17   Hazard rate out of the labor force for women

Next, we would like to verify whether the recent trends in the patterns of retirement are also consistent with the structure of incentives that we have derived. It is pointless to apply our calculations to years before 1985. In fact, owing to the slow implementation of the 1985 reform, only very recent years may reveal anything informative with respect to the working of the current system.

Table 8.13 (based on social security administrative data) reports the distribution, according to the age of the pensioner, of the new retirement pensions awarded by the general scheme (RGSS) during the years 1991 and 1994. For workers aged sixty-four or younger, we also report the percentage of the new pensioners who, for reasons detailed earlier, were exempted from the 8 percent penalty generally applicable for each year of early retirement.

The results are startling: in spite of the fairly heavy penalties associated with early retirement, more than 40 percent of individuals retire at age sixty or earlier. Furthermore, the percentage of those retiring earlier than age sixty-five has been increasing steadily in the last few years, from 64 percent in 1991 to 70 percent in 1994. The intermediate years (not reported) are perfectly consistent with this trend.

To sum up, the Spanish social security system makes retirement at earlier ages than sixty-five the only rational strategy. Indeed, for workers with earning profiles below the median or with incomplete earning histories (a situation particularly frequent among women), the incentive to retire as early as possible, that is, at age sixty, is particularly strong. The available data on hazard

Table 8.13   **Age Distribution of New Pensioners, 1991 and 1994**

Age	1991			1994		
	Penalty	No Penalty	Total	Penalty	No Penalty	Total
≤60	38.61	1.81	40.42	37.84	2.89	40.73
61	5.91	.32	6.23	7.20	.34	7.54
62	5.72	.27	6.00	7.39	.35	7.74
63	4.71	.51	5.22	6.13	.34	6.46
64	4.22	1.83	6.04	5.22	2.25	7.47
65	. . .	. . .	31.38	. . .	. . .	26.39
66	. . .	. . .	1.71	. . .	. . .	1.17
67	. . .	. . .	.93	. . .	. . .	.72
68	. . .	. . .	.58	. . .	. . .	.50
69	. . .	. . .	.41	. . .	. . .	.39
≥70	. . .	. . .	1.07	. . .	. . .	.89
<65	59.17	4.74	63.92	63.79	6.16	69.95
≥65	. . .	. . .	36.08	. . .	. . .	30.05

rates and the recent retirement patterns are completely consistent with this prediction.

8.4 Conclusions

The Spanish pension system has witnessed a remarkable evolution in the last twenty-five years, moving away from a collection of dispersed and uncoordinated professional schemes toward a more uniform and comprehensive public system. Such a process has generated a tumultuous growth in the size and nature of public pension schemes as well as a rapid increase in the number of retirees with short contribution histories receiving the minimum public pension. Together with the dramatic demographic changes affecting Spain since the late 1970, the continuous enlargement of the public pension system has been a major cause of the large financial imbalances that have come about in the last decade. This evolution is not yet complete, and the recently enacted (June 1997) changes suggest that further rationalization and uniformization of treatments will be taking place between now and the beginning of the next century.

A third factor underlying the emergence of financial distress is the strong reduction in labor force participation rates among individuals aged fifty-five to sixty-five, which began between 1975 and 1980 and is still taking place. This paper examines the interplay between the incentives generated by the public pension system and the decision to retire after age fifty-five. We quantify such incentives by computing measures of social security wealth and of the implicit tax/subsidy to keep working generated by the current system.

Our findings support the intuitive idea that pension-induced incentives matter for the labor supply behavior of Spanish workers. While the Spanish system does not pay a particularly generous average pension relative to GDP per capita, its "generosity" concentrates in providing relatively large minimum pensions to individuals with below-average working histories and/or low wages. We show how this fact generates very strong incentives for people to retire as early as possible. At the same time, the pension system provides workers earning average or above-average salaries and having complete working histories relatively weak financial gains from not retiring after age sixty. These financial gains completely disappear and become losses around age sixty-three, particularly for workers who have already reached thirty-five years of contributions. We have also shown how the disability insurance system is being used "strategically" by individuals who cannot legally anticipate retirement (e.g., the self-employed and farmers) actually to achieve early retirement.

The combination of these three salient features of the Spanish legislation seems to account well for the observed increase in the percentage of early retirees among Spanish new pensioners during the 1990s.

It should be stressed, however, that the possibility of retiring before age sixty-five is, according to current legislation, restricted to those workers who began their contribution histories before 1967. While this group represents today the bulk of the labor force nearing the age of retirement, its quantitative relevance will decrease rapidly in future years.

It is yet unclear whether such a privilege will be progressively extended as well to individuals who began contributing after that date. Political pressure toward such an extension is currently being applied from various quarters, and the final outcome is hard to predict.

Legislation recently enacted (26 June 1997) is ambivalent on this matter. On the one hand, it links more closely initial pensions to lifetime contribution histories, thereby starting to cut down on opportunities for "pension purchases," especially among the self-employed. On the other hand, it mildly reduces the penalization for retiring younger than age sixty-five for individuals with long contribution histories, and it leaves untouched both the disability and the minimum pension mechanisms, which we have singled out as the most powerful incentives for early retirement.

If anything, in fact, the extension from eight to fifteen of the number of years over which the benefit base is computed may have the effect of increasing the number of individuals for whom the minimum pension is binding. As we have documented, workers expecting to receive a minimum pension have a strong incentive to anticipate retirement. The final outcome of the recent legislation may therefore be that of just increasing the proportion of the workforce to whom such incentives matter.

Appendix A
Data Appendix

In what follows, we briefly describe the most important data sources employed in this chapter. We also mention some other potentially useful data sources.

Micro Data

Encuesta de Población Activa (EPA)

This is a quarterly CPS-like survey of roughly sixty thousand Spanish households carried out by the Spanish National Statistical Institute (INE). It contains fairly detailed information on labor force status, education, and family background variables but, unfortunately, no information on wages and incomes. This feature is common to most European-style labor force surveys. Publicly released cross-sectional files are available from 1976.

From 1987, the INE also releases the Encuesta de Población Activa Enlazada, which is the panel version of the EPA obtained by exploiting the rotating cross-sectional nature of the survey. It contains fewer variables, but it permits one to follow individuals for up to six quarters.

Encuesta de Presupuestos Familiares (EPF)

This is a cross-sectional household budget survey carried out by INE in 1973–74, 1980–81, and 1990–91, with reference to income and expenditure in the previous calendar year. The 1990–91 sample, used in this paper, contains 21,155 households and 72,123 persons.

Administrative Records from Social Security

The third micro-data set used in this paper is a random sample of one of every two hundred pensioners on file at the INSS in January 1993. The sample consists of 32,366 observations of a universe of 6,473,200 pensioners. The data provide information on initial and current pensions. The difference between these two concepts is broken down into revalorization and complement to minimum pension, which permits us to construct a measure of social security generosity.

Other Micro Data

The Encuesta de Estructura Salarial was carried out by the INE in 1995. It provides detailed information on wages, working hours, and personal characteristics for about 175,000 workers in 19,000 establishments.

The Encuesta Continua de Presupuestos Familiares is a rotating household survey carried out quarterly by the INE since 1985. It collects data on income, consumption, and personal characteristics for about three thousand households. One eighth of the sample is replaced at each rotation.

Aggregate Annual or Monthly Data

The *Boletín de estadísticas laborales,* published by the Ministry of Labor (MTSS), contains data from 1981 on the most important social security programs.

The *Boletín informativo de la seguridad social,* published by the Dirección General de la Seguridad Social, MTSS, contains detailed information on social security expenditures, including medical care, from 1981.

The Encuesta de Salarios en la Industria y los Servicios is a quarterly survey on wages and hours worked carried out by the INE at the establishment level.

Appendix B
An Overview of the Literature on Social Security and Retirement in Spain

We have been able to trace the existence of only one investigation of the effect of the Spanish social security system on labor supply and, in particular, retirement decisions. Martín and Moreno (1990) look at weekly work hours over the period 1964–84 using net and gross social security wealth as explanatory variables. A fairly simple econometric analysis leads to the conclusion that the negative income effect associated with social security contributions more than compensates for both the substitution effect toward leisure and the increase in expected wealth induced by the promise of a pension payment, thereby increasing the overall labor supply.

The rest of the existing literature concentrates almost exclusively on two issues: (1) the financial evolution of the system and the dramatic increase in its current account deficit as a consequence of both the system's generosity and the adverse demographic evolution; (2) the redistributive features of the system and, in particular, the existence of a wide dispersion in the internal rates of return across different programs.

Analysis of Long-Run Sustainability

Recent years have witnessed the publication of a large number of studies concerned with the long-run viability of the Spanish public pension system and with its capability to sustain the ongoing demographic changes. Among them are the monographs by Barea (1995), Barea and Gonzáles-Páramo (1996), Herce et al. (1996), INVERCO (1996), Ministerio de Trabajo (1995), and Piñera and Weinstein (1996) as well as the interesting papers by Herce (1997) and Jimeno and Licandro (1996). While the various authors reach different conclusions about the most appropriate type of reform, they express similar concerns about the economic viability of the existing system.

Normalizing at zero the deficit of the social security system in 1995, the estimates for 2010 range from −0.8 to −3.5 percent of GDP, with an average of −1.5 percent. For 2025, the average deficit prediction is of −2.6 percent of GDP, with a range going from −1.0 to −4.2 percent of GDP. Most studies are based on a set of macroeconomic predictions that, while not overly optimistic, are nevertheless not obviously realistic. In general, a 3 percent per year average growth rate of GDP is assumed, together with a substantial increase in labor force participation rates (up to 70 percent in 2010) and a reduction in the unemployment rate from the current 23 percent to about 16–18 percent. Barring substantial structural reforms, these predictions are hardly realistic in the light of the performance of the Spanish economy over the last twenty years.

Analysis of the Redistributive Effects

Most studies concentrate on the period prior to the 1978 reform, and only a few cover more recent years. The unit of investigation is always the individual agent, not the household, and income is very often measured as an annual flow, not as total lifetime income.

For the earlier period, there is widespread consensus on the regressive nature of the combined social security and fiscal system (see, e.g., Castellano 1977; and Vereda and Mochón 1978). The studies that we have examined, however, are imprecise and naïve in their theoretical apparatus, the quality of the data available, and the econometric techniques adopted. We find their conclusions dubious.

After 1978, things look quite different. While an early study (Argimón and González-Páramo 1987) still finds evidence of a regressive effect in the structure of contributions, this is not the case when pension expenditures are taken into consideration (Medel, Molina, and Sánchez 1988). More recently, a number of fairly complete studies (Monasterio and Suárez 1992; Melis and Díaz 1993; and Bandrés and Cuenca 1996) unequivocally document the very strong and progressive redistribution accomplished by the post-1978 and post-1985 Spanish pension systems.

These more recent studies do not restrict their analysis to annual income flows but manage to construct relatively credible indices of lifetime contributions and payments according to professional status and decile position in the overall distribution of earnings and to compute internal rates of return for different social security programs and income profiles.

Their (fairly uniform) conclusions can be summarized as follows: (*a*) For most social security programs, both past and current contribution/payment profiles give rise to a large intergenerational transfer. For example, the ratio of net transfers to the total present value of pensions for individuals affiliated with

REEH went from 61.2 percent before the reform to 52 percent after (using a discount rate of 3 percent). (*b*) The only important exception to this rule is given by the general scheme before and, especially, after the 1985 reform. In this case, net lifetime social security wealth was positive (and equal to about 30 percent of total pension present value) before the reform only if a real discount rate of 1 percent was used. It turned negative when a 3 percent discount rate was applied, and it remained negative in either case after the reform. It turns out to be particularly large (50 percent of total pension present value) when discounted at 3 percent. (*c*) Both the old and the current Spanish social security systems generate very large intragenerational transfers from the general to all the special schemes. Domestic workers and small farmers are by far the largest beneficiaries of such transfers. (*d*) If one looks at the intragenerational transfers occurring not across programs but across income deciles, the Spanish social security system turns out to be a very progressive one: up to 90 percent of the total present value of pensions to which individuals in the first decile of the earnings distribution are entitled represent a pure transfer. This transfer's percentage decreases rather slowly as one moves up with earnings and changes sign only for the very last decile (or the last two, depending on the details of the calculations).

References

Argimón, I., and J. M. González-Páramo. 1987. Translación e incidencia de las cotizaciones sociales por niveles de renta en España, 1980–84. Documentos de Trabajo (Working Paper) no. 1. Madrid: Fundación para la Investigacion Economica y Social.

Bandrés, E., and A. Cuenca. 1996. Capitalización y transferencias en las pensiones de la seguridad social. In *II simposio sobre igualdad, y distribución de la renta y la riqueza,* vol. 7. Madrid: Fundación Argentaria.

Barea, J., ed. 1995. *El sistema de pensiones en España: Análisis y propuestas para su viabilidad.* Madrid: Circulo de Empresarios.

Barea, J., and J. M. González-Páramo, eds. 1996. *Pensiones y prestaciones por desempleo.* Bilbao: Fundación. Banco de Bilbao Vizcaya.

Castellano, F. 1977. Distribución por niveles de ingreso de la cuota patronal de la seguridad social en España. *Investigaciones economicas* 2: 103–24.

de las Fuentes, J. M., and B. Gonzalo. 1996. Modelos de aseguramiento en España del riesgo de pérdida de la renta derivada de la actividad laboral a causa de la vejez. Documento de Trabajo (Working Paper), Serie Economía Pública. Bilbao: Fundación. Banco de Bilbao Vizcaya.

Durán, A. 1995. Politíca de pensiones: Situación y perspectivas. In *Las actividades económicas de la personas mayores.* Madrid: SECOT.

Fernández Cordón, J. A. 1996. Demografía, actividad y dependencia en España. Documento de Trabajo (Working Paper), Serie Economía Pública. Bilbao: Fundación. Banco de Bilbao Vizcaya.

Herce, J. A. 1997. La reforma de las pensiones en España: Aspectos analíticos y aplicados. *Moneda y crédito,* no. 204:105–43.

Herce, J. A., S. Sosvilla, S. Castillo, and R. Duce. 1996. *El futuro de las pensiones en España: Hacia un sistema mixto.* Colección de Estudios e Informes 8. Barcelona: Caja de Ahorros y Pensiones de Barcelona.

INVERCO. 1996. *Análisis de los sistemas de pensiones.* Madrid: Asociacion de Instituciones de Inversion Colectiva y Fondos de Pensiones.

Jimeno, J. F., and O. Licandro. 1996. El equilibrio financiero de un sistema de reparto de pensiones de jubilación: Una aplicación al caso español. Documento de Trabajo (Working Paper) no. 96-21. Madrid: Fundación de Estudios de Economia Aplicada.

Martín, A., and L. Moreno. 1990. Efectos de las pensiones de la seguridad social sobre la oferta de trabajo en España. *Investigaciones económicas* 14:291–303.

Medel, B., A. Molina, and J. Sánchez. 1988. Los efectos distributivos del gasto público en España. Documentos de Trabajo (Working Paper) no. 28. Madrid: Fundación para la Investigacion Economica y Social.

Melis, F., and C. Díaz. 1993. La distribución personal de salarios y pensiones en las fuentes tributarias. In *I simposio sobre igualdad, y distribución de la renta y la riqueza,* vol. 2. Madrid: Fundación Argentaria.

Ministerio de Trabajo. 1995. *La seguridad social en el umbral del siglo XXI: Estudio económico actuarial.* Madrid.

Monasterio, C., and J. Suárez. 1992. Gasto social en pensiones. *Hacienda publica española* 120–21:119–43.

Piñera, J., and A. Weinstein. 1996. *Una propuesta de reforma del sistema de pensiones en España.* Madrid: Circulo de Empresarios.

Vereda, J., and F. Mochón. 1978. Efectos redistributivos de la seguridad social. *Hacienda pública española* 52:83–93.

Villagarcía, T. 1995. Esiste un sesgo de inactividad en la encuesta de población activa? Documento de Trabajo (Working Paper) no. 95-04. Universidad Carlos III, Madrid.

9 Social Security, Occupational Pensions, and Retirement in Sweden

Mårten Palme and Ingemar Svensson

The social insurance system plays a very important role in the Swedish economy. In 1994, benefits paid out by this system represented 20 percent of Sweden's GDP, or about 32 percent of all public spending. Table 9.1 shows the size of the different parts of the social insurance system. From this table, it is apparent that the largest share of social insurance spending is directed toward individuals who have permanently left the labor market, mostly older people. Social security spending consists of three main parts: the basic pension, the supplementary pension (ATP), and the partial retirement pension. The payments from these systems amounted to 42.4, 55.3, and 1.3 percent, respectively, of total pension payments in 1994. The supplementary pension and the basic pension can be paid as an old age pension, a survivor pension, or a disability pension. People who have permanently left the labor market in Sweden are largely dependent on payments from social security. On average, about 74 percent of the income of individuals older than age sixty-five consists of payments from the social security system.[1]

Forecast financial problems in the system led to a major reform to be fully implemented by 2001. The majority in the Swedish parliament agreed on the principles of the new pension system in 1994, although all the details have yet to be determined. There are two causes for the forecast financial problems of the current system: demographic change and slow growth in the Swedish econ-

Mårten Palme is associate professor of economics at the Stockholm School of Economics. Ingemar Svensson is a researcher at the National Social Insurance Board in Stockholm.

The authors are grateful to participants in the NBER International Social Security project, in particular Jonathan Gruber and David Wise, for comments. They also thank Anders Björklund, Joakim Palme, Ed Palmer, and Eskil Wadensjö for comments on earlier drafts of this paper. Mårten Palme acknowledges financial support from the Swedish Council for Social Research. The authors take full responsibility for errors or shortcomings.

1. Figures are our own calculations from the 1994 Household Income Survey provided by Statistics Sweden. Appendix A contains information on the sample properties of this survey.

Table 9.1   Social Insurance Expenditures in Sweden, 1994

	Expenditures in SKr Million	Percentage Share of Total Social Insurance Expenditures	Percentage Share of GDP
Pension insurance	195,814	64.0	13.8
National basic pension	82,933	27.1	5.8
National basic old age pension	52,602	17.2	3.7
National basic disability pension	14,156	4.6	1.0
National supplementary pension	108,371	35.4	7.6
Nation supplementary old age pension	75,240	24.6	5.3
Nation supplementary disability pension	20,665	6.8	1.5
Part-time pension	2,564	.8	.2
Sickness and parental insurance	53,800	17.6	3.8
Work injuries insurance	7,999	2.6	.6
Allowances	32,204	10.5	2.3
Other	15,920	5.2	1.1
Total	305,737	100	21.5

omy. The ratio between the number of persons over age sixty-five to the number aged sixteen to sixty-four rose from 0.184 in 1950 to 0.278 today. This ratio is projected to rise to 0.35 by 2050 and to 0.37 by 2070. There are two aspects of changes in the demographic structure: the increase in life expectancy and the aging of the baby-boom generation. The increase in life expectancy increases the financial pressure—for the basic pension system, which is a pure pay-as-you-go scheme, and for the supplementary pension system, which is a mixture of a funded and a pay-as-you-go scheme. The aging of the baby-boom generation creates extra financial pressure in the basic pension system. But, because the supplementary pension system is a partly funded system, this source of financial pressure could be alleviated if the fund is built up when this generation is active in the labor market.

The continuing slow economic growth in Sweden causes problems primarily for the supplementary pension system. National Social Insurance Board studies show that this scheme is not viable if the long-run rate of growth falls below about 2 percent (see National Social Insurance Board 1993).

Another important component of the pension system is the centrally bargained occupational pension schemes. As is well known, Sweden has a highly unionized labor market. Occupational pension schemes are determined in central agreements between the central unions and the employers' confederations. Although the unionization rate is about 81 percent, the occupational pensions are compulsory for most workers and cover about 95 percent of the labor market. The influence of the centrally bargained pension plans is growing.

An explicit goal of pension reform is to increase work incentives (especially for older people). However, very little is known about what economic incentives to leave the labor market the current social insurance system provides and the extent to which the system affects the behavior of older workers since very few empirical studies have been conducted in this area.[2] The aim of this paper is to provide an overview of the incentives erected by the social security system for older people to participate in the labor force. We also consider the occupational pension scheme for blue-collar workers. We compare the estimates of these incentives with the observed pattern of labor force participation of older people historically and by age groups.

The paper is organized as follows. Section 9.1 describes the labor market behavior of older workers in Sweden, the present situation, and development over time. Section 9.2 provides an overview of the social security system and the occupational pension schemes. Section 9.3 presents the results from a simulation model designed to reveal the economic incentives implied by the Swedish social security system and the occupational pension scheme for blue-collar workers (STP) for a representative individual. Section 9.4 concludes.

9.1   The Labor Market Behavior of Older Persons in Sweden

Figures 9.1 and 9.2 show the historical trends in labor force participation rates since 1963 for men and women over age forty-four. Four different age groups are studied: forty-five to fifty-four, fifty-five to fifty-nine, sixty to sixty-four, and sixty-five to seventy-four. Considering the entire historical period, figure 9.1 shows that the labor force participation rate of older men decreased in all age groups. But, in the youngest age group, forty-five to fifty-four, the decrease is comparatively small. Labor force participation for the age group fifty-five to fifty-nine goes from about 95 to about 82 percent in 1995. There is a comparatively large decrease in labor force participation for the age group sixty to sixty-four: from 85 percent in 1963 to 55 percent in 1995, or 30 percentage points. Figure 9.1 also shows that labor force participation in the three youngest age groups decreased more in the most recent recession in the Swedish economy (1991) than in the years preceding the recession. The largest decrease is in the age group sixty to sixty-four for this period as well. The historical trend in labor force participation of the age group sixty-five to seventy-four reveals that the change in mandatory retirement age, from age sixty-seven to age sixty-five in 1976,[3] was preceded by a steady decrease in labor force participation of the age group affected by the reform; that is, here, the actual effect of the reform was small.

The trend in the labor force participation of older women, shown in figure 9.2, is very different from that of men: for the entire period 1963–90, labor

---

2. The economic literature on the labor supply of the elderly and its relation to social insurance spending is reviewed in app. B.
3. Section 9.2 below provides a more detailed description of labor market institutions and mandatory retirement ages.

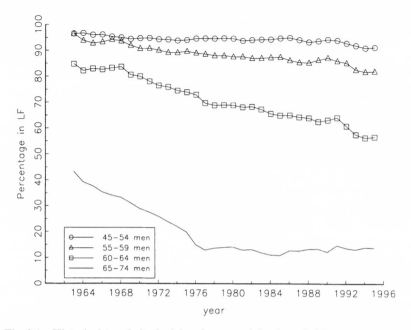

Fig. 9.1   Historical trends in the labor force participation of older men

Source: Various reports of the Swedish Labor Force Survey, provided by Statistics Sweden, adjusted to be comparable between different points of time.

Note: LF = labor force.

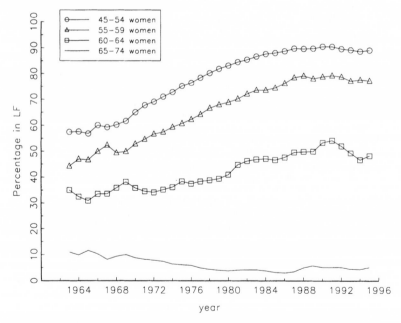

Fig. 9.2   Historical trends in the labor force participation of older women

Source: See fig. 9.1 above.

Note: LF = labor force.

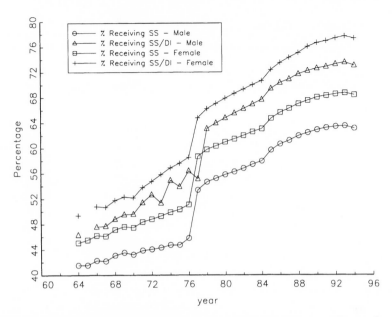

**Fig. 9.3   Share of Swedish men and women age fifty-five and over who receive
disability pension and old age pension**
Source: Different issues of *Allmän Försäkring* (National Insurance Board, Stockholm).
Note: SS = social security; DI = disability insurance.

force participation rates increased for all age groups between forty-five and
sixty-four, although at a decreasing rate. The smallest increase is in the age
group sixty to sixty-four, viewed over the entire period. Labor force participation decreased somewhat in all three groups after the 1991 recession. The
largest decrease for women, about 7 percentage points between 1991 and 1994,
is in the age group sixty to sixty-four.

Of course, the extent to which social security might have affected the observed pattern of labor force participation depends on the coverage and generosity of the schemes. Ever since the introduction of the compulsory old age
pension (*folkpension*) in 1913, all Swedish citizens are entitled to an old age
pension. Figure 9.3 shows the percentage share of men and women older than
fifty-five years who actually receive an old age or disability pension for the
period 1964–94. It reveals that the share of women in this age group who
receive an old age or disability pension is somewhat higher (about 4 percentage points) than it is for men in this age group—throughout the entire period.
It is interesting to compare the big *leap* for the number of men who received
an old age pension in 1976 with the smooth decrease in labor force participation before 1976. The difference was caused by the change in mandatory retirement age, which was preceded by agreements between the trade unions and
the employers' confederations on occupational pensions that offer benefits between age sixty-five and age sixty-seven.

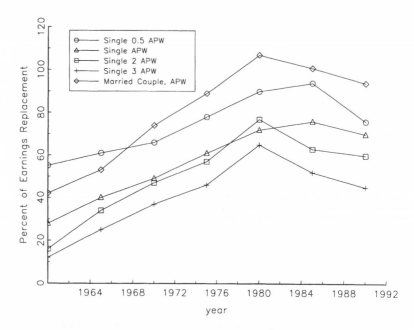

Fig. 9.4 Replacement rates of old age pension from the national pension system for a production worker with average wage
Source: Palme (1990).

But the most striking fact in figure 9.3 is the dramatic increase between 1964 and 1994 in the share of men and women receiving old age or disability pensions: an increase of about 25 percentage points for men and about 28 for women. About 6 percentage points of this increase for men and women can be attributed to the increased number of disability pensions; the number of old age pensions increased by about 8 percentage points after the 1976 pension reform, when the mandatory retirement age was decreased from sixty-seven to sixty-five; a very small part of the increase can be attributed to a small increase in the early withdrawal of social security benefits. The rest, about 11 percentage points for men and 14 percentage points for women, might be caused by changes in the demographic structure, primarily, the increase in life expectancy.

Figure 9.4 shows the replacement level from the national Swedish pension system,[4] that is, the amount of the first year's pension as a share of the preceding year's earnings provided that the worker continues to work until he or she reaches the age of mandatory retirement.[5] The calculation is made using the

4. This includes the basic pension and the supplementary pension (ATP) schemes. Occupational pension schemes are not included.

5. The source of the estimates of the compensation levels shown in fig. 9.4 is Palme (1990), where the compensation levels in eighteen OECD countries are compared, and Kangas and Palme (1989), where the compensation levels in the Nordic countries are compared.

earnings history of an *average production worker* (APW).[6] The compensation levels are calculated for net income; that is, income taxes are considered in the calculations. Figure 9.4 shows the compensation level for four hypothetical single workers: (1) one who has an earnings history amounting to half the earnings of the APW in each year; (2) one who has always earned the same as the APW; (3) one who has earned double the APW; and (4) one who has always earned three times as much as the APW.

Figure 9.4 also shows the compensation level for a married couple, where the husband is assumed to have had the same earnings as the APW. Here, it is assumed that the wife never worked.[7] The worker is assumed to retire at age sixty-five. The replacement rate is generally different if the individual elects to retire earlier than the mandatory retirement age—as sections 9.2 and 9.3 below show. Figure 9.4 shows that the replacement level increased a great deal in the years between 1960 and 1980. The maturing of the supplementary pension system explains the largest part of the increase.

9.1.1 Labor Market Behavior in 1995

To get a more detailed picture of the current pattern of exiting from the labor force, the 1994 and 1995 Labor Force Surveys are used.[8] Figure 9.5 shows labor force participation by age and sex for individuals older than forty-five years. To improve the precision in the estimates, the 1994 and 1995 Labor Force Surveys are combined. Figure 9.5 shows two properties of the labor force participation of older workers. First, labor force participation decreases with age, except for women in their late forties and for some age groups between sixty-five and sixty-nine for men and women.[9] It could also be seen that the decrease in labor force participation is fairly moderate until workers reach age fifty-seven. Labor force participation for, for example, fifty-six-year-olds is above 80 percent for men and women. Among individuals in their late fifties and early sixties, labor force participation rates fall every year and at an increasing rate. Labor force participation for individuals age sixty-four, one year before the mandatory retirement age, is about 30 percent for women and 43 percent for men. Second, labor force participation rates are higher for men in all age groups. But the difference is very small for people in their late forties, increasing gradually with age. At age sixty-four, the difference is as large as about 13 percentage points.

Figure 9.6 distinguishes among the employed, unemployed, disabled,[10] and

6. The *average production worker* is a concept frequently used for comparing wages in different countries (see, e.g., U.S. Department of Labor 1996). The Swedish APW is used for the calculations in fig. 9.4
7. But note that this situation is very uncommon in Sweden.
8. Appendix A describes these surveys.
9. The latter finding should be interpreted with care since, in the Labor Force Survey, the sample sizes for individuals older than age sixty-five are very small (for details, see app. A).
10. Because the Labor Force Survey does not distinguish between the individuals who receive an old age pension and those who receive a disability pension, we used the number of individuals who receive a disability pension provided by the National Social Insurance Board to obtain figures on the share of the disabled in each age group.

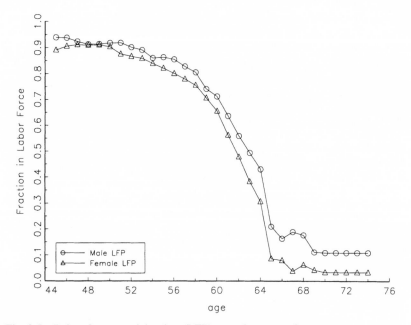

Fig. 9.5   Labor force participation (LFP) rates by age and sex
Source: Authors' calculations based on the Swedish Labor Force Survey, 1994 and 1995 (provided by Statistics Sweden), combined.

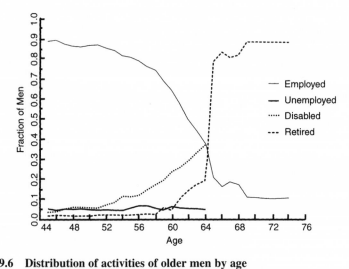

Fig. 9.6   Distribution of activities of older men by age
Source: Authors' calculations based on the Swedish Labor Force Survey, 1994 and 1995 (provided by Statistics Sweden), combined. For the graph of the share of individuals receiving a disability pensions, we have used statistics from the entire Swedish population published in *Allmän Försäkring 1995* (National Social Insurance Board, Stockholm).

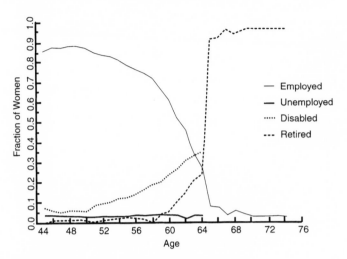

Fig. 9.7   Distribution of activities of older women by age
Source: See fig. 9.6 above.

retired, by age, for older men. Figure 9.7 provides the same information for women. Figures 9.6 and 9.7 show that the graphs for the unemployed and for the disabled continue only to age sixty-four. This is because the Labor Force Survey counts only people younger than the mandatory retirement age, sixty-five, as unemployed. People older than age sixty-five are not entitled to unemployment insurance. Our definition of *disabled* is an individual who receives a disability benefit from the national pension system, which is only possible for those under sixty-five years of age.[11]

By comparing the graphs for the retired and the disabled, figures 9.6 and 9.7 show that in all age groups between forty-five and sixty-four, the most common way to leave the labor market for men and women is to become a disability pensioner. At age sixty-four, as many as about 37 percent of all men and 35 percent of all women receive a full-time disability pension. A comparison of figures 9.6 and 9.7 shows that women, on average, retire somewhat earlier than men: at age sixty-four, about 20 percent of men and 25 percent of women are retired. A study of the graphs for the unemployed shows that unemployment is about equal in all age groups. A comparison of figure 9.6 with figure 9.7 shows that the unemployment rate is somewhat higher for men than for women for the entire age range considered in the figures.

11. Section 9.2 below describes the rules for selecting delayed payments from the basic and supplementary pension schemes (including possible economic gains from the selection).

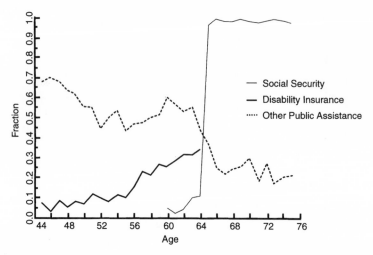

Fig. 9.8   Share of older men who receive different kinds of support from the public sector by age
Source: Authors' calculations based on data from 1994 Household Income Survey, provided by Statistics Sweden.

9.1.2   Income Sources of Older Persons

Figures 9.8 and 9.9 reveal the incidence of private, occupational, and public pensions among older persons in 1994. The data source for these calculations is the Household Income Survey (HINK) provided by Statistics Sweden.[12]

Figure 9.8 shows the share of all men between the ages of forty-five and seventy-five, divided into one-year age groups, who receive an old age pension, a disability pension, or any other form of public assistance. The graphs for a disability pension confirm what is already known from figure 9.6 above, although another data source is used for these figures: about 35 percent of the sixty-four-year-olds receive a disability pension, and the rate of receipt increases rapidly starting from about age fifty-seven.

When comparing the share of retired men in figure 9.6 with the estimates of the share of men receiving an old age pension shown in figure 9.8, two things should be noted: First, for men aged sixty to sixty-four, the rate of take-up of old age pensions is about 10 percentage points lower than the rate of retired men in this age group. So about half the men who retire before the mandatory retirement age of sixty-five do not claim an old age pension from social security until age sixty-five. Second, according to the data in figure 9.8, almost all people claim old age pension benefits at age sixty-five, although, as shown in figure 9.6, only about 85 percent are retired at that age. The rate of all other public transfers is very high for men in the younger age groups considered in

12. For a detailed description of this survey, see app. A.

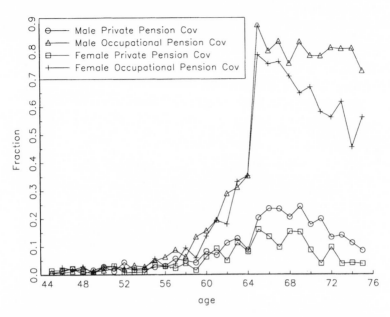

Fig. 9.9   Share of all Swedish men and women who receive occupational and private pensions by age
Source: See fig. 9.8 above.

figure 9.8: about 70 percent for men age forty-five.[13] This graph decreases steadily in older age groups.

Figure 9.9 shows the proportion of men and women between the ages of forty-five and seventy-five, again divided into one-year age groups, who receive occupational and private pensions. As expected, the proportion receiving private and occupational pensions increases rapidly at age sixty-five. But figure 9.9 also shows that the proportion decreases steadily after age sixty-five. This is due to the increase in the coverage of both occupational and private pensions in younger birth cohorts. The increased gender gap that is most evident for occupational pensions in older age groups is also due to changes in the work patterns of younger birth cohorts, that is, the increased rate of labor force participation of women.

Figure 9.10 displays the average shares of different sources of household income by the age of the head of the family. Although, as explained in appendix A, these figures should be interpreted with caution because the sample sizes for some components of household income are very small, it is interesting

13. Note that this figure includes *all* public transfers, e.g., payments from the compulsory sickness insurance and income support programs directed primarily toward households with dependent children, like housing allowances.

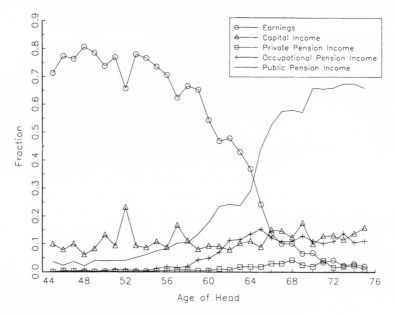

Fig. 9.10   Average shares of different sources of family income by age of family head
Source: See fig. 9.8 above.

to note that the observations made in figure 9.9 above are confirmed. The importance of private and occupational pensions is decreasing among older pensioners. The share consisting of earnings is decreasing from about 75 percent at age fifty to about 65 percent at age fifty-eight. After that age, the share of earnings is decreasing at an increasing rate. The share of capital income is around 10 percent in the younger and around 15 percent in the older age groups considered.

9.2   Key Features of the Social Security System

9.2.1   A History of the Social Security System in Sweden

In 1913, the first compulsory old age pension insurance was implemented. It was a fully funded system consisting of two parts: a means-tested basic pension and a supplementary pension, which was related to individual contributions. Although the compensation levels from the means-tested part of this pension scheme were very low—only 11.3 percent of the earnings of an industrial worker (Elmér 1960)—the 1913 reform was fundamentally important: all Swedish citizens were covered by an old age pension scheme. This Swedish system was the first pension system in the world to cover all citizens regardless of occupation.

In 1935 and 1946, two major reforms were implemented. Criticism from conservatives and liberals about large, state-controlled pension funds, which influenced capital markets, dominated the political debate preceding the 1935 reform. The Social Democrats wanted to increase benefit levels without increasing expenditures for the pension system. This debate led to a switch to a *pay-as-you-go* system in the 1935 reform. The financing of the system was changed to employers' contributions, and the levels of pensions were substantially increased.

In 1941, the minimum pension was about 29.4 percent of the earnings of an industrial worker (Elmér 1960). Because of means testing, the increase in the replacement rates also implied that the share of the population that actually received pension payments increased from about 70 to 90 percent after the reform. In the 1946 reform, the basic pension replaced the old means-tested pension. A housing supplement in the areas where the cost of living was the greatest was also introduced.

The supplementary pension (ATP) was implemented after a 1959 referendum. The two main alternatives in the referendum were a compulsory system (which was finally implemented), proposed by the blue-collar trade union and the Social Democratic Party, and a voluntary system, proposed by the employers' confederation and the conservative and liberal parties. The first birth cohort affected by the supplementary pension was that born in 1896. The first year when pension right income for a supplementary pension was recorded was 1960.

In 1976, the mandatory retirement age was decreased from sixty-seven to sixty-five, and the right to a *partial retirement* pension was introduced. In 1990, a gender-neutral survivor pension replaced the widow's pension.

In 1994, a majority in the Swedish parliament reached an agreement on principles for a new old age pension. Details of the new system will be determined in 1998. The first cohort to be affected by the new system is that born in 1938. Twenty percent of the pension coverage provided to this group will be determined under the rules of the new system and 80 percent under the rules of the old. The new system determines 5 percent more of the pension coverage of each successive cohort. Hence, 25 percent of the coverage provided to the cohort born in 1939 will be determined under the new system and 75 percent under the old. The coverage provided to the cohort born in 1954 will be determined entirely under the new system. No pensions will be paid out under the new system until 2001.

9.2.2   Current Features of the Social Security System

Employer contributions levied on wages finance the social security system. In 1994, the level of *all* social contributions was 31.36 percentage points on gross earnings. The level of the contribution for the national basic pension was 5.86, for the supplementary pension (ATP) 13.00, and for the part-time pension 0.20 percentage points. In the current system, there is no ceiling on contributions. General tax revenues partially finance the national basic pension.

All Swedish citizens and all persons living in Sweden are entitled to a basic pension. In principle, all receive the same amount irrespective of previous earnings. There is a reduction of the amount if the time of residence in Sweden is under forty years and the number of years with income in Sweden is under thirty years.

Like all social insurance, the basic pension is related to the *basic amount* (BA). The BA is linked to the CPI. As the BA is decided each year by the government, it is possible for a majority in the Swedish parliament to make discretionary changes that do not follow the development of the CPI. This has happened on several occasions since 1960. During the period between November 1980 and November 1982, the BA was temporary linked to another price index, which to a lesser extent than the CPI reflected large increases in oil and electric prices during that period. In addition, the price increases that resulted from the large devaluation of the Swedish currency in 1982 were not fully reflected in the BA. And, during the 1990s, pensions have not been fully aligned with price indexing owing to several measures meant to cut the government budget deficit. In 1995, the BA was SKr 34,986 (U.S.$4,907), and the annual wage of an average production worker was SKr 189,488 (U.S.$26,576).[14]

The basic pension for a single old age pensioner is 96 percent of the BA. The basic pension is reduced to 78.5 percent if the person is married. Before 1995, it was reduced only if the person was married to someone who also received the basic pension. Individuals with no, or low, ATP are entitled to a special supplement. The special supplement is independent of marital status and is 55.5 percent of the BA. The special supplement is reduced on a one-to-one basis against the supplementary pension. Thus, a single old age pensioner with only a basic pension and a special supplement receives 151.5 percent of the BA. In 1995, that was SKr 53,004 (U.S.$7,434) in annual pension, or 28.0 percent of the annual earnings of an average production worker. In 1994, about 20 percent of all old age pensioners did not have a supplementary pension; that is, they received only a basic pension and a special supplement. This group mainly consists of older women; for example, 63 percent of female old age pensioners older than age eighty-five did not receive a supplementary pension. The corresponding figures for male and female old age pensioners between the ages of sixty-five and sixty-nine were 1.7 and 13.8 percent, respectively.

As previously mentioned, the survivor pension was changed in 1990, and women born before and after 1945 follow different rules for the survivor pension. For women born before 1945, the rules for the widow's pension still apply. They get 90 percent of the BA until they reach age sixty-five. The rules

---

14. To convert Swedish krona to U.S. dollars, we have used the exchange rate of SKr 7.13 = U.S.$1.00, which was the average selling price of Swedish krona in 1995. This exchange rate is used throughout this paper.

for the new gender-neutral *transitional* survivor benefit apply to those born after 1 January 1945. According to these rules, the survivor benefit is paid to the insured individual's spouse within twelve months of the death. From 1 January 1997, the period is reduced to six months. It could be prolonged under special circumstances (widows with dependent children). This means that, for most women born before 1945, a survivor benefit is a possible source of supplementary income for about the next ten to fifteen years.

The supplementary pension (ATP) is related to the individual's earnings history. The benefit level is determined in three steps. The first step is to determine the *pension-rights* income for each year from age sixteen. The calculation of pension-rights income is based on income from labor recorded in the annual tax return. Pension-rights income is the share of income exceeding the BA, and it is set to zero if the annual income from labor does not exceed the BA.[15] Besides earnings and income from self-employment, transfer payments from social insurance, such as income from sickness and unemployment insurance, the parental cash benefit, and the partial retirement pension, are included in pension-rights income. Three years of pension-rights income greater than zero between the ages of sixteen and sixty-five are required to receive an old age pension under the ATP scheme. Income above 7.5 times the BA, the social security ceiling, is not included in pension-rights income.[16]

The second step is to calculate the average pension points. This is done by dividing the pension-rights income by the corresponding year's BA to obtain the pension points for each year. Thus, with the social security ceiling at 7.5 times the BA, the maximum number of pension points an individual could get in a particular year is 6.5. The average pension point becomes the average from the individual's best fifteen years of pension points.

The final step is to calculate the individual's ATP pension income (Y_i) by applying the formula

$$Y_i = 0.6 \cdot AP_i \cdot \min\left(\frac{N_i}{30}, 1\right) \cdot BA,$$

where AP_i is individual average pension points, BA is the basic amount, and N_i is the number of years the individual has recorded a pension-rights income greater than zero. The number of years with pension points required for a full ATP pension is thirty for individuals born in 1924 or later. Using the amount of the BA in 1995 in the ATP formula gives us a maximum pension amount from the Swedish national pension system in 1995 of SKr 170,032 (U.S. $23,847), which is about 90 percent of the annual wage of an average production worker.

15. Since 1993, two different basic amounts have been in use. The BA, which is linked to the CPI, is used to calculate pension-rights income (SKr 35,700 in 1995), and a reduced (by 2 percent) BA is used to calculate pension benefits.

16. But the proportional payroll tax that finances the ATP pension is also paid on the share of the income exceeding 7.5 times the BA.

There is no dependents' benefit within the ATP scheme; that is, the amount of the pension is independent of marital status, and there are no rules for splitting future ATP benefits in a divorce. As previously mentioned, the survivor benefit in the ATP scheme has recently changed. Those who were born before 1945 receive 35 or 40 percent of the deceased husband's ATP pension until they reach the normal retirement age of sixty-five: 35 percent if there are children in the household who are eligible for a children's pension and 40 percent otherwise. After the widow reaches age sixty-five, her ATP pension is reduced, taking into account her own ATP pension. The rules are somewhat different for different birth cohorts. The survivor pension for those born after 1 January 1945 is gender neutral. The surviving spouse of an individual who has qualified for an ATP pension is entitled to the ATP survivor benefit within twelve months of the death according to the rules implemented in 1990. The amount is 20 percent of the deceased spouse's ATP pension—if there are also surviving children entitled to the children's pension—and 40 percent otherwise.

The principal rules of the new pension system, which will replace the basic and ATP pension schemes, were decided in 1994. The main changes are the following: Earnings from the entire life cycle are counted when the individual's pension income is determined, rather than only the fifteen best years. The pension is related to the real growth rate in the entire economy—rather than price indexed. Changes in life expectancy also affect individual pension income; that is, increased life expectancy and lower economic growth rates decrease individual pension income at a given retirement age.

9.2.3 Social Security and Pathways to Early Exit from the Labor Market

Sweden has a normal retirement age of sixty-five years.[17] Older workers are not covered by the employment security law;[18] that is, workers older than age sixty-five are excepted from the seniority rules, and, if a firm wants to scale down, these workers are the least protected. Furthermore, workers older than age sixty-five are not entitled to support from unemployment insurance. On the other hand, the wage cost for employers is lower for workers older than age sixty-five because the employers do not pay part of the payroll tax for the national or occupational pensions.

Central and municipal government employees automatically lose their jobs at age sixty-five. But exceptions to this rule are permitted for one year. In the private sector, there are often collective agreements between the trade unions and the employers' confederations, prescribing strict rules for mandatory retirement at age sixty-five. As the number of these agreements is very large, it is hard to get an overview of how strict the rules for mandatory retirement are.

---

17. Wadensjö (1989) examines this issue in detail.

18. If the employee is not covered by a central agreement between the union and the employers' confederation—and only about 5 percent of the Swedish labor market is—workers up to age sixty-seven are covered by the employment security law.

There may also be a social convention to stop working at age sixty-five, at least in areas with high unemployment.

The basic pension and the ATP can be claimed as early as age sixty and as late as age seventy. If the individual chooses to claim early, the amount of the benefit is permanently reduced by 0.5 percent for each month of early withdrawal. For example, if the individual retires at age sixty, the permanent reduction is 30 percent (5 × 12 × 0.5). If the individual decides to begin to receive a pension later than at age sixty-five, the pension income is permanently increased by 0.7 percent for each month of postponement.

Beside the national old age pension scheme, there are two other pathways to early retirement: the partial retirement pension and the disability pension.

A partial retirement pension allows workers age sixty and older to reduce their hours of work and receive a benefit to replace the lost earnings. To be eligible for part-time retirement, the worker must have had ten years of pension-rights earnings after age forty-five and must work at least twenty-two hours before the reduction. The benefit is 65 percent of the difference in earnings between before and after part-time retirement.

The most common means of leaving the labor market before age sixty-five is through a disability pension. Figure 9.6 above for men and figure 9.7 above for women illustrate this. In 1994, 37 percent of men and 35 percent of women in the age group sixty-four years received a full-time disability pension.

The disability pension consists of the basic pension and the income-related ATP supplement. Pension income is determined in the same way an old age pension benefit is, without the actuarial reduction for withdrawal in advance. A disability pension can be received from age sixteen. To be entitled to one, an individual must have a physician's certification that his or her capacity to work is permanently reduced by at least 25 percent owing to sickness or some similar cause. If the capacity to work is reduced for a long period but not permanently, the individual is entitled to a *temporary* disability pension. If the individual's working capacity is reduced by at least 25 percent but not by 50 percent, he or she is eligible to receive 25 percent of the full disability pension benefit. If it is reduced by at least 50 but not by 75 percent or by at least 75 but not by 100 percent, he or she is eligible to receive 50 and 75 percent, respectively, of the full pension benefit. To obtain a full disability pension, an individual must be completely unable to work.

In practice, the strictness of medical screening has varied over time. Successive, significant tightening of the eligibility rules was legislated in July 1993, October 1995, and January 1997. Figure 9.11[19] shows the number of new disability pensions granted between 1971 and 1995. Studies of the long-term variation in the number of new disability pensions granted between the mid-1970s

---

19. New part-time disability pensions have been recalculated as the *equivalent* number of full-time disability pensions.

Fig. 9.11   Number of new disability pensions, 1971–95
Source: National Social Insurance Board (1996).

and 1992 (see, e.g., Hedström 1987; or Wadensjö 1985) suggest that it can be explained by variation in access to such pensions and increased compensation. Between 1970 and 1991, it was possible to receive a disability pension for *labor market reasons.* In order to be eligible to receive such a pension, the insured individual had to be over sixty years old and to have exhausted his or her right to unemployment insurance.[20] During 1992 and 1993, the number of new disability pensions granted was very high. This was because, during these years, the social security administration tried to decrease the number of ongoing long periods with sickness benefits. In some cases, the individual was granted a disability pension because of these measures.

9.2.4   Occupational Pensions

There are basically four different centrally bargained pension plans for Swedish workers: *(a)* two separate pension plans for employees in the private sector, one for white-collar workers (ITP) and one for blue-collar workers (STP), and *(b)* two separate plans for public-sector employees, one for those employed by the central government and one for those employed by municipalities and counties.

In 1985, ITP covered about 32.6 percent of all insured workers, STP 39.8

---

20. Workers were generally entitled to unemployment insurance for twenty-one months.

percent, the pension for those employed in central government 10.7 percent, and the pension for those employed in municipalities 16.9 percent (Kangas and Palme 1989). Like social insurance, all the occupational pension schemes are price indexed. Pension rights are portable among these four main occupational pension schemes.

STP

The STP pension scheme was introduced after a central agreement between LO (the blue-collar workers' union) and SAF (the employers' confederation in the private sector) in 1971. It is entirely a pay-as-you-go pension plan, and it is financed through employers' contributions. In 1996, the rate of the employers' contribution was 3.15 percent of gross earnings. STP was radically reformed in 1996: for workers born after 1931, a new, partially funded pension was established. The main reason for the reform of STP was the long-term decrease in the number of blue-collar workers in the private sector.

The size of the individual STP pension depends on the number of years the worker has contributed to the scheme and annual earnings between the ages of fifty-five and fifty-nine. Receipt of a full STP pension requires that the insured worker have contributed for at least thirty years between the ages of twenty-eight and sixty-five and for at least three years between the ages of fifty-five and sixty-five. Provided that the insured worker has contributed for the maximum number of years, the STP pension is 10 percent of the average earnings below 7.5 times the BA of the three best years between age fifty-five and age fifty-nine. The STP pension cannot be collected before the month of the individual's sixty-fifth birthday, nor can payments be postponed. But pension payments are not reduced if the worker decides to continue to work after age sixty-five. To summarize, the worker's pension wealth is not reduced at all, or by only a comparatively small amount, if he or she decides to quit at age fifty-eight or later, but he or she will not receive a pension at all if he or she quits before age fifty-seven.

ITP

The ITP pension plan existed before the introduction of ATP in 1960. But then it covered only about 50 percent of the white-collar workers in the private sector. Since that time, it has been gradually expanded to cover almost all private-sector white-collar workers. It is financed through an employer contribution, which, in 1996, was 1.15 on gross earnings for employees and contributions made between the ages of twenty-eight and sixty-two for the insured individual.

The size of the individual ITP pension depends on the number of years between the ages of twenty-eight and sixty-five that the individual has contributed to the ITP pension and on the salary the year before he or she starts to collect the pension. In general, receipt of a full ITP pension requires thirty years of contributions. Otherwise, the pension is reduced proportionally. Provided that the individual has contributed the required number of years, the pension is 10 percent of last year's salary up to 7.5 times the BA, 65 percent of the salary between 7.5 and 20 times the BA, and 32.5 percent between 20 and 30 times the BA. The pension-rights age for the ITP pension is sixty-five. But the pension can be claimed from age sixty-two with a lifetime reduction of 0.6 percent for each month it is collected early. It can also be postponed until age seventy, with a lifetime increase of 0.6 percent for each month the pension is postponed. The ITP pension can also be claimed before age sixty-two; the amount of the pension is then determined individually depending on the sum of the individual's contributions to the pension scheme. Because the individual contributes to the scheme only until age sixty-two, the reduction is generally larger if he or she decides to quit before rather than after age sixty-two.

State Employees' Pensions

The supplementary occupational scheme for employees in the central government consists of two parts: one basic pension and one supplementary pension. The basic pension is entirely a pay-as-you-go scheme, and pensions are paid directly from the central government budget. But the supplementary pension is a fully funded system, and 1.7 percent of the annual salary is redirected to a pension fund. The size of the basic pension is determined in a way very similar to that in which the ITP pension is. Thirty years of work in central government are required for receipt of a full pension, and the same rules as for the ITP pension are applied if the individual does not fulfill this requirement. Apart from this requirement, the average of the five years preceding the year the individual decides to collect pension payments determines the size of the pension, which is 10 percent of this five-year average up to 7.5 times the BA, 65 percent between 7.5 and 20 times the BA, and 32.5 percent between 20 and 30 times the BA.

The retirement age is sixty-five for most people employed in central government. But there are several exceptions—most important are military personnel, who are in general pensioned at age fifty-five and receive a full occupational pension from that date. A pension can be claimed voluntarily before the pension-rights age. The amount of the pension is then decreased by 0.4 percent for each month the pension is collected early for the rest of the individual's life and by 2.4 percent on the share of the income below 7.5 times the BA when the individual turns age sixty-five. Pension payments can also be postponed. This increases the pension by 0.4 percent for the rest of the person's life for each month the pension is postponed after the pension-rights age.

Local Government Employees' Pensions

The pension plan for employees in the municipalities is administered by an insurance company owned by Sweden's 288 municipalities. Receipt of a full pension requires thirty years of employment in the local government sector between the ages of eighteen and sixty-five; otherwise, the pension is reduced proportionally. The size of the pension is determined by the average of the five best years of the seven years preceding the year before the year the individual decides to retire. This pension scheme is fully coordinated with the basic and the ATP pensions from the national scheme. Including the two national schemes, the pension is 96 percent of the average calculated salary (as previously described) below the BA, 78.5 percent between the BA and 2.5 times the BA, 60 percent between 2.5 and 3.5 times the BA, 65 percent between 7.5 and 20 times the BA, and 32.5 percent between 20 and 30 times the BA.

The pension-rights age is sixty-five for most people employed by municipal governments. But pension payments can be collected from age sixty and postponed until sixty-seven. If the individual decides to retire before age sixty-five, the pension is reduced for the rest of the individual's life by 0.3 percent per month between age sixty-three and age sixty-five, by 0.4 percent between age sixty-two and age sixty-three, and by 0.5 percent per month between age sixty and age sixty-two. The pension is increased by 0.1 percent for each month the individual decides to continue working after age sixty-five.

9.2.5   Income Taxes and Housing Allowances

Besides the social security system, retirement incentives are also affected by income taxes.[21] Sweden has an integrated income tax system. Individuals pay local and national income tax. The national government determines the tax base for national and local taxes. The tax base is divided into *earned* and *capital* income. All income from the social insurance system is included in earned income—together with wages and salaries. Income from capital is subject to a national proportional tax of 30 percent. Earned income is subject to national and local taxes. The tax rate for the local tax is determined independently by each of Sweden's 288 municipalities. But there is a clustering of these tax rates at around 31 percent.

Local income taxes are proportional, while the national income tax is progressive. After the major income tax reform in 1991, the national income tax was set to zero below a certain breakpoint (about U.S.$25,000 in 1996) and to 20 percent on all income above that level. In 1995, this tax was temporarily increased to 25 percent. This may give the false impression that there are only two possible marginal tax rates on earned income. But there is a basic deduction that varies among different brackets of earned income. There are special rules for the basic deduction for old age pensioners that largely determine their marginal tax rates.

For a single pensioner with only a basic pension, the basic deduction is equal to the amount of his pension income; that is, he pays no income tax at all. If the pension income is higher than the amount of a basic pension (in 1995, SKr 53,000, or U.S.$7,434), the deduction is reduced by 65 percent of

---

21. For a more detailed description of the Swedish tax system, see Aronsson and Walker (1997).

the amount in excess of SKr 53,000. But earnings, self-employment income, and private pension insurance income do not reduce the deduction. High-income pensioners are covered by the rules of basic deduction for nonpension-ers. The basic deduction for nonpensioners has a humped-shaped relation to income: For income below SKr 66,800 (U.S.$9,369) it was SKr 8,900 in 1995; it increased linearly with taxable income to SKr 18,100 at SKr 103,200; then it decreased linearly for taxable incomes between SKr 108,700 and SKr 199,700 to once again, SKr 8,900 for higher taxable incomes. At income levels where the deduction for nonpensioners is not applicable, the deduction for a married pensioner is SKr 10,100 lower—compared to a single pensioner at a given income level. A pensioner has a right to the deduction for nonpensioners if it is higher.

Low-income old age, disability, and survivor pensioners are entitled to a housing allowance. In 1995, this allowance was at most 85 percent of the housing cost up to a certain ceiling and above a certain floor. It was reduced by 40 percent (45 percent at high income levels) of income in excess of a basic pension and special supplement and by 2 percent of wealth. In 1994, about 30 percent of all old age pensioners received housing allowances, and the average amount was about SKr 17,673 (U.S.$2,479), that is, 33 percent of the amount of the lowest pension from the national pension system.

9.2.6   Retirement Behavior

Figures 9.12 and 9.13 depict the hazard rate out of the labor force for men and women, respectively. These figures are obtained by comparing the size of each one-year age group in the 1994 and 1995 Labor Force Surveys.[22] The small negative estimates that are obtained for some of the age groups can thus be explained by sample error. The sample size does not permit us to present calculations for the age groups beyond age sixty-five. But a clear pattern emerges in figures 9.12 and 9.13: the hazard rate out of the labor force increases slowly until age sixty, when there is a marked increase in the rate of exiting from the labor force, that is, for the ages between sixty and sixty-four. At age sixty-five, the mandatory retirement age, there is a spike that indicates that almost 70 percent of the remaining labor force, both men and women, decide to exit at this age.

9.3   Retirement Incentives

9.3.1   Simulation Modeling of Retirement Incentives

This part of the paper provides an overview of the economic incentives for labor force participation generated by the Swedish social security and occupational pension systems for blue-collar workers in the private sector. In order to

---

22. Appendix A gives a description of this sample.

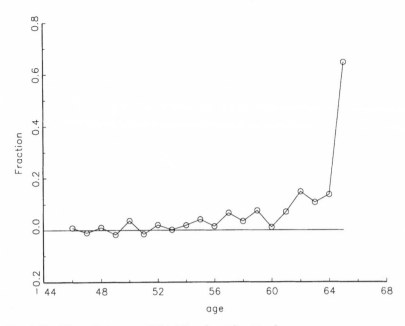

Fig. 9.12   Hazard rate out of the labor force for men by age
Source: Authors' calculations based on the Swedish Labor Force Survey, 1994 and 1995, provided by Statistics Sweden.

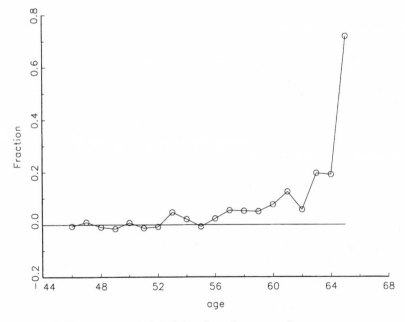

Fig. 9.13   Hazard rate out of the labor force for women by age
Source: See fig. 9.12 above.

provide this overview, we simulate the social security outcome for a representative individual. First, we assume that the representative individual is a man born on 1 January 1930. As a *base case,* we assume that his life-cycle earnings path will follow the earnings of the median income earner in each age among men born in 1930. We also examine the case where the representative individual earning path for each year corresponds to the earnings of the tenth and ninetieth percentiles of this birth cohort. To obtain the synthetic earning history of our representative individual, we use administrative records of the National Social Insurance Board. The sample we use includes all individuals born on the fifth, fifteenth, or twenty-fifth of each month, that is, about 10 percent of the Swedish population. We selected men born in 1930 for the estimation of the tenth, fiftieth, and ninetieth percentile incomes. This sample contains about forty-two hundred people. Between 1978 and 1994—except for the year 1983—we have data that are obtained from tax records, which include income shares below the floor and above the ceiling for pension-rights income. For the entire period 1960–94, we have data on the individual's pension points, which are registered at the National Social Insurance Board.

Figure 9.14 shows the earnings histories that we obtained from the data for the median earner and the tenth and ninetieth percentiles, respectively. These figures show the results from the tax records and the pension point records. The potential problem of using pension points for measuring earnings is that earnings below the social security floor are excluded, as are earnings above the social security ceiling. For the birth cohort that we selected, it turned out that the median earner has about the same income measured by pension points as measured by the corresponding variable from tax records in the period 1978–94. This means that the number of men with income below the floor (i.e., the BA) is so small that it does not affect the measure of median income by pension points. But, for individuals at both the tenth and the ninetieth percentiles, there is, as expected, a substantial difference between the results from these two data sets. For the simulations for individuals at the tenth and ninetieth percentiles, we have imputed incomes for the years where only pension points are observed. This is described in appendix C.

In our data, we found a decline in real earnings in ages fifty-one to fifty-six due to the recession experienced by the Swedish economy in the early 1980s. We also found a sharp decline in earnings after age sixty for the median earner and the earner of the tenth percentile. A decline could also be seen for the ninetieth percentile earner, but one less marked. This is probably explained in part by the fact, which could not be observed in the data, that many people decrease the number of hours of work after age sixty. But, in the calculations, we assume full-time earnings. To deal with this problem, we make our calculations for two cases. In the first, case, we assume that, after age fifty, the individual's income increases at the same rate as the change in the real hourly wage rate for the entire Swedish economy, obtained from the national accounts. This is treated as the base case in our calculations. These imputed incomes are shown by a dotted line in figure 9.15. As a sensitivity analysis, we also

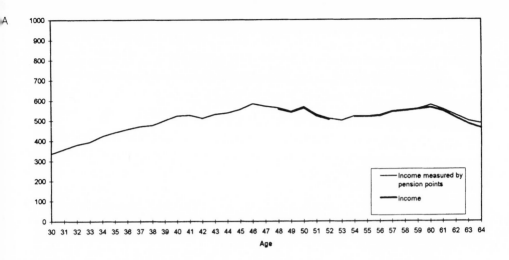

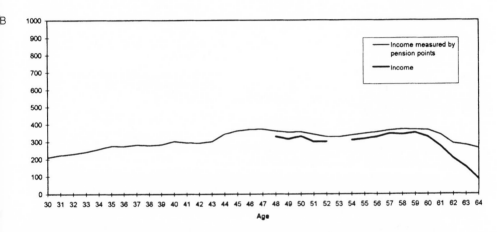

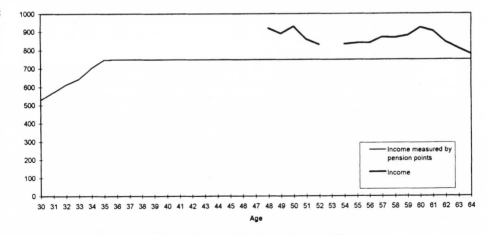

Fig. 9.14   Men born 1930: *a*, median earner; *b*, tenth percentile earner;
c, ninetieth percentile earner

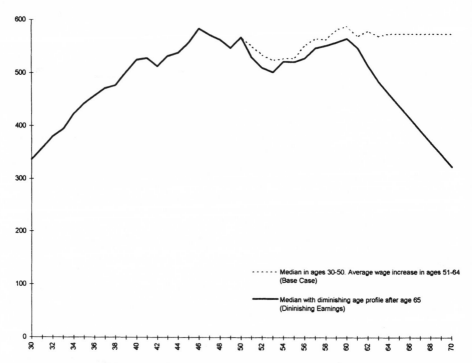

Fig. 9.15   Base case and diminishing earnings case

calculate the *actual synthetic* earnings history for the individual with median income in each year until age sixty-four and with the diminishing trend in ages sixty-three to sixty-four prolonged to age seventy. As figure 9.15 shows, the difference between the two earning profiles is rather small for ages fifty-one to sixty-one. After age sixty-one, the difference increases considerably. This is partly due to the fact that men born in 1930 reached the age of sixty-two to sixty-four during the recession experienced by the Swedish economy in the early 1990s.

Section 9.2 above explains that the Swedish social insurance system provides benefits for two different pathways of early exiting from the labor market: a disability pension and an old age pension. Figure 9.6 above shows that the most frequent means utilized of leaving the labor market is to become an old age pensioner. But, as is also evident from figure 9.6, the most common way of *early* exit, that is, exit before the normal retirement age at sixty-five, is to start to collect disability insurance payments: about 9 percent of sixty-four-year-old men have taken the opportunity for early withdrawal from the old age pension, compared to 37 percent who receive benefits from disability insurance.[23]

23. It should, however, be noted that those who were sixty-four years old in 1994 had the oppor-

According to Swedish law, an individual is eligible for a full disability pension if for health reasons he is completely unable to work. If this rule were interpreted and applied in a strict sense, and if true working ability were easy to observe, there would be no point in calculating economic incentives for continued work for an eligible person since he could not work anyway. However, neither of these conditions applies. It is not plausible that 37 percent of sixty-four-year-old men are completely unable to work.[24] In the United States, the corresponding disability rate among sixty-four-year-olds is 8 percent (see Diamond and Gruber, chap. 11 in this volume). And, even if the intention of the legislation had been that a full disability pension should not be granted unless the individual is completely unable to work, the economic incentives would be of interest because the evaluation of working ability is not perfectly reliable. For these reasons, we begin the simulations by considering the case of an individual who is judged eligible to receive a full disability pension and who considers working full-time one additional year. However, in the base-case calculations, we will also consider the national old age pension. For both these base cases, we also include the STP pension scheme and income tax rules and housing allowance. The reason for choosing the STP scheme is that this occupational pension scheme covers the largest number of workers.

To reduce the complexity of the calculations, we applied the 1995 rules for all ages between fifty-five and seventy. This implies that we disregard several minor changes in benefit rules and the 1990–91 tax reform. The simulations show the incentives inherent in the 1995 rules, not those actually confronting a man born in 1930. But, apart from taxes, the structure of the system has been constant.

Applying the rules to the earnings history of the hypothetical individual, calculating the monthly payments conditional on the date the hypothetical individual chooses to leave the labor market is fairly straightforward. But the main objective of the simulations is to calculate social security wealth (SSW), and for this we need additional information. Social security wealth is defined, for each point of time, as the net present expected value of future payments from the social security system (net of income taxes) less the present expected value of future contributions to the system. So we need three additional pieces of information: (1) the mortality rates of the hypothetical individual and his wife; (2) the individual's discount rate; and (3) the contributions to the system that the hypothetical individual is expected to pay. The formula for computing social security wealth is provided in appendix D.

In the base-case calculations, we assume that the hypothetical individual is married and that his wife is exactly three years younger, that is, born on 1

---

tunity to obtain a disability pension before the legislative tightening of requirements during the 1990s. The present legislation is considerably more restrictive and can be expected to result in lower disability rates in the future.

24. For a short summary of Wadensjö (1996), which analyzes how Swedish disability insurance works in practice, see app. B.

January 1933. We also assume that she never worked. As described in section 9.2 above, benefit levels differ between a married and a single pensioner. So, when calculating the social security wealth for this couple, we must consider the probabilities for three different states for each year: (1) both spouses are alive; (2) the husband is alive and the wife dead; and (3) the wife is alive and the husband dead. To do this, we used gender-specific life tables (provided by Statistics Sweden), which are conditional on the individual living to age fifty-five. We assumed independence in mortality rates between the spouses. Note that we use the unconditional mortality risk beyond age fifty-five. So there is always some mortality risk for all ages older than age fifty-five. Our calculations thus give the economic incentives (implied by the social security system) that face the representative worker at age fifty-four. But this is not appropriate if we are interested in the economic incentives for year-to-year behavior.

As section 9.2 explains, the Swedish social security system is primarily financed through payroll taxes. In the simulations, we assume that the incidence of these payroll taxes is such that the entire cost is directly passed on to wages.[25] The basic pension is partly financed by income taxes. We deduct this part of the expenditures and payroll taxes for old age, survivor, and occupational pensions in the calculation of net social security wealth. In the disability option case, we also deduct payroll taxes for a disability pension. In the base case calculations, we assume a discount rate of 3 percent.

Besides social security wealth, we present three different concepts from the simulations: (1) *the replacement rate,* defined as the pension benefit net of taxes as a share of the earnings net of taxes during the last year of work; (2) *the accrual rate,* defined as the percentage change in social security wealth compared to the previous year; and (3) *the tax/subsidy rate,* defined as the absolute change in social security wealth from an additional year of work divided by net earnings during the year. If the absolute change in social security wealth is zero, the expected present value of the hypothetical individual's contributions to the system equals the increase in the present value of the amount he expects to receive from the system. Thus, the combined effect of the social security system, income taxes, occupational pensions, and housing allowances implies neither an implicit tax nor a subsidy on one year's additional work. But, if the change in social security wealth is negative, that is, the individual's contribution to the social security system of one additional year of work exceeds the increase in expected benefits from the social security system, it could be interpreted as an implicit tax on one additional year of work induced by the systems that we analyze. If the increase in what the individual expects to receive from the system from one year of additional work exceeds his contributions to the system, it could be interpreted as a subsidy of additional work. By relating this amount to the individual's net earnings, it could be interpreted as a tax (or subsidy) rate.

Before continuing, let us take a closer look at the various effects of addi-

---

25. Empirical studies (e.g., Palmer and Palme 1989) find that this assumption is highly realistic.

tional work at the early retirement ages on the social security wealth in our calculations: (*a*) The share of the payroll tax that constitutes the fee to the pension system will decrease the worker's social security wealth if he continues to work. This is not the case after age sixty-five because employers need not pay payroll taxes for these workers. (*b*) There is some risk that the worker will die for each year he decides to continue to work. This will lower his social security wealth. (*c*) If the worker decides to continue to work beyond age sixty, his monthly pension payments from the public pension scheme will increase by 0.5 percent for each month that he continues to work beyond age sixty until age sixty-five and by 0.7 percent beyond age sixty-five until his seventieth birthday. This actuarial adjustment will increase the individual's social security wealth. Note that the adjustment of the pension benefit does not occur if the individual receives disability insurance. (*d*) An additional year of work means fewer years when pension benefits can be claimed, which decreases social security wealth. However, as it is not possible to claim benefits before age sixty in the old age pension scheme, this applies only in the disability insurance case before age sixty. (*e*) Because the *net* income streams constitute social security wealth, income taxes on pension incomes will decrease social security wealth. The housing allowance will also affect net income. If an individual decides to work one additional year, he may increase his annual pension income. But this might reduce his housing allowance, net income, and thereby his social security wealth.[26] (*f*) The ATP and STP benefits are related to the worker's previous earnings. The requirement for receipt of a full ATP benefit is thirty years of earnings and for receipt of a full STP pension twenty-eight years of earnings starting from 1965.[27] Furthermore, the STP scheme requires three years of earnings between the ages of fifty-five and sixty-four if the individual is to be eligible for any benefit at all. Apart from these requirements, the ATP pension is determined by the average of the individual's best fifteen years, the STP pension by the best three years between the ages of fifty-five and fifty-nine. So the levels of the pensions from both schemes could be affected depending on when the individual decides to leave the labor force.

Besides the base-case simulations, we perform simulations where we alter the assumptions of the second *base case*. In this context, we investigate the results assuming that our representative individual follows the earnings path of the tenth and ninetieth percentile earners for each year—rather than the median. We also use an earnings path for the median earner with decreasing earnings toward the end of the career. We alter the composition of the household of the hypothetical individual, that is, assume a single hypothetical individual. Finally, we investigate what happens if the hypothetical individual has an incomplete earnings history starting at age thirty-five.

For the simulations with these alternative assumptions, we use the rules for

---

26. Section 9.2 above provides a short description of the Swedish income tax system and the housing allowance scheme.

27. This rule applies to individuals born in 1930. For those born in 1932 and later, the requirement was thirty years.

Table 9.2   Incentive Calculations—Base Case with Disability Pension Option

Last Age of Work	Replacement Rate	SSW	Accrual	Accrual Rate	Tax/ Subsidy
54	.842	2,020,280	. . .	. . .	. . .
55	.841	1,864,510	−155,770	−.077	1.171
56	.814	1,717,957	−146,553	−.079	1.058
57	.805	1,674,099	−43,858	−.026	.309
58	.810	1,536,893	−137,205	−.082	.971
59	.792	1,409,862	−127,032	−.083	.870
60	.789	1,281,354	−128,507	−.091	.870
61	.810	1,147,275	−134,079	−.105	.939
62	.798	1,022,147	−125,129	−.109	.860
63	.808	900,608	−121,539	−.119	.850
64	.729	785,497	−115,111	−.128	.799
65	.785	780,345	−5,152	−.007	.036
66	.841	768,133	−12,212	−.016	.085
67	.897	749,632	−18,501	−.024	.128
68	.953	725,280	−24,353	−.032	.169
69	1.011	697,510	−27,769	−.038	.193

the old age pension rather than the disability pension. The reason for choosing the old age pension scheme for the sensitivity analyses is that the actuarial adjustment in this scheme generally provides us with a richer set of results because it interacts with the income tax system and the housing allowances.

9.3.2 Base-Case Results

Tables 9.2 and 9.3 show the *base case* results. Table 9.2 shows the results for a worker who is eligible for a disability pension, table 9.3 the results for one who is not. Each row in these tables gives the various results provided that the representative individual works until the age depicted in the first column, that is, provided that he retires on his next birthday. The second column gives the replacement rate. As it is not possible to start to receive payments from the national old age pension scheme before age sixty, the first five numbers in table 9.3 are left out in the second column.

Comparing column 3 in tables 9.2 and 9.3, we see that there is a large difference in social security wealth depending on whether disability is an available option: the value of the individual's social security wealth on his fifty-fifth birthday is SKr 2,020,280 (U.S.$283,349) with disability pension and SKr 1,168,183 (U.S.$163,841) without. This 73 percent difference in social security wealth represents the present value of the gain the representative worker can obtain if he decides to retire at age fifty-five and is eligible for disability insurance.[28] By comparing column 4 in tables 9.2 and 9.3, it can also be seen

28. These figures include only the present expected value of future benefits; contributions up to this age are not deducted. But the following rows account for changes in benefits and contributions. In order to obtain the figure of a 73 percent difference, we have used the same conditional

Table 9.3   **Base-Case Incentive Calculations**

Last Age of Work	Replacement Rate	SSW	Accrual	Accrual Rate	Tax/ Subsidy
54	...	1,168,183	...	...	...
55	...	1,137,465	−30,717	−.026	.231
56	...	1,106,826	−30,640	−.027	.221
57	...	1,098,951	−7,874	−.007	.056
58	...	1,077,393	−21,558	−.020	.153
59	.459	1,056,086	−21,307	−.020	.146
60	.485	1,004,338	−51,749	−.049	.350
61	.545	953,215	−51,123	−.051	.358
62	.572	916,429	−36,786	−.039	.253
63	.620	874,964	−41,465	−.045	.290
64	.729	829,879	−45,086	−.052	.313
65	.785	824,727	−5,152	−.006	.036
66	.841	812,515	−12,212	−.015	.085
67	.897	794,014	−18,501	−.023	.128
68	.953	769,662	−24,353	−.031	.169
69	1.011	741,892	−27,769	−.036	.193

that the change in social security wealth is equal in the two *base cases* if the representative worker decides to work his last year at age sixty-four or later. This is because the worker is not eligible for disability insurance after age sixty-five and the *base cases* are therefore equivalent beyond this age.

By studying the column giving tax/subsidy rates in tables 9.2 and 9.3, several interesting properties of the two schemes can be noted. First, both systems provide a tax rather than a subsidy of additional work throughout the entire period considered. Second, the level of the tax rate is much higher over the entire period for the case where we treat disability insurance as an old age pension option. This result is not surprising since, unlike the old age pension scheme, disability insurance has no actuarial adjustment of the benefit if the individual begins to claim benefits early. This explains the difference in the tax rate between age sixty and age sixty-five. Furthermore, if an individual retires without a disability pension before age sixty, he cannot start to claim benefits until age sixty anyway; that is, if the individual decides to work one additional year before age sixty, the number of pension payments he receives will not be affected, and the tax on additional work will be smaller than it would have been were this not the case. This is not true for disability insurance at any age. For each additional year the worker decides to work, he will have to give up disability insurance payments.

---

survival probabilities as we did for the old age pension case. This represents a case where the individual manages to get disability insurance without any severe physical handicap. We have, however, also made calculations where we use an estimate of the survival probabilities for the population of those who receive disability insurance. In this case, social security wealth is SKr 1,908,873 (U.S.$267,724) if the worker retires at age fifty-five, i.e., 5.5 percent lower.

Table 9.4   **Tax/Subsidy Rate: Base Case with Disability Pension Option**

Last Age of Work	Gross Public Pension	Gross Public Pension + STP	Net Public Pension + STP	Net Public Pension + STP + BTP
55	1.250	1.502	1.170	1.171
56	1.166	1.341	1.056	1.058
57	.977	.204	.295	.309
58	1.020	1.228	.967	.971
59	.922	1.085	.863	.870
60	.893	1.095	.865	.870
61	.987	1.214	.941	.939
62	.918	1.104	.861	.860
63	.904	1.097	.852	.850
64	.851	1.028	.800	.799
65	−.006	−.007	.036	.036
66	.062	.070	.085	.085
67	.123	.139	.128	.128
68	.178	.202	.169	.169
69	.227	.257	.193	.193

For the disability pension case, the tax rate on one year of additional work at age fifty-five is above 100 percent. This means that the accrual in social security wealth is larger, in absolute value, than the net income of the representative worker. The tax rate on additional work remains in general very high, above 70 percent, until the representative worker reaches age sixty-five.

To facilitate the analysis of which parts of the institutional system generate the variations in the tax/subsidy rates and of the results in general, we present for the sake of comparison tables 9.4 and 9.5. Column 4 in these tables gives the tax/subsidy rate where we have not considered the housing allowance. Column 3 shows the tax/subsidy rate where we have considered neither the housing allowance nor income tax. Column 2 gives the tax/subsidy rate, but without considering the STP pension scheme. The last column gives the total effect of all parts of the system. The results of the four columns are also shown in figures 9.16 and 9.17.

The tax on additional work decreases somewhat for one year of additional work after the fifty-seventh birthday for both base cases. Item *f* above explains this. The STP scheme requires at least three years of work between age fifty-five and age sixty-four; that is, one additional year of work at age fifty-seven leads to a lifetime increase in monthly pension payments of about 10 percent. This can be more carefully examined in tables 9.4 and 9.5 as well as in figures 9.16 and 9.17. Comparing the results obtained when we took the STP benefit into account with those obtained when we did not, we can see that the STP benefit creates a dramatic shift in the graph of the tax/subsidy rate. The graphs in figures 9.16 and 9.17 also show that the incentive to stay in the labor force

Table 9.5   Tax/Subsidy Rate: Base Case

Last Age of Work	Gross Public Pension	Gross Public Pension + STP	Net Public Pension + STP	Net Public Pension + STP + BTP
55	−.006	.022	.147	.231
56	−.017	.010	.137	.221
57	−.035	−.984	−.421	.056
58	−.044	−.044	.056	.153
59	−.066	−.064	.046	.146
60	.055	.079	.195	.350
61	.130	.153	.214	.358
62	.173	.194	.249	.253
63	.233	.254	.287	.290
64	.280	.300	.311	.313
65	−.006	−.007	.036	.036
66	.062	.070	.085	.085
67	.123	.139	.128	.128
68	.178	.202	.169	.169
69	.227	.257	.193	.193

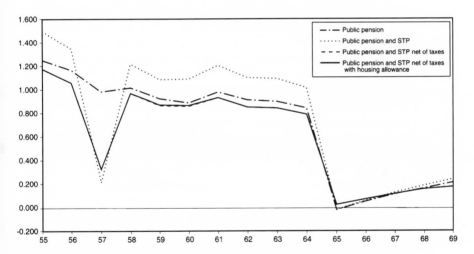

Fig. 9.16   Tax/subsidy rate, base case with disability pension option

created by STP is to a large extent counteracted by income taxes and the housing allowance: for the disability pension case, the tax rate increases from 16.9 percent when we do not consider income taxes and housing allowances to 27.5 percent when we do.

Turning to the case without a disability pension, we can see that the accrual and tax/subsidy rates vary between three phases: between age fifty-four and age fifty-nine, when there is a relatively low tax on continued work; between

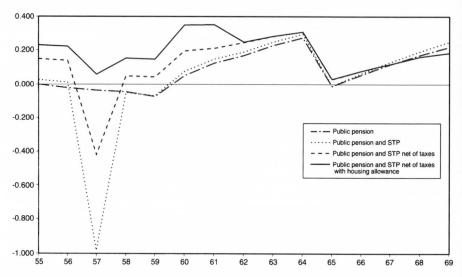

Fig. 9.17   Tax/subsidy rate, base case

age sixty and age sixty-four, when there is a relatively high tax rate; and between age sixty-five and age sixty-nine, when there is a somewhat lower tax
rate compared to the preceding phase, but a rate that increases within the phase.
The pattern of these three phases can be explained by the six institutional factors that determine social security wealth, which the previous section summarized. The fact that the number of monthly pension payments will not be affected by whether the individual chooses to work one extra year between age
fifty-five and age fifty-nine because neither the national nor the STP pension
can be collected before age sixty (item *d* above) explains why there is a difference between the tax/subsidy rate in this age group compared to the age group
sixty to sixty-four. The difference in the tax/subsidy rate between age sixty to
sixty-four and age sixty-five to sixty-nine is attributed to the fact that employers need not pay payroll taxes for employees beyond age sixty-five.

Figure 9.17 also gives some background as to why the old age and survivor
pension systems provide a tax rather than a subsidy on additional work
throughout the rest of the age interval considered. Following the graph, where
we consider only the old age national pension schemes, we can see that the
system is about actuarially fair until age sixty. After that, the tax/subsidy rate
turns positive, that is, turns to a tax on additional work, and increases. This
result shows that the 0.5 percent reduction in the monthly pension payments
for each month of early withdrawal before age sixty-five for the basic pension
and the ATP and the 0.7 percent increase in the payments from these pension
schemes for each month of delayed withdrawal after age sixty-five are not
enough to offset the pension payments given up and the contributions paid by
working additional years. This result depends on the choice of discount rate.

Choosing a discount rate greater than 3 percent makes the decrease in social security wealth even greater, while choosing a smaller discount rate makes this decrease smaller. Also note that these results are, at least to some extent, dependent on the option of using unconditional mortality risk beyond age fifty-five. A lower mortality risk gives a higher value to future pension payments and therefore a smaller increase in the implicit tax rate.

Figure 9.17 also shows the importance of income taxes and housing allowances. By comparing the graph where we consider income taxes and housing allowances with the graph where we have not, we can see that income taxes and rules for the housing allowance lead to a large part of the taxes on additional work under age sixty-four.

9.3.3 Other Cases

Table 9.6 gives the same information as table 9.3 above for a worker who, instead of following the earnings of the median earner, follows those of the tenth percentile during his work life. We follow the same principles for the imputation of earnings beyond age fifty as we did in the *base-case* calculations. Table 9.7 and figure 9.18 give the corresponding information as table 9.5 and figure 9.17 above for this earnings history. A comparison of tables 9.3 and 9.5 above and tables 9.6 and 9.7 show that the implicit tax rate largely follows the same pattern as for the *base-case* calculations. The main difference is that the implicit tax rate on additional work is higher in this case (being above 50 percent for those who decide to work one additional year at age sixty-one). The high tax rate also continues for ages sixty-five and sixty-six. By studying the difference between the graphs for the tax/subsidy rate where we have and have

Table 9.6   **Incentive Calculations: Tenth Percentile**

Last Age of Work	Replacement Rate	SSW	Accrual	Accrual Rate	Tax/ Subsidy
54	. . .	1,103,805	. . .	. . .	. . .
55	. . .	1,080,498	−23,307	−.021	.222
56	. . .	1,057,808	−22,691	−.021	.210
57	. . .	1,044,762	−13,046	−.012	.119
58	. . .	1,024,217	−20,545	−.020	.188
59	.513	1,003,353	−20,864	−.020	.186
60	.536	949,159	−54,194	−.054	.479
61	.577	893,650	−55,510	−.058	.503
62	.597	846,566	−47,083	−.053	.421
63	.632	799,586	−46,980	−.055	.425
64	.797	749,420	−50,167	−.063	.452
65	.825	718,450	−30,969	−.041	.278
66	.856	685,647	−32,803	−.046	.294
67	.910	668,093	−17,555	−.026	.158
68	.965	648,227	−19,866	−.030	.178
69	1.021	624,777	−23,450	−.036	.210

Table 9.7   **Tax/Subsidy Rate: Tenth Percentile**

Last Age of Work	Gross Public Pension	Gross Public Pension + STP	Net Public Pension + STP	Net Public Pension + STP + BTP
55	−.020	.008	.136	.222
56	−.041	−.014	.120	.210
57	−.053	−.925	−.331	.119
58	−.065	−.059	.088	.188
59	−.041	−.034	.097	.186
60	.064	.087	.339	.479
61	.132	.154	.363	.503
62	.177	.199	.279	.421
63	.236	.256	.285	.425
64	.280	.299	.312	.452
65	−.007	−.007	.047	.278
66	.061	.069	.097	.294
67	.123	.138	.138	.158
68	.179	.200	.178	.178
69	.228	.255	.210	.210

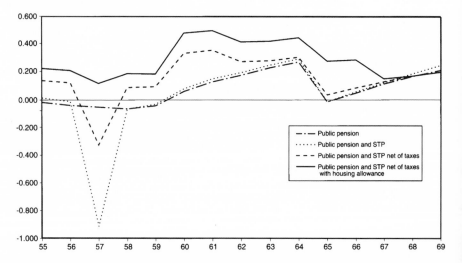

Fig. 9.18   **Tax/subsidy rate, tenth percentile**

not considered income taxes and housing allowances, we can conclude that this higher tax—compared to the *base case*—can be explained by the high marginal effects of housing allowances and income taxes.

Table 9.8 and 9.9 and figure 9.19 explore the results for a worker following the earnings of the ninetieth percentile. Although the pattern of the changes in the accrual rate over the period considered is similar to that of the *base case,*

Table 9.8   **Incentive Calculations: Ninetieth Percentile**

Last Age of Work	Replacement Rate	SSW	Accrual	Accrual Rate	Tax/Subsidy
54	. . .	1,284,308	. . .	. . .	. . .
55	. . .	1,233,428	−50,881	−.040	.246
56	. . .	1,181,194	−52,234	−.042	.245
57	. . .	1,237,965	56,771	.048	−.262
58	. . .	1,199,582	−38,382	−.031	.178
59	.389	1,161,857	−37,725	−.031	.171
60	.415	1,102,060	−59,797	−.051	.268
61	.455	1,039,183	−62,877	−.057	.289
62	.480	970,742	−68,441	−.066	.310
63	.516	899,324	−71,419	−.074	.328
64	.613	824,144	−75,180	−.084	.343
65	.660	820,681	−3,463	−.004	.016
66	.699	791,431	−29,250	−.036	.133
67	.731	746,173	−45,258	−.057	.206
68	.763	697,441	−48,732	−.065	.222
69	.795	645,793	−51,648	−.074	.235

Table 9.9   **Tax/Subsidy Rate: Ninetieth Percentile**

Last Age of Work	Gross Public Pension	Gross Public Pension + STP	Net Public Pension + STP	Net Public Pension + STP + BTP
55	.071	.104	.171	.246
56	.070	.102	.173	.245
57	.064	−.831	−.441	−.262
58	.052	.082	.157	.178
59	.049	.078	.151	.171
60	.177	.205	.268	.268
61	.217	.244	.289	.289
62	.259	.284	.310	.310
63	.294	.319	.328	.328
64	.327	.350	.343	.343
65	−.005	−.006	.016	.016
66	.052	.060	.133	.133
67	.105	.119	.206	.206
68	.151	.173	.222	.222
69	.193	.220	.235	.235

there are two interesting differences. First, the spike at age fifty-seven remains when we also consider income taxes and housing allowances. A comparison of figures 9.17 above and 9.19 shows that this difference is primarily due to the fact that the representative individual in this case is not eligible for a housing allowance. Second, the implicit tax on additional work is much higher for all

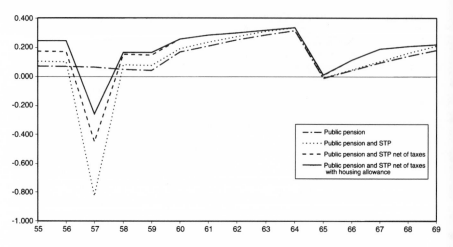

Fig. 9.19   Tax/subsidy rate, ninetieth percentile

Table 9.10   Incentive Calculations: Single Worker

Last Age of Work	Replacement Rate	SSW	Accrual	Accrual Rate	Tax/ Subsidy
54	. . .	953,956	. . .	. . .	. . .
55	. . .	920,488	−33,468	−.035	.252
56	. . .	886,960	−33,528	−.036	.242
57	. . .	866,485	−20,475	−.023	.144
58	. . .	835,941	−30,544	−.035	.216
59	.487	807,084	−28,857	−.035	.198
60	.510	750,163	−56,921	−.071	.386
61	.556	692,330	−57,833	−.077	.405
62	.584	654,754	−37,577	−.054	.258
63	.633	612,872	−41,882	−.064	.293
64	.743	566,912	−45,960	−.075	.319
65	.800	561,656	−5,256	−.009	.036
66	.857	549,014	−12,642	−.023	.088
67	.914	530,163	−18,852	−.034	.131
68	.971	505,350	−24,813	−.047	.172
69	1.031	477,573	−27,777	−.055	.193

ages beyond age sixty-two—compared to the *base case*. For ages sixty-six to sixty-eight, the difference is explained by the fact that the representative nineti-eth percentile individual has a higher marginal tax rate compared to the base case. For ages sixty to sixty-one, the median individual has a higher tax on additional work due to the reduction of the housing allowance.

Tables 9.10 and 9.11 and figure 9.20 give the results where we assume that the representative worker is single. We can see that, here, the implicit tax rate

Table 9.11   **Tax/Subsidy Rate: Single Worker**

Last Age of Work	Gross Public Pension	Gross Public Pension + STP	Net Public Pension + STP	Net Public Pension + STP + BTP
55	.053	.081	.192	.252
56	.042	.070	.182	.242
57	.026	−.923	−.308	.144
58	.017	.017	.144	.216
59	−.002	.000	.124	.198
60	.068	.092	.236	.386
61	.139	.162	.265	.405
62	.185	.206	.258	.258
63	.244	.264	.293	.293
64	.290	.310	.319	.319
65	−.005	−.005	.036	.036
66	.065	.073	.088	.088
67	.127	.143	.131	.131
68	.184	.207	.172	.172
69	.233	.263	.193	.193

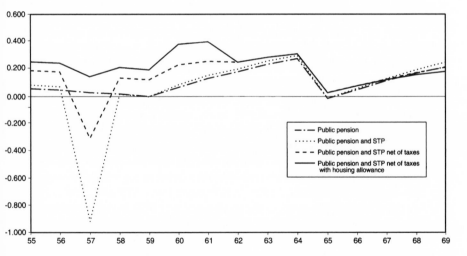

Fig. 9.20   Tax/subsidy rate, single worker

is generally higher, especially if the individual chooses to work one additional year between age fifty-seven and age sixty. This difference is due to the fact that one year of additional work at this age gives a higher survivor pension from both the ATP and the STP schemes. But additional work after age sixty will have no effect on the STP survivor pension and have very little effect on the ATP pension; this is why the difference between this case and the base

Table 9.12   Incentive Calculations: Diminishing-Earnings Profile

Last Age of Work	Replacement Rate	SSW	Accrual	Accrual Rate	Tax/ Subsidy
54	. . .	1,164,845	. . .	. . .	. . .
55	. . .	1,135,751	−29,094	−.025	.221
56	. . .	1,106,538	−29,214	−.026	.219
57	. . .	1,096,397	−10,141	−.009	.074
58	. . .	1,074,918	−21,479	−.020	.155
59	.475	1,054,706	−20,212	−.019	.144
60	.498	1,002,527	−52,179	−.049	.368
61	.554	949,421	−53,107	−.053	.385
62	.628	905,100	−44,320	−.047	.341
63	.705	865,587	−39,513	−.044	.322
64	.870	824,399	−41,188	−.048	.351
65	.982	819,128	−5,271	−.006	.047
66	1.106	807,074	−12,054	−.015	.113
67	1.242	788,860	−18,213	−.023	.180
68	1.394	765,220	−23,641	−.030	.247
69	1.565	737,077	−28,142	−.037	.312

case diminishes with age. Had we selected a larger age difference between the representative worker and his wife in the *base-case* calculations, that is, had the wife belonged to a younger birth cohort, the difference in the accrual rate between the case with a single worker and the *base case* would have been smaller because the transition rules for the survivor pension would have reduced the survivor pension within the ATP.

In tables 9.12 and 9.13 and figure 9.21, we evaluate the sensitivity to the imputation of incomes after age fifty in the synthetic earnings history in our *base-case* simulations by using the median earnings history after age fifty as well, that is, the *actual synthetic* earnings history. A comparison of the tax/ subsidy rate for this case with that for the *base case* reveals two effects that work in different directions. Lower earnings between age fifty-five and age fifty-nine means (as pointed out in item *f* above) lower ATP and, more important for this particular phase in the work life, lower STP. But the contribution through the payroll tax is lower. The tables show that the implicit tax rate is somewhat lower when we use the actual synthetic earnings history compared to the *base case,* although the difference is very small. This means that the second effect dominates with a small margin.

Tables 9.14 and 9.15 and figure 9.22 show what happens if we decrease the number of years in the labor force of the representative individual. We now assume that he starts to work at age thirty-five, that is, meets the requirement for a full ATP pension of thirty years of contributions to this pension scheme at age sixty-four compared to the base case, where the worker meets the requirement at age fifty-nine. Thus, the only phase where we expect the incen-

Table 9.13   **Tax/Subsidy Rate: Diminishing-Earnings Profile**

Last Age of Work	Gross Public Pension	Gross Public Pension + STP	Net Public Pension + STP	Net Public Pension + STP + BTP
55	−.046	−.017	.126	.221
56	−.017	.010	.136	.219
57	−.036	−.979	−.401	.074
58	−.042	−.039	.060	.155
59	−.056	−.053	.048	.144
60	.072	.096	.216	.368
61	.173	.195	.244	.385
62	.221	.243	.285	.341
63	.275	.296	.322	.322
64	.329	.349	.351	.351
65	−.008	−.009	.047	.047
66	.081	.091	.113	.113
67	.170	.192	.180	.180
68	.260	.294	.247	.247
69	.352	.397	.312	.312

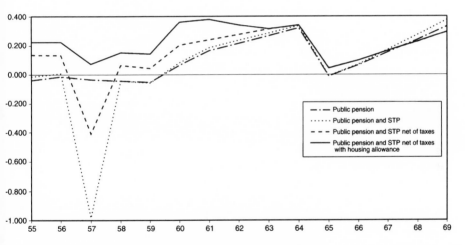

Fig. 9.21   Tax/subsidy rate, diminishing-earnings profile

tives of the social security system to differ between this case and the *base case* is between age sixty and age sixty-four. This is also exactly what we see if we compare tables 9.3 and 9.5 above and tables 9.14 and 9.15. The implicit tax rate on additional years of work is substantially higher between age sixty and age sixty-four. For the rest of the period, it is more or less the same.

Table 9.14   Incentive Calculations: Incomplete Earnings History

Last Age of Work	Replacement Rate	SSW	Accrual	Accrual Rate	Tax/ Subsidy
54	...	1,126,679	...	...	...
55	...	1,095,855	−30,824	−.027	.232
56	...	1,065,278	−30,577	−.028	.221
57	...	1,047,490	−17,788	−.017	.125
58	...	1,019,839	−27,652	−.026	.196
59	.422	992,748	−27,090	−.027	.185
60	.449	954,794	−37,954	−.038	.257
61	.503	912,882	−41,911	−.044	.294
62	.546	872,770	−40,113	−.044	.276
63	.606	853,506	−19,264	−.022	.135
64	.729	829,879	−23,627	−.028	.164
65	.785	824,727	−5,152	−.006	.036
66	.841	812,515	−12,212	−.015	.085
67	.897	794,014	−18,501	−.023	.128
68	.953	769,662	−24,353	−.031	.169
69	1.011	741,892	−27,769	−.036	.193

Table 9.15   Tax/Subsidy Rate: Incomplete Earnings History

Last Age of Work	Gross Public Pension	Gross Public Pension + STP	Net Public Pension + STP	Net Public Pension + STP + BTP
55	−.003	.025	.149	.232
56	−.012	.015	.138	.221
57	−.028	−.977	−.349	.125
58	−.038	−.038	.101	.196
59	−.057	−.054	.089	.185
60	−.166	−.142	−.050	.257
61	−.116	−.093	.074	.294
62	−.076	−.054	.072	.276
63	−.024	−.003	.110	.135
64	.026	.046	.140	.164
65	−.006	−.007	.036	.036
66	.062	.070	.085	.085
67	.123	.139	.128	.128
68	.178	.202	.169	.169
69	.227	.257	.193	.193

9.4   Conclusions

The simulations of how social security wealth is affected when a representative worker decides to retire carried out in section 9.3 above reveal huge differences in the economic incentives for leaving the labor force provided by dis-

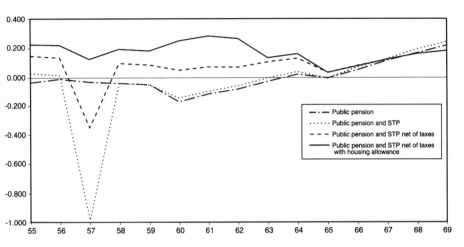

Fig. 9.22   Tax/subsidy rate, incomplete earnings history

ability insurance and the old age pension: the implicit tax on additional work generated by disability insurance is above 100 percent of the representative worker's net income. Still, the overview of the rates of labor force participation in section 9.1 shows that, despite these economic incentives, labor force participation is very high until about age fifty-eight and the hazard rate out of the labor force is moderate before this age. This observation supports the findings obtained in previous research (see Hedström 1987; and Wadensjö 1996) that the rate of people receiving disability insurance is determined by access to this insurance, that is, by the strictness in the law determining eligibility and the application of this law in the social insurance administration, rather than by individual economic incentives. Further research using micro data is, however, required to resolve this issue.

On the other hand, the economic incentives generated by the old age pension scheme seem to have an effect on retirement behavior. A striking observation that can be made from section 9.1 above is that labor force participation in the age group fifty-five to fifty-nine is very high compared to that in the age groups sixty to sixty-four and sixty-five and over. The historical trends in labor force participation for men also suggest that the decrease in labor force participation in this age group is smaller than that in the age group sixty to sixty-four. It is unlikely that this difference between these age groups can be explained entirely by biology. In this context, it is interesting to note that the simulations presented in section 9.3 above indicate that the pension system, especially the occupational pension scheme for blue-collar workers, provides stronger economic incentives not to leave the labor force up to age fifty-seven than after this age. The explanations for the very low labor force participation of persons aged sixty-five and older are dominated by the rules for mandatory retirement at age sixty-five.

Another interesting observation that can be made on the basis of the simulations presented in section 9.3 is the importance of income taxes and housing allowances. When we consider only the rules for the national pension system in the simulations, the system is close to being actuarially fair regarding when the individual decides to exit from the labor market and start to claim benefits. But, when we also consider the effect of income taxes and housing allowances, there is an implicit tax on continued work. The economic incentives provided by the STP occupational pension scheme are also largely counteracted. The political objective of the highly progressive income taxes, in particular for old age pensioners, and housing allowances is to provide an equal income distribution among old age pensioners. Obviously, this objective of equity in the distribution of economic outcome conflicts with the objective of equity inherent in the actuarial fairness of the pension system.

Appendix A
Data Sources

The statistical source of the figures about labor force participation is the Swedish Labor Force Survey. This survey has been conducted since 1961, and comparable figures are available since 1963. From 1963 until 1969, the survey was conducted four times every year, and the sample size was twelve thousand individuals (i.e., forty-eight thousand each year). Since 1970, the sample size is about twenty thousand, and the survey is conducted every month. We used annual averages in the figures, except for the age group sixty-five to seventy-four between 1986 and 1995, for which we used the average for the last three months of every year because this age group is only included in the population of these surveys. The rate of nonresponse is about 10 percent in each survey.

Four different measures of attachment to the labor market are reported in the figures: labor force participation, employed, full-time employed, and working. Individuals who did some kind of paid work for at least one hour in the week of the survey are defined as *employed*. Those actively searching for a job or expecting to start a job within four weeks are defined as *unemployed*. The *employed* and *unemployed* constitute the labor force. Students and participants in labor market programs are not considered as members of the labor force. Individuals who regularly work thirty-five hours per week are defined as *full-time employed*. Employed persons who were not absent all days in the week preceding the time of the survey are defined as *working*.

Statistics Sweden provided the Household Income Survey 1994. The data from this survey consist of three parts; information from (1) interviews about, for example, employment, housing, and household composition, (2) tax returns from household members on different components of household income, and (3) administrative records on taxes and transfers from the government. The rate of nonresponse is about 11 percent. The sample size of this survey is about ten thousand households. The total number of observations in single-year age groups varies between about 100 and 250. This means that some of the estimates in figures 9.11–9.13 above are based on very few observations.

Appendix B
Review of Previous Empirical Studies on Social Security and Retirement

The effect of the Swedish social security system on labor force participation was analyzed in a few empirical studies. The most general is Hansson-Brusewitz (1992), which estimates a life-cycle and an atemporal labor supply model on cross-sectional data for men aged between fifty-five and seventy. Modeling the dichotomous choice of labor force participation jointly with the choice with hours of labor supply enables Hansson-Brusewitz to study the effect of the introduction of the partial pension scheme on desired retirement age and desired number of hours of work for those who are not retired. Using the life-cycle model, he finds that this scheme actually has a positive effect on total hours of work. He also simulates the effect of other, hypothetical reforms in the Swedish income tax and social security systems. Again using the life-cycle model, he finds that a 10 percentage point decrease in the marginal income tax rates will increase the labor supply of elderly men by about 2.5 percentage points. A simulation of the effects of replacing current rules for calculating the benefits in the ATP scheme with a pension benefit that is equal to 60 percent of lifetime earnings shows a small positive effect on desired labor supply for those who have not retired, although a small negative effect on the desired retirement age.

Sundén (1994) estimates a conditional/multinomial logit model and considers the individual choice among four different options: (1) fully retire at age sixty; (2) retire with disability insurance at age sixty; (3) partially retire at age sixty; and (4) do not retire at all before age sixty-five. Sundén estimates this model using cross-sectional data for 1974 and 1981, that is, before and after the introduction of the partial retirement scheme in 1976. She finds that the introduction of the partial pension resulted in a small decrease in the number of individuals receiving benefits from disability insurance. By decomposing the overall change in retirement behavior between 1974 and 1981 in changes attributed to estimated coefficients (preferences) and individual characteristics (among these, changes in individual pension wealth), she concludes that the largest share of the change in retirement behavior seen between 1974 and 1981 can be attributed to changes in preferences. Changes in rules, reflected in the variables of individual characteristics, have a very small effect.

By studying the rules governing the receipt of benefits from disability insurance and the social security system for different pathways to early retirement, Kruse and Söderström (1989) find that, primarily, disability insurance and the partial retirement scheme provide large subsidies for early retirement and part-time work among the elderly. They suggest that the decreased labor supply among the elderly and the increased dependency ratio in the social security system to a large extent can be attributed to these generous benefits.

Wadensjö (1996) takes a closer look at how the legislation for disability insurance works in practice. Wadensjö shows that fluctuations in the number of new disability pensions between 1972 and 1991 can largely be explained by variations in the unemployment level (with a lag of about two years). He describes a common pathway to early retirement from the Swedish labor market. A company wants to reduce its personnel. In general, the older workers are best protected by seniority rules in Swedish legislation. But the company wants to retain at least some of its young workers. A standard procedure is then to investigate whether any of the older workers are eligible to receive a disability pension. The necessary medical examination is often conducted by the company doctor. Including extra severance payments, the compensation level for the dismissed older workers, who are eligible for disability pension, could be more than 100 percent of forgone earnings. The local unions are then often willing to deviate from the seniority rule. The implementation of new, stricter rules governing eligibility for a disability pension has made it more difficult for firms to use this option for reducing personnel. But a market for insurance (guarantee pensions), offered by private insurance companies, that retains the same early labor market exit option for older workers has been introduced.

Eriksen and Palmer (1997) examine the concept of disability as it is employed in Sweden and find that the increasing rate of disability since 1960 is largely a result of changes in factors other than health, concluding that labor market factors are predominantly responsible for the trend.

Appendix C
Imputations of Income

For the tenth percentile income earners, we had to impute incomes for ages thirty to forty-seven. For ages forty-eight to fifty-nine, the observed difference between true income and income measured by pension points is about 10 percent on average. We assumed that the corresponding difference decreases from

20 percent at age thirty to 10 percent at age forty-seven, which reflects a larger share of earners with income below the BA at lower ages. For the ninetieth percentile income earner, we can observe true income only in ages under thirty-six and above forty-seven because income is above the social security ceiling between these ages. We assumed that income increases linearly between age thirty-five and age forty-eight.

Appendix D
The Formula for Computing Social Security Wealth (SSW)

a_0 = the worker's age at evaluation of social security wealth (set to fifty-five in the base-case calculations);

r = the worker's age at retirement;

maxage   = maximum potential age;

$p(a|a_0)$ = probability of survival of the worker at age a conditional on survival at age a_0;

$q(a|a_0)$ = probability of survival of the spouse at the worker's age a conditional on survival of the spouse at the worker's age a_0.

$BM(a, r)$ = amount of the worker's pension benefit at age a if he retires at age r and is married at age a;

$BS(a, r)$ = amount of the worker's pension benefit at age a if he retires at age r and is not married at age a;

$S(a, r)$ = amount of survivor benefit the year when the worker would have been of age a if he retires at age r;

$C(a)$ = amount of the worker's contribution to social security at age a; and

ρ = discount rate (set to 3 percent in the base-case calculations).

$$PB(a_0, r) = \sum_{a=r}^{a=\text{maxage}} \left\{ \frac{p(a|a_0)q(a|a_0)BM(a, r)}{(1 + \rho)^{a-a_0}} + \frac{p(a|a_0)[1 - q(a|a_0)]BS(a, r)}{(1 + \rho)^{a-a_0}} \right.$$

$$\left. + \frac{[1 - p(a|a_0)]q(a|a_0)S(a, r)}{(1 + \rho)^{a-a_0}} \right\},$$

$$SSC(a_0, r) = \frac{\sum_{a=a_0}^{a=r-1} p(a|a_0)C(a)}{(1 + \rho)^{a-a_0}},$$

$$SSW(a_0, r) = PB(a_0, r) - SSC(a_0, r).$$

References

Aronsson, Thomas, and James R. Walker. 1997. The effects of Sweden's welfare state on labor supply incentives. In *The welfare State in transition,* ed. R. B. Freeman, B. Swedenborg, and R. Topel. Chicago: University of Chicago Press.

Elmér, Åke. 1960. *Folkpensioneringen i Sverige* (with a summary in English). Lund: C. W. K. Glerups.

Eriksen, Tor, and Edward Palmer. 1997. The concept of work capacity. In *Social policy and the labour market,* ed. P. R. De Jong and T. R. Marmor. Andershot: Ashgate.

Hansson-Brusewitz, Urban. 1992. Labor supply of elderly men: Do taxes and transfers matter? Ph.D. diss., Department of Economics, University of Uppsala.

Hedström, Peter. 1987. Disability pension: Welfare or misfortune? In *Welfare states and welfare research,* ed. Robert Erikson et al. New York: Sharp.

Kangas, Olli, and Joakim Palme. 1989. Public and private pensions: The Scandinavian countries in a comparative perspective. Working Paper no. 3. Institute for Social Research, Stockholm University.

Kruse, Agneta, and Lars Söderström. 1989. Early Retirement in Sweden. In *Redefining the process of retirement,* ed. W. Schmähl. Berlin: Springer.

National Social Insurance Board (Riksförsäkringsverket). 1993. ATP och Dess Finansiering i det Medel- och Långsiktiga Perspektivet. RFV Anser 1993:1. Stockholm.

———. 1996. Nybeviljade Förtidspensioner 1971–1995. Statistikinformation Is-I 1996:1. Stockholm.

Palme, Joakim. 1990. Pension rights in welfare capitalism: The development of the old-age pension in 18 OECD countries, 1930–1985. Ph.D. diss., Department of Sociology, Stockholm University.

Palmer, Edward, and Mårten Palme. 1989. A macroeconomic analysis of employer-contribution financed social security. In *The political economy of social security,* ed. B. A. Gustafsson and N. A. Klevmarken. Amsterdam: North-Holland.

Sundén, Annika. 1994. Early retirement in the Swedish pension system. Ph.D. diss., Department of Economics, Cornell University.

U.S. Department of Labor. 1996. *International comparisons of hourly compensation costs for production workers in manufacturing, 1975–1995: Supplementary tables for BLS Report 909.* Washington, D.C.: Bureau of Labor Statistics.

Wadensjö, Eskil. 1985. Disability pensioning of older workers in Sweden: A comparison of studies based on time-series and cross-section data. Meddelande 15/1985. Swedish Institute for Social Research, Stockholm University.

———. 1989. Varför har vi normal pensionsålder? In *Vingarnas trygghet: Arbetsmarknad, ekonomi och politik,* ed. Eskil Wadensjö, Åke Dahlberg, and Bertil Holmlund. Lund: Dialogos.

———. 1996. Early exit from the Swedish labour market. In *The Nordic labour markets in the 1990's,* ed. E. Wadensjö. Amsterdam: Elsevier Science.

10   Pensions and Retirement in the United Kingdom

Richard Blundell and Paul Johnson

Unlike those of most other European countries, the United Kingdom's pension system is not well described by an analysis of the social security element. For thirty years or more, around half the workforce has been covered by occupational pensions. Something like half the income of pensioners comes from non–social security sources, and this proportion is growing. Of the workforce in the mid-1990s, three-quarters are "contracted out" of the second-tier State Earnings-Related Pension Scheme (SERPS) into private occupational or personal pensions.[1]

In fact, one can probably divide the population nearing state pension age into two groups—those with and those without significant private provision. For those with private provision, state benefits are likely to be relatively unimportant in understanding retirement behavior; the rules of their pension scheme will be rather more important. For the rest, the state system might be much more relevant, but especially the *effective* availability of benefits, which appears to differ somewhat from what one might understand from a simple reading of the rules governing benefit availability.

Partly as a result of these facts, the United Kingdom also differs from many other countries in one other important respect—its state pension system is solvent. Tax rates necessary to pay for it are not predicted to rise despite the fact

Richard Blundell is director of research at the Institute for Fiscal Studies and professor of economics at University College London. Paul Johnson is deputy director of the Institute for Fiscal Studies.

The authors would like to thank Sarah Tanner and Jayne Taylor for their invaluable help in preparing this paper. Thanks are also due to the editors of this volume and authors of other papers in it for their advice and comments. Funding for the research on which this paper is based was provided by the Economic and Social Research Council through its support of the Centre for the Microeconomic Analysis of Fiscal Policy at the Institute for Fiscal Studies.

1. For an overview of the U.K. pension system, see Dilnot, Disney, Johnson, and Whitehouse (1994).

that the number of people over state retirement age is predicted to rise from 10.4 million in the mid-1990s to 11.5 million in 2020 and 14 million in 2050, representing an increase from 15.7 percent of the whole population to over 24 percent.[2]

In this paper, we begin by describing the past and current labor market behavior of individuals around pension age. We also consider the coverage of the various parts of the social security system. We go on to explain the structure of state pensions in the United Kingdom, before computing the incentives for retirement that the structure creates. We end by considering some of the evidence on retirement behavior, especially with regard to the effects of occupational pensions.

10.1 The Labor Market Behavior of Older Persons in the United Kingdom

The labor market behavior of older persons in the United Kingdom has been characterized by a severe fall in the participation of men, with younger cohorts showing distinctly less attachment to the labor market after age fifty-five. The rate of participation among recent cohorts falls sharply below 80 percent after age fifty and declines rapidly thereafter. In contrast, the secular rise in the participation of women has resulted in a small upward trend in participation among women in the age bracket fifty-five to sixty, with participation rates approaching those for men in that age group.

Three micro-data sources are used in the following discussion. One important primary data source is the U.K. Family Expenditure Survey (FES), which is available in consistent annual form for the period 1961–94. This is a continuous sample survey of some seven thousand households collecting information on expenditures, incomes, labor market activity, and demographics. A second source is the U.K. Labour Force Survey, published by the Office of National Statistics and covering some eighty thousand individuals for the period from the 1970s through to the present day. Finally, we make use of a new data source, the Family Resources Survey, a new household-level data set set up by the Department of Social Security that contains detailed income information for a sample of twenty-six thousand households. It is more than three times the size of the FES, which we traditionally use, and is specifically designed to provide good-quality information on income and benefits.

10.1.1 Historical Trends

To show how activity rates by age group have changed over time, we make use of data from the U.K. Labour Force Survey (*Labour Market Trends* [May 1996]). This covers the period from 1971 to 1995 and shows the proportion

---

2. These figures include the effect of the equalization of state pension age at sixty-five for both men and women, a change that will be phased in between 2010 and 2020.

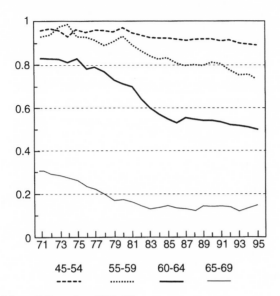

Fig. 10.1   Male activity rates, 1971–95

in each age group counting as economically active—in employment or self-employment or unemployed and actively seeking work (ILO definition). The information that we need is split into four age groups—forty-five to fifty-four, fifty-five to fifty-nine, sixty to sixty-four, and sixty-five to sixty-nine.

In figure 10.1 we present the picture of activity rates for men. Here, the drop in participation rates is clear. Falls are recorded for each of these groups, although much less dramatically for the youngest group, among whom 90 percent were still recorded as being active in 1995, a drop of 5 percentage points since 1971. For the other age groups, falls in activity rates are much more dramatic—from well over 90 to 74 percent for fifty-five- to fifty-nine-year-olds and from 83 to 50 percent for sixty- to sixty-four-year-olds. The changes are not smooth. There are very dramatic falls in activity rates, especially for sixty- to sixty-four-year-olds, in the early 1980s. This seems strong evidence that the structural change in the labor market with the loss of many jobs in traditional industries where there was a predominance of older workers played an important part in the initial reduction in activity rates, although they never recovered with the economic upturn. It is also interesting to note that there have been big activity drops among sixty-five- to sixty-nine-year-olds but that these occurred earlier, in the mid-1970s.

The pattern of changes in activity rates for women over time is very different from that of males, as is evident in figure 10.2. Among the youngest age group, activity rates grew virtually constantly over the period from 62 to 75 percent. Among fifty-five- to fifty-nine-year-olds, activity rates were uneven over the period but generally increasing. Among sixty- to sixty-four-year-olds, the pat-

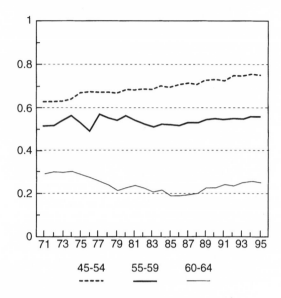

Fig. 10.2   Female activity rates, 1971–95

tern seems to be slightly U shaped, falling in the 1970s and then rising in the early 1990s.

These time-series figures by age group cloud some important date-of-birth cohort effects. We do not have an adequate run of panel data to look at an actual cohort's behavior, but we can use the long run of cross-sectional data that we have to create "pseudocohorts" and thereby see what happens to labor market activity within a particular date-of-birth cohort as the cohort ages.

Figure 10.3 shows labor market activity rates between the ages of fifty-five and sixty-five for three cohorts of men—the first born in 1913, reaching age sixty-five in 1978; the second born in 1921, reaching age sixty-five in 1986; and the third born in 1928, reaching age sixty-five in 1993. The data are drawn from the FES over the period 1968–94. *Activity* is defined as working or seeking work.

The oldest group had higher activity rates at each age, with activity falling from two-thirds to 20 percent between the ages of sixty-four and sixty-five for this group. For a very large portion of this cohort, retirement started at the state pension age. For the middle cohort, the big fall in activity occurred between the ages of sixty-one and sixty-five, while, for the youngest cohort, labor market withdrawal started earlier still.

10.1.2   Benefit Coverage

Coverage of the U.K. state pension system is now virtually universal for people under the state pension age. Anybody in work and earning more than £60.00 per week (about 15 percent of average male earnings) is covered, as is

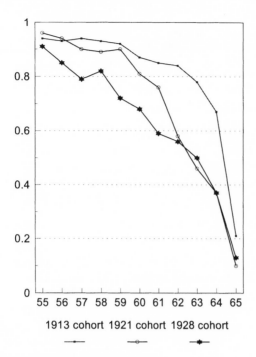

1913 cohort 1921 cohort 1928 cohort

Fig. 10.3   Male activity rates in three cohorts

anybody not working who is unemployed or disabled or who is at home looking after children of school age. (A more detailed exposition of the relevant
rules is set out in sec. 10.2 below.) Among men, universal coverage has been a
fact virtually since the introduction of the current regime in the late 1940s. For
women, the movement toward full coverage is only just reaching completion.
This is the result of three separate changes. The first is just the greatly increased levels of economic activity among women. The second is the introduction, in 1978, of Home Responsibilities Protection, which effectively credits
contributions for women with dependent children. The third is the phasing out
of what is known as the *married women's rate* of national insurance contributions. This latter feature of the system allowed married women to pay much
reduced social insurance contributions in return for forgoing rights to the basic
pension in their own right. Since 1978, no new entry to this lower-rate national
insurance band has been allowed. As a result of this, by 2010 virtually all
women reaching the state pension age will have some entitlement to a state
pension.

In sum, there has been virtually 100 percent coverage of male workers over
the past thirty years. Coverage for women has been less but is now almost 100
percent. No published statistics are available that allow this trend to be graphed
over time.

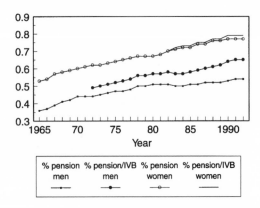

Fig. 10.4   Pension and invalidity benefit (IVB) receipt among over fifty-fives

Finally, in this historical section, we show how the proportions of men and women aged fifty-five and over receiving retirement pensions or invalidity pensions have changed over time. These trends are illustrated in figure 10.4, from which a number of interesting facts emerge. First, a rather higher proportion of women than men receive a pension. This fact—at first sight surprising— arises from the lower pension age for women, the higher proportion of women over age fifty-five who are also over age sixty, and the receipt by married women and widows of pensions entitlement to which was gained through their husband's contributions. Second, there has been a rise over time in the proportion of men and women with retirement pensions. Third, for men, there has been a very substantial increase in the proportion receiving invalidity pensions from a mere 1 or 2 percent in the early 1970s to 10 percent by the early 1990s. There has been no such increase for women, although there are signs of this changing by the start of the 1990s.

10.1.3   Labor Market Behavior in 1994–95

Participation rates by age and sex are presented in figure 10.5. The vast majority (80 percent or so) of men in their late forties are (full-time) workers. This proportion drops to around 40 percent by age sixty. For women, the pattern is similar, but it should be emphasized that one sees much lower full-time working and higher levels of part-time work. Work participation among women tails off quite rapidly for the fifty-year-old women, falling from about 60 percent in the late forties to 40 percent in the mid-fifties, 30 percent in the late fifties, and 20 percent at age sixty.

Figure 10.6 provides somewhat more detail than this using data from the Family Resources Survey. It considers four subsets of men: those employed working full-time (including the self-employed), those unemployed and seeking work, the disabled, and the retired. We ignore part-timers, who never make up more than 3 percent of any male age group.

The vast majority (80 percent or so) of men in their late forties are full-time

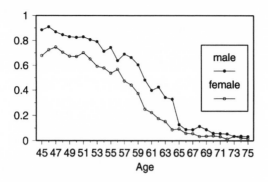

Fig. 10.5   Participation rates by age and sex (fraction in labor force)

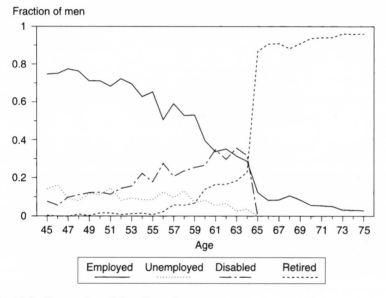

Fig. 10.6   Economic activity of men by age

workers; 7–10 percent consider themselves unemployed, and a further 7 percent are unoccupied, sick, or retired. The proportion in full-time work falls steadily, reaching 75 percent of those in their early fifties, dropping to 60 percent of those in their late fifties, and dropping sharply again to 40 percent of sixty-year-olds. This drops again to 30 percent by age sixty-four and then to under 10 percent at age sixty-six. By age sixty-one, the majority of men consider themselves unoccupied, retired, or long-term sick. Ninety percent are in this position at age sixty-six. Among those over seventy, fewer than 5 percent of those in our sample are in full-time work.

Figure 10.7 shows the corresponding distribution of activities for women.

Fraction of women

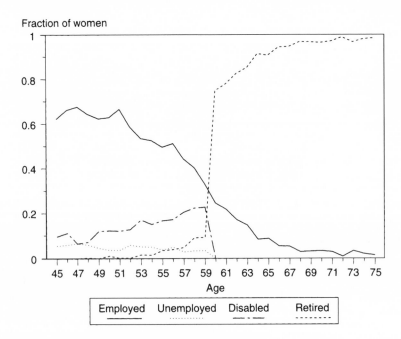

Fig. 10.7   Economic activity of women by age

Participation in work tails off quite rapidly in the fifties, falling from about 60 percent in the late forties to 40 percent in the mid-fifties, 30 percent in the late fifties, and 20 percent at age sixty. The proportion unoccupied or retired at age fifty-nine is 59 percent, rising to 72, 75, and 80 percent at ages sixty, sixty-one, and sixty-two, respectively. Given that the state pension becomes available at age sixty, the increase in inactivity at that age is not surprising.

The state pension age is five years younger for women than for men, but a higher proportion of women work past the state pension age. There are a number of possible reasons for this. One is that there is some tendency for husbands and wives to retire at the same time, with the result that wives might not retire until their husband reaches age sixty-five. A second is that some occupational pension schemes have normal leaving ages for both men and women of sixty-two or sixty-three. Finally, because many women reach age sixty without entitlement to a full basic pension, they might work more years in order to defer receipt and thereby raise their eventual entitlement.

For comparison, figures 10.8 and 10.9 present the hazard rates out of the labor force for men and women, respectively. The relatively small sample sizes in the Family Resources Survey, which has been used to construct these figures, lead to exaggerated variation. Nevertheless, the growing rate of exit for men beginning in their early fifties is clear, as is the strong peak at the official retirement age of sixty-five. Although there is a clear rise in the hazard, there

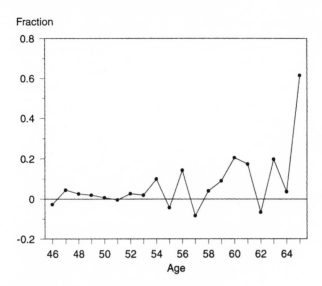

Fig. 10.8   Hazard rate out of the labor force for men

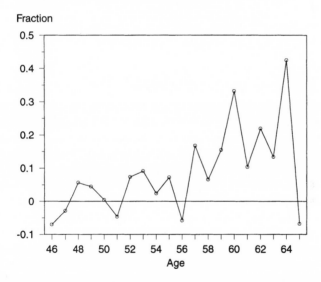

Fig. 10.9   Hazard rate out of the labor force for women

is no evidence of a peak at age fifty-five due mainly to the very different early retirement schemes available across occupations. There is, however, a peak at age sixty corresponding to the retirement age in many public-sector occupations and to the rules of the social security system, which stop entitlement to welfare benefits being dependent on work availability from age sixty. This is something we discuss further below. For women, the picture has similar overall

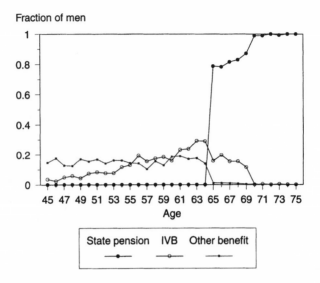

Fraction of men

Fig. 10.10   Public income receipt for men (IVB = invalidity benefit)

shape but displays a swift increase in the hazard up to the retirement age of sixty.

10.1.4   Income Sources of Older Persons

Overall rates of public income receipt for men by age group are shown in figure 10.10. More detail is provided in table 10.1. These figures are based on data from the Family Resources Survey. The table shows the proportion of men in age bands from forty-five up receiving particular types of state benefits[3] (excluding private pensions). The columns sum too more than one hundred because it is possible to be in receipt of more than one benefit at a time. The proportion receiving some benefit (we exclude the child benefit) rises gradually with age. Over 40 percent of sixty- to sixty-four-year-olds receive some benefit: one-quarter receive the invalidity benefit, 13 percent the minimum means-tested income support, and 10 percent other sorts of sickness benefits. The fact that we do not see virtually 100 percent of sixty-five- to sixty-nine-year-olds receiving a retirement pension is simply because 17 percent are receiving the invalidity benefit. Between the ages of sixty-five and seventy, it is possible to choose which to receive if the invalidity benefit was being received prior to age sixty-five. Because the invalidity benefit was nontaxable until 1995, there was an incentive to continue receiving it.

Above age seventy-five, more than one man in ten receives means-tested

---

3. The housing benefit is not included. *Other* includes such categories as war pensions, special payments, and a host of small-scale benefits.

Table 10.1   **State Benefit Receipt among Males (percentages by age band)**

	45–49	50–54	55–59	60–64	65–69	70–74	75+
None	80	75	70	57	1	0	0
Pension	0	0	0	0	81	99	99
Invalidity benefit	4	8	17	25	17	0	0
Income support	9	8	8	13	5	5	11
Other sick	5	7	7	10	7	3	1
Other	10	9	9	9	8	13	16

Source: Family Resources Survey, 1994–95.

Table 10.2   **Number of Male Invalidity Benefit Recipients by Age (numbers given in thousands)**

Men	1979–80	1984–85	1989–90	1993–94
45–49	39	53	64	105
50–54	56	75	108	134
55–59	108	128	171	224
60–64	171	239	266	322
65+	47	72	177	235
All ages	506	673	917	1,217

income support (the rate of receipt among women is more than double that). This reflects the fact that income support rates are actually higher than basic pension rates, especially for older pensioners. Administrative statistics reveal that, in addition to these benefits, a further 11 percent of those over age seventy receive the housing benefit—designed to help low-income individuals afford rented accommodation.

Within the state welfare system itself, the most dramatic changes with respect to numbers receiving benefits have been in the number of individuals, particularly pre–pension age, receiving benefits initially designed for the long-term sick and disabled. The invalidity benefit is the most important of these. It is a contributory benefit payable to long-term sick individuals who can show that they are incapable of working owing to illness or disability and have been unable to work for at least twenty-eight weeks. Until recently, claimants have only been required to provide a certificate from their own doctor stating that they are incapable of working as a result of sickness. Since 1995 and the replacement of the invalidity benefit by the incapacity benefit, the rules for entitlement have been tightened with the express intention of halting the increase in numbers of recipients shown in table 10.2.

This growth in the numbers appears to be related directly to growth in unemployment rates (see Disney and Webb 1991). Until the early 1990s, the benefit provided income levels significantly in excess of such other social security benefits as the unemployment benefit and income support because earnings-

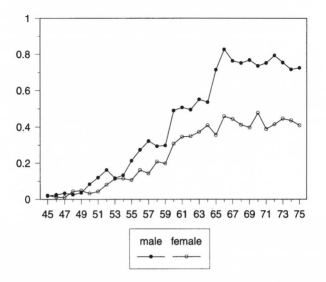

Fig. 10.11   Private pension receipt by sex

Table 10.3   Percentage of Birth Cohorts Recording Occupational Pension Receipt, by Birth Cohort, Gender, and Marital Status (men aged 65–69, women aged 60–64)

Cohort	Male Pensioners	Married Female Pensioners	Single Female Pensioners
1900–4	48	2	19
1905–9	50	2	23
1910–14	58	5	28
1915–19	64	10	31
1920–24	65	15	41
1925–29	68	23	48
1930–33	. . .	24	45

Source: Johnson and Stears (1995), based on the 1961–93 FESs.

related pensions were payable in the same way as for SERPS for those over the state pension age. Given that about a quarter of all men aged between sixty and sixty-four received the invalidity benefit in 1994, there can be little doubt that the invalidity benefit has been used as an early retirement vehicle.

In figure 10.11, we provide a description of the proportion of men and women at each age who are receiving a private pension. As in the United States, this rises fairly rapidly after age fifty-five, with a large gap opening up between men and women after age sixty-five. Table 10.3 gives a similar picture of the proportion of various cohorts who were receiving occupational pensions in the first five years after the state pension age. An increase in pension coverage for each successive cohort is evident, rising from around half to two-thirds

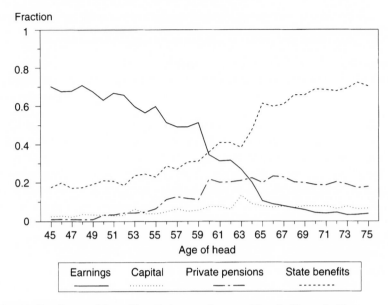

Fig. 10.12   Composition of family income by age of head of household

of men, roughly doubling to just under a half of single women, and rising from very few to about a quarter of married women. Average receipt has also risen. Among recipients, mean real occupational pension levels have doubled to nearly £90.00 per week for men and £60.00 for women. This important development in private, largely occupationally based pensions in the United Kingdom is documented in further detail below.

Finally, in figure 10.12, we present a picture of the distribution of family income by source. Earnings remain the main source of family income until around age sixty, when the importance of public and private pension sources begins to play a dominant role.

10.2   Key Features of the U.K. Pension and Social Security System

As we have made clear, it is hard to consider the U.K. state pension system in isolation from the private sector. For one thing, among recently retired pensioners, private pensions make up close to half of total income in retirement—with the mean occupational pension payment (among those receiving some payment) approaching £90.00 per week, which compares with a basic state pension of £61.15 per week. This is just about 16 percent of male average earnings. More important for understanding the structure of the system, one needs to take account of the relation between SERPS and the private sector for the majority (over three-quarters) of workers at any time are "contracted out" of SERPS into private schemes.

Traditionally, the state in the United Kingdom has offered just a basic pension at close to "subsistence" levels. First introduced in 1906, and reformed into something approaching its current form following the last war, the basic pension provides a flat-rate benefit, unrelated to earnings levels, which was £61.15 per week for a single person in 1996. Although unrelated to earnings levels, it is nonetheless a "contributory" benefit, at least in principle. Entitlement to a full benefit depends on contributions being made (or credits received) for 90 percent of a working life. This requires forty-four years of contributions or credits for men and thirty-nine years for women (rising to forty-four when pension ages are equalized at sixty-five in 2020).

These contributory conditions are nowhere near as onerous as they appear. Any time spent unemployed or sick/disabled gains credits—which count in just the same way as contributions—and time spent looking after children has, since 1978, reduced the effective number of years of contributions required through a system called Home Responsibilities Protection (HRP). Virtually all men aged sixty-five and over receive a full basic pension on the basis of their own contributions. The coverage of women currently over sixty is less comprehensive. Fewer than 60 percent receive a full pension, and the majority of them do so only on the basis of contributions made by their deceased husband. However, married women without rights of their own are entitled to a dependent's addition to their husband's pension, worth £36.60 per week in 1996.

Low rates of entitlement among married women reflect long periods spent out of the labor market by older cohorts, along with an option that married women used to be able to exercise whereby their national insurance contributions were reduced in return for a loss of pension rights. Later generations have benefited from the introduction of Home Responsibilities Protection (in 1978); they have also seen higher levels of female labor market participation. The consequence is that, by the early years of the next century, the vast majority of women as well as of men will retire with entitlement to a full basic pension (see Johnson and Stears 1996).

Perhaps the most important feature of the basic pension is its low level. It represents just 16 percent of average male earnings. With indexation in line with the retail price index, its level *relative to* earnings is falling—it was 20 percent of the male average in the late 1970s. With continued price indexation, we can expect it to fall to just 7 or 8 percent of the male average by 2030.

Currently, entitlement to the basic pension depends only on contributory record and age—there is no retirement test. It is possible, however, to defer pension receipt by up to five years to "state retirement age" (sixty-five for women, seventy for men). Deferral results in an increase in pension entitlement of 7.5 percent per year. This is more valuable to women than to men because of their higher life expectancy. Possibly as a result of this, 17 percent of female pensioners and 11 percent of males receive increments to their basic pensions as a result of deferral. There is no provision for the payment of retirement pensions before age sixty-five (men) or sixty (women).

Deferral is becoming less widespread following the abolition, in 1989, of the "earnings rule," which effectively meant that those (women aged sixty to sixty-four and men sixty-five to sixty-nine) earning more than £75.00 per week (in 1989) had their pension entitlement reduced. The reduction was fifty pence for every £1.00 between £75.00 and £79.00 of earnings and £1.00 for every £1.00 thereafter. Virtually all those affected deferred their pension receipt rather than taking a reduced amount. The fact that nearly a quarter of men and a third of women over age eighty, with pension entitlements in their own right, have pension increments as a result of deferral indicates that this was a relatively important provision when many younger pensioners worked, as they did in the 1960s and 1970s.

One might have expected the complete abolition of this rule to lead to significantly changed behavior among those in the relevant age ranges. However, as Whitehouse (1990) points out, there was limited evidence that the rule was having much effect during the 1980s. We present new evidence here based on earnings distributions in the FES in 1987–88 and in 1991–92. It should be stressed that we have only very small samples of men in work in these age groups—just seventy-two individuals in the two years 1987 and 1988 and sixty-six individuals in 1991 and 1992.

The graphs are presented with earnings shown in nominal terms. The maximum on each graph is set such that it is effectively scaled up by nominal earnings growth—of 40 percent over the period. In other words, £165 in 1991–92 becomes £115 in 1987–88 when deflated by nominal earnings growth. For ease of presentation, the graphs exclude those individuals earning over these maxima. This excludes 20 percent of the working individuals in 1987–88 but a third of those in 1991–92.

Even with this small sample, there is clear evidence (shown in fig. 10.13) of bunching at the earnings-rule level of £75.00 per week in 1987–88. The majority of those in work were, however, earning well below this level and, as we noted, about a fifth were earning well in excess of it. There is no such obvious peak in figure 10.14. The increased proportion earning over £170 might also be evidence of people being freed from the effects of the earnings rule. However, such conclusions should be treated with considerable caution, given the sample sizes in the data.

The basic pension remains by far the most important element in social security spending on the elderly. There are also, however, important income-related benefits. Of the 10 million pensioners in the United Kingdom, 1.5 million are dependent on the minimum means-tested benefit income support, which is available at higher levels than the state pension. In addition, a similar number receive means-tested help with their housing costs. This means that the minimum social security income for a single sixty-five-year-old is not the £61.15 available from the basic pension but the £67.05 available from income support *plus* the housing benefit to cover any rent.

The contributory benefit system was originally designed as a purely flat-rate

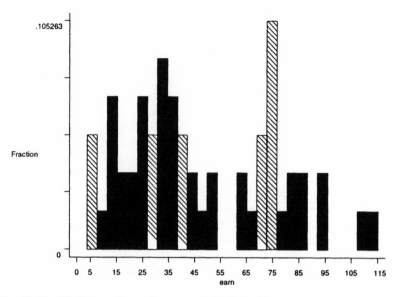

Fig. 10.13   Weekly earnings of men aged 65–69 in 1987 and 1988 FES

arrangement intended to provide only a bare minimum income level. Until the early 1960s, contributions were also paid at a flat rate. As they became partially income related, an earnings-related "graduated pension" was introduced. No further accruals were earned after 1975. Never generous, this pension is now a virtual irrelevance as its design purposely failed to allow for indexation. Although 7.5 million pensioners receive it, average receipt is just £2.00 per week. It can be safely ignored.

The same is not true of its successor, SERPS—the State Earnings Related Pension Scheme. SERPS was introduced only in 1978, with the intention that it would start paying out full benefits twenty years hence. Between 1978 and 1999, there would be a very gradual building up of maximum SERPS benefits as each successive cohort of retirees would have built up one more year of benefit entitlement.

It was originally designed, broadly speaking, to provide a pension equal to one-quarter of earnings during the best twenty years of earnings, with full inheritance by surviving spouses. The earnings on which the pension is calculated are bounded by the lower earnings limit (approximately equal to the basic pension) and the upper earnings limit (£455 per week, or just 20 percent above male average earnings, in 1996). Along with the basic pension, these earnings limits move up each year in line with prices. The result is that an increasing proportion of contributors has earnings above the upper earnings limit, which is itself not far in excess of male average earnings. Current contribution rates are 10 percent for employees and 10.2 percent for employers. The upper earnings limit caps contributions from employees but not from employers.

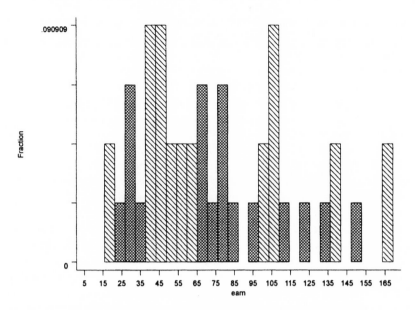

Fig. 10.14   Weekly earnings of men aged 65–69 in 1991 and 1992 FES

At present, SERPS entitlements are calculated as follows. Earnings above the national insurance upper earnings limit are ignored. Earnings in each financial year since 1978 are revalued to the year in which the individual reaches pensionable age by an index of economywide average earnings. From this figure, the national insurance lower earnings limit in the year prior to retirement is deducted. The total revalued earnings net of the lower earnings limit are then multiplied by an accrual factor to arrive at the additional pension entitlement. The accrual rate is determined by the year in which pension age is reached. It is currently 25/20 (1.25 percent or 1/80th). It is this accrual rate that determines the relation between level of SERPS entitlements and earnings levels. The current one-eightieth accrual rate is what allowed the scheme when introduced to provide a pension of a quarter of earnings over twenty years. In other words, the calculation would be number of years entitled divided by eighty and multiplied by the total level of revalued average earnings.

From 1999 on, the SERPS accrual factor will gradually fall, reaching 20/49 (0.41 percent or 1/244th) by 2027–28. So, for people retiring after 2027–28, SERPS will be 49/244 (= 20 percent) of average revalued earnings over their entire working life if they work for each of the available forty-nine years between sixteen and sixty-five. Shorter working lives will reduce the numerator accordingly and thereby reduce the proportion of revalued earnings, which will form the SERPS payment.

This fall in accrual rate was introduced in the Social Security Act of 1986 following concerns about the generosity of SERPS and the aging population resulting in unsustainable levels of expenditure in the future. The main effect of the changes will be to move from a benefit formula producing a pension worth 25 percent of best twenty years earnings to one producing 20 percent of lifetime average revalued earnings and a reduction in survivor benefits from 100 percent of the SERPS payment to 50 percent of it.

As with the basic pension, there is no provision for the early receipt of SERPS, but receipt can be deferred on the same basis as can the basic pension. Deferral, however, is rare.

The result of the introduction of SERPS, especially for the generation retiring in the years around 2000, will be significantly to increase the social security income, and thus the total income, *of those without a private pension.* The retirement income of those in occupational pension schemes will have been largely unaffected by its introduction, however, because, from its inception, such schemes have been able to *contract out* of SERPS. People in schemes that guarantee a certain level of benefit can give up rights to SERPS and pay lower national insurance contributions as a result. Since 1988, not only have traditional final salary occupational pensions been able to contract out in this way, but so also have group money purchase and personal pension schemes. So now about three-quarters of eligible workers (i.e., those earning over the lower earnings level) are not covered directly by SERPS. Half are in occupational schemes, and another quarter are in personal pensions. The coverage of personal pensions is particularly high among young men, for whom the advantages of joining, given a rebate that is not age related and a SERPS system that is becoming less generous, are considerable. Occupational pension coverage is less clearly associated with a particular age group, although those who are covered tend to work for large employers and to be relatively well off.

These facts must be borne in mind when considering the effect of social security on retirement. There can be no question that, for many people, it is the size of, and policies followed by, their particular occupational schemes that matter. In the future, personal pensions will become much more important (very few have reached maturity) in this context.

10.3   Retirement Incentives

In this section, we look at the retirement incentives within the U.K. social security system by considering sample workers with specific sets of characteristics that are relevant to the calculation of state benefit income entitlement in retirement. The analysis reveals a number of interesting features of the U.K. retirement benefit system. In particular, it demonstrates the role of benefits available before the state pension age and the rather wide range of incentives created for different individuals depending on their earnings, age, and marital status.

In our simulations, we consider the incentives facing a man born in 1930 and so reaching the state retirement age of sixty-five in 1995.

In order for us to make the calculations, the first thing that matters is a work and earnings history. We actually need this only from 1978. We do not need to look beyond that because state pension entitlement became dependent on earnings only after that date.[4] For our base case, we take the median earnings of a male worker up to age fifty and then project these forward by average earnings growth over the following twenty years.

This results in a smooth increase in real earnings over time. But it does fail to take account of the falls in real earnings that one does observe in a cohort once the early to mid-fifties are reached. To some extent, this fall is a result of selection. Those with occupational pensions and higher earnings are more likely to retire early. This means that the lower earnings recorded for older individuals are probably closer to the ones actually faced by those people most dependent on the state system. We also considered an individual facing the actual median earnings of his cohort through to age sixty-five. The results were very similar, except that the lower earnings resulted in higher replacement rates. The results are set out in the appendix.

With this information, we can calculate the amount of SERPS plus the basic pension to which the individual would be entitled in the first and subsequent years of retirement. Given life tables (supplied by the government actuary's department) and an assumed discount rate, we can then calculate an expected net present discounted value of social security wealth. This is done, in the base case, for a married man. Under current rules, he would be entitled to a dependent's addition to the basic pension if (as we assume) his wife had no rights of her own. If she outlived him, his wife—who, we assume, is three years his junior—would inherit the full amount of his benefits (including SERPS benefits and excluding the dependent's addition). We take account of this by using mortality data on women as well and looking at the joint probabilities of one or both of them living to any age (up to one hundred).

The rules for SERPS that we use are those pertaining to people reaching pension age in 1995. That means that they receive one-eightieth of revalued earnings for every year of work from 1978. The spouse is assumed to have rights to the full SERPS pension on the death of her husband. The effects of changes in policy reducing the value of SERPS for individuals retiring after the year 1999 are not considered.

So our base case individual, results for whom are shown in table 10.4, is a married man, with cohort median earnings up to age fifty and with earnings then rising with the national average. For the moment, we assume that he would receive no early retirement benefit were he to retire before age sixty-five, as is implied, in theory, by the structure of the benefit system. We later consider the effects of relaxing this assumption by looking at the case of an individual who becomes entitled to the incapacity benefit at age sixty. We have

---

4. As we have already noted, the previous "graduated pension" scheme resulted in benefits so small as not to be worthy of consideration.

Table 10.4   **Base-Case Incentive Simulations**

Last Year of Work	Replacement Rate	SSW (£)	Accrual (£)	Accrual Rate	Tax/ Subsidy
54	. . .	66,464	. . .	. . .	. . .
55	. . .	66,232	−233	−.004	.02
56	. . .	66,154	−78	−.001	.01
57	. . .	65,830	−323	−.005	.03
58	. . .	65,499	−331	−.005	.03
59	. . .	65,179	−320	−.005	.03
60	. . .	64,878	−300	−.005	.03
61	. . .	64,708	−171	−.003	.02
62	. . .	64,526	−182	−.003	.02
63	. . .	64,309	−216	−.003	.02
64	. . .	64,108	−201	−.003	.02
65	.464	64,011	−97	−.001	.01
66	.491	63,818	−193	−.003	.02
67	.519	63,489	−329	−.005	.03
68	.549	63,004	−485	−.008	.05
69	.581	62,345	−659	−.011	.07

already seen that a very high proportion of individuals receive this benefit before age sixty-five.

In table 10.4, five measures are presented. The first is simply the replacement rate. This is a measure of pension income in the first year of retirement divided by available *net* earnings in that year. So, if the individual concerned could earn £10,000 (after tax) at age sixty-five and could receive £5,000 in pension benefits, he would have a replacement rate of 50 percent. For years before it is possible to draw a state pension, the replacement rate is not defined.

The second is a measure of *social security wealth* (SSW). At all points, this is wealth considered from the point of view of a fifty-five-year-old, so it is discounted to age fifty-five. It is calculated by adding together pension entitlement from each year of assumed retirement to age one hundred, conditioned on the probability of living to that age. Since the probability of living to such an old age is small, the contribution of discounted wealth at these ages is negligible. Survivor benefits are also included in this calculation conditioned on probability of death of the husband and survival of the wife.

Social security wealth is itself a net concept, in this case net of projected national insurance contributions. If someone retires at sixty-five, he receives benefits from that year on but will have paid national insurance contributions in each year up to then. We measure net social security wealth as the difference between the discounted sum of projected benefits and the discounted sum of projected national insurance contributions (including employer contributions).

The third measure is social security wealth *accrual*. This, very straightforwardly, is the difference between social security wealth in the year before retirement and social security wealth in the year of retirement. It is just a measure of how social security wealth changes. A positive number means that an extra year of work will increase social security wealth, a negative number that an earlier retirement date would maximize it. Accrual *rate* is just the *proportionate* change in social security wealth between the same two years.

The final numbers presented are tax/subsidy rates, which are the absolute accrual amount divided by the earnings available in that year. So, if your social security wealth were to rise by £1,000 over the year and your earnings were £10,000, you would have a 10 percent subsidy on your earnings to work that extra year. Positive numbers, arising from negative social security wealth accruals, effectively indicate a tax on the projected earnings. Positive is tax, negative subsidy.

Taking our base case first, table 10.4 shows the results for a married man born in 1930, with a wife three years younger and entitled to no pension in her own right, and with the base-case smoothed-earnings profile described earlier.

The pattern of results is quite striking. In each year up to age sixty-five, the accrual of social security wealth is slightly negative. Net social security wealth conditional on retiring at age sixty-five is about £2,000 less than that conditional on retiring at age fifty-five. This difference is small. It reflects two features of the U.K. system and of our calculations. Until age sixty-five, this individual will be paying 10 percent of his earnings in nation insurance contributions each year, and his employer will be paying an additional 10 percent. So the cost to working an extra year is substantial. The benefit of working an extra year, in terms of social security wealth, comes through extra SERPS being accrued. Basic pension entitlement, which makes up the greater part of the total state pension, is unaffected by extra years of work. The loss in net income to higher national insurance contributions is significant for each extra years of work but adds on only once. The extra amount of SERPS earned is small for each year but payable for many years, especially given the existence of a younger wife. These values come close to canceling each other out, but the negative effect of extra national insurance contributions is just the greater.

The accrual *rate* is small—social security wealth falls at less than 1 percent per year. The effective tax on employment averages out at about 2 percent of salary each year.

This pattern is constant up to the state pension age. Further pension deferral increases the available pension, both basic and SERPS, by 7.4 percent. This increase would be inherited by the widow of our sample man in the (likely) event that he were to die first. But, of course, a full year's pension is sacrificed. By the time the man reaches his late sixties, the cost of not claiming the pension is beginning to become more substantial, although still not great.

In this example, and in what follows, we see no great change in accrual rates at age sixty-five that would be likely to explain the very great observed retirement hazards at this age. This would seem to be evidence of the impor-

Table 10.5   Incentive Calculations—Single Worker

Last Year of Work	Replacement Rate	SSW (£)	Accrual (£)	Accrual Rate	Tax/ Subsidy
54	...	33,951	...	...	...
55	...	32,875	−1.077	−.03	.10
56	...	31,944	−930	−.03	.09
57	...	30,794	−1,150	−.04	.10
58	...	29,626	−1,169	−.04	.10
59	...	28,465	−1,161	−.04	.10
60	...	27,339	−1,126	−.04	.10
61	...	26,330	−1,008	−.04	.09
62	...	25,333	−997	−.04	.09
63	...	24,328	−1,005	−.04	.09
64	...	23,356	−971	−.04	.09
65	.358	22,478	−879	−.04	.09
66	.379	20,491	−1,986	−.10	.20
67	.401	18,404	−2,087	−.11	.21
68	.424	16,220	−2,185	−.13	.22
69	.449	13,942	−2,278	−.16	.23

tance of social norms, of employer-determined retirement dates, and of the fact that all employment protection comes to an end once people pass their sixty-fifth birthdays.

It is also worth noting here that the assumption that the spouse has no rights of her own is important. If she had full rights of her own, then she would not be able to inherit her husband's full rights in the event of his death.

In table 10.5, where we consider the case of a single man, the importance of marital status for these calculations is demonstrated quite clearly. Pension wealth at any age is only around half that for the married man. This reflects both the higher pension rights of the married man and the higher survival expectations of his (younger) spouse, who is in a position to inherit the whole of his pension. In addition, accruals from extra work are substantially more negative at all ages; each extra year of work costs just as much in national insurance contributions, but the return is lower because there is no spouse to inherit SERPS. Before age sixty-five, these negative accruals effectively impose an extra tax rate of about 10 percent on earnings in each extra year of work.

Accruals and tax rates become much more negative after age sixty-five as the deferment rules are not generous enough to compensate the single man for the loss of each year's pension. Again, the fact that deferral rates are the same for men and for women, married and single, places single men at a significant disadvantage.

The other comparison between the single and the married man that is worthy of note is that between replacement rates. Replacement rate at age sixty-five for the married man is 46 percent, for the single man 36 percent. This is the

Table 10.6   **Incentive Calculations—Ninetieth Percentile Earnings**

Last Year of Work	Replacement Rate	SSW (£)	Accrual (£)	Accrual Rate	Tax/ Subsidy
54	. . .	75,942	. . .	. . .	. . .
55	. . .	75,543	−489	−.01	.03
56	. . .	75,107	−345	−.00	.02
57	. . .	74,468	−639	−.01	.03
58	. . .	73,736	−732	−.01	.04
59	. . .	72,930	−806	−.01	.04
60	. . .	72,133	−798	−.01	.04
61	. . .	71,511	−622	−.01	.03
62	. . .	70,955	−556	−.01	.03
63	. . .	70,330	−624	−.01	.03
64	. . .	69,748	−583	−.01	.03
65	.333	69,300	−447	−.01	.03
66	.353	68,503	−797	−.01	.05
67	.373	67,557	−946	−.01	.06
68	.394	66,442	−1,116	−.02	.07
69	.417	65,134	−1,308	−.02	.08

Table 10.7   **Incentive Calculations—Tenth Percentile Earnings**

Last Year of Work	Replacement Rate	SSW (£)	Accrual (£)	Accrual Rate	Tax/ Subsidy
54	. . .	61,046	. . .	. . .	. . .
55	. . .	61,143	98	.00	−.01
56	. . .	61,394	250	.00	−.03
57	. . .	61,427	33	.00	−.00
58	. . .	61,450	23	.00	−.00
59	. . .	61,469	19	.00	−.00
60	. . .	61,482	13	.00	−.00
61	. . .	61,309	−173	−.00	.02
62	. . .	61,353	44	.00	−.01
63	. . .	61,363	10	.00	−.00
64	. . .	61,369	5	.00	−.00
65	.631	61,204	−165	−.00	.02
66	.668	61,318	114	.00	−.02
67	.706	61,310	−8	−.00	.00
68	.747	61,163	−147	−.00	.02
69	.791	60,862	−301	−.00	.05

effect of the dependent's addition to the basic pension, which is available to the married man.

As tables 10.6 and 10.7 show, the incentive effects for high and low earners are remarkably similar to those for middle earners. Tax/subsidy rates for extra years of work are very similar. Levels of social security wealth are also much

Table 10.8   **Incentive Calculations, Counting Incapacity Benefit at Age 60 as an Early Retirement Benefit**

Last Year of Work	Replacement Rate	SSW (£)	Accrual (£)	Accrual Rate	Tax/ Subsidy
54	...	90,346	...	...	...
55	...	98,878	532	.006	−.05
56	...	91,566	688	.007	−.06
57	...	91,994	428	.005	−.04
58	...	92,424	431	.005	−.04
59	...	92,869	444	.005	−.04
60	.521	93,319	450	.005	−.04
61	.484	84,814	−8,505	−.100	.75
62	.456	76,555	−8,258	−.108	.73
63	.441	68,529	−8,026	−.117	.72
64	.425	60,761	−7,767	−.128	.71
65	.412	53,256	−7,505	−.141	.71
66	.436	52,978	−278	−.005	.03
67	.461	52,584	−393	−.007	.04
68	.488	52,061	−524	−.010	.05
69	.517	51,389	−672	−.013	.07

alike, largely as a result of the mainly flat-rate nature of the U.K. benefit system. Replacement rates, however, are very different, being very much higher for the low earner.

In table 10.8, we consider the most important divergence from the base case, one that may better describe the incentives facing most individuals who would be dependent on the state for their pension income. Thus far, we have taken the rules of the U.K. social security system literally and modeled incentives as though there is no early retirement option. However, the reality is that virtually anybody dependent just on the state provision would be able to leave work earlier and receive state benefits. This is made explicit to some extent in the social security system in that, from age sixty on, there is no "availability for work test" that must be satisfied before income support will be paid out. Furthermore, as we saw in the previous section, a very large fraction of men in their early sixties receives the incapacity benefit (previously the invalidity benefit).

With this in mind, we have performed the same calculations as above, but on the assumption that benefits become available at age sixty. In particular, we have assumed that the incapacity benefit becomes available, although it is similar enough in level to income support that the results are almost identical if one chooses to model income support instead.

The effects of introducing this possibility are dramatic, indeed. Once age sixty is reached, each extra year of work means forgoing a full year's benefits with only a small future increase in SERPS as compensation. The pattern until age sixty is familiar. After age sixty, the effects of an extra year of work are to reduce social security wealth by about £8,000 per year. This is equivalent to a tax rate of more than 70 percent on the year's earnings and means a fall in social security wealth of around 10 percent or more for each year of work.

Until now, it has been hard to understand why the benefit system might create significant incentives to leave work early. Introducing this extra element of realism makes it much easier to see its potential role. The penalty for working past age sixty can be great, indeed. To the extent that individuals are able to claim invalidity pensions before age sixty, these arguments could, for some people, extend back even further. It is also worth saying that, until the beginning of the 1990s, SERPS additions were payable with respect to invalidity pensions as well as with respect to retirement pensions. So, for the period up to then, incentives to retire before age sixty-five would have been greater still.

For low earners, the effects of being eligible for benefits at age sixty are even more spectacular. The tax rate on an extra year's work reaches 91 percent at age sixty-one for a married man at the tenth percentile of earnings. For high earners, the effects are somewhat less dramatic, with the effective tax rate reaching a maximum of 60 percent. The potential incentives for low to middle earners to leave the labor market are very considerable indeed.

These observations raise interesting issues about the structure of the U.K. benefit system and appear to fit rather well with the observed behavior of many older men. Especially for the low paid, there are significant incentives to retire early. But it is harder to implicate the social security system alone in the *change* in activity rates since the 1970s for there have been no major changes that could have had such an effect. Put together with the fall in demand for lower-skilled workers, however, the relative generosity of social security for older groups, especially through apparently easy access to the invalidity benefit, can explain the observed fall in participation rates among older, less skilled workers.

10.4 Occupational Pensions

As we have stressed throughout, for a large part of the population, social security pensions play only a secondary role in providing retirement income and presumably also in the retirement decision. In the private sector, the standard occupational pension offers a pension equal to one-sixtieth of the final salary for each year of membership in the scheme. This was true of nearly two-thirds of private-sector schemes in 1990. So, after forty years of service, one could expect a pension of two-thirds of final earnings. Of course, very few people actually stay in schemes that long.

There are a variety of postretirement indexation provisions. Only about 20 percent of members of private schemes were guaranteed postretirement benefits to match inflation, a third could expect inflation matching subject to a maximum of 5 percent, and a further quarter were promised inflation indexation up to 3 or 4 percent. This variety of indexation promises is further complicated

Table 10.9   Proportion of Scheme Members Covered by Particular Early
                    Retirement Rules (1990)

	Early Retirement at Request of Employer (%)	Voluntary Early Retirement (%)
No provision	2	9
Accrued pension actuarially reduced	11	58
Accrued pension reduced favorably	15	14
Accrued pension with no reduction	20	8
Accrued pension plus extra payment	24	. . .
Other	28	11

Source: National Association of Pension Funds.

by the fact that many schemes operate with a degree of discretion in the actual awards made.

In the public sector, a number of schemes provide a pension of one-eightieth of the final salary for every year of service but are payable from age sixty and guarantee full inflation indexation.

This range of schemes makes a "typical" pension promise hard to value. The job is made infinitely harder by the range of early retirement provisions. Here, *early* means prior to the scheme's "normal pension age." This normal pension age has traditionally been sixty-five or sixty—largely sixty for women and sixty-five for men. European equal treatment legislation has resulted in equalization between men and women, often at the lower age. Voluntary early retirement usually offers less generous terms than early retirement at the employer's request. Early retirement for health reasons is often extraordinarily generous: "Many schemes calculate the pension on the basis of the member's earnings at the time of retirement, but as if employment had continued until normal retirement age. This produces a substantially greater benefit than an ordinary early retirement" (Pension Law Review Committee 1993, 2.2.39). Employers have made use of these generous provisions to ease older individuals out of work (Pension Law Review Committee 1993, 4.15.10). Given that the rules defining exactly what counts as ill health grounds for early retirement are often unclear, there is also scope for employees to make use of them.

In cases other than ill health, the complex situation is summarized in table 10.9. Where retirement is at the request of the employer, at least 44 percent receive their fully accrued pension with no actuarial reduction, or better. Given that this is often offered as part of a voluntary redundancy package, the fact that this is designated "at the request of the employer" should not be taken to indicate that the employee has no scope for decision making in the face of such incentives. Even where the retirement decision is purely voluntary, at least a fifth of employees face better than actuarially fair reductions in benefits.

When early retirement is available, it is often available on generous terms that clearly result in losing pension wealth by working longer. The only group for whom this is unlikely to be true are those who might expect substantial pay increases in the years approaching normal retirement age. Otherwise, there is clear potential for redistribution of resources in occupational schemes toward earlier retirees as well as toward those whose earnings do increase sharply right at the end of their careers.

10.4.1 Occupational Schemes and Retirement Behavior

Given the detail we have shown on the effects of state pensions on incentives and the fact that occupational schemes clearly provide different incentives, there is clear value in considering the actual retirement behavior of each group.

The differing nature of the rules governing occupational pension schemes and those governing state pensions clearly induces different incentives to retire before the standard retirement age. On becoming eligible, the most obvious effect of occupational pension schemes operates through a wealth effect. Individuals eligible for early retirement are less likely to work when their pension income is higher. However, occupational pensions may also give an incentive to work longer since continued employment increases eventual pension entitlement when pensions are typically linked to final earnings.

These differential incentives should show themselves in observed transition rates out of employment for those nearing retirement. To analyze this, we consider results from the 1988–1989 U.K. Retirement Survey.[5] This data source covers some twenty-five hundred households in the age range fifty-five to sixty-nine. It gives detailed employment and pension life histories. It is a retrospective work history data set unique in the United Kingdom, recording all job spells for each individual in the household and carrying health information based on a detailed description of medical symptoms.

Figure 10.15 shows *retirement probabilities* for men at each age between forty and sixty-five, separately for those with and without an occupational pension. (These are *not* retirement hazards.) *Retirement* is defined as leaving work and never reentering before age sixty-five. It is clear that the probability of retirement before age fifty-five is greater for those without an occupational pension. From age fifty-five, those with a pension are more likely to retire at each age. This pattern in part reflects the composition of the two groups— those without an occupational pension tend to be less skilled and more likely to be forced out of the labor market very early. Those with occupational pensions start to be able to take attractive levels of pensions from age fifty-five. The spike at age sixty is much more apparent for those with occupational pensions, reflecting the substantial proportion for whom this is the scheme's normal retirement age.

The equivalent picture for women is shown in figure 10.16. Here, the biggest

---

5. For more information on this data, see Bone et al. (1992) and Disney, Grundy, and Johnson (1997). Examples of use of the panel element of these data include Tanner (1998), Disney, Johnson, and Stears, and Johnson, Stears, and Webb (1998).

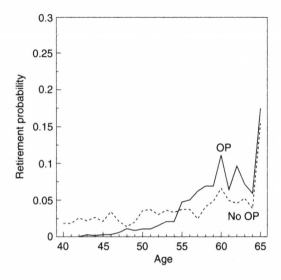

Fig. 10.15   Retirement probabilities for men (OP = occupational pension)

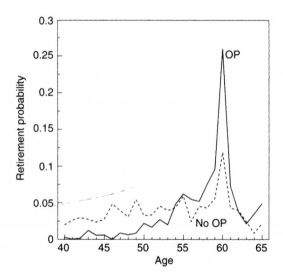

Fig. 10.16   Retirement probabilities for women (OP = occupational pension)

difference is in the size of the spikes at age sixty. Those with occupational pensions are more than twice as likely as those without to retire at age sixty. At first sight, this appears surprising given that those without occupational pensions are dependent just on the basic pension, for which the normal pension age is exactly sixty. But many will not have full entitlement in any case; within occupational pensions, the most common normal retirement age for women is

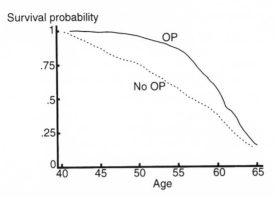

Fig. 10.17   **Survival functions for men (OP = occupational pension)**

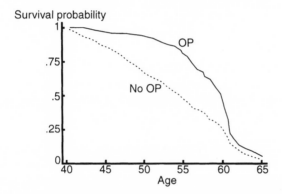

Fig. 10.18   **Survival functions for women (OP = occupational pension)**

sixty, and general attachment to the labor market is likely to be much lower for those without an occupational pension. The gains from working until age sixty for those with occupational pensions are much greater than for those without.

Disney, Meghir, and Whitehouse (1994) demonstrate similar effects using retirement hazards from the same data. They, too, find that the structure of pension benefits shifts the retirement probabilities, deterring individuals from retiring just prior to the earliest potential receipt of benefits. Once an individual is eligible for benefits, the hazard rate and probability of labor market exit are significantly increased.

Survival functions for men are plotted in figure 10.17 and for women in figure 10.18. The figures show the probability of survival in the labor force at each age from forty to sixty-five according to occupational pension status. They demonstrate very clearly for both men and women that those with occupational pensions are much more likely to remain in the labor market at least until age sixty than are those without. From age sixty, the survival probabilities converge for both men and women.

The labor market experience of the two groups is shown to be profoundly different. The lower retirement hazards at earlier ages among the occupational pension sample, resulting from both a lower exit rate and a lower probability of never subsequently working, mean that a large gap opens up between the two pension groups. After age fifty-five, the gap begins to close. These survival functions confirm the importance of the incentives provided by occupational pension schemes: the survival probability is considerably higher just before retirement benefits may become due (either "full" or early retirement), and thereafter the survival probability falls much more rapidly than that of those not covered by pension schemes. For those without occupational pensions, retirement behavior is considerably more heterogeneous. Retirement ages cover a larger age range and have a broader distribution. These differences in this survival to retirement functions are consistent with what we would expect given the incentive structure built in occupational pensions.

10.5   Conclusions

There have been significant changes in labor market behavior among older individuals in the United Kingdom since the 1970s. Participation and activity rates, especially among men over age fifty-five, have fallen dramatically. While it is hard to see any *changes* to the social security system that might have caused this, the social security system does provide significant incentives to retire early if, as is often the case, benefits can be received before age sixty-five. For those who can get invalidity benefits—and these individuals account for more than 40 percent of nonworking sixty- to sixty-four-year-olds—the system comes close to working as providing early retirement benefits with no actuarial reduction. The same is true for individuals who are entitled to income support in this age group. One in eight men receives this benefit. The relative generosity of these benefits and the incentives that they create, combined with the reduced demand for unskilled labor, must play a part in explaining the observed fall in labor market participation.

Among those with occupational pensions, significant increases in pension wealth could have had an important effect on increased early retirement, as could the relatively generous treatment of early retirement by many occupational schemes. We have shown that the retirement behavior of occupational pensioners differs significantly from that of those without occupational pensions in ways that are consistent with the former taking advantage of generous early retirement benefits.

Appendix
Evidence of the Effect of State Pensions on Retirement

Although there is a large international literature that has addressed the issue of estimating models of retirement behavior,[6] there is little evidence for the United Kingdom. Here, we draw on the recent study by Meghir and Whitehouse (1997) using the U.K. Retirement Survey data described above to examine the effect of various features of the pension system as well as earnings and demographic and health variables on the transition into retirement. The only previous econometric study for the United Kingdom was that by Zabalza, Pissarides, and Barton (1980), which used an earlier retirement survey but presented a purely static model of labor market participation at retirement in relation to the "earnings rule" discussed in section 10.2 above.

It is difficult to argue that retirement in the United Kingdom can be modeled as a well-defined labor market state distinct from other spells out of work. On the one hand, men within the state pension scheme can draw a pension only after age sixty-five; even this can be deferred at any point in time at a (more or less) actuarially fair rate. However, as we have seen, in addition to own savings, the state social security system, including the invalidity benefit, provides an important source of income for those out of work before that age. Those with occupational pensions are not prohibited from working even after drawing a pension early so long as they change employers. Thus, the obvious approach to modeling the age at which individuals leave the labor market is to study the transitions in and out of work up to age sixty-five, beyond which only very few men work. This is the approach followed in Meghir and Whitehouse (1997) and Disney, Meghir, and Whitehouse (1994). It was also followed recently by Blau (1994) for the United States.

In their reduced-form equations, Disney and Whitehouse show that, among other variables, health and the aggregate unemployment rate both have a strong and negative effect on the exit rate and that education increases the exit rate. The occupational variables included relate to the ones observed in the previous job. Professional/managerial workers have lower exit rates back to work and clerical workers higher vis-à-vis manual workers; nevertheless, these differences seem completely insignificant. When unobserved heterogeneity is taken into account, the effects of health and the unemployment rate increase. The exit rate elasticity with respect to aggregate unemployment for a manual worker at the start of the spell with mean education and age fifty-four is -1.16.

These results imply that age, health, and labor market conditions are important determinants of early retirement, as defined above. They affect the exit rate from jobs and change the rate of return to work in opposite directions. Thus, older men and men in poor health are likely to retire earlier, and the

---

6. Including Berkovec and Stern (1988), Stock and Wise (1990), and Rust (1989) on the United States and Borsch-Supan (1993) on Europe.

incidence of early retirement becomes more prevalent in periods of high unemployment. It is possible that both these effects are operating through the wage. But it is very likely that the aggregate unemployment rate and health both operate through the job arrival rate. Further, health is also likely to change the tastes toward work.

"Structural" transition equations, including earnings and benefits out of work, were also estimated. Social security benefits were shown to have a negative effect on the rate of return back to work, while earnings have a negative effect in the transition out of work and a positive effect on the rate of return back to work. The most significant effect was that of earnings on the job exit rate. Again, health and age have important effects.[7]

These results do indicate that incentive effects may play an important role in determining the age of retirement. The overall effect of benefits on the probability of retirement at a particular age (i.e., job exit at that age and nonreturn to work thereafter) can be calculated from a combination of the two estimated transition models. On the basis of the results, which control for unobserved heterogeneity, the elasticity with respect to benefits is about -0.36. In terms of these results, the job exit rate elasticity with respect to earnings (-0.54) is the strongest indication that economic incentives may affect the retirement age even for individuals without an occupational pension, indicating that lower-paid individuals do drop out of the labor market first.

References

Berkovec, J., and S. Stern. 1988. Job exit behaviour of older men. *Econometrica* 56.
Blau, David, 1994. Labour force dynamics of older men. *Econometrica* 62:117–56.
Bone, M., J. Gregory, B. Gill and D. Lader. 1992. *Retirement and retirement plans.* London: H. M. Stationery Office/Office of Population Census and Surveys.
Borsch-Supan, A. 1993. Retirement behaviour and social security design in Germany. Paper presented to the Institute for Fiscal Studies session on pensions and retirement, Royal Economic Society conference.
Dilnot, A., R. Disney, P.Johnson and E. Whitehouse. 1994. *Pensions policy in the UK: An economic analysis.* London: Institute for Fiscal Studies.
Disney, R., E. Grundy, and P. Johnson. 1997. The dynamics of retirement. Department of Social Security Research Report no. 72. London: H. M. Stationery Office.
Disney, R., P. Johnson, and G. Stears. 1998. Asset wealth and asset decumulation among households in the Retirement Survey. *Fiscal Studies* 19, no. 2:153–74.

---

7. Health could partly capture the effect of eligibility for the invalidity benefit (for a discussion of the importance of the invalidity benefit, see sec. 10.2 above) since the reduced-form benefit equations do not include health; the FES, from which the benefits are imputed, does not contain health information.

Disney, R., C. Meghir, and E. Whitehouse. 1994. Retirement behaviour in Britain. *Fiscal Studies* 15, no. 1:24–43.

Disney, R., and S. Webb. 1991. Why are there so many long-term sick in Britain? *Economic Journal* 1011:252–62.

Johnson, P., and G. Stears. 1995. Pensioner income inequality. *Fiscal Studies* 16, no. 4:69–94.

———. 1996. Should the basic state pension be a contributory benefit? *Fiscal Studies* 17, no. 1:105–12.

Johnson, P., G. Stears, and S. Webb. 1998. The dynamics of incomes and occupational pensions after retirement. *Fiscal Studies* 19, no. 2:197–216.

Meghir, C., and E. Whitehouse. 1997. Labour market transitions and retirement of men in the UK. *Journal of Econometrics* 79:327–54.

Pension Law Review Committee. 1993. *Pension law reform: The report to the Pension Law Review Committee.* London: H. M. Stationery Office.

Rust, J. 1989. A dynamic programming model of retirement behaviour. In *The Economics of Aging,* ed. D. Wise. Chicago: University of Chicago Press.

Stock, J., and D. Wise. 1990. Pensions, the option value of work and retirement. *Econometrica* 58:1151–80.

Tanner, S. 1998. The dynamics of male retirement behaviour. *Fiscal Studies* 19, no. 2:175–96.

Whitehouse, E. 1990. The abolition of the pensions earnings rule. *Fiscal Studies* 11:55–70.

Zabalza, A., C. Pissarides and M. Barton. 1980. Social-security and the choice between full-time work, part-time work and retirement. *Journal of Public Economics* 14:245–76.

11   Social Security and Retirement in the United States

Peter Diamond and Jonathan Gruber

The largest entitlement program in the United States today is the social security program. Social security benefits payments in 1993 amounted to $267.8 billion, which is over 18 percent of the federal budget and over 4 percent of U.S. GDP in that year; this represents a doubling as share of GDP in the past thirty years. Social security in the United States is also a system in fiscal imbalance. The convergence of three trends in the early twenty-first century will cause problems with the long-run solvency of the program. Two of these trends are the aging of the "baby-boom" cohort and the drop in the fertility rate of U.S. families. As a result, the ratio of persons over age sixty-five to those aged twenty to sixty-four has risen from 0.14 in 1950 to 0.21 today and is projected to rise to 0.36 by 2030 and to 0.41 by 2070. The final trend is the reduction in the rate of growth in real wages in the United States, which has lowered the base of earnings on which social security benefits commitments can be financed. As a result, current estimates imply that, if the structure of the program remains unchanged, payroll taxes to finance this program, currently at 12.4 percent of payroll, would have to rise to over 18 percent (Steuerle and Bakija 1994).

As a result of this fiscal imbalance in the social security program, a number of alternatives for reform have been considered, ranging from benefit reductions or tax increases to the increased taxation of social security benefits, raising the age of normal or early retirement, or even shifting partly or wholly into

Peter Diamond is professor of economics at the Massachusetts Institute of Technology and a research fellow of the National Bureau of Economic Research. Jonathan Gruber is professor of economics at the Massachusetts Institute of Technology and director of the Children's Program at the National Bureau of Economic Research.

The authors are grateful to Alain Jousten and Karl Critz for exceptional research assistance, to David Wise and the participants in the International Social Security Comparisons project for helpful comments, and to the National Institute of Aging and the National Science Foundation for financial support.

a funded (privatized) system. A critical input into understanding the efficiency implications of each of these alternatives is a model of how social security affects retirement decisions. Social security is a dominant feature of the opportunity set facing older households in the United States. Ranking households where the head is over age sixty-five by the share of their income from social security, social security represents 51 percent of total family income at the median; for 16 percent of such households, social security is the only source of family income.[1] As a result, it seems likely that the structure of the social security program has important effects on the life-cycle savings and labor supply decision making of households and, in particular, on their retirement decisions.

The purpose of our paper is to provide an overview of the interaction between social security and the labor force behavior of older persons in the United States. We do so in four steps. First, in section 11.1, we document the pertinent facts about the labor market behavior of older persons in the United States, both today and over time. Then, in section 11.2, we describe the structure of the social security system in the United States, summarizing the relevant institutional details for thinking about retirement behavior. Finally, in section 11.3, we present the results of a simulation model designed to document the retirement incentives inherent in social security for current cohorts of retirees. We conclude our analysis in section 11.4.

11.1   The Labor Market Behavior of Older Persons in the United States

One of the most striking trends in the U.S. labor market over the twentieth century has been the declining attachment to the labor force of older persons. In 1950, almost 60 percent of men aged sixty-five to sixty-nine were participating in the labor force. By 1990, this figure had fallen to 26 percent. This dramatic shift in the lifestyles of older men has prompted a large literature on its proximate causes, and a leading candidate is the growth of the social security program over this same time period. But, before addressing the effects of social security, it is useful to provide some more background on the labor market behavior of older men and women.

The historical and contemporaneous facts presented in this section are drawn from a number of different data sources. These are summarized in appendix A. In that appendix, we also provide a brief overview of the databases that are used by researchers in the United States to study retirement behavior.

11.1.1   Historical Trends

Figures 11.1 and 11.2 graph the labor force participation rates of men and women in different age groups since 1960. We focus on four age groups: forty-five to fifty-four; fifty-five to fifty-nine; sixty to sixty-four; and sixty-five and

---

1. Authors' tabulations from March 1994 and 1995 Current Population Survey.

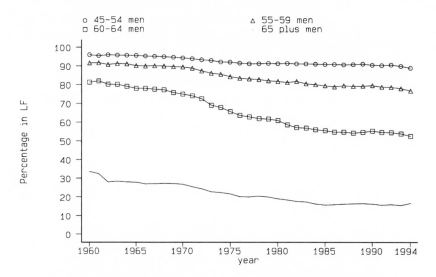

Fig. 11.1   Historical trends in labor force (LF) participation of older men

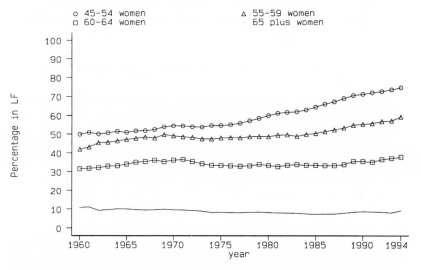

Fig. 11.2   Historical trends in labor force (LF) participation of older women

over. For men, there is a decline in the labor force participation of all these groups. The decline for the youngest group is slight, while the decline for sixty- to sixty-four-year-olds is much more precipitous. There is also a large percent-age decline, albeit from a smaller base, for the oldest group.

For women, the pattern is quite different: any trend toward earlier retirement is dominated by increased labor force participation across cohorts. Even for

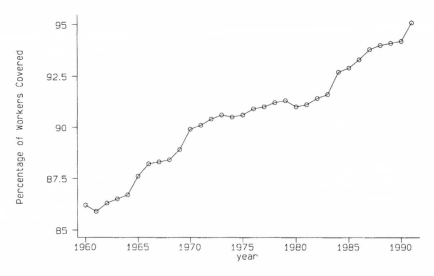

Fig. 11.3   Percentage of workers covered by the social security system

those aged sixty to sixty-four, participation is rising; for the oldest group, participation declines slightly.

One first-pass approach to considering whether social security is associated with these labor force trends is to examine related trends in social security generosity. We do so in three ways. First, in figure 11.3, we show the share of the workforce covered by the social security system. By 1960, a very high share of the workforce was already covered by social security, although that share grew steadily over the next thirty years. An important break in the series is after 1983, when a major reform brought several new sectors into the social security system; this reform is described further below.

Second, in figure 11.4, we show the share of men and women over age fifty-five receiving social security benefits as well as the share receiving social security or disability insurance benefits.[2] There was a dramatic increase in the share of the older population receiving payments from these public schemes over time. In 1960, fewer than 40 percent of older men and fewer than 20 percent of older women received social security and disability insurance benefits. By 1993, over 55 percent of older men were receiving social security, and over 65 percent were receiving either social security or disability insurance. For women, the percentage growth has been even more dramatic, with the result that by 1993 roughly 40 percent of women are receiving social security or disability insurance; the net contribution of disability insurance is much smaller for women than for men.

---

2. *Social security benefits receipt* refers to receipt of retired worker benefits only, which is restricted to those age sixty-two and over. *Disability insurance receipt* refers to receipt of disabled worker benefits, which is not age restricted; but we use disability insurance recipients of age fifty-five and over in the numerator of our calculation.

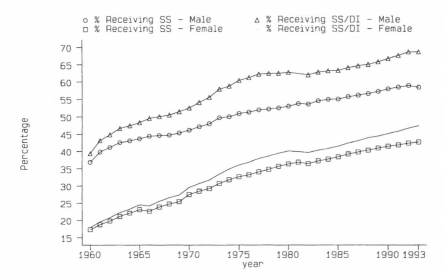

Fig. 11.4   Social security (SS) and disability insurance (DI) benefits receipt—age 55 and over

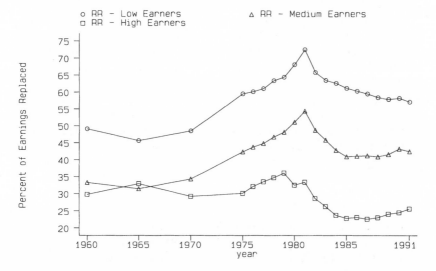

Fig. 11.5   Social security replacement rates (RRs) over time

Third, we show the change in generosity of benefits payments over time in figure 11.5. We show the replacement rate from 1960 to 1991 for low-earnings, medium-earnings, and high-earnings workers. These replacement rates are computed for a sixty-five-year-old single worker. In fact, social security replacement rates were roughly constant until 1970 for all three groups. Replacement rates then grew dramatically from 1970 to 1980, for reasons that are

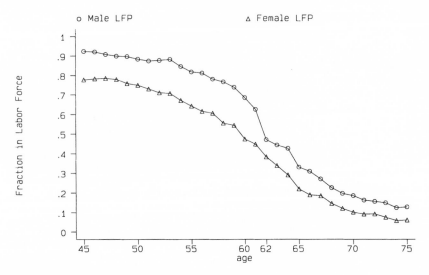

Fig. 11.6   Labor force participation (LFP) rates by age and sex

described below; this growth was especially dramatic for low earners, who saw their replacement rates rise by 50 percent, to 75 percent of their previous earnings level. Replacement rates then fell fairly precipitously beginning in 1981. For high earners, replacement rates are now actually lower than they were in 1970, while, for average earners and low earners, they remain somewhat higher.

These time-series patterns yield a mixed picture of the influence of social security. Clearly, there is a strong correlation between the size of the program and the labor force participation rate of older men. But the decline in participation of older men has continued unabated in the 1980s and 1990s, even as program generosity has declined. For women, any effects of social security are swamped by secular trends in time-series behavior.

11.1.2   Labor Market Behavior in 1995

For a more detailed understanding of the time pattern of labor force participation in recent times, we turn to the March 1994 and 1995 Current Population Survey (CPS). The CPS is a large, nationally representative survey that asks individuals about their labor force attachment at both the point of the survey and the previous year as well as about income in the previous year. We pool two years of the CPS for added precision in our estimates of labor force participation by age.

The age pattern of nonparticipation for men and women is depicted in figure 11.6. At age forty-five, the participation of men is significantly higher, although almost 80 percent of forty-five-year-old women are working in 1994–95. There is then a gradual parallel decline for men and women until age fifty-five, at

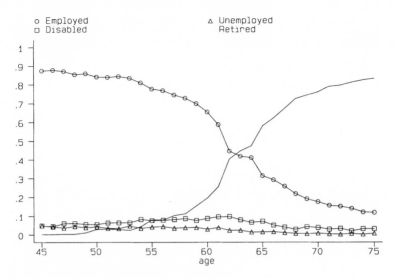

Fig. 11.7   Distribution of activities of men by age

which point the age pace steepens; this is particularly true for men, with the result that the participation gap closes substantially by age sixty-two. By age seventy-five, participation has dropped quite low, with fewer than 20 percent of men and 10 percent of women participating in the labor force.

Figure 11.7 considers in more detail the allocation of time among men as they age, by dividing activities at each age into employment, unemployment, disability, and retirement. The top line, showing the share of men employed, mirrors the age trend in figure 11.6 above. There is very little age trend in either unemployment or disability, although both categories do shrink over time. The dominating trend here is increased retirement with age. This same exercise is repeated for women in figure 11.8; the patterns are very similar to those for men, although a much larger share of women is in "other" activities that are not captured by these four metrics (as can be seen by taking one minus the sum of the four values).

11.1.3   Income Sources of Older Persons

Figures 11.9 and 11.10 examine the incidence of public and private retirement income for older persons. Figure 11.9 graphs three series for men only: the rate of social security receipt; the rate of receipt of disability insurance and supplemental security income; and the rate of receipt of income from other public assistance programs.[3] Before age sixty-two, there is relatively little receipt of public assistance income among men. There is a declining pattern of

---

3. Supplemental security income is cash welfare for low-income elders; the other categories represented here are unemployment insurance, workers' compensation, and cash welfare (through the AFDC program or state welfare programs).

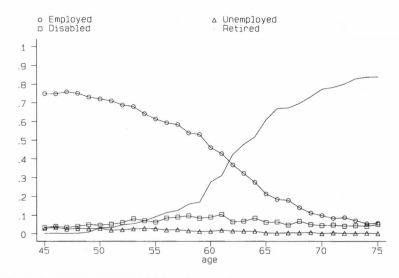

Fig. 11.8   Distribution of activities of women by age

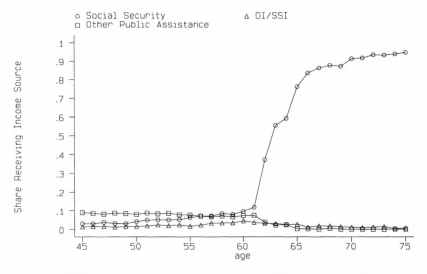

Fig. 11.9   Public income receipt for men (DI = disability insurance; SSI = supplemental security income)

other public assistance receipt, which is offset by a rising pattern of disability insurance/supplemental security income receipt. It is somewhat surprising that, under age sixty-two, a large number of men actually report receiving social security benefits. Some of this may be due to miscoding of disability insurance or supplemental security income; indeed, the reported number of age sixty recipients of disability insurance in the CPS data is only about two-thirds of

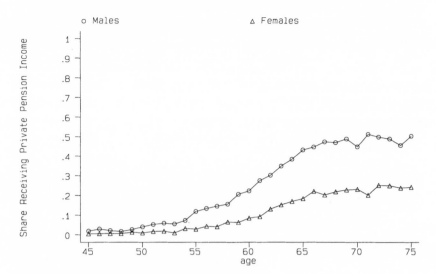

Fig. 11.10   Private pension receipt by sex

the administrative totals. Some of this may be due to miscoding of family social security receipt as own receipt among men with older wives, but this can
explain only a small share of the total. And some may be due to simple miscoding, either of age or of the type of income being received.

   In any case, beginning at age sixty-two, the rate of receipt of social security
skyrockets, until it is over 95 percent for those over age seventy-five. It is interesting to note that this increase in social security receipt is associated to a small
extent with a decline in disability insurance/supplemental security income receipt. This suggests that the net government cost of increased social security
receipt after age sixty-two is somewhat smaller than the social security budget
alone would suggest.

   Figure 11.10 displays the percentage of men and women at each age who are
receiving private pension income on their own account (as opposed to survivor
benefits from a spouse's pension). This grows fairly rapidly from age fifty-five
on, particularly for men, with the result that there is a rapidly growing gender
gap; by age seventy-five, the rate of receipt for men is twice that for women.
At the same time, however, some older women will be benefiting from survivor
benefits paid through their husband's pension.

   Finally, figure 11.11 shows the distribution of income sources for couples,
arrayed by the age of the head of the family.[4] We consider the distribution of
income across four sources: earnings, capital income, private pensions, and
public transfers (predominantly social security for older couples, as shown in

---

4. This differs somewhat from previous figures, where the unit of observation is the older person; we do this since these income concepts are best measured at the family level.

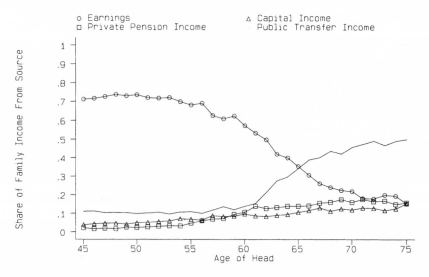

Fig. 11.11   Distribution of family income by source

fig. 11.9). Earnings are the dominant source of family income until age sixty, although, even for this younger subset of the sample, over 30 percent of income comes from other sources. Beginning at age sixty, earnings and capital income decline in proportional terms, and private pensions and public income (especially the latter) grow as shares of income. The high share of income accounted for by public-sector income at older ages highlights the importance of social security for workers making their retirement decisions.

11.2   Key Features of the Social Security System

11.2.1   History of the Social Security System in the United States

The landmark Social Security Act of 1935 created social security as well as the Aid to Dependent Children program, which was the start of today's cash welfare system. Originally, the act required that all workers in commerce and industry (except railroads) under age sixty-five be covered by social security. Over the years, the coverage of workers has steadily expanded; today, the only significant group of workers not covered by social security is some state and local government employees. At first, benefits for workers were available only for retired workers over age sixty-five. In 1956, benefits (reduced for early retirement) were made available to women between the ages of sixty-two and sixty-five. In 1961, the same treatment was extended to men. Dependent and survivor benefits were introduced in 1939, with benefits for wives and widows over age sixty-five and children under age eighteen. In 1950, benefits were extended to dependent husbands and widowers over age sixty-five. In 1965, divorced wives became eligible for benefits provided the marriage had lasted at least ten years, with similar treatment extended to divorced husbands in 1983. In 1956, benefits were extended to disabled workers over age fifty, with extension to disabled workers of all ages in 1960.

Until 1972, it took an act of Congress to increase benefits. Tiring of the repeated struggle over how much to increase benefits, the 1972 act introduced automatic increases in benefits with increases in the consumer price index. This was done by continuing to base benefits on a lifetime average of earnings in nominal terms but increasing the benefit formula (as a function of lifetime earnings) in step with inflation. Unfortunately, since inflation affects both life-time nominal earnings and the relation between benefits and earnings, this act overindexed benefits. While this overindexing might have been roughly offset by the nonlinearities in the benefit formula had inflation remained low, with the large increase in inflation in the 1970s this overindexing led to a large, unintended increase in benefits that placed the financing of social security in trouble.

In 1977, the current benefit structure was adopted. After reaching retirement age, there is continued adjustment of benefits for increases in the CPI. Deter-mination of the level of benefits when reaching retirement age is now based on lifetime earnings using wage indexing. For each worker, there is calculation of the worker's average indexed monthly earnings (AIME)—an average of a worker's earnings (indexed by the average level of wages in the economy each year) over the highest thirty-five years of his or her career. The indexing is still not done quite right, with a gap of two years between the year used for the wage indexing of earnings (when the worker turns age sixty) and the year that CPI increases begin (when the worker turns age sixty-two) and no indexing of earnings after age sixty. This gap would become important if we had large and varying inflation rates. There has been controversy over the generations (re-ferred to as the *notch babies*) affected by the transition to the new system.[5]

The last major reform of social security came in 1983, in the face of an imminent shortage of funds. This act addressed both short- and long-run fi-nancial problems. The most notable of the changes affecting long-run consid-erations is a phased increase in the normal retirement age, from the current level of sixty-five to sixty-seven, which is reached for workers reaching age sixty-two in 2022 and later. As legislated in 1983, the change in the normal retirement age does not change the age at which people can first claim retire-ment benefits, which remains at age sixty-two. But the amount of benefits re-ceived at age sixty-two, or at any other age, is made smaller if the normal retirement age is older. When the normal retirement age is sixty-seven, a worker retiring at age sixty-two will receive 70 percent of the benefit formula amount (the PIA, or primary insurance amount), rather than the 80 percent received now. Taxation of part of social security benefits began with the 1983 legislation. Also, the incentive to continue working past the normal retirement age was increased. Someone first claiming benefits after the normal retirement

5. For a further discussion of the notch babies, see Krueger and Pischke (1992).

age has benefits increased by a delayed retirement credit. The 1977 legislation raised this credit to 3 percent per year, while the 1983 legislation phased in increases until the credit reaches 8 percent per year.

The social security system was created by the same act that also created a program to provide aid to the poor elderly. In the early days, the elderly received more income from the welfare portion of this act than from social security. Over time, social security has outstripped aid to the aged; currently, the social security program is roughly ten times as large as the program of welfare for the low-income elderly and disabled (Supplemental Security Income).

11.2.2   Current Features of the Social Security System

The social security system in the United States today is financed by a payroll tax that is levied on workers and firms equally. The total payroll tax paid by each party is 7.65 percentage points; 5.3 percentage points are devoted to the old age and survivors insurance program, with 0.9 percentage points funding the disability insurance system and 1.45 percentage points funding Medicare's hospital insurance program. The payroll tax that funds old age and survivors insurance and disability insurance is levied up only to the first $62,700 (in 1996) of earnings (the taxable maximum); the hospital insurance tax is uncapped.[6] Like many other earnings figures in the law, this earnings limit is indexed to increase with average earnings in the economy. Part of the revenue from the income taxation of social security benefits goes to social security. Social security also receives interest (at market rates) on its holdings of Treasury debt.

Individuals qualify for an old age insurance pension by working for forty quarters in covered employment, which encompasses most sectors of the economy in recent years.[7] The process of determination of the level of benefits proceeds in several steps. The first step for qualifying workers is computation of the worker's averaged indexed monthly earnings (AIME), which is one-twelfth of the average of the worker's annual earnings in covered employment, indexed by a national wage index. This real wage history is averaged over the highest thirty-five years of earnings. Earlier, a shorter averaging period was used to reflect the immaturity of the system. A key feature of this process is that additional higher-earnings years can replace earlier lower-earnings years since only thirty-five years are used in the calculation.[8]

---

6. This cap is 2.4 times the median earnings of a full-year (forty-eight weeks or more), full-time (thirty-five hours or more per week) worker; 92 percent of such workers earn less than this amount.

7. Notable exceptions are state and local employees, some of whom are covered and some not. The current Social Security Advisory Council has recommended mandatory coverage in this sector, starting with newly hired workers. Many of these workers will receive benefits anyway because of covered work, before, after, or as a second job during their current employment.

8. In particular, while earnings through age fifty-nine are converted to real dollars for averaging, earnings after age sixty are treated nominally. There is a two-year lag in availability of the wage index, calling for a base in the year in which the worker turns age sixty in order to be able to compute benefits for workers retiring at their sixty-second birthday. While it would be possible to

The next step of the benefits calculation is to convert the AIME into the primary insurance amount (PIA). This is done by applying a three-piece linear progressive schedule to an individual's average earnings, whereby ninety cents of the first dollar of earnings is converted to benefits while only fifteen cents of the last dollar of earnings (up to the taxable maximum) is so converted. As a result, the rate at which social security replaces past earnings (the "replacement rate") falls with the level of lifetime earnings. For a worker with no dependents whose earnings had grown at the same rate as average earnings in the economy and who retired at age sixty-five in 1995 with a 1994 level of earnings of $15,000, the replacement rate is 50 percent. For 1994 earnings levels of $25,000, $35,000, and $45,000, the replacement rates are 43 percent, 37 percent, and 30 percent, respectively. For someone who always earned the maximum amount subject to taxation, the replacement rate is 24 percent. While 85 percent of social security benefits are subject to tax for retirees with sufficiently high incomes (couples with incomes above $32,000 in 1993), all earnings are taxed (including the employee portion of the payroll tax), raising the effective replacement rate of the program. Also, many social security recipients are in a lower tax bracket than they were before retirement.

Adjustments to the level of the PIA are made on the basis of the age at which benefits are first claimed. For workers claiming before the normal retirement age (currently sixty-five but legislated to increase slowly to sixty-seven), benefits are decreased by five-ninths of 1 percent per month, so that the benefits of those claiming on their sixty-second birthday are 80 percent of what they would be if they waited until the normal retirement age. The size of the reduction factor will be only five-twelfths of 1 percent for months beyond thirty-six months before the normal retirement age, which will become relevant once the delay in the normal retirement age becomes effective. The reduction is called the *actuarial reduction factor.* Individuals can also delay the receipt of benefits beyond age sixty-five and receive a *delayed retirement credit.* For workers reaching age sixty-five in 1996, an additional 5 percent is paid for each year of delayed receipt of benefits. Under current legislation, this amount will steadily increase until it reaches 8 percent per year in 2009.

While one can claim as early as age sixty-two, receipt of social security benefits is conditioned on the "earnings test" until the worker reaches age seventy: if one earns more than a certain floor level, social security benefits are reduced for each additional dollar of earnings, until, at high earnings levels, one cannot qualify at all. In order to receive all his or her benefits, in 1995 a worker must have earnings below $8,280 if between the ages of sixty-two and sixty-five and below $12,500 if between the ages of sixty-five and seventy. These figures increase each year with average earnings in the economy. Bene-

---

make adjustments as data become available, this is not done, with all later years entering the AIME calculation without any adjustment for further growth in the national average wage index. This gap would become important if we had large and varying inflation rates.

fits are reduced for any earnings above this limit, $1.00 for each $2.00 of earnings for workers between the ages of sixty-two and sixty-five and $1.00 for every $3.00 for workers between the ages of sixty-five and seventy. There is a special monthly retirement test for workers in their first year of retirement. In 1996 legislation, the earnings limit for those between the ages of sixty-five and sixty-nine has been increased in a series of steps, reaching $30,000 in 2002. Months of benefits lost through the earnings test are treated as delayed receipt, entitling the worker to a delayed retirement credit on the lost benefits when he does claim benefits.

There are also important additional benefit provisions based on family structure. Spouses of social security beneficiaries receive an additional benefit, which is 50 percent of the PIA, beginning at age sixty-two, although a spouse receives only the larger of this and her own entitlement as a worker.[9] Dependent children are also each eligible for 50 percent of the PIA, but the total family benefit cannot exceed a maximum that varies with PIA level but is roughly 175 percent of the PIA. Surviving spouses receive 100 percent of the PIA, beginning at age sixty, although there is an actuarial reduction for claiming widow benefits before age sixty-five or if the worker had an actuarial reduction. The benefits for dependents are somewhat complicated by the fact that both spouses may qualify for social security benefits as retired workers. For previous generations, where wives generally earned substantially less over their lifetimes than their husbands, this was not such an important consideration. But, in recent times, it is quite frequent that wives will earn enough so that they would have a PIA of at least half that of their husbands and so will not automatically use the default of dependent benefits; benefits are the maximum receivable under different provisions. Currently, of the 20 million female beneficiaries of social security, 7.5 million are entitled solely as workers, 5 million are entitled both as workers and as dependents/survivors, and another 7.5 million are entitled solely as dependents or survivors.

Benefit payments are adjusted for increases in the consumer price index after the worker has reached age sixty-two. Thus, social security provides a real annuity to its recipients. Social security benefits are largely tax favored: they are taxed only if the sum of other income and half of social security benefits exceed $32,000 for a joint return, and even at that point they are only partially taxed.

Finally, it is important to note that the social security program does not operate in a vacuum. There are a number of other public assistance programs for which elderly persons are eligible that may also have effects on their labor market behavior. One such program is disability insurance, which provides income insurance to workers physically unable to participate in the labor force. Given the difficulty of distinguishing true career-ending disability, particularly in the near elderly population, this program also potentially has an effect on

---

9. Spousal benefits can begin earlier if there is a dependent child in the household.

the retirement decisions of older workers. Indeed, there is a large empirical literature in recent years that suggests that variations in disability insurance program parameters do affect labor force participation among those aged forty-five to sixty-five (see, e.g., Bound 1989, 1991; Gruber 1996; Gruber and Kubik 1997; Leonard 1986; and Parsons 1980, 1991a, 1991b).

Moreover, there is an important interaction between disability insurance and social security. As noted above, if individuals receive social security benefits before the normal retirement age of sixty-five, they are reduced by five-ninths of 1 percent per month. However, if an individual with the same earnings trajectory qualifies for disability insurance, then he or she receives the full social security entitlement with no reduction.[10] It is unclear how substitutable social security early retirement and disability insurance are, but this potentially reduces any savings to the government from lowering the benefits for early retirement, or raising the age of early eligibility, without changing the benefit structure for disabled workers. This is highlighted by figure 11.9 above, which showed the interaction between the rise in social security receipt and the decline in disability insurance receipt around age sixty-two.

Another public assistance program that potentially interacts with social security is the supplemental security income program, which provides income support to the low-income elderly (defined as at least age sixty-five) and disabled individuals. Unlike social security or disability insurance, benefits and eligibility for supplemental security income are conditioned on point-in-time income rather than lifetime income. The size of the supplemental security income recipient population is small relative to social security recipients; fewer than 4 percent of social security recipients age sixty-five and older also receive supplemental security income. On the other hand, over two-thirds of supplemental security income recipients do receive some social security income. So supplemental security income is serving both as an alternative to social security for very low-income elderly and as a supplement for those with very low social security income.

There are also large private incentives for retirement embedded in firm pension plans. Pension coverage has grown dramatically in the postwar period, and, in 1994, roughly 45 percent of workers aged twenty-one to sixty-five were covered by a pension plan at work.[11] Given the age structure in the pattern of job holding relative to pension provision, a noticeably larger fraction of workers is covered by pension provisions at some time in their careers than this number suggests. On the other hand, some fraction of workers cashes out their pension accumulations when changing jobs, leaving no accumulation when reaching retirement. In 1994, 35 percent of retired workers over age sixty-two who were receiving social security were receiving pension income as well. A

---

10. This calculation is complicated, of course, by the fact that additional work can affect the benefits computation.

11. Authors' tabulations from March 1995 Current Population Survey.

number of papers in recent years have suggested that pension incentives play an important role in determining retirement behavior among covered workers; this may interact with the social security incentives described below (see Stock and Wise 1990; or Samwick 1993).

Finally, for understanding the role of social security, it is important to consider this program in the broader context of the treatment of older workers in the labor force. The United States has a broad set of protections in place preserving the rights of older workers through the 1967 Age Discrimination in Employment Act, including legal restrictions on age-of-hire rules and on mandatory retirement (Parsons 1996). This levels the playing field between older and younger workers for labor supply decision making, highlighting the potential importance for retirement decisions of financial incentives such as those through social security.

11.2.3   The Retirement Effects of Social Security—Theory and Evidence

There is a large U.S.-based literature that describes both the expected effects of the social security system on retirement and evidence on the actual retirement effects of the program. The motivation for examining the effects of social security can be seen clearly by examining the hazard rate out of the labor force for men and women. This is measured as the increase in the rate of labor force leaving from the previous age, relative to the stock of workers participating at the previous age. Figure 11.12 shows the hazard rate for labor force leaving for men. The striking fact about this figure is the dramatic increase in labor force leaving at age sixty-two, which is the age of eligibility for early retirement under social security, and at age sixty-five, which is the normal retirement age. These spikes are very suggestive of a role for social security in explaining

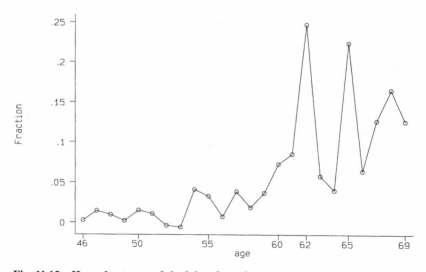

Fig. 11.12   Hazard rate out of the labor force for men

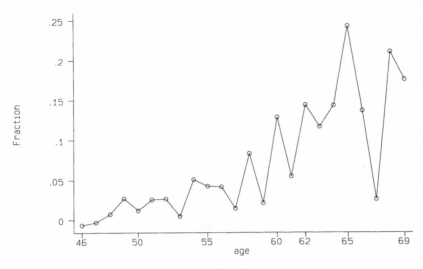

Fig. 11.13   **Hazard rate out of the labor force for women**

the retirement behavior of men. There is also a small spike around age fifty-five, which may reflect the early retirement provisions at that age under many pension plans. There is also another spike around age sixty-eight; the cause here is not clear, although the small denominator of the participation hazard after age sixty-five makes it hard to interpret this finding.[12]

The hazard rate for women is plotted in figure 11.13. The spike at age sixty-five is apparent here as well, but the spike at age sixty-two is not as pronounced. This may reflect the fact that female retirement is determined more by joint timing with husbands than by social security incentives.

In appendix A, we discuss theoretically the various effects that social security has on retirement behavior and then review the extensive U.S.-based literature on social security and retirement. We highlight the sources of agreement and disagreement in the existing literature and conclude that there is fairly broad agreement that the overall structure of social security is an important determinant of retirement, even while there remains disagreement over the effects of variations in program generosity within this structure.

11.3   Retirement Incentives

In this section, we use a model of social security benefits determination to assess the incentives of social security on retirement through accrual rate effects.

---

12. That is, the spike at age sixty-five represents a 9.5 percentage point change in labor force participation, while the spike at age sixty-eight represents only a 4.5 percentage point change; the latter appears almost as large as the former because the denominator is so much smaller.

11.3.1   Simulation Modeling

The basis for our analysis is the Social Security Administration's ANYPIA program.[13] This program inputs a set of worker characteristics: age, wife's age, earnings history, and date of retirement. It then computes the benefits entitlement for a given month in the future. To do so, we use the social security base-case assumptions about price and wage growth in the future. The program computes the benefits for the worker, dependent benefits for married workers, and survivor benefits for the case where the worker has died.

The next step in our simulation is to take these monthly benefit entitlements and compute an expected net present discounted value of social security wealth (SSW). This requires projecting benefits out until workers reach age one hundred and then taking a weighted sum that discounts future benefits by both the individual discount rate and the prospects that the worker will live to a given future age.[14] Our methodology for doing so is described in appendix A. For the worker himself, this is fairly straightforward; it is simply a sum of future benefits, discounted backward by time preference rates and mortality rates. For dependent and survivor benefits, it is more complicated since we must account for the joint likelihood of survival of the worker and the dependent. In our base case, we use a real discount rate of 3 percent. To adjust for mortality prospects, we use the sex/age-specific U.S. life tables from U.S. Department of Health and Human Services (1990). Finally, to compute net social security wealth, we subtract out social security payroll tax payments that the individual would make during any continued work. We add both the employee and the employer shares of the payroll tax, under the assumption that the employer share is fully borne by the worker in the form of lower wages. All figures are discounted back to age fifty-five by both time preference rates and mortality risk.

For the output of the simulations, we calculate three different concepts. The first is the net of tax replacement rate, the rate at which social security replaces the (after-tax) earnings of the worker should he continue working in that year. It is important to do this calculation on an after-tax basis in order to account for the fact that social security benefits are not taxed for most families while earnings are. We do so by modeling the average tax rate faced by earners of different earnings levels in each year and whether they are subject to taxation of their social security benefits. The second concept is the accrual rate, the percentage change in social security wealth from the previous year.

Finally, we compute a tax/subsidy rate, which is the absolute change in social security wealth over the potential earnings from working that next year.

---

13. We are grateful to Steve McKay of the Social Security Administration for his assistance in applying this program to our purposes.

14. We have experimented with extending the model to account for ages up to 120 since this is the extent of the life-table information available. This had little effect on the results, however, since so few persons are alive beyond age one hundred.

This represents the implicit tax on or subsidy to continued work in terms of the net change in social security wealth that is implied by that additional year of work. The numerator of this tax/subsidy rate is the opposite of the change in social security wealth from working the additional year. The denominator is the potential earnings over that additional year. Thus, if this figure is positive, it implies that the social security system causes a disincentive to additional work through forgone social security wealth. This is the relevant concept for the worker who is trading off leisure (on social security) against continued work.

Note that, in computing these concepts, we use the unconditional mortality risk beyond age fifty-five; that is, there is some probability that the worker may be dead at each year after his fifty-fifth birthday. An alternative approach would be to use conditional life tables at each year, with the result that, for the worker considering retiring on his sixty-third birthday, we discount the future by the age sixty-three–conditional life table. The correct approach here depends on the perspective from which this computation is taken. Our approach is appropriate if the computation is taken from the perspective of the forward-looking fifty-four-year-old who is considering the retirement incentives at all future ages. The alternative would be appropriate for year-by-year decision making about retirement. Since we discount all our dollar figures back to age fifty-five by both time preference and mortality risk, both concepts yield the same tax/subsidy effects (since both numerator and denominator are deflated); however, they will yield somewhat different values of social security wealth and therefore different accrual rates.

For the purposes of the simulations outlined below, we assume that workers claim social security benefits either at the point of their retirement or when they become eligible if they retire before the point of eligibility. In fact, this is not necessarily true; retirement and claiming are two distinct events, and, for certain values of mortality prospects and discount rates, it is optimal to delay claiming until sometime after retirement (owing to the actuarial adjustment of benefits). In fact, a nontrivial share of individuals who retire before age sixty-two delay claiming their benefits for at least one year. We plan to explore this issue further in future work.

To produce our base-case numbers, we use a typical individual who was born in January 1930 and thus turned sixty-five in January 1995. In theory, to calculate benefits for a worker, we would need his entire earnings history. In practice, we use a "synthetic" earnings history, which uses the median earnings of a cohort through time. As a first step in creating this synthetic earnings history, we use information on the median earnings by calendar year and age cohort from U.S. Department of Health and Human Services (various years). More specifically, we use the median earnings of a sixty-one-year-old in 1991 (the last available year of data) as our base point and then follow this cohort back through time (using the median for sixty-year-olds in 1990, fifty-nine-year-olds in 1989, and so on). We then update this to ages beyond age sixty-

Table 11.1   **Base-Case Incentive Calculation**

Last Year of Work	Replacement Rate	SSW	Accrual	Accrual Rate	Tax/ Subsidy
54	. . .	110,574	0	0	0
55	. . .	111,033	458	.004	−.022
56	. . .	110,126	−906	−.008	.046
57	. . .	108,994	−1,133	−.010	.060
58	. . .	107,734	−1,259	−.012	.069
59	. . .	106,474	−1,260	−.012	.072
60	. . .	105,294	−1,180	−.011	.071
61	.403	104,275	−1,019	−.010	.064
62	.440	104,701	426	.004	−.028
63	.476	104,766	65	.001	−.005
64	.703	104,335	−432	−.004	.031
65	.749	101,882	−2,452	−.024	.188
66	.798	99,109	−2,773	−.027	.225
67	.845	95,964	−3,145	−.032	.269
68	.872	91,131	−4,833	−.050	.439
69	.898	86,412	−4,718	−.052	.455

one by using the age-earnings profile for 1991, along with actual inflation data and base-case inflation assumptions.

In pursuing this calculation, we found a relatively steep decline in median earnings after about age fifty, which presumably reflects the fact that more and more of the earning population is working only part-time. However, our synthetic individual is considering the decision to work full-time for an additional year, so this skews the true nature of the underlying earnings history. As a result, we use this synthetic earnings profile through age fifty and then assume that earnings stay constant in real terms from age fifty-one on.

We assume initially that the worker's wife is exactly three years younger than he. We also assume that she has never worked, with the result that she claims as a dependent spouse only and not as a worker as well.

11.3.2 Base-Case Results

Table 11.1 shows our base-case results. Each row represents the age of the worker in the last year that he works; that is, the first row represents the effect of working during the fifty-fourth year and retiring on the fifty-fifth birthday (1 January 1985). The first column shows the net replacement rate. This concept is not defined until the worker can actually claim benefits, which occurs if his last year of work is at age sixty-one and he retires at age sixty-two.

At that first point of possible claiming, the replacement rate is roughly 40 percent.[15] This rises somewhat over time as workers increase their social secu-

---

15. This is lower than the replacement rates used in fig. 11.5 above since our base-case worker has higher earnings than the "average" worker used in that figure.

rity benefits by delaying claiming. The major change occurs for retirement on the sixty-fifth birthday, when the wife turns age sixty-two, since at that point the spouse becomes entitled to dependent benefits. This jump in replacement rates is somewhat artificial in that the worker who retires at age sixty-two will also see a jump at his sixty-fifth birthday, when his wife turns age sixty-two. That is, the replacement rate rises at age sixty-five regardless of the age of retirement. For the worker who works through his sixty-ninth year and collects on his seventieth birthday, social security replaces almost 90 percent of his after-tax earnings.

The next three columns show the evolution of social security wealth over time. In order to understand these results, it is useful to recap the four mechanisms through which additional work affects the computation of social security wealth: (1) The worker must pay social security taxes on his earnings, lowering net social security wealth. (2) The additional year of earnings is used in the recomputation of social security benefits. For workers who have not yet worked thirty-five years, this additional year will be replacing a zero in the benefits computation; for workers who have worked thirty-five years, it will potentially be replacing a previous low-earnings year. For both these reasons, additional work raises net social security wealth. (3) The additional year of work, for work at ages sixty-two and beyond, implies a delay in claiming. This raises future benefits through the actuarial adjustment, but it implies fewer years over which benefits can be claimed. As a result, there is an ambiguous effect on net social security wealth. (4) For each year into the future that we consider, there is some chance that the worker will die, lowering his net social security wealth. This is related to mechanism 3; the probability of mortality raises the required actuarial adjustment to make the worker indifferent to delayed claiming. Thus, it is unclear ex ante whether the social security system will tax or subsidize additional work in any given case.

As table 11.1 shows, a worker who retires on his fifty-fifth birthday has accumulated roughly $110,000 in social security wealth. There is then a small increase in social security wealth for work during the fifty-fifth year; this is because that next year "completes" the worker's earnings history, with that year of earnings therefore replacing a zero in the benefits computation. After this point, additional earnings affect the benefits computation only to the extent that they replace earlier, lower-earnings years. With a more variable earnings history, as we show below, this "completion" effect will lower the tax rate at older ages as well.

For work in the fifty-sixth to sixty-first years, social security wealth uniformly declines. This decline is driven by two factors: the fact that the worker has some (small) chance of dying[16] and, more important, the fact that the

---

16. That is, since we discount mortality from the perspective of age fifty-five, a worker who is considering retiring at age fifty-six relative to age fifty-seven has a slightly higher chance of receiving his benefits, increasing his social security wealth.

worker is paying the social security payroll tax if he continues to work. As a result, the accrual rate is negative; there is roughly a 1–1.2 percent decline in social security wealth each year from continued work.

The final column shows the tax/subsidy rate. There is a slight subsidy to work in the fifty-fifth year, as noted above, and then taxes on work in the fifty-sixth through sixty-first years. This tax, however, is lower than the statutory social security payroll tax rate. This differential arises because these additional years of earnings are replacing lower-earnings years in the benefits computation. Thus, there is some tax/benefit linkage in this age range.

There is then a slight subsidy to work during the sixty-second year. This subsidy arises because the worker receives an actuarial adjustment for delaying claiming benefits, which offsets both the payroll tax and the fact that the worker is claiming one year later. That is, for work during the sixty-second year, the system is roughly actuarially "fair."[17] The fact that the tax rate on continued work actually declines at age sixty-two while retirement jumps up at that age (fig. 11.12 above) is striking and casts some doubt on the full rationality/perfect markets model often used to explain the effects of social security on retirement. This spike at age sixty-two is more likely associated with either the market imperfections or individual irrationalities discussed in the theory section of appendix B.

During the sixty-third year, the actuarial adjustment is roughly sufficient to compensate for the taxes paid and the smaller number of years of collecting benefits, and there is no net tax or subsidy. There is then a nontrivial tax rate in the sixty-fourth year. For work during the sixty-fifth year, the tax rate jumps up dramatically. For this worker, working during his sixty-fifth year means forgoing over $2,450 in social security wealth, which amounts to almost 19 percent of what he would earn during that year. This is because the delayed retirement credit is actuarially unfair, given the forgone year of social security benefits. This tax rate rises further with age, with the result that, for the decision to work during the seventieth year, forgone social security wealth amounts to almost half of what he would earn during that year. There is an explicit jump for work in the sixty-eighth year due to spousal claiming behavior. For the spouse, as for the worker, there is a penalty to delaying claiming past age sixty-five. Since we assume that both the worker and his spouse claim when the worker retires, then his working during his sixty-eighth year means that his spouse will not claim until after age sixty-five and so will be penalized. It is important to note, however, that future changes in the delayed retirement credit put in place by the 1983 legislation substantially lower these work disincentives.

---

17. *Actuarial fairness* here refers to the net of taxes and benefits, not to the structure of benefits only.

Table 11.2   **Incentive Calculation—Single Worker**

Last Year of Work	Replacement Rate	SSW	Accrual	Accrual Rate	Tax/ Subsidy
54	. . .	60,934	0	0	0
55	. . .	60,083	−851	−.014	.043
56	. . .	58,574	−1,510	−.025	.081
57	. . .	57,007	−1,567	−.027	.087
58	. . .	55,366	−1,640	−.029	.095
59	. . .	53,782	−1,585	−.029	.095
60	. . .	52,290	−1,492	−.028	.094
61	.430	50,885	−1,405	−.027	.093
62	.465	49,682	−1,203	−.024	.083
63	.503	47,704	−1,978	−.040	.143
64	.540	45,385	−2,319	−.049	.177
65	.568	41,324	−4,061	−.089	.327
66	.598	37,192	−4,132	−.100	.352
67	.627	32,939	−4,253	−.114	.385
68	.657	28,651	−4,288	−.130	.412
69	.687	24,334	−4,317	−.151	.442

11.3.3   Other Cases

Table 11.2 explores these same results for a single worker. In this case, there are slightly higher tax rates before the sixty-second year—for two reasons. First, in the married case, if the worker dies, his wife will still get survivor benefits, and the discounting for mortality is therefore not as severe as it is for the single worker. Second, the gains from benefits recomputation are smaller for the single worker since higher benefits affect only him and not both him and his spouse. That is, recomputing benefits for the married worker has a much larger effect both because each additional dollar of benefits turns into an additional $1.50 through the spousal benefit and because that extra dollar becomes an extra dollar of benefits to the surviving spouse as well. Yet both the married and the single worker pay the same payroll tax, so this results in a larger net disincentive for the single worker.

Interestingly, for the single worker, this disincentive does not diminish noticeably for work during the sixty-second year. Here, the system is actuarially unfair; the extra benefits in future years from delaying claiming are outweighed by the forgone year of claiming and the taxes paid. So, for work during ages sixty-two to sixty-seven, the system offers much larger disincentives to single than to married workers; by age sixty-seven, the implicit tax rate is over 40 percent. On the other hand, for work during ages sixty-eight and sixty-nine, the tax rate is actually lower for single workers owing to the unfairness of the delayed retirement credit for both spouses in the married worker case (as described above).

Tables 11.3 and 11.4 show the effect of considering different earnings histor-

Table 11.3 **Incentive Calculation—Tenth Percentile Married Earners**

Last Year of Work	Replacement Rate	SSW	Accrual	Accrual Rate	Tax/ Subsidy
54	...	60,936	0	0	0
55	...	61,141	205	.003	−.024
56	...	60,753	−389	−.006	.049
57	...	60,329	−424	−.007	.055
58	...	59,820	−509	−.008	.069
59	...	59,320	−499	−.008	.071
60	...	58,866	−454	−.008	.067
61	.530	58,448	−418	−.007	.065
62	.577	58,841	393	.007	−.064
63	.627	59,310	470	.008	−.080
64	.926	59,504	194	.003	−.035
65	.990	58,521	−983	−.017	.187
66	1.056	57,331	−1,190	−.020	.238
67	1.119	55,232	−2,099	−.037	.445
68	1.156	52,234	−2,997	−.054	.673
69	1.193	49,465	−2,769	−.053	.660

Table 11.4 **Incentive Calculation—Ninetieth Percentile Married Earners**

Last Year of Work	Replacement Rate	SSW	Accrual	Accrual Rate	Tax/ Subsidy
54	...	124,421	0	0	0
55	...	122,647	−1,775	−.014	.047
56	...	119,903	−2,743	−.022	.076
57	...	117,159	−2,745	−.023	.078
58	...	114,309	−2,850	−.024	.084
59	...	111,498	−2,811	−.025	.087
60	...	108,800	−2,698	−.024	.087
61	.247	106,436	−2,364	−.022	.081
62	.267	105,760	−676	−.006	.024
63	.290	105,362	−398	−.004	.015
64	.432	104,647	−715	−.007	.028
65	.465	101,810	−2,837	−.027	.117
66	.501	98,602	−3,209	−.032	.140
67	.536	95,054	−3,548	−.036	.165
68	.559	89,545	−5,508	−.058	.272
69	.583	84,203	−5,343	−.060	.281

ies for a married worker. We consider two additional cases: that of a worker at the tenth percentile of the earnings distribution and that of a worker at the ninetieth percentile of the distribution. Since we do not have true longitudinal data, we assume that the age/earnings profile is the same at the tenth and ninetieth percentiles as at the median and just use data on the 1995 differences across these percentiles to scale the profiles up and down.

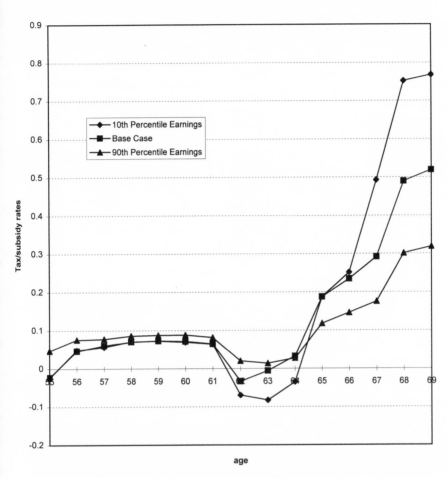

Fig. 11.14   Tax/subsidy rates across earnings profiles

These changes have important effects on the retirement incentives inherent in social security. As the first column of table 11.3 shows, the replacement rate is much higher for the low-earnings worker, confirming the findings of figure 11.5 above. The time pattern of tax/subsidy rates across earnings groups is also shown in figure 11.14. Before age sixty-two, there is a somewhat higher tax rate on high-wage workers since the tax/benefit linkage is reduced by the redistributive nature of benefits computation. From age sixty-two to age sixty-four, there is a large subsidy to continued work for the low-earnings workers, while there is a tax on the high earners. This reflects the fact that the low-earnings workers are getting a much higher return from their social security contributions at this age. This pattern reverses from age sixty-five on, however, as the large negative accruals implicit in social security at older ages are much larger on the smaller base of earnings at the tenth percentile. By age sixty-

Table 11.5   **Incentive Calculation—Incomplete Earnings History for Married Workers**

Last Year of Work	Replacement Rate	SSW	Accrual	Accrual Rate	Tax/ Subsidy
54	. . .	97,300	0	0	0
55	. . .	97,776	476	.005	−.023
56	. . .	98,274	498	.005	−.025
57	. . .	98,635	362	.004	−.019
58	. . .	98,922	287	.003	−.016
59	. . .	99,303	380	.004	−.022
60	. . .	99,732	429	.004	−.026
61	.391	100,419	687	.007	−.043
62	.434	102,617	2,198	.022	−.145
63	.476	104,280	1,662	.016	−.115
64	.703	103,848	−432	−.004	.031
65	.749	101,395	−2,452	−.024	.188
66	.798	98,622	−2,773	−.027	.225
67	.845	95,477	−3,145	−.032	.269
68	.872	90,644	−4,833	−.051	.439
69	.898	85,926	−4,718	−.052	.455

nine, the implicit tax rate on low-earnings workers is over twice that on high earners.

Table 11.5 considers a different permutation to the earnings history: assuming that the worker did not start work until 1929 and therefore has an incomplete earnings history (fewer than thirty-five years of work) until he works during his sixty-third year. This has a striking effect on the incentives before age sixty-four. In the place of sizable tax rates on continued work before age sixty-two, there are now small subsidies; and, in the place of a small subsidy at age sixty-two, there is now a much larger subsidy. That is, for a worker with this incomplete earnings history, working during the sixty-second year receives a subsidy of 15 percent owing to the value of replacing a zero in the average monthly earnings computation. Once this worker reaches age sixty-four, however, the incentives are identical to those for the base case since the earnings history has been completed.

11.4 Conclusions

The social security program is an important feature of the opportunity set of workers making their retirement decisions. There is clear evidence from both previous work and hazard rate diagrams that the broad structure of the social security program influences retirement timing. Evidence on the effects of variation in the benefits provided by this program is less clear, however. In this paper, we have explicitly documented the implicit tax rates on continued work from this system. We find that, on average, for married men with nonearning spouses, there is little net tax on continued work around the age of early eligibility for social security but that the tax becomes quite large at the normal retirement age. There is important heterogeneity in these incentives across workers, however, according to features such as marital status and earnings.

The implications of these findings depend critically on the elasticity of the response of retirement behavior to the implicit tax rates of the social security program. As we have noted, this elasticity remains a source of empirical controversy. Future work in this area could employ recent high-quality data on social security entitlements and retirement behavior to resolve this controversy.

Appendix A
Data Sources

Historical Data

Labor force participation by age and sex (figs. 11.1 and 11.2 above) is taken from U.S. Bureau of Labor Statistics (various years). Share of workers covered and replacement rates (figs. 11.3 and 11.5 above) are taken from U.S. Congress (1993). Receipt of social security/disability insurance by age and sex (fig. 11.4 above) and median earnings by cohort over time (simulations) are taken from U.S. Department of Health and Human Services (1995).

Contemporaneous Data

All contemporaneous figures are tabulated by the authors from March CPS data for 1994 and 1995.

Studying Retirement in the United States

There are two types of data available for studying retirement in the United States:

1. The first are cross-sectional data on participation at a point in time. The CPS is one of a variety of cross-sectional surveys available. Another of note is the National Health Interview Survey (NHIS), which also has health information.

2. The second are longitudinal data that follow individuals over time, providing information on demographics, labor force attachment, and income sources. Some examples here are (*a*) the Survey of Income and Program Participation (SIPP, 1984–present), which follows a large sample of persons over a period of two to three years; (*b*) the Panel Study of Income Dynamics (PSID, 1968–present), which has followed a smaller sample of persons since 1968; (*c*) the Retirement History Survey (RHS, 1969–79) and the National Longitudinal Surveys of Older Men and Women (NLS, 1968–present), which follow large samples of older persons over time, the former survey containing detailed in-

formation on the worker's entire earnings history; and (*d*) the Health and Retirement Survey (HRS, 1992–present), which updates the RHS with a new cohort of older persons that will be followed for at least ten years. The HRS has the richest data yet available from a retirement survey, including detailed information on earnings histories and firm pension plans.

Appendix B
The Effect of Social Security on Retirement— Theory and Evidence

Theory

The major role that social security plays in determining the well-being of the elderly, as well as the dramatic spikes in labor force participation and retirement at exactly the ages of social security entitlement in figures 11.12 and 11.13 above, suggest that social security is a key determinant of retirement behavior. But, in practice, it is quite complicated to model the effects of social security on retirement. In this section, we provide an overview of the effects of the system on retirement. This discussion draws heavily on Crawford and Lillien (1981); for a related discussion, see Burtless and Moffitt (1986).

The discussion proceeds in three steps. First, we consider the effects of social security on retirement in a perfect market/full rationality setting. Then we examine the implications of effects coming from imperfections in the credit and insurance markets. Finally, we consider the implications of behavioral responses that do not correspond to the full rationality model.

In a full rationality/perfect markets setting, one has two types of effects of social security on retirement: income effects and substitution effects. Insofar as the system increases the lifetime wealth of an individual, it will tend to induce earlier retirement (assuming that leisure is a normal good). Such redistributions happen across generations, particularly from the large benefits coming with an underfunded pay-as-you-go system. Such redistribution also happens within a generation, reflecting both deliberate redistributions and the redistributional effects of other policies. For example, the progressivity in the benefit formula is a redistribution to lower earners, for a given life expectancy (although life expectancy does vary systematically with income level). The presence of spouse benefits represents a redistribution from the never married to couples with different earnings histories. The use of an approach based on giving a maximum of an earned benefit and a spouse or surviving spouse benefit redistributes among couples, giving more to couples that have very different earnings levels, particularly one-earner couples. The presence of child benefits helps those having children late in life (so that the children are still young when the worker retires). Since benefits are paid as an annuity, with the same formula for all, the system redistributes toward those who, ex ante, have greater life expectancies. There are similar effects from the disability insurance portion of the program. In terms of substitution effects, one needs to consider the financial implications of continuing work once eligible for retirement benefits, as documented above.

Once one moves away from a perfect market setting, one cannot infer the effects of social security solely from their implications for the shape of the lifetime budget constraint. There are two effects that have been recognized in the literature. Insofar as it is difficult to borrow against future earnings, some young workers will be liquidity constrained, consuming less than they would if they could borrow against future earnings. The payroll tax tightens this constraint, resulting in even lower consumption among such workers. As a result of having consumed less when young, these workers may have more wealth when reaching retirement age, resulting in an income effect leading to earlier retirement.

With imperfect individual annuity markets, social security is providing real annuities that are not available in the market. Correction of this market failure has two effects. One is that the greater efficiency in planning lifetime consumption associated with annuitization works like an income effect, resulting in earlier retirement. Second, the link between work and the size of these annuities is an incentive for additional work at retirement age. Moreover, the inability to tap this source of wealth until reaching the early retirement age will lead some of those who would otherwise have chosen to retire before this age to continue to work until retirement age.

Turning to individual irrationalities, it is a premise of social security systems that many individuals would not save enough to finance retirement in the absence of compulsion. Forcing people to save more than they would (myopically) choose to results in greater wealth at retirement age and therefore an income effect leading to earlier retirement. Also relevant is the possibility of myopia in making the retirement decision itself, based on evaluating only the consumption possibilities in the near term rather than over the full remaining life span. This might result in some people retiring too soon.[18] Limiting eligibility until the early retirement age reduces this effect.

A further element comes into focus once one considers a couple. Poverty rates among widows are roughly three times as high as among married women of the same age. This suggests that many couples are not choosing sizable joint life annuitization. Insofar as social security requires partial joint life annuitization that would not have been chosen by the couple, it lowers consumption of the workers at retirement age and may lead to more work.

18. One must be careful here in measuring the degree of rationality about retirement decisions. For example, from the perspective of maximizing family social security wealth, a given husband may appear to retire too early. However, if he downweights his wife's consumption in his utility function, his decision may be individually rational.

Evidence

There is an enormous empirical literature that attempts to evaluate the effects that social security has had on retirement behavior. There are two broad strands of this literature. The first uses aggregate information on the labor force behavior of workers at different ages over time to infer the role that is played by social security. Hurd (1990) and Ruhm (1995) emphasize the spike in the age pattern of retirement at age sixty-two; as Hurd (1990, 597, no. 42) states, "There are no other institutional or economic reasons for the peak." Moreover, both authors show that this peak has grown over time as social security generosity has increased; and Burtless and Moffitt (1986) show that this peak was not present in 1960, before this early retirement option was available. As Ruhm (1995) notes, however, the existence of this peak does not prove that social security is lowering participation rates among all older workers; in fact, it may be inducing longer work among those aged sixty and sixty-one in order to qualify for early retirement at age sixty-two.

Moreover, for workers for whom the actuarial adjustment, additional tax, and AIME recomputation is fair on average, there is no reason for social security per se to induce a spike at age sixty-two; it is only an interaction of social security with liquidity constraints that would yield this response. Indeed, this is exactly what Kahn (1988) finds; there is a spike in retirement at age sixty-two for low-wealth workers but not for very high-wealth workers.

There is also a large spike in retirement at age sixty-five, as noted by many analysts, that would be consistent with the traditionally unfair actuarial adjustment made by social security for additional work beyond age sixty-five. Indeed, using more precise quarterly data, Blau (1994) finds that almost one-quarter of the men remaining in the labor force at their sixty-fifth birthday retire within the next three months; this hazard rate is over 2.5 times as large as the rate in surrounding quarters. However, Lumsdaine and Wise (1994) document that this penalty alone cannot account for this "excess" retirement at age sixty-five; nor can the incentives embedded in private pension plans or the availability of retirement health insurance through the Medicare program. This does not rule out a role for social security here; by setting up the "focal point" of a normal retirement age, the program may be the causal factor in explaining this spike.

The second strand of this literature attempts specifically to model the role that potential social security benefits play in determining retirement. The general strategy followed by this literature is to use micro-data sets with information on potential social security benefit determinants (earnings histories) or expost benefit levels to measure the incentives to retire across individuals in the data.[19] Then retirement models are estimated as a function of these incentive

---

19. The data used are generally the Retirement History Survey (Boskin and Hurd 1978; Burtless 1986; Burtless and Moffitt 1984; Hurd and Boskin 1984; Fields and Mitchell 1984; Blau 1994), although some authors have relied on the National Longitudinal Survey of Older Men (Diamond and Hausman 1984), and recent work uses the Survey of Consumer Finances (Samwick 1993).

measures. While the exact modeling technique differs substantially across papers,[20] the conclusions drawn are fairly similar: social security has large effects on retirement, but they are small relative to the trends over time documented in figures 11.1 and 11.2 above. For example, Burtless (1986) found that the 20 percent benefit rise of the period 1969–72 raised the probability of retirement at age sixty-two and age sixty-five by about 2 percentage points. Over this period, however, the labor force participation of older men fell by over 6 percent, and social security can therefore explain only about one-third of the change.[21]

This literature suffers from two important limitations. First, the key regressor, social security benefits, is a nonlinear function of past earnings, and retirement propensities are clearly correlated with past earnings levels. This problem is common to the social insurance literature in the United States.[22] But, for other social insurance programs, there is often variation along dimensions arguably exogenous to individual tastes, such as different legislative regimes across locations or within locations over time, that can be used to identify behavioral models. There is no comparable variation in social security, which is a nationally homogeneous program. Of course, this criticism does not necessarily imply that the estimates of this cross-sectional literature are flawed; as Hurd (1990) emphasizes, the nonlinearities in the social security benefits determination process are unlikely to be correlated with retirement propensities. But there has been little serious effort to decompose the sources of variation in social security benefits in an effort to assess whether the determinants that drive retirement behavior are plausibly excluded from a retirement equation.[23]

This criticism is levied most compellingly by Krueger and Pischke (1992), who note that there is a unique "natural experiment" provided by the end of double-indexing for the "notch generation" that retired in the late 1970s and early 1980s. For this cohort, social security benefits were greatly reduced relative to what they would have expected on the basis of the experience of the early to mid-1970s. Yet the dramatic fall in labor force participation continued

20. The earliest studies (Boskin and Hurd 1978; Fields and Mitchell 1984) used standard linear or nonlinear regression techniques. Later research (Burtless 1986; Burtless and Moffitt 1984) used nonlinear budget constraint estimation to capture the richness of social security's effects on the opportunity set. The most recent work (Diamond and Hausman 1984; Hausman and Wise 1985; Samwick 1993; Blau 1994) uses dynamic estimation of the retirement transition.

21. One exception is Hurd and Boskin (1984), who claim that the large benefits increases of the period 1968–73 can explain all the change in labor force participation in those years.

22. For a careful discussion of this issue in the context of unemployment insurance, see Meyer (1989).

23. At a minimum, one would want to include the level of lifetime earnings as a regressor, but most studies include only earnings in a recent year (i.e., Boskin and Hurd 1978; Burtless 1986). In addition, even using a somewhat longer time frame for measuring the earnings control (as Diamond and Hausman [1984] do) does not solve the problem; one could imagine that certain features of the lifetime pattern of earnings are correlated with both benefit levels and retirement decisions, such as the ratio of earnings around age sixty-two to earnings at earlier ages (since individuals who have relatively high earnings at older ages may have better labor market opportunities around the age of retirement and therefore work longer).

unabated in this era. This raises important questions about the identification of this cross-sectional literature.

The second problem with this literature is that it generally focuses on only one of the two key social security benefits variables, including social security benefits or wealth but ignoring the social security tax/subsidy rate documented above. In theory, as discussed above, both these factors plays an important role in determining retirement behavior. Studies that included this regressor found it to have a significant role in explaining retirement (Fields and Mitchell 1984; Samwick 1993); indeed, even in Krueger and Pischke's (1992) paper, the accrual rate is often right signed and significant even as the wealth effect is insignificant. More recently, Stock and Wise (1990) noted that the correct regressor for considering both social security and pension incentives for retirement is not the year-to-year accrual rate but the return to working this year relative to retiring at some future optimal date.

Thus, to summarize, the past empirical evidence has produced mixed conclusions as to the effect of social security policy on retirement. The abnormal spikes in retirement at the ages of early and normal retirement under social security suggest that the structure of the program plays a fundamental role in retirement timing decisions. Within this framework, however, there is only mixed evidence that changes in the overall generosity of the system have much effect on retirement behavior, although the evidence seems clearer for social security accrual rates than for social security wealth levels.

Redistribution

The other aspect of social security that has been emphasized by previous work is redistribution. Hurd and Shoven (1985), Boskin et al. (1987), and, more recently, Steuerle and Bakija (1994) document empirically the redistribution within and across generations that we discussed earlier. Table 11B.1 presents a summary of the results from Stuerle and Bakija on redistribution across and within generations. Each figure is the expected lifetime net transfer from the social security system, which is total received postretirement minus taxes paid during the working life. These net transfers are calculated for four demographic groups, for three levels of lifetime earnings, for three dates of retirement. In the first three columns, the expected values use average mortality assumptions; in the last two columns, the authors allow mortality to be income related, accounting for longer lives for higher-income individuals. All figures are in thousands of 1993 dollars.

A number of interesting findings emerge from table 11B.1. First, there is a secular decline in the net transfers from the social security system for newer cohorts; net transfers are positive for all groups retiring in 1960 but negative for most groups for those retiring in 2030. Second, the system transfers resources differentially to females relative to males since the tax structure is the same but females live longer. Third, the system transfers resources disproportionately to couples through spousal and survivor benefits and even more so to

Table 11B.1   Redistribution through the Social Security System (figures are net transfers in thousands of 1993 dollars)

Wage	Average Mortality			Income-Specific Mortality	
	1960	1995	2030	1995	2030
Single male:					
Low	26.1	12.5	−4.1	5.1	−13.8
Average	36.5	−5.1	−56.2	−5.1	−56.2
High	36.8	−37.1	−248.5	−20.8	−224.3
Single female:					
Low	41.4	33.4	22.5	27.0	13.0
Average	59.4	28.1	−13.8	28.1	−13.8
High	62.1	6.5	−187.3	20.4	−162.9
Single-earner couple:					
Low	62.3	89.5	99.3	86.0	94.2
Average	89.9	122.5	117.0	122.5	117.0
High	97.2	134.7	24.2	144.6	36.2
Two-earner couple:					
Low	68.4	62.6	36.5	53.1	30.0
Average	88.7	78.6	29.4	78.6	29.4
High	98.7	37.1	−173.5	53.5	−154.9

Source: Steuerle and Bakija (1994).

single-earner couples since no taxes are paid by the spouse but he or she gets benefits. Fourth, despite its ostensibly redistributional structure, the system traditionally transferred more resources toward higher-income earners than toward lower-income earners; this is largely because social security was a good investment and the higher-income earners were more heavily invested. But, by 1995, and even more so by 2030, net transfers are progressive for average mortality prospects. Finally, introducing differential mortality prospects somewhat offsets this progressivity.

Appendix C

In this appendix, we provide the formulas for our computation of social security wealth.

Notation

AM	= worker's age;
AF	= spouse's age;
YM	= year of worker's birth;
YF	= year of spouse's birth;
a	= month of worker's birth;

maxage	= maximum potential age that we consider for both worker and spouse;
ρ	= discount rate;
t	= number of months after attaining age sixty-two that the worker decides to wait before first claiming benefits;
m	= number of months after t that the worker decides to continue working just below the earnings test limit (so that he is still eligible for full benefits despite continued work);
s	= number of months that a spouse, aged less than normal retirement age, decides to wait until starting to claim benefits;
$\{s_k\}, k$	= $1 \ldots, 12 \times (\text{maxage} - \text{AM})$ = number of months that a widow aged less than her normal retirement age, and whose partner died k months after attaining age sixty-two, decides to wait before claiming her survivor benefits;
B_x	= amount of benefits that the worker is entitled to in month x;
D_x	= amount of benefits that the spouse is entitled to claim in month x on the basis of the worker's earnings history;
C_x	= amount of benefits that the surviving spouse is entitled to claim in month x in case the worker dies (before retiring) in month x;
E_x	= amount of benefits that the surviving spouse is entitled to claim in month x in case the worker dies (after retiring) in month x;
θ_i^1	= dummy variable, which is one if $12 \times \text{AF} + k \geq 12 \times 60 + s$ and zero otherwise;
θ_i^2	= dummy variable, which is one if $12 \times \text{AF} + k \geq 12 \times 60 + s_k$ and zero otherwise;
$p_x(\cdot\vert\text{YM}, \text{sex})$	= cohort- and sex-specific conditional probability measure expressing the probability that the worker is still alive in month x, conditional on being alive in month $x - 1$ (by definition, $p_{12\times62} = 1$);
$q_x(\cdot\vert\text{YM}, \text{sex})$	= cohort- and sex-specific conditional probability measure expressing the probability that the spouse is still alive in month x, conditional on being alive in month $x - 1$ (by definition, $p_{12\times\text{AF}} = 1$);
w	= $[12 \times (\text{YM} + \text{AM} - 1) + a + i]/12$;
v	= $[12 \times (\text{YM} + \text{AM} - 1) + a + k]/12$;
BI_x	= increase in benefits in December of year x;
SSC_x	= contributions to social security system in month x; and
i, l, j, k	= simple counting variables

The construct of interest for our analysis is the net present discounted value (NPDV) of social security benefits. This is the sum of four components:

PB   = NPDV of worker's benefits;
SpB = NPDV of spousal benefits;
SuB = NPDV of survivor benefits; and
SSC = NPDV of social security contributions.

$$PB \equiv \sum_{i \cdot t}^{12 \cdot (maxage=AM)} [B_{12 \cdot AM+i} \times p_{12 \cdot AM+i}(YM, sex) \times (1 + \rho)^{-i}],$$

$$SpB = \sum_{i \cdot t}^{12 \cdot (maxage=AF)} \left(D_{12 \cdot AM+i} \times \theta_i^1 \right.$$

$$\left. \times \left\{ \prod_{j=0}^{i} [q_{12 \cdot AF+j}(\cdot|YF, sex) \times p_{12 \cdot AM+j}(\cdot|YM, sex)] \right\} \times (1 + \rho)^{-i} \right),$$

$$SuB \equiv \sum_{k=0}^{t-l} \left[\sum_{i=k}^{12 \cdot (maxage-AF)} \left(C_{12 \cdot AM+i} \times \theta_i^2 \times \left\{ \prod_{j=0}^{k-l} [p_{12 \cdot AM+j}(\cdot|YM, sex)] \right\} \right. \right.$$

$$\times [1 - p_{12 \cdot AM+j}(\cdot|YM, sex)] \times \left\{ \prod_{j=0}^{j} [q_{12 \cdot AF+j}(\cdot|YF, sex)] \right\}$$

$$\left. \times \left[\frac{\prod_{t=v}^{w} (1 + BI_l)}{(1 + BI_v)} \right] \right) \right] \times \left\{ \left[1 - p_{12 \cdot AM+j}(\cdot|YM, sex) \right] \right.$$

$$\times \left(\prod_{j=0}^{i} \right) [q_{12 \cdot AF+j}(\cdot|YF, sex)] \times \frac{\left[\prod_{l=v}^{w} (1 + BI_l) \right]}{(1 + BI_v)} \right\}$$

$$+ \sum_{k=t}^{12 \cdot (maxage-AM)} \left[\sum_{i=k}^{12 \cdot (maxage-AF)} \left(E_{12 \cdot AM+i} \times \theta_i^2 \times \left\{ \prod_{j=0}^{k-l} [p_{12 \cdot AM+j}(\cdot|YM, sex)] \right\} \right) \right],$$

$$SSC \equiv \sum_{i=0}^{t+m} SSC_{(12 \cdot AM)+i}.$$

The net present discounted value of social security benefits (NPDVSSC) is thus

$$NPDVSSC \equiv PB + SpB + SuB + SSC.$$

References

Blau, David M. 1994. Labor force dynamics of older men. *Econometrica* 62:117–56.
Boskin, Michael J., and Michael D. Hurd. 1978. The effect of social security on early retirement. *Journal of Public Economics* 10:361–77.
Boskin, Michael, John Shoven, Lawrence Kotlikoff, and Douglas Puffert. 1987. Social

security: A financial appraisal across and within generations. *National Tax Journal* 40:19–33.

Bound, John. 1989. The health and earnings of rejected disability insurance applicants. *American Economic Review* 79:482–03.

———. 1991. The health and earnings of rejected disability insurance applicants: Reply. *American Economic Review* 81:1427–34.

Burtless, Gary. 1986. Social security, unanticipated benefit increases, and the timing of retirement. *Review of Economic Studies* 53:781–805.

Burtless, Gary, and Robert Moffitt. 1984. The effect of social security benefits on the labor supply of the aged. In *Retirement and economic behavior,* ed. H. Aaron and G. Burtless. Washington, D.C.: Brookings.

———. 1986. Social security, earnings tests, and age at retirement. *Public Finance Quarterly* 14:3–27.

Crawford, Vincent P., and David M. Lillien. 1981. Social security and the retirement decision. *Quarterly Journal of Economics,* no. 385:505–29.

Diamond, Peter, and Jerry Hausman. 1984. Retirement and unemployment behavior of older men. In *Retirement and economic behavior,* ed. H. Aaron and G. Burtless. Washington, D.C.: Brookings.

Fields, Gary S., and Olivia S. Mitchell. 1984. *Retirement, pensions, and social security.* Cambridge, Mass.: MIT Press.

Gruber, Jonathan. 1996. Disability insurance benefits and labor supply of older persons. Massachusetts Institute of Technology. Mimeo.

Gruber, Jonathan, and Jeffrey D. Kubik. 1997. Disability insurance rejection rates and the labor supply of older workers. *Journal of Public Economics* 64:1–23.

Hausman, Jerry, and David Wise. 1985. Social security, health status, and retirement. In *Pensions, labor, and individual choice,* ed. D. Wise. Chicago: University of Chicago Press.

Hurd, Michael. 1990. Research on the elderly: Economic status, retirement, and consumption and saving. *Journal of Economic Literature* 28:565–637.

Hurd, Michael, and Michael Boskin. 1984. The effect of social security on retirement in the early 1970s. *Quarterly Journal of Economics* 99:767–90.

Hurd, Michael, and John Shoven. 1985. The distributional impact of social security. In *Pensions, labor, and individual choice,* ed. D. Wise. Chicago: University of Chicago Press.

Kahn, James A. 1988. Social security, liquidity, and early retirement. *Journal of Public Economics* 35:97–117.

Krueger, Alan, and Jorn-Steffen Pischke. 1992. The effect of social security on labor supply: A cohort analysis of the notch generation. *Journal of Labor Economics* 10: 412–37.

Leonard, Jonathan S. 1986. Labor supply incentives and the disincentives for disabled persons. In *Disability and the labor market: Economic problems, policies, and programs,* ed. M. Berkowitz and M. A. Hill. Ithaca, N.Y.: ILR Press.

Lumsdaine, Robin, and David Wise. 1994. Aging and labor force participation: A review of trends and explanations. In *Aging in the United States and Japan: Economic trends,* ed. Y. Noguchi and D. Wise. Chicago: University of Chicago Press.

Meyer, Bruce D. 1989. A quasi-experimental approach to the effects of unemployment insurance. Working Paper no. 3159. Cambridge, Mass.: National Bureau of Economic Research.

Parsons, Donald. 1980. The decline of male labor force participation. *Journal of Political Economy* 88:117–34.

———. 1991a. The health and earnings of rejected disability insurance applicants: Comment. *American Economic Review* 81:1419–26.

————. 1991b. Self-screening in targeted public transfer programs. *Journal of Political Economy* 99:859–76.

————. 1996. Retirement age and retirement income: The role of the firm. In *Assessing knowledge of retirement behavior,* ed. Eric A. Hanushek and Nancy L. Maritato. Washington, D.C.: National Academy Press.

Ruhm, Christopher. 1995. Secular changes in the work and retirement patterns of older men. *Journal of Human Resources* 30:362–85.

Samwick, Andrew. 1993. The joint effect of social security and pensions on the timing of retirement: Some new evidence. Massachusetts Institute of Technology. Mimeo.

Steuerle, Eugene C., and Jon M. Bakija. 1994. *Retooling social security for the 21st century: Right and wrong approaches to reform.* Washington, D.C.: Urban Institute Press.

Stock, James, and David Wise. 1990. Pensions, the option value of work, and retirement. *Econometrica* 58:1151–80.

U.S. Bureau of Labor Statistics. Various years. *Employment and earnings.* Washington, D.C.

U.S. Congress. House Committee on Ways and Means. 1993. *Overview of entitlement programs.* Washington, D.C.: U.S. Government Printing Office.

U.S. Department of Health and Human Services. Various years. *Annual statistical supplement to the Social Security Bulletin.* Washington, D.C.: Social Security Administration.

Contributors

Didier Blanchet
INSEE
15, boulevard Gabriel Péri
BP 100
92244 Malakoff Cédex, France

Richard Blundell
Department of Economics
University College London
Gower Street
London WC1E 6BT United Kingdom

Michele Boldrin
Departamento de Economia
Universidad Carlos III de Madrid
28903 Getafe
Madrid, Spain

Axel Börsch-Supan
Department of Economics
University of Mannheim
D-68131 Mannheim, Germany

Agar Brugiavini
Dipartimento di Economia
Università Ca 'Foscari de Venezia
S. Gibbe, 873
30121 Venezia, Italy

Peter Diamond
Department of Economics
Massachusetts Institute of Technology
Cambridge, MA 02139

Jonathan Gruber
U.S. Treasury Department, Rm 3450
1500 Pennsylvania Avenue
Washington, D.C. 20220

Sergi Jimenez-Martin
Departamento de Economia
Universidad Carlos III de Madrid
28903 Getafe
Madrid, Spain

Paul Johnson
Institute for Fiscal Studies
7 Ridgmount Street
London WC1E 7AE United Kingdom

Arie Kapteyn
Center for Economic Research
Tilburg University
Warandelaan 2
5000 Le Tilburg, The Netherlands

Takashi Oshio
9-10 Taniguchi-Sonomachi, Ukyo-ku
Kyoto 616 Japan

Mårten Palme
Handelhogskolan
Stockholm School of Economics
Box 6501
113 53 Stockholm, Sweden

Louis-Paul Pelé
INSEE
15, boulevard Gabriel Péri
BP 100
92244 Malakoff Cédex, France

Franco Peracchi
DMQTE
Università d'Annunzio
I-65127 Pescara, Italy

Pierre Pestieau
Université de Liège
Faculté d'Economie
Boulevard du Rectorat 7 (B31)
4000 Sart Tilman, Liège 1 Belgium

Javier Ruiz-Castillo
Departamento de Economía
Universidad Carlos II de Madrid
28903 Getafe
Madrid, Spain

Reinhold Schnabel
Department of Economics
University of Mannheim
P.O.B. 10 34 62
D-68131 Mannheim 1 Germany

Jean-Philippe Stijns
Université de Liège
Faculté d'Economie
Boulevard du Rectorat 7 (B31)
4000 Sart Tilman, Liège 1 Belgium

Ingemar Svensson
National Social Insurance Board
Adolf Fredriks Kyrkogata 8
S-103 51 Stockholm, Sweden

Klaas de Vos
Center for Economic Research
Tilburg University
Warandelaan 2
5000 Le Tilburg, The Netherlands

David A. Wise
National Bureau of Economic Research
1050 Massachusetts Avenue
Cambridge, MA 02138

Naohiro Yashiro
Institute of International Relations
Sophia University
7-1 Kioi-Chō, Chiyoda-Ku
Tokyo 102 Japan

Author Index

Subject Index

Benefits
  benefit accrual pattern, 8
  Belgium: disability, 40–41; payments
    (1990), 37; unemployment, 40, 57, 61–64
  Canada: disability, 89
  France: unemployment, 126–27
  Germany: disability, 10, 141, 144–45, 153,
    167–68; public spending for social secu-
    rity (1993), 135; survivor, 149, 153–54;
    tax-free, 149; unemployment, 10; work-
    related old age, 151–53
  Italy: computation of and minimum benefit,
    198–200; disability, 187–88, 201–4; early
    retirement, 198; severance pay fund,
    214–15; survivors, 214; taxation of,
    215–16
  Japan: amounts determined, 251–52
  Netherlands: disability, 271, 277; supple-
    ments to pension, 278
  Spain: computation for general social secu-
    rity, 322–23; disability, 312, 315–16, 318,
    331–36; survivor benefits, 311–12,
    327–28; unemployment, 336
  Sweden: disability, 359–60, 400; payments
    (1994), 355
  United States, 437
  See also Disability insurance; Survivor ben-
    efits

Canada/Quebec Pension Plan (CPP/QPP), 73,
  76–80, 85–86

Data sources
  Belgium, 44, 65–67

Germany, 137, 176–78
Italy, 228–30
Netherlands, 298–99
Spain, 349–50
Sweden, 361, 364, 398–99
United States, 463–64
Demographic issues
  Germany: old age dependency ratio, 136;
    population aging, 136, 147
  Italy, 181–84
  Japan, 239, 250
  Netherlands, 269–70
  Spain, 306–7
  Sweden, 355–56
Disability insurance
  retirement incentives in, 9
  Belgium, 40–41
  Canada: through CPP/QPP, 89
  Germany: benefits, 10, 141, 144–45, 153,
    167–68; benefits for all age groups, 153;
    old age disability, 149–50
  Italy: benefits (1975–95), 187–88; benefits
    under pre- and post-1984 legislation,
    201–4
  Netherlands, 271, 277
  Spain: eligibility criteria (1985), 318; men
    as recipients of (1945–75), 315–16; popu-
    lation receiving (1965–95), 312; tempo-
    rary and permanent, 331–36
  Sweden: empirical work related to concept
    of, 400; older men and women receiving
    benefits (1960–96), 359–60; pension,
    362f, 363f, 371–72, 381